TELEPEN
80 7209377 5
DILEWYD O STOC
WITHDRAWN FROM STOCK
AF841950
ABERYSTWYTH

L

PUBLIC FINANCE

PUBLIC FINANCE

UNIVERSITY COLLEGE OF WALES
LIBRARY
ABERYSTWYTH

Bruce F. Davie
Georgetown University

Bruce F. Duncombe
Georgetown University

HOLT, RINEHART AND WINSTON, INC.
NEW YORK CHICAGO SAN FRANCISCO ATLANTA
DALLAS MONTREAL TORONTO LONDON SYDNEY

THE UNIVERSITY COLLEGE OF WALES
ABERYSTWYTH
ACC. No. B72-9377
CLASS No. HJ 131 D2.

An earlier version of Chapters 11 and 12 was separately published under the title *Modern Political Arithmetic* by Holt, Rinehart and Winston, Inc., 1970.

Copyright © 1972 by Holt, Rinehart and Winston, Inc.
All Rights Reserved
Library of Congress Catalog Card Number: 72-162645

ISBN: 0-03-077240-0

Printed in the United States of America
0 1 2 3 038 9 8 7 6 5 4 3 2 1

PREFACE

Government expenditures are a means of attaining policy objectives rather than burdens to be financed. We begin this study of public finance by considering rationales for government expenditures. Two major analytical problems are investigated: Altering resource allocation to provide public goods and to adjust for externalities; choosing among alternative expenditure programs and selecting means of producing public goods. Government expenditures must be financed, and are the principal reason for taxation and raising other revenues. We define public finance as the use of government expenditures and revenues to pursue policy objectives. Policy objectives are seen as emerging from the welfare-increasing actions of individual citizens, private groups, and public officials. The effects of government expenditures and revenues on individual welfare are examined through their impact on allocation, distribution, and macroeconomic stability. When public policies directed at specific objectives are under investigation, we recognize implicit impacts on others. For instance, government provision of secondary education involves resource allocation but also has distributive implications; the real

U.C.W. ABERYSTWYTH LIBRARY

income of pupils, their families, and others is affected. Similarly, tax increases designed to stabilize the price level have distributive implications if unemployment results. Equity questions are raised throughout, including equity in the distribution of public goods. Our personal stands on particular issues are distinguished from those that follow from analysis.

As teachers, we felt that certain topics usually omitted from, or only briefly mentioned in, public finance textbooks should have extensive treatment. We have devoted a chapter to benefit-cost analysis because this technique of public policy analysis is widely used by federal, state, and local governments. Too often discussions of public spending are limited to government purchases of goods and services and transfer payments. Federal credit policies involve the public sector in the nation's capital markets, and are the subject of a separate chapter. Similarly, a discussion of government expenditures is not complete without considering private expenditures purposely encouraged by special features of the tax laws; this topic is treated under the rubric of tax expenditures. In addition to developing the fiscal policy models usually found in public finance texts, we have included a more detailed, noneconometric model illustrating a wider range of fiscal policy actions. The federal budget is usually in surplus or deficit; we focus on the means of financing budget surpluses and deficits and the macroeconomic consequences of such financing in our discussion of postwar fiscal policy. This provides links between the federal budget, fiscal policy models, and changes in the size of the national debt. Many tax and expenditure programs entail international transactions or affect private international transactions; we have given these aspects of public finance special attention.

Treatment of the federal, state, and local governments in four national economic accounts—national income accounts, flow of funds accounts, the balance of payments account, and input-output tables—receives special attention. Because argumentation regarding public economic policy is often buttressed with data from these accounts, it is important that they be understood. Data from the federal *Budget* are also examined in detail. We often refer to other data and have provided references to their sources and interpretation. Extensive bibliographic footnotes are placed throughout the text.

Today's leading public policy debate may be only a dim memory as new issues surface tomorrow. Thus, we have not written this text with a focus on any one issue. However, particular policy questions are discussed. Issues related to education and the environment are frequently used as examples of theoretical points. The value added tax is analyzed and considered as an alternative to the corporate income tax; the border tax issue is appraised. The urban crisis was a concern as this book was written: two policy proposals are considered: revenue sharing in the chapter on intergovernmental fiscal relations, and the negative income tax and welfare reform in the chapter on maintaining personal income.

We have designed this text for students of economics who have completed the basic principles of economics course. Generally the theoretical analysis is at the level found in intermediate micro- and macroeconomic theory courses, but these are not assumed to be part of the student's background. Since our analysis does rest on firm theoretical foundations, the text is also suitable for beginning graduate students. Graduate students will also find useful the material not usually found in other theoretical texts.

Each of us is convinced that any errors, omissions, or confusions are the responsibility of the other.

January 1972

B. F. Davie
B. F. Duncombe

CONTENTS

1

PUBLIC ECONOMIC POLICY

Public policy touches the life of everyone living in an organized society. It is formed by the actions of governments, and embodied in statutory laws, administrative decisions, and judicial interpretations. In the United States there are approximately 80,000 separate governments —federal, state, and local—engaged in the continually evolving process of formulating public policy.

Economic problems stem from the fact that man's desires for goods and services exceed his ability to fulfill them. In the face of scarcity, governments adopt *public economic policies* that direct the allocation of resources, promote stability in the allocative process, and approach equity in the distribution of output to the end that man's desires for goods and services are better met. Some goods and services that would not be produced and sold in the private market-place, such as national defense, are provided as a result of public economic policy. A few goods and services that consumers demand and producers would gladly sell—narcotics, for example—may be prohibited. Methods of production may be altered by policies that restrict the use of certain factors of production, such as child labor laws, or limit the range of permissible technologies, such as air and water pollution control. Public economic policy can promote technological change by supporting basic research or by subsidizing new developments as in the discovery of atomic energy. Resources that might otherwise be unemployed are put to work as the result of stabilization policies. Many government actions are taken to alter the distribution of benefits from economic activity; incomes may be redistributed through social security, for example, or the ownership of factors of production may be changed by small business loans. *Public finance* is the use of the revenues and expenditures of government to implement public economic policy.

Public economic policies, whether they are primarily concerned with allocation, distribution, or stabilization, must be discussed in the context of a particular society, for the policies adopted by any government are influenced by the values of that society. Public economic policy in the United States is formulated within a federal structure of government that is dedicated to maintaining personal freedom and a market economy. Awareness of these values is essential for interpreting American policy actions and provides some normative grounds for policy decisions. Different values would have to be enumerated for other nations.

INDIVIDUAL WELFARE FUNCTIONS

To understand public economic policy in a democratic society we must focus our attention on the welfare of individuals. The individual must be the starting point because public policies affect the individual, and because in a democracy individuals are a vital part of the political processes by which public policy is formed and implemented. Governments adopt policies to increase individual welfare. Only the most naive would expect that public economic policies always "promote the general welfare"; a policy may in fact be designed to increase the welfare of public officials or the members of a lobby group. Whether citizens are deserving or self-serving, individual welfare is the underlying motive.

To lend some precision to a discussion of welfare that might otherwise become an excursion into generalities, we regard each individual as attempting to maximize his lifetime welfare, subject to certain constraints. Lifetime welfare, W, of an individual, i, is the summation of his welfare in each time period, t, running from the present, $t = 1$, to death, $t = d$.

$$W_i = \sum_{t=1}^{d} W_{it} \qquad [1.1]$$

The variable, W_{it}, which denotes the welfare of individual i in time period t, may be expressed as a function of several variables

$$W_{it} = f(C_{it}, A_{it}, L_{it}, G_t, W_{jt}, N_t) \qquad i, j = 1, \ldots, n; \; i \neq j \quad [1.2]$$

where C_{it} is private consumption by i of goods and services; A_{it} designates his privately held assets; L_{it} designates his leisure; G_t is consumption of goods and services provided by governments; W_{jt} is the welfare of others; and N_t is intangibles. The principal constraints within which individuals attempt to maximize their welfare are present and future income, past levels of welfare, and the time interval remaining until death. Each of the variables in Equation (1.2) requires additional explanation.

Private consumption of goods and services is conceptually the easiest to deal with. Individuals consume what they purchase because the particular items either make a direct contribution to their welfare or, as in the case of commuting to work or buying tools, enable them to earn income. Current and expected future disposable income constrains the amount which can be spent on consumption during any one time period. Individuals may of course consume more than their current income by borrowing against future income or reducing their stock of assets. Such action reduces the possibilities of future consumption, usually by a greater dollar amount, because interest must be paid when borrowing against future income. When current consumption is less than current income, assets are accumulated through saving.

Assets play at least a double role in an individual's welfare function. Assets yield income either in money terms, if they are financial assets, or in kind (as current consumption) if they are real assets. In addition, assets contribute to an individual's welfare as long as he attaches positive value to bequeathing an estate. Assets also constitute a hedge against uncertainty. Practically no one knows his future income with certainty nor can he anticipate circumstances that might call for unexpected consumption expenditures. Having assets to draw upon (or borrow against) in an emergency contributes to welfare even though such a contingency may never arise.

Most individuals consider additional hours of leisure a contribution to their welfare. However, if to increase leisure income must be given up along with additions to either private consumption or assets, the nature of individual preferences is less clear. Leisure that is the consequence of involuntary unemployment or underemployment presumably does not enhance welfare. Historical evidence does suggest that Americans buy more leisure as their incomes rise; there has been a long-term downward trend in the average number of hours worked per week and per year and a tendency for workers to retire earlier. Certain patterns of private consumption and asset holding tend to go along with additional leisure—expenditures for travel and entertainment, boats and summer cottages.

The contribution to individual welfare made by government provision of goods and services is central to the study of public finance. Typically these public goods are consumed jointly with many other individuals, hence we use the notation G_t rather than G_{it}.[1] Everyone consumes national defense but each individual is likely to perceive differently the contribution (perhaps even negative) that current defense spending and stocks of weapons make to his own welfare. Other types of government-provided goods and services, such as public education and parks, have a more immediate impact on individual welfare. Lifetime welfare is affected not only by present consumption of these goods and services but also by the possibility of their consumption at some future date. The development of a new national park contributes to a person's welfare even though he may not visit the park this year, if he values the option of being able to do so in the future. Of course not all the goods and services provided by governments contribute to an individual's welfare, and some are undoubtedly welfare reducing.

The consequences for individual welfare that typically result from government activity are not attributable to public expenditures alone. If the economy is fully employed, the resources required to provide these goods and services must be diverted from some alternative use. If taxes are imposed as a means of financing this resource transfer, individual disposable incomes are reduced; the constraint within which one must operate to maximize welfare is narrowed. With diminished disposable income the individual must either reduce private consumption and asset accumulation or give up some leisure and work longer in an attempt to maintain his level of after-tax income. Each individual can weigh the additions to his welfare that come from the consumption of public goods against the decrease in his welfare associated with the tax, and thus judge the efficacy of government programs.

It would be a mistake to expect that public officials only adopt programs supported by a majority while acting on the basis of their own material welfare. The mistake stems from ignoring two other variables in the welfare function and the political processes by which decisions are reached. The first is the welfare of every other individual. Private philanthropy develops from the donor's concern with the well-being of others. How significant the welfare of others is to our own welfare is a difficult matter to discuss, and is perhaps a matter best left to the moral philosophers. But we cannot avoid the issue because of its importance in understanding public finance. There is also ample precedence for treating the subject; the separate intellectual discipline we now call economics grew out of eighteenth century moral philosophy. Adam Smith, after all, was Professor of Moral Philosophy at the University of Glasgow when, well before the appearance of *The Wealth of Nations*, he wrote a treatise on this subject, *The Theory of Moral Sentiments*. How strongly another's welfare affects our own undoubtedly depends on who the other fellow is. Our neighbor's welfare concerns us more than a distant

---

[1] In this chapter and the next, public goods refers to all those goods and services provided by government. The term is defined with greater precision in Chapter 3.

stranger. Many individuals develop a special concern for the welfare of groups of people—the mentally retarded, promising artists, or perhaps a particular ethnic or cultural group. In some cases it is a decrease in another's welfare that increases our own. We may gain satisfaction in seeing wrongdoers punished.

The last variable in the welfare function, the catch-all of "intangibles," includes a vast array of items that affect the individual. Personal factors such as good health and a loving spouse can be listed here, but more important for our present purposes are the widely held values of a society that set the limits within which governments operate. For the United States these values are expressed as personal freedom within the context of a market economy and a federal structure of government.

Personal freedom has many dimensions. When alluded to in a political party's platform or Fourth of July speech, the term is defined by the ringing phrases of the American tradition: "Life, Liberty, and the Pursuit of Happiness," or "Freedom from Fear, Freedom from Want, Freedom of Expression, and Freedom of Worship." More specifically, personal freedom includes guaranteed civil and property rights that yield, as a consequence, freedom of movement in both a geographical and social sense, freedom of occupational choice, and freedom of consumer choice.

In a democracy personal freedom is both the means and end of public policy. Men must be free if a democratic government is to function, and such a government should maintain and extend personal freedom. In a complex society no individual can enjoy complete freedom because his actions affect the ability of others to enjoy theirs. Governments therefore limit freedom so that it can be enjoyed, and herein lies the foundation for much of public economic policy. The constraint on personal freedom imposed by a traffic light increases the welfare of all drivers because they fear the consequences of unlimited freedom. But to prevent single males under the age of twenty-five from driving because they have relatively high accident rates would be judged too great a limitation on personal freedom, although such a law would increase the welfare of some drivers.

Americans traditionally support the retention of an economy organized largely on the basis of competitive markets. A market economy is one in which (1) the individual as owner of his own labor as well as capital and natural resources is unrestrained in allocating these resources to whatever employment he chooses, and (2) the individual recipient of income from the sale of these factor services is unrestrained in apportioning this income to various uses. The terms (prices) at which resources and goods and services are exchanged are set by the combined action of unrestrained buyers and sellers. Hence a market economy implies the existence of personal freedom. As individuals exercise free consumer choice a market economy responds by producing the goods and services that consumers demand. Demand is limited by consumer income and cultivated by advertisers. New types of goods and services will only continue to be produced if they increase consumer welfare. Edsels and midis didn't seem to increase consumer welfare and their production ceased. Monopoly elements limit the degree to which consumer demands are met. A nonmarket economy may permit freedom of consumer choice—free selection among those goods and services that are produced—but this falls short of the consumer sovereignty that characterizes a market economy where consumers also dictate what will be produced.[2]

The relationship between federalism and personal freedom is not so strong as that between the market economy and personal freedom. A federal system of government, with states possessing a large measure of sovereignty, emerged after American independence and was embodied in the Constitution. Federalism has continued to evolve since 1789; the relative power of the states *vis à vis* the federal government has waxed and waned in response to changing political attitudes and sheer economic and population growth. Adherence to a federal system is not based solely on historical tradition, however. Powerful arguments have been made for its relevance in the twentieth century. Despite the growth in the relative importance of the federal government since the 1930s, states, and their political subdivisions, have a vital responsibility for those government activities that affect individual citizens most directly—schools, police and fire departments, libraries, and welfare programs. Personal freedom, it is argued, can be more easily maintained and expanded when citizens have close contact with the local elected officials responsible for these functions of government. In addition, one single unit within a multiplicity of state and local governments is more likely to innovate—to initiate a new type of government program, to experiment in the field of social legislation, or to tap a new source of revenue—than a unitary government. In this sense, federalism limits the range of permissible public economic policy. At the state and local level, for example, governments cannot take action that would limit interstate commerce even though such action might be consistent with the welfare of their citizens. The federal government cannot change state and local tax rates in an effort to achieve macroeconomic stability. In other nations federalism need not constrain public policy, but Americans find it essential.

INDIVIDUAL ACTIONS TO INCREASE WELFARE

Surely no one methodically writes out his own welfare function, consults it upon arising each morning, and judges his every action in accordance with it.

---

[2] For two views of this process, *see* Milton Friedman, *Capitalism and Freedom* (Chicago: The University of Chicago Press, 1962), and Oscar Lange, "On the Economic Theory of Socialism," in Benjamin E. Lippencott (ed.), *On the Economic Theory of Socialism* (Minneapolis: University of Minnesota Press, 1938).

But just as surely, no one consciously takes steps to diminish his own welfare, though his actions may appear to do so in the eyes of others. We may assume that all voluntary actions taken by individuals are, at least at the moment they are taken, thought to be welfare increasing. Two types of individual actions concern us here—market transactions and political participation.

Market transactions. Individuals increase their welfare through market transactions. If this were not so, markets would not exist; marketing involves information-acquisition costs and the expenditure of time to complete transactions. In a market where resources are bartered we may visualize a transaction in assets between two persons. For example, if one has paintings of the Renaissance and another a collection of Impressionists, agreement between them to exchange assets implies that gains in welfare will result. However, most transactions in a modern economy are monetized. When a person surrenders leisure by selling his labor services for money, it is because working increases his welfare, yielding income he then exchanges for commodities and securities. The person who pays money for another's labor services benefits from the exchange because he values the labor services more highly than the money payment.

The voluntary market actions of individuals are said to be *Pareto optimal*.[3] A Pareto optimal situation is one in which it is impossible to take any action to increase a person's welfare without at the same time decreasing the welfare of another. Any action is Pareto optimal that benefits at least one person while not making any other person worse off. This welfare criterion is widely used because it makes no judgment as to total welfare; thus there is no need for additive welfare units and making interpersonal comparisons of utility.

The concept of Pareto optimality is illustrated geometrically in Figure 1.1. For two-dimensional analysis we assume an economy with only two products—A and B—which are in fixed supply. The horizontal dimension represents the fixed quantity of A and the vertical dimension the fixed quantity of B. We suppose that these products are distributed between only two persons, X and Y. Consumption by X is measured from the lower left corner of Figure 1.1, and point X is the origin for X's indifference map. Two of X's indifference curves, X_1 and X_2 are shown. Similarly, consumption by Y is measured from the upper right corner of the box, and point Y serves as the origin for Y's indifference map. Two of Y's indifference curves, Y_1 and Y_2, are shown.

[3] This term comes from the writings of the twentieth century Italian economist and sociologist Vilfredo Pareto, particularly his *Manuel d'Economie Politique* (Paris: V. Giard & E. Brière, 1909). For a discussion of pareto optimality in the context of modern welfare economics, *see* Francis Bator, "The Simple Analytics of Walfare Maximization," *American Economic Review,* March 1957.

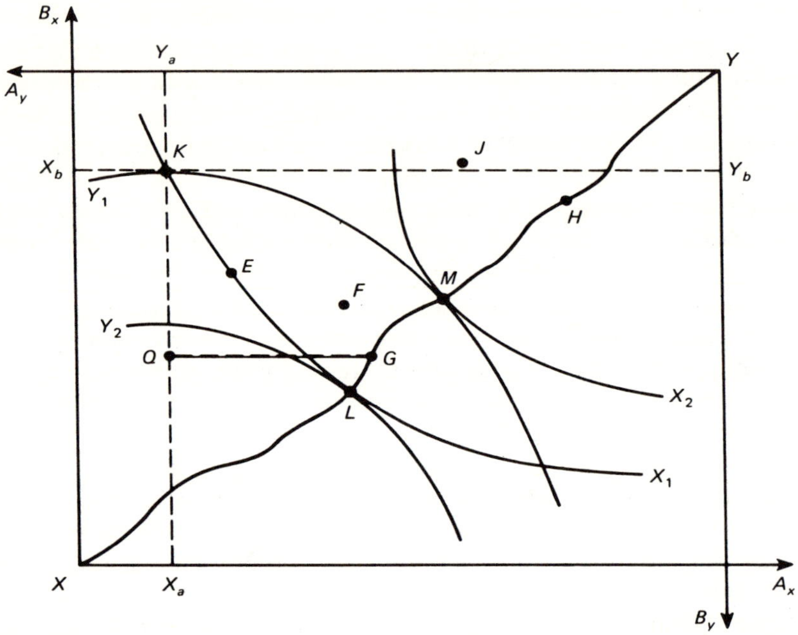

Figure 1.1 Pareto optimality.

When all of products A and B are distributed, any point within Figure 1.1 is associated with six pieces of information—the quantities of A and B consumed by each individual and each individual's welfare. Thus, at point K consumer X derives welfare level X_1 from x_a units of A and x_b units of B, while consumer Y obtains welfare level Y_1 from y_a units of A and y_b units of B. The sum of these individuals' consumption of A and B ($x_a + y_a$ and $x_b + y_b$) exhausts the available quantities. Point K is not a Pareto optimal situation for it is possible to redistribute the unchanged total amounts of A and B to make both persons better off or to make one person better off at no expense to the other: moving from K to either L or M makes one person better off while the other's welfare remains unchanged; moving from K to G makes both persons' welfare greater. A market transaction between X and Y where X exchanges KQ units of B for QG units of A would be a Pareto optimal action.

Points L and M are Pareto optimal and once obtained one person's welfare may be increased only at the expense of the other's. Starting with situation L, for example, it is possible to increase X's welfare only by decreasing Y's, for there is no higher X indifference curve that has a common point with Y_2. The infinity of points where the X and Y indifference curves are tangent is all Pareto optimal, and is geometrically shown as the curve $XLGMHY$, known as the contract curve. Thus, starting with situation K, any movement to or toward $XLGMHY$ that falls within the areas bounded by X_1 and Y_1 is a Pareto optimal action because one or both persons benefit while no person is adversely affected. A movement from K to H, however, is not a Pareto optimal action, for while situation H is itself optimal, its attainment, when starting from K, involves a welfare loss for Y. What is optimal in the Pareto sense is not necessarily acceptable in an equity sense. Optimal situation L, for instance, may give an inequitably large welfare to Y and an unacceptably small welfare to X. When the criterion of Pareto optimality is used, only allocative efficiency is implied and no judgment as to the distributive equity of such an outcome is made.

The welfare function in Equation (1.2) made one person's welfare a function of the welfare of others. While the two-dimensional geometry of Figure 1.1 does not permit its illustration directly, this interdependence of persons' welfare might lead Y, starting from an initial Pareto optimal distribution at L, to donate some of his A and B to X, moving the distribution to say, G. This move increases X's material welfare from A and B at the expense of Y's welfare from the two material goods. But if Y knows that this redistribution alleviates X's hunger, for example, then Y may be happier even though he has less food for himself. The fact that persons make voluntary contributions, in goods, money, or time, to private charities suggests that redistributive actions can be Pareto optimal.

Political participation. By participation in the nation's political life, at the local, state, or national levels, a person may also take welfare-increasing action. For many the act of participation itself, as a voter, party worker, or candidate for office, contributes to welfare. More important for our purposes, participation gives a voice in the formulation and implementation of public policies, for political parties and individual candidates espouse different policies, and one's vote, lobbying, or candidacy may help shape public policy. Welfare-maximizing citizens will want government economic action for several reasons. Some goods and services, including national defense and the control of communicable diseases, cannot be acquired by persons through individual market actions and must be collectively provided.[4] Other goods and services, such as education, libraries, medical care, and welfare programs, can be individually provided and, to one degree or another, are found in the private sector. But persons who cannot afford these as individuals or who believe that they may be had at less cost to themselves if collectively provided, will campaign for government action, and, if successful, the need for private provision is modified. In addition, some may feel that the welfare of others, and thus their own welfare, is increased when

---

[4] Collective provision does not require government action. Welfare-maximizing persons form private associations such as clubs, churches, and professional organizations that collectively provide goods and services to their members. Government action differs from the collective action of private associations since it makes participation compulsory; most public action is supported by the taxing authority of the state.

government affects the private provision of goods and services. Such attitudes underlie support of child labor laws, control of narcotics, and government guarantee or insurance of home mortgages.

The democratic process itself plays a role in determining the scope of public action. There are many types of government activity in which the majority may have little or no interest—conservation, museums, supersonic transports, and possibly the space program. All of these could be privately provided if individuals formed associations for their collective provision. Yet the public sector provides these. This is partially because of the impact of one person's welfare on another's—one may support conservation programs because others feel strongly. Equally important is the necessity for trading power, influence, and votes in a pluralistic society. The conservationist and the art lover know that they would never obtain their objectives without supporting each other's programs. Political leadership is even more important. In a democracy political leaders are responsive to the will of the electorate but, as leaders, they also influence that will and are instrumental in the molding of public opinion. This leadership is undoubtedly important in shaping public opinion to support programs such as space exploration, where individual perceptions of enhanced welfare are, at best, remote.

The concept of Pareto optimality can also be used to illustrate political participation. In the real world we know that public action is seldom, if ever, unanimously supported, and government economic activity is, therefore, not Pareto optimal. Seen within the framework of Figure 1.1, any action to shift from situation *K* to *E*, *F*, *G*, *L*, or *M* will receive the unanimous vote of *X* and *Y*. Such a political action is, in each case, Pareto optimal. The movement from *K* to *E*, *L*, or *M* allocates all the welfare gain to one person, and the nongainer, realizing this, might employ a strategy to block action until he also benefits. But even in this case there is some move from *K* that should be able to receive the unanimous consent of *X* and *Y* and result in a Pareto optimal government action. Alternatively, any move from *K* to either *J* or *H* will be supported by *X* but denounced by *Y*, and would never receive a majority.

Suppose that *X* and *Y* represent groups rather than individuals, and that there are more voters in group *X* than in group *Y*. In the absence of strategies, any move from *K* within the area bounded by X_1 and Y_1 will again receive unanimous support and be Pareto optimal. It is tempting to conclude that group *X* would employ strategies to move the selected action toward *M*. If a simple majority determines public action, when all members of group *X* vote identically, they need not be satisfied with *M* but may take *J* or *H* or even *Y*. Political activity may lead to actions that are not Pareto optimal.

We have considered individual actions to increase personal welfare. Can we similarly discuss those actions that will increase social welfare? Democratically supported actions need not be welfare increasing unless unanimously approved, and since government action seldom receives unanimous consent, some individuals do not benefit from them. An action that receives majority support guarantees only that those who are pleased with the action are more numerous than those who are displeased. Since no account is taken of the intensities of feelings there may be little meaning to the concept of a *social welfare function* analogous to the individual welfare function. Thus, we discuss public policy largely within the framework of personal welfare maximization and do not attempt to deal with a social welfare function.

EXPLICIT AND IMPLICIT POLICIES

Public economic policies may be of two types. First, and most important, is the *explicit economic policy* that occurs when government action is taken deliberately to affect allocation, distribution, or stability. The federal social security program is an explicit economic policy designed to affect the distribution of income. Alternatively, *implicit economic policy* occurs when government action taken for some other purpose has an allocative, distributive, or stabilization effect. Municipal construction of an airport may affect, as an implicit policy, the use of adjacent land. Discussion of public economic policy largely revolves around the formulation and implementation of explicit economic policies, and these are the principal subjects of this volume. Yet we must be aware of the implicit dimensions of public policy since they may be a factor in determining whether or not an action is taken.

Although we discuss allocation, distribution, and stabilization policies separately in the remainder of this chapter, they are not necessarily independent.[5] The allocation of resources in a market economy depends on the distribution of income and the ownership of productive factors; public action to equalize income distribution would probably reduce the demand for such luxuries as caviar and fur coats and increase the demand for beef and for cloth coats. At the same time, distribution policy will have an implicit impact on economic stability; broadly based social security and unemployment programs guarantee that personal income, and hence consumption spending, will fluctuate less than in their absence. The interdependence of the allocation, distribution, and stabilization dimensions of public economic policy will become more apparent as the discussion proceeds.

ALLOCATION POLICY

Governments adopt policies to change the mix of goods available to the private and public sectors, they adopt policies that change the ways that factors of production are combined to produce output, and they adopt policies

[5] *See* Richard A. Musgrave, *The Theory of Public Finance* (New York: McGraw-Hill, Inc., 1959) for a treatment of public finance which makes a fairly rigid division between these three types of public economic policy.

that change the terms (prices) on which goods and services and factors of production are exchanged. Such policies are *allocation policies.*

Consider first allocating the economy's output between the private and public sectors. This may be illustrated with a nation's production possibility curve as in Figure 1.2. On the vertical axis we measure goods and services

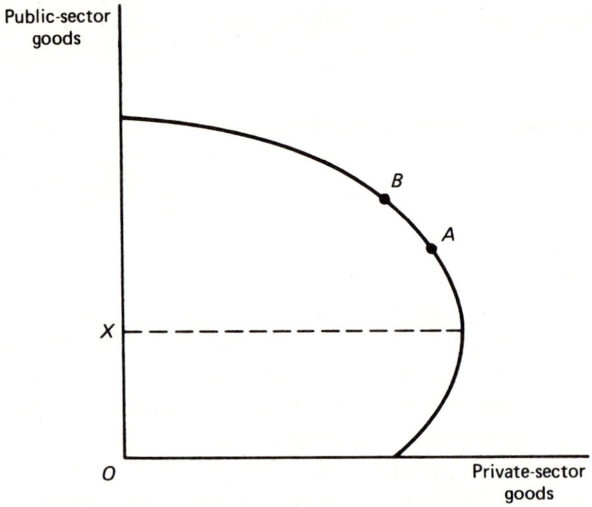

Figure 1.2 Production possibility curve.

produced for use by the public sector and on the horizontal axis, goods and services produced for private sector use. Some minimal level, OX, of public goods is needed to produce the maximum possible amount of private goods. Without, for example, a system of courts and some law enforcement, output of private goods would be less than the maximum possible. Only an anarchist would want to choose a mix of public and private goods that involved less than OX amount of public goods. In a fully employed economy, output is limited to points along the production possibilities curve, and the allocative decision is to decide between mixes such as A and B. Selection of B means larger amounts of such public goods as national defense, public libraries, education, and public health clinics than would be available at A. But to attain B the economy must divert resources from the production of private automobiles, housing, education, and medical care, and these also add to personal welfare. This decision depends, in part at least, on the type of allocation that occurs in the absence of public policy. If the medical profession privately provided adequate medical care to all, then public health services would make little or no contribution to welfare and would probably not be a public policy issue. If the intensities of desires for additional public goods exceed the intensity of desires for private goods, the political process will move public policy to the upper left along the production possibility frontier.

Next is the question of what goods to provide within these sectors. This is clearly not an independent question; the level of defense expenditure determines the share of output going to the government sector as well as allocation within that sector. Likewise, the level of private primary, secondary, and university education determines the public-private sector mix as well as allocation within the private sector. If we regard the mix between the sectors as fixed, we may examine the intrasectoral allocative policies. Within the public sector more hospital construction may be provided if resources are diverted from space exploration, highways, or defense. Welfare expenditures may be shifted among programs for the young, the disadvantaged, or the aged. Educational expenditures may be oriented toward preschool children, vocational education, or scientific training; public monies are fungible. Welfare-maximizing citizens, as influenced by their political leaders, support many government expenditures and oppose others. Because citizens cannot possibly vote on each and every public action, public officials have some latitude in determining the actual programs adopted; making this determination is a major allocative problem. Similarly public economic policy affects allocation within the private sector. Here public policy may easily encroach on personal freedom and the operation of the market mechanism. Public policy restricts production of products such as narcotics and pornography, limits consumption of alcoholic beverages and firearms, and encourages the production of watches by tariff protection, merchant ships by direct subsidy, and periodical literature by special mailing rates. In all these examples the self-interest of some is evident; the implications of the allocative policies for total welfare are frequently debated.

The economy's product mix is only part of the allocation question. Equally important is the choice of technology that determines how things are produced. Within the public sector national defense may be provided in a labor intensive manner by reliance on military personnel, or by capital intensive weapons systems such as intercontinental missiles, bombers, and spy-in-the-sky satellites. In an economy where defense expenditures absorb nearly ten percent of gross national product, the technological dimension of allocative policy assumes enormous importance. The number of persons in the armed forces significantly affects the size of the civilian labor force, and the production of military hardware limits the availability of private sector durables. Similarly, welfare programs may take the form of income supplements, payments in kind, or professional counseling of welfare recipients; education depends on teachers, buildings, and equipment. Public economic policy also has an effect on how goods are produced within the private sector. Welfare is believed to be increased by prohibitions on the use of child labor, the enforcement of labor's right to organize, maintenance of antitrust policies, and specification of minimum safety standards in mines and factories. Public policy in the 1960s altered the way automobiles were produced for safety reasons and, in the 1970s, should dictate even greater changes as environmental pollution is attacked.

Economic growth is an important dimension of allocation policy. The issue has emerged since the Depression and World War II and has been exacerbated by the ideological struggle between the Communist world and the West. Economic growth is usually associated with investment in fixed and human capital. Capital formation implies that some of the economy's current output is diverted from satisfying today's wants so that greater output may be obtained tomorrow; since welfare depends on current and expected future consumption of private and public goods, citizens are willing to make such sacrifices. Public economic policy can alter the allocation of resources between current consumption and capital formation and influence the type of capital formation that occurs. Some capital is formed within the public sector, such as the construction of highways and schools, but in the United States the dedication to market capitalism largely precludes public ownership of the means of production and government capital formation is thus limited. In most other Western countries, public ownership of capital is more extensive than in the United States; in socialist countries most capital is government owned.

Public economic policy is also concerned with the allocation of resources among nations. International agreements regarding rights to resource use have been developed because nations have found that their citizens' welfare from the seas and the air is enhanced by such agreements on use rights. Thus, fishing agreements have been negotiated, atomic explosions in the atmosphere have been outlawed, and nations usually permit the aircraft and communications of others to use their air space. In addition, nations have entered into international agreements regulating the production and marketing of basic commodities such as wheat, coffee, and sugar.

DISTRIBUTION POLICY

Factor payments equal to the value of marginal products determine the distribution of income in an economy organized solely on the basis of purely competitive markets. Governments adopt policies to alter the distribution of income dictated by market forces because the welfare of others enters into individual welfare functions. These attitudes toward the welfare of others are the basis for the equity dimension of public economic policy. No single, immutable concept of equity can be offered because these elements of individual welfare functions are changeable, hard to define, and must be translated through political processes into policy. In these processes divergent attitudes must either be reconciled or a majority position determined.

Political leadership is usually a major factor in both shaping the attitudes of individuals and translating them into policy guidelines. Any concept of equity involves two elements, the object, such as income, the distribution of which is in question, and the subjects or the groups of individuals among whom the distribution of the object is being considered. We can discuss equity in terms of these two elements even though we cannot specify with finality a single equity criterion.

Individual welfare cannot be taken as the object of equity because the welfare of individuals cannot be measured and compared. Typically, income is treated as the object of equity, and one talks about an equitable distribution of income. Various policies may be proposed to achieve a more equitable distribution of income. When considering a specific policy—an antipoverty program, for example—income must be carefully defined. Antipoverty policies might be aimed at reducing the number of families with incomes below a certain level. But problems such as adjusting that level for family size and age structure, adjusting for geographical differences in prices, and treatment of income in kind such as homegrown food and the value of owner occupied housing, must be faced. Closely allied to the specification of income as the object of equity is wealth as the object; one may speak of an equitable distribution of wealth. Here the problem of definition is even more difficult. If wealth is defined simply as the market value of assets, its distribution is different from wealth defined to include the present value of future labor income. In addition, the market value of many types of wealth, paintings and rare books, for example, is difficult to assess.

The incidence of taxes is another traditional object of equity. The terms progressive and regressive are used to denote the relationship between taxes paid by individuals and their incomes. Indeed the progressivity or regressivity of a tax system is one of the major ways political processes implement basic societal attitudes toward equity in the distribution of disposable income. The existence of rising marginal tax rates in the system of federal personal income taxes is evidence that the individual welfare functions that underlie the politics of writing tax laws support the use of taxation as a means of rendering the distribution of the after-tax income less unequal than the distribution of before-tax income. A progressive tax takes a larger fraction of higher than lower incomes. Individuals may support such taxes because they make an interpersonal utility comparison and conclude that an extra dollar yields less welfare to the man with a high income than it does to a man with a low income. Additionally, individuals may support progressive taxes because a reduction in the welfare of a man with a high income diminishes their own welfare less than a reduction in the welfare of a man with a low income.[6]

---

[6] *See* Walter J. Blum and Harry Kalven, Jr., *The Uneasy Case for Progressive Income*

Income, wealth, and taxes are traditional terms in which to discuss the concept of equity. Equally important in the study of public finance is the treatment of public goods as an object of equity. It would be a mistake, for example, to discuss the equity of a particular tax without considering the distribution of the benefits from the public goods being provided with the proceeds of the tax. The joint consideration of both taxes and expenditures may lead to a judgment that the implications of both result in a more or less equitable distribution than the effect of just the tax. Such government-provided goods and services as national defense are jointly consumed by all citizens.[7] But in many cases only some people benefit directly from a particular government program or the benefits are distributed unequally. In the context of public education we use the phrase "equality of educational opportunity" to express the equity goal in that area of public finance. But what does the phrase mean? Does it mean equal dollar expenditures for every pupil in a single school, a school district, a state, the whole nation? Or does equality of educational opportunity mean every child is guaranteed access to schools which meet certain minimum standards? Perhaps it means that groups of children having the same distribution of abilities should achieve the same level of educational performance even though the per pupil costs of bringing some groups (the disadvantaged) up to that level might well be greater than the costs for others. What does equality of educational opportunity mean in terms of the mentally retarded or the exceptionally bright? A great deal of debate over policy for public education is based on conflicting concepts of equity, or even failure to define a term such as equality of educational opportunity. No single definition will be agreed to by all precisely because the education of others affects the welfare of different individuals differently.

So far this discussion of equity has focused on the objects of distribution—income and wealth, taxes and public goods. Just as important to an understanding of this policy goal are the subjects of distribution—the groups of individuals whose income, wealth, taxes, and consumption of public goods are being considered. Individuals are considered in groups because policy actions affect groups and not single individuals, and because that is typically the way we think of the welfare of others influencing our own welfare. It is the welfare of the blind, of Indians, or of the poor that concerns us when we don't personally know the other individuals. Thus, in a discussion of

---

Taxation (Chicago: University of Chicago Press, 1953) for a consideration of the mixture of legal, economic, and ethical issues involved in progressive taxes.

7 We are speaking here of national defense *per se*, not the effects of defense purchases or manpower policies. Some regional economies, and hence the people living in those regions, may benefit more than others from defense contracts; some individuals and not others are drafted.

equity, we typically refer to the distribution of income (or wealth, or taxes, or public goods) among income classes, that is, among individuals grouped in accordance with the amount of their income. But this is by no means the only way to consider questions of equity. There are many other meaningful and useful ways individuals may be grouped, for example, a simple urban-rural distinction. Equity in the provision of public goods may require special action to overcome the high costs of maintaining some kinds of public services—roads, schools, libraries, hospitals, and postal services—in sparsely populated areas. Further examples of groupings are those of sex, race, and ethnic background. Legislation outlawing wage and salary differences based solely on sex is a clear manifestation of policy action directed toward equity. The civil rights movement has shifted the focus of policy debates away from the traditional groupings of individuals by income class to racial and other demographic groupings. Government manpower policies are now addressed to such problems as unemployment among young Negro men living in cities. These subject groupings as the focus of public policy are aimed at approaching interpersonal equity.

Individuals are often grouped geographically for the purpose of considering equity. Programs for the development of particular regions, such as Appalachia, may be supported on interregional equity grounds even though allocative issues may also be considered. A similar mix of allocation and equity considerations is involved in foreign aid where the subjects are grouped in geographic terms.

Demographic groupings by age deserve more detailed discussion because such groupings formulate issues in terms of intergenerational equity. A variety of government programs involve income redistribution from a younger, working generation to an older, retired generation. Existing tax laws give special advantages to those over the age of 65. Intergenerational equity was one of the factors responsible for the enactment of Medicare. Slightly different from age considerations are groupings by time—current and future generations. This type of intergenerational equity becomes a factor in evaluating public investment projects where benefits accrue for many years. Intergenerational equity is involved in taxing today's citizens in order to provide benefits for the newborn. Concepts of intergenerational equity are often appealed to when a local government proposes to finance capital expenditures through a bond issue. For example, if a high school is to be built today what portion of its costs ought to be shifted to future taxpayers, the parents of children who will be using that facility in the future? In many instances then intergenerational equity becomes one of the many factors influencing public economic policy even though this concept of equity often is not explicitly stated.

STABILIZATION POLICY

Stabilization policy does not evolve as directly from the welfare functions of individuals as allocation and distribution policies do. While individuals may clearly perceive the benefits of an allocative action such as building a rapid transit system in the city where they live, or the equity involved in increasing social security payments to the elderly, they may have difficulty seeing the relevance of tax rate changes designed to achieve economic stability. This difficulty can be traced to the relatively recent origin of stabilization policy and the more technical reasoning required to evaluate proposals specifically intended to achieve stability. Only since the 1930s has stabilization become an avowed aim of public policy, and only since the late 1950s has equilibrium in the balance of international payments joined aggregate employment and the price level as a concern of stabilization policy in the United States.

With as much as 25 percent of the labor force unemployed, the Depression convinced Americans that the federal government should adopt policies designed to maintain full employment. During the nineteenth century, individual cities adopted public works programs to relieve unemployment, and after the establishment of the Federal Reserve System in 1914, the federal government accepted increased responsibility for maintaining stability in financial markets. It was not until the catastrophic economic conditions of the 1930s that the federal government assumed responsibility for maintaining the aggregate level of employment. This responsibility was codified following World War II by the passage of the Employment Act of 1946.

Wartime demands on the economy had virtually eliminated unemployment, which had hovered around ten percent just prior to the war, but most economists expected a postwar depression such as the one following World War I. The Employment Act expressed Congressional concern and contained this broadly worded declaration of policy:

> The Congress declares that it is the continuing policy and responsibility of the Federal Government to use all practicable means consistent with its needs and obligations and other essential considerations of national policy, with the assistance and cooperation of industry, agriculture, labor, and State and local governments, to coordinate and utilize all its plans, functions, and resources for the purpose of creating and maintaining in a manner calculated to foster and promote free competitive enterprise and the general welfare, conditions under which there will be afforded useful employment opportunities, including self-employment, for those able, willing, and seeking to work, and to promote maximum employment, production, and purchasing power.

At times the goal of full employment has been expressed more explicitly. The *Economic Report of the President* submitted to Congress by President

John F. Kennedy in January 1962 viewed a "four percent unemployment rate as a temporary target" at a time when actual unemployment was about six percent.[8] Debate has raged over the definition of maximum employment. This dispute need not concern us here. What is abundantly clear is that modern governments do direct economic policies toward full employment.

The phrase "maximum production" in the Employment Act has never received much attention, and achieving stability in aggregate output is generally not listed as a policy goal but rather treated as part-and-parcel of achieving full employment. Although there is much truth in the common sense proposition that employment and production go hand-in-hand, the uses to which unemployed labor are put do have an impact on the additional production associated with increased employment. Employment, production, and welfare do not necessarily move together. Maximum employment and production must be defined within a sociological framework that defines labor force participation rates and the length of the work week. Employment (and production in the short run) could be increased by ending public schooling at age 12, and by providing day care centers for small children to permit, or possibly even require, more women to enter the labor force. Production could be increased by stretching the work week at the expense of leisure. The unemployed can be put to work raking leaves and building pyramids, manufacturing consumer goods, and constructing schools, or they can be conscripted. The results in terms of production would be different. This point illustrates the relationship between stabilization and allocation. The essence of stabilization policy is to put the economy on the production possibility frontier. Allocative considerations are involved in what types of goods and services are going to be produced with currently unemployed resources. Some answers to the allocative part of the question could result in full employment of labor but leave other factors of production—machines, for example—not fully utilized. We think it best to treat full employment of labor as the appropriate stabilization goal, and to consider the impact of employment policy on the output of goods and services as an allocative problem.

Price level stability was not explicitly enumerated as a policy goal by the Employment Act of 1946 though the phrase "maximum purchasing power" is sometimes interpreted in that manner. Individuals are concerned about particular prices—of the things they buy, of their assets, and of the factor services they control—more than about a general indicator of prices. The Consumer Price Index, for example, is based on the prices of a specific list of goods and services, and these prices are weighted in a prescribed manner. An individual's consumption would have to exactly mirror the spending pattern on which the Consumer Price Index is based, and there would have

[8] *Economic Report of the President, January, 1962* (Washington, D.C.: Government Printing Office, 1962), p. 8.

to be no change in the prices of the assets and factor services owned by that individual for the index to be a measure of the effect of price changes on his own welfare. Suppose the costs of medical care are rising very rapidly and exerting an upward pressure on the Consumer Price Index. The man who enjoys perfect health is unaffected except when his welfare depends on the welfare of the sick. This failure to translate changes in measures of the level of aggregate prices into perceived changes in individual welfare is likely to be typical when the rate of change in the aggregate price level is not very great. Individuals are also likely to have very dim perceptions of the effect of price level changes on the welfare of others; certainly the fact that another person is unemployed will be thought by an individual to have a much greater effect on the person's welfare, and hence on his own, than the knowledge that the prices of some of the things that a person buys have gone up. For these reasons we rank price stability below full employment as a policy goal. Only during periods of acute changes in aggregate prices, a ten percent increase in prices over two years, for example, is price level stability likely to become a major political concern.

Balance of payments equilibrium is the most abstruse of all stabilization goals. The issues involved are not widely understood and it is hard to imagine balance of payments equilibrium entering into many individual welfare functions. The issue is, rather, a concern of federal officials. There is danger that chronic disequilibrium in the United States balance of payments will threaten the international monetary system and the world trade that depends on its stability. Governments can affect the inflow and outflow of international payments in an attempt to bring these flows into an appropriate equilibrium relationship.

CONFLICTS AMONG PUBLIC ECONOMIC POLICIES

Any particular act of public economic policy is likely to conflict with other public economic policies. Measures taken to reallocate resources toward the production of some public goods may conflict with generally held attitudes toward equity in the distribution of income. When governments demand the labor services of those possessing skills that are in short supply, the incomes of these individuals will tend to rise relative to other incomes. At some point that rise might conflict with notions of equity. The initial effects of Medicare and Medicaid on the incomes of doctors is a case in point. Taxes imposed for stabilization reasons may affect the allocation of resources if they alter relative prices. In wartime, for example, taxes sufficiently high to release resources required for the war effort from alternative, civilian uses may reduce work incentives. This is the basic reason why, in the United States during World War II, personal income and other taxes were increased but not high enough to finance total wartime expenditures. Had taxes been significantly higher, defense workers might not have been willing to work longer hours. Rationing had to be used along with taxation to reduce civilian demands.

Conflicts among goals in the area of stabilization policy are an especially troublesome problem. Postwar experience indicates the great difficulty in achieving full employment and price level stability at the same time. Actions designed to reduce unemployment often tend to increase the aggregate price level. When confronted with a balance of payments problem a nation is not completely free to follow policies aimed at domestic stabilization. For balance of payments reasons a low interest rate policy could not be pursued in the United States during the early 1960s, even though such a policy would have been appropriate given domestic levels of unemployment.

2

THE MEANS OF PUBLIC ECONOMIC POLICY

A typical university's offering in the department of economics includes courses entitled "Government Regulation of Business," "Monetary Economics," "Public Finance," and "Planning." The subject matter of these courses overlaps because they all involve a substantial discussion of public economic policy. The majority of this chapter is devoted to a definition of public finance which is one means of public economic policy. The chapter concludes with brief discussions of regulatory policy, monetary policy, and planning, as alternative policy means.

PUBLIC FINANCE

To study public finance is to analyze the effect of government revenues and expenditures on allocation, distribution, and the stability of the economy. It is essential to emphasize that public finance entails the study of both government revenues and expenditures. Public finance texts have traditionally emphasized government revenues with many chapters devoted to different types of taxes, and sometimes a detailed analysis of tax legislation. Discussion of public revenues would then be followed by an analysis of fiscal policy and public debts; the fact that revenues were usually raised to finance expenditures was merely recognized. Historically, economists paid scant attention to public expenditure theory, perhaps reflecting the maxim that "the government which rules least rules best." Although undoubtedly an oversimplification, the prevalent attitude was that government expenditures were "unproductive" and the result of political exigencies, but had to be financed. Thus, the role of public revenues was to finance these "unproductive" expenditures in the least painful manner, and an extensive literature developed on the subject of tax and debt burdens. Since World War II economists have been increasingly concerned with analysis of public expenditures; their investigations have given rise to a theory of public goods, benefit-cost and cost-effectiveness analysis, and program budgeting. Modern treatments of public finance begin by seeing public expenditures in a productive light and treating public revenues as the means of financing productive expenditures. Reflecting this view, in the chapters that follow we deliberately omit use of the burden label in our discussion of public revenues.

Although they are clearly related, it is pedagogically convenient to divide the study of public finance into two major divisions: public expenditures and public revenues. Public expenditures and revenues by themselves are vehicles governments may use to pursue the allocative and distributive goals of public economic policy. Stabilization policy as a dimension of public finance is usually referred to as *fiscal policy* and is the combined impact of public expenditures and revenues on economic stability. This definition of fiscal policy is elaborated and refined following our discussion of the public expenditures and revenues. The public finance section of this chapter concludes with a brief introduction to debt management as a special case of public expenditures and revenues.

Public expenditures. Even the most casual observer is aware that modern governments make many expenditures that have a direct bearing on his life. Yet these expenditures are often seen within a framework that praises or damns government spending because of a political predilection on the part of the observer, and without complete understanding of their ramifications and the alternatives. How often do motorists bemoan inadequate highway facilities as they wait in evening rush hour traffic and then, when reading the evening newspaper, comment on excessive government spending? Visceral citizen responses to government expenditures are common. In this section we hope to begin rational analysis of government expenditures, not by presenting a reasoned argument for or against any particular type of expenditure, but rather by examining the different forms public expenditures may take. This task has utility for two reasons: (1) it points out that many types of government activities, often popularly thought to be quite different, are basically the same—expenditures, and (2) it examines the various forms expenditures may take and presents alternative courses of action to achieve a particular objective.

Government expenditures for goods and services are defined in national income accounts and input-output tables as a sector of final demand for the nation's gross national product. This category of public expenditures includes local government expenditures for education, state government expenditures for highways, and the salary of the President of the United States. These expenditures are alike in that they all absorb part of the nation's gross national product, but they differ in at least one important respect. Some of these, including the instruction (teacher salaries) component of local educational expenditures and the President's salary, represent *public production.* Others, including the building and supplies component of local educational expenditures, and the construction costs of a new highway, represent *public purchase* from private producers; output is produced within the private sector and sold to government. In some instances, such as the executive and judicial services of all levels of government and the conduct of foreign affairs, the very nature of government requires public production by government employees. Other activities, such as police and fire protection, primary and secondary education, and national defense, are usually produced by government but need not be. The enforcement of laws could be contracted to private police forces; citizens could hire fire protection. Public grants could be made to reimburse parents for tuition payments to private schools of their choice. Historically, national defense was sometimes purchased from mercenary armies rather than produced by government employees. The United States engaged mercenaries during the Vietnam war. Approximately 50 percent of all government purchases of goods and services in the United States, as recorded in national accounts, is compensation of government employees and represents public production.

In some instances public production might be wasteful of resources. For example, military aircraft that the federal government purchases from private aircraft companies could be produced by government employees in government arsenals. However, if publicly produced, private aircraft producers would not have the expertise to produce military aircraft, and private production could not readily be adapted to military needs during national emergencies. Thus, government arsenals would require the capacity to produce at peak wartime levels, and during peacetime there would be idle capacity. By the same token, private aircraft companies during wartime would have idle capacity since aircraft materials would be rationed. Under these conditions public production would duplicate resources. Competition among private producers should promote more efficient production and lower costs than if a government agency were a monopoly supplier.[1] Discussion of public expenditures for goods and services must, at some point, deal with whether public production or purchase is a desirable form for the expenditure to take. American preference for market capitalism limits public production.

Mixed provision is an alternative to either public production or public purchase. *Mixed enterprises*, such as the Communications Satellite Corporation (Comsat), the partnership between Boeing Aircraft and the federal government to develop supersonic, commercial aircraft, and the Federal National Mortgage Corporation, operate in the United States.[2] All these ventures are jointly undertaken by the federal government and private interests. In a less direct sense government and private industry are jointly engaged in production where there is *public ownership and private operation* of the means of production. An example is the nation's air space that is in the public domain. The federal government grants use rights to private broadcasters and airlines (commonly regarded as an aspect of regulatory policy). This practice differs from that in most Western countries where state-owned and -operated airlines, radio, and television have monopoly or near monopoly rights to air use. In the nineteenth century several European nations provided rail service with government ownership of the right-of-way, and private ownership and operation of the rolling stock. In the United States since the 1930s, states and municipalities have issued industrial development bonds to finance plants that are then leased to private industry. *Private ownership and public operation* is also possible. During World War I the federal government operated the railroads though they were still privately owned. Governments frequently lease office space and rent equipment from private owners (who are sometimes the close friends and relatives of government officials).

Transfer payments are an important expenditure of any modern govern-

---

[1] Economic efficiency sometimes plays a subsidiary role in government procurement. As a matter of interregional equity the federal government in the 1950s and 1960s attempted to assist the development of regions within the United States; support of a region's development might involve purchasing goods there that are less expensive elsewhere. For similar reasons state or local governments might buy from local manufacturers at prices above the minimum available. As a matter of national policy to promote balance in the United States international payments, the federal government has encouraged a "Buy America" campaign aimed at substituting domestic for imported goods. Finally, other dimensions of public policy may enter as a noncost consideration in government purchases; subsequent to passage of the Civil Rights Act of 1964 the federal government was committed to purchasing from firms that did not discriminate in employment practices.

[2] The precedent for mixed enterprises goes back to the eighteenth century. The Bank of the United States, established in 1791, was a combination of a private enterprise and a government agency. The second Bank of the United States, 1816–1836, was similarly organized.

ment. In the United States transfer payments to persons include social security benefits, various public welfare payments such as aid to families with dependent children and aid to the blind, and the pensions of retired government employees. Transfer payments do not absorb the economy's gross national product as the expenditures are made. Instead, they are received by households as a component of personal income enabling consumption expenditures or savings to exceed what they would have been in the absence of the payment. Transfer payments are also made between governments. The federal government, for instance, makes payments for highway construction to state governments, and state governments make payments in support of education to local governments. These intergovernmental transfer payments are known as *grants-in-aid.*

Governments also make *expenditures for real and financial assets.* Purchase of real assets is, in one sense, merely a special case of government spending on goods and services. It is particularly important if these are assets such as newly produced highways or office buildings, because such asset acquisition constitutes capital formation. Governments may acquire real assets for other reasons, such as the acquisition by the Department of Defense and the General Services Administration of stockpiles of critical materials as part of the nation's contingency defense planning. Governments also purchase financial assets. Several federal agencies purchase securities issued by the United States Treasury; the Social Security Administration invests its surpluses in United States government securities as does the federal government employee retirement fund. State and local governments often hold surplus funds in short-term federal government securities. The employee retirement funds of state and local governments purchase both public and private securities. *Government loans* are an important type of public expenditure. As the loan is made the lending government purchases financial assets as the borrower incurs a liability.

Tax expenditures became part of the lexicon of the economist toward the end of the 1960s. These expenditures—or more correctly, nonexpenditures—are made when a government does not collect tax monies because a household or firm has taken deduction or credit for an expenditure they have made, thus reducing their income tax liability. Rather than directly subsidize certain nonprofit organizations via transfer payments, a government permits citizens to make contributions that are tax deductible. The government in effect participates in the contribution by not raising revenue, thus reducing the out-of-pocket expense of the contribution to the donor. Income tax deductions could be eliminated; with an unchanged schedule of tax rates a government would then have greater receipts that could be utilized to make direct expenditures.

Public revenues. For governments to make disbursements they must first have receipts. Governments may raise revenues for other reasons, such as to dampen aggregate demand for stabilization purposes, but certainly the major role of public revenue is financing government expenditures. There are a number of different ways that revenues may be acquired.

Benjamin Franklin once quipped that the only certain things are death and taxes. Everyone in organized society pays taxes and these are certainly the primary source of any modern government's revenue. There are many different types of taxes—income, commodity, and property taxes to mention three important categories—and each type will affect citizen welfare differently. Taxes are levied usually without reference to the financing of any particular expenditure. Some government operations, however, are organized primarily to sell services directly to citizens. This is the case with the Tennessee Valley Authority, municipally owned water and electric departments, and toll bridges and highways. Furthermore, these operations are expected to be self-financing; when this is the case the operation is designated as a *public enterprise* and revenues are referred to as *user charges* rather than taxes. Profits earned by public enterprises are sometimes available as general government revenues. Tuition payments at state universities or admission charges to national parks are not considered to be user charges because these operations are not expected to be completely self-financing from *fees*.

Sale of real and financial assets also provides governments with revenue. When the General Services Administration sells materials from the national stockpile, the federal government receives revenue. Similarly, the sale of military bases by the Department of Defense, used automobiles by state governments, or obsolete school buildings by local governments, brings revenue to the public sector. The sale of public land was an important source of revenue for the federal government during much of the nineteenth century. The revenue received from the 1967 sale of Leonardo da Vinci's "Ginevra dei Benci" by the Prince of Liechtenstein to the National Gallery of Art, reportedly for five million dollars, was expected to finance Liechtenstein's government for several years. A government also receives revenue as its loans are repaid.

Sale of financial liabilities—bonds and other securities representing the government's indebtedness—are an additional source of public revenue. Since taxes are a compulsory levy whereas bonds are usually voluntarily purchased, these types of financing are fundamentally different. Lottery tickets are sometimes sold by governments to raise revenue; perhaps the most famous lottery is the Irish Sweepstakes. New Hampshire and New York inaugurated state lotteries in the 1960s to raise additional revenue.

The Constitution of the United States provides (Article 1, Section 8) that "The Congress shall have the power to lay and collect Taxes, . . . to borrow Money, . . . [and] To coin Money. . . ." The first two of these revenue powers have already been discussed; the same powers are also available to most state and local governments. The final power, to coin money, is limited to national governments. Historically, money creation, by debasing the coin of the realm, was a common means by which sovereigns raised revenue. In the 1970s the *Budget of the United States Government* still shows direct money creation as a source of revenue; the Treasury's profit that results from issuing coins whose money value exceeds their intrinsic metallic value is known as *seigniorage* and annually appears as a line entry in the *Budget*. In modern times governments also have more sophisticated means of money creation. When a government sells its securities to the central bank its receipts are in the form of new deposits at that bank. When disbursements are made out of these deposits the money supply is increased. In this respect money creation is a special case of the sale of government liabilities, but for analytical purposes the sale of securities to monetary authorities and sale to the public should be distinguished.

In the previous section grants-in-aid were cited as a transfer payment type expenditure made by some governments. These grants-in-aid are receipts of the receiving government. Governments also obtain receipts from a variety of miscellaneous sources: fines imposed by the courts; gifts and bequests made by a few citizens; and regulatory fees, such as those charged by licensing bureaus. The licensing of drivers and automobiles provides the states with substantial receipts. A unique receipt of the federal government is the deposit of earnings by the Federal Reserve System. The Federal Reserve System is not a government agency; most of its revenues are derived from the interest payments the Treasury makes on United States government securities it owns. Any excess of receipts over expenditures by the Federal Reserve System must, by law, be paid to the Treasury, which treats them as a miscellaneous receipt.

Fiscal policy. Public expenditures for goods and services, either as public production or public purchase, are a component of aggregate demand; changes in these expenditures will constitute a change in the economy's aggregate demand. Transfer payments are received by households as a part of personal income and are related to aggregate demand through household consumption functions. When governments raise revenue from sources other than money creation, funds are shifted from private to public use, and affect the private sector's ability to spend. We may tentatively conclude that making public expenditures increases aggregate demand, and raising public revenue reduces aggregate demand in amounts determined by the multiplier process. Depending on economic conditions existing in the economy, the combined impact of public expenditures and revenues will affect prices, employment, and, through the marginal propensity to import and changes in relative prices, the balance of international payments. Fiscal policy is this combined impact of public expenditures and revenues on economic stability.

Prior to the 1930s, governments generally did not explicitly consider the fiscal policy impact of their expenditures and revenues that primarily reflected allocative and distributive policies. Nevertheless, these revenues and expenditures had implications for economic stability and were an implicit fiscal policy. In a federal system, it is important to recognize that all levels of government are involved in implicit fiscal policy. In the United States we think of the federal government as the fiscal policy agent and not, for example, the state of Nebraska. Yet Nebraska and all of the approximately 80,000 other units of state and local government, as well as the federal government, make expenditures and raise revenue, and the implicit fiscal policy embodied in these expenditures and revenues must not be neglected.

Debt management. At the beginning of the 1970s the combined debts of the federal and all state and local governments amounted to approximately $500 billion. Changes in the size of the debt reflect decisions regarding the public revenues and expenditures. Debt management decisions affect the composition of public debts rather than their size. Suppose current government decisions with respect to expenditures and revenues entail no change in the size of outstanding government indebtedness. Nevertheless, some securities may mature and new securities must be issued to refund them. One dimension of debt management is the length of time to maturity of newly issued securities. Probably no government whose outstanding debt is of any consequence would like to have all securities mature at the same time. Debt management attempts to stagger maturity dates so that no overwhelming volume of securities will have to be refunded at any one time. Short-term interest rates are usually below long-term interest rates and, from the viewpoint of minimization of interest costs, this might suggest placing the public's debt in short-term securities. But short-term securities must be refunded more frequently than long-term issues and there may be offsetting advantages to a long-term placement. An increase in the size of the debt requires a decision regarding the timing of the issue, the yield offered, and its maturity date. Similarly, decreasing the size of the debt requires a management decision regarding which outstanding securities to call or purchase, or which maturing securities not to refund.

REGULATION

Regulation, as a means of public economic policy, affects allocation, distribution, and economic stability through government decree. Suppose the goal of public economic policy is to redirect consumer expenditures so that citizens will not purchase narcotics. Public finance would pursue this goal by the levy of excise taxes that make narcotic prices prohibitive. Regulatory policy, by contrast, makes it a crime to possess such products. To allocate resources to snow removal on sidewalks, a government might use its employees to shovel snow. Alternatively, regulatory policy would require property owners to keep their sidewalks clear. Federal antitrust legislation, decisions by the Federal Aviation Agency and the Interstate Commerce Commission regarding carriers' routes, municipal smoke control laws, and state and federal safety requirements for automobiles, are all instances of regulatory policies designed to affect the allocation of resources. Regulatory policy employs the authority of the state to require citizens to follow a course of action they probably would not otherwise take. Because citizens are required to act (or not to act) in a particular way, regulatory policy is a direct infringement of personal freedom.

Minimum wage legislation is a regulatory policy adopted in the pursuit of equity. By making wages different from what they would be under competitive market conditions, minimum wage legislation changes relative input prices and thus involves an implicit allocation policy. As an alternative to minimum wage legislation, public finance could be employed to accomplish the same goal; transfer payments equal to the difference between the market wage and the minimum wage could be made. Many other government regulations, such as mine safety and child labor laws, are a combination of allocation and distribution policies. Regulatory policies may also bear on economic stability. Wage and price controls may be adopted to prevent inflation. Variation in the required size of the down payment on homes financed with loans guaranteed by the Federal Housing Administration and the Veterans' Administration alter conditions in the construction industry, and through this, the macroeconomic stability of the economy. International commodity agreements have, as one of their goals, regulation of prices to stabilize the foreign exchange earnings of less developed nations. Quotas may be employed to promote balance in a nation's international payments and, thus, to contribute toward economic stability.

Regulation as a means of public economic policy dictates personal and business behavior and provides penalties for noncompliance. In some instances regulations may interfere with the more ultimate aims of society. Regulatory policy restricts personal freedom in the sense that it requires or prohibits certain behavior; the same objective might be pursued by making subsidies to encourage one type of behavior or, by the levy of taxes, to discourage another. Public finance, in this case, is more compatible with personal freedom than is regulation, because public finance encourages, by financial incentives, rather than prescribes. On the other hand, some regulatory policies may promote these ultimate aims better than public finance. In the area of safety standards for automobiles, for example, rather than have government produce and market safe automobiles, automobile safety regulations are promulgated. This leaves the means of production in private hands and permits consumer sovereignty subject only to the safety constraint. Similarly, antitrust legislation leaves the means of production in private hands and permits a maximum of personal freedom subject to certain limitations on business practices.

MONETARY POLICY

Monetary policy originates with the central bank and operates through the money supply, credit availability, and interest rates. It is a policy means available only to national governments. In the United States the Federal Reserve System is the monetary policy agent; the discussion of monetary policy in the remainder of this section assumes the institutional arrangements of the United States.

Some tools of monetary policy, such as reserve requirements for commercial banks, are similar to regulatory policy. They limit the ability of the commercial banking system to make loans and therefore affect the money supply. Other aspects are difficult to separate from public finance: When new issues of government securities are purchased by the Federal Reserve System this is a source of revenue for the Federal government, and a dimension of public finance. As the government spends these funds the money supply is affected and the entire transaction may be taken as a dimension of monetary policy. The Federal Reserve System aims at maintaining an orderly market for government securities and this sometimes requires open market transactions that are a vehicle for monetary policy. These similarities and connections with other means of policy need not concern us here. Instead we examine some techniques by which the Federal Reserve System may affect allocation, distribution, and stabilization as objects of economic policy.

The Federal Reserve System can affect the money supply and interest rates by altering member bank reserve requirements and by changing the discount rate. By making open market purchases and sales of government securities, the money supply and interest rates are also influenced. Policies that affect the interest rate bear on both allocation and stability. Interest rates are presumed to influence the decision to invest and to purchase those consumer durables that are bought on credit. Through this allocative effect on consumption and investment, monetary policy alters aggregate demand and hence has repercussions for economic stability. In the early 1960s the United States monetary authorities instituted "Operation Twist." This policy was designed to raise short-term rates relative to long-term rates in order to draw short-term capital to the United States, for balance of payments reasons, while keeping long-term interest rates low to encourage domestic investment. If the Federal Reserve System holds both long- and short-term securities in its portfolio, such an adjustment in relative interest rates could be accomplished by open market sale of short-term securities (driving down their price and increasing their yield) and purchase of long-term securities (increasing their price and reducing their yield). Since monetary policy may, in some respects at least, be considered as a substitute for fiscal policy, decisions must be made regarding which policy means is preferred.[3]

During the late 1960s debate was renewed over the relative efficacy of monetary and fiscal policy as tools of stabilization policy. Led by Professor Milton Friedman of the University of Chicago, a growing group of economists argued that, in Friedman's phrase, "money matters most"; the money supply should be increased via the policy action of the Federal Reserve System by a constant percentage each year, about equal to the rate of growth in real terms of gross national product. This prescription for long-run stability was offered as an alternative to the more widely held view that discretionary monetary policy, "leaning against the wind," and avowedly countercyclical fiscal policy are the appropriate means by which stabilization objectives can be achieved. Much of the debate hinges upon the time lags between policy actions and macroeconomic results. Those following Friedman's lead hold that the lags are relatively long, and by the time the effects of a policy action are felt they are no longer appropriate. Actions requiring Congressional approval are particularly likely to involve delay.[4]

Monetary policy also has an impact on economic equity. The monetary authorities probably do not adopt policies motivated primarily by equity considerations, but their allocation and stabilization policies have direct bearing, as implicit policies, on equity. A stabilization program that increases interest rates reduces aggregate demand in those sectors where spending is sensitive to interest rates. Thus, less residential housing will be constructed and fewer consumer durables such as automobiles will be purchased due to monetary policy, but the effect on, let us say, retail groceries, clothing, and entertainment may be negligible. Is it equitable for the stabilization program to bear more directly on the suppliers of factor services to one segment of the economy than another? Similarly, an easy money policy that leads to a reduction in interest rates and increased availability of loanable funds, whether it be primarily for allocative or stabilization purposes, provides the most direct benefit to those persons and firms deemed credit worthy by commercial banks and other financial institutions. Is this equitable?

---

[3] Myron H. Ross, "Operation Twist: A Mistaken Policy?" *Journal of Political Economy,* April 1966. Concerning the trade-off between monetary and fiscal policy for stabilization objectives, *see* Robert A. Mundell, "The Appropriate Use of Monetary and Fiscal Policy for Internal and External Stability," *International Monetary Fund Staff Papers,* March 1962. Mundell argues that monetary policy is the correct policy means to achieve balance in international payments, and that fiscal policy should be employed to achieve domestic stability.

[4] For a sample of the debate, *see* Milton Friedman and Walter W. Heller, *Monetary vs. Fiscal Policy* (New York: W. W. Norton and Company, Inc., 1969).

PLANNING

To plan means to have a conception of the future and to direct one's current actions toward achievement of that objective. Households make long-range plans for the education of children and the retirement of the breadwinner. Future expansion of plant and equipment requires businesses to plan. All governments plan and citizens expect them to do so: Once a public economic policy has been adopted it must be carried out; the implementation of the policy is planned. Planning itself is something we all do, yet in the United States, national economic planning is ordinarily not accepted as a means of public economic policy. It is regarded with suspicion by many.

In the United States one type of formal national economic planning does occur. This is associated with the federal government's contingency defense plans; if the need for general mobilization arises the allocation of resources for national defense has been preplanned. Planning was required for mobilization during two earlier world wars and, in view of the national emergency, was accepted by the citizenry. National emergency planning during World War II was in the hands of several federal agencies. The War Production Board set allocative guidelines to assure the necessary flow of materials to the war effort, and the Office of Price Administration controlled wages and prices, and rationed consumer goods. To plan for the possibility of mobilization, the Office of Emergency Preparedness regularly evaluates the economy's needs, potentials, and performance.[5] One example of this planning is government policy with respect to the national stockpile. The Strategic and Critical Materials Act of 1947 provides for the purchase and storage of materials—from such metals as lead, copper, and platinum to quartz, shellac, and goose down—that might be in short supply during a national emergency. The Office of Emergency Preparedness regularly reevaluates these needs and the federal government is a frequent purchaser and sometimes a seller of these products. In one respect, management of the national stockpile is nothing more than an instance of government purchase and sale of real assets. In another sense, however, it constitutes one dimension of a national economic plan. Emergency planning draws heavily on the technique of input-output analysis to predict requirements on particular industries under various conditions; if capacity is inadequate to meet these requirements the planners must find alternatives, such as holding materials in stockpiles, or encouraging production. The Defense Production Act of 1950, which permits payment of above market prices to some producers of selected minerals, is an instance of such

[5] The Office of Emergency Preparedness is also responsible for planning relief from such disasters as floods, tornadoes, and earthquakes. In 1969 the Nixon administration changed its name from the Office of Emergency Planning to the Office of Emergency Preparedness.

encouragement, as is the federal subsidy to the American Merchant Marine and the building of warships in American shipyards, although they might be constructed at lower cost elsewhere.

In a less formal sense the United States also engages in national economic planning. We typically do not regard our economy as planned, and in the rigid sense of a planned economy it certainly is not. Furthermore, public policy usually does not specify the required performance of any individual firm (except perhaps in the regulatory sense). But many of the acts of public economic policy that are widely accepted and are categorized as public finance, regulation, or monetary policy entail planning. Starting with a conception of how the economy ought to perform, these policies advance achievement of that norm. When the Council of Economic Advisors recommends an explicit fiscal policy to promote achievement of an estimated, full employment level of gross national product, this stabilization program must be regarded as national economic planning. In this instance the performance of the total economy is being managed although personal freedom, market capitalism, and federalism are maintained. In 1962 the Council of Economic Advisors promulgated *wage-price guideposts* that indicated to the private sector appropriate wage and price adjustments that, in view of productivity growth, would leave the aggregate price level unchanged. Although no statutory authority to enforce the guideposts was available, the federal government was able to bring substantial pressure in support of compliance. The guideposts were abandoned in 1966 because it was no longer reasonable to expect compliance given the general inflation that began about then, due primarily to increasing war expenditures.[6] The guideposts were designed to promote distributive equity and economic stability; had the federal government possessed the legal authority to enforce, the guideposts would have constituted an *incomes policy* similar in intention to those employed by several European governments.[7] The Johnson administration's "voluntary" balance of payments program to check capital outflows may be considered part of a national plan where the specific parties to international transactions were directed to comply voluntarily with the plan. Thus, there is some evidence that national economic planning is employed in the United States. In some instances, such as the wage-price guideposts and the voluntary balance of payments program, actions were taken that infringed on citizen freedom and market forces. In other instances, such

---

[6] For a discussion of these, *see* John Sheehan, *Wage-Price Guideposts* (Washington, D.C.: The Brookings Institution, 1967), and George P. Schultz and Robert Z. Aliber (eds.), *Guidelines, Informal Controls and the Market Place* (Chicago: University of Chicago Press, 1966).

[7] Andrew Shonfield, *Modern Capitalism: The Changing Balance of Public and Private Power* (New York: Oxford University Press, 1965). This discussion emphasizes the planning involved in modern capitalistic economics.

as the use of fiscal policy to obtain full employment, such departures from basic American principles are not required.

The American people experimented with another form of national economic planning during the Depression. The National Industrial Recovery Act called for each industry to establish a code of fair practices, specifying minimum prices and wages, setting production quotas for individual firms, and regulating competitive practices. It was an attempt to pull the economy out of the Depression based on the assumption that industry-wide cooperation would restore the level of employment. In the two years of operation under this act, the National Recovery Administration approved hundreds of codes proposed by trade associations and other industry groups; public support for the program was encouraged by using the blue eagle symbol to identify products produced and firms operating under these codes. In effect cartels were being formed in major industries with the consent and encouragement of federal policy. The Supreme Court held the act unconstitutional on the grounds that Congress could not delegate what were essentially legislative powers to an administrative agency. The New Deal then reversed direction and returned to a more traditional regulatory policy by vigorous enforcement of the antitrust laws. Those sections of the National Industrial Recovery Act that set labor standards—minimum wages and maximum hours—and dealt with labor unions were reenacted in the National Labor Standards Act and the Wagner Act.

At the other end of the planning spectrum is the planned economy. Typically the means of production are government owned, and producers, as government employees, take the course of action dictated by the planners. The national economic planners, in view of their information regarding capacities in various sectors, make the allocative decisions necessary to achieve their objectives. Perhaps the most important allocative decision made in a planned economy is the division of resources between consumption and investment, as this decision has important ramifications for economic growth. Citizens may be free to choose among those consumer goods marketed by government enterprises, at the government-dictated price, but consumer sovereignty that might require an allocation different from that envisioned by the plan is not permitted. For example, even if resources were available to produce the automobiles demanded by consumers, planning might not permit this allocation if the plan specifies that in the next decade subways and railroads will be the principal mode of travel. In extreme cases national economic planning may command citizens with respect to occupational choice and consumer purchases. By and large, however, planned economies, including the Soviet Union and its Eastern European allies, do not carry planning to this extreme. Rather, citizens are attracted to various occupations, as needed to fulfill plans, by incentive wages, or other rewards, and the consumer goods markets are cleared by adjusting prices so as to absorb, through free market choice, the mix of products that the planners have decided to offer.[8]

French planning, sometimes known as *indicative planning*, is an example of planning that is more formal than planning in the United States, but that continues to permit a large measure of personal freedom and market capitalism. The French plans, prepared under the direction of the *Commissariat au Plan*, have a grand design for the French economy; they specify, sector by sector, what is expected, although no firm is mentioned by name. The means of production in some industries are owned by government—electricity, coal, and railroads, for example—and in these sectors the plan may be readily implemented. For other industries government participation is less direct and the government may only suggest or indicate what is expected. However, because the government controls most credit facilities, building permits, and in some instances raw materials and the markets for products, it may make it very attractive or unattractive for business to engage in various types of economic activity; thus the government may encourage compliance with *Le Plan*. Subject to these limitations, however, the majority of the nation's means of production remain in private hands and French citizens and firms are perfectly free to cooperate or not; in this sense French planning does not infringe on personal freedom or market forces and basic allocative decisions remain in the private sector.[9]

A form of planning, similar in many ways to French indicative planning, has become increasingly popular in Western economies, including the United States, since World War II. This is urban and regional planning. Even in nations where there is no formal national economic plan, public policy has planned for urban renewal and development and for the total economic development of regions, especially depressed areas. In the United States in the 1950s and 1960s, urban planning became a widely accepted policy; urban planners attempt to work with community organizations in identifying total community needs and seek to promote balanced growth among such

---

[8] For a discussion of planned economies and the planning process, *see* Jan Tinbergen, *Central Planning* (New Haven: Yale University Press, 1964) and M. F. Millikan, *National Economic Planning* (New York: Columbia University Press, 1967). For a discussion of the Soviet economy, *see* Robert W. Campbell, *Soviet Economic Power,* 2d ed. (Boston: Houghton-Mifflin Company, 1966). On planning in Yugoslavia, *see* Snetozar Pejovich, *The Market-Planned Economy of Yugoslavia* (Minneapolis: University of Minnesota Press, 1966), and in China, *see* Jan S. Prybila, *The Political Economy of Communist China* (Scranton: International Textbook Company, 1970). On the modifications leading toward less rigid centralized planning in Soviet-type economies, *see* George R. Feivel (ed.), *New Currents in Soviet-Type Economies* (Scranton: International Textbook Company, 1968).

[9] P. Bahchet, *Economic Planning: The French Experience* (New York: Frederick A. Praeger, Inc., 1964).

sectors as transportation, housing, industry, and recreational facilities. To promote this end zoning ordinances are enacted, low interest rate loans are sometimes provided, and public construction is undertaken. New industries may be granted exemption from local taxes for a period of time. Similarly, American regional planners study the economic base of a region and identify sectors that have economic promise; the development of these sectors is encouraged through advertising and other promotional activities, by providing transportation facilities, and sometimes by securing financial backing for new or expanding firms. These efforts are much like French planning since they permit personal freedom and market forces to operate in most instances, but at the same time make, through market oriented incentives, implementation of the plan attractive.[10]

National economic planning is particularly important for less developed nations. The gap between rich and poor nations is widening and the latter feel the need to advance rapidly. For this to occur, careful attention to resource allocation is required, especially among alternative investment projects. The necessary financing must also be planned, particularly when capital is provided by foreign governments and international organizations. To qualify for aid or loans the developing nation must convince donors and lenders that assistance will be used productively; a national economic plan is often required as part of the evidence.[11] Such a requirement was made explicit for Latin American countries receiving aid under the Alliance for Progress.

---

[10] J. Brian McLoughlin, *Urban and Regional Planning: A Systems Approach* (New York: Frederick A. Praeger, Inc., 1969). *Also see* Walter Isard, *Methods of Regional Analysis* (Cambridge: Massachusetts Institute of Technology Press, 1960) for an introduction to the methodology of regional economic analysis.

[11] For a discussion of planning in underdeveloped nations, *see* Everett E. Hagen (ed.), *Planning Economic Development* (Homewood, Ill.: Richard D. Irwin, Inc., 1963) and Louis J. Walinsky, *The Planning and Execution of Economic Development* (New York: McGraw-Hill, Inc., 1963).

3

THE THEORY OF PUBLIC GOODS

Many goods and services, such as education, medical care, welfare programs, and the fine arts, are both publicly and privately provided. Although consumer sovereignty is usually the rule in a market economy, welfare-maximizing individuals sometimes support public provision of goods and services that could be marketed by private firms because they believe their own welfare or the welfare of others will thereby be enhanced. Goods and services that may be efficiently provided in the private sector but are provided by the public sector because of the normative belief that all should be able to benefit from them have been called *merit wants*.[1] Merit wants are deemed so desirable that they are provided publicly in order that consumption of these goods and services will not be limited by the distribution of income. In some instances laws stipulate that merit wants such as primary and secondary education, smallpox vaccinations, and fluoridated water must be consumed. Other merit wants are merely made

[1] Richard A. Musgrave, *The Theory of Public Finance* (New York: McGraw-Hill, Inc., 1959), chapter 1.

available, including most public health services, libraries, and museums. Notions of equity, historical precedents, and the politics of paternalism all explain why these goods are publicly provided.[2]

Certain products are deemed so undesirable by some citizens that their consumption has been prohibited, irrespective of consumers' welfare-maximizing wishes. These products we term *forbidden goods*. Perhaps the best example is narcotics that may be legally consumed only for medical purposes under the direction of a physician. Here society is taking action to alter the allocation of resources from what it would be under market conditions. A similar, but less extreme type of public action is the levy of taxes to discourage a product's consumption; such taxes are referred to as *sumptuary taxes*. It is sometimes argued that excise taxes on tobacco and alcoholic beverages are efficacious because they raise prices and discourage consumption, and those who defend this position regard these products as morally offensive or injurious to health. Protective tariffs are akin to sumptuary taxes; they are levied to alter the free market allocation of resources. The welfare-maximizing motivation of a segment of the population is obvious in these examples.

Merit wants, forbidden goods, and sumptuary taxes encompass many products, and there is little doubt that public policy toward these products affects welfare. Hence, these policies are often the subject of heated public debate—for example the controversies over fluoridated water and cigarettes—and whatever public policy is adopted is clearly not Pareto optimal. In fact, in many cases the policies are explicitly intended not to improve the efficiency of the allocative process because allocative efficiency is incompatible with welfare objectives. How then can economic analysis illuminate the rationale of government expenditures? We now turn to the main topic of this chapter—a discussion of pure public goods and externalities where, strictly by the criterion of economic efficiency, a positive case for government provision of goods and services can be made.

PURE PUBLIC GOODS

The production and use of various goods and services affect members of society differently. If an apple is purchased and consumed, the market transaction is mutually satisfactory to both the buyer and seller and is Pareto optimal; aside from making the apple and the resources used in its production

[2] The arts are a particularly interesting example. In the United States it is not uncommon for art galleries to be publicly supported while the performing arts, typically, are privately financed. For a discussion of the economics of the performing arts, *see* William J. Baumol and William G. Bowen, *Performing Arts—The Economic Dilemma* (New York: Twentieth Century Fund, 1966) and Thomas Gale Moore, *The Economics of the American Theater* (Durham: Duke University Press, 1968).

unavailable, the transaction has no effect on others. Most market transactions are like this, and a traded product that becomes unavailable to others is defined as a *pure private good*.[3] An alternative type of product is mosquito control. Mosquito control entails reducing the probability of mosquito bites from, let us say, 0.7 to 0.1 per hour during the month of August. If a citizen drains or sprays the mosquito breeding areas in the vicinity of his residence his welfare is increased as he consumes the reduced probability of mosquito bites. However, his neighbors' welfare is also increased, for their probability of being bitten is also reduced, and by the same amount. Mosquito control is an example of a product that is jointly consumed in equal amounts by more than one person. This type of product is called a *pure public good*. To say that persons consume pure public goods in equal amounts does not imply that they assign equal values to the product. What is meant is that when a product is jointly consumed, consumption by one person does not alter the availability of the product to another person. This contrasts sharply to the pure private good where consumption by one made the product unavailable for consumption by another.

Pure public goods are not subject to the *exclusion principle*; it is impossible to prevent their consumption by many while permitting their consumption by some. Thus, mosquito control is not only jointly consumed by many persons in equal amounts, it is impossible to exclude persons in the control area from consuming this product. A number of products, such as beaches, concerts, plays, and athletic events, may be jointly consumed, up to the point where congestion becomes a problem, and in this sense they are pure public goods. However, exclusion is possible and they are privately provided although they are sometimes found in the public sector as merit wants. Radio and television programming is also jointly consumed although scramblers or cables may yet be technologically and economically feasible so that radio and television reception may be made subject to exclusion and marketed. In the United States radio and television are in the private sector, despite the publicness of the product, because programming is jointly produced with advertising that covers all costs.

Examples of pure public goods are difficult to find. Perhaps the most commonly used example is national defense.[4] The electorate may differ as to

---

[3] Pure private goods may be publicly provided; most of the services of public enterprises are pure private goods.

[4] Mosquito control was used as the example to introduce the concept of pure public goods because, at least on a localized basis, a single citizen may derive so much utility from the product that he will privately cover its entire cost; thus without any collective action whatsoever, mosquito control might be provided. In the case of national defense, at least in the nuclear age, single-person action is unlikely because the cost of nuclear weapons is greater than any individual could possibly bear. For a discussion of public goods individually and collectively provided, *see* Mancur Olson, Jr., *The Logic of Collective Action* (Cambridge: Harvard University Press, 1965). For a discussion of mosquito control, *see* Gordon Tulloch, "Problems in the Theory of Public Choice:

the desired level of defense expenditures but once national defense is provided it is consumed in equal amounts by all. Defense is clearly not subject to the exclusion principle: It is not feasible to deploy antiballistic missiles to protect only part of a city. Another example of a pure public good is the police protection of persons on the streets. In the absence of any obvious way of distinguishing pedestrians to be protected from those not to be protected, the services of the local police are equally available to all.[5] Police and fire protection of property are frequently cited as examples of pure public goods, but here the issue is less clear. It is conceivable that property could be marked to indicate whether or not that property is excluded from protection. This, in fact, was done in the eighteenth and nineteenth centuries when private fire companies sold their services and issued plaques to identify protected property. Property is often protected by private security forces.

Other candidates for pure public goods are municipal streets, sidewalks, and parks. These are unacceptable for several reasons. First, streets, sidewalks, and parks conceivably could be made subject to the exclusion principle. Turnstiles might be erected and toll booths set up at street intersections, as is done on limited-access, toll highways. However the nuisance and real costs of such controls suggest that exclusion for nonpayment is administratively absurd, although technically possible. This is an instance where marketing costs are so high that nonmarket means for providing the product are usually found. Second, a further problem arises in the case of sidewalks, streets, and parks because use of these facilities may affect the ability of others to derive welfare from them. On the one hand, their use enhances safety, thus increasing the welfare of other users. On the other hand, use may cause congestion which decreases other users' welfare. Although streets, sidewalks, and parks are jointly available to all, one's welfare from these facilities is not independent of their utilization by others, as was the case with personal police protection, mosquito control, and national defense. Finally, while jointly available, streets, sidewalks, and parks may not be utilized by all. Thus, there are dimensions to such municipal services that make them dubious candidates as pure public goods, although they do exhibit many public good characteristics and are treated as such.

Demand for public goods. Having defined pure public goods our next task is to investigate their provision. We first consider pure private goods and then pure public goods in contrast.

Social Cost, and Governmental Action," *American Economic Review,* May 1969. *See also,* Harold Demsetz, "Private Production of Public Goods," *Journal of Law and Economics,* October 1970.

[5] The black community might disagree since skin color does provide a means of dividing the population.

Market demand is the summation of individual demands. Two individuals' demand curves, d_1 and d_2 are shown in Figure 3.1. Suppose, first, that these individuals are buying a pure private good. If the community consisted of only these two persons the market demand curve, $D_{\Sigma Q}$, would be the horizontal summation of their demands; at $10 per unit 15 units are demanded.[6] The market supply curve is the horizontal summation of the marginal cost schedules of producers when the market is competitively organized. With supply curve, S, the equilibrium price is $10 per unit and the first consumer buys five units while the second consumer buys ten. The benefits from consumption accrue solely to the buyers whose marginal valuations are reflected along the market demand curve.

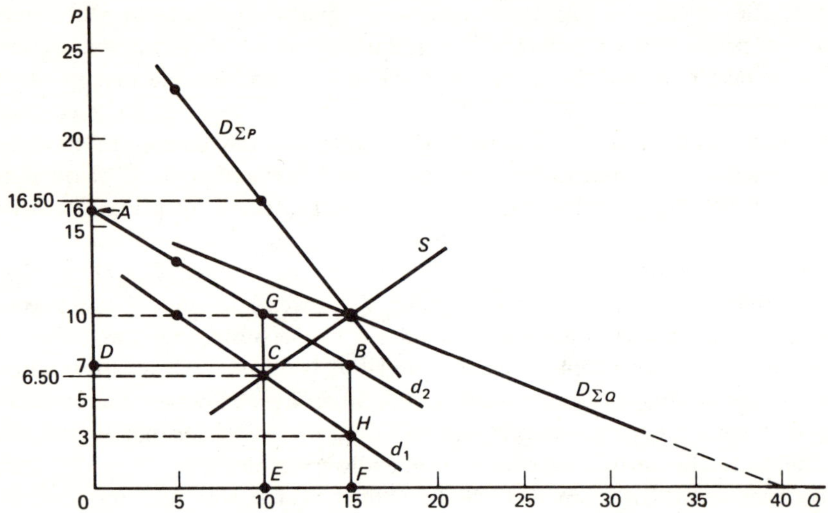

Figure 3.1 Individual and market demands for private and public goods.

Assuming perfect competition, the value of factors in alternative uses determines their prices; marginal cost equals the value society places on inputs in alternative uses. When competitively organized markets are in equilibrium the price paid by consumers, which is their marginal valuation of the product, is equal to the marginal factor costs of production. This competitive market allocation is Pareto optimal. In the example of the

[6] Simple addition of individual demands to obtain market demand requires that individual tastes be independent of one another. For the discussion of this section we make this assumption despite our including the welfare of others in the individual welfare functions as in Equation (1.2).

previous paragraph, \$10 represents the marginal valuation of consumers and is also the marginal cost of the factors used in production when 15 units are produced. If marginal valuation by consumers exceeds marginal production cost, as when less than 15 units are produced, there is a divergence between what buyers are willing to pay for additional factor services and what sellers must receive to induce them to supply those factor services. As long as this divergence exists increasing the quantity traded is Pareto optimal, because either buyers or sellers or both benefit. Competition expands the quantity traded until an equilibrium is reached where the equality of marginal valuations and costs permits no further Pareto optimal transactions.[7]

Before examining the demand for a pure public good consider the pricing of a product whose marginal cost is zero. This might be sidewalks, streets, or parks; as long as congestion does not develop, once a sidewalk is built the cost of an additional pedestrian's use is the wear and tear on the pavement which essentially equals zero. In the context of Figure 3.1, since marginal cost is zero, the optimal price and quantity are determined by the intersection of the demand curve with the horizontal axis. Only at this equilibrium is the marginal value of the product to consumers equal to marginal cost of production, giving a Pareto optimal allocation of resources. The difficulty with pricing in this manner is that while marginal costs are zero the service is not free because there are fixed costs; streets, sidewalks, and parks are costly despite the fact that the marginal cost of their use is zero. Optimal pricing will not cover fixed costs and profit-maximizing private producers may not provide these goods and services in optimal quantities. It may be necessary for governments to provide such goods.

An objection to pricing at marginal cost equal to zero is that information is lost about preferences for the zero-priced good. As is explained shortly, persons will understate their valuation for pure public goods if they will be charged on the basis of the valuations they reveal. Knowing that they can have unrestricted use of a bridge once it is built, they will not declare their valuation of it if they are to be charged accordingly. Zero pricing of the bridge, although optimal, thus gives no information about its social value. This may be suitable if no additional facilities are contemplated, but if an additional bridge is being considered how should the decision be made?

There are instances where optimal allocation, in the face of zero marginal cost, probably occurs through private provision. Take the case of a private golf, tennis, or swimming club. Fixed costs are incurred as the recreational facility is constructed, but once available the marginal cost of an additional unit of use is negligible. Clubs typically make a lump-sum

[7] The amount of benefit going to buyers and sellers as the Pareto optimal marketing of products occurs is known as consumers' and producers' surplus, respectively. For an elaboration of this welfare criterion, *see* James E. Meade, *Trade and Welfare* (London: Oxford University Press, 1955).

dues assessment on their members and do not make a charge each time the club's facilities are used. Essentially the same means of pricing is used when the public sector provides recreational facilities. The difference is that the taxing authority of the state requires each taxpayer to defer part of the fixed costs even when the taxpayer perceives no particular benefit. With private provision citizens defer the fixed costs of those facilities from which they receive benefits; when the benefits do not justify the costs, facilities are not provided. Local telephone service is another instance where the private sector makes lump sum charges to defer fixed costs and then sets a marginal cost price equal to zero.

Now consider the demand for a pure public good. The demand curve d_1, in Figure 3.1, shows that the first consumer will pay—and here we could substitute "be taxed" for "pay"—$10 for each of 5 units, $6.50 for each of 10 units, and $3 for each of 15 units. The curve d_2 shows that the second consumer will pay $13 for each of 5 units, $10 for each of 10 units, and $7 for each of 15 units. Thus, if 10 units were provided, the first consumer would be willing to pay $6.50 for each of the 10 units, and together they would be willing to pay $16.50 since the product is jointly consumed. In the case of pure public goods the market demand curve, $D_{\Sigma p}$, is the vertical summation of individual demands: at a market price of $10 per unit, 15 units are demanded with the prices paid by each consumer being $3 and $7 per unit respectively.[8] Given the market supply curve S the equilibrium price and quantity is $10 for each of 15 units. Each consumer takes the full 15 units and makes a payment as determined by his own marginal valuation. At this equilibrium the marginal value of the product to society is equal to marginal cost, but each citizen receives products whose marginal cost exceeds his marginal valuation.

It may seem surprising that citizens who consume equal amounts of a product will each make different payments. In the private sector this does occur, as illustrated by private support of educational (noncommercial) television. Once aired television is jointly consumed by all within range of the station and no one can be excluded. Thus, all members of the community take the same amount of the service but some pay larger amounts than others; a few make large contributions, others make token contributions, and many viewers make no contribution.

Conceptually, optimal quantities of public goods may be determined as in Figure 3.1. However, this analysis requires that all consumers voluntarily reveal their true preferences and make the appropriate payments. In the

---

[8] This approach to the aggregate demand for public goods is discussed by Howard Bowen, *Toward Social Economy* (New York: Holt, Rinehart and Winston, 1948), chapter 18. For a fuller discussion of consumer equilibrium with public goods, *see* James M. Buchanan, *The Demand and Supply of Public Goods* (Chicago: Rand McNally and Co., 1968).

case of private goods, such as an apple, this must be the case: if apples cost $10 each, a consumer must pay this price or go without. In the case of pure public goods this is not true because, by definition, consumption by any one person requires consumption in equal amounts by all. This fact means that if individuals are charged (taxed) their marginal value for public goods they have an incentive to understate their valuation in order to reduce their share of the costs. At the same time, public goods will be available to them since, once provided, no one may be excluded from consumption. Suppose the second consumer in Figure 3.1 failed to reveal his preferences and only the first consumer's demands were considered. In this case 10 units would be provided at $6.50 per unit; the full cost falls on the first consumer either as he makes market purchases or is taxed in accordance with his marginal valuations. But once provided these 10 units are also available to the second consumer. The total value to him of these 10 units is the area *AGEO* under his demand curve; since he incurs no cost, this area represents his consumer's surplus. When the second consumer does reveal his preferences the value of the public good to him is the area *ABFO* and his cost is given by the area of the rectangle *DBFO*; his consumer's surplus is *ABD*. Thus, by not revealing his preferences the second consumer loses *GBC* in consumer's surplus and obtains *DCEO* in exchange. Whenever such an exchange increases his consumer's surplus, the rational consumer will understate his preferences for public goods. If the community is sufficiently large, each member, if rational, would deny any demand for public goods.[9] Thus, whenever citizens will be charged or taxed an amount equal to their true marginal valuations, the demand for public goods will be understated. This understatement stems from the collective consumption of each unit, once provided.

When the number of persons consuming public goods is large an analogy may be drawn between the provision of public goods and the behavior of a perfectly competitive market for private goods. In the perfectly competitive private market the number of buyers and sellers is so large that the action of one is inconsequential to the entire market. Since no seller can exert any influence on market price, rationality dictates that the profit-maximizing seller expand sales up to the point where marginal cost is equal to price (marginal revenue). However, the collective action of all sellers may so increase supply that market price falls and if market demand is inelastic the total revenue of the industry will decrease. In this event the group of sellers is collectively irrational although the behavior of each is rational by the profit-maximizing criterion.

The demanders of public goods are in much the same position. If one of many individuals fails to reveal his preferences there is no perceptible

---

[9] The size of the group is very important to the revelation of preferences. *See* Olson, *op. cit.*, pp. 53–65.

effect on total demand, and the total quantity available to the individual who withheld his preferences is unaffected; he is now in a position to consume these goods without cost to himself. An illustration of the problem may be taken from the tale of the king who asked each of his subjects to contribute one quart of wine to a community vat from which all might partake at his daughter's wedding feast. Since the king had many subjects, each reasoned that his quart was inconsequential and contributed water instead of wine. And on the wedding day all expected wine but drank water.

In some instances, perhaps in the case of mosquito control, one individual may derive so much welfare from a public good that he will individually provide some. This might be the case of the first individual purchasing 10 units at $6.50 per unit as in Figure 3.1. Here we clearly have suboptimal allocation of resources for the marginal value to society is $16.50 which exceeds marginal cost. But at least some of the good is provided. Suppose, however, that d_1 is a total demand curve for 100 type-one individuals, each willing to pay 6.5 cents per unit for each of 10 units. Further suppose that each individual's demand curve lies entirely below the supply curve so that in the absence of collective action none of the product is provided because each individual's marginal valuation—even for the first unit—is less than the marginal cost of production. This would be the case with defensive radar systems. Now none of the product—not even suboptimal quantities—will be provided by individual action and collective action is thus required. However, since the product is not subject to the exclusion principle individuals have an incentive to understate the product's value and provision of this public good then requires collective action perhaps enforced by the authority of the state. Solely by the criterion of economic efficiency a case may be made for government action to allocate resources to the production of public goods to enhance citizen welfare. Faced with public goods, the "government which rules least rules best" is an incorrect proposition because competitive market forces cannot adequately allocate society's scarce resources. That a positive case may be made for government action does not specify what form that action should take, nor does it guarantee that government will do a better allocative job and increase welfare. Government, for example, will have the same difficulty obtaining allocative information as does the market.

EXTERNALITIES

In the previous section we discussed the provision and use of pure public and private goods, such as mosquito control and apples. Now consider two additional products, the services of a rock band and a tuberculosis examination. If a person engages a rock band to perform at his garden party the transaction is Pareto optimal to both the buyer and seller and, in this respect, is like the sale of apples. But this transaction gives rise to *externalities* if the music can be heard by others.[10] If a neighbor enjoys the music, he derives welfare at no cost to himself; this type of externality is known as a *third party benefit,* the first two parties being the participants in the transaction itself. Alternatively, if a neighbor dislikes the music he bears a cost, known as a *social cost,* for which he is not compensated and which reduces his welfare. The band's services thus involve externalities which are not marketed.[11]

Chest x-rays or Mantoux tests illustrate another type of transaction. Both detect the presence of tuberculosis, a disease which, if detected in its infancy, can usually be contained, permitting the carrier to live a full and normal life. Since tuberculosis cannot be prevented by inoculation, individuals derive clear benefits from periodic examinations. Tuberculosis is communicable; one citizen's periodic examination also benefits others since detection will lead to the carrier's isolation until the disease is contained, thereby reducing the probability of others being infected. These third party benefits are impossible to market.

Externalities associated with detection and treatment of communicable diseases have a number of interesting economic properties. The case of tuberculosis is used because, since inoculations are not available, no individual may by himself take the necessary action to guarantee that he will not contract the disease. This is not the case with polio or smallpox, for example, where vaccines are available that guarantee immunity to a vaccinated person. For these diseases the individual receiving medical treatment has less reason (except as a merit want) to be concerned with the medical treatment received by others, although third party benefits are also available to the unvaccinated person. In the control of communicable disease once a substantial percent of the population—but clearly less than 100 percent—has been vaccinated, the disease virtually disappears because the number of potential carriers is small. Thus, public health programs to administer polio vaccine in the 1960s made little effort to vaccinate the entire population; once most citizens had been vaccinated the benefits of additional vaccina-

---

[10] Other terms for the externality phenomena (as opposed to "internalities" that are exchanged in the market place) are "interdependencies," "spillovers," "side effects," "social costs," and "third party benefits." For additional discussion of goods exhibiting these properties, *see* Roland N. McKean, *Public Spending* (New York: McGraw-Hill Inc., 1968), especially chapter 5. *See also,* E. J. Mishan, "The Postwar Literature on Externalities: An Interpretative Essay," *Journal of Economic Literature,* March 1971.

[11] Externalities affect the distribution of real income. A person's real income is clearly increased if he is permitted freely to consume third party benefits, and his real income is decreased if social costs are not compensated for. Some externalities are, in fact, marketed: A person may buy a scenic easement across his neighbor's property. When externalities are marketed—that is, when they are internalized by purchase or sale—no adjustments in the allocation of resources are necessary.

tions did not justify the costs of a door-to-door canvass. Yet the success of the polio program is apparent since the disease has all but disappeared from the United States; those who are unvaccinated derive benefit from the fact that others are.

Optimal provision of goods and services in the presence of externalities can now be examined. First consider the rock band's services. Disregarding externalities, the price and quantity for musicians' services would be determined as in Figure 3.2 with price P_1 and quantity Q_1. At this equilibrium

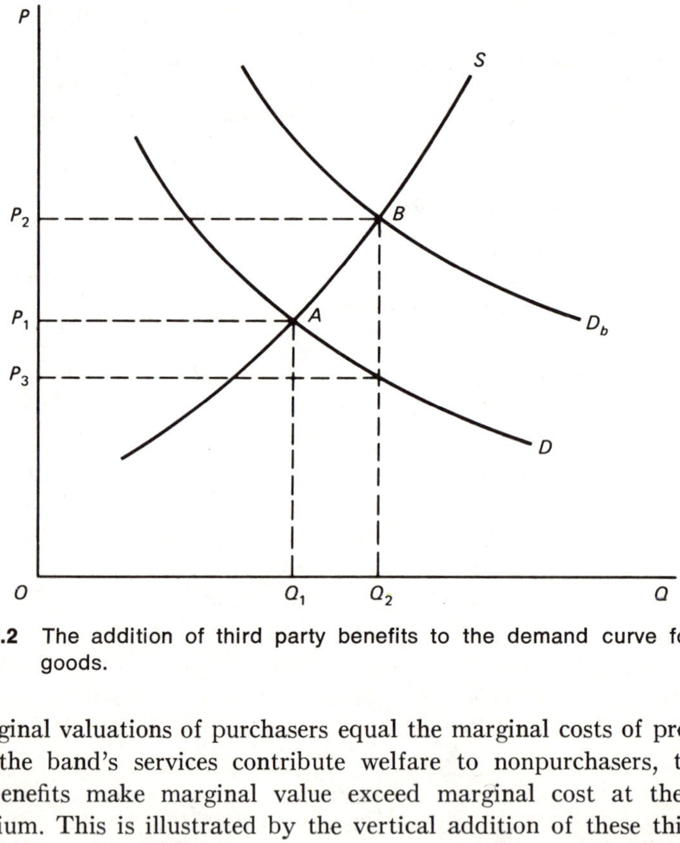

Figure 3.2 The addition of third party benefits to the demand curve for private goods.

the marginal valuations of purchasers equal the marginal costs of production. But if the band's services contribute welfare to nonpurchasers, the third party benefits make marginal value exceed marginal cost at the market equilibrium. This is illustrated by the vertical addition of these third party benefits to the market demand curve, D, to give the demand curve, D_b. The third party benefits are vertically added to obtain D_b since they reflect a pure public good characteristic of this basically private good. Thus, the market underprovides musicians' services and results in a misallocation of resources. The ideal allocation of resources would be determined by the equilibrium B, where D_b and S intersect. Here quantity Q_2 would be purchased at price P_2. Each private purchaser would pay P_3 per unit and the difference between market price and the purchasers' price, $P_2 - P_3$, would be paid (or publicly subsidized) by benefitting third parties in accordance with each one's marginal benefit.

Suppose, alternatively, that rock music annoys nonpurchasers. Their disutility is essentially a cost of providing this service, but this is a nonfactor cost and is not reflected in the market supply curve. At the market equilibrium *A* illustrated in Figure 3.3, marginal cost exceeds benefits by the

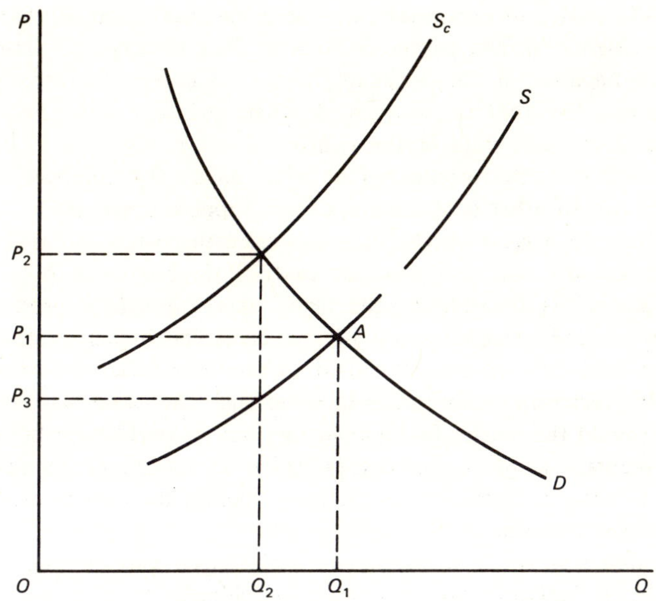

Figure 3.3 The addition of social costs to the supply curve for private goods.

amount of these social costs. These social costs must be vertically added to the factor-cost supply curve, *S*, to give the supply curve S_c that reflects all the costs involved in the production of this service.[12] Thus, at equilibrium *A* this service is overprovided; optimal resource allocation requires reducing output to Q_2 and increasing price to P_2. The price, P_2, paid by consumers would be paid only partially to producers; musicians would receive price P_3 and the difference, $P_2 - P_3$, would be paid to those who incur disutility due to unwanted consumption of rock band services.

The argument of the preceding paragraph is not as straightforward as it appears at first sight. In cases where externalities are injurious to third

[12] Social costs may be more tangible than the psychological costs of the annoyance caused by loud music, low flying aircraft, or foul odors. Air pollution can result in increased laundry or medical bills, and water pollution increases the factor cost of potable water. These costs, if fully accounted for, may be seen as the costs of additional inputs involved in the production of the polluting good or service.

parties, preventing the social cost is injurious too: If *A*'s actions harm *B*, then preventing *A*'s actions, while beneficial to *B*, is harmful to *A*. At issue here is personal freedom, for as *A*'s actions infringe on *B*'s freedom, preventing *A*'s action restricts *A*'s freedom. There are no clear solutions to this problem. Littering, for example, is socially unacceptable; it is also prohibited by law, although enforcement is costly and rare. Persons are permitted to own and keep dogs although many localities have leash laws designed to maintain the personal freedom of nonowners. At the same time, local ordinances may not permit citizens to own pet lions because their ownership is seen as too great an infringement on the personal freedom of others. In many instances individuals who feel that the actions of others infringe upon their freedom are able to bring civil suits in the courts.[13]

Externalities in the production of some goods and services may alter the resource cost of other goods and services. Suppose upstream firms deposit waste products in a river so that the downstream cost of potable water is increased. Seen in terms of our earlier analysis these costs of potable water would be added via taxation to the firms' marginal costs; product prices would increase and outputs would be reduced. The higher prices paid by consumers would only partially be paid to producers; the remainder would be paid to downstream communities to cover their increased water treatment costs. But should the matter be handled this way? Would it be better public policy to regulate firms to prevent pollution at its source? Suppose such regulation forces some firms out of business. Should the owners of the factor services be compensated?

More importantly the existence of social costs may not be assignable to any specific individual or group of individuals. In the case of water pollution, for instance, the effluent from one firm may be harmless, as may be the effluent from another. But the two of these in combination may interact and be harmful. In a similar vein, environmental pollution may not be attributable to any individual's actions. The operation of a single internal combustion engine does not cause air pollution; instead it is the simultaneous operation of thousands of automobiles, plus buses, aircraft, incineration of rubbish, the generation of electricity, and the heating of residences that combine to pollute the air. In the 1970s few Americans will deny the existence of this social cost, but determining responsibility and the proper course for public policy is difficult.

Let us pursue this issue further by considering air pollution. Suppose

---

[13] These issues are discussed by R. H. Coase, "The Problem of Social Cost," *Journal of Law and Economics,* October 1960; Harold Demsetz, "The Exchange and Enforcement of Property Rights," *Journal of Law and Economics,* October 1964; and "Some Aspects of Property Rights," *Journal of Law and Economics,* October 1966. *See also* E. J. Mishan, *Technology and Growth: The Price We Pay* (New York: Frederick A. Praeger, 1970).

a single, identifiable source of air pollution—the operation of the internal combustion engine in automobiles—is discovered. Suppose, also, that all automobile owners recognize that air pollution exists and is undesirable. Further suppose that social costs have been measured and that increased laundry bills, house painting costs, medical expenses, and so on, total $100 per person per year. Households derive obvious benefits from operation of the family automobile and none are likely to abandon vehicle operation when confronted with the fact that vehicles pollute. This is especially true because any one family's actions are inconsequential; if one family ceases driving air pollution remains. Suppose, now, that an antipollution device costing $50 is available that is easily installed on any vehicle's exhaust system and completely eliminates the polluting emissions. Thus, for an expenditure of $50 each family stands to reap $100 worth of benefits, and rationality would dictate that all vehicles be equipped with antipollution devices. But this will not happen; if only one vehicle is equipped its owner incurs a $50 expense but pollution continues and he thus reaps no benefits. Further, if all other members of the community install the antipollution device, pollution will disappear and the individual may reap $100 worth of benefits at no cost to himself. What is rational for the community is inconsistent with individual rationality and, as a result, resources are misallocated. Faced with this problem what is the proper course for public policy?

The Nixon administration proposed in 1970 to tax the lead used in the production of gasoline in order to increase the price of leaded, relative to the price of lead-free fuel. This is an example of the use of sumptuary taxes, clearly for nonrevenue purposes. Alternatively, the installation of antipollution devices on automobiles could be subsidized. A third possibility is to use the regulatory power of the state to require that all vehicles be equipped with antipollution devices. The public interest in some action to improve the allocation of resources is obvious; the ideal direction that action should take is less obvious.

Optimal resource allocation requires consideration of externalities but this consideration is not easily accomplished. Just as individuals will not reveal their preferences for pure public goods, so third parties will undervalue third party benefits and overstate social costs if payments and charges are actually to be made.[14] Because externalities are a public goods component

---

[14] There is a controversy in welfare economics concerning the compensation principle. An action is said to be Pareto optimal if those who gain are able to compensate those who are made worse off by the action. But does the compensation actually have to be paid? In one view it does, otherwise those who are adversely affected will overstate the value of their loss in order to block action, as discussed in Demsetz, "Some Aspects of Property Rights," *op. cit.* Other authors for a variety of reasons, argue that the compensation does not have to be paid. For these views and a fuller discussion of the entire issue, *see* E. J Mishan, "A Survey of Welfare Economics, 1939–1959," *Economic Journal,* June 1960.

of private goods, revelation of preferences for them encounters the same difficulties as does determining the demand for pure public goods.

There is an additional dimension to these externalities. Obtaining information and marketing goods is costly. If the costs of accounting for externalities exceed their value should they be considered at all?[15] Potentially, a third party could sell rights to have social costs inflicted on him or third party benefits might be marketed but in each case there are costs involved in obtaining the proper information (presuming it could be obtained), organizing the market, and completing the transaction. Whenever these marketing costs are substantial, attempting to achieve efficiency by marketing externalities may reduce total social product. Now consider the distinction between the rock band and the tuberculosis examination. Both these products are essentially private in the sense that one person's use makes them unavailable for use by others, but there also is no doubt that consumption of these products has externalities. These externalities might conceivably be marketed; third parties might agree to help hire the musician or might pay (bribe) a buyer not to hire him, and one person might pay for the medical examinations of others. Undoubtedly instances may be found of externalities actually being marketed, but, by and large, they are not. Thus, the externalities associated with musicians are usually ignored unless, in the case of disutility, they become so great as to be banned under a "disturbing the peace" ordinance. They are ignored because the externalities are likely to be minimal and highly localized, and because the marketing costs are prohibitive: efficient resource allocation dictates that no corrective effort be made. With the tuberculosis examination, however, the externalities are not as localized and their value may be substantial. It is difficult, if not impossible, to identify the recipient and even if identified, because of their publicness, marketing the externalities would be out of the question. Thus, tuberculosis examinations are partially or wholly provided through collective action at a low or zero cost to the examinee by public health services and privately supported health services such as the x-ray units sponsored by the National Tuberculosis Association.

There is no guarantee that government action to improve the allocation of resources by accounting for externalities will increase total welfare; the point is that Pareto optimal action is possible as long as the expected value of the benefits exceeds the expected real cost of the corrective action. The form government action should take and the level of its application is still to be investigated. To support this investigation we now turn to a discussion of the production functions for public goods.

---

[15] Roland N. McKean and Jora R. Minasian, "On Achieving Pareto Optimality—Regardless of Cost!" *Western Economic Journal,* Fall 1966.

4

PRODUCING PUBLIC GOODS

The term economic efficiency, when used in conjunction with public goods, often triggers a response conditioned by basic attitudes and preconceptions. Some believe that greater amounts of public goods are always efficient and continually seek additional schools, public health services, and public housing. Others view the production of most public goods as inefficient and certainly regard as wasteful the provision of any public good that reduces their own welfare. In determining what level of public goods to provide, reasonable men disagree about the efficiency of a particular program because they do not agree on measures of benefits and costs. But there is an additional dimension to economic efficiency about which there should be no disagreement. This is efficiency in the use of resources so that, irrespective of the level of output selected, production takes place at the lowest possible cost per unit. Efficiency in this sense does not determine the desirability of producing nor does it imply that any particular quantity should be produced. In this chapter we first review production theory and then discuss production functions for public goods. Discussion of production functions is essential to an analysis of public expenditures because much controversy arises from the failure to specify correctly what is being produced. A formidable obstacle here is quantifying output.

PRODUCTION FUNCTIONS AND COSTS OF PRODUCTS

There is a tendency to confuse the quantity of public goods with their cost of production—to presume that an expenditure of \$600 per pupil represents 20 percent more education than an expenditure of \$500 per pupil, or that spending twice as much for cancer research doubles the effectiveness of the research effort. Whether or not this is the case depends on the nature of the production function and the behavior of factor prices as levels of output change. This section investigates the properties of production functions and their implications for costs of production.

The production of any good or service requires resource inputs, usually a combination of factor services and intermediate products (raw materials or semifinished products). Factor services are generally classified in terms of labor effort, the use of capital goods, and the use of land. A *production function* expresses the technological relationship between the quantity of output achieved during the period of production and inputs of factor services and intermediate products. This relationship can be illustrated by Figure 4.1. A two-dimensional representation can only consider two inputs, F_1 and F_2, though the principles that follow can be generalized to any number of inputs. Each level of output is represented by an *isoquant* showing all of the efficient combinations of F_1 and F_2 that can be used to produce that level of output. Consider the isoquant for output level Q_1. This level of output can be produced by using OA units of F_1 and OD units of F_2, or OB of F_1 and OC of F_2, or any other combination of F_1 and F_2 described by a point on the Q_1 isoquant. The Q_1 level of output presumably could also be produced by using OA of F_1 and more than OD of F_2, but to do so would clearly waste the additional amount of F_2. This illustrates an important point: Isoquants show efficient combinations of inputs, and clearly inefficient or wasteful methods of production have been eliminated.

Determining the least cost method of producing a particular level of output is an economic decision (in contrast to the engineering decision to rule out the clearly inefficient methods of production). To minimize the unit cost of producing a product, inputs must be employed in combinations that put their marginal physical productivities in the same proportion as their prices. If the marginal physical productivities and prices of inputs F_1 and F_2 are given by MPP_1, MPP_2, P_1, and P_2, respectively, then the unit cost minimizing condition is $MPP_2/MPP_1 = P_2/P_1$. The ratio MPP_2/MPP_1 is given in Figure 4.1 by the slopes of the isoquants. The steeper the isoquant the larger the amount of F_1 employed per unit of F_2 and, as given by the law of diminishing returns, the smaller the marginal productivity of F_1 relative

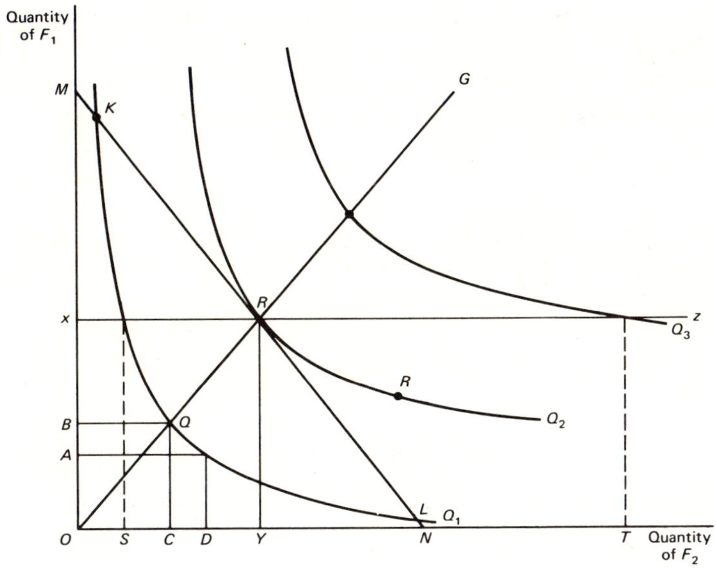

Figure 4.1 A production function.

to F_2. Conversely, as we move along the isoquant to the lower right, the amount of F_2 employed in conjunction with a unit of F_1 becomes larger and larger, and the marginal physical product of F_2 declines relative to the marginal physical product of F_1. Thus, moving along the Q_2 isoquant from R to R', MPP_1 increases as MPP_2 decreases, and the ratio MPP_2/MPP_1 decreases.

Just as an isoquant shows the different input combinations that may be used to produce some level of output, an *isocost* shows the different combinations of inputs that may be purchased for the same total expenditure. In our two-input case, total expenditure on inputs, E, is given by the sum of the expenditures on each of the two inputs,

$$E = F_1P_1 + F_2P_2 \qquad [4.1]$$

where F_1 and F_2 are the quantities of the inputs purchased. Solving Equation (4.1) for F_1 gives

$$F_1 = \frac{E}{P_1} - \frac{P_2}{P_1}(F_2) \qquad [4.2]$$

Equation (4.2) is the equation for a straight line whose vertical intercept is E/P_1 and whose slope is $-P_2/P_1$, the ratio of input prices. An isocost described by such an equation is given by the line MN in Figure 4.1, showing the different amounts of F_1 and F_2 that may be purchased for the same cost,

E, when input prices remain unchanged at P_1 and P_2. Point R, where MN is tangent to isoquant Q_2, determines the least cost means of producing that level of output. At R, the slope of Q_2 equals the slope of MN and $MPP_2/MPP_1 = P_2/P_1$. Other combinations of F_1 and F_2, such as those given by K and L, could be purchased for the same cost but they would give a smaller output and clearly would be an inefficient use of resources. The total cost of producing Q_2 at point R is equal to E, and is given by $OX(P_1) + OY(P_2)$. This determines a point on a total cost function, such as point H on the total cost function LTC_C shown in Figure 4.2. This total cost E

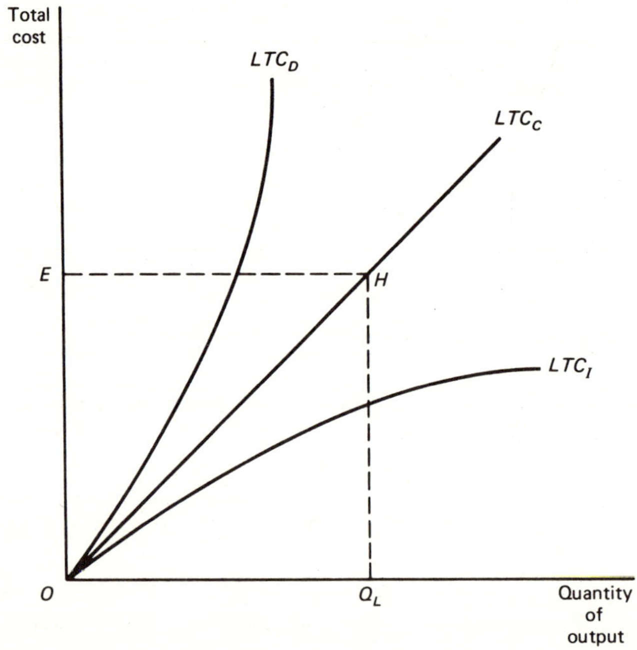

Figure 4.2 Long-run total cost functions.

is affected by the absolute price levels of F_1 and F_2, whereas the selection of the least cost combination of F_1 and F_2 (point R in Figure 4.1) depends only on their relative prices. To put the matter another way, if the prices of F_1 and F_2 increased proportionally, point R would still represent the least cost method of producing Q_2 but the total cost function in Figure 4.2 would shift up.

Given the relationship between the prices of F_1 and F_2, shown by the slope of line MN in Figure 4.1, any number of isocosts—one for each level of expenditure on inputs—could be drawn having that same slope. One of these isocosts would be tangent to each isoquant showing the least cost combination of F_1 and F_2 sufficient to produce each level of output. Connecting these points of tangency gives the line OG in Figure 4.1; this locus of tangency points—the *expansion path*—shows what combinations of inputs must be used if cost minimization is to be maintained as output changes. For every possible ratio of prices for F_1 and F_2 there would be a separate expansion path. For every point along the expansion path OG, total cost, such as for Q_2, can be derived and an entire total cost function, such as LTC_C in Figure 4.2, can be drawn. It should be emphasized that each point on LTC_C represents the minimum total cost for producing each quantity of output; more expensive methods could be selected due to a failure to make engineering decisions that rule out clearly inefficient alternatives, or failure to choose points along the expansion path.

The *long run* is defined as the condition where all inputs are variable. *Constant returns to scale* is the condition where varying all inputs in some proportion results in output variation in the same proportion. Thus, if inputs are doubled, output is also doubled; if in Figure 4.1, inputs F_1 and F_2 are doubled from OB and OC units to OX and OY units, respectively, output would double from Q_1 to Q_2, and, geometrically, the distance QR would equal the distance OQ. *Increasing returns to scale* occur when increasing all inputs in some proportion increases output by a proportionally greater amount. In this case doubling inputs from OA and OB to OX and OY would more than double output, and Q_2 would represent an output more than twice as great as Q_1. Conversely, *decreasing returns to scale* occur when increasing all inputs in some proportion leads to a proportionately smaller increase in output. In this case doubling inputs would less than double output and Q_2 would represent an output less than twice as great as Q_1.

The implications of constant, increasing, and decreasing returns to scale for long-run total and average costs may be quickly inferred: If input prices do not change as the output level is varied, doubling inputs will always double total cost. With constant returns to scale, doubling inputs doubles outputs, total cost increases in the same proportion as output, and long-run average total cost is constant. Long-run total and average total costs under conditions of constant returns to scale are shown by the curves LTC_C and $LATC_C$ in Figures 4.2 and 4.3, respectively. With increasing returns to scale, output increases proportionally more rapidly than inputs; since total cost varies in the same proportion as inputs, total cost increases proportionally less rapidly than output, and long-run total and average total costs are illustrated by the curves LTC_I and $LATC_I$ in Figures 4.2 and 4.3. Conversely, with decreasing returns to scale, total cost increases proportionally more rapidly than output and long-run total and average total costs are given by the curves LTC_D in Figure 4.2, and $LATC_D$ in Figure 4.3.

The *short run* is defined by the existence of a fixed input; in the short run at least one input cannot be varied. Short-run analysis is also possible utilizing the production function of Figure 4.1. The horizontal movement

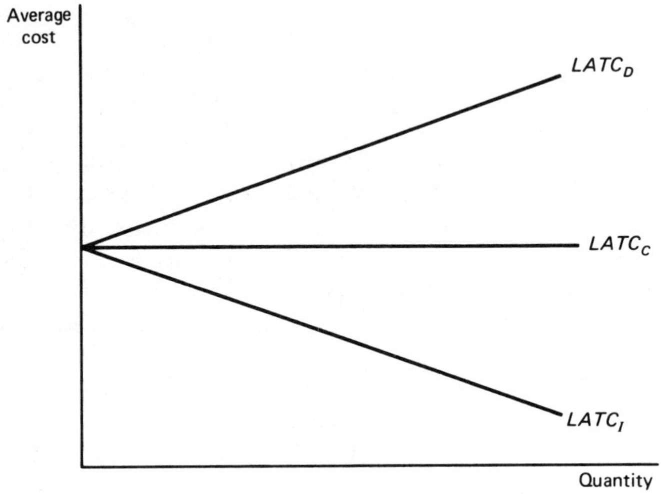

Figure 4.3 Long-run average cost functions.

along the path XZ shows that, when F_1 is fixed at OX units, output may be varied by employing different amounts of F_2 in connection with this amount of F_1. Assume (for convenience, not necessity) constant returns to scale with isoquants Q_1, Q_2, and Q_3 representing 1, 2, and 3 units of output, respectively. The *law of diminishing returns* is illustrated here by the successively larger and larger amounts of the variable input F_2 needed to produce an additional unit of output, and by the decreasing slopes of the isoquants as we move to the right along XZ. The horizontal expansion across the production function along line XZ shows that OS units of F_2 are needed to produce the first unit of output, an additional, larger amount, SY of F_2, is needed to produce the second unit, and a still larger additional amount, YT units of F_2, is required to produce the third. Thus, larger and larger additional amounts of the variable input F_2 are employed in conjunction with OX units of F_1 to produce each additional unit of output. The short-run total product curve is shown in Figure 4.4; on the horizontal axis the number of units of the variable input F_2 employed in conjunction with the fixed OX units of F_1 is measured, and on the vertical axis the level of output associated with each isoquant attained as F_2 is increased is measured. Because of diminishing returns, total product increases at a diminishing rate. Given this short-run production function, the short-run costs may be ascertained, again assuming input prices do not change as the level of output is varied. The costs associated with the fixed OX units of F_1 do not vary with output; these are fixed costs. As the amount of F_2 is increased, since output increases at a diminishing marginal rate, variable costs will increase more rapidly than output. Short-run total cost, the sum of the fixed and variable costs, is illustrated in Figure 4.5. Here total cost is shown increasing at an increasing rate, due to diminishing returns to the

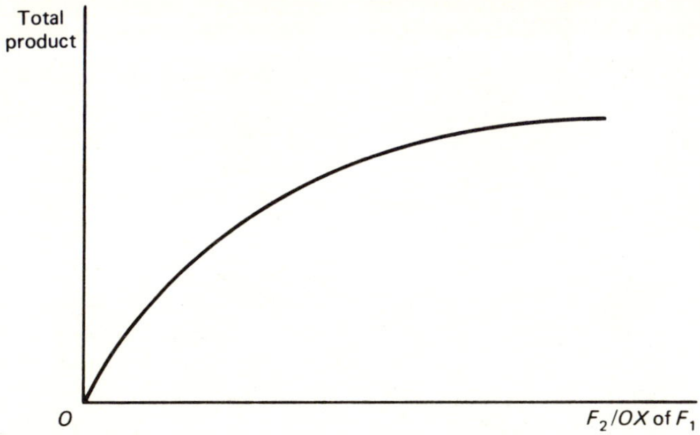

Figure 4.4 Diminishing returns.

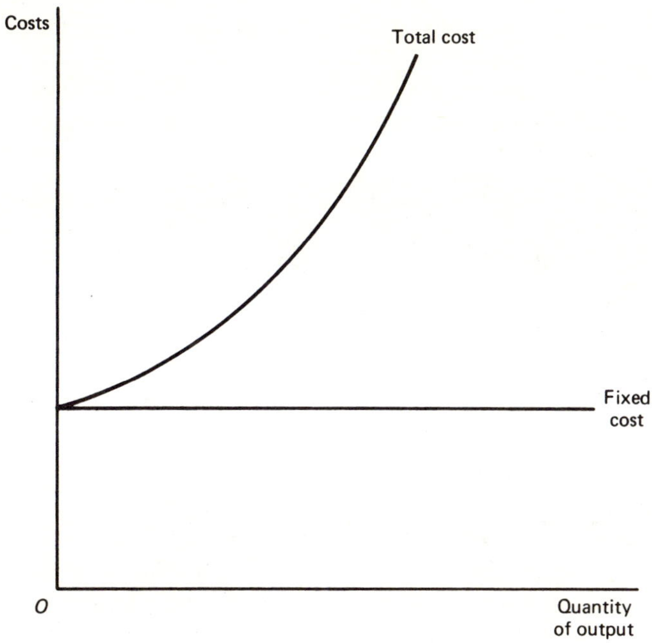

Figure 4.5 Short-run total cost function.

variable input F_2. Variable cost is not shown separately, but is equal to the vertical distance between total and fixed cost for each level of output. From the cost curves shown in Figure 4.5 we may derive average and marginal costs; these are geometrically shown in Figure 4.6 where *SATC*, *SAVC*, and *SMC* are short-run average total cost, short-run average variable cost, and short-run marginal cost, respectively.

This exercise by no means exhausts the treatment of production functions

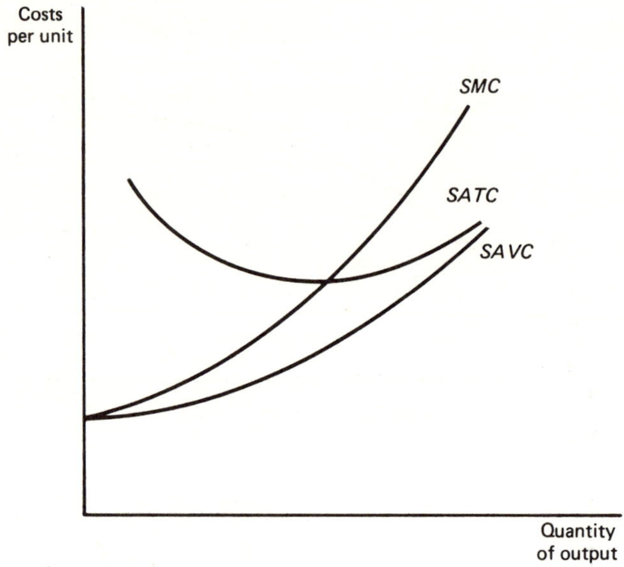

Figure 4.6 Short-run average, variable, and marginal cost functions.

and costs, but it does illustrate two important points. First, cost must be discussed with reference to production functions; costs are incurred because inputs are employed and costs may be determined only after input requirements are known. This input information is provided by production functions. Second, the production function describes only efficient input requirements and the costs considered here are the lowest possible costs per unit for each of the output levels. It would be feasible to employ OX and OY of F_1 and F_2 to produce Q_1 level of output. (See Figure 4.1.) If resources were used in such a wasteful manner costs would be above those shown for each level of output in the figures. With this review of production and costs behind us we now discuss the production functions and costs of public goods.

PRODUCTION FUNCTIONS FOR PUBLIC GOODS

The central problem in applying microeconomic production theory to public goods is one of measurement: how to quantify the output of the productive process. A police department uses a variety of factor inputs, the time of policemen, the services of some capital goods, and so on, but what is the quantity of police protection produced? With factor prices unchanged could that quantity be increased while keeping the police budget constant? This is equivalent to asking if the current mix of factor inputs represents a point along the expansion path in Figure 4.1. Would the quantity of protection be increased more than proportionally, less than proportionally, or even decreased, if additional units of one factor were used? This is comparable to questioning the shape of the function that describes the reaction of output to variation in the use of a single input, such as described by line *XZ* in Figure 4.1. If all factor inputs are increased proportionally what is the effect on the quantity of production? This is the economies of scale question. The mind rebels at questions like these precisely because we do not know how to define the quantity of police protection. The analysis of most types of public goods creates the same conceptual problems, and an initial step in tackling them is to break public goods, like police protection, down into component parts: for example, traffic control, protection of property, maintaining a jail. Indeed categories like these can probably be broken down further into more specific subcategories. The analysis of the more narrowly defined public good can then proceed by specifying the type of output: physical quantities or the degree to which certain goals are achieved.

In the atypical instances where a public good can be measured in physical terms the production function concept can be applied directly. Most of the clerical functions of government, such as issuing checks, recording births, marriages, and deaths, and handling the mail, are of this sort. In many of these cases there is no significant issue as to whether or not the public good should be produced or in what quantity; there is simply a given volume of output to be produced (checks to be issued, for example) and the analytical problem is finding the least cost combination of factor inputs. However, as this is done, the government agency in question should not consider only the costs of inputs charged against the agency's budget. The least cost method may impose costs on other agencies, costs that might be reduced if some other combination of factor inputs were used. Suppose that a government's check writing agency attempts to lower its costs by using more automated equipment and less manpower. If such a change requires more paperwork, and hence more costs by other government agencies that submit accounts to the check writing agency, these costs may overshadow the apparent savings introduced by using the automated equipment. In addition, in seeking a cost-minimizing factor mix a government agency may also foist significant costs on the public. For example, the filing and processing of tax returns entails costs for the taxpayer as well as the tax collecting agency. Economic efficiency should not be appraised by examining only the budgetary costs of government agencies.

More commonly the output of a government program can be quantified in terms of the degree to which certain goals are attained. The appropriate specification of quantifiable goals is often the most difficult aspect of public expenditure analysis. In education, for example, if a school district adopts as its goal "development, to their fullest potential, of the children of today so that they will become the responsible citizens of tomorrow," analysis is stymied from the start. No agreement can be reached on a means of measuring the degree to which the development of children reaches its full potential, let alone agreeing on the meaning of responsible citizenship. However, a school board might adopt as one of its goals "the ability of 90 percent of all nine-year-olds to achieve a score of 70 percent on a particular standardized reading test." Expressed in this fashion, analysis of alternative instructional techniques can proceed in order to determine the least cost solution. Suppose 27 randomly selected groups of primary school children were given reading instruction in the ways depicted in Figure 4.7. The teaching method for each group

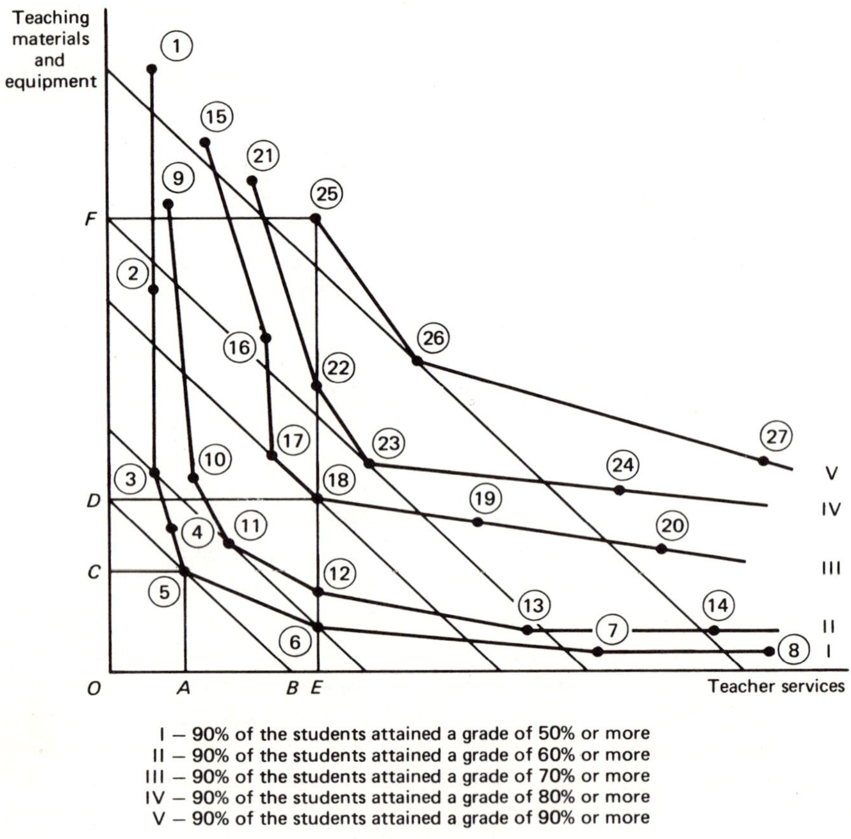

Figure 4.7 A production function for education.

varies with respect to the inputs of teacher services and the amounts of teaching materials and equipment used. Group five, for example, represents the use of *OA* amount of teacher services and *OC* amount of teaching materials and equipment. Output is measured by the test score 90 percent of the pupils in each group attained or exceeded. Groups one through eight all yielded the same test results—90 percent of each group scored 50 percent or better—though each utilized different combinations of factor inputs. Note that groups one, two, and three all used the same quantity of teacher services but differing amounts of teaching materials and equipment. The additional inputs of materials and equipment for groups one and two, as compared with group three, did not result in any improvement in the educational product; the marginal product of the additional inputs was zero. Similarly, the additional teacher services devoted to group eight, in comparison to group seven, made no contribution to output. Line 1–8 is in effect an isoquant for a particular level of test results; that is, 90 percent of the pupils score 50 percent or better and lines 9–14, 15–20, 21–24, and 25–27 are isoquants for progressively higher levels of educational output. Line *DB* represents all the combinations of the two factor inputs that could be purchased with same total expenditure. The isocost lines in Figure 4.7 parallel to *DB* have similar meanings. The combination of factor inputs used in group five is the least cost method of instruction that yields the result that 90 percent of the students score 50 percent or above on the test.

The model of an educational production function in Figure 4.7 can also be used to illustrate diminishing returns to additional applications of one factor when the other is held at a constant level. If the use of teacher services is held constant at *OE*, one can trace out the response, in terms of test results, to larger inputs of teaching materials and equipment. To increase the level of performance from 90/60 to 90/70 (12 to 18) requires a greater additional input of teaching materials and equipment than the inputs needed to raise the level from 90/50 to 90/60 (6 to 12). The entire relationship, illustrating the principle of diminishing returns, can be seen in Figure 4.8. Successive improvements in test results require greater and greater inputs of (or expenditures on) materials and equipment, given a constant input of (or expenditures on) teacher services.

The least cost combination of factor inputs for each performance level can be determined by finding the point of tangency between each isoquant and an isocost representing a constant level of total expenditures. Groups 5, 11, 23, and 26 represent such points but, for the 90/70 isoquant, groups 17 and 18 fall on the same isocost; hence there is no reason to prefer one over the other. These points of tangency show the efficient means of producing the public good. At each point of tangency, total costs (which are the minimum total costs for each level of output) can be calculated by multiplying the quantity of each factor used by its price and adding the resulting dollar amounts. The total cost function derived in this manner is displayed in Figure 4.9, where dollar amounts are measured on the horizontal axis; such relationships are sometimes referred to as *cost-effectiveness* functions.[1] The analysis

[1] Without specifying actual quantities of the factors used and the absolute level of their

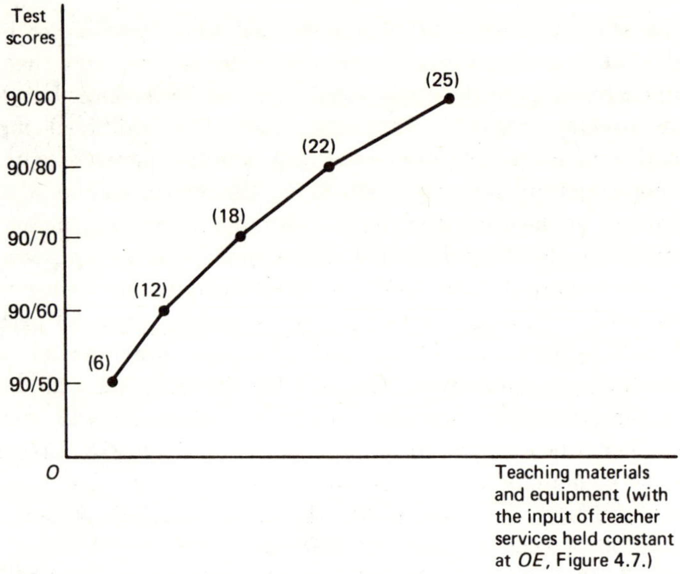

Figure 4.8 Diminishing returns in education.

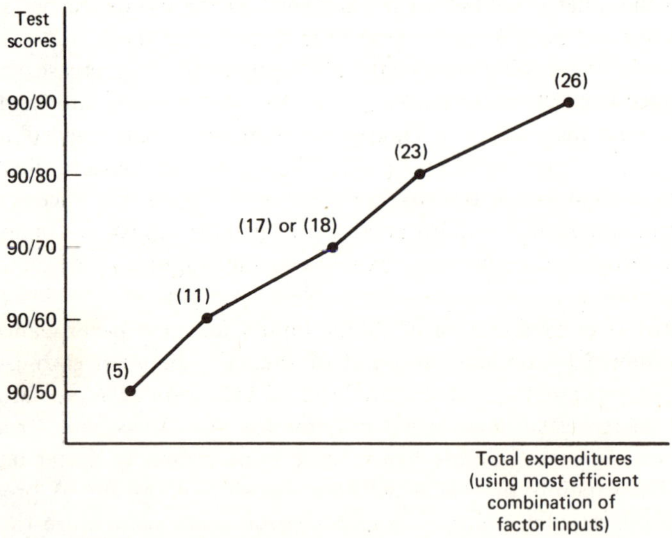

Figure 4.9 A total cost function for education.

prices, no scale values can be put on the horizontal axis of Figure 4.9. Such specification would not affect the shape of the minimum total cost function.

The most widely known applications of the production function concept to the provision of public goods have been in the area of national defense. *Cost-effectiveness analysis,* in the jargon of the Pentagon, means achieving the most defense from a itself cannot be used to answer the question of what level of output (and corresponding level of total expenditure) is preferred. Is a goal of 90 percent of the students achieving a test score of at least 70 percent appropriate, given its cost, or should alternative goals be considered? Should the goal be relaxed to 90 percent of the students scoring 60 percent and the subsequent savings in expenditures be used elsewhere in the school system (or total school spending be reduced by that amount)? Would it be worth the additional cost to assure that 90 percent of the students score at least 80 percent? Analysis using the production function concept cannot answer these questions; it can only indicate those methods of achieving particular goals that should be ruled out on efficiency grounds.

This analysis is merely illustrative of the application of production function theory to the field of education. It does show, however, the rational approach to problems such as the proper mix of teachers, and what, in the days of computer assisted instruction, has come to be called educational hardware and software. One of the virtues of this form of analysis is the attention focused on the really basic problems in public expenditure decisions; has the goal been correctly specified; have all of the relevant costs been identified; have all the alternatives been examined? Our hypothetical example can be pushed further to consider these problems.

Of the three, specification of goals is usually the most critical. The goal, 90 percent of all nine-year-olds scoring at least 70 percent on a standardized reading test, can be examined in more detail. Even assuming no question about the validity and reliability of the examination there are still important issues

---

given level of resources or determining the least cost for a specified level of defense. The fundamental limitations on the nation's resources dictate rejecting the notion that our national security goals must be pursued whatever the cost. When defense problems come to be viewed in terms of objectives specified in an operationally meaningful way—such as the probability of target destruction or the ability to move troops and equipment certain distances within a certain time span—alternative weapons systems can be compared. Costs and performances can be brought into focus. Cost-effectiveness analysis is used by the Department of Defense in the framework of *systems analysis,* broadly defined by E. S. Quade as "inquiry to aid a decision-maker choose a course of action by systematically investigating his proper objectives, comparing quantitatively where possible the costs, effectiveness, and risks associated with the alternative policies or strategies for achieving them, and formulating additional alternatives if those examined are found wanting." E. S. Quade (ed.), *Analysis for Military Decisions* (Chicago: Rand McNally, 1966), p. 4.

See also C. J. Hitch and Roland McKean, *The Economics of Defense in the Nuclear Age* (Cambridge: Harvard University Press, 1960); Murray Kamrass and Joseph A. Navarro, "An Analysis of Tactical Air Systems," in Thomas A. Golden (ed.), *Cost-Effectiveness Analysis: New Approaches in Decision-Making* (New York: Frederick A. Praeger, 1967); and Gene H. Fisher, "Illustrative Example of Cost-Utility Considerations in a Military Context," in David Novick (ed.), *Program Budgeting: Program Analysis and the Federal Budget* (Cambridge: Harvard University Press, 1965), appendix to chapter 4.

to raise. One must be careful that the examination is measuring the results of of the educational program and not something else. In describing this hypothetical analysis it was noted that the experience of similar groups of children was being studied; it is essential to the analysis that the reading performance of all groups of students be on the same average level at the beginning of the experiment.[2] That issue aside there is a fundamental point to be made about the quantification of goal achievement. Measures of goal achievement are most often ordinal rather than cardinal in nature; that is, performance can be ranked but differences between ranks cannot be interpreted. Beauty contestants can be ranked but one cannot say that the winner is more beautiful than the runner-up by precisely the same amount by which the runner-up is more beautiful than the third-place contestant. In our example we cannot say that the difference between the 90/60 result and the 90/70 result is the same as the difference between 90/80 and 90/90. The matter is further complicated by the nature of the quantitative measure used. To specify 90 percent of students scoring at least a certain mark as the measure of output ignores differences among those scoring both above and below the specified mark. Is a 90/70 result where in addition 50 percent of the students score 80 percent really to be preferred to a case where 90 percent score 60 percent but where 70 percent also score 80 percent? Again a choice must be made: what is more important, maximizing the total score of all students in the group or making sure that practically all score above some acceptable level?

Difficulties exist on the cost side of an analysis as well. The time of students is the major factor input to the educational process not paid for by the school system. In seeking efficient means of achieving desired educational outcomes alternative methods should not be evaluated solely in terms of the costs of the factor inputs that have to be purchased. The hypothetical example used above would only be valid if all alternative methods required the same amount of student time. Typically, however, choices must be made between methods that are more expensive and require less student time, and methods that are less expensive but require more student time. As decision-makers ponder the trade-off between time and money they should consider the value of student time in terms of its best alternative use. The additional real cost

---

[2] Consider this analogy: Which is the best high school in the city? Popular opinion judges high schools on the basis of the percentage of graduates going on to college. The school ranked best by this criterion may simply have much better entering students than any other. The more appropriate criterion would focus on the difference between entering and leaving students, not on the absolute level of performance of the graduates. Needless to say this same point applies to evaluation of colleges and universities. Some school districts have let contracts to private, profit-making firms where compensation is to be based, in part at least, on the actual improvement in student performance resulting from the firm's activities.

then of a reading program that takes more student time is the value of the art classes, recreation, or whatever else, that will have to be missed.

A separate problem is the possible change in the prices of inputs. The isocosts in Figure 4.7 were drawn on the assumption that the relative prices of teacher services and teaching materials and equipment remain unchanged as the volume of services purchased increases. When the production of a public good requires very large purchases of particular factor inputs—large in comparison to the total market supply of these inputs—it is very likely that the price of those inputs will increase as additional quantities are purchased. In the example, suppose that the prices of teaching materials and equipment are not affected by the quantity purchased, but that the price of teacher services does go up as larger quantities are purchased. The isocosts would become curved indicating that the price of teacher services is increasing relative to the price of teaching materials and equipment, as more and more teacher services are purchased. The expansion path would tend to shift away from the axis for the factor with an increase in price, and the minimum total-cost function, as in Figure 4.9, would tend to shift to the right.

The application of production functions to the output of public goods is likely to broaden the range of alternatives considered by decision makers. Rules-of-thumb (spend $5 per pupil on the school library) and qualitative guidelines issued by professional organizations (a good school has a pupil-teacher ratio no higher than 25:1, and all teachers are fully certified) lose their appeal and come to be sharply questioned once production function theory is applied. New alternatives outside the traditional range of choice are more likely to be suggested. Consider the following example from the water resources area. On hot summer days the estuary of a river begins to stink; local residents, political leaders, and editorial writers agree that something must be done as the tourist business is endangered. Scientists agree that the problem is attributable to the low oxygen content in the water that limits the ability of the river to absorb natural and man-made pollutants. The public works commission is directed to devise a plan for solving the problem. After intensive study the public works commission recommends the construction of a series of upstream dams that could store water during the winter and release water during periods of low flow in the summer. Their objective is to assure that the water flow can be maintained at least x gallons per minute, because flows of that magnitude will assure adequate oxygen content in the estuary's water. Engineering, hydrological, and economic studies are conducted to determine the least cost system of dams capable of providing that level of low-flow augmentation. The alternative solution—of pumping air directly into the water of the estuary (through perforated hoses laid on the floor of the estuary)—is not considered by the public works commission because they have not built a project like that before (while they have built many dams), or because they lack legislative authority to construct such a project. As an alternative means of achieving the objective of maintaining an adequate oxygen content in the water, the pumping system is far less expensive than even the least cost system of dams. Specifying oxygen content in the estuary's water as the means of measuring output leads to the consideration of more alternatives than specifying output in terms of river flows. Thinking about a problem in terms of production function theory is more likely to lead to the consideration of all the relevant alternatives.[3]

APPLICATIONS TO EDUCATION

The theoretical principles of applying the production function concept to education were discussed above; we now turn to empirical studies attempting to identify the relationships between factor inputs and educational outcomes. Large-scale studies of these relationships rely upon statistical analysis of educational data rather than carefully controlled experiments. Several investigators have approached the problem by seeking to measure the extent to which variations in scores on standardized tests are related to various measurable characteristics of schools and pupils.

In 1966 the U. S. Office of Education published the results of a study of American elementary and secondary public education attempting primarily to assess the degree of inequality of educational opportunity.[4] The data gathered included information on some 645,000 pupils and the 3100 schools they attended. The educational achievements of pupils were measured as were various pupil and school characteristics. The report concluded that per pupil expenditures and other indices of school facilities and curriculum had very little relation to achievement, given the social background and attitudes of individual students and their peers. Indeed the effect of a student's peers on his own achievement was found to be more important than any other school variable.[5] On the question of the effects of racial integration, the *Coleman Report* found that "although the differences are small, and although the degree of integration within the school is not known, there is evident, even in the

---

[3] Robert K. Davis, *The Range of Choice in Water Management: A Study of Dissolved Oxygen in the Potomac Estuary* (Baltimore: Johns Hopkins Press, 1968). Altering the flow of pollutants must, of course, also be considered.

[4] James S. Coleman *et al.*, *Equality of Educational Opportunity* (Washington, D.C.: Government Printing Office, 1966). *See also* Lewis C. Solomon, "A Note on Equality of Educational Opportunity," *American Economic Review,* September 1970.

[5] The interpretation of such survey data is at best difficult; for a critique of the report *see* Samuel Bowles and Henry M. Levin, "The Determination of Scholastic Achievement—An Appraisal of Some Recent Data," *Journal of Human Resources,* Winter 1968. *See also* the response of Coleman; contributions by Marshall S. Smith and Glen G. Cain, and Harold W. Watts; and the rebuttal by Bowles and Levin in the Spring and Summer 1968 issues of that *Journal.*

short run, an effect of school integration on the reading and mathematics achievement of Negro pupils."[6] Drawing largely on the results of the *Coleman Report,* the U. S. Commission on Civil Rights argued for a public school policy stressing racial and economic integration over compensatory education policies where relatively more is spent per pupil in schools predominantly attended by students from disadvantaged backgrounds.[7]

Herbert J. Kiesling studied data from 97 New York school districts on average pupil achievement in basic subjects, average pupil intelligence, the socioeconomic characteristics of the community in which a school district is located, per pupil expenditures, and school district size.[8] He found only a very weak relationship between performance and expenditures for the total group of school districts. When average scores of students grouped by their socioeconomic characteristics were examined, a negative relationship was found between performance and expenditures. The performance of pupils from the highest socioeconomic group was not significantly affected by the level of per pupil expenditures; they did well regardless of the amount spent. The relationship between the size of school districts and performance was negative. As would be expected, performance was positively related to measures of intelligence.

A somewhat similar study of input-output relationships in high schools in Chicago and Atlanta has been made by Jesse Burkhead.[9] Socioeconomic variables, principally median family income in the census tracts from which students came, were found to be of the greatest importance in determining differences in school outputs. Within the range of variation existing in the Chicago school system, class size was not important in producing different test score results. The experience of teachers had an important impact on reading scores and was generally a more significant determinant of educational outcomes than either class size or the formal education of teachers. The size of the high school was shown to have no perceptible effect. Findings for Atlanta were essentially similar.

One major difficulty in drawing implications for public policy from studies like these is that the range of variation of the variables representing school inputs, such as average class size, is rather narrow. Whereas small changes in these variables may not make much of a difference in terms of

---

[6] Coleman, *op. cit.*, p. 29.

[7] U. S. Commission of Civil Rights, *Racial Isolation in the Public Schools* (Washington, D.C.: Government Printing Office, 1967).

[8] Herbert J. Kiesling, "Measuring a Local Government Service: A Study of School Districts in New York State," *Review of Economics and Statistics,* August 1967.

[9] Jesse Burkhead, *Input and Output in Large-City High Schools* (Syracuse: Syracuse University Press, 1967). *See also* Richard Raymond, "Determinants of the Quality of Primary and Secondary Public Education in West Virginia," *Journal of Human Resources,* Fall 1968.

educational results, large changes, changes outside the pattern of current experience, may still have a very marked effect. Much additional research clearly needs to be done in this area. School administrators should have some empirically verified theory of the educational production function as a guide to their allocation of resources.

5

BENEFIT-COST ANALYSIS

Everyone would agree that benefits derived from public goods ought to exceed their costs. The formal comparison of benefits measured in dollar terms and costs of public expenditure programs is called *benefit-cost analysis*, and is a means of refining the allocative decision-making process. Many of the programs that implement a government's allocative policy are of an investment nature where benefits (and sometimes costs, too) extend into the future. The treatment of time, therefore, is a special and very important part of benefit-cost analysis.

The first applications of benefit-cost analysis were made in the 1930s when the federal government undertook many investment type programs, particularly in the water resources area. The Flood Control Act of 1936 set forth the criterion for evaluating water resources projects, that "the benefits to whomever they may accrue [be] in excess of the estimated costs." In response, federal agencies adopted techniques for estimating benefits and costs, but in many cases their analyses were window-dressing for projects undertaken for political reasons and designed purely in engineering terms. After World War II several attempts were made to establish analytical procedures that would be common to all agencies engaged in water resources projects, and at the same time benefit-cost analysis spread to agencies having program responsibilities in other areas. In 1962 President Kennedy approved a set of techniques for benefit-cost analysis to be used by all federal agencies.[1] By the late 1960s benefit-cost analysis was being applied to a wide range of government activities both at the federal and state-local levels, although there were still great inconsistencies among the analytical techniques used by various agencies.[2]

MEASURING BENEFITS

Public investment projects are usually undertaken because they possess at least some of the characteristics of public goods discussed in Chapter 3. For this very reason measuring benefits in dollar terms inevitably involves serious analytical problems. Can the output of the project be identified? Can the future amounts of output from that project be estimated? Can the proper price be established to convert these quantities into dollar amounts? Answers to these three questions are at the heart of the analytical problems involved in measuring benefits.

In some cases the output of a public investment project can be clearly identified because that output will be marketed—electric power and irrigation water will be produced by a dam; vehicle miles of transportation services will be rendered by a toll road. To treat the revenue generated by the sale of electricity and water and the revenue from tolls as the only benefits of these projects would be myopic. There are likely to be externalities involved, such as the dam protecting an area from floods or the toll road reducing traffic congestion on nontoll routes. Flood control and reduced congestion are not subject to the exclusion principle and therefore these benefits cannot be marketed. Nevertheless these important benefits should be identified as a part of the output of such projects. There may also be externalities

---

[1] For a brief history of benefit-cost analysis, *see* Stephen A. Marglin, *Public Investment Criteria: Benefit-Cost Analysis for Planned Economic Growth* (Cambridge: M.I.T. Press, 1967), pp. 15–18. The book applies the logic of benefit-cost analysis to the problems of economic planning in underdeveloped countries.

[2] Three volumes stand out in the growing literature related to benefit-cost analysis: John V. Krutilla and Otto Eckstein, *Multiple Purpose River Development* (Baltimore: The Johns Hopkins Press, 1958); Robert Dorfman (ed.), *Measuring Benefits of Government Investments* (Washington, D.C.: The Brookings Institution, 1965); and Samuel B. Chase, Jr. (ed.), *Problems in Public Expenditure Analysis* (Washington, D.C.: The Brookings Institution, 1968). For another view, *see* A. R. Prest and R. Turvey, "Cost-Benefit Analysis: A Survey," *Economic Journal,* December 1965.

that are marketed: The dam may increase the generating capacity of a downstream hydroelectric facility.

Once all the outputs of a public investment project are identified the future quantities of these outputs must be estimated. Where outputs are marketed the problem is to estimate the quantity to be purchased during each future time period. Confusion between the physical capacity of the project and amounts to be sold should be avoided. Physical capacity, such as the maximum killowatt hours of electricity that a hydroelectric plant can generate, represents only an upper limit; not all of that electricity will necessarily be sold and, of course, the amount sold will not be independent of the price charged—a problem we will return to shortly. By their very nature, estimates of future sales involve uncertainty, so the analyst may want to project a range of quantity estimates or attach probabilities to his forecast; he may be 90 percent confident that in the fifth year after completion one million vehicle miles of toll road services will be demanded, but only 50 percent certain that two million vehicle miles will be traveled. Appropriate quantities of nonmarketed public good outputs and externalities will generally be more difficult to project. Lacking Noah's inside information, estimating the probable flood damage that a dam will prevent requires careful analysis of available hydrological data and development of a river basin model. If recreational facilities are a by-product of a dam project, estimates of future visitor days of recreational services should probably be based on projections of the surrounding area's population and income, plus availability of alternative recreational facilities. An externality such as reduced transportation costs may be a good deal easier to estimate.

The word intangible has been used in the literature to describe benefits that either cannot be quantified or, if quantified, cannot be priced. Advances in the analytical techniques of benefit-cost analysis have tended to reduce the areas within which benefits can only be considered as intangible; the use of shadow prices (which will be discussed later) has been especially useful in this regard. What remains are such questions as aesthetics—benefits in the form of an improved landscape or preservation or restoration of historic sites or buildings. In some cases intangibles are judged sufficiently important to merit undertaking a project even when a negative conclusion is reached on the basis of benefits and costs measurable in dollar terms.

Market prices. When project outputs are to be marketed, estimated future prices can be multiplied by the estimates of future quantities as a starting point for estimating dollar amounts of future benefits. If the output in question will be small in relation to the total quantity bought and sold in a competitive market, then that competitive price can be used accurately to convert estimated quantities into dollar estimates of benefit. For example, if the electricity to be generated by a public hydroelectric project will be a small fraction of the total electricity generated and sold in a market area, this additional output cannot be expected to have any influence on the market price, and that price is the appropriate one to use in the analysis. Benefits from the generation of electricity in this case are simply equal to price times quantity, because that is the amount people will be willing to pay for that quantity of electricity.

If the quantity of output from the public project is large relative to the total market, the effect of that increase in supply on the market price must be considered. This case is illustrated by Figure 5.1. Suppose *DD* represents

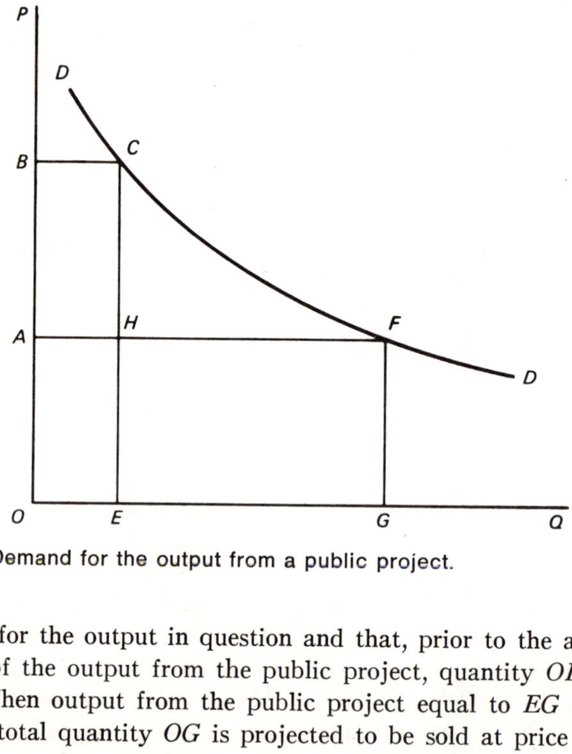

Figure 5.1 Demand for the output from a public project.

the demand for the output in question and that, prior to the appearance on the market of the output from the public project, quantity *OE* was sold at price *OB*. When output from the public project equal to *EG* comes on the market, the total quantity *OG* is projected to be sold at price *OA*. What is the benefit from the public project? Is it simply the amount received from the sale of the output, an amount equal to *EHFG?* Since this additional output had the effect of reducing the price, it can be argued that benefits are equal to the entire amount people would be willing to pay for the added output—an amount equal geometrically to the area *ECFG*. *Consumer surplus* is the difference between what consumers are willing to pay for the total output and what they in fact do pay. The difference between *ECFG* and *EHFG*, the area of triangle *CHF*, is the consumer surplus obtained from the additional output of the public project. Additional consumer surplus, *ABCH*, is also obtained as the output from the public project decreases price from *OB* to *OA*. If it were feasible for the output of the public project to be sold using *discriminatory pricing*—selling at different prices to different consumers—then the entire consumer surplus could be absorbed as revenue from the sale of the output.[3] On these grounds many analysts argue that consumer surplus ought to be considered as part of total benefits.[4]

One should beware of the consumer surplus argument. Consider again the rectangle *ABCH*. This represents revenue lost by the suppliers of *OE* amount of output. When *OE* was the only output sold at price *OB*, total revenue to the sellers of *OE* was equal to *OBCE;* with the market price reduced to *OA*, the producers of *OE* now have a total revenue of only *OAHE* and have lost an amount equal to *ABCH*. To sharpen the argument, suppose that total costs to the producers of *OE* are *OAHE* so that *ABCH* formerly represented their economic profits. In the new situation they lose these profits as consumers gain consumer surplus. Whatever one may think of the recipients of economic profit as individuals, they themselves will consider this change a reduction in their welfare. Only if one is willing to make the value judgment that the welfare gained by consumers is more important than, or exceeds, the welfare lost by the producers of *OE* should one be willing to count the consumer surplus as part of total benefits.[5] Now consider the triangle *CHF*. The resources used in this public investment project could have been alternatively employed to yield consumer surplus elsewhere. To count consumer surplus, such as *CHF*, on the benefit side and ignore it on the cost side is to bias the analysis.

Shadow prices. Many government projects yield outputs that may be measured but are not traded in markets. Since market prices are unavailable these outputs, if they are to be put in dollar terms, must be evaluated using shadow prices. When goods are bought and sold in markets, prices indicate the rates at which different goods may be substituted. If apples cost five cents and oranges cost ten cents, two apples exchange for one orange. When one thing exchanges for another at a fixed ratio but with no market transaction, prices are implicit or *shadow prices*.[6] Leisure is not traded in a market, but if a man refuses to work an extra hour at $5.00 per hour we may

---

3 In the case where an average cost curve lies everywhere above the demand curve, discriminatory pricing may yield a total revenue sufficient to equal or exceed total costs for some level of output.

4 Prest and Turvey, *op. cit.*

5 If *ABCH* did not represent pure economic profit to the producers of *OE* then of course reducing the market price to *OH* will force those producers to incur losses and in the long run drive them out of the industry. For a discussion of this point, *see* Robert M. Dunn, Jr., "A Problem of Bias in Benefit-Cost Analysis: Consumer Surplus Reconsidered," *Southern Economic Journal,* January 1967.

6 *See* Roland N. McKean, "The Use of Shadow Prices" in Chase, *op. cit.,* pp. 33–65.

conclude that he values that hour of leisure at at least $5.00 and can call that the shadow price of his leisure. The analysis of transportation projects often calls for the use of a shadow price to value time saved. A new highway may produce some benefits that are directly measurable in dollar terms, such as fuel savings, but a major output will be reduced travel time. When asking whether, on grounds of economic efficiency, the proposed highway should be built, one element of the benefit-cost analysis would involve applying a shadow price to the saving of time. This can be fairly straightforward in the case of commercial traffic such as trucking; truckers' wage rates can be used as a shadow price for the time saved. In addition, shadow prices may be estimated reflecting the value of time saved since the truck may now be available to carry additional loads. For other types of highway users, the family on vacation or the commuter, the appropriate shadow price is not clear. Some analysts base the shadow price on wage rates; others ask the question: What are people willing to pay to save time? This latter approach seeks relevant information from cases where drivers can choose between a slow, free route or a fast, toll route. Another area where benefits take the form of nonmarketed outputs is recreation. Water resources projects often create new recreational facilities as a by-product of flood control, irrigation, or hydroelectric plants. If no fees, or nominal fees, are charged for the use of these facilities, no market information that can be used to value the output is generated; a shadow price is required.[7]

In addition to valuing nonmarketed outputs, shadow prices are sometimes used as substitutes for market prices. This is conceptually different from the problem of estimating future market prices. The analyst may be convinced that market prices, either current or future, do not accurately reflect true values. There are two principal reasons for arguing that market prices are inappropriate. Output marketed by a government agency may be sold at consciously subsidized prices. Water for irrigation may be sold at prices well below what farmers would be willing to pay; a policy decision has been made to set prices equal to marginal costs or to charge low prices as part of a strategy of regional development. On equity grounds it may have been decided that low water prices will raise farmers' incomes to a more desirable level.[8] In this case the analyst would argue that revenue from the sale of irrigation water understates benefits and that a shadow price equal to what farmers would willingly pay should be used. This problem is illustrated by Figure 5.2 where a commodity, such as electricity or irrigation water, is assumed to be in completely inelastic supply. Given the demand

---

[7] Jack L. Knetsch, "Economics of Including Recreation as a Purpose of Eastern Water Projects," *Journal of Farm Economics,* December 1964. This is an example of a technique by which such a shadow price may be derived.

[8] Arguments such as this are often made in the context of evaluating government investment projects in underdeveloped countries. *See* Marglin, *op. cit.*

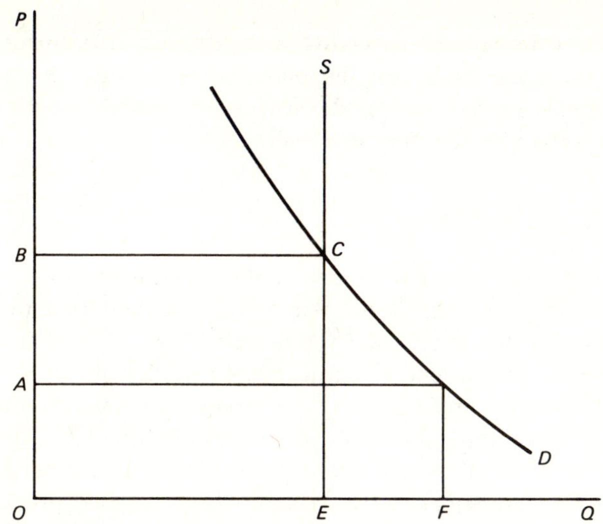

Figure 5.2 Demand for and inelastic supply of output from a public project.

function, *D,* a price of *OB* would clear the market. Suppose, however, that the price were set at *OA;* at that price consumers would be willing to purchase an amount equal to *OF*. Since no greater supply is forthcoming there will have to be some formal or informal system to ration the available supply *OE*. The public agency may adopt regulations that accomplish the required rationing; for example, licenses can be issued to firms using substantial amounts of electricity or each farmer may be limited to irrigating 160 acres. In this situation it would be appropriate to use *OB* as a shadow price in valuing the output. At this juncture the analyst must beware. It would involve double counting to use both *OB* as a shadow price and to treat added profits accruing to firms and farmers, because they use electricity or water being sold at below market-clearing prices, as project benefits. This method of pricing a commodity in fixed supply may or may not be associated with subsidization of the public price. For example, suppose price *OA* covered average cost; there would be no subsidy yet the shadow price, *OB,* should still be used in measuring the dollar values of benefits.

Some cases calling for the use of shadow prices instead of market prices stem directly from the theory of public goods. There may be externalities associated with the outputs marketed by the public agency. The per unit amount of the benefits or costs should be added to, or subtracted from, the price charged by the public agency in order to calculate benefits. Consider, for example, the construction of a public sewage system to replace private septic tanks, and suppose that after some treatment the effluent from the sewer system is dumped into a river. In addition to the benefits received by the households served, others might benefit by the elimination of health hazards as the septic tanks are removed. But there is no reason to suppose that all of the externalities associated with a public investment project are positive. In the above example, the public sewer system, by polluting the river, could create social costs for downstream communities and water users. The shadow price should reflect externalities.

MEASURING COSTS

In the broadest sense, the cost of any public investment project is the value of the best alternative uses of the real resources committed to the project. Since all possible alternatives, and the benefits to be derived from each, can seldom if ever be known, one relies instead on market prices to measure the value of the resources used. Most of the issues raised above with respect to market prices for outputs also apply when considering costs. Ideally, market prices for the real resources used in a public project, such as the wage rate for labor services, are equal to the value of their marginal products in alternative uses. Shadow prices can be used where there is a persuasive reason to doubt the validity of market prices. The prices of these resources might be artificially low; for example, the stipend paid to trainees in a manpower development program may be below their opportunity wage. Where the demands made by the projects are large relative to the total market for particular inputs, market prices can be expected to be bid up when the project is initiated. Input prices as measured in the market place might be too high if, for example, unemployed resources were used; resources might be compensated, but that compensation would be above their value in the alternative of unemployment.

This last point requires further elaboration.[9] Should one assume full employment and use those prices that would prevail at full employment when estimating the costs of public investment projects? This question is bound to arise in two contexts. In a developed economy, such as the United States, public works projects may be proposed as a major component of a set of policies designed to combat a recession or to develop a depressed region. If these projects will put the unemployed back to work, should the estimated cost be set below actual wage and other payments on the grounds that in the absence of the projects workers and other resources would remain idle? We think not. Modern fiscal and monetary policies are capable of averting depressions of the magnitude of the 1930s and minimizing the duration of recessions. The cost of idle resources should be considered in terms of alternative uses; the alternative to a particular public investment project is not continued idleness but rather the output of private goods and

---

[9] For a complete treatment of this issue, *see* Robert H. Haveman and John V. Krutilla, *Unemployment, Idle Capacity, and the Evaluation of Public Expenditures: National and Regional Analysis* (Baltimore: The Johns Hopkins Press, 1968).

services, the demand for which can be stimulated by tax cuts or lower interest rates, or spending on other public goods. Valuing resources at the prices that would prevail at full employment gives some assurance that temporarily idle resources will not be devoted to projects that generate relatively few benefits. In a less developed economy, where there is no assurance that unemployed or underdeveloped resources will be used in the absence of a public investment project, there may be some justification for valuing inputs at prices below market values.

This by no means exhausts the list of possible circumstances in which market prices may not reflect true opportunity costs. There is sometimes a tendency to neglect the costs of resources not paid for by the public agency sponsoring and analyzing the project in question. Often an agency has the free use of facilities no longer needed by another public agency; for example, when a training school is proposed on the site of an unused military base. The agency running the training project may not be required to rent the facility but that does not, in any fundamental sense, make that resource free. There always exist alternative uses of the facility, including its sale, and an appropriate cost figure should be calculated. There can also be intangible costs of a project just as there can be intangible benefits. Analysts often show more ingenuity in identifying intangible benefits than they do in considering intangible costs. When a unique natural site is being altered by a project, such as building a dam in the Grand Canyon, intangible costs are a primary concern. In less spectacular instances the issue is also important, but likely to be overlooked.[10]

THE ANALYSIS

Once the future benefits and costs of potential public investment projects have been expressed in dollar terms, comparisons of the benefits and costs of each project can be made and decisions reached. This task requires the application of formal mathematical models and appropriate decision rules. No conclusion can be reached by the simple comparison of aggregate benefits and costs in large part because the element of time enters in. Let us first, then, consider the treatment of time in benefit-cost analysis.

Time patterns, time horizons, and discounting. For purposes of mathematical simplicity time may be divided into years, rather than considered continuously, and future benefits and costs viewed as accruing in

---

[10] For an ecologist's discussion of the failure to do this in conjunction with the construction of the Aswan High Dam (and for a skeptical view of the economist's work with benefit-cost analysis in general), *see* Garrett Hardin, "To Trouble a Star: The Cost of Intervention in Nature," *Bulletin of the Atomic Scientists,* January 1970.

Table 5.1 Hypothetical Benefit-Cost Analysis (Dollar figures in millions)

Year	Benefits	Costs	Net Benefits	Discount Factor: Expression	Discount Factor: $i = 5\%$	Present Value of Net Benefits
(1)	(2)	(3)	(4)	(5)	(6)	(7)
1	$0	$4	$—4	$1/(1+i)$	.9524	$—3.8
2	0	4	—4	$1/(1+i)^2$	.9070	—3.6
3	1	1	0	$1/(1+i)^3$	.8638	0.0
4	2	1	1	$1/(1+i)^4$	.8227	0.8
5	3	1	2	$1/(1+i)^5$	.7835	1.6
6	4	1	3	$1/(1+i)^6$	.7462	2.2
7	4	1	3	$1/(1+i)^7$	.7107	2.1
8	4	1	3	$1/(1+i)^8$	.6768	2.0
9	3	1	2	$1/(1+i)^9$	.6446	1.3
10	2	1	1	$1/(1+i)^{10}$	.6139	0.6
Total	$23	$16	$7	$\sum_{t=1}^{10} \frac{1}{(1+i)^t}$		$2.3

specific years. Table 5.1 shows, in column 2, the time pattern, over an interval of ten years, for the dollar benefits of a hypothetical public investment project. It is assumed here that no benefits accrue until the third year, since two years are required for initial construction. Benefits at first increase, then level off, and finally decline. The third column in Table 5.1 shows costs for the hypothetical project—construction costs in the first two years and operating costs for the remaining years. In the fourth column net benefits—benefits minus costs—are shown: negative during the two-year construction phase, zero in the third year when benefits equal operating costs, and positive in the last seven years.

We have used a ten-year time horizon in our example. In many empirical situations the appropriate time horizon is readily apparent, for example, the engineering life of a physical project or the time remaining in the labor force for trainees. In other cases the appropriate time horizon may not be clear; the engineering life of a project may be unknown. If, in our example, net benefits are simply summed over the ten-year period, they total $7 million. But one cannot simply conclude that this figure accurately represents the excess of benefits over costs and that the project is therefore desirable. Future dollar amounts must be discounted to reflect the fact that dollars in the future are always worth less than dollars in the present.[11] In a

[11] This statement and the argument that follows have nothing to do with the possibility that future dollars may have less real purchasing power than current dollars because of inflation.

fundamental sense discounting reflects the value of resources in an alternative use. To take a simple example, \$100 one year from now is worth less than it is today; the \$100 could be deposited in an interest-paying bank today and one year from now it would be worth $\$100(1+i)$, where i is the rate of interest expressed in decimal terms. If the rate of interest paid by the bank were five percent we would have \$105 at the end of the year. To evaluate the worth today of \$100 to be paid to us one year from now we would have to divide that amount by the discount factor $(1+i)$, or multiply by $1/(1+i)$. Thus the present value of \$100 one year from now is $\$100/(1+i)$. With a five percent rate of interest that present value is approximately \$95.24. Looking at the matter another way, if we put \$95.24 today into a bank paying five percent interest, we would have \$100 in our account at the end of a year. When calculating the present value of an amount two years in the future we must raise the discount factor to the second power—$(1+i)^2$; similarly for the third year the discount factor must be raised to the third power—$(1+i)^3$, and so on. This compounding of the discount factor is identical to the concept of compound interest: money deposited in a bank earns interest at a compound rate so that at the end of a second year an initial \$100 deposit would grow to $\$100\ (1+i)^2$ or, at a five percent rate, \$110.25. Thus, the present value of \$110.25 two years hence is \$100 when the rate of discount is five percent. The bank account example should not conceal the essential phenomenon that today's real resources can be invested to enlarge the quantity of real resources available in the future. The fundamental reason for discounting, therefore, is to reflect the current value of resources in alternative investment uses.

The problem of choosing an appropriate time horizon is often a moot one because of the pervasive effects of discounting. The present value of either benefits or costs becomes very small when dollar amounts in the distant future are discounted. Consider, for example, the following table showing the present value of one dollar at various years in the future, discounted at rates of three, five, and ten percent.

Years in the Future	Present Value of One Dollar Discounted at		
	3%	5%	10%
10	\$.744	\$.614	\$.386
20	.554	.377	.149
50	.228	.087	.008
100	.052	.008	*

* less than .5 mills

Excluding far distant years from the analysis will typically have little effect on the results, especially if a relatively high discount rate is used. What may be a major problem to a future generation, such as the silting up of a storage reservoir behind a dam 200 years after construction, will be of little consequence to the current policy maker. On the other hand, time horizons should not be set so short as to miss significant benefits or costs. A ten-year time horizon would be inappropriate if, as in the case of a new subway system, benefits grow at a rapid rate after the tenth year.

We can return now to our hypothetical example. The last column in Table 5.1 shows the present values of net benefits. Net benefits were discounted at a five percent rate using the discount factors shown in column 6. This procedure is expressed mathematically as

$$PV = \sum_{t=1}^{n} \frac{B_t - C_t}{(1+i)^t} = \frac{B_1 - C_1}{(1+i)^1} + \frac{B_2 - C_2}{(1+i)^2} + \ldots + \frac{B_n - C_n}{(1+i)^n}$$

In comparison with the undiscounted sum of net benefits, $7 million, the sum of the present values of net benefits is significantly smaller, $2.3 million, though still positive. Had a sufficiently high discount rate been used, say ten percent, the present value of net benefits would be negative.

Formulas and decision rules. If every proposed public investment project where the present value of net benefits is positive could be undertaken there would be no need for the following discussion. But there are two fundamental reasons why such is not the case. First, some projects are mutually exclusive—you cannot build both a large dam and a small dam at the same site; you cannot train the same group of hard-core unemployed in two different programs at the same time. Second, and more important, a government agency operates in the context of budget constraints; in any one year it may be impossible to fund all projects with a positive present value of net benefits. Given a budget constraint projects must be ranked by an appropriate criterion. The three criteria which have been developed in the literature—the present value of net benefits, the rate of return, and the benefit-cost ratio—are illustrated in Table 5.2, where an example has been carefully prepared to show that the three criteria do not necessarily yield identical results.[12]

The present value of net benefits criterion is familiar from the discussion above. The rate of return criterion, sometimes referred to as the internal rate of return, has a long tradition in economic theory. Keynes, for example, used the concept to develop his marginal efficiency of capital function in the *General Theory*. The *rate of return* is defined as that rate of discount that

[12] E. J. Mishan, "A Proposed Normalization Procedure for Public Investment Criteria," *Economic Journal*, December 1967, suggests a reconciliation, given certain assumptions, of the three criteria.

Table 5.2 Comparison of Three Evaluation Criteria

The Three Criteria

I Present Value of Net Benefits: $\sum_{t=0}^{n} \frac{B_t - C_t}{(1+i)^t}$

II Rate of Return: $\sum_{t=0}^{n} \frac{B_t - C_t}{(1+r)^t} = 0$

III Benefit-Cost Ratio: $\dfrac{\sum_{t=0}^{n} \frac{B_t}{(1+i)^t}}{\sum_{t=0}^{n} \frac{C_t}{(1+i)^t}}$

where B_t = total benefits in year t
C_t = total costs in year t
n = number of years spanned by the analysis
i = social discount rate
r = rate of return

The Three Decision Rules

I Choose projects having the highest present values of net benefits; reject any project having a negative present value of net benefits.

II Choose projects having the highest rates of return; reject any project that has a rate of return less than the social discount rate.

III Choose projects having the highest benefit-cost ratios; reject any project having a benefit-cost ratio less than one.

The Example ($i = 5\%$)

Project	Cost $t=0$	Benefits $t=1$	Benefits $t=2$	Total Undiscounted Net Benefits	Criteria Measure I	Criteria Measure II	Criteria Measure III
A	$200	$106	$112.36	$18.36	$2.86	$r = 6\%$	1.014
B	100	107	—	7.00	1.90	$r = 7\%$	1.019
C	50	—	57.14	7.14	1.20	$r = 6.9\%$	1.024

will set the present value of net benefits equal to zero.[13] The *benefit-cost ratio* expresses explicitly the relative magnitudes of the present value of benefits and the present value of costs, rather than being derived from net benefits as is the case with the first two criteria.

[13] Certain time patterns exist for benefits and costs for which no rate of return can be calculated or for which multiple solutions for the rate of return are derived. *See* J. H. Lorrie and L. J. Savage, "Three Problems in Capital Rationing," *Journal of Business*, October 1955.

The example in Table 5.2 shows how the three criteria can give contradictory ranking of projects. For simplicity projects *A*, *B*, and *C* have been assumed to incur all costs during the present time period ($t = 0$) and benefits are limited to the two following time periods. Using a discount rate of five percent the present value of net benefits for each project can be determined. With the discount rate of five percent, project *A* is ranked highest using the present value of net benefits criterion. Project *B* is preferred using the rate of return criterion. Project *C* is ranked highest using the benefit-cost ratio technique. All three projects are acceptable in terms of each of the criteria; in each case the present value of net benefits is positive, the rate of return is greater than the discount rate, and the benefit-cost ratios are greater than unity.[14]

Suppose that a budget constraint of \$200 prevents all three projects from being funded. Which criteria should be used? By the present value of net benefits criterion, project *A* ranks highest but would absorb the entire \$200 available for investment. If, alternatively, the projects are replicable, the \$200 could be used to fund four project *C*'s and the present value of net benefits from the four would be \$4.80, a greater amount than the \$2.86 from project *A*. Two project *B*'s would have a combined present value of \$3.80, also greater than that for project *A*. As long as projects are replicable, ranking by the benefit-cost ratio criterion yields a set of projects that maximizes the present value of net benefits for the level of investment dictated by the budget constraint. Even if projects *B* and *C* were not replicable, undertaking both *B* and *C* would be preferable to undertaking *A*; the total present value of net benefits would be \$3.10, again greater than that for project *A*. This would leave \$50 of the agency's budget unspent; perhaps that would be bureaucratically unacceptable. In cases where projects are mutually exclusive the present value of net benefits criterion should be used. Suppose projects *A*, *B*, and *C* represent large, medium, and small dams that could be built at a single site. If the dam with the highest benefit-cost ratio were constructed the additional present value of net benefits from the large dam ($\$2.86 - \$1.20 = \$1.66$) could never be reaped.

The nature of the budget constraint is the key consideration in ranking a complex set of potential investment projects. If an agency invests in projects whose benefits are in a marketable form and the receipts are available to that agency for reinvestment, then ranking by the rate of return criterion is appropriate. By always selecting projects with the highest rate of

---

[14] At higher discount rates the rankings by the present value criterion would change. At a discount rate of six percent the present value of net benefits for either project *B* or project *C* exceeds the present value of project *A*; by the present value criterion a different project would be selected at a six percent discount rate than would be selected at a five percent discount rate. At discount rates in excess of seven percent none of the projects would be acceptable by any of the three criteria.

return the agency can, by reinvesting its receipts, establish the future stream of net benefits having the largest possible present value. This presumes that receipts may be reinvested to earn the same rate of return. More typically, however, an agency cannot invest in projects with marketable benefits and its budget is likely to be constrained over the foreseeable future. A commitment in the present to investment projects with relatively high operating costs may mean that future budgets will be largely absorbed by these operating costs, severely limiting (or even excluding) the possibility of initiating new projects in the future. When no receipts outside the budget appropriated by the legislature are available to cover future operating costs, the benefit-cost ratio criterion is the more appropriate one; it explicitly compares in absolute terms the present value of benefits and costs rather than the difference between them. Glancing back at Table 5.1 may help to make this point. If $10 million were added each year to both benefits and costs, net benefits and the present value of net benefits would be unaffected. With these added benefits and costs the benefit-cost ratio would be lower. Ranking projects by the ratio criterion is more likely to lead to the selection, over many budget years, of a set of projects that maximizes the present value of net benefits from the investment of that entire budget.

The proper discount rate. The discount rate used has a critical impact on any benefit-cost analysis. The question naturally arises, what is the proper discount rate? In part, there are different answers to this question because the discount rate has two problems to solve: proper allocation of resources between the private and public sectors, and the allocation of resources between the provision of current and future goods and services.[15] The rate used to solve this latter problem is usually referred to as the *social rate of time preference*. Observing interest rates that prevail in the securities market is not much help because there are a bewildering variety of securities, and a corresponding multiplicity of interest rates. The only market determined interest rate of special significance is the yield on long-term, federal government securities because these securities are essentially riskless. Barring some holocaust, in which case such matters would be the least of our problems, we are all confident that interest and principal payments on United States government securities will be met.[16] The fact that individuals

---

[15] William J. Baumol, "On the Social Rate of Discount," *American Economic Review,* September 1968. *See also* the several comments on Baumol's article and his reply in *American Economic Review,* December 1969.

[16] Included in the rate of interest on long-term federal government securities may be compensation for bearing a risk of a different sort—the risk that, because of inflation, the real purchasing power of the dollars received in the future as interest and principal payments may be worth less than current dollars. The inflation problem in benefit-cost analysis is discussed in the following section.

and institutions are willing to hold these securities at prevailing yields (interest rates) indicates that they prefer the stream of future payments that ownership of these securities guarantees rather than the sum that could be realized if they sold them at prevailing market prices. This rate of interest is, therefore, the best measure we have of the social rate of time preference, and is the reason why many economists argue that the yield on long-term federal government bonds should be used as the discount rate in benefit-cost analysis. If the market gives this evidence of the relative preferences of individuals for current versus future income then, it is argued, that rate should be used for discounting the future costs and benefits of public investment projects. To use a higher rate rules out some projects that generate future benefits of a dollar magnitude that the public must prefer in comparison to the dollar magnitude of the costs of that project. Conversely, to use a lower rate wastes current resources by accepting projects whose future benefits the public values less highly than the current value of those resources.

The decision to undertake a public investment project involves not only the question of comparing present and future values but also the allocation of resources between the public and private sectors. Using allocative criteria, resources should not be used in the public sector if the benefits they generate are less than the benefits that would accrue from their application in the private sector. Therefore it can be argued that the rate of return on private uses of resources should be used as the discount rate for the purposes of benefit-cost analysis.[17] Again evidence from the marketplace confuses us because different rates of return are earned on investments in different sectors of the economy; differentials in private rates of return must, in part at least, reflect degrees of risk. We can, however, think in terms of the minimum rate of return required to reward an investor in a private project when, alternatively, that investor could have purchased a long-term government bond at the prevailing yield. There is, however, no unique rate of return on the net receipts attributable to riskless investments in the private sector due to the tax laws regarding the treatment of interest and depreciation in the calculation of corporate tax liabilities. The actual rate depends on the mix of equity and debt financing used in a hypothetically risk-free corporate investment, and the rate at which depreciation is charged. Using an average rate of return on actual streams of net receipts from private investments in calculating present values for benefit-cost analyses seems inappropriate also. If such a rate were used to evaluate investments in the private sector whose

[17] Some writers at this point make a distinction between consumption and investment uses of resources in the private sector. Krutilla and Eckstein, *op. cit.*, chapter IV, for example, developed a schema for weighting rates of return on corporate investments and the interest rates faced by consumers by the relative importance of corporate and personal income taxes in the federal tax structure to estimate a proper discount rate for benefit-cost studies.

rates of return fall below the average, such private investments would be judged a waste of resources. Clearly not all these types of investments will be ruled out by private investors; it would, therefore, be a mistake to use such a high rate in evaluating all public investment projects. Similarly, it would be a mistake to judge as wasted resources used in the private sector that failed to earn a rate of return as high as the average rate of return on projects in the public sector. For resource allocation purposes it is the lowest rate of return on streams of net receipts on private investments, which can be undertaken without losses to investors, that should be used in evaluating public investment projects. Our tax laws operate to exclude the possibility of uniquely determining that rate.

During 1968 a subcommittee of the Joint Economic Committee made a study of the discount rates actually used by the various federal agencies.[18] Some agencies, including those in the water resources area, were required by law to use a rate based upon the average [coupon] rate of interest payable by the Treasury on interest-bearing marketable securities of the United States outstanding at the end of the fiscal year preceding such computation, which upon original issue, had terms to maturity of 15 years or more. That rate was calculated to be about 3.2 percent at a time when actual market yields on long-term Treasury bonds were above 5 percent. Other agencies were reported to use rates varying from zero to 20 percent. As the Comptroller General said in a report to the subcommittee, "It is possible that the wide disparity in agency practices and discount rates may produce a more serious misallocation of resources than would exist in the absence of discounting." The subcommittee recommended on the basis of its study "that no public investment be deemed 'economic' or 'efficient' if it fails to yield overall benefits which are at least as great as those which the same resources would have produced if left in the private sector. Currently the rate of return on alternative minimum risk private spending is at least five percent."[19] Further, the subcommittee judged that the current yield on long-term federal government securities is the lowest possible rate consistent with the minimum risk opportunity cost of displaced private spending. A few months after the appearance of that report the Bureau of the Budget announced that, following a recommendation of the Water Resources Council, discount rates used to evaluate water resources projects would in the future be based on the

---

[18] *Interest Rate Guidelines for Federal Decisionmaking*, Hearings before the Subcommittee on Economy in Government of the Joint Economic Committee Congress of the United States Ninetieth Congress (Washington, D.C.: Government Printing Office, 1968); *Economic Analysis of Public Investment Decisions: Interest Rate Policy and Discounting Analysis*, a report of the Subcommittee on Economy in Government of the Joint Economic Committee Congress of the United States Ninetieth Congress (Washington, D.C.: Government Printing Office, 1968).

[19] *Interest Rate Guidelines, op. cit.*, p. 34.

average yield during the preceding year on Treasury securities having 15 years or more to maturity. For the fiscal year 1969, a rate of 4⅝ percent would be used compared with an old rate of 3¼ percent. Given the theoretical indeterminacy of the social discount rate, this new method of specifying the discount rate seems acceptable.

Risk, uncertainty, and price level changes. Public investment projects are just as subject to risk and uncertainty as private sector investments. Risk means the probabilities that can be attached to future events. The probability that revenue from the sale of electricity will be reduced because of drought can be estimated; mortality tables can be used to estimate the most probable life spans for a group of trainees in a manpower program. Prevention of floods is another area where a probabilistic approach must be taken to estimate program benefits.[20] Uncertainty is more difficult to handle than risk. Unlike risk no data from the past permit the quantification of uncertainty. When a manpower training program is initiated one is uncertain about the outcome—how many trainees will complete the program, how many will successfully acquire new skill, how many of these will use these skills in future employment, and so on. One can guess on all these points and perform the benefit-cost analysis before the program starts, but the results are inherently subject to uncertainty. An analysis based on actual information gained sometime after the completion of the program is not plagued by as many of these uncertainties.

Probably the most pervasive uncertainty is the impact of future technological change. A public investment project that appears desirable when the benefit-cost analysis is made may turn out to be a waste of resources because new technology creates a lower cost alternative. A hydroelectric project may look desirable today but technological change may make it possible to use atomic power to generate electricity at one-tenth the cost of current atomic generating plants. The technology of the future may render today's pollution control systems obsolete. Decisionmaking in such cases is extremely difficult; one has to consider the consequences of postponing action. In cases where action is imperative the consequences of future technology may well be ignored. Today's garbage must be collected. Benefit-cost analysis can be used to evaluate alternative methods of collection and disposal; a particular system may be selected even if there is a strong possibility of a dramatic technological breakthrough in the near future that will provide a far less costly solution to the problem. On the other hand if immediate action is not imperative but may be required in the more distant future—desalination of water for use in Southern California, for example—

[20] For a treatment of this matter, *see* Howard Raiffa, *Decision Analysis* (Reading, Mass.: Addison-Wesley, 1968).

then no current action to construct a large scale project may be the wisest decision.

One aspect of the future about which people generally may have strong expectations is the course of the aggregate price level. In all western economies there has been at least some inflation since the end of World War II. At the start of the 1970s most Americans probably expect at least a two to three percent annual rise in price level. This raises the question of how to treat future prices in benefit-cost analysis. The general practice is to assume a constant price level when measuring future benefits and costs since analysts may be loath to make their price expectations explicit, particularly those who are employed by governments committed to price stability as a matter of policy. Beyond this understandable predilection for such an assumption there is a theoretical reason for it. A measure of benefits made high by the use of inflated prices would exaggerate the difference between real costs and benefits of a project. Price level expectations, widely held by participants in the economy, are likely to affect the general level of interest rates. Lenders will demand compensation in the form of higher interest rates for taking the risk that the real purchasing power of money will be lower when the principal of a loan is returned to them. To the extent that, say, one or two percentage points in the yield on long-term government bonds reflects this phenomenon, using that yield as the discount rate in benefit-cost analysis gives a downward bias to estimates of the present value of benefits and costs in cases where future benefits and costs have been estimated assuming a constant price level.

Equity considerations. We started this chapter by suggesting that benefit-cost analysis was a means to refine a government's allocative policy. But, as is so often the case, it is impossible to completely divorce allocative policy from equity considerations. Many public investment projects provide benefits to particular groups within the total population—residents of a specific area, a particular group of labor force trainees, or a single age group. Should a dollar's worth of benefits going to each subgroup be treated equally? Should a project that raises the income-earning capacity of a group of poor farmers be considered differently from a project that yields an equal present value of net benefits in the form of recreational facilities that will be enjoyed by the relatively affluent? There are no simple answers to questions like these.[21] In part the political process reflects societal judgments on these equity problems by allocating different budget amounts to specific agencies so that agencies responsible for investment projects affecting the poor will be able to fund projects with lower benefit-cost ratios than other agencies.

---

[21] One of the few considerations of this problem in the literature is by Burton A. Weisbrod, "Income Redistribution Effects and Benefit-Cost Analysis," in Chase, *op. cit.*

A single agency may still, however, face the problem of choosing among projects that have different distributional impacts. It is wiser for the analyst to confront decision makers with specific estimates of the distributional effects of alternative projects than to ignore the issue altogether.

A concluding statement. Benefit-cost analysis does not solve all decision-making problems in the area of public investment projects. The analysis itself is full of conceptual pitfalls as indicated above. What the technique does do is provide a framework for narrowing the range within which policy makers have to make more or less subjective judgments. Some projects can easily be ruled out and others found clearly to be acceptable. Where the relationships of benefits to costs among alternative projects are less certain, the key areas of uncertainty that call for the application of judgment can be identified. *Sensitivity analysis* tests the significance of major assumptions by recomputing benefits and costs as alternative versions of the assumptions are specified. To show, in a less abstract way, how benefit-cost analysis can be used, the following section applies the technique to the area of investment in human resources.

BENEFIT-COST ANALYSIS OF INVESTMENTS IN HUMAN CAPITAL

In the 1950s economists began to appreciate investments in human capital, investments that enhance the future income-producing capacity of individuals. Research, both theoretical and applied, demonstrated that expenditures for education and health could yield substantial returns in terms of increasing the productivity of the labor force. Along with these developments in economics, and not independent of them, federal, state, and local governments expanded existing programs and initiated new ones in the areas of vocational education, vocational rehabilitation, manpower training, Job Corps, and so on. All such programs have as one of their primary goals increasing the earning power of individuals. Benefit-cost analyses have been made of many specific programs in an effort to evaluate their effectiveness. Since all programs in this area have certain common features the following discussion is presented in rather general terms—a framework of analysis that, with a few modifications, would fit any human capital investment project. One conclusion that emerges from the discussion is that projects that look desirable from a societal viewpoint may not appear desirable in the eyes of the individuals expected to participate.

From a societal vantage point the primary benefit of a human capital investment project is the additional output of goods and services attributable to the project. Actual increases in goods and services resulting from the training can be measured by the additional future earnings of the trainees; employers will be willing to pay higher wages and salaries, including all fringe benefits, in amounts equal to their contribution to added output.[22] In performing the analysis care must be taken not to confuse employment histories before and after training with the conceptually relevant employment experience with and without training. If workers averaged $1.50 per hour before participation in the training program, and $2.00 per hour afterwards, the increase in wages is not necessarily attributable to the training. General developments in the labor market are relevant also; the degree of unemployment may have declined and the general level of wages gone up. The best estimating procedure then would be to have employment data for a control group as well as for workers who underwent training. If the control group, similar to the trainees in terms of age, sex, education, and so on, experienced an increase in average earnings from $1.50 to $1.75 per hour, then one can conclude that an increase in average earnings of only $.25 per hour was attributable to the program. Such an estimate of additional earnings becomes the starting point for estimating the benefits of the program. Since policy makers are interested in analyses of current programs, the analyst cannot sit back and wait for trainees to complete their lifetime participation in the labor force to compute these benefits; he must take evidence of increased wages based on initial post-training employment experience and project these increases into the future so that the present value of the estimated stream of benefits can be calculated.

From a societal viewpoint there may be other benefits from a manpower training program. As the trainees become employed they may increase the productivity of other workers. For example, many manpower projects have been designed specifically to train the unemployed or underemployed as "subprofessionals": engineering aides, medical and hospital technicians, nurses' aides, and the like. Such employees are likely to increase the productivity (and hence incomes) of the professional engineers, medical personnel, and nurses with whom they work. Effective training programs may also lead to a reduction in welfare and other transfer payments, and often this is a prime political factor lending support to such programs. This issue must be treated with a good deal of analytical care. Welfare and unemployment payments must be viewed as transfers from taxpayers to recipients. As such, output of goods and services is not affected though the distribution of income is altered. To count reduced transfer payments as a benefit one would have to make an interpersonal comparison of the utility of income and conclude that the income is more highly valued by taxpayers than by recipients.[23] But, the value of any resource used to administer transfer payments

---

[22] Additional earnings may also accrue to nonlabor factors of production in the form of profits and rents. These are empirically difficult to identify and are generally ignored in the literature.

[23] On equity grounds one might argue that transfer payments from income-earning taxpayers to employable recipients should be minimized. One other argument can be

that are freed for some alternative use as a result of a successful training program would be a genuine benefit of the program.[24]

Other benefits are also possible. The productivity of future generations may be increased as trainees with additional education and income induce their children to become better educated. The trainees themselves may have new options open to them in the form of additional education and training because they successfully completed a particular program. Trainees may become better citizens and reduce the costs to society of their former behavior. While it is interesting to raise these points, the central issue in measuring benefits is still the extent of additional earnings attributable to the program.

Individual trainees will take a view of the benefits other than the societal one. Their primary concern will be with the anticipated additional after-tax earnings attributable to the program. Their expectations may exceed or fall short of the additional earnings that actually materialize. They may gain some psychic income from their future employment but surely they will not be concerned with the effect that their training has on the income-earning capacity of others. If trainees receive some stipend during the period of training they will, of course, view that payment as a benefit to them; whereas they are actually transfer payments.

The costs of a manpower development program are traditionally thought of as the instructional and other expenses borne by the sponsoring agency. Some costs may additionally be borne by other agencies, but the major real cost, usually far exceeding direct agency expenses, is the income (output of goods and services) foregone by trainees during the period of their training.[25] Even though some, or all, trainees may have been unemployed at the beginning of the program, in practically all cases it would be unrealistic to assume that all trainees would be unemployed for the entire period in the absence of the program.

Just as trainees view benefits differently from society, so their conception of costs will differ. A trainee considers any tuition payment and out-of-pocket expenses as a personal cost of the program; he also considers foregone

---

raised: If the taxes required to finance transfer payments have a disincentive effect (see Chapter 7) so that income earners work less (produce fewer goods and services) than they would in the absence of that tax, then reducing the welfare rolls may generate added benefits as the previously taxed workers supply additional labor services. Although a theoretical possibility, the argument is too strained to be of empirical significance.

[24] Here we have an interesting anomaly. The salaries of bureaucrats administering the system of transfer payments are included in gross national product (see Chapter 11) and their salaries in some alternative occupations would also be included. Thus while there is no change in gross national product (ignoring any changes in salary levels) additional real output results.

[25] Every college student should be aware that foregone income is the greatest part of the cost of his education.

earnings (net of taxes) and any reduction in transfer payments received as costs.

When computing the present value of future societal benefits the analyst will use a social rate of discount. Individual trainees may discount future expected income at much higher rates because the rates at which they borrow are relatively high or because their implicit rates of time preference are very high. Individuals may view the future with a greater degree of uncertainty than the analyst. These arguments suggest that many training programs seen as desirable by society—that is, their benefit-cost ratios are greater than unity—may, quite rationally, from the individual trainee's vantage point, appear undesirable. This reasoning forms the basic rationale for paying stipends to trainees primarily to offset the opportunity costs of foregone income.

One of the best benefit-cost studies evaluating investments in human capital is a study of graduates from a two-year post-secondary technical school in North Carolina.[26] The earnings for graduates over a four-year period after graduation were compared with those of demographically and educationally similar high school graduates to estimate the additional income attributable to the two years of technical education. These average earnings differentials increased from $555 per year in the first year after graduation to $1,038 per year in the fourth year. By projecting these differentials into the future and making a comparison with educational costs, including foregone earnings, an internal rate of return of 16.5 percent was calculated. The present value of these net benefits, discounting at five percent, was $33,713 per graduate; discounting at ten percent it was $11,494. The benefit-cost ratios were 4.5:1 (at a five percent discount rate) and 1.5:1 (at a ten percent discount rate). This kind of analysis can be very helpful to policy makers attempting to plan future human capital investment projects. One final word: Equity considerations should not be forgotten. On equity grounds a training project having a 1.5:1 benefit-cost ratio might be preferable to a project having a ratio of 5:1 if the former resulted in additional income to a particularly disadvantaged segment of the population.

---

[26] Adger B. Carroll and Loren A. Ihnen, "Costs and Returns for Two Years of Post-secondary Technical Schooling: A Pilot Study," *The Journal of Political Economy,* December 1967. For two collections of papers devoted to this topic, *see* Gerald Somers (ed.), *Retraining the Unemployed* (Madison: University of Wisconsin Press, 1968) and G. G. Somers and W. D. Wood (eds.), *Cost-Benefit Analysis of Manpower Policies* (Kingston, Ontario: Industrial Relations Center, Queen's University, 1969).

6

PROGRAM BUDGETING

Most government agencies have a multiplicity of functions and thus face the problem of analyzing their entire program consisting of many individual projects. In addition legislators and high-level administrators must analyze the relationships among the programs of many separate agencies. A government's budget comprises a framework within which analysis of an agency's entire program takes place, or within which legislative and administrative review occurs. The entire budgetary process, from initial development of requests by the lowest levels of government organizations, through administrative and legislative review to final approval, is a mechanism through which major public expenditure decisions may be made. The nature of that budgetary process and the format of the budget have a significant impact on the ability of a government to meet efficiently citizen demands for public goods.

Any organization with decentralized decision-making requires a budget as a means of controlling expenditures. The budget for a government agency specifies the amount and type of spending that agency can undertake during an accounting period. Without budgetary limits spending is likely to exceed available financial resources as each official with the authority to expend funds feels he can do a better job by spending more—hiring more personnel, renting more space, carpeting the floor, or buying the best equipment. No wonder then that organizations force managers to live within their budgets. This control of spending may be accomplished using budget formats such as those of the federal government described in Chapter 12, but such control is only one of the functions of a budget. Of more concern to us here is the means by which a government's budget can explicitly show the relationship between the objectives of public economic policy and the resources used by a government. We wish to view budgeting as a means of rational decision-making. Our purpose in this chapter is to describe program budgeting, a modern budgeting technique suited for economic analyses of public expenditures.[1]

PROGRAMS

Budgets typically enumerate expenditures in terms of object categories such as personnel, equipment, supplies, or construction. Keeping budgets and accounts in terms of object categories is sensible as a means of fiscal control, but is of limited use in analyzing the contributions made by expenditures toward attaining the goals of public policy. Alternatively, one can think of total agency expenditures for the set of programs for which that agency has responsibility. Instead of (or, more realistically, in addition to) having a budget in which salary and equipment expenditures are enumerated, the budget would specify spending to advance attainment of a particular objective—health for instance. These expenditures would constitute the health program. Most agencies devote their resources to a number of programs and some programs draw support from many agencies. Thinking about budgeting in the context of programs automatically raises several questions. How are

---

[1] An initial bibliography on program budgeting would include the following: "Planning-Programming-Budgeting Symposium," *Public Administration Review,* December 1966; "Symposium on PPBS Reexamined," *Public Administration Review,* March/April 1969; Harry P. Hatry and John F. Cotton, *Program Planning for State, County, City* (Washington, D.C.: George Washington University Press, 1967); Joint Economic Committee, 91st Congress, 1st Session, *The Analysis and Evaluation of Public Expenditures: The PPB System,* Volumes I, II, and III (Washington, D.C.: Government Printing Office, 1969); David Novick (ed.), *Program Budgeting, Program Analysis and the Federal Budget* (Cambridge: Harvard University Press, 1965); Harold A. Hovey, *The Planning-Programming-Budgeting Approach to Government Decision-Making* (New York: Frederick A. Praeger, 1968); and Fremont J. Lyden and Ernest G. Miller (eds.), *Planning Programming Budgeting: A Systems Approach to Management* (Chicago: Markham Publishing Company, 1968).

programs defined? What are the objectives of each program? What is the total commitment of resources to each program?

The starting point in the development of a program budget is relating programs to broad objectives of public policy. This relation is done through a *program structure* and is best understood by way of example. Elimination of poverty became a widely voiced goal of public policy during the 1960s. Many new programs were initiated by the federal government and a new executive agency, the Office of Economic Opportunity, was established. Many existing programs were of course related to the war on poverty. Figure 6.1

Figure 6.1 A program structure for the War on Poverty.

GENERAL OBJECTIVE: ELIMINATION OF POVERTY

Specific Objective: Enhancement of Earning Power

- Programs
    - Student Scholarships and Other Aid
    - Work-Study Programs
    - Vocational Education
    - "Anti-dropout" Programs
    - Elementary and Secondary School Programs
    - "Head Start"
    - Labor Mobility and Relocation
    - Job Placement
    - Provision of Skills
    - Adult Literacy

Specific Objective: Income Maintenance

- Programs
    - Unemployment Insurance
    - Retirement and Disability Benefits
    - Public Assistance
    - Health Programs for the Poor
    - Federal Tax System
    - Food Stamps

Specific Objective: Community and Environmental Improvements

- Programs
    - Low Income Housing
    - Community Action Programs
    - Area Redevelopment

illustrates the principles of a program structure, relating a wide variety of programs to the general goal of eliminating poverty. Programs are grouped under three more specific objectives, enhancement of earning power, income maintenance, and community and environmental improvement. Administrative responsibility for the various programs rests with a variety of federal agencies and many involve explicit relationships between the federal government and agencies of state and local governments. Many of these programs have other objectives as well. A program designed to enhance the earning power of the poor through vocational education, for example, will—presuming that it is an effective program—enhance the earning power of the nonpoor as well, for not all vocational education students are members of poor families. To state the matter alternatively, vocational education also contributes to a specific educational objective: equipping students with occupational competency in those jobs for which employment opportunities exist. As new goals of public policy emerge from the political process, new program structures are conceived. This process forces the reexamination of old programs in the light of new objectives. The food stamp program, for example, emerged from an older program of surplus food disbursements administered by the Department of Agriculture. Food stamps may be purchased by poor people at a designated fraction of their face value and are spent at their face value for groceries. The consequences of viewing this program as a means of attacking the problem of malnutrition among the poor are quite different from viewing it as a method for disposing of excess farm production.

The programs listed for illustrative purposes in Figure 6.1 are themselves specified in broad terms. A more detailed program structure would break each down into a number of *program elements*. The level of detail can become fine, but in general a program element is treated as the smallest unit of analysis. In the area of vocational education a program element would be a specific curriculum, say to train operators of data processing equipment, in a particular school. A fully developed system of program budgeting requires that expenditures be budgeted in terms of program elements. Spending decisions should be based on each program element's contribution to policy objectives. The connection between program budgeting and benefit-cost analysis should be obvious: Benefit-cost analysis can be used to evaluate different types of program elements as alternative means of accomplishing a particular policy objective.

The difference between a budget expressed in terms of object categories and in terms of programs is illustrated by Table 6.1. Here the Department of Defense budget for the 1969 fiscal year is presented both ways. The program structure used by the Department of Defense was first introduced by Secretary McNamara in 1961. Although budget planning and the analysis of alternative weapons systems are conducted within the framework of this program structure, Congress still acts upon the defense budget on the basis of object categories, considering appropriation bills for military personnel, procurement, and so on. In August 1965, President Johnson, by executive order, required most federal agencies to emulate the Department of Defense budgetary system and apply a "Planning, Programming, Budgeting" (PPB) system to their own activities. Initial response at most agencies was far from enthusiastic. Results have not measured up to the hopes of those who looked for significant improvements in the efficiency of the federal government. However, despite shortcomings, the system has provided an

Table 6.1 **Department of Defense Budget, 1969 (Millions of dollars)**

Object Categories	**Actual Budget Authority**
Military personnel	21,427
Operation and maintenance	22,349
Procurement	20,542
Research, development, test, and evaluation	7,629
Military construction	1,168
Family housing	512
Civil defense	60
Revolving and management funds and other	961
Military trust funds	8
Deductions for offsetting receipts	—128
Total	76,970
Programs	
Strategic forces	8,174
General purposes forces	29,132
Intelligence and communications	5,585
Airlift and sealift	1,497
Guard and reserve forces	2,126
Research and development	4,595
Central supply and maintenance	9,312
Training, medical and other general personnel activities	12,369
(Retired pay included in category above)	(2,450)
Administrative and associated activities	1,308
Support to other nations	2,041
Total distributed to programs above	76,138
Undistributed nonprogram financing adjustments	833
Total	76,970

SOURCE: *The Budget of the United States Government, Fiscal Year 1971* (Washington, D.C.: Government Printing Office, 1970), pp. 285–298 and *Special Analyses Budget of the United States, Fiscal Year, 1971* (Washington, D.C.: Government Printing Office, 1970), p. 273.

improved environment for decisionmaking and, in a number of instances, analytical studies growing out of the PPB system have caused different decisions to be made than would have been without them.[2]

[2] *See* Jack W. Carlson, "The Status and Next Steps for Planning, Programming and Budgeting" in *The Analysis and Evaluation of Public Expenditures: The PPB System, op.cit.*, Vol. II.

BUDGETING

Categorizing expenditures by program is only half of the program budgeting concept. The process by which budgets are determined is equally important. In any government that process includes initial formulation, review, and enactment; naturally the larger the unit of government the more complex and time-consuming that process becomes. We discuss here a few basic propositions.

Multiyear budgets are better than annual budgets. Practically all government programs are either ongoing or at least last over several fiscal years. When budgets are prepared, reviewed, and enacted on an annual basis there may be a tendency to ignore the consequences of current expenditure decisions on future budgets. The foot-in-the-door technique can be used more easily with annual budgeting; a program involving modest expenditures in the first year may be introduced without fully examining the implied expenditure levels in future years. Construction and research projects usually last several years and commitments in one year imply carry-over costs for future years. These future costs should be explicitly considered in the budgetary process. For an example of the difficulties that can arise, consider the experience of many federal research programs during the 1960s. When new research programs were initiated there was a natural tendency on the part of program officers in the administering agencies to make research grants and contracts in the first year to show Congress that the funds were being used. Since most of these grants and contracts involved funding over several years, demands were implicitly being placed on future research budgets. When, in the late 1960s, those budgets were not increased because of Vietnam spending, carry-over costs absorbed a very large part of the available funds. The administering agencies were then in the position of being unable to fund many new projects just at the point when full staffs had been hired to administer the program, and when individual researchers and research organizations were responding to pleas for the submission of proposals. Some of this staff demoralization and antagonizing of the research community might have been avoided if more attention had been paid to the long-run impact of the initial funding decisions. Most federal agencies now prepare five-year budget forecasts, revising the whole set of forecasts each year and adding on a new year in preparation for the annual review by the Office of Management and Budget. These forecasts are not, at the start of the 1970s, included in the budget documents submitted to Congress. Their consideration in the budgetary process depends on the predilections of the various subcommittees of the Senate and House Appropriations Committees.

Total budget requests should be reviewed, not simply incremental changes. There is a tendency in the process of reviewing budgets, either at the administrative or legislative level, to give close scrutiny to the changes proposed for particular budget items rather than examining programs in their entirety. Focusing on increases and reductions—called *incremental budgeting*—can well lead to hardening of the bureaucratic arteries, maintaining old programs that go unexamined simply because no substantial changes are called for in the budget. The alternative—called *zero base budgeting*—is more likely to insure that total expenditures are regularly examined in the light of current objectives. This does not mean that every program must be viewed *de novo* each year, as many surely should; rather long periods of time should not pass with programs going unscrutinized.[3]

Segregating current and capital expenditures can be a useful budgetary device. Governments that make this distinction in a formal way are said to use *capital budgeting*.[4] When, for example, a small school district builds a new high school, its expenditures for a two- or three-year period will be unusually large; special revenues will be required, probably from a bond issue. Separating these extraordinary receipts and expenditures from the current operating budget helps to clarify the budgetary situation. Making the separation is likely to force explicit recognition of the future consequences of the capital projects undertaken. In addition to recognizing construction costs that will carry-over to future-year budgets, operating costs that will most likely be higher once the new projects are completed may be anticipated.

Less developed countries commonly use capital budgets. Where governments play a major role in the development process by financing a large number of capital projects, a separate budget showing the sources of investment funds is useful. Some of these funds will come from domestic taxation and borrowing and others from foreign sources—loans and grants from other governments and international agencies like the World Bank or the Inter-American Development Bank. Presumably the current operating expenditures of the government will be met out of domestic taxation, and capital budgets permit domestic lenders as well as foreign suppliers of funds to make this evaluation. There is a possible drawback. Capital projects are thought to be particularly important in the development process since they render productive services on into the future. If planners emphasize these projects at the expense of other government operations, that is, if they attempt to keep the operating budget at a minimum and shift funds to the capital budget, such services as education and health may be slighted. There is some danger then that capital budgeting may bias the allocation of resources

---

3 *See* Murray L. Weidenbaum, "Budget 'Uncontrollability' as an Obstacle to Improving the Allocation of Government Resources" in *The Analysis and Evaluation of Public Expenditures: The PPB System, op. cit.*, Vol. I, for a discussion of these rigidities in the federal budgetary process.

4 Richard Goode and Eugene A. Birnbaum, "Government Capital Budgets," *International Monetary Fund Staff Papers*, February 1956.

Table 6.2 Federal Budget Investment and Current Outlays, 1969 (Millions of dollars)

Investment-Type Outlays	
Additions to Federal Assets—Civil:	
Loans and other financial investments	3,374
Physical Assets:	
Public works	2,186
Major commodity inventories	353
Major equipment and other physical assets	370
National Defense	26,645
Additions to State, Local, and Private Assets:	
Civil	6,659
National Defense	17
Development Outlays:	
Civil	15,482
National Defense	9,186
Total	64,272
Current Outlays	
Current Expenses for Aids and Special Services:	
Civil	23,355
National Defense	1,705
Retirement and Social Insurance Benefits—Civil	38,571
Other Services and Current Operating Expenses—Civil:	
Interest	16,716
Interest on capital in enterprises (—)	—628
Interest on capital in enterprises (—)	—11
Interest received by trust funds (—)	—3,099
Other	44,912
Total	126,065
Unclassified items	—5,770
Total Budget Outlays	184,556

SOURCE: *Special Analyses, Budget of the United States, Fiscal Year, 1971* (Washington, D.C.: Government Printing Office, 1970), pp. 46–47.

toward bricks and mortar projects and away from investments in human capital.

The federal government does not use formal capital budgeting. The suggestion has been periodically made that such a format would improve the federal budgetary process. The Office of Management and Budget in recent years has presented a breakdown between investment-type and current outlays. (See Table 6.2.) Definitional problems abound, particularly in the treatment of the defense budget. In what sense is adding bombs and

LIBRARY

missiles to the weapons stockpile an investment? Such military procurement is included as investment-type outlays in budget figures. This type of information is certainly of interest; many of the long-range implications of federal activity hinge on the distinction. Yet, it does not seem appropriate, nor is there much sentiment for, revising the federal budgetary process so as to treat current and capital budgets separately.[5]

PROGRAM BUDGETS FOR HIGHER EDUCATION

The utility of program budgeting is best illustrated by detailed example; for this purpose we consider its application in colleges and universities.[6] All our readers probably have some familiarity with the structures and operations of an institution of higher education and may thus appreciate this example more than one pertaining to an unfamiliar government agency. In many ways the problems of a college or university are similar to those of government agencies; in some instances the educational institution itself is a government agency. Institutional objectives and priorities are difficult to specify in operational terms; resources are limited and the demands on those resources are varied, growing rapidly, and often conflicting. Decisions must be made allocating resources among various programs. Program budgeting can provide educational decision makers with needed information and permit them to analyze the implications of alternative courses of action.

Universities have traditionally been viewed for administrative purposes as a collection of academic and nonacademic departments, such as the English Department and the Mathematics Department, Buildings and Grounds, and the Admissions Office. For the preparation of annual budgets, each department makes requests in terms of object categories—academic salaries, nonacademic salaries, equipment, supplies. As budgets are reviewed and approved, incremental changes are likely to receive detailed examination. The budgets of operating departments might be supplemented with a capital budget if physical facilities are expanded. This system of budgeting, while adequate for purposes of fiscal control, is not well suited to the problem of relating resources to the real purposes of the university. These purposes can be categorized as instruction, research, and public service; a wide variety of

---

[5] For a discussion of this matter, *see* Maynard S. Comiez, *A Capital Budget Statement for the U.S. Government* (Washington, D.C.: The Brookings Institution, 1966).

[6] *See* Harry Williams, *Planning for Effective Resource Allocation in Universities* (Washington, D.C.: American Council on Education, 1966). Beginning in the mid-1960s several universities began developing, some with assistance from the Ford Foundation, the type of program budgeting and planning techniques discussed in this section. *See also*, James Farmer, *Why Planning, Programming, Budgeting Systems for Higher Education?* (Boulder, Colo.: Western Interstate Commission for Higher Education, 1970).

program elements serve one or more of these purposes. It is in terms of these purposes that the objectives and priorities of a university can be meaningfully expressed. Not all conceivable academic programs will be offered and some will be given priority over others. Some types of research may be encouraged and supported and others—classified military research, for example—may be eschewed. Public institutions are more likely to stress public service, such as agricultural extension stations, than private institutions. Arriving at a completely specified set of objectives and ordering of priorities is a difficult process because so many groups have an interest in the outcome—faculty, administration, students, alumni, trustees, the local community, and the public at large. Nonetheless, thinking in terms of programs and their relationship to purposes is much preferred to the pontifical prose one usually finds in college catalogs.

Instructional programs can be defined in terms of a prescribed curriculum followed by an identifiable group of students; thus freshmen enrolled in a liberal arts curriculum would be one program, senior English majors another, and graduate students in economics a third. Each instructional program typically draws upon the resources of a number of academic departments and other organizational units in the university. The relationships between the organizational units (departments) of a university and its programs are shown in a schematic fashion in Figure 6.2. A variety of data can fit this matrix. The most fundamental would show the distribution of enrollments, indicating the demands for courses (or credit hours) placed by each instructional program on the various academic departments. A second set of data organized in this fashion would indicate the allocation of expenditures by each organization unit to the various programs. Of course, the expenditures of some units would be allocated to only one or a few programs. This allocation of expenditures becomes, then, a program budget statement for the university.

The allocation of expenditures from organization units to programs requires care. The first requirement is to identify the costs of individual activities, such as a single course. Then shares of the cost of a course are allocated to programs on the basis of each program's share of the total enrollment in the course. The costs of research programs are particularly difficult to identify. The matter is clear enough when the research is funded by an agency outside the university, but less measurable when research is unfunded. When a faculty member is explicitly released from teaching duties to do research, and is given a sabbatical leave or a summer grant, an appropriate portion of his salary can be assigned to a research program. However, it is nearly impossible to attribute a portion of a faculty member's salary to the research that he does in addition to regular teaching duties.

The matrices of relationships between organizational units and programs can form the basis of a simulation model of the university. (See Figure

Programs

Organizational units	Instructional															Research				Public service							
	Undergraduate									Graduate						Basic science	Applied science	Public policy	Humanities	Nondegree instruction				Dissemination of knowledge			
	Liberal arts			Engineering			Education			Arts & sciences			Medicine		Law												
Academic departments																											
XXXX	✓	✓	✓	✓	✓	✓				✓									✓				✓			✓	
XXXX	✓		✓	✓	✓	✓		✓			✓					✓	✓										
XXXX		✓	✓									✓															
XXXX							✓	✓	✓									✓		✓	✓	✓			✓		
XXXX				✓	✓	✓						✓				✓	✓									✓	✓
Academic administration																											
Deans offices																											
XXXX	✓	✓	✓																								
XXXX				✓	✓	✓																					
XXXX							✓	✓	✓																		
Admissions	✓	✓	✓	✓	✓	✓	✓	✓	✓	✓	✓	✓	✓	✓	✓												
Registrar	✓	✓	✓	✓	✓	✓	✓	✓	✓	✓	✓	✓	✓	✓	✓												
Student services																											
Health	✓	✓	✓	✓	✓	✓	✓	✓	✓																		
Athletics	✓	✓	✓	✓	✓	✓	✓	✓	✓																		
XXXX										✓	✓	✓	✓	✓													
XXXX	✓	✓	✓							✓	✓	✓															
XXXX							✓	✓	✓																		
Library	✓	✓	✓	✓	✓	✓	✓	✓	✓	✓	✓	✓	✓	✓	✓	✓	✓	✓	✓					✓	✓	✓	✓
Computer center				✓	✓	✓										✓	✓	✓	✓								
Buildings and grounds	✓	✓	✓	✓	✓	✓	✓	✓	✓	✓	✓	✓	✓	✓	✓	✓	✓	✓	✓	✓	✓	✓	✓	✓	✓	✓	✓
General administration	✓	✓	✓	✓	✓	✓	✓	✓	✓	✓	✓	✓		✓	✓	✓	✓	✓	✓	✓	✓	✓	✓	✓	✓	✓	✓

The check marks indicate a relationship between the indicated organizational unit and program, for example, enrollments by students in a program in courses offered by an academic department.

Figure 6.2 A program structure for a university.

6.3.) With the help of a large computer and an adequate data bank a simulation model can be used to analyze a wide variety of resource allocation problems. From the bank of actual data on students, faculty, facilities, and financial information, current values for the parameters of the simulation model can be calculated. Examples of these parameters are listed in Figure 6.3, but require some further explanation. To project enrollment and cost data for future years, assumptions about admissions and transition rates—

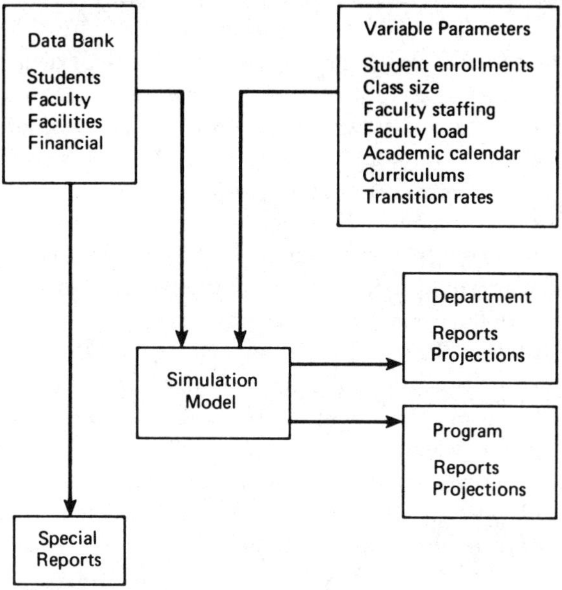

Figure 6.3 Simulation model for a university.

the movement of students from one program to another or their withdrawal—must be made. For example, out of 100 freshmen admitted to the liberal arts college, how many continue to the sophomore year, how many sophomores go on as junior majors in economics, English, history, and so on, and finally how many of these juniors in each major go on to complete their senior year? The admission of transfer students would also be specified. Future costs will be affected by the course load taken by students, the number and mix by rank of faculty, faculty salaries, and teaching loads. Putting the matter alternatively, for any given level of faculty salaries, costs per student are largely determined by the student-faculty ratio. This ratio, along with student course loads and faculty teaching loads, determines average class size. The relationships among the major variables are indicated by the following equation:

$$C = \frac{\frac{S}{F} \cdot L_S}{L_F}$$

where average class size, C, is determined by the student-faculty ratio, S/F, the student course load, L_S, and the faculty teaching load, L_F. For example, with a student-faculty ratio of 15:1, if students take five courses per semester and faculty members teach three courses, the average size of classes will be

25.[7] The curriculum for each program is summarized by the proportion of total courses (or credit hours) demanded from individual departments. When values for the parameters are introduced into the model, the output takes the form of future year budget statements and other summaries of data for each organizational unit and program. For example, if university policy calls for doubling freshman admissions over a five-year period, one can project the number of additional staff members needed, by department, if current curriculums, teaching loads, student course loads, and average class size are to be maintained. One could also inquire of the model how many additional faculty members would be needed if the average class size were allowed to increase by ten percent. In short, such a model permits the analysis of a wide variety of changes in academic policy (curriculum, student and faculty course loads, class size), changes in enrollments, salary levels, and so on. A well developed model would show the full implications of proposed changes on all parts of the university over a number of future years and at a variety of levels of detail. The future effects of alternative policies can be examined before decisions are made, ways to economize on physical facilities will become obvious, requests for funding from either public or private sources can be substantiated, and areas spotted where resources are being wasted.

A new or rapidly growing institution is more likely to find program budgeting and simulation techniques valuable than established, stable universities. Quite a wrench in thinking and practice is required for the latter institutions to move to a system where budget requests are substantiated in terms of changing program demands placed on departments, and where the discipline of program budgeting forces the proponents of any particular change to consider its impact on all parts of the university over a series of future years. We would be among the last to suggest that higher education can be run on a business-like basis, that programs should be scrapped if their costs exceed their receipts. Program budgeting and the use of simulation models are aids to the decision-making process, not substitutes for it. There must be a place for academic entrepreneurship—the development of new programs, changes in teaching techniques, and flexibility in both the courses of study followed by students and the manner in which faculty

---

[7] There are two different measures of class size: average size of courses taught and the average size of courses enrolled. The former looks at class size from the faculty's viewpoint and the latter from the vantage point of the student. The average size of courses taught is simply the total number of enrollments divided by the total number of courses and is not affected by the size distribution of courses taught. The average size of courses enrolled weights the size of each course by the number of enrollments in each course. The weighted sum is then divided by the total of enrollments. If there were only two courses, one size 99 and the other size 1, the average size of courses taught would be 50 and the average size of courses enrolled would equal 98.

members structure their professional activities. But, during the 1970s, American colleges and universities will continue to feel the financial pinch they experienced in the late 1960s when several private institutions sought the fiscal shelter of state college and university systems, and many public institutions found state legislatures no longer willing to appropriate budgets at the levels requested. The soul-searching induced by student protest has led many institutions to cut back their research done under contract with government agencies and private firms; much of this activity was profitable because the overhead item in the contracts brought in substantial revenues to the institution itself. The many demands on the post-Vietnam budget of the federal government will offer stiff competition to funds for higher education. In addition, there is greater public awareness of the equity questions involved in higher education.[8] Why, it is argued, should increasing amounts of tax revenues go to support higher education when so many of the benefits accrue directly to the student in the form of higher future income? Cannot the student be expected to pay a substantial part of the costs of his education, perhaps through a loan program? All of this suggests, then, that the public as well as private institutions will, during the 1970s, find themselves faced with the perennial problem of economics—scarcity of resources—and are well-advised to adopt the type of budgeting and planning techniques discussed in this section.

---

[8] For a study that concludes that public support of tuition-free higher education taxes the poor for the benefit of the nonpoor, *see* W. Lee Hansen and Burton A. Weisbrod, "The Distribution of Costs and Direct Benefits of Public Higher Education: The Case of California," *Journal of Human Resources*, Spring 1969.

7

TAXES AND RESOURCE ALLOCATION

Under ordinary circumstances modern governments derive the overwhelming majority of their revenues from taxation; the ubiquity of taxation is obvious to every citizen. In this chapter and the next we examine the effects of taxes on resource allocation and income distribution. Taxation has, as its basic intent, the reduction of private purchasing power and its transfer to the public sector so that resources may be reallocated from private to public use. In this very obvious sense the intent of all means of raising public revenue is to affect allocation, but this basic transfer of resources is not what is generally meant by the allocative effects of taxes. By the allocative effects of taxes we mean how they alter relative prices, and hence the mix of goods and services produced and the income received by owners of the factors of production.

The allocative effects of taxes come from the role taxes themselves play in the economic decisionmaking of the private sector. We define a *neutral tax* as one that does not affect relative prices. A tax that does not alter relative prices cannot be a factor in the economic calculus of private decision makers and therefore plays no part in the allocation of resources within a market economy. A *nonneutral tax* is one that does affect relative prices. An example of a nonneutral tax would be the levy of a $500 tax on the owners of automobiles with engines having more than 200 horsepower: Such a tax increases the cost of owning high-powered automobiles relative to other types, and is clearly a variable in the allocative process since some potential purchasers will undoubtedly pick a nontaxed substitute. The allocative effects of four basic types of taxes—income, commodity, wealth, and lump sum—are considered from a theoretical view in this chapter.[1] For the most part, a discussion of taxes actually used in the United States is postponed until Chapters 13 and 14. Prior to considering these four basic types of taxes, the concepts of tax liability, shifting, and incidence must be understood.

TAX LIABILITY, SHIFTING, AND INCIDENCE

Tax liabilities are determined by a combination of tax rates and tax bases. Legislation authorizing the raising of tax revenue must include a definition of the *tax base* against which the tax is assessed. Typical tax bases are the value of retail sales, taxable corporate profits, or the assessed valuation of real estate. The *tax rate* may take two forms: *specific taxes,* those that raise a fixed amount of revenue from each unit of the tax base, and *ad valorem taxes,* those that yield revenue as a percent of the value of the tax base. The possessor of the tax base—the merchant making retail sales, the corporation earning taxable profits, or the owner of real estate—actually remits revenue to the taxing authority and, in a nominal sense, pays the tax. The *tax liability* is his.

Tax shifting and tax incidence are central concepts in an analysis of the allocative effects of taxation. *Tax shifting* occurs when the tax is borne by someone other than the possessor of the tax base. Since the principal purpose of taxation is to divert resources from private to public sector use, a tax must reduce the availability of resources to private users. The *tax incidence* of a particular tax falls on those citizens whose access to resources is actually

---

[1] The distinction sometimes made between direct and indirect taxes is not made in this text since the definitions are unclear. *Direct taxes* are sometimes taken to be taxes on persons while *indirect taxes* are taxes on things purchased; other times direct taxes are said to be nonshiftable, while indirect taxes are shifted. *See* The National Bureau of Economic Research and The Brookings Institution, *The Role of Direct and Indirect Taxes in the Federal Revenue System* (Princeton, N.J.: Princeton University Press, 1964), and Otto Eckstein, "Indirect versus Direct Taxes: Implications for Stability Investment," *Excise Tax Compendium,* Committee on Ways and Means, House of Representatives, Congress of the United States (Washington, D.C.: Government Printing Office, 1964), pp. 43–55.

reduced by the tax. If the tax incidence rests on the possessor of the tax base there is no shifting and the tax liability and incidence coincide. If the incidence of the tax falls wholly or partially on someone other than the possessor of the tax base who bears the liability, then the tax is wholly or partially shifted. *Forward shifting* is said to occur if the incidence of the tax lies on a buyer of the tax base. For example, if the tax leads to an increase in the price of the tax base, the buyer, because of the higher price, is able to purchase fewer products than in the absence of the tax. The seller, who is liable for the tax, retains part of the price paid by the buyer and remits the remainder to the public sector as tax revenue. Part of the buyer's income, which represents his market command of resources, has been transferred to the government since he bears the incidence of the tax.[2] *Backward shifting* occurs when the tax causes a reduction in the money income paid to the owners of factors of production employed in the production of the tax base. Here the owners of factors have less purchasing power than in the absence of the tax: When the possessor of the tax base fulfills his obligation the public sector is able to command resources that otherwise would have been available for private use.

Tax liabilities are often referred to as tax burdens. In this volume we refer to tax incidence or tax liability rather than tax burden, since most taxes are raised to finance public expenditures and in this sense are the prices citizens pay for public goods. Just as product prices are not typically referred to as burdens, so the prices of public goods should not be termed burdens even though these prices are involuntary levies authorized by tax legislation.

Shifting and incidence must be analyzed to determine the allocative effects of taxes. Product and factor prices are variables in the economic calculus of decision makers in a market economy. As a tax alters these prices, the terms on which alternatives are evaluated change and the tax itself becomes an allocative variable and is nonneutral. If one assumes an optimal allocation of resources in the absence of the tax, the nonneutral tax levy will lead to a less than optimal allocation of resources—a reduction in economic efficiency. In the absence of optimal resource allocation, nonneutral taxes may lead to an improved allocation.

The necessary analysis of tax shifting and incidence can rest on several theoretical foundations. One may assume profit-maximizing perfect competitors, and undertake the analysis within a traditional, and theoretically certain, world where the effects of various types of taxes are reasonably clear.

---

[2] When a tax is paid by drawing down assets, the analysis of shifting and incidence becomes more complex. Payment of taxes by reducing assets does not affect private purchasing power over current output, and unless the public sector wishes to acquire assets rather than current output, additional revenue may be required.

But even here a distinction must be made between partial and general equilibrium analysis. Suppose, for example, that a tax is levied on a single product leading to an increase in its price and a decrease in the quantity sold. *Partial equilibrium analysis* of shifting and incidence would end here stating that the tax was wholly or partially shifted forward. However, since the tax results in a reduction in the quantity produced, fewer factors of production are employed than before the tax was imposed. Do these factors remain unemployed and, if not, what changes will take place in factor markets as they are reemployed? *General equilibrium analysis* deals with these questions and the additional impact, if any, the subsequent change in factor prices will have on production costs and product prices. General equilibrium analysis may be carried even further to investigate the effect spending public revenues will have on the economy. If public spending is a perfect substitute for private spending, the distribution of output and employment by industry will remain unchanged; if the public sector demands goods and services different from those that would have been purchased by the private sector, the tax induced transfer of resources will lead to a change in the distribution of employment and output. In the analysis that follows we assume that the public sector spends its tax revenue, but no effort is made to carry the general equilibrium analysis far enough to ascertain what happens to the industrial composition of output and employment.[3] In some cases we consider the impact of taxes beyond the immediate effect on the tax base and to this extent general equilibrium analysis is utilized.

Despite its pedagogic convenience, the purely competitive economy inhabited by profit maximizers cannot serve as the only basis for a theoretical analysis of tax shifting and incidence. Most markets are not perfectly competitive and there is evidence that firms may not follow profit-maximizing behavior.[4] Shifting and incidence, in the discussion that follows, are therefore viewed with traditional assumptions as well as others.

TAXES ON INCOME

Corporate income taxation. First we consider taxes on corporate incomes and assume that the tax is assessed on the profit (income) of the corporation.

---

[3] Where taxes are collected for stabilization rather than allocative purposes tax revenues may not be spent, perhaps with the specific intention of reducing demand for factor services. Stabilization policy is discussed in Chapters 15–17.

[4] R. L. Hall and C. J. Hitch, "Price Theory and Business Behavior," *Oxford Economic Papers,* May 1939; Harvey Leibenstein, "Allocative Efficiency vs. 'X' Efficiency," *American Economic Review,* June 1966; Richard M. Cyert and James G. March, *A Behavioral Theory of the Firm* (Englewood Cliffs, N.J.: Prentice-Hall, 1963); and Oliver E. Williamson, *The Economics of Discretionary Behavior: Managerial Objectives in a Theory of the Firm* (Chicago: Markham Publishing Company, 1967).

The tax base is defined, for purposes of this theoretical analysis, as profit in the economic sense—total revenue minus total cost. Total cost includes purchases of raw materials and other intermediate products, a capital consumption allowance (depreciation), and all factor payments including the normal return to invested capital just sufficient to keep that capital employed in the firm. Economic theory teaches that under conditions of perfect competition the profit-maximizing firm in the long run will earn no pure economic profit and the corporate income tax will therefore raise no revenue and have no long-run effect. Therefore, we assume imperfectly competitive, profit-maximizing corporations where the firm may earn long-run economic profit and thus incur corporate income tax liabilities.

The corporate income tax is not a cost of doing business in the ordinary sense. It is not a variable cost directly related to the firm's output and it is not a fixed cost. In fact, a tax liability may be avoided by not earning economic profit. Traditional analysis of the corporate income tax concluded that the tax cannot be shifted, at least in the short run, because the profit-maximizing firm produces and sells that output where marginal cost is equal to marginal revenue. Marginal revenue depends on consumer demand, which is unaffected by this tax. Marginal cost equals the additional costs that must be paid for variable inputs as the firm varies its output; since this tax is levied on profit and not any particular unit of output, marginal cost is unaltered by the tax. Therefore price and output are unaffected and the incidence of the corporate income tax falls entirely on the firm's owners who find their after-tax, pure economic profit reduced. Since the tax is some portion (less than 100 percent) of profit, maximizing before-tax profits will also maximize after-tax profits.

The foregoing argument is illustrated in Figure 7.1. The firm will maximize profits by producing and selling the output Q_1 at price P and will earn a pure economic profit equal to the area of the rectangle $PTRS$. If a 50 percent corporate income tax is now levied, since the tax leaves marginal revenue and cost unaffected, price and quantity are not affected. Maximum profit $PTRS$ constitutes the base against which the tax assessment is made, and the tax liability is 50 percent of these total profits, illustrated by the shaded portion of the rectangle; the unshaded area represents the after-tax profit of the corporation and is maximized when $PTRS$ is maximized. In this case, the corporate income tax is said to have no short-run allocative effects.

In the long run there may be allocative effects of the corporate income tax. This is because the tax will affect the after-tax rate of return on investment by corporations.[5] If there are unincorporated businesses that are taxed

[5] Arman Alchian, "Costs and Outputs," in Moses Abramovitz (ed.), *The Allocation of Economic Resources* (Stanford, Calif.: Stanford University Press, 1959), pp. 23–41; and L. L. Pasinetti, "Changes in the Rate of Profit and Switches of Techniques," *Quarterly Journal of Economics,* November 1966.

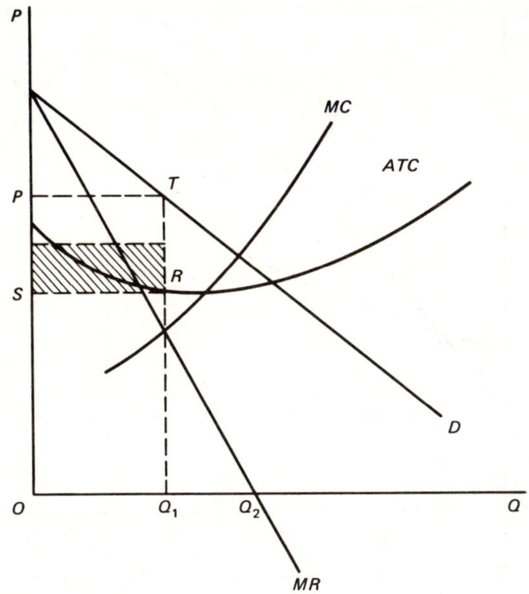

Figure 7.1 Profit maximization.

differently from corporations, resources may shift between these two types of business organizations because of a tax. If firms in one industry are typically incorporated and in another are unincorporated, the corporate income tax will be nonneutral since it results in a reallocation of resources from one industry to another.

More importantly, firms may not maximize profits. One approach to nonprofit-maximizing behavior has been suggested by Professor Baumol, who argues that firms, and especially large corporations where there is separation of ownership and management, attempt to maximize sales subject to a minimum acceptable profit constraint.[6] The minimum profit constraint is measured after taxes and provides the firm with sufficient funds to finance investment from retained earnings, to meet contingencies, to pay dividends, or to fulfill other managerial goals. Once executives have specified the level of profits needed to fulfill these goals Professor Baumol believes they aim at maximizing their sales value—total revenue—as long as profits remain satisfactory. Revenue maximization requires the firm to produce and sell that quantity where demand for the firm's output is unit elastic. This is the output Q_2 in Figure 7.1.[7] Because marginal revenue is less than marginal cost

[6] William J. Baumol, *Business Behavior, Value and Growth*, rev. ed. (New York: Harcourt, Brace and World, 1967), Chapters 6 and 7.

[7] The relationship between marginal revenue, price (or average revenue), and the

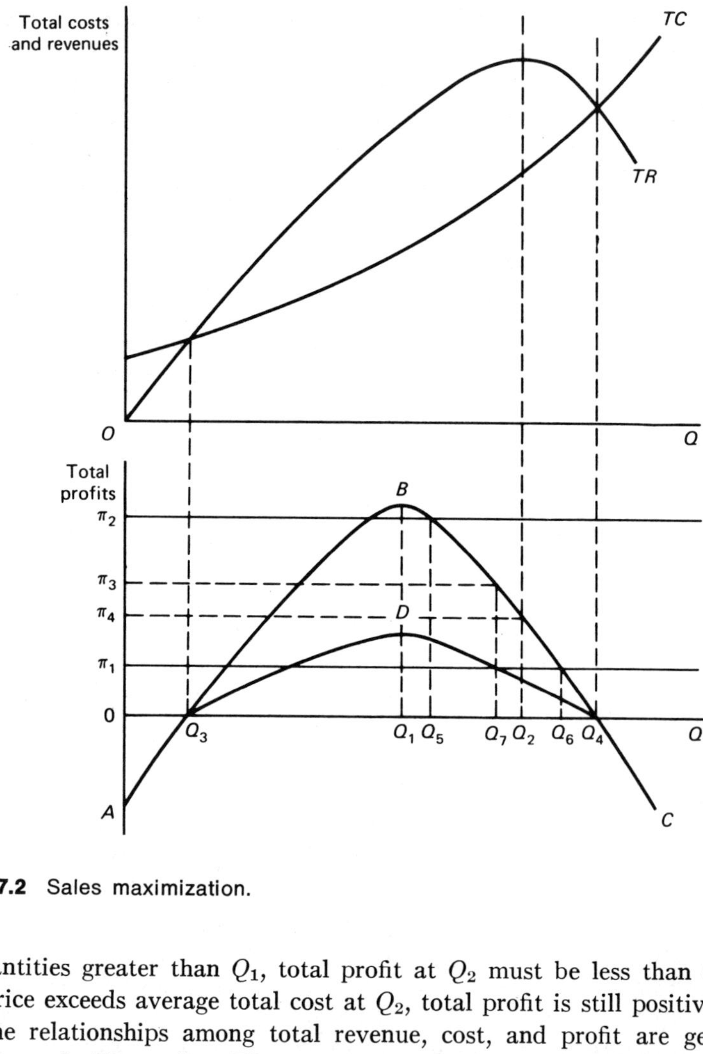

Figure 7.2 Sales maximization.

for quantities greater than Q_1, total profit at Q_2 must be less than Q_1 but, since price exceeds average total cost at Q_2, total profit is still positive.

The relationships among total revenue, cost, and profit are geometrically shown in Figure 7.2. The upper part of Figure 7.2 includes the total cost curve, *TC*, from which the average total cost and marginal cost curves in Figure 7.1 were derived. The total revenue curve, *TR*, is derived from the demand curve *D* in Figure 7.1. The total profit curve AQ_3BQ_4C in the lower portion of Figure 7.2 is derived by subtracting total cost from total revenue

---

elasticity of demand is given by the expression $MR = P(1 + 1/E_D)$, where E_D is the elasticity of demand. When demand is unit elastic the elasticity coefficient is equal to -1 and marginal revenue is equal to zero. *See* Richard H. Leftwich, *The Price System and Resource Allocation,* 4th ed. (New York: Holt, Rinehart and Winston, 1970), pp. 235–236.

for each quantity. For quantities less than Q_3 and greater than Q_4, total cost is greater than total revenue and economic profit is negative. At quantity Q_1 marginal revenue is equal to marginal cost and total profit is maximized; at quantity Q_2 total revenue is maximized where demand is unit elastic. If the profit constraint is set at π_1, the firm will produce and sell the quantity Q_2 where sales value is maximized and actual profit, π_4, is greater than the minimum required. If the profit constraint were, alternatively, set at π_2, the firm would produce and sell quantity Q_5 where sales value is as large as possible, subject to the minimum profit constraint. If sales maximization meant maximizing the physical volume of sales subject to the profit constraint, and if the profit constraint were set at π_1, the firm would sell Q_6. The corresponding prices for these quantities can be obtained from the demand curve in Figure 7.1.

If this firm is now subject to a corporate income tax, tax shifting will occur whenever the profit constraint is effectively limiting; if the profit constraint is not limiting, the tax may be absorbed by the owners of the firm out of their excess profits. This effect is geometrically illustrated in the lower portion of Figure 7.2. The corporate income tax shifts the after-tax profit curve downward, by a percentage amount equal to the tax rate, to AQ_3DQ_4C.[8] If the firm regards π_1 as the minimum acceptable profit and was, before tax, maximizing the physical volume of sales by producing and selling output Q_6, the firm will now cut back production to Q_7, earn before-tax profit π_3, and have the same after-tax profit, π_1, as before. The full amount of tax paid, equal to $\pi_3 - \pi_1$, has been shifted forward to consumers in the price increase that resulted from the cutback in quantity from Q_6 to Q_7. Alternatively, if the firm had been producing and selling the revenue-maximizing output Q_2 subject to the profit constraint π_1, the tax will induce the firm to cut back production and sales from Q_2 to Q_7. The total tax paid is the same, $\pi_3 - \pi_1$, but, in this case, it is paid partially by the owners of the firm through a reduction, $\pi_4 - \pi_1$, in their after-tax pure economic profit and partially by consumers, $\pi_3 - \pi_4$, via the price increase that results when output and sales are reduced from Q_2 to Q_7.

The analysis must be carried a step further when there is a short-run reduction in output. As corporations adjust to the corporate income tax, variable factors of production are now unemployed and their search for alternative employment may affect factor prices. If the corporate sector is extensive, so that the tax causes variable factor layoffs from many firms, and if factor markets are competitive, this net reduction in employment will lead to competitive reductions in factor prices resulting in a decrease in production costs for all levels of output. This decrease in costs will, geometrically, shift

---

[8] For quantities less than Q_3 and greater than Q_4 after-tax and before-tax profits are the same because the corporation has no profit to be taxed.

the before-tax profit curve upward and, therefore, the after-tax profit curve upward. Unchanged demand conditions may then make it possible to sell the original output at an unchanged product price. Thus, as there is a general equilibrium adjustment to the corporate income tax, the tax may possibly be shifted backward to owners of factors of production as factor prices fall with product prices remaining unchanged.

This discussion of the corporate income tax leaves the analyst uncertain as to what shifting of the tax is expected. On the assumption of profit maximization there can be no short-run shifting of the tax and the incidence falls entirely on the owners of the fixed factors. What long-run shifting occurs will depend on the economy's structural organization and rates of profit earned elsewhere in the economy. When the assumption of profit maximization is abandoned a variety of results are possible and the incidence of the tax may fall on the owners of the firm, may be shifted backward to factors, may be shifted forward to consumers, or some combination of these. The incidence of the corporate income tax would seem, therefore, to be an empirical question; empirical evidence is considered in Chapter 13.

Personal income taxation. Our second consideration is taxes on personal income. Defining the tax base for the personal income tax is more complicated than for the corporate income tax. First, the taxpaying unit is less obvious than for corporations where the taxable unit is defined by corporate charters. Is the personal income tax unit the person or the family? If it is the family, what constitutes a family, and how are the incomes of more than a single member of the family to be treated? Second, should the tax base be income received by the individual or income earned by the factor of production? If the tax base is income earned by the factor of production, there may be a separate schedule of tax rates for each type of factor income a taxpayer receives; if the tax base is income received by the individual then income from all factors owned by a taxpayer are combined and taxed at a single, individual income tax rate.[9] The discussion in this chapter assumes

---

[9] The former type of personal income tax, common in Spanish-speaking nations, is known as a *schedular tax.* This means that there is a different schedule of tax rates for each type of factor income—wages, rents, interest, and so on—and each of these is taxed as though it were the only source of income to its recipient. *See,* for example, Richard Goode, "Personal Income Tax in Latin America," in *Fiscal Policy for Economic Growth for Latin America* (Baltimore: Johns Hopkins Press, 1965), pp. 157–196. In the United States an individual's income from all sources is summed and a single schedule of tax rates is applied against this tax base. The existence of provisions in the Internal Revenue Code for special treatment of capital gains income, exemption from tax of interest paid on state and local securities, and mineral depletion allowances in fact creates different schedules of tax rates depending on the source of income, and is in this respect similar to the schedular tax system. A number of states levy severance taxes on extractive industries that may supplement state corporate income taxes,

that the tax base is the income of the individual and that all income is derived from the sale of labor services. Whether income taxes should be assessed on income received or income accrued is also disputed. On balance, intellectual sentiment prefers accrued income as the tax base, but administrative efficiency dictates an income received measure.[10]

A third problem in defining the personal income tax base is determining what part of a taxpayer's receipts to classify as income. Personal expenses incurred earning income must be distinguished from household consumption expenditures out of income. Expenses of the self-employed, such as doctors or lawyers, and expenses of employees must somehow be separated from personal consumption expenditures when one decides what, for tax purposes, may be subtracted from gross receipts in determining personal income for income tax purposes. The problem of determining expenses that are a cost of earning income and are deductible from gross receipts is different from the question of what deductions from income, if any, will be permitted in arriving at the tax base. Both issues are relevant to the question of tax neutrality; just as deductions from income may induce taxpayers to organize their affairs to avoid the tax, so permissible deductions from gross revenues may induce taxpayers to incur these deductible expenses to avoid the tax. In both cases the explicit provisions of the tax law become a variable in economic decisionmaking, thus making the income tax nonneutral.

The personal income tax is levied on personal contributions to, rather than extractions from, the economy. Income is earned when factors provide services that increase the total product available; when this income is spent products are absorbed, making them unavailable to others. Some experts have argued that a more appropriate tax base would be extractions rather than contributions, and have, therefore, proposed that consumption rather than income be used as the personal tax base.[11] In the case where all income is spent, the consumption and income tax bases are identical.

In this section we investigate two issues from a theoretical viewpoint: What is the effect of the personal income tax on the decision to earn income that will be subject to tax? What is the effect of the tax on consumption?

The allocative effects of a personal income tax on a self-employed person may be much the same as those of the corporate income tax on the

---

substitute for the corporate income tax in extractive industries, or simply be special levies on the extractive industries. *Severance taxes* may be assessed on the value or volume of products extracted but, whatever their form, they constitute a schedular type of business tax. Mineral depletion allowances, and other taxes that have separate schedules of taxes on income from different factors of production, may lead to tax capitalization. Tax capitalization is discussed below in connection with taxes on wealth.

10 Henry Simons, *Personal Income Taxation* (Chicago: University of Chicago Press, 1938). In this text, note the discussion in Chapter 13.

11 Nicholas Kaldor, *An Expenditure Tax* (London: George Allen and Unwin, 1955).

sales maximizing firm. Consider a person whose goal is the after-tax personal income, π_1, in Figure 7.2. In this case the total revenue schedule is interpreted as the total receipts of the individual, the total cost schedule shows the total deductible costs incurred earning these receipts, and the profit schedules are the before- and after-tax personal income of the self-employed taxpayer. If the taxpayer is selling a before-income tax volume of services equal to Q_6, realizing his net income goal π_1, then the levy of the personal income tax, which shifts the schedule of after-tax personal income downward, will decrease the quantity of services rendered to Q_7. The price of these services will be correspondingly increased as the tax is shifted forward.[12] The self-employed taxpayer, because he sells less services after tax, will supply fewer hours of labor services; the income tax thus has a disincentive effect on labor. This forward shifting of the personal tax and the resulting disincentive effect assume, as in the case of corporate income tax, that the taxpaying unit was not maximizing income (profit) prior to levy of the tax. If income were maximized to start, forward shifting of the tax would be impossible because maximization of before-tax income would also maximize after-tax income, provided tax rates are less than 100 percent.

The incentive effects of personal income taxation may alternatively be approached with analysis of consumer behavior. Taxpayers may be seen as endowed with a fixed number of hours that may be retained as leisure or spent at work in exchange for income. The hourly wage rate fixes the rate at which leisure may be transformed into income, and the allocative problem is to decide how much leisure and income to consume in order to maximize satisfaction. This is geometrically illustrated in Figure 7.3 where a citizen is shown endowed with some fixed number of hours, *O*, that may be retained as leisure or may be wholly or partially surrendered in exchange for income. The budget lines *OA*, *OB*, *OC*, and *OD* show four possible transformations of leisure into income, the slope of each being equal to the hourly wage rate. Hours of work are ascertained by reading to the left from *O*, since a decrease in the amount of leisure represents time spent at work. The optimal behavior for this consumer is shown by the point of tangency between his budget constraint and the highest attainable indifference curve. As the wage rate is increased, satisfaction maximizing combinations of income and leisure shift from *Q* to *R* to *S* and to *T*; hours of work first increase from *Oq* to *Or*

[12] The additional assumption is required here that the self-employed individual will provide the maximum quantity of services consistent with his income goal. Strong unions would lead to a similar result. If union leaders are concerned with the level of after-tax earnings of their members, an income tax increase may lead to union pressure for higher money wages that would result in increased variable costs of production and thus higher product prices. Labor in this sense would be shifting the income tax forward to the consumers of labor's product.

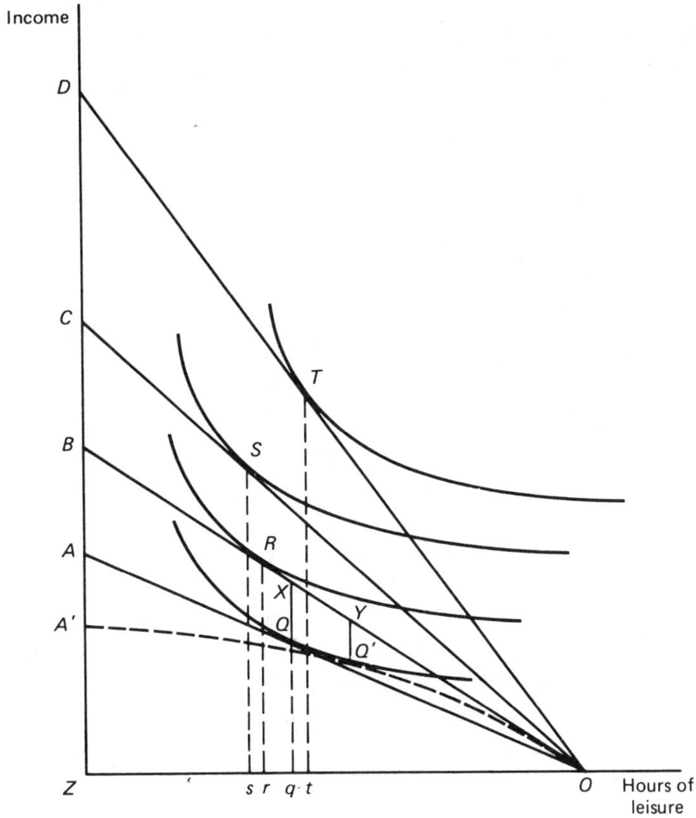

Figure 7.3 Incentive effects of personal income taxation.

to *Os* and then decrease to *Ot*. This analysis suggests that an increase in wage rates may either increase or decrease effort.

The effect of a proportional income tax is to reduce the net return to the taxpayer for each hour of work, and may be geometrically shown by a rotation downward around *O* of the budget constraint. If the original budget constraint were *OD* and a proportional personal income tax is now levied, the taxpayer will perceive this as a reduction in his net earnings per hour, rotating his budget constraint from *OD* to *OC*; as shown, the proportional rate of tax is *DC*/*ZD*. This taxpayer would shift from equilibrium *T* to equilibrium *S* increasing his work effort. Alternatively, if the taxpayer had originally faced budget constraint *OB*, the effect of a proportional income tax would be to rotate his budget constraint, net of taxes, downward to *OA*. In this case the proportional rate of tax is *AB*/*ZB* and the taxpayer shifts from equilibrium *R* to equilibrium *Q*, decreasing his labor effort. Thus, the theoretical analysis gives ambiguous results concerning the incentive effect of personal income taxation, and either an increase or decrease in work effort may be expected to result from the levy of a proportional tax on personal income. The outcome depends ultimately on the individual's preferences that set the indifference curves.

With slight modification Figure 7.3 may be used to investigate the effect of a progressive income tax. A *progressive tax* is one where the marginal tax rate varies directly with taxable income, and the average tax rate on high incomes is larger than the average rate on lower incomes. Starting with the budget constraint *OB* and equilibrium *R*, a proportional income tax rotates the net budget constraint downward to *OA*, while a progressive income tax would rotate the net budget constraint downward to *OA′*; the taxpayer's satisfaction maximizing equilibrium would shift from *R* to *Q′*. In the case of the proportional income tax the amount of revenue raised is *QX*; in the case of the progressive tax the amount of revenue raised is *Q′Y*.[13] Because of the diminishing marginal rate of substitution along indifference curves, and the increasing marginal rate of tax under the progressive income tax, the progressive income tax has a disincentive effect in comparison to the proportional income tax that leaves the taxpayer on the same indifference curve. No general theoretical solution can, however, be given to the problem of the disincentive effects of progressive personal income taxes when their effect is compared with the situation prior to the levy of any tax.

The foregoing discussion suggests that the personal income tax may be nonneutral with respect to effort. We now consider the effects on consumption as the personal income tax reduces disposable personal income. The consumption effect of the personal income tax is geometrically illustrated in the commodity space *X*, *Y* in Figure 7.4. In the absence of taxes the consumer spends his entire income on the products *X* and *Y* and, given some set of prices for these products, his consumption possibilities are illustrated by the budget line *MN* whose slope is P_x/P_y, whose vertical intercept is money income/P_y, and whose horizontal intercept is money income/P_x. A satisfaction maximizing consumer will purchase the bundle of products *A* determined by the tangency between the budget line *MN* and the highest attainable indifference curve I. If this consumer now incurs a personal income tax liability, without any change in before-tax personal income, his disposable income will fall by the amount of the tax. This is geometrically illustrated by the budget constraint's shift from *MN* to *RS*, where *MR* is equal to the tax liability/P_y, and *NS* is equal to the tax liability/P_x. *MR* measures the transfer of resources to the public sector in terms of product

---

[13] The proportional and progressive taxes have been illustrated giving the same after-tax level of satisfaction to the taxpayer. A different illustration would be required to show equal amounts of revenue raised by the government.

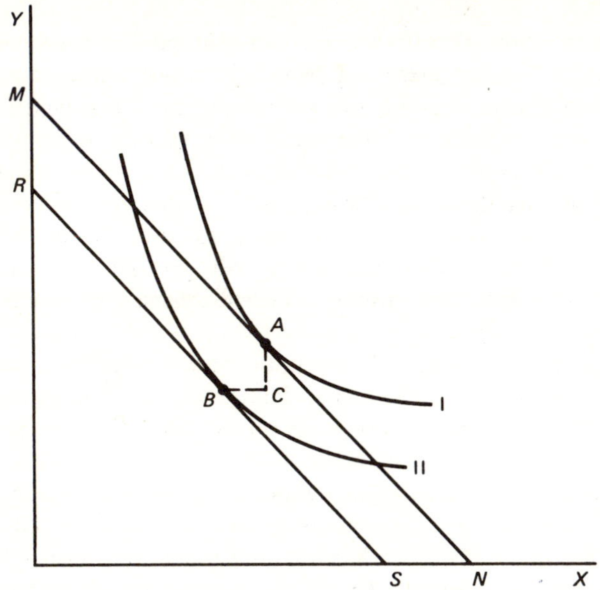

Figure 7.4 Effects of personal income taxation on consumption.

Y, and *NS* measures the transfer of resources in terms of product *X*. The satisfaction maximizing consumer will now consume the bundle of commodities *B* where his after-tax budget line *RS* is tangent to the highest attainable indifference curve II. In this example, as a result of the personal income tax, the taxpayer decreases his purchases of *X* by *BC* and decreases his purchases of *Y* by *AC*.[14]

From the viewpoint of consumption the personal income tax is neutral because it leaves the relative prices of *X* and *Y* unchanged; it has not affected the terms on which market decisions are made and the tax is not a variable in economic decisionmaking. The sole impact of the tax on this taxpayer's behavior is due to an income effect as resources are transferred to public use. Ultimately, relative prices may change because the public sector may not purchase *BC* units of *X* and *AC* units of *Y* with its tax revenue.

TAXES ON COMMODITIES

Commodity taxes are taxes whose base is specified in terms of units or value of commodities produced or sold. For purposes of exposition, two

[14] No effort has been made to judge what advantage the taxpayer derives from the public expenditures financed with tax monies. Presumably these public expenditures will affect his well-being, but ordinal welfare criteria do not permit us to add welfare from public expenditures to welfare from private expenditures to make a comparison with the taxpayer's happiness before the tax was levied.

major types of commodity taxes and two examples of each are considered. *Single stage commodity taxes* are levied on a commodity only once as it passes through the productive process to the final consumer, for example the manufacturer's excise and the retail sales taxes commonly used in the United States. *Multiple stage commodity taxes* are levied on a commodity more than once as it passes through the productive process to the final consumer, for example the tax on value added and the turnover tax commonly used in Europe. Other commodity taxes are similar to one or more of these and the four examples provide sufficient models for their evaluation.

Single stage taxes. The fundamental distinction between excise and sales taxes is the broadness of their bases. The *excise tax* is narrowly based; enabling legislation will specify precisely which products are taxed, as well as the tax rate. *Sales taxes* are more broadly based; their tax base comprises many commodities and legislation designates those commodities not subject to tax. For example, retail sales taxes may be based on all commodities except food and personal services, while excise taxes are assessed on automobiles, cigarettes, or gasoline. Excise taxes may be either specific or *ad valorem*; broadly based sales taxes must be *ad valorem* taxes since the tax is assessed on many products where the only basis for comparison and assessment of taxes is their value.

A specific excise tax collected from the manufacturer may be treated as a nonfactor variable cost of production. For each unit of product produced the manufacturer is obligated to remit a fixed sum of money to the government, and the excise tax will make the average variable, average total, and marginal costs of production greater than in the absence of the tax. Because the profit-maximizing firm equates marginal cost to marginal revenue in determining its output, and because the excise tax affects marginal cost, the excise tax will have a short-run impact on price and output.

The amount of shifting and the incidence of the excise tax depend on the competitive structure of the taxed industry and the demand and supply elasticities of the taxed product. Consider first the case of perfect competition illustrated in Figure 7.5. The industry begins in long-run, perfectly competitive equilibrium with price P_1 determined by the intersection of market supply, S_1, and market demand, D. For the single, perfectly competitive profit-maximizing firm, marginal revenue is equal to marginal cost at the minimum point on the firm's average total cost curve, and normal profit, but no pure economic profit, is earned. If a specific excise tax is now levied, marginal and average total costs increase (shift vertically upward) by the full amount of the tax from MC_1 and ATC_1 to MC_2 and ATC_2. Because market supply is the horizontal summation of each firm's supply, and because the firm's supply curve is that part of the marginal cost curve above average variable cost, this vertical shift upward of firms' marginal cost curves shifts

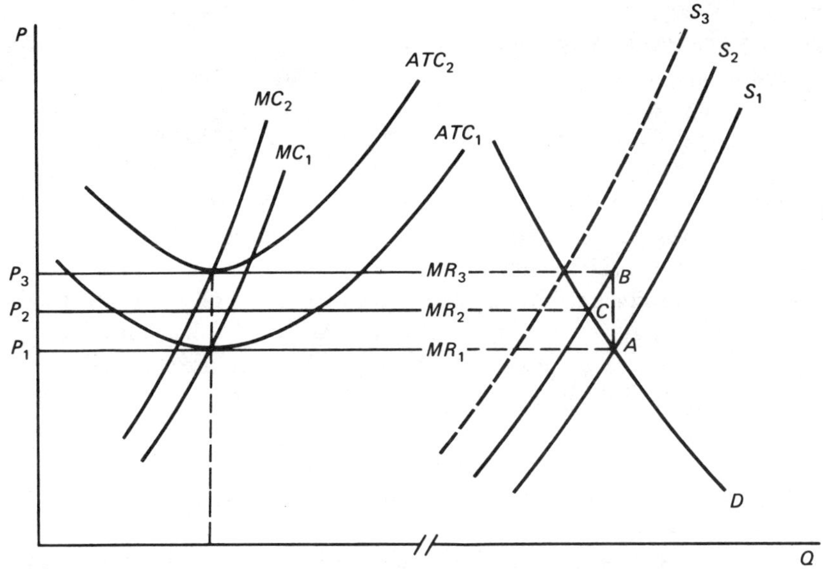

Figure 7.5 Shifting and incidence of an excise tax: The case of imperfect competition.

the market supply schedule vertically upward by the full amount of the tax, from S_1 to S_2. The per unit amount of the tax is geometrically equal to the vertical distance AB. Given the indicated shift in the market supply curve, the short-run impact on price and quantity will depend on the elasticity of demand and supply. The greater the elasticity of demand at point A the lesser will be the increase in market price, and the lesser the demand elasticity the greater will be the increase in price; in the limiting case of perfectly elastic demand, market price will remain unchanged; in the case of perfectly inelastic demand, market price will rise by the full amount of the tax. Conversely, the greater the elasticity of supply at point A the greater will be the increase in price, and the lesser the elasticity the smaller will be the increase in price; in the limiting case of perfectly elastic supply, price will rise by the full amount of the tax, and in the case of perfectly inelastic supply, market price will be unaffected by the tax. For any elasticities other than these limiting cases the market price of the product rises in the short run by less than the amount of the tax, the new market equilibrium is determined by C, and the typical producer in this industry now maximizes profit by producing that output where $MC_2 = MR_2 < ATC_2$. Thus, in the short run, part of the tax is shifted forward to consumers in the form of higher prices, and the tax incidence partially falls on the owners of firms as their economic profit (which is now negative) is reduced.

This short-run reduction in the return to fixed factors induces a further long-run adjustment in this industry. Because revenue no longer covers all costs, including a normal return to fixed factors, resources will leave the industry. As the number of firms selling in the industry decreases, market supply will shift further to the left—eventually to S_3—raising price to P_3, where $MC_2 = MR_3$ at minimum ATC_2. When this has been accomplished, those resources remaining in the industry will earn a return equal to their opportunity cost and no additional exit from the taxed industry will occur. Since the tax increased the firms' costs by the full amount of the tax, the new long-run equilibrium is established when the price of the taxed product has risen by the full amount of the tax and the tax is fully shifted forward to consumers. Because the excise tax increases the price of one product only, relative prices are altered, the tax is nonneutral, and is a variable in market decisionmaking.

Levy of a specific excise tax on the product of a profit-maximizing imperfect competitor would have a similar effect but the long-run adjustment may be different. As illustrated in Figure 7.6, the effect of the excise tax is to increase short-run price from P_1 to P_2, but with the price increase less than the amount of the tax.[15] In the short run the tax is partially shifted forward to the consumers and partially absorbed by the owners of the firm since their pure economic profit is reduced. The long-run adjustment will depend on the willingness of owners to absorb this reduction in pure economic profit; this is partially a function of the rate of pure economic profit in other industries. If the tax induces resources to leave the industry in the long run, prices would rise even further and more of the tax would be shifted forward to consumers; to the extent that producers are willing to accept this reduction in their pure economic profit, the incidence of this tax remains partially on the owners of the fixed factors of production even in the long run. For the tax not to be fully shifted forward there must be some before-tax, pure economic profit out of which owners of fixed factors may absorb the tax.

The foregoing analysis of shifting and incidence could have been handled differently. A demand curve specifies consumer willingness to make purchases at various prices, irrespective of who receives the price paid by the consumer. When a consumer buys a product subject to tax, part of the price paid is retained by the seller as his revenue and part of the price is

---

[15] That price will increase by less than the amount of the tax may readily be proved with the linear demand and marginal revenue curves illustrated in Figure 7.6. The slope of the demand curve is less than the slope of the marginal revenue curve; hence the vertical displacement along the marginal revenue curve exceeds the vertical change along the demand curve for the same horizontal movement Q_2Q_1. The tax shifts MC vertically upward by the full amount of the tax; the vertical ordinate of the intercept of MC_2 with MR lies above the vertical ordinate of the intercept of MC_1 with MR by less than the amount of the tax. Thus, price must increase by less than the amount of the tax.

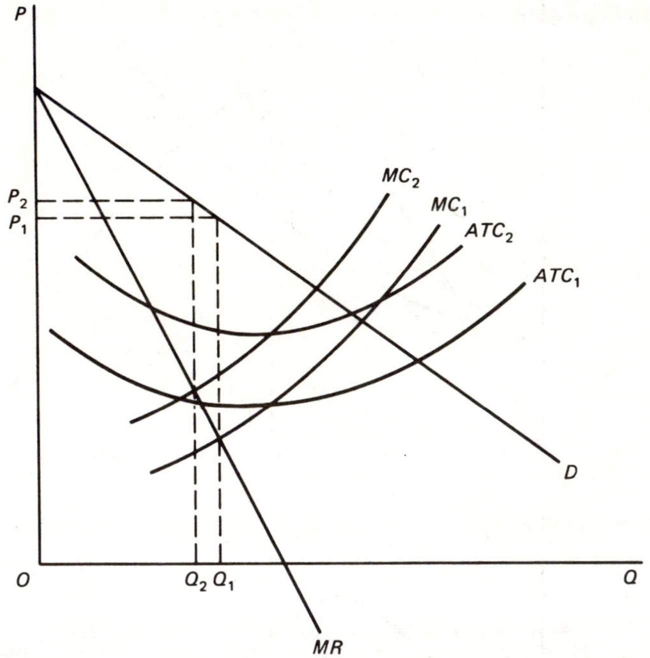

Figure 7.6 Shifting and incidence of an excise tax: The case of imperfect competition.

remitted by the seller to the government as he fulfills his tax liability. Thus, if we subtract the amount of the tax per unit from the price paid by consumers we may estimate a net demand curve that shows the price received and retained by sellers for various levels of sales. Such a net demand curve would indicate revenue to the seller for various quantities sold, and the marginal revenue derived from this net demand curve would be equated with marginal cost to determine the firm's most profitable output. Associated with this profit-maximizing output is a net price retained by the seller and a higher price paid by the consumer. Analytically these results would be similar to those described in the text. In analysis of some types of tax problems this approach may prove useful.

Sales-maximizing analysis may be used to evaluate the shifting and incidence of excise taxes. As illustrated in Figure 7.7, TC_1 is the before-tax total cost curve and ABC is the before-tax profit schedule. The levy of an excise tax rotates the total cost schedule upward to TC_2; the vertical distance between TC_1 and TC_2 increases as quantity increases because the larger the quantity sold the larger the total tax liability. The tax thus geometrically rotates the profit schedule downward to ADE. If the firm's minimum profit constraint is given by π_1, and before tax the firm was maximizing revenue by selling quantity Q_1 with profit π_2, then the effect of the

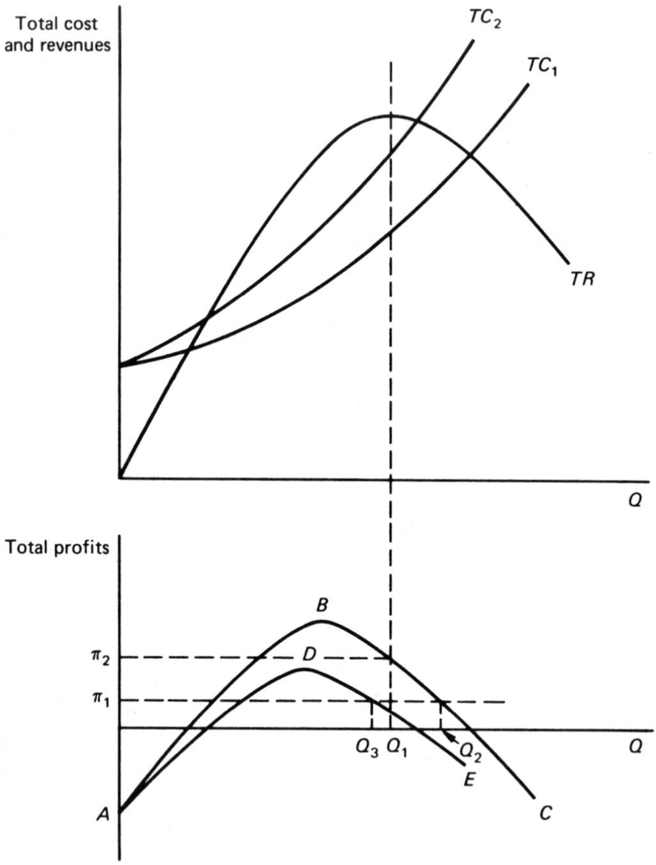

Figure 7.7 Shifting and incidence of an excise tax: The case of sales-maximizing behavior.

tax is to cut back sales to Q_3. In this case the incidence of the tax lies partially on producers whose after-tax economic profit is reduced (π_2 to π_1) and partially on consumers who pay higher prices. If, alternatively, the firm, before tax, had been maximizing sales volume by selling the quantity Q_2, then the effect of the tax is to cut back quantity to Q_3, and the tax incidence falls entirely on consumers as prices rise.

The excise tax is thus nonneutral. In the short run it is partially shifted forward to consumers and partially absorbed by the owners of fixed factors of production under most assumptions. In the long run the tax will be fully or partially shifted, depending, additionally, on the nature of competitive conditions in the taxed industry and the rate of pure economic profit being earned in the taxed industry and other industries.

This analysis of excise taxation may be used to illustrate an argument

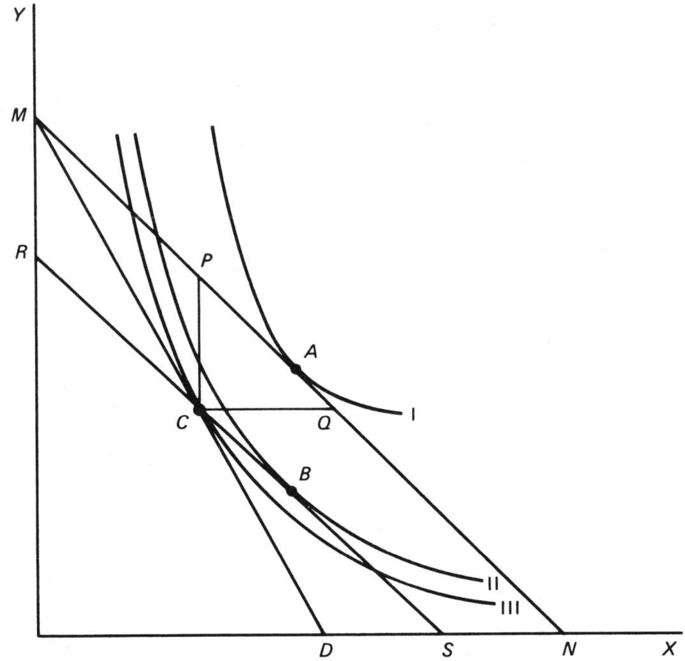

Figure 7.8 Excise taxation and consumer welfare.

in welfare economics that has implications for the formulation of public policy. Suppose the consumer illustrated in Figure 7.8 spends his entire income on the products *X* and *Y* and buys the combinations of products given by *A*. Now suppose that product *X*, but not product *Y*, is made subject to a specific excise tax that is wholly or partially shifted forward; the increase in the price of *X* will geometrically rotate the consumer's budget line around the point *M*, resulting in the budget line *MD*. The satisfaction maximizing consumer will now purchase commodity bundle *C* on indifference curve III. Since the consumer actually purchases bundle *C*, the amount of tax revenue raised by the government is sufficient to buy either *CP* units of *Y* or *CQ* units of *X*. This is because with the same money income, but no tax, the consumer buying bundle *C* would be able to move to the budget line *MN* and buy either *CP* additional units of *Y* or *CQ* additional units of *X* (or some intermediate combination), and these amounts, which he could have purchased in the absence of the tax, measure the amount of transfer to the public sector that results from the tax. The closer point *C* is to *D* the greater are *CP* and *CQ*, because the more the consumer purchases of the taxed good, the more revenue the government will receive. The same is true conversely, and the closer point *C* is to *M* the smaller are *CP* and *CQ*. In the limiting case where the consumer does not purchase any of the taxed good, the government will receive no revenue, as shown by the coincidence of point *M* on budget lines *MN* and *MD*.

To raise the same amount of revenue with a personal income tax, the consumer's disposable income would have to be reduced so that his budget constraint shifts to the left passing through *C*. The distance between the original budget constraint *MN* and the new after-income tax budget constraint *RS* is vertically equal to *CP* and horizontally equal to *CQ* for all possible combinations of *X* and *Y*. In other words, the effect of an income tax that raises the same revenue as the excise tax on *X* is geometrically shown by shifting the consumer's budget constraint parallel to the left, passing through point *C*. Because *RS* is parallel to *MN*, when the taxpayer is located anywhere on *RS* the government raises the same amount of revenue as was raised when the consumer purchased bundle *C* on *MD*. But the budget constraint *RS* is not tangent to indifference curve III at point *C*, and, with the income tax, the consumer would purchase bundle *B* instead, obtaining the higher level of satisfaction indicated by indifference curve II. Thus the personal income tax leaves the consumer better off, measured in terms of the level of satisfaction attained, than a specific excise tax, based on only one product, that raises the same amount of revenue.

It is alleged that there is an excess burden of commodity taxation.[16] The preceding analysis shows the excise tax to be inferior to the income tax because the nonneutral excise tax leads to a change in relative prices and, as an allocative variable, induces product substitution as well as reducing the real income of the taxpayer. The personal income tax is neutral and, hence, raises the same revenue as the excise tax, with a smaller reduction in the taxpayer's real income; it is thus thought to be preferred to the excise tax on allocative efficiency grounds. But suppose both *X* and *Y* had been subject to excise taxes and their relative prices, as a result, remained unchanged.[17] Raising an excise on product *Y* would geometrically have the effect of rotating the consumer's budget constraint downward around its horizontal intercept and the proper combination of nonneutral excises on products *X* and *Y* would yield the same after-tax budget constraint, *RS*, as is yielded by the personal income tax. Furthermore, as was shown above, the income

---

[16] This argument was first presented by Myron Joseph, "The Burden of Indirect Taxation," *Review of Economic Studies,* June 1939. This argument is also referred to as "The Classical Indictment of Indirect Taxation." *See* the article of the same title by H. P. Wald, *Quarterly Journal of Economics,* August 1945.

[17] The tax rate on *X* and *Y* would not necessarily be the same. The taxes would have to be raised so that the relative after-tax prices of the two products would be in the same proportion as relative before-tax prices. As the earlier discussion suggested, the amount of shifting depends on market structures and demand and supply elasticities, and because these are not the same in all industries there is no presumption that the tax rate would be the same on both products.

tax is nonneutral in its effect on effort because it is a variable in the decision to work or take leisure. Thus, for relative prices—including the price of leisure—to remain unaffected, income as well as commodity taxes on all products may be required. This suggests that welfare will be maximized by generating taxes on all tax bases that are related to an economic variable.[18]

The discussion of the excise tax has implicitly assumed that the tax will not lead to a change in factor prices. When the specific excise illustrated in Figures 7.5, 7.6, and 7.7 leads to a reduction in quantity produced and sold, the amount of variable factors employed in the taxed industry is decreased. Partial equilibrium analysis assumes that these resources are released in such small amounts, relative to the entire factor market, that factor prices remain constant as these resources are absorbed elsewhere. Analysis of the general sales tax does not permit this assumption because the tax is more broadly based, leading to the release of resources from many industries. Thus, while the sales tax is analytically similar to the excise tax when discussed in connection with a single commodity, when taken as a whole it must be seen in a somewhat different light.

Suppose a truly general sales tax were levied on all goods and services. The analysis of shifting and incidence given in connection with the excise tax suggests that this will lead to an increase in the prices of all goods and services as the tax is shifted forward to consumers. The levy of the tax would empirically appear as an economy-wide increase in retail prices. If factor prices, and thus factor incomes, remain unchanged because there is no untaxed product that may be substituted for taxed products to avoid the tax, the sales tax will reduce the real volume of purchases made by income recipients. Thus, the volume of variable factors employed producing goods and services for private buyers is reduced. If the public sector, with its sales tax revenues, makes purchases sufficient to increase total product demand and absorb the output of these factors, no unemployment will result and there will be no adjustment of factor prices.[19]

The general sales tax may alternatively be seen as shifted backward to factors of production. Suppose the monetary authorities, opposed to inflation, pursue a policy that does not permit a general price increase. Then, because the sales tax reduces the net return to the seller he will attempt to cut his output; as this happens resources become unemployed. The only way factors may again be fully employed, with constant product prices including

---

18 This policy recommendation is an illustration of the theory of the second best. *See* Robert G. Lipsey and Kelvin Lancaster, "The General Theory of the Second Best," *Review of Economic Studies,* 1956–57.

19 The value of products produced differs from the value of the same products consumed because of the tax that does not reflect a payment to a factor of production. This illustrates the difference between gross national product and national income due to indirect business taxes, as discussed in Chapter 11.

tax, is with a general reduction in factor prices. As per unit factor costs decrease, marginal and average factor costs will decrease for all levels of output; as the economy adjusts to a new general equilibrium at unchanged product prices, all factors may again be employed. This is because with a reduction in factor prices the original level of output may be produced at lower factor cost; this lower factor cost, plus tax, will permit the product to be sold at its original before-tax price.

The incidence of the general sales tax is similar with either forward or backward shifting. With backward shifting owners of factors of production have reduced money incomes but pay constant product prices; the real income of factor owners is reduced and the public sector has access to products that otherwise would have been available for private use. With forward shifting consumers receive unchanged factor incomes but pay higher product prices; consumer real income is reduced and the public sector has access to resources that otherwise would have been available for private use. Since consumers derive their income from the sale of factor services the ultimate incidence of the truly general sales tax is the same in that it falls on persons who are simultaneously sellers of factor services and buyers of goods and services.[20] In both cases the tax effectively constitutes a tax on income either as the income is spent by consumers or as it is earned by factors of production.

A truly general sales tax, because the decision maker may not rearrange his economic activities to avoid the tax, is a neutral tax provided its shifting does not lead to changes in relative prices. Because supply and demand elasticities differ, avoiding relative price changes will require different rates of tax on each product and it is thus unlikely that the truly general sales tax will be neutral. There are additional reasons to expect the general sales tax to be nonneutral. First, a sales tax is never truly general: Food and personal services are often excluded from the sales tax base. Second, the sales tax base does not include saving and leisure, and the tax may be avoided by increasing one's consumption of these two items. The fact that one may accumulate savings that are not subject to tax may provide an inducement for citizens to substitute saving for present consumption. With these qualifications in mind, however, we conclude that the more broadly based the sales tax, the more nearly neutral it is likely to be, and the more narrowly based the sales tax the less likely it is to be neutral.

Multiple stage taxes. Commodity taxes in the United States are primarily of the type described in the previous section: Excise taxes are used by the

---

[20] For this to be strictly true, prices of all factors or the prices of all products would have to change in the same proportions and saving would have to be included in the tax base. Otherwise, on equity grounds, forward shifting differs from backward shifting.

federal and state-local governments and are usually collected from the manufacturer or the wholesaler; sales taxes are employed in many states, and by some cities, and are collected at the retail level. Both are single stage taxes since products are taxed only once by each taxing authority.[21] Multiple stage taxes, in contrast, are levied on the commodity more than once by a taxing authority as the product is fabricated and distributed. Two important multiple stage taxes are the turnover tax and the value-added tax, both of which play major roles in national government revenue systems outside the United States.[22] The turnover tax is collected each time a transaction occurs and is clearly a multiple stage tax since most products have several intermediate places of fabrication and distribution before reaching their final consumer. The value-added tax is less easily classified.[23] The tax base is value added but this, of itself, does not make the value-added tax a multiple stage tax. It would be possible to collect this tax only once, at the retail level, and the tax would be virtually the same as the retail sales tax since the price of products equals value added. In European practice the value-added tax is collected from producers and distributors at many points and is treated as a multiple stage commodity tax.

---

[21] A cigarette excise, for example, is collected by the federal government from the manufacturer, and by state governments from the wholesaler. Although the product is taxed twice this is not regarded as a multiple stage tax.

[22] The value-added tax was once part of Michigan's revenue system. In 1970 neither the value-added nor the turnover tax was levied in the United States. For a discussion of Michigan's value-added tax, *see* C. W. Lock, D. J. Rau, and H. D. Hamilton, "The Michigan Value-Added Tax," *National Tax Journal,* December 1955. For a discussion of all types of commodity taxes, including the European experiences with the turnover and value-added taxes, *see* John Due, *Sales Taxation* (Urbana, Ill.: University of Illinois Press, 1957). Both these taxes were used prior to 1968 in the Common Market nations. In 1968 the Common Market nations began to harmonize their fiscal systems by adopting the value-added tax; for a discussion of the value-added tax and tax harmonization, *see* Carl S. Shoup (ed.), *Fiscal Harmonization in Common Markets* (New York: Columbia University Press, 1967), Volumes I and II. The turnover tax is the major tax in the Soviet Union; it is not only a part of the Soviet revenue system but also is manipulated to make the quantity demanded for particular commodities equal to the available supply. Robert W. Campbell, *Soviet Economic Power,* 2d ed. (Boston: Houghton Mifflin, 1966), pp. 87–93.

[23] *The Role of Direct and Indirect Taxes in the Federal Revenue System, op. cit.,* especially pp. 89–100. Depending on the definitions adopted the value-added tax is seen as a tax on all factor incomes (equal to value added) or a general tax on production (equal to value added).

It is not entirely clear that the value-added tax is even a commodity tax. Value added, in some sense, is like profit in that it is not assignable to any particular unit of product, but it is a function of the entire level of operation of the productive unit. In practice, however, the value-added tax is treated as a commodity tax, and in France is separately invoiced as the product passes through several stages of fabrication, subject to tax at each stage. *See* John Due, *op. cit.,* p. 130.

Consider first the allocative effect of the turnover tax. The turnover tax is collected each time a transaction occurs, and for any single transaction may be treated as though it were a retail sales or excise tax in appraising its shifting and incidence. If we consider, as an example, the manufacture and distribution of ornamental iron products the following transactions may occur: sale of iron ore and coal as inputs to a primary metal producer; sale of primary metal products to a metal fabricator; sale of fabricated metal products to a distributor; and sale of the final product by the distributor to the consumer. The two columns at the left in Table 7.1 describe the produc-

***Table 7.1* Turnover vs. Value-Added Taxes**

			10 Percent Turnover Tax			30 Percent Value-Added Tax		
	Value Added	No-Tax Price	Tax Base	Tax	Price (inclusive of tax)	Tax Base	Tax	Price (inclusive of tax)
Iron ore	$50	$ 50	$ 50	$ 5	$ 55	$50	$15	$ 65
Coal	50	50	50	5	55	50	15	65
Primary ferrous metals	50	150	160	16	176	50	15	195
Fabricated ferrous metals	50	200	226	22.60	248.60	50	15	260
Distributor	50	250	298.60	29.86	328.46	50	15	325

tion and pricing of this product. Here the value of the iron ore and coal from the miners is $50 each (all value-added in mining—no intermediate inputs) and these intermediate inputs are processed into a primary metal product as the primary metal producer adds $50 to their value and sells his output for $150 per unit. The fabricator purchases an intermediate input for $150, adds $50 in value, and sells a fabricated metal product for $200, which is the price paid by the distributor. The distributor adds $50 in value and the final sale price to the consumer is $250 per unit. If a 10 percent turnover tax is now levied, for each transaction the tax base is the price of the product and, assuming full forward shifting of the tax, the final price to the consumer will be affected as follows. The iron ore is taxed at 10 percent, increasing its price from $50 to $55; the same is the case for the coal. Thus, the cost of mined inputs to the primary metal producer is now $110. The primary producer adds $50 in value to these inputs and has a primary metal product valued at $160, subject to the 10 percent tax, and sold to the fabricator for $176; the fabricator's input now costs $176; he adds $50 of value and sells his product for $248.60, fully shifting forward his tax liability of

$22.60. The distributor has purchased a product for $248.60, to which he adds $50 in value-making the before-tax retail price $298.60. If the turnover tax is also collected at the retail level this product is subject to an additional tax assessment of $29.86, which, when fully shifted forward to the consumer, leaves the consumer paying a final price, including all taxes, of $328.46. The total tax collected by the government equals $78.46. Were the same amount of revenue to be collected with a single stage retail sales tax, the tax rate would have to be 31.4 percent on a product valued at $250.00. The turnover tax, therefore, raises a given amount of revenue at lower statutory tax rates than would be possible with a retail sales tax. If political objection to taxes is a function of the height of the rate rather than the size of total tax liabilities, this tax is attractive from the government's viewpoint.

For there to be a turnover tax liability a transaction must occur and the tax may be avoided by not making transactions. Thus, the turnover tax is said to encourage vertical integration. In the example, suppose the mining, primary metal, and fabrication stages of production are vertically integrated.[24] The before-tax price (equal to value added) of the fabricated metal product remains $200 and the product is sold to the distributor with full forward shifting of the tax, for $220. When the distributor adds his $50 value to the product his before-tax retail price is $270. When the product is sold to the consumer, the price, including all taxes, is $297. Vertical integration clearly gives the integrated firm a competitive advantage over the non-integrated producer. Therefore, the turnover tax is an allocative variable.[25]

The turnover tax will have different proportional effects on product prices. If the turnover tax is a fixed *ad valorem* rate on all transactions, the amount of tax raised per unit of final product will depend on the number of transactions involved in production and distribution as well as value of the product. For example, in the 1950s and 1960s the German turnover tax was collected at the basic rate of 4 percent and was estimated to raise the average price of final products by 7.4 percent: The actual increase in price ranged from a low of 3.2 percent to a high of 12.5 percent.[26] Thus, the turnover tax is also an allocative variable as it changes relative product prices.

Tax pyramiding occurs when commodity taxes are levied at other than the retail level, and when firms follow a markup pricing policy. Suppose the

---

[24] When the tax base accumulates from one stage of fabrication to another, as in the case of the turnover tax, the tax is referred to as a *cascade tax*. It is cascade taxes that are said to encourage vertical integration; the term is widely used in the European literature on taxation.

[25] The Canadian manufacturers' sales tax originally was a turnover tax assessed on all transactions at other than the retail level. The argument that this tax favored vertical integration resulted in its being changed to a single stage tax on manufacturers at the final stage of a product's fabrication. *See* John Due, *op. cit.*, chapter 8.

[26] John Due, *op. cit.*, pp. 60–61. For prices to rise by less than 4 percent, full forward shifting did not occur.

inputs to a product cost the manufacturer \$100 and the manufacturer adds a 20 percent markup to cover his costs and produce some profit. The distributor then buys for \$120 and with a 50 percent markup would sell to the consumer for \$180. Now suppose that this product is subject to a 10 percent turnover tax; without considering the effect of the turnover tax on the input costs of the producer, the producer sells to the distributor for \$120 plus \$12 tax. The distributor thus pays \$132, adds his markup of 50 percent, and charges a before-tax price of \$198 and an after-tax price of \$217.80. Thus, the effect of the tax is to increase the price to the consumer from \$180 to \$217.80, a price increase of \$37.80. But the revenue to the government is only \$12 plus \$19.80, or \$31.80. This difference arises because the distributor has taken his 50 percent markup on the \$12 tax as well as the \$120 before-tax cost of the product and the tax is thus pyramided. If a retail tax only had been used, the same amount of revenue could be raised at a lower product price to the consumer (a 17.67 percent retail tax on \$180 will produce \$31.80 for the government, at a price to the consumer of \$211.80) or for the same price to the consumer, the government could have had a larger revenue (a 21 percent retail tax on \$180 will yield \$37.80 in tax revenue at a \$217.80 price to the consumer).

The allocative effects of the value-added tax are quite different. The tax base for this tax is value added in production rather than value of sales: Since value added is unaffected by the tax, it does not matter in determining the tax liability whether or not production is vertically integrated. Suppose, in the context of the example in Table 7.1, that each unit of product is subject to a 30 percent value-added tax that is wholly shifted forward. The value added by the iron ore producer (\$50) is subject to the 30 percent tax (\$15) and the price, including tax, of the iron ore is \$65. The same is true for the coal. Thus, the price paid by the primary metal producer for raw materials is \$130; he adds \$50 to their value and the before-tax price of the output of the primary metal producer is \$180. The primary metal producer is subject to the 30 percent value-added tax and his tax liability (\$15) when added to \$180 makes his price, including tax, \$195. This is the price paid by the fabricator for his raw materials; he adds \$50 to the value of the product, incurs a \$15 value-added tax liability, and sells at a price, inclusive of tax, of \$260. The distributor then adds \$50 to the value of the product, incurs a tax liability of \$15, and sells to the consumer at \$325 per unit. The government has collected revenue of \$75, raised in \$15 units from each of the five firms. The 30 percent value-added tax was selected in this example to make the after-tax price and tax revenue approximately the same as in the example of the 10 percent turnover tax. To raise equivalent amounts of revenue, the value-added tax rate must be greater than the turnover tax rate.[27]

[27] The French value-added tax is assessed differently, though the results are similar. The

The value-added tax cannot be avoided through vertical integration. If the mining through fabrication stages of production are vertically integrated, value added by the metal fabricator is $200 and his tax liability would be $60, making the price to the distributor, inclusive of tax, $260, the same as in the absence of vertical integration. Furthermore, since the value-added tax cannot be avoided by vertical integration and in no other way depends on the number of firms involved in production and distribution, the effective rate of tax on different products will be the same and the value-added tax, provided it is fully shifted forward, does not have the nonneutral effect of inducing changes in relative product prices. Finally, the value-added tax treats all factors of production alike. In comparison, the corporate income tax is levied only on the return to capital; to the extent it reduces the return to capital, the corporate income tax may induce the substitution of other factors for capital and in this respect be nonneutral. The value-added tax, alternatively, is assessed equally on the contributions of all factors of production and thus avoids this possible nonneutrality. The value-added tax may be assessed on all businesses; since it need not discriminate between incorporated and unincorporated businesses, it may avoid the nonneutral effect of the corporate income tax that arises when that tax is a variable in the decision to incorporate.

We have discussed personal income, sales, and value-added taxes in a way that leaves the impression that they are quite different from one another. In many ways they are similar. In fact, in a world without corporations, savings, investment, and income tax deductions and exemptions, the personal income, value-added, and truly general sales taxes all have the same tax base—national income. The personal income tax is assessed on income as it is received by factors of production; the value-added tax is assessed on the same income as it is generated in production; and the general sales tax is assessed as the income is spent. Because of the ways in which these taxes are raised in the context of a specific revenue system, they usually have different rate structures and appear different from one another. But all are broadly based taxes that in this limiting case have the same base. The specific provisions of these taxes as they are enacted into law will determine the basic differences in their allocative effects.

French tax is a turnover tax in that its base is the total value of each transaction. However, the tax is separately invoiced and each taxpayer may take a credit against his tax liability for taxes paid on his inputs. The tax credit effectively makes the French tax one whose base is value added at each stage of production and distribution. For a discussion of the French tax on value added and value-added taxation in general, *see* Clara K. Sullivan, *The Tax on Value Added* (New York: Columbia University Press, 1965).

TAXES ON WEALTH

Wealth taxes take assets as their tax base. In the United States wealth taxes are assessed on a number of bases, including real estate, personal property, inventories, bank balances, and estates. An obvious way to avoid wealth taxes is not to own assets, and wealth taxes are allocative variables as individuals arrange their purchases to avoid holding taxable assets. Wealth taxes are usually assessed on the value of an asset, and determining asset values is a major problem. In the case of real estate and personal property, for example, the asset may clearly have value, but since it is not for sale or has not been sold recently, determining this value may be difficult. Making judgments on the value of assets is known as *assessment*, a topic discussed in Chapter 14.

The most important wealth tax levied in the United States is the tax on business and household property (primarily real estate). Consider first a tax levied on business property. In the short run, at least, the tax will be regarded by the owners of the firm as a fixed cost; it is assessed on their fixed factors of production and does not in any way relate to the volume or value of their output. If we assume profit-maximizing firms, a change in fixed cost will affect neither marginal cost nor marginal revenue; the tax cannot be shifted and its incidence will fall on the owners of the firm who take a reduction in their economic profit. If, alternatively, we assume the sales-maximizing firm, the increase in fixed costs will reduce profits for all levels of output (the total profit schedule in Figure 7.2 would shift vertically downward as the total cost schedule shifts vertically upward); if the sales of the firm were constrained, before tax, by the minimum profit constraint, then the tax would be fully shifted forward to consumers in the short run. If the short-run incidence of the property tax falls wholly or partially on the owners of the firm, their profits are reduced, and in the long run resources will leave the industry if there are nontaxed alternatives with higher rates of return.

A related but somewhat different issue is *tax capitalization*. Assets produce income, and the property tax reduces the net income from the taxed asset. Income-producing assets will not be able to command a price any greater than the present value of their income streams given by

$$PV = \sum_{t=1}^{n} \frac{R_t}{(1+i)^t}$$

where PV denotes the present value of the income stream, R_t the net income produced in year t, n is the number of years over which the assets will produce income, and i the appropriate rate of discount.[28] If the property tax

[28] Chapter 5 includes a discussion of the method of computing present values, net returns, and the appropriate rates of discount.

is not fully shifted forward the net return is reduced in each year it is imposed. Reduction in the flow of net returns will lower the present value of the income stream and reduce the market price that the asset commands. This effect of the tax on asset values is known as tax capitalization; other things remaining equal, increases in taxes on assets that are not fully shifted will reduce the market value of the asset, and reductions in such taxes will increase the market value of the asset.[29]

A tax on owner-occupied housing, as opposed to business property, cannot be shifted, because the possessor of the tax base is not selling a service to others. But the personal property tax may be capitalized since it is a cost involved in owning property. Owners of residential housing receive an imputed income from their homes although there is no actual payment involved.[30] In making the decision to purchase property, the prospective buyer estimates the benefits he will derive from the asset, considers the costs involved in owning the asset, and on the basis of his estimated net return makes a decision on the value of property to himself.[31] The property tax is a cost of owning the asset and will therefore affect the value of the estimated returns and the amount the buyer is willing to pay for the asset. Thus, the property tax leads to tax capitalization.

LUMP SUM TAXES

Lump sum taxes include head (poll) taxes on persons and license fees on businesses; for these taxes the tax base is the physical existence of the person or business rather than any particular economic characteristic of the person or business. Poll taxes were once common in the United States but have virtually disappeared at the start of the 1970s. In 1963 the Supreme Court declared them unconstitutional as a prerequisite for voting in federal elections; their constitutionality as a prerequisite for voting in state and local elections has also been challenged. The poll tax is in no way related to any personal economic variable and is therefore incapable of being

---

[29] Other taxes may also lead to tax capitalization. The personal income tax, for example, taxes income received from assets and thus reduces the net return derived from the asset. This reduction in net return may well reduce the price which is paid for the asset. If taxes have a differential impact on incomes produced by different factors of production, tax capitalization will lead to changes in relative factor prices.

[30] The national income accounts include the net imputed rental value of owner occupied housing as part of personal income and gross national product. In 1969 the gross imputed rental value of owner occupied nonfarm housing in the United States was $48.0 billion: after subtracting depreciation allowances, taxes, and interest payments the net rental value imputed to owners of these homes was $12.7 billion. *Survey of Current Business,* July 1970, Table 7.3, lines 51 and 55.

[31] Wallace E. Oates, "The Effects of Property Taxes and Local Public Spending on Property Values: An Empirical Evaluation of Tax Capitalization and the Tiebout Hypothesis," *Journal of Political Economy,* November/December 1969.

shifted. Because the tax is not related to hours of work, level of income, wealth held, or any other variable characteristic of the person, the poll tax is said to have no allocative effects. Discussions of the allocative effects of taxation in public finance texts sometimes cite this tax as the ideally neutral tax with which other taxes are then compared. Even this ideally neutral personal tax may have allocative effects. Consider the person whose goal is a fixed level of after-tax disposable personal income. The poll tax affects the ability of such a person to achieve his goal and becomes a variable affecting his economic behavior. Also, one might consider the levy of poll taxes on persons in a less developed nation who live outside a monetized, market economy. If the poll tax must be paid in money, this will induce the taxpayer to enter the monetized economy to meet his tax liability; in this case the poll tax is nonneutral.

The lump sum business tax, such as the license fees imposed by many local governments, may be treated as a fixed cost; it is unrelated to the level of operation of the firm, its profitability, or the value of its assets, and may be avoided only by withdrawing from the business. For analytical purposes it may be handled in the same way as the business property tax; as a fixed cost it may or may not be shifted depending on the type of behavior assumed for the firm; it may be capitalized.

TAX NEUTRALITY

The preceding discussion has investigated the allocative effects of four types of taxes. The general conclusion to be drawn from this investigation is that taxes are likely to be nonneutral and, therefore, play a role in the allocation of resources. Nonneutrality as such, however, has no normative significance. Our earlier discussion showed that efficient resource allocation requires that price equal marginal cost. In the absence of externalities, perfectly competitive markets will obtain this result and public policy cannot increase allocative efficiency. But in the real world all prices do not equal marginal cost for several reasons. First, nonmarketed externalities exist, and even when price (marginal value) equals marginal cost between the parties to the transactions, this is not the case for the entire community. Second, firms have various degrees of monopoly power and, if they are profit maximizers, will not aim at setting price equal to marginal cost. Third, even if monopoly power could be contained, in the event of decreasing cost industries (where average cost is falling and, therefore, marginal cost is less than average cost) price cannot equal marginal cost and cover all private costs of production.[32] In these events public policy may increase allocative

[32] *See* Francis Bator, "The Anatomy of Market Failure," *The Quarterly Journal of Economics*, August 1958, for a systematic treatment of the conditions for allocative efficiency and some reasons for their nonattainment.

efficiency and nonneutral taxes may result in improved resource allocation. In addition, allocative goals are not the only goals of public economic policy, and not all allocative goals are designed to promote allocative efficiency; economic policy may require conscious departures from neutrality to promote the attainment of goals other than those related to allocative efficiency.

Departures from neutrality to improve resource allocation. The prices that consumers pay for products reflect, at the margin, their valuation of those products. The price of factors of production equals, at the margin, what those factors could receive in alternative employments and this, in turn, is the value society places on them in alternative uses. When a product's price is greater than its marginal cost, consumers are paying more for additional factor services in that use than they value those factor services in a sector where price equals marginal cost; Pareto optimal actions to reallocate resources are possible. As an illustration of how nonneutral taxes may promote allocative efficiency we consider an economy with both a perfectly competitive sector and a monopoly sector. Producers in both sectors are assumed to be profit maximizers; their products are assumed to be substitutes.

In the perfectly competitive sector the interaction of market supply and demand determines a market equilibrium where the marginal value of the product, measured by the price paid by consumers, is equal to the marginal factor cost of production (which determines the market supply curve). In the monopoly sector the price paid by the consumer, representing the product's marginal value, is above marginal factor cost. If resources are mobile and were somehow reallocated from the perfectly competitive to the monopoly sector, consumers would receive additional amounts of monopoly produced products, whose value exceeds their marginal cost, and less competitively produced products, whose value equals their marginal cost for the same total resource employment. For some reallocated increment of inputs, products with increased value to consumers could be produced and this reallocation is welfare increasing. As less of the competitive product is produced marginal value will begin to exceed marginal cost in that sector and the divergence will grow as the reallocation progresses. The reallocation will continue to be welfare increasing until the divergence between marginal value and marginal cost is equal in both sectors.[33]

Suppose an excise tax is levied on the competitively produced product and further assume the tax is shifted forward. Because of the increased price of the taxed product relative prices are altered and consumers will substitute the monopoly product for the competitively produced product. Since they are

---

[33] This analysis presumes the ability to measure utility and to make interpersonal comparisons of utility. For a fuller discussion of this approach to welfare economics, *see* James E. Meade, *Trade and Welfare* (Oxford: Oxford University Press, 1955), Part I.

assumed to be substitutes, the levy of the nonneutral tax on the competitive product leads to a shift to the right in the demand for the monopoly product. Because of the price increase, less of the competitive product is sold and, because of the demand shift, more of the monopoly product is sold: The welfare increasing resource allocation occurs as the result of the levy of a nonneutral tax.[34]

The previous example is an illustration of the *theory of the second best*.[35] Earlier in the chapter we argued that if a nonneutral excise tax were levied on one product, then for that level of resource transfer to the public sector, welfare may be maximized by the simultaneous levy of nonneutral taxes in other sectors so that the resource transfer occurs without any changes in relative prices. What both these examples have in common is the fact that when the price paid by the consumer differs from marginal resource cost in one sector of the economy, then having price equal to marginal resource cost in other sectors of the economy may not be desirable; a second-best optimum may require violation of this marginal condition in other sectors of the economy as well. This theory has implications for the formulation of public policy since it shows that the levy of nonneutral taxes may improve the allocation of resources, and that tax policy is a means of accomplishing allocative goals even when no transfer of resources from the private to the public sector is intended. We thus see that nonneutral taxes may be used to improve the allocation of resources. But allocative efficiency is not the only goal of public policy, and nonneutral taxes may be employed to reallocate resources in pursuit of other goals as well.

Departures from neutrality for reasons other than promoting allocative efficiency. Nonneutral taxes are commonly employed to promote allocative goals not based on achieving optimal resource allocation. Historically, tax literature discussed *sumptuary taxes*, excise taxes levied on products to discourage their consumption because society believes their use is undesirable.[36] Liquor and tobacco excise taxes are sometimes regarded in this light; they raise the price of these products relative to others in the hope that the higher price will moderate their use.[37] A similar tax is the protec-

---

[34] We avoid having to deal with the transfer of resources to government as tax revenue is raised by assuming that tax receipts are distributed as transfer payments to the buyers of the competitively produced product.

[35] *See* Lipsey and Lancaster, *op. cit.*

[36] With the development of movie ratings in the late 1960s, a Texas state legislator introduced a bill to make the state admissions excise tax a function of the rating. Thus, X rated movies would be taxed more heavily than G rated movies; the legislator's intents were sumptuary.

[37] Taxation of alcoholic beverages and tobacco may also be designed to promote allocative efficiency. Excessive use of alcohol results in intoxication which, in turn, calls for

tive tariff whose intent is to discourage the consumption of imports in favor of domestic products. Tariffs may also play a part in a nation's stabilization policy since variation in tariff rates will affect the level of imports and thus the tariff-levying nation's balance of payments. For balance of payments purposes the United States levied the interest equalization tax on portfolio foreign investment in 1962, and the United Kingdom levied an across-the-board 15 percent surcharge on all imports in 1964; in both instances the tax was deliberately nonneutral and designed to discourage international transactions in order to pursue stabilization goals.[38]

The tax mechanism is sometimes employed to promote economic growth. Economic growth is partially an allocative question since the division of gross national product between consumption and investment will affect the size of the economy's capital stock and its ability to generate gross national product in the future. Of concern here is the effect of taxes on the saving needed to finance investment, and the effect of taxes on the decision to invest. As suggested earlier in the chapter, the truly general sales tax would tax saving as well as commodities; the fact that sales taxes typically exclude savings from the tax base indicates that these taxes may encourage saving. But more important, it is proposed that nations adopt an expenditure or consumption tax explicitly designed to encourage saving.[39] Such a tax could replace or supplement income and retail sales taxes. The tax base for the expenditure tax is income less change in asset holdings. In the case where the taxpayer increases the value of his assets during the year (excluding changes in asset values that result from changes in an asset's price), his consumption is less than his income and he has taken from the economy less than he has contributed during that year. For the individual whose asset holdings decrease during the year, consumption exceeds income and the individual has consumed more than his annual contribution. The expenditure

---

additional law enforcement expenditures; use of tobacco increases the probability of fire and thus requires additional expenditures for fire protection. The externalities associated with these products may require taxation of their use on grounds of allocative efficiency.

[38] As first enacted, the interest equalization tax was levied on the market value of portfolio foreign investment at variable rates up to 15 percent in order to reduce the effective yield to buyers by about one percentage point; this tax is discussed further in Chapter 22. The British import surcharge was a 15 percent increase in the rate of duty on nearly all products. It was introduced in October 1964, was lowered to 10 percent in April 1965, and removed in May 1966. There is evidence to suggest that it had very little impact on the British balance of payments. *See* J. Johnston and M. Henderson, "Assessing the Effects of the Import Surcharges," *Manchester School of Social and Economic Studies,* May 1967.

[39] Kaldor, *op. cit.* Expenditure taxes have been employed in India, Ceylon, and Ghana. Regarding India, *see* Walter W. Brundo, Charles K. Cobb, Jr., and Nani A. Palkhivala's *Taxation in India* (Boston: Little, Brown, 1960).

tax takes as its base extractions from rather than contributions to the economy and the schedule of rates is applied against this base. It is argued that the schedule of rates for the expenditure tax may be highly progressive (and marginal rates may be greater than 100 percent), and that such a tax, because it increases the cost of consumption at the margin, will discourage consumption and thus encourage the saving required to finance investment. Quite aside from the equity argument that a tax on extractions is preferred to a tax on total income, proponents of the expenditure tax see it as a conscious departure from neutrality designed to encourage saving.[40]

Alternatively, taxes may be specifically designed to encourage investment. The decision to invest is based on a number of factors, one of which is the after-tax rate of return on investment.[41] Any variation in taxes that affects the after-tax rate of return on investment is likely to affect the volume of investment. The adoption in the United States of the investment tax credit in 1962 (see Chapter 17), its removal in the last quarter of 1966, its restoration in the first quarter of 1967, and its repeal in 1969, is a clear example of the use of nonneutral taxes to accomplish allocative and stabilization goals through their impact on investment.

ADMINISTRATIVE EFFICIENCY

The actual raising of public revenues requires that costs be incurred. By the *administrative efficiency of taxation* we mean minimizing the collection costs per dollar of tax revenue collected. This must be examined from two viewpoints, the cost to government of collecting taxes and the compliance costs incurred by the taxpayer for which he is not remunerated.

In the United States voluntary taxpayer compliance makes collection costs less than in some nations where compliance is only grudgingly given. In some instances the intention of raising taxes is not revenue but regulation, and here collection costs may not be an important consideration. Most taxes, however, are for revenue purposes and as long as they are not overridden by

---

40 The British purchase tax is a wholesale sales tax levied at different rates depending on whether the taxed product is a necessity or a luxury. During World War II the purchase tax had rates as high as 125 percent on some products. The purchase tax is like the progressive expenditure tax in the sense that it taxes luxury goods, which are presumably purchased by those making large consumption expenditures, at higher rates than the necessities purchased by those making only small amounts of consumption expenditures. The difference arises because the expenditure tax is levied on total spending rather than on each unit of spending, and thus the wealthy consumer who gorges himself on "necessities" may be made subject to progressive rates under an expenditure tax.

41 *See* D. W. Jorgensen and C. D. Siebert, "A Comparison of Alternative Theories of Corporate Investment Behavior," *American Economic Review*, September 1968, for a discussion of investment behavior and a listing of additional bibliography.

other considerations, minimizing the per unit collection costs is a desirable goal for the tax authorities.

Payment of taxes imposes costs on the taxpayer other than the payment itself. Payment of personal income taxes requires keeping extensive records of receipts and expenditures, especially if the taxpayer chooses to itemize deductions. Corporate income taxes also require keeping extensive records, although such record keeping is likely to be done by the modern, efficiently run corporation anyway. The requirement that employers withhold income and social security taxes from employee earnings imposes bookkeeping costs on employers. Collection of retail sales taxes requires the merchant to assess the taxes and make periodic remittances. Cash registers that compute the tax and keep totals on taxes collected are an example of compliance costs imposed on taxpayers. A well thought out and administered tax system will be cognizant of these compliance costs and attempt to make them minimal, if for no other reason than to encourage voluntary compliance with the tax laws. A point to note is that minimizing the budgetary cost of the revenue collecting agency does not necessarily minimize the administrative cost of taxation. Increasing the budgetary cost of the revenue collecting agency may also involve a reduction in taxpayer compliance costs and, conversely, reducing the budgetary cost of the revenue agency may increase uncompensated taxpayer compliance costs. It is sometimes suggested that tax authorities should increase their collection activities to the point where their marginal collection costs equal marginal revenue collections. As long as the revenue agents do not consider taxpayer compliance costs as part of the costs of collection this rule is allocatively inefficient.

SUMMARY

Whenever taxes are shifted or capitalized they affect prices and resource allocation. Our discussion of income, commodity, wealth, and lump sum taxes showed that all taxes are likely to have allocative effects; since we are uncertain as to which theoretical model best describes a modern market economy we are unable to state conclusively what these allocative effects will be. Finally, we examined the theory of the second best and the allocative goals of public economic policy, and saw that the levy of nonneutral taxes is a means of accomplishing some of these goals.

8

TAXES AND EQUITY

Equity is the subject of heated debate. Part of the debate over policies to promote economic equity stems from a confusion of criteria. In a competitively organized market economy, economic efficiency is achieved when, among other things, factors of production receive a real return equal to their marginal physical product. But this distribution of product, although allocatively efficient, is not necessarily equitable; nor is it necessarily inequitable and to argue equity from it, as is sometimes done, is to misuse the efficiency criterion. Because policies to promote equity usually alter the distribution of income or wealth, approaching equity may, in the short run at least, benefit some at the expense of others. Since criteria are not easily defined, reasonable men differ about what is equitable and from this disagreement, and not the goal of equity itself, the public policy debate results. In this chapter a number of issues are raised and discussed relating to equity in taxation; unfortunately, firm answers as guidelines to public policy are difficult to find.

Adam Smith devoted the fifth and final book of *The Wealth of Nations* to a discussion of "The Revenue of the Sovereign or Commonwealth." There he set forth four maxims regarding taxes; the first, which is most important to a discussion of tax equity, began as follows:

> The subjects of every state ought to contribute towards the support of the government, as nearly as possible, in proportion of their respective abilities; that is, in proportion to the revenue which they respectively enjoy under the protection of the state.[1]

This passage reflects two strands of thought with respect to tax equity. Smith first asserts that citizens should pay in accordance with their abilities; this proposition is embodied in the modern ability to pay principle of taxation. The second portion of Smith's statement—"in proportion to the revenue which they respectively enjoy"—contends that citizens should be taxed on the basis of the benefits they derive from their government. This proposition is at the heart of the benefit principle of taxation. These two principles of taxation are at the foundation of a modern discussion of tax equity. Throughout the chapter we will be referring to the distribution of the incidences of taxes rather than tax liabilities; it is tax incidence that affects equity.

BENEFIT PRINCIPLE

Under the *benefit principle of taxation* taxes are regarded as the prices citizens pay for the goods and services they buy through their government, and are assessed on each citizen according to the benefits he directly and indirectly receives. Direct sale to buyers, as through the United States Post Office or municipal water departments, where the department making the sale is, by and large, expected to be self-supporting from revenues, represents charging on the benefit principle; their receipts are usually referred to as *user charges* rather than taxes.[2] The federal motor fuel excise tax and most state gasoline excise taxes are earmarked for highway construction and maintenance; although the connection between payment and service is less direct than with user charges, these taxes are basically assessed on the benefit principle. When externalities are minimal and the beneficiaries of government expenditures are easily identified, taxation on the benefit principle has con-

1 Adam Smith, *An Inquiry into the Nature and Causes of the Wealth of Nations* (New York: Random House Modern Library Edition, 1937), Book V, Chapter 2, p. 777.

2 Postal charges may not be levied entirely on the benefit principle. The cost of rural deliveries and collections may exceed the unit costs of collection and delivery in metropolitan areas although both groups of postal users pay the same fees. This is an instance where society regards low-cost rural access to postal services as a merit want, and rural users are subsidized.

siderable appeal, provided the goal of public policy is not to redistribute the fruits of economic activity. When pure public goods and externalities are involved, taxation on the benefit principle is difficult because it is impossible to observe who benefits and by what amount in order to assess charges.

Demand analysis may serve as a guide to taxation on the benefit principle. As income changes, citizens will vary their purchases of goods and services. The income elasticity of demand specifies how purchases vary with income, assuming prices are constant. The coefficient of income elasticity of demand for the *i*th product, E_i, is equal to the percent change in quantity of i demanded, divided by the percent change in income or

$$E_i = \frac{\Delta Q_i/Q_i}{\Delta Y/Y}$$

where Q_i designates quantity of product i and Y designates money income. If E_i is positive, the quantity of i purchased increases with income and, because prices are assumed constant, the amount spent on i increases. If E_i equals unity, the share of income spent on product i is constant; if E_i exceeds unity, the share of income spent on i increases as income increases; and if E_i is positive but less than unity, the share of income spent on i decreases as income increases. If E_i is negative, the quantity of i purchased varies inversely with income, and as income increases the amount spent for product i decreases. This last case defines an *inferior good.*

Taxes are often evaluated with reference to income: a *regressive tax* is one where the share of income going to tax decreases as income increases; a *proportional tax* is one where the share of income going to tax is a constant proportion of income; and a *progressive tax* is one where the share of income going to tax rises as income rises. If the income elasticity of demand for public goods is less than unity, regressive taxes are required on the benefit principle. This conclusion does not specify the appropriate regressiveness of rates, which at the margin would have to be negative if public goods are inferior goods, but it does provide a guideline for structuring the tax system. If the income elasticity of demand for public goods equals unity, proportional taxes are required, and if the income elasticity of demand for public goods exceeds unity the benefit principle requires a progressive tax structure. These tax structures may be achieved with income, commodity, or wealth taxes; selecting the type of taxes used requires consideration of their allocative effects as well as their structure.

Taxation perfectly in accord with the benefit principle would leave the distribution of real incomes unchanged. Disregarding the difficulties involved in determining who benefits from public expenditures in the event of public goods and externalities, assessing taxes on the benefit principle would make citizen marginal valuations equal marginal production costs and would result in a Pareto optimal allocation of resources. Provided society's distributive objectives are met, pursuit of allocative efficiency is a desirable direction for public policy; taxation on the benefit principle is a step in this direction.

We are accustomed to thinking of citizens as the beneficiaries of government activity, and our discussion has thus far looked implicitly at personal taxes and personal benefits. In the real world taxes are assessed on businesses as well as individuals. Can business taxes also be based on the benefit principle? Businesses benefit from the social overhead capital and the legal protection provided by government. Without local and interstate highways, airports, and harbor facilities, direct business costs would be increased. Without the police and fire protection provided by governments at all levels, business costs would undoubtedly be increased. Business taxes shifted forward to buyers may be seen as the cost of inputs provided by government. If the incidence of business taxes falls on owners their income is not necessarily reduced; without government, direct business costs would be higher and, with the same product prices, profits would be reduced. In addition, many business operations give rise to social costs; industrial smoke increases the laundry and home painting costs of citizens, and water pollution increases the cost of potable water. Businesses pay taxes in return for the benefit they reap by imposing unmarketed social costs, and citizens pay these social costs in return for lower product prices and taxes.

Government investment projects require current public expenditures that do not result in current benefits. Highway or school construction, for example, requires expenditures as the assets are built, but benefits are realized only as the assets are used. If the revenues to finance public construction are raised from taxes, current taxpayers finance expenditures from which they derive no current benefits; hence, such taxes are inconsistent with the benefit principle. The benefit principle requires that public capital be financed from the sale of bonds—deficit financing. Citizens who buy bonds acquire financial assets with their savings and make no current sacrifice as the public assets are financed. Interest is paid and bonds are retired over the life of the asset, while citizens are receiving benefits from the use of the asset. Current taxes used to service the debt are consistent with the benefit principle.

The effects investment projects have on the capitalized value of private property may require modification of this conclusion. For instance, the price a family is willing to pay for residential property depends on the discounted inputed values the property is expected to yield. If a piece of property includes a swimming pool from which the family expects to benefit, the value of the property is increased by the capitalized value of the swimming pool's use. A nearby municipal swimming pool may be a close substitute for a private pool, and the value of local government services may be a capitalized component of property values. If the municipal pool is financed from the sale of bonds, taxes to service these bonds must be raised over the life of the asset. When property taxes are used to meet debt service charges these taxes will also be capitalized, reducing private property values. Presuming the government investment has a benefit-cost ratio greater than unity, the capitalized value of benefits will exceed the capitalized value of the taxes and lead to a net increase in private property values for which the present owner does not pay. Is this equitable?

Debt financing of government investments may be contrasted with financing from current taxes. A one-time increase in property taxes to cover an asset's capital costs could not be capitalized. Property values increase only by the capitalized value of expected future benefits, and the increase should be more than if government investments were financed from the sale of bonds. In this case the property owner makes a one-time current payment and buys this larger capitalized increase in property values. Is this equitable?

According to the benefit principle citizens who consume equal amounts of public goods should pay equal taxes just as citizens who send the same number of letters pay the same postal fees. Quite aside from our inability to ascertain consumption of benefits from most public expenditures, this method of taxation is regarded as inequitable in the United States. Our belief in equality of opportunity in a democratic society requires, for example, that all citizens have access, as a merit want, to primary and secondary education. Although there are undoubtedly substantial externalities from education, the pupil certainly benefits most, and on the benefit principle large families, who are often poor families, would be heavily taxed to finance education. One reason why the benefit principle does not have widespread appeal is that most Americans see government economic activity accomplishing distributive objectives.

ABILITY TO PAY

The *ability to pay principle of taxation* takes the position that the benefit approach is irrelevant. First, benefits cannot operationally be used as the basis for taxation in a world with public goods and externalities because it is impossible to determine who benefits from most public expenditures and in what amounts. Second, since beneficiaries cannot be identified and charged, taxes become compulsory payments, unrelated to benefits, extracted from the citizenry, and must be levied only with consideration to an equitable incidence of their liabilities. At the core of this principle is the capacity of persons to pay taxes. How is this capacity measured?

In a modern economy taxes are paid in money rather than in kind, and income is usually used as the measure of ability to pay taxes. By this criterion the larger a taxpayer's income the greater his capacity to pay taxes, and two persons with equal incomes have equal ability to pay. But is this correct? Detailed discussion of the federal and state-local tax systems is deferred until Chapters 13 and 14. However, the provisions of these tax laws suggest that Americans believe some qualified portion of income rather than gross income is the appropriate measure of ability to pay. From gross income taxpayers are permitted to subtract exemptions depending on family size. Personal exemptions are compatible with the proposition that the exempted income is the minimum needed for subsistence and is not a reflection of ability to pay. Medical expenses in excess of some percent of income may also be subtracted from gross income in computing taxable income because persons with costly medical problems are judged to have less ability to pay taxes. Many states exempt food purchases from retail sales taxation (or tax food at lower rates than other products) on the grounds that food is a necessity whose purchase does not reflect the buyer's ability to pay taxes. Some states also exempt clothing for the same reasons. Thus, it is taxable income rather than gross income that is taken as a measure of ability to pay taxes and, as we shall see in Chapter 13, the adjustments, and not the appropriateness of income as a measure of ability to pay, are most often questioned in evaluations of the equity of the tax system.

Other objects than income may be used as measures of ability to pay. The most important of these is wealth. A person who owns substantial assets is, in some respects, better able to pay taxes than the person who owns no assets. Assets may be in a form that does not produce current income, such as growth stocks or timber lands, and paying taxes based on wealth may require their liquidation. If this happens, wealth as an indicator of ability to pay may be questioned. The major wealth tax in the United States is the local property tax whose base is the value of real estate and, sometimes, personal (moveable) property. Because tax liabilities vary directly with the value of property, wealth is being used as an indicator of ability to pay. Increases in property taxes may create financial difficulties—especially for retired persons living on fixed income—because this form of asset holding often reflects a former rather than a current ability to pay measured in terms of income.

Horizontal equity. The Declaration of Independence proclaims that all men are created equal before the law. Carried over to taxation this fundamental principle of American democracy is embodied in the concept of *horizontal equity* which, as a canon of taxation, requires that equals be taxed equally. One conception of horizontal equity might be that all citizens should pay equal amounts of taxes. Another, embodied in the benefit principle, is that citizens who benefit equally from public expenditures should pay equal amounts of taxes. Neither of these positions is widely accepted. Instead, the principle of horizontal equity requires that taxpayers with equal abilities to pay should bear equal taxes. The primary difficulty in making this principle operable is determining ability to pay. In the United States, citizens with equal taxable incomes pay equal amounts of federal income taxes. But is this necessarily equitable? There are cost of living differences between rural and urban areas, and among different regions of the nation. Thus persons with identical taxable incomes may have different capacities to pay taxes because of these differences in real purchasing power. Should an equitable tax system reflect these differences?

Accepting the proposition that income is the proper basis for determining which citizens have equal capacity to pay taxes, an additional question is whether or not income received is the appropriate concept. Should income be measured on a cash receipt or an accrual basis? An additional dimension to this question arises when taxes have allocative effects so that gross income flows before and after taxation differ.[3] The presence of such allocative effects may create confusion about the definition of income to be used in an evaluation of horizontal equity.

Suppose citizens receive income from the sale of labor and capital services where capital may be employed in either incorporated or unincorporated businesses. Income received from capital invested in unincorporated businesses is conventionally added to labor income to determine personal income. Assume that all corporate profits (income from capital) are paid out as dividends that citizens receive as personal income. Personal income, for this example, equals all income received from the sale of labor and capital services and includes all corporate and unincorporated business income. Assuming no differences in risk between these two types of business, capital will be allocated so that rates of return are equalized in the corporate and unincorporated business sectors. Thus, two taxpayers with equivalent skills and equal capital resources will have identical personal incomes even though one has his capital in corporate investments and the other his capital in an unincorporated business. With identical personal incomes (and disregarding personal exemptions and deductions) horizontal equity requires that they pay equal amounts of taxes.

Now levy a corporate income tax whose base is corporate profits before payment of dividends, and assume there is no forward shifting of the tax to consumers or backward shifting to variable inputs. In the short run there will be no change in the gross earning of corporations, and gross personal income (from sale of labor services and corporate profits) does not change. Since the incidence of corporate income tax falls on the owners of corporate capital, citizens whose capital is in unincorporated investments pay less taxes than citizens with corporate investments; the incidence of tax liabilities is,

---

[3] The following argument, which sees tax equity in a general rather than a partial equilibrium framework, is discussed by Arnold Harberger, "The Incidence of the Corporation Income Tax," *Journal of Political Economy,* June 1962; and by John Isbister, "On the Theory of Equitable Taxation," *National Tax Journal,* September 1968.

in the short run, inequitable because corporate income is taxed twice. Since the net return on corporate investments is reduced the tax will be capitalized and corporate shareholders realize a short-run decrease in asset values.

The long-run effects may be quite different. With tax induced difference in net yields, resources already employed in the corporate sector may attempt to shift to the unincorporated sector; when new investment is made investors will prefer unincorporated to incorporated business. Thus, in the long run, resources will be allocated in increasing amounts to unincorporated businesses, reducing the gross yield on capital devoted to those businesses. At the same time, resources will shift away from corporate investment, increasing the gross return on corporate investments until it is high enough to make the after-tax net return on corporate investment equal to the untaxed return on investment in the unincorporated business sector.

If personal income is defined as income received, then citizens with investments in the corporate sector receive dividends equal to the after-tax profits of corporations (assuming no undistributed profits), which is a yield on investments equal to the yield that would have been received had the investments been alternatively made in unincorporated businesses. Payment of equal amounts of taxes based on income received by citizens whose investments are in corporate and unincorporated businesses is equitable by the criterion of horizontal equity. Payment of equal amounts of taxes based on gross factor earnings would be inequitable because these gross capital earnings have been altered by the levy of the corporate income tax to equalize the after-tax return on investment in the two sectors. It is commonly argued that the United States tax laws are inequitable because corporate income is taxed twice—once when it is received by the corporation and once again when it is received as the dividend component of personal income. If there were no allocative effects of the tax, this equity argument might have some appeal; but if resources are reallocated in the way suggested, equal taxation on the basis of gross factor earnings would violate the principle of horizontal equity. Of course, if the corporate income tax is shifted forward to consumers, then rates of return in the corporate and unincorporated sectors are unaffected, and without the suggested reallocation of resources double taxation would not result.

Over what time span should horizontal equity be achieved? Public capital acquisition yields benefits to future generations and reintroduces the benefit principle into the discussion of horizontal equity. If all public expenditures are financed from current taxes, any expenditures that produce a flow of future benefits provide future generations of taxpayers with benefits for which they are not assessed; taxes on these future generations will be lower than they would be if the same quantity of public benefits were all financed from current taxes. Thus, for a particular level of educational services, current taxpayers may authorize the construction of school facilities. If these are financed from taxes all the costs of the capital facilities are borne by current taxpayers although benefits will be available for many years. Taxes on taxpayers when the assets are acquired will be greater than taxes on the generation of citizens who reap the benefits, and persons with equal ability to pay in these two periods will pay different amounts of taxes. If the demand for public goods increases from one generation to the next it is equitable for taxpayers in one generation to pay more taxes than taxpayers in the other, but for a particular level of public goods such differences are contrary to the principle of horizontal equity. Thus, horizontal equity, as well as the benefit principle, suggests that debt financing of public capital is appropriate on intergenerational equity grounds.

An additional timing problem arises when taxpayers have uneven flows of income and when tax rates are not proportional. With progressive (or regressive) tax rates, citizens with uneven annual income flows pay different amounts of taxes than citizens with the same lifetime earnings received in equal annual amounts. Before determining the horizontal equity of a tax it is first necessary to decide whether capacity to pay should be measured annually, by decades, over the entire lifetime of the taxpayer, or over some other time span. This issue is further considered as we take up income averaging in Chapter 13.

Vertical equity. The principle of horizontal equity requires that taxpayers with equal abilities pay equal amounts of taxes. A logical extension of horizontal equity is that taxpayers with different abilities should pay different amounts of taxes. This is usually interpreted to mean that as a citizen's ability to pay increases so should his taxes; *vertical equity* requires that citizens with large incomes pay more taxes than citizens with small incomes. That it is equitable for a rich man to pay more taxes than a poor man is seldom questioned. Rather, controversy centers around the structure of a tax's effective rates.

Regressive, proportional, and progressive taxes are defined with reference to the share of income taken by the tax. Proportional and progressive taxes always require citizens with high incomes to pay larger amounts of taxes than citizens with low incomes. It would be almost impossible to design a regressive tax that does not require the rich to pay more than the poor. The principle of vertical equity is no help in determining the appropriate structure of tax rates, and guidance on this particular point must be sought elsewhere. Many pages have been written attempting scientifically to make the case for progressive taxes but the results of this literature are inconclusive. As one author put it: "The moment you abandon . . . the cardinal principle of exacting from all individuals the same proportion of their income or their property, you are at sea without rudder or compass and there is no amount of injustice or folly that you may not commit."[4] The scientific case for progression in tax rates rests on diminishing marginal utility of income, and minimizing the total sacrifice that citizens make when they pay taxes. If for no other reason, these arguments have little appeal because they require making interpersonal comparisons of utility. The case for a particular structure of tax rates is best made in reference to political decisions regarding equity in the distribution of after-tax income. If society regards the degree of inequality in the distribution of before-tax incomes as excessive, then progressive tax rates are one means of reducing this inequity; the case for progressive taxation is best seen from this viewpoint. In the mid-twentieth century the belief is widespread that progressive taxation is equitable, although this belief is by no means as prevalent as the belief that it is equitable for the rich to pay more taxes than the poor. Even among those who advocate progressive taxation there is little agreement as to what degree of progression is equitable.

USING TAXES TO ACHIEVE DISTRIBUTIVE OBJECTIVES

The structure of tax rates determines whether before- and after-tax income distributions are the same. Although wealth is sometimes discussed as an object of distributive equity it is ignored in this section and the discussion centers on equity in the distribution of income. If incomes were equitably distributed before any taxes were collected, then the tax system should not alter that distribution; before- and after-tax income distributions should be the same. In this event the most equitable tax structure would be one where all taxes combined absorb equal proportions of citizens' before-tax incomes.

Taxes do not, in fact, leave the after-tax income distribution the same as the before-tax distribution. In some instances this redistribution was intended as the tax laws were written. Redistributive intent is certainly the foundation on which the progressive rate structure of the federal and state personal income taxes rests. Further, the base for these income taxes is not gross income but taxable income which is smaller. This means that even if personal income taxes were raised with proportional rates applied to taxable income, the effective structure of rates on gross income would be progressive and after-tax inequalities would be less than before-tax inequalities in the distribution of income. This feature of income taxation reinforces the progressive rate structure. If all income were taxed under the same schedule of

---

[4] McCulloch, *Taxation and the Funding System* (1845), cited in Walter J. Blum and Harry Kalven, Jr., *The Uneasy Case for Progressive Taxation* (Chicago: The University of Chicago Press, 1963), p. 45. Blum and Kalven give a brief history of income taxation, including its legal foundation, and discuss the major arguments in the controversy over progression in income tax rates.

rates, and if deductions and exemptions were made solely on the basis of family size, then proportional as well as progressive taxes on taxable income would have the effect of narrowing the inequalities in the after-tax income distribution. In Chapters 13 and 14 these features of the federal and state income tax laws that tend toward equalization of the after-tax income distribution are further examined, as are some features that tend toward greater inequality. State exemption of food, drugs, and clothing from retail sales taxation rests on the same equity foundation. A truly general sales tax with only these exemptions would be progressive with respect to total income and reduce inequalities in the after-tax income distribution. The fact that retail sales taxes typically exclude personal services and saving from the tax base means that they are in fact regressive, thus increasing inequality in the after-tax distribution of income.

Throughout this discussion we have not defined what is equitable although we have hinted that making the after-tax distribution of income more equal than the before-tax distribution of income is a step in that direction. This is frequently asserted, and receives some empirical support from several features of Western tax laws that are deliberately enacted to accomplish redistribution, but no one has yet succeeded in scientifically proving this case. As is shown in the following chapter, what is democratically selected reflects collective choice under a particular set of decision-making rules, and welfare-maximizing voters may support actions that increase their individual welfare without increasing total welfare or without being equitable. If majority decision is equated with equity this problem collapses, but making this equation seems presumptuous. This chapter has attempted to set out several criteria that may be useful in evaluating the equity of a tax system, but since equity is an elusive concept we are unable to arrive at firm conclusions. Before turning, in the next chapter, to a discussion of collective choice and the rationale that motivates voters in supporting tax and expenditure programs, we conclude this chapter with a discussion of possible conflicts that may arise between the allocative and equity dimensions of taxation.

CONFLICTS BETWEEN ALLOCATIVE AND EQUITY CRITERIA

Our discussion, in Chapter 7, of tax neutrality led us to the conclusion that while the allocative effects of taxes are uncertain they are likely to exist since no tax is clearly neutral. Thus, evaluation of any tax must consider both its allocative effects and its equity; taxes that are designed to accomplish a particular allocative goal may not necessarily be equitable. Similarly, taxes that are designed to promote society's distributive objectives may have undesirable allocative effects. Hence, there are possible conflicts between the allocative and equity goals of taxation. Two examples of such conflicts are considered here.

First take the national objective of increasing the rate of real economic growth. There are many dimensions to an analysis of economic growth but central to any effort to enhance economic growth is the requirement that there be an increase in the nation's capital stock. Directing resources to capital formation is an allocative problem. To increase the capital stock requires that net private domestic investment be positive and, provided investment is to remain private in accordance with our institutional constraint of market capitalism, private saving must be available to finance this private investment. To encourage additional investment, income from capital might be taxed at preferential rates by lowering corporate income taxes, permitting accelerated depreciation, or exempting from taxation portions of income derived from especially desired types of investment—for example, mineral depletion allowances (see Chapter 13). To encourage saving, commodity taxes may be raised to increase saving and discourage consumption at the margin, or personal income taxes on savers may be reduced in order to increase after-tax income and saving. Programs to increase the amount of resources allocated to investment might require these tax actions, and it is precisely these tax actions that are frequently cited as the inequitable features of the tax laws. All these tax proposals are likely to widen the degree of inequality in the distribution of income and thus they run counter to the concepts of distributive equity held by many Americans. At the same time if these programs are successful in increasing the rate of economic growth, new jobs will become available, and in a rapidly growing economy wages will rise as productivity advances. Job availability and rising real wage rates will increase the income of the low income segment of the population and may be a major step in the direction of accomplishing society's welfare objectives. There are these many dimensions to most public economic policies and when these conflicts arise priorities have to be established.

As a second example, suppose that a more equitable after-tax distribution of income is sought by the levy of a highly progressive tax on personal incomes. Although the theoretical case is uncertain (see Chapter 7), as is the empirical case (see Chapter 13), income taxes may have the effect of decreasing incentives; the more progressive the tax rates the greater is the likelihood that a decrease in incentives will result, reducing gross national product. This decrease may thus have effects on persons other than those who are made subject to the progressive tax. Are these allocative effects desired? How does the equity objective relate to allocative efficiency? Which goal should receive priority? Policies to achieve economic stability may also be in conflict with allocative and distributive policies and priorities again have to be considered. In the next chapter we view the policy-making process from the perspective of economic reasoning.

9

CHOOSING PUBLIC ECONOMIC POLICIES

All citizens, whether they remain private individuals or become public officials, have welfare functions, and can be expected to take what they, as individuals, regard as welfare-increasing actions. The point is important because the fact that public officials are citizens with personal welfare functions of their own is not often recognized. Rather, public policy is usually said to be in the public interest where some norm is presumed and where selfless public servants further this interest. But how is this public interest revealed to public officials? What factors other than the public interest are reflected in their welfare functions? There are two problems at hand. The first is to determine what government actions citizens seek to increase their welfare; the assumption that the public interest is known, while necessary for the implementation of public economic policy, does not shed light on the formulation of that policy. The second is to determine how public officials conceive the public interest and what motivates their actions.

In simpler times citizens participated regularly in democratic government; the Greek city state and the New England town meeting are examples. Even today popular democracy is found: Some towns still hold meetings and referenda are often placed on ballots. But democratic processes in the 1970s seldom permit direct citizen participation, even at the local level. Instead, the electorate chooses representatives—congressmen and senators, state representatives and senators, and local councilmen, aldermen, and school board members—who are organized into legislatures that enact laws and authorize policies that are then implemented by executives and bureaucrats. Bureaucracies are headed by executives—the President, governors, mayors, and other officials such as cabinet officers, bureau chiefs, or commissioners—who are popularly chosen by the electorate or appointed by elected executives. By and large, however, bureaucracies are staffed by public employees, civil servants, not chosen by the electorate. Some are appointed by elected officials to whom they are immediately responsible; most, however, are employees functioning in ways essentially similar to employees of any large organization, and are not in a position to influence policy. In this chapter we discuss how individuals, as private citizens and government officials, see public policies and act to influence their formulation.[1] The task is a necessary one if we are to understand the process by which a pluralistic society, organized as a democracy, makes collective decisions.

As public policies are conceived, formulated, and implemented, private citizens and public officials interact. Citizens periodically pass judgment on their government at the polls, and the necessity of standing for election surely molds public officials' perceptions of welfare-increasing actions. People respond to political leadership; the statements of public figures influence citizen perceptions of their interests. Individuals and groups seek to influence public policies in a myriad of ways apart from the ballot-box. Within government itself there are interactions among public officials: Administrations must have their programs and budgets approved by legislatures; within legislatures the division of opinion requires vote trading as each legislator seeks enaction of his program; and within administrations various departments and agencies will have conflicting interests to be reconciled or complementary programs to be coordinated. As public officials plan and implement public policies they must not lose sight of the governed whose welfare these policies affect and who ultimately judge their government. These dynamics are at the core of the determination of public policy. In the following discussion we focus on the behavior of one group at a time as we investigate citizen actions to influence public policy; this should not obscure these dynamic interactions. One student of government has compared this process with that of producing and marketing: The voters are the buyers of a product sold by

---

[1] Throughout this discussion we are thinking only of legal means of influencing public policy. Illegal means, such as bribing or blackmailing public officials, are also available.

government where the legislature is the manufacturer, and the bureaucracy retails the product.[2] We begin by examining citizen perceptions of the effects public economic policies have on their own welfare.[3]

CITIZEN PERCEPTIONS

As we understand how citizens perceive public policies we may understand citizen motivations to take political action to advance their interests. Within the context of the welfare function developed in Chapter 1

$$W_{it} = f(C_{it}, A_{it}, L_{it}, G_t, W_{jt}, N_t) \qquad [9.1]$$

a citizen will perceive benefits and costs arising from economic policies; his reading of these benefits and costs will influence his reaction to his government and may determine the welfare-increasing actions he will take.

Benefits. Many government expenditures directly benefit citizens. The recipient of transfer payments almost certainly will regard them as welfare increasing. Similarly, transfer payments to others will be seen as welfare increasing by those citizens who deem the recipient worthy of support. Transfer payments do not appear directly in the welfare function of Equation (9.1) because they are received by households as a component of personal income, and as such bear on a household's consumption expenditures for goods and services, asset holdings, and the decision to work or take leisure; it is through these variables that transfer payments affect welfare. As expenditures for goods and services are made, citizen welfare is also affected. Fire protection enhances welfare since citizens feel safer than in its absence. Public education makes it unnecessary for parents personally to finance their children's education. Governments provide street lights near a citizen's home and traffic lights where his children cross the street. As governments provide medical care and food, the welfare of the sick and the hungry, and those who believe they should be aided, is enhanced.

---

[2] Roland N. McKean, *Public Spending* (New York: McGraw-Hill, 1968), p. 16. *See also* "Costs and Benefits from Different Viewpoints," in Howard G. Schaller (ed.), *Public Expenditure Decisions in the Urban Community* (Washington, D.C.: Resources for the Future, 1963).

[3] There are a number of sources that discuss both economic and political factors associated with the formulation and implementation of public policy. For a discussion by a former Director of the Bureau of the Budget, *see* Charles L. Schultz, *The Politics and Economics of Public Spending* (Washington, D.C.: The Brookings Institution, 1968). For a discussion from a political science viewpoint, *see* Joyce Mitchell and William C. Mitchell, *Political Analysis and Public Policy* (Chicago: Rand McNally, 1969) and R. L. Curry and L. L. Wade, *The Theory of Political Exchange* (Englewood Cliffs, N.J.: Prentice-Hall, 1968).

Government expenditures may also be regarded as welfare reducing.[4] Some perceive an expanded police force or the use of wiretaps as actual or potential infringements on their personal freedoms and thus, welfare reducing. The construction of a public playground adjacent to one's property, or an airport whose approaches pass over one's property, will be seen as welfare reducing by the property owner, although he approves of these facilities when located elsewhere; he merely wants another to bear their social costs. There are also public expenditures that some citizens see as welfare reducing because of outright opposition on ideological grounds to that type of government activity. Any particular expenditure may be understood to be the first step in a major new direction for public economic policy and thus be warmly welcomed or violently opposed irrespective of its merits. Supporters of a national health service might have been grossly dissatisfied with the Medicare bill enacted in 1965 but, as a foot-in-the-door measure, they perhaps saw the bill as welfare increasing. At the same time, citizens who did not find the Medicare bill offensive in itself may have perceived substantial negative benefits because of their fear of what it might ultimately entail.

Some citizens may stand to benefit from government expenditures because they will be employed as the expenditure is made. Construction companies or construction workers may support housing or highway programs simply because they expect employment as the facilities are built. Conversely, termination of some government expenditures may lead citizens to perceive negative benefits because of loss of employment opportunities; local protests regarding abandonment of government shipyards or military installations usually do not reflect opposition to efficiency in government operations or to reductions in military expenditures *per se*, but rather reflect the perception of welfare losses by those who may become unemployed.

Costs. We are accustomed to thinking about costs in a financial sense—the amount of money required to make a purchase. Real cost, however, is the alternative foregone when a particular action is taken. The financial cost of public expenditures is reflected in government budgets; their real cost is the welfare sacrifice that citizens make as the expenditures are financed. This sacrifice can take the form of foregone benefits from alternative public expenditures or, when resources are diverted from private use with a tax, the real cost of public expenditure falls on those citizens who bear the incidence of a tax. Citizens perceive welfare losses as their disposable income, assets, leisure, or consumption of public goods is reduced. Citizens may be unaware they are paying taxes, when they are shifted, and will perceive no real costs.

[4] Such policies might alternatively be considered as costs but they are discussed here as negative benefits since they stem from the expenditure process itself.

If financing is done through money creation, in a fully employed economy, inflation will give a different distribution of real costs; in a less than fully employed economy, inflation may not occur and citizens will perceive no real costs. When the resources employed in making public expenditures are paid less than their market price a still different incidence of real costs results. Conscription, for example, reduces the budgetary cost of the armed forces at the cost of the personal freedom of the draftee. This means of financing public expenditures involves shifting to the draftee some of the real cost from those who would bear it if volunteer military personnel were paid competitive market wages. The same consideration applies to the judicial system where citizens are required to be available for jury duty, often at considerable expense to themselves.

There are additional real costs that citizens associate with particular public policies. There are information costs that arise as people spend time and money becoming informed about public policy issues. Unlike the costs associated with taxes or conscription, these are avoidable costs; there are no legal penalties for being uninformed. Costs may also be perceived when the adoption of one course of action forecloses other courses of action: Constructing dams to provide electricity may make rivers unsuited for navigation or white-water canoeing, and some may see the loss of this future option as welfare reducing. Finally, an individual may find his welfare reduced when the incidence of the real costs of public policy falls on those whom he believes should not have to bear these costs. Citizens not subject to the draft may oppose conscription; regressive taxes are opposed by those who believe that distributive equity requires the incidence of taxes to fall more heavily on the affluent; deflationary policies may be rejected as a means of eliminating inflation since the real cost of the economy's adjustment falls primarily on those who become unemployed.

Public revenues are not directly associated with any particular expenditure except in the case of earmarked revenues, user charges, and fees. The public is willing to incur the real costs associated with general public revenues because they receive benefits from the expenditures that these revenues finance. Thus, citizens' perceptions of the real costs associated with their taxes are compared with the total benefits they see coming from government expenditures; the resulting comparison will influence voter expressions of satisfaction or dissatisfaction with their government. At the time of general elections, individuals may support or oppose the government in office for a wide variety of reasons, including their reading of the total benefits and costs to them of that government's public economic policies. In fact, governments that raise taxes or, at the national level, face rapid price increases, are often defeated on the tax or the inflation issue. When this occurs the electorate is paying attention to the total cost of their government when making a decision at the polls. We shall return to this point in our discussion of public officials.

Citizens regard many government expenditures as costless and may actively support them because they expect to benefit. It is even more likely that they are indifferent; as individuals they see no particular cost or gain. Most government expenditures provide no direct, recognizable benefit to most citizens: The expenditure of federal monies to build a post office certainly affects few other than those in the town where the post office is located and the employees of the construction company that builds the facility; the construction, by a local government, of a sidewalk on one street is of direct interest to only a few people. How is it that citizens may see such expenditures as costless? For most public expenditures the share of the cost born by any single person is insignificant: For example, a twenty million dollar federal project could be financed by assessing each American approximately ten cents. Thus, even if a citizen realized that his taxes could be reduced if the expenditure were not made he is unlikely to be particularly concerned.

CITIZEN ACTIONS

Having perceived a positive or negative stream of net benefits associated with public economic policies, a citizen may act to influence government to maintain or modify existing policies or to adopt new policies. Individuals have several means of influencing governments. By voting for legislators and elected executives who are associated with particular platforms, citizens play a role in shaping public policy. In some instances they may even vote on a specific policy as in town meetings, bond elections, and referenda. As lobbyists, citizens try to influence legislators, executives, and bureaucrats. An individual lobbies by writing letters, picketing, making contributions to campaign funds, and personally visiting officials. He may also act through a group that engages paid, professional lobbyists to promote the group's position. Thus citizens join the National Rifle Association, the Sierra Club, or the National Association for the Advancement of Colored People to attempt, collectively, to influence government. Labor unions, churches, and professional associations such as the National Association of Manufacturers and the American Medical Association also lobby. Citizens can also belong to a political party and as party workers be in a position to influence the formulation of public policies. Individuals may seek and hold elective office, or they may seek employment as bureaucrats or consultants. Finally, a citizen votes with his feet as he moves from one jurisdiction to another. His move may be a symbolic act designed to influence public policy, or a conscious selection of a community where his views toward public economic policy are in harmony with others. Since voting is the most common of all these means we begin our discussion of citizen actions with a consideration of democratic voting.

Democratic voting. Elections provide two types of voting opportunities to the individual. First, he votes for public officials—either executives or legislators—who will then act to formulate and implement public policies. Very seldom are public officials elected on the basis of a single policy issue; a citizen sometimes agrees and at other times disagrees with his candidate. A voter's choice of one candidate over another may simply mean that the total net benefits he expects to accrue from the supported candidate's policies exceed the net benefits expected from others. The election of a public official, however, rarely means automatic adoption of his platform; even if elected he must operate through a bureaucracy and legislature to enact his program. Thus, even when the voter is certain regarding a candidate's views, he is uncertain of the stream of net benefits to be obtained from voting. In addition, becoming informed costs both time and money, and these information costs must be compared with the stream of expected net benefits. If the real cost of information exceeds the expected value of the net benefits from casting an informed vote, remaining ignorant is rational.

Direct voting on a specific public policy, as in town meetings, local bond elections, or referenda, is the second type of voting opportunity available. The issues are clear since only a single, specific policy is considered; once the vote is counted the policy is accepted or rejected. Since only one issue is involved, the voter can more clearly gauge the expected benefits and costs associated with this policy and reach an informed decision. Information costs may therefore be less than in the case of voting for candidates.

Direct voting on policy issues is common enough to make it worthy of further consideration. In addition, candidates are occasionally elected or rejected on the basis of a single, leading, campaign issue; voting for candidates may sometimes be regarded as citizen expression of preference regarding a particular public policy. Since legislators vote for specific public policies, much of the following discussion applies to the voting process within legislatures. Thus, we consider the voting process itself as a mechanism by which the electorate reveal their preferences for public policies. Such revelation of preferences is one means by which public officials may perceive the public interest.

If all citizens had identical tastes then the public interest would be clear to public officials, for what they, as individuals, see as welfare increasing will also be seen by the remainder of the citizenry as welfare increasing.[5] In a democracy identical citizen preference functions guarantee that each public policy proposal will be either unanimously accepted or rejected. Any action unanimously adopted must be Pareto optimal and welfare increasing.[6]

---

[5] Presuming, also, equal incomes or constant, identical, income elasticities of demand for all citizens.

[6] We assume, throughout the discussion of this section, that citizens whose welfare is not affected by a public policy abstain, thus giving the unanimous consent of those voting.

Knut Wicksell, the eminent Swedish economist of the late nineteenth and early twentieth century, recognized this and argued that the unanimous consent of the governed was desirable for reaching collective decisions. At the same time, Wicksell recognized that unanimous consent is seldom practical and thus concluded that a qualified majority of the voters, with the limiting case of 100 percent as the ideal, was appropriate for determining the public interest.[7]

There are several objections to unanimity. In the event of pure public goods and externalities citizens may gain from collective action, but collective action entails organizational costs that must be offset against the expected gains. The larger the percentage of the population that must accede to collective action, the greater the organizational costs—because of the necessity to convince larger and larger numbers of persons who, at the margin, are uncertain.[8] When the marginal organizational costs exceed the marginal benefits from collective action welfare will not be improved. Further, unanimity implies single person rule because one citizen is able individually to block action and impose his will on the community in the negative sense of preventing any policy from being adopted. Under the rule of unanimity one man would be in a position to withhold his consent until the remainder of the community was willing to "pay" him the entire social gain from public action in return for his consent.

At the other extreme is simple majority voting. When a simple majority of the voters is obtained more people believe they will benefit from public action than believe they will be hurt by the action. For a public policy selected by a simple majority to increase total welfare, the welfare gain to those in the majority must exceed the welfare loss to those in the minority. For any total welfare judgment to be made about public policies that are not Pareto optimal, utility must be measurable and interpersonally comparable. If the welfare gain to each member of the majority is equal to the welfare loss of each citizen in the minority, the proposed public action will increase social welfare. However, if the intensities of feelings of individuals are not equal on the two sides of the issue, majority voting may lead to the adoption of policies that reduce total welfare. This may be the case, for example, when those in the minority feel strongly about the issue while those in the majority have but slight preference for the proposed public action. It is this condition that led Wicksell, while recognizing the impracticality of una-

In the event a citizen is truly indifferent, among the alternatives, failure to exercise the franchise is socially responsible action.

[7] Knut Wicksell, "A New Principle of Just Taxation," in Richard A. Musgrave and Alan T. Peacock (eds.), *Classics in the Theory of Public Finance* (New York: Macmillan, 1958).

[8] James M. Buchanan and Gordon Tulloch, *The Calculus of Consent* (Ann Arbor: University of Michigan Press, 1965), especially chapters 6–8.

nimity, to argue that a qualified majority rather than a simple majority be required for public policy decisions.[9]

The expression of the public interest through simple majority voting may be ambiguous.[10] Consider a decision to be made by three voters—X, Y, and Z—by simple majority vote. Suppose the issue concerns the construction of an urban subway system where the alternatives are A, no subway; B, a small subway that serves the center of the city; and C, a comprehensive system that would provide rapid transit for the entire metropolitan area. Further assume that while each voter knows that all three alternatives are available, a decision is made by voting upon only two at any time. This assumption fits the vote on a referendum or the problem faced by a legislator who, when an issue is called, must vote "yes" or "no"; regardless of whatever other alternatives may be available when the vote is taken the measure is either adopted or, if the negative votes are in the majority, the *status quo* is maintained. Suppose the preferences of the voters are as follows (where $>$ should be read "is preferred to"):

$$\begin{array}{ll} X & A > B > C \\ Y & B > C > A \\ Z & C > B > A \end{array}$$

In this case, if a vote is taken to choose between A and B, B wins; if the choice is between A and C, C wins; and if the vote is between B and C, B wins. Therefore, irrespective of the sequence in which the alternatives are presented to the voters, B will finally be selected and majority voting will unambiguously select the public policy desired by the majority.

Now suppose Z's evaluation of the alternatives were different and the voters' preferences were

$$\begin{array}{ll} X & A > B > C \\ Y & B > C > A \\ Z & C > A > B \end{array}$$

If A is voted against B, A wins; if A is voted against C, C wins; and if B is voted against C, B wins. In this case the result of the voting process is that

---

[9] *See* Anthony Downs, *An Economic Theory of Democracy* (New York: Harper and Row, 1957), especially pp. 55–60, for a discussion of coalitions of minorities. Downs argues that a passionate minority (pp. 64–69) may so influence political parties that public action does, in fact, reflect a qualified majority vote. Vote trading or log rolling may also be important; *see* Downs, and note Buchanan and Tulloch, *op. cit. See also* Robert Wilson, "An Axiomatic Model of Logrolling," *American Economic Review,* June 1969.

[10] Kenneth Arrow, *Social Change and Individual Values* (New York: John Wiley & Sons, 1951) and J. S. Coleman, "The Possibility of a Social Welfare Function," *American Economic Review,* December 1966. For comments on Coleman's position, see *American Economic Review,* December 1967.

the majority prefers *A* to *B*, prefers *B* to *C*, but also prefers *C* to *A*. The community's preferences in this case are said to be intransitive and the outcome of the majority voting process depends solely on the order in which the vote is taken. There is an alternative that the majority always prefers over any particular program, and majority voting does not unambiguously reveal social preferences. This outcome is possible in communities where opinion is evenly divided and where some voters prefer all or nothing courses of public action; in this example voter *Z* prefers metropolitan rapid transit, but also feels that no action is preferred to action that will not (in his opinion) adequately deal with the metropolitan area's transportation problems.

Although only two of many alternatives are actually voted on at a time, citizens may be aware of the other alternatives and employ strategies when casting their ballots. In our second example, when *A* and *B* are paired, *Z* may actually vote for *B* rather than *A* despite the fact that this is the non-preferred outcome. This is a rational strategy if *Z* believes that the major battle is getting some program enacted that may subsequently be amended to give outcome *C*. Likewise, *X* might actually vote for *B* rather than *A* if he believes that enactment of *B* will foreclose the possibility of *C*.

Such problems as non-Pareto optimal decisions and intransitive social orderings do not mean that democratic voting is an inappropriate means of reaching collective decisions. Decisions do have to be made, and voting, although by some criteria imperfect, does permit collective choice and is in keeping with the philosophical ideals of Western societies. Winston Churchill once observed "No one pretends that democracy is perfect or all wise. Indeed it has been said that democracy is the worst form of government—except all those other forms which have been tried from time to time." The alternative to majority voting may be failure to make collective choices, and there is no reason to believe that this is a preferred course of action. Further, decisions reached by majority action may be reversed by a subsequent reconsideration of the issue. Voting is a means by which collective choices are made, and imperfections in the voting mechanism hardly seem an adequate reason to discard the system.[11]

Other citizen actions. There are means other than voting available for exerting influence, and most of these are probably more effective. These include lobbying, joining and financially supporting political parties, and becoming either elected or employed public officials. Because the real costs associated with these activities probably exceed the costs associated with voting, it is not surprising that fewer citizens employ these means of influencing public policy. Writing letters to congressmen or attending city

---

[11] James M. Buchanan, "Social Choice, Democracy, and Free Markets," *Journal of Political Economy,* April 1954.

council hearings are means of directly presenting one's position to a government; these usually cost very little money although both entail substantial commitments of time. Political activity requires time as well as money. Moving government through churches, labor unions, professional organizations, or *ad hoc* committees created for a single, temporary purpose may take a great deal of the activist's time. Working through political parties may require giving financial support as well as volunteering services. Finally, the most costly activity of all is probably seeking office; this requires a substantial commitment of time, and often money, from the candidate.

There is a public goods dimension to group action. Many public policies—building a new school, for example—probably cannot be adopted as the result of one citizen's effort; rather the sentiment for the policy must come from a group representing constituents that public officials believe are too numerous to ignore. Once a group decision to lobby for a particular public policy is reached, individual members of the group, as well as sympathetic nonmembers, can rationally provide no or nominal financial support and commitments of time simply because their contributions are inconsequential as a share of the total effort, provided all others are active. The "publicness" of group action means that individual citizens may find it rational not to be active partisans of causes they favor. Those members of the group who have particularly strong feelings or interests in the desired course of action, or who merely derive welfare from activity itself, may have to bear the major part of the costs, in terms of both time and financial commitment.[12]

The rational citizen will actively attempt to influence government as long as the net benefits he anticipates exceed activity costs. For example, one citizen reads that the federal government plans to construct a hydroelectric project on a western river and shrugs his shoulders; he anticipates no benefits from this, sees no cost, and is indifferent. At the same time, a conservationist learns of this proposal and is enraged; the water rising behind the dam will inundate a scenic canyon. For the conservationist this piece of news may produce a stream of letters to government officials and a flood of contributions to conservation lobbies because the expected welfare loss justifies the activity costs. Conversely, the first citizen may read of hearings to determine the need for additional school buildings; the prospects of this expenditure will send him to the next school board meeting since he has school-age children. At the same time, the conservationist, whose children are grown, shrugs his shoulders. Some citizens even derive welfare from activity itself, often irrespective of the cause. Being a public figure, receiving attention from the press or TV cameras, or even being arrested by the police

[12] For a discussion of group action, *see* Mancur Olson, Jr., *The Logic of Collective Action: Public Goods and the Theory of Groups* (New York: Shocken Books, 1968).

is welfare increasing for some, and the benefits that activity itself entails are sufficient rewards to justify the costs of action. Life on the hustings is a calling for some!

Incurring activity costs usually does not guarantee the desired result. When a citizen "purchases" influence over government his intent is to increase the likelihood of a particular outcome. Citizens make a subjective judgment of the expected value of the benefits resulting from their activity that are weighed against the cost of that activity when determining if an activist position is appropriate. Often citizens do not act, even though they know government plans to take actions that reduce their welfare (let us say, construction of an airport whose approach passes over their homes) because a reading of the costs of action and the probability of success makes activism irrational. Likewise, when government action is proposed that is welfare increasing, citizens fail to act; most of us would probably reap substantial benefits from peace but daily do nothing to promote this end because we believe our actions, as individuals, will not affect the likelihood of peace or war. Thus, on most issues that come before government only a very small segment of the population shows any interest and, as we shall see, this may lead to a faulty reading of the public interest by public officials.

PUBLIC OFFICIALS

Public officials are citizens. As public officials they formulate and implement public policies more directly than as private citizens. Many public employees hold positions that do not bear on policy formulation; this is probably true of public school teachers, enlisted men in the armed forces, and lower-ranking civil servants. We are here concerned with executives, legislators, and the higher-ranking civil servants (as well as government consultants) who constitute a government's expert, professional staff. These public officials govern and bear the responsibility for formulating and implementing public economic policy. As citizens with welfare functions of their own, they will perceive public policy affecting their well-being and will seek policies that they regard as welfare increasing. In this respect public officials are the same as other citizens, but included among the variables that contribute to welfare are the rewards of holding office, having influence, or exercising power. These variables may be of great importance; the exercise of power, for example, may be the goal of some public officials, and the particular policies that are affected may be of secondary importance.

Elected officials must first be elected and must stand for reelection; thus, their performance must be responsive to their constituents', as well as their own, preferences. When the chips are down, the welfare-maximizing politician usually takes his stand, as a leader, on the side that his reading of popular sentiment shows is supported; the benefits of holding office and the costs of defeat are great. Once elected he must continue to respond, for within his party certain positions are expected and the cost of breaking ranks may be the scorn of colleagues and financial backers. This is particularly important, for the "wrong" stand on one issue may be taken at the cost of needed support on another; the isolated legislator, for instance, may not be able to deliver to his constituents when their interests are clear and this does not augur well for his reelection prospects. In addition, letters from constituents and the necessity of reply, as well as his press, may determine an official's welfare-maximizing action not only because of the implications for reelection, but also because of the psychic costs of adverse reaction. After all, politicians are human and few of us thrive on disparagement. Thus, while the importance of political leadership in forming public opinion must be recognized, so must the importance of public opinion in shaping the course of political leadership.

Appointed public officials are also expected to take welfare-increasing actions; because they do not have to stand for election their welfare is probably affected by a different set of variables than those who must. These variables will certainly include praise from superiors, promotions, and salary increases, as well as influence and respect both within and outside government. The cost of unsatisfactory performance includes being passed over for promotion, transfer to a less desirable position, criticism, and dismissal. We do not mean to imply that public officials have no concern with broader interests. Many devoted public servants act in accordance with their understanding of the public interest and derive personal satisfaction from their actions. Occasionally a man even sacrifices his career because his understanding of the public interest requires a course of action not pleasing to his superiors. We suggest only that public officials, as citizens, will, like all of us, take welfare-increasing actions.

We argued earlier that many citizens are unlikely to express any interest in a particular public policy because of the remoteness of the benefits, the unimportance of the costs, and the costs of taking action. How, then, are public officials to perceive the public interest? Except for major decisions that have significant bearing on the great majority, and where popular opinion can be polled, they must either personally judge what the public interest is or must act in the interest of those few who actively attempt to influence policy. If a policy entails substantial benefits to a few, and costs are so diffused that the vast majority of citizens are unconcerned, then public reaction will emanate from those few who stand to benefit; they may determine the course of public policy since they are the only ones who reveal their preferences. Conversely, some expenditures may benefit many by a small amount but be very costly to a few. If the many who benefit find their individual gain too small to justify activity costs, while the few who perceive real costs are actively opposed, then a program that, by benefit-cost analysis, is in the public interest, may not be adopted if public officials respond to those who reveal their preferences. Ultimately either public officials themselves or the interested few who act may determine the course of public policy.

Legislators play a key role in public economic policy as they authorize expenditures and provide for raising revenues. Legislative acts constitute directions to executives and bureaucrats. Legislatures are not independent of the bureaucracies that prepare the budgets submitted to them; proposals for new expenditure programs and tax changes are frequently contained in these budgets. The public revenues are of great concern to legislatures. A major issue leading to the American Revolution was taxation without representation. Under the American system of government, the authority to levy taxes is vested with legislatures and they jealously guard this right; the power of the purse constrains the appetites of the palace. Tax increases are frequently major issues in general elections since they amplify citizen perceptions of the real cost of government. Legislators thus agonize more over the decision to increase taxes than over public expenditures not requiring new revenues. Since all legislators must periodically stand for reelection, their concern with the public revenues is thus understandable.

Economic growth, by expanding tax bases, automatically yields additional revenues to governments without any change in tax rates.[13] As population increases and personal incomes rise, tax receipts, fees, and user charges will increase permitting government to fund additional expenditures. This phenomenon may be illustrated with the aid of the economy's production boundary in Figure 9.1. In year 1 the economy's production boundary is shown as *AA*, and point *X* illustrates the mix of public and private goods in that year. Provided net investment was positive during year 1, the nation's capital stock will be larger in year 2; it is also reasonable to expect the labor force to increase. Thus in year 2 the economy's production boundary will have shifted to *BB* as larger amounts of resources and technological change permit greater levels of output. With an increase in tax bases due to economic growth, government will have additional receipts in year 2; additional expenditures may be authorized without also enacting new revenue measures. In moving from *X* to *Y*, the economy yields more public and private goods without any change in tax rates.[14]

The public may regard this increase in public expenditures as costless.[15]

---

[13] This expansion in tax receipts due to economic growth was, in the 1960s, labeled a *fiscal dividend*. The fiscal dividend is further discussed in connection with stabilization policy in Chapters 16 and 17.

[14] The movement from *X* to *Y* has been shown, for simplicity, along a linear expansion path through the origin. Depending on the type of revenues and the balance in the public sector's budget, other paths are possible.

[15] Of course the increase in public expenditures is not costless. By reducing tax rates,

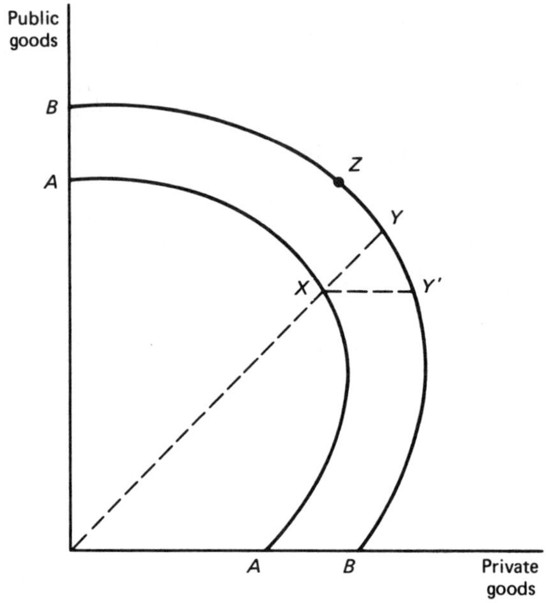

Figure 9.1 Production boundaries.

Citizens seem more attuned to tax rates than to tax liabilities, and as long as the economy expands along the expansion path XY, they will not perceive costs of additional public spending, although tax liabilities will rise. It is when, over time, the economy moves from X to Z that citizens are made aware of costs of additional public expenditures, for this movement entails increased tax rates or broader tax bases. At Z citizens may still have more total private goods than at X but, because they pay taxes at higher rates or on broadened bases, they individually see additional costs of public policy. The manner in which additional public revenue is raised determines which segment of the population bears the real costs of increased public expenditures. States, and especially local governments, have less elastic revenues than does the federal government, and the financing of additional state and local expenditures may require periodic tax increases or expansions of tax bases. At the federal level, major shifts, such as those shown by movements from X to Z, occur during wartime; the only two federal income tax increases since the Second World War came during the Korean and Vietnam Wars.

When public expenditures are not financed on the benefit principle

narrowing tax bases, and holding the line on public expenditures, the economy could move from X to Y', having an even larger amount of private goods in the second year. If citizens realize this then they may perceive costs of increased public expenditures.

citizens may consume government provided goods and services for which they need not bear any cost; simultaneously, others will be incurring real costs as they finance expenditures from which they do not benefit. In a world where unanimity of choice is not required, one citizen does not have to be concerned with the support of all others, and one group may recommend policies that further its interests at the expense of others. Even when this is not the motive, one group may appear to be furthering its interests at the expense of another because of differences in their respective readings of benefits and costs. The unevenness of the distribution of income in the United States makes it likely that policies will be voted that place a disproportionate share of the financial cost on the minority that is located at the upper end of the income distribution. This distribution of costs may be in keeping with the welfare-maximizing interests of all, including those with high incomes. This condition led Buchanan to argue that citizens should be permitted to vote on distributive issues only once in their lifetime; the possibility of moving from low to high level income positions should constrain voting for redistributive programs.[16] On the other hand, the high income minority often exerts a disproportionate amount of influence in democratic government. Those at the upper end of the income distribution tend to be better educated and thus better informed regarding alternatives and the means of moving government. They are better able to lobby and finance campaigns. For these reasons the wealthy are better able to promote their interests and to prevent the adoption of measures they oppose.

Within administrations executives may be in conflict with one another despite the appearance of a united front before the electorate. This is because financial resources are limited. Programs already enacted may be relatively secure but new or expanded programs require additional financing. If there is to be no legislative battle to raise additional revenues, budgetary requests must fall within the financial limits dictated by existing tax rates and bases. These do provide a margin for increases in government expenditure as economic growth automatically increases tax bases. However, this increment to public revenues is competed for by many different agencies, each of which feels its program should receive top priority. As budgets are prepared for legislative submission, department and agency executives submit proposals that, probably with few exceptions in modern history, exceed the financing available from existing revenue sources. Within the administration each executive aims to advance his own objectives. A single agency chief will seek funds for many reasons: He may genuinely believe his programs are in the public interest and this belief may be supported by economic analysis; he may believe programs are in his personal interest including the interest

---

[16] James M. Buchanan, *Public Finance in Democratic Processes* (Chapel Hill: University of North Carolina Press, 1966).

he sees in having his agency expand for expansion's sake; he may believe that budget officers are bound to reduce his requests (perhaps budget officers derive satisfaction from cutting requests) and therefore deliberately inflates his initial estimates. Whatever the motives, they will all reflect welfare-increasing activity for the executive and, subject to financial limitations, the well-being of one executive can be enhanced only at the expense of another.[17] Therefore, priorities must be established and the conflicting claims to resources must be reconciled. The major budget decisions may be incremental ones; out of the additional revenues automatically available from economic growth, what expansion should be made in existing programs and what new programs should be funded? A special problem arises when adoption of a program forecloses other actions; policy makers may hesitate to take actions that limit their options. Within the legislature this conflict continues. Legislators will be partisans of particular types of programs and some will thus favor transfer payments while others will favor parks, police services, or public works. The successful executive will be aware of these interests and maximize his welfare by not recommending clearly unacceptable programs. Because of conflicting interests and claims within government, compromise is needed for policy decisions to be reached. Fortunate indeed is the program that is favored by the administration and has a clear, unquestioning, majority in a legislative body.

A government's experts are among the bureaucrats. This is a matter of consequence when it comes to public economic policy. Economists, with few exceptions, are not politicians, and the expertise of the economist in the formulation and implementation of public economic policy is provided by those economists employed by government agencies. It is these bureaucrats, first and foremost, who bring economic analysis to bear on public policy. Benefit-cost analyses and studies of externalities are done within government agencies. Treasury officials concern themselves with questions of tax shifting, incidence, and equity. The results of these analyses often constitute the basis for public policy recommendations; they are of interest to legislators and executives who typically do not perform the analysis and would not be competent to do so. Legislatures may hold hearings to get the advice of additional experts and may even hire analysts of their own, but analysis remains primarily with bureaucrats, and their role in the formulation of public economic policy is thus important.

[17] If the financial limitation cannot be overcome, increasing the total allocation of funds to one agency comes at the expense of monies allocated to others. The bargaining that will take place as budgetary requests are prepared may be seen in the context of a zero-sum game where the fixed payoff is the available financial resources. For an introduction to the theory of games, *see* John D. Williams, *The Compleat Strategist* (New York: McGraw-Hill, 1954).

The professional consultant is an important complement to bureaucratic expertise. The 1950s and 1960s saw government at all levels turning to the nongovernment professional for advice. The consultant presumably is devoid of partisan interests and is not responsive to those variables that motivate public servants. Rather, he is temporarily employed to render his professional opinion on a particular subject, or to give an impartial evaluation of the work that is being done by permanent government employees.

10

GROWTH OF THE PUBLIC SECTOR

The first serious internal threat to the federal government arose over taxation. Treasury Secretary Alexander Hamilton sought, and convinced Congress to enact, domestic excise taxes to supplement the federal government's revenue from customs duties. Hamilton's excise tax package included an eight cent per gallon tax on whiskey. Backwoods farmers resented the tax; they felt discriminated against because whiskey was practically the only form in which surplus grain could be marketed. In the less than fully monetized economy of the western mountains, whiskey was used as a medium of exchange, valued at twenty-five cents a gallon. The revenue agents appointed by Hamilton to ferret out stills and collect the tax were given rough treatment, and the militias from four states were called on to suppress the Whiskey Rebellion of 1794. Subsequent taxpayer revolts have usually taken a milder form though feelings may have been no less intense. The history of American public finance since Hamilton's day is the focus of this chapter; our intent is not simply to chronicle changing patterns of taxation and expenditures, but to provide tentative explanations for some of the major features that characterize the growth of the public sector in the United States.[1]

THE PUBLIC SECTOR TO 1860

The political leaders of the post-revolutionary period had grown up in the climate of mercantilism. Although mercantilism embodied a great variety of economic policies, two characteristic objectives of seventeenth- and eighteenth-century European mercantilism were of particular importance for Americans.[2] First, the domestic economy was to be unified and made responsive to the needs of the nation state. Second, international economic affairs were to be regulated to enhance the nation's economic and military strength; colonial empires were to be exploited for the benefit of the mother country. Under mercantilism, the welfare of the state, rather than its citizens, was the object of governmental policies. This was sometimes thought to imply a favorable balance of trade—exports greater than imports—and an influx of precious metals. Other times, the overriding concern was that colonies provide raw materials and markets for finished products. An example of British mercantilism is the Navigation Acts that, beginning in 1651, regulated commerce between the North American colonies and England, among the various colonies in the empire, and between British colonies and foreign powers. The colonists resented many specific aspects of English mercantilist policy—resentments that fueled the fires of revolution—but did not, by and large, reject the principle that the state should play an active role in economic affairs. Men like Jefferson, who argued for a more restricted view of government activity, were in the minority. Adam Smith's attack against mercantilism had not as yet attracted many converts on the western side of the Atlantic.

---

[1] The most convenient source of statistical data concerning the history of American public finance is U.S. Bureau of the Census, *Historical Statistics of the United States, Colonial Times to 1957* (Washington, D.C.: Government Printing Office, 1960). For a general work in this area, *see* Paul Studenski and Herman E. Krooss, *Financial History of the United States,* 2d ed. (New York: McGraw-Hill, 1963). For more specialized studies, *see* Solomon Fabricant, *The Trend of Government Activity in the United States Since 1900* (New York: National Bureau of Economic Research, 1952); M. Slade Kendrick, *A Century and a Half of Federal Expenditures,* Occasional Paper 48 (New York: National Bureau of Economic Research, 1955); Lewis H. Kimmel, *Federal Budget and Fiscal Policy, 1789–1958* (Washington, D.C.: The Brookings Institution, 1959); and Paul B. Trescott, "The United States Government and National Income, 1790–1860," in *Trends in the American Economy in the Nineteenth Century,* Studies in Income and Wealth, Vol. 24, National Bureau of Economic Research (Princeton: Princeton University Press, 1960).

[2] *See* Eli F. Heckchser, *Mercantilism* (New York: The Macmillan Company, 1935).

Most Americans expected their new governments to assist the nation's economic growth; in this respect they were still mercantilists.

The first instance of strict versus liberal interpretation of the new Constitution showed Alexander Hamilton to be in the mercantilist tradition. The issue concerned his plan to establish a national bank. No clause in the Constitution specifically gave Congress the power to charter such a bank; Madison and Jefferson argued, from what has come to be called the strict constructionist position, that such action was unconstitutional. Hamilton, convinced that a national bank was essential to the economic development of the new nation, persuaded President Washington that in the absence of a specific prohibition the Constitution granted Congress the implied power to act. Washington sided with his Secretary of the Treasury and The Bank of the United States was established in 1791.

The bank was a key feature in Hamilton's plan for economic development: He saw scarcity of money and credit as a major obstacle to growth, and sought solutions through refunding the nation's debt and creating the national bank. The first step was to refund the debts of the United States government, left over from the Revolutionary War, and for the federal government to assume the debts of the states. Gold and silver coins were the only form of legal tender during our early history and were quite scarce in the 1790s. As long as the federal government paid interest on its securities, they would have value and perform an economic function quite similar to hard money, since merchants and other entrepreneurs would accept these securities in lieu of specie as payment for goods and services. Further, the securities would be instrumental in establishing the national bank; capital stock in the bank could be purchased in part with these securities and only partly in specie. As the bank made loans, by giving bank notes to borrowers, additional money would be created. This part of Hamilton's plan was carried out.

The rest of Hamilton's plan, incorporated in his *Report on Manufacturing,* called for a variety of government actions, protective tariffs in particular, to stimulate the nascent industrial sector of the American economy. His thinking here is very clearly in the mercantilist tradition. The proposals contained in the *Report* were not enacted by Congress. By the middle of the 1790s American entrepreneurs were caught up in a wave of commercial prosperity induced by the European wars following the French Revolution. They had little interest in manufacturing enterprises when handsome profits could be made in international trade and shipping. That part of Hamilton's grand plan was largely forgotten until after the War of 1812 when renewed interest in protectionism became manifest in the Tariff of 1816. Despite the lack of protectionist sentiment, however, tariffs raised most of the federal government's revenue in the early years of our history.

When Jefferson brought the Republicans to power in the election of 1800, public economic policy was altered. Expenditures were cut back and the debt reduced (see Figure 10.1). Jefferson also hoped to avoid United States

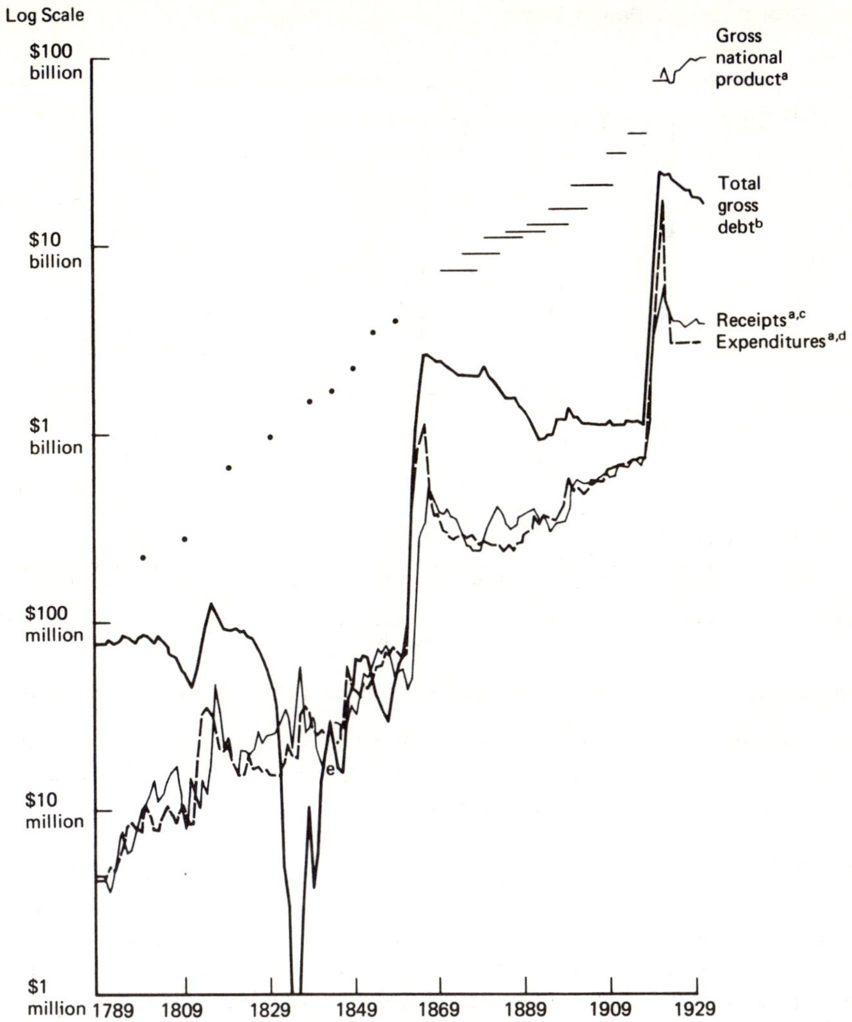

[a]Gross National Product estimates for 1800-1830 based on Paul A. David, "The Growth of Real Product in the United States Before 1840: New Evidence, Controlled Conjectures," *Journal of Economic History*, June 1967. Estimates for 1839-1908 are taken from Robert E. Gallman, "Gross National Product in the United States, 1834-1909," in *Output, Employment, and Productivity in the United States after 1800,* National Bureau of Economic Research, Studies in Income and Wealth, Vol. 30 (New York: Columbia University Press, 1966). Estimates for 1907-1929 taken from the *Historical Statistics* using the Department of Commerce concept. All gross national product estimates are in current dollars.

[b]For 1789-1842, years ending December 31; 1844-1929, June 30; 1843 figures are for January 1 - June 30.

[c]Excludes receipts from borrowing.

[d]Excludes debt repayment.

[e]For January 1 - June 30, 1843. Receipts were $8,303 million and expenditures were $11,858 million.

SOURCE: Bureau of the Census, U. S. Department of Commerce, *Historical Statistics of the United States, Colonial Times to 1957* (Washington, D. C.: Government Printing Office, 1960), pp. 139, 711.

Figure 10.1 Summary of federal government finances, 1789–1929 and gross national product estimates.

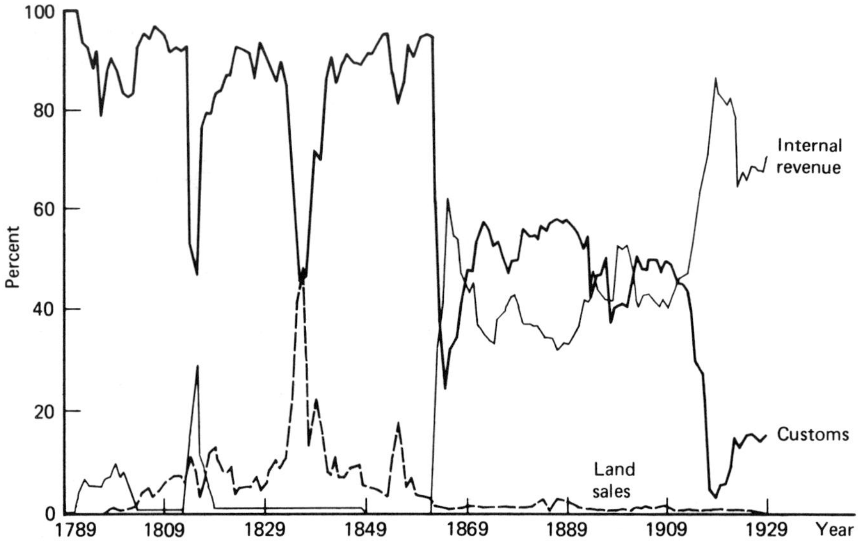

SOURCE: U.S. Department of Commerce, Bureau of the Census, *Historical Statistics of the United States, Colonial Times to 1957* (Washington, D.C.: Government Printing Office, 1960), p. 712.

Figure 10.2 Federal revenues, by type, as a percent of total receipts, 1789–1929.

involvement in the Napoleonic wars. Thus the Embargo Act of 1807 prohibited trade with the European powers, frustrating Jefferson's financial plans; revenues from customs duties fell (see Figure 10.2) resulting in budget deficits. Military expenditures were increased over the next few years and during the War of 1812 the government was forced to borrow heavily. By the end of Madison's second administration, after 16 years of Republican rule, the debt exceeded the amount inherited from the Federalists. However, the Republican policy should not be interpreted as a complete rejection of the mercantilist tradition. They envisioned an extensive program of federal support for internal improvements to be undertaken once the debt had been retired. Albert Gallatin, Jefferson's Secretary of the Treasury, drew up an elaborate proposal for federally sponsored canal, road, and river improvement projects.

At least some contemporaries had a clear conception of internal improvements—the term used in the early nineteenth century for transportation projects—as a pure public good. The following argument was made in 1818 by Henry Clay from the floor of Congress, in support of the proposition that budget surpluses should be eliminated by increased public works expenditures rather than financed through debt retirement.

> Some principles drawn from political economists have been alluded to, and we are advised to leave things to themselves, upon the ground, that, when the condition of society is ripe for internal improvements—that is, when

> capital can be so invested with a fair prospect of adequate remuneration, they will be executed by associations of individuals, unaided by government . . . . In regard to internal improvements, it does not follow, that they will always be constructed whenever they will afford a competent dividend upon the capital invested. It may be true generally that, in old countries, where there is a great accumulation of surplus capital, and a consequent low rate of interest, they will be made. But, in a new country, the condition of society may be ripe for public works long before there is, in the hands of individuals, the necessary accumulation of capital to effect them; and, besides, there is generally, in such a country, not only a scarcity of capital, but such a multiplicity of profitable objects presenting themselves as to distract the judgement. Further, the aggregate benefit resulting to the whole society, from a public improvement, may be such as to amply justify the investment of capital in its execution, and yet that benefit may be so distributed among different and distant persons, that they can never be got to act in concert . . . . I think it very possible that the capitalist, who should invest his money in one of these objects, might not be reimbursed three per centum annually upon it; and yet society, in various forms might actually reap fifteen or twenty per centum.[3]

The focus of public sector economic activity shifted, after the War of 1812, from the federal government to the states. Citizen demand for improved transportation facilities would not wait for the national debt to be repaid. The state of New York led the way by constructing the Erie Canal between 1817 and 1825. It was, and remained, in modern terminology, a public enterprise, financed, owned, and operated by the state. The overwhelming success of the Erie Canal, by opening up trade and more rapid communication with the Ohio River Valley, stimulated other states to act. There followed in the 1830s a wave of canal and railroad projects supported, and in many cases initiated and carried out, by state and municipal governments. Bonds were issued to finance these ventures. About three-quarters of total canal investment and about one-third of the total railroad investment before the Civil War were financed by state and local governments. In addition to internal improvements, many states actively promoted and in a few cases owned and operated banks.

The flurry of promotional activity on the part of the states came to an abrupt halt in the early 1840s when a depression forced many governments to default on interest payments and a few to repudiate bond issues. States had come to rely upon foreign (primarily British) capital markets for the sale of their bonds facilitating the flow of foreign capital into the American economy during the 1830s. With the depression of the early 1840s, and the

---

[3] Henry Clay, "Address on Internal Improvements" (March 13, 1818), in William Letwin (ed.), *A Documentary History of American Economic Policy Since 1789* (Garden City: Doubleday & Company, Inc., 1961), pp. 62–64.

resulting defaults and repudiations, the foreign market for American securities dried up. The confluence of these developments led many states to reverse their policy of active involvement in economic development. Constitutions were amended and legislation passed prohibiting state ownership of business enterprises and the use of state funds to aid private business ventures. A few states did continue to support canal and railroad projects, but the focus shifted to private corporations. Through the remainder of the nineteenth century states adopted progressively more liberal laws regarding corporations.[4]

The federal debt was a major policy issue during the early years of our nation's history. Hamilton's funding plan created a debt more than fifteen times as large as receipts and expenditures (see Figure 10.1). As a consequence interest payments absorbed a major share of total expenditures, more than half in several years, and military expenditures accounted for practically all of the remainder (see Figure 10.3). The Republican policy of debt reduction was successful until the War of 1812 required expenditures substantially in excess of revenues and hence an increase in the debt past the $100 million mark. Following the war the outstanding debt was reduced, at a particularly rapid rate during the decade following 1825. By the mid-1830s substantial surpluses were being accrued but there was no longer any debt to be repaid. In modern terminology, how can a government finance a budget surplus when there are no outstanding securities to retire? The surpluses could have been eliminated by either increasing expenditures or decreasing revenue but there were powerful political forces that prevented both of those alternatives. The Jacksonians conceived the federal government's role in the area of internal improvements to be limited, and manufacturers, protected by tariffs, did not want customs receipts (the major source of the government's revenue) reduced. The solution was to distribute a $37 million budget surplus to the states in proportion to their representation in Congress. Three of four scheduled installments were paid in 1837. These payments foreshadowed the revenue sharing proposals of the 1970s. The financial panic of that year combined with a dramatic fall in land sales drastically altered the federal government's financial position and the fourth installment was never paid. The problem of surpluses in the absence of debt to be retired has never reoccurred for the federal government.

Federal land policy was a dominant public finance issue throughout the

---

[4] Many cities and counties continued the policy of government aid to business enterprises, particularly railroads, including those in some states that had prohibited such action on the part of the state government. The depression following 1873 was in this sense similar to the depression of the early 1840s, causing a wave of defaults on municipal bonds and inducing the adoption of statutes limiting the power of city and county governments to aid private businesses.

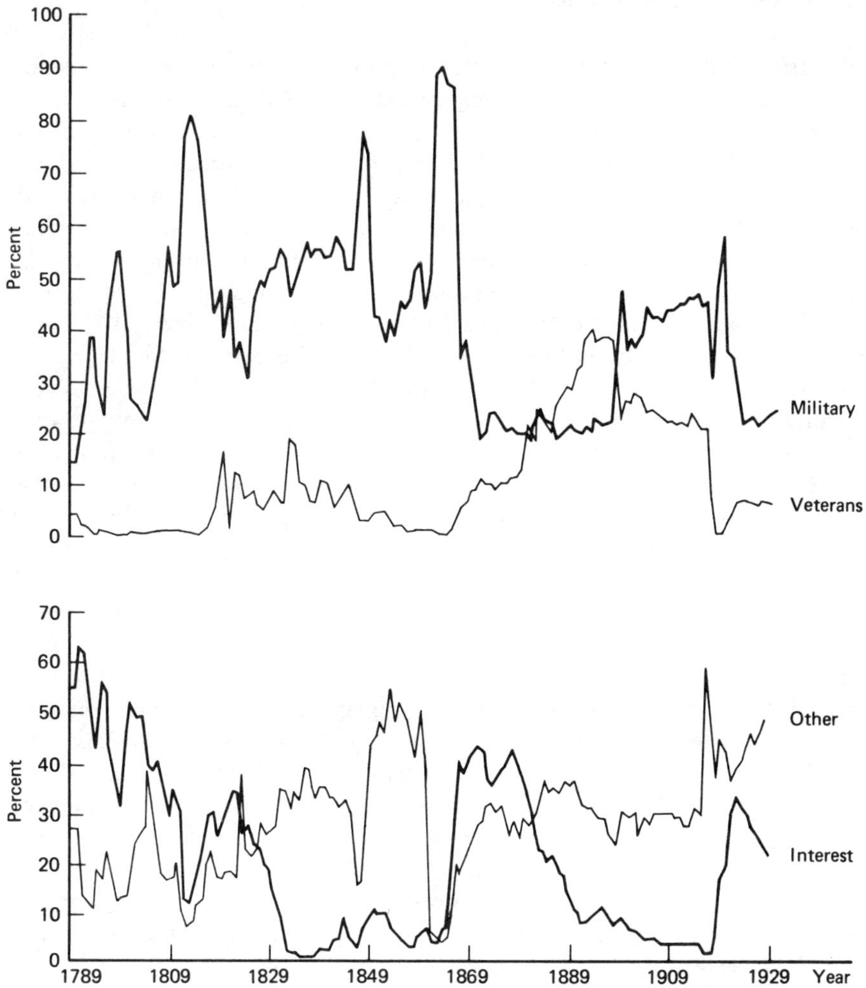

SOURCE: U.S. Department of Commerce, Bureau of the Census, *Historical Statistics of the United States, Colonial Times to 1957* (Washington, D.C.: Government Printing Office, 1960), pp. 718–719.

Figure 10.3 Federal expenditures, by type, as a percent of total expenditures, 1789–1929.

nineteenth century.[5] The *public domain,* land owned by the federal government, presented the American people with an historically unique opportunity. Originally created in the 1780s as former colonies renounced their claims to western lands in favor of the central government (at that time operating

[5] For a history of federal land policy, *see* B. H. Hibbard, *A History of the Public Land Policies* (New York: The Macmillan Company, 1924), or Roy Robbins, *Our Landed Heritage* (Princeton: Princeton University Press, 1942).

under the Articles of Confederation), the public domain was augmented by the Louisiana Purchase and other acquisitions. The federal government faced a problem of asset management. There was no serious challenge to the proposition that much of the land should become the property of private individuals, but the terms under which land might be sold were disputed. Some viewed the public domain primarily as a source of revenue that would minimize the need for taxation; others wanted the land put in private hands, particularly farmers, as quickly as possible even if that implied sale at relatively low prices. From the Northwest Ordinances of 1785 and 1787, which first specified terms for the disposition of the public domain, to the Homestead Act of 1862, the general trend of land policy was one that progressively liberalized the terms under which acreage could be acquired. Only toward the end of the century did the conservation of public lands for the enjoyment of future generations become a major policy concern. Public lands were also used as a catalyst for economic development. From 1850 to 1871 the federal government made land grants to stimulate railroad construction. Here is a case where it would be an obvious mistake to view public finance merely in terms of receipts, expenditures, and debt. Land was (and still is) a publicly owned real asset, the disposition and management of which was (and is) a major national concern.

Modern readers, accustomed to thinking in terms of billions of dollars, find it difficult to view total federal expenditures in historical perspective. To gain such perspective, estimates of gross national product have been placed in Figure 10.1 beginning with $230 million for 1800. Federal expenditures were approximately 4 percent of gross national product at that time; the ratio fell to around 2 percent in 1840, and to about 1.7 percent in 1859. Custom duties were the dominant source of federal receipts throughout the pre-Civil War era; revenue from land sales was particularly significant during the 1830s (see Figure 10.2).

FROM THE CIVIL WAR TO 1929

War strains any system of public finance. A major war creates a crisis. Neither the Union nor the Confederacy was fiscally prepared for the magnitude or duration of the Civil War. Federal expenditures increased about 20-fold between fiscal years 1860 and 1865 (see Figures 10.1 and 10.3).[6] At the height of the war, federal expenditures probably equaled 20 percent of

---

[6] By comparison, there was about a 25-fold expansion of expenditures during World War I, and during fiscal year 1945, at the height of World War II, expenditures were only ten times what they had been in 1940.

gross national product in the northern states.[7] The basic problem facing the Union government was the reallocation of the economy's resources. The market system was relied upon; most goods and services required for the military effort were purchased from private producers. The major exception was manpower.

Conscription was introduced in 1863 after two years of war. Unlike the modern draft, service could be avoided by the payment of $300 (a figure somewhat higher than per capita gross national product) or provision of a substitute. Four days of rioting in New York City working-class neighborhoods followed the first drawings, in reaction to the inequities of the measure. The draft provided, however, a very small proportion of the Union army.

To buy needed goods and services from the private sector, the Union government resorted to a combination of monetary expansion, taxation, and borrowing. Noninterest-bearing Treasury notes (greenbacks) were issued and declared legal tender. Internal revenues joined customs as important tax receipts (see Figure 10.2). An income tax was introduced in 1862, the structure of which was quite similar to the modern income tax. Rates were progressive, though only slightly so, and a limited system of withholding was put in effect. The relatively high level of exempt income ($600) coupled with widespread evasion resulted in smaller than expected receipts; about 1 out of 15 gainfully employed persons paid the tax. Various stamp, excise, and license taxes were imposed. In addition, a general *ad valorem* tax was assessed on manufactured goods at rates of 3 to 6 percent; it exhibited the general characteristics of a turnover tax. In all, taxes financed about 20 percent of total war expenditures.

The debt expanded rapidly as budget deficits were covered by borrowing. Two primary strategies were used to market this flood of securities. The banking system was reformed by the National Banking Act which permitted banks to receive charters from the federal government. Such national banks would have the privilege of issuing national bank notes (which circulated along with greenbacks as the principal source of paper currency) in amounts equal to 90 percent of the U.S. government securities that the banks purchased. A market was thus created for government bonds. To encourage the

---

[7] Gallman's estimate of gross national product in the entire United States for 1859 is $4.17 billion (see note to Table 10.1). If the southern states, with about one-third of the total population (including slaves), produced one-quarter of the nation's gross national product, and if federal expenditures of $1.3 billion in 1865 are reduced by one-half to reflect wartime inflation, then these expenditures in real terms would equal about 20 percent of gross national product produced in the northern states. The effects of the drain of labor into the army may have been offset by growth in the labor force (because of natural population increase and immigration) and increasing productivity so that real gross national product in the North may not have declined during the war.

purchase of bonds by individuals, the Treasury entered into an agreement with the Philadelphia financier Jay Cooke, who formed a nationwide organization to sell bonds in small denominations to the farmer and working man, as well as in larger amounts to businesses and the wealthy. Since so much of the war effort was financed by money creation and borrowing, and since about one-sixth of the labor force was in uniform, it is easy to understand how inflationary pressures developed. Wholesale prices doubled between 1860 and 1865.[8] Some of the required resource reallocation was achieved as consumers reduced their real standards of consumption in the face of rising prices and lagging wages.

The Confederacy faced the same fundamental problem as the Union government—reallocation of resources to support a prolonged military effort. The Confederacy's problem was made more severe by its relatively small industrial base and the effects, toward the end of the war, of widespread destruction of fixed capital and dislocation of agriculture as more and more southern territory became a battleground. Even in the first years of the war the Confederate government had difficulty buying needed goods and services. It had little power to impose taxes, relying heavily on newly printed Confederate currency. Prices rose quickly—more than 200-fold during the course of the war—partially because of the expansion of the money supply, but also because of reductions in the level of real output. The Confederacy adopted military conscription in 1862, and also attempted to control directly the allocation of particularly scarce and needed resources.[9]

Federal receipts and expenditures declined after the Civil War but not to their antebellum levels. Both interest payments and veterans' benefits accounted for substantial fractions of total expenditures (see Figure 10.3). Although there were reductions of the Civil War internal revenues, such taxes remained an important source of federal receipts throughout the remainder of the nineteenth century; in most years, however, customs duties returned to their accustomed place as the single most important revenue source (see Figure 10.2). The income tax was discontinued after 1872 and declared unconstitutional by the Supreme Court in 1880, on the grounds that it was a direct tax in violation of Article I, Section 9 of the Constitution which states that "no Capitation, or other direct, Tax shall be laid, unless in Proportion to the Census or Enumeration herein before directed to be taken." This constitutional hurdle was surmounted by the adoption of the Sixteenth Amendment in 1912. During most of these years receipts exceeded expenditures and the debt was reduced; as a result income was being transferred in

---

[8] The inflation during World War I was of the same relative magnitude.

[9] For a collection of essays that deal, in part, with public finance during the Civil War, both North and South, *see* Ralph Andreano (ed.), *The Economic Impact of the American Civil War,* rev. ed. (Cambridge, Mass.: Schenkman Publishing Co., 1967).

the form of interest and principal payments. It has often been argued that this implicit fiscal policy encouraged investment since bondholders as a group were much more likely to invest than taxpayers. Even if true, the amounts involved were relatively small in comparison with the aggregate amount of investment in the post-Civil War era. As percentages of estimated gross national product, federal expenditures fell from about 3.4 percent in the 1870s to about 2 percent on the eve of World War I. In particular geographic areas, such as in the West, federal expenditures were relatively more important than the aggregate figures indicate.

During the period between the Civil War and World War I, state and local governments were active participants in the economy. The initiation and expansion of public school systems was their most important activity at the local level; highway and road construction became a major focus of state governments around the turn of the century. The statistical record for the latter part of the nineteenth century is much more fragmentary for state and local governments than it is for the federal government. The censuses did collect some information:

	State and Local Government	
	Taxes (Millions)	Debt (Millions)
1850	$ 43	$ n.a.
1860	94	n.a.
1870	281	869
1890	585	1135

n.a. – not available

These figures are probably not precise. State and local government taxes increased from about 2 percent of gross national product in 1850 to about 4.7 percent in 1890, and were larger than federal spending in 1880 and 1890. Aggregate state and local government debts were about equal to the federal debt in 1890. In 1890 public school expenditures equaled about 25 percent of total state and local government spending. The variation among states was extreme; per pupil expenditures ranged from a low of $1.50 in North Carolina to a high of $23.79 in Nevada.[10]

The first census of governments was conducted in 1902, and three more were made during the period under review—1913, 1922, and 1927.[11] These censuses provide more accurate data concerning state and local governments.

---

[10] *Abstract of the Eleventh Census*, 2d ed. (Washington, D.C.: Government Printing Office, 1896), p. 209.

[11] Summaries of these data can be found in the *Historical Statistics, op. cit.*, pp. 694–730.

	State and Local Government		
	Expenditures (Billions)	Revenue (Billions)	Debt (Billions)
1902	$1.1	$1.0	$ 2.1
1913	2.3	2.0	4.4
1922	5.7	5.2	10.1
1927	7.8	7.8	14.9

State and local government spending increased to about 8 percent of gross national product by 1927. Spending on education absorbed a growing share of the total, up from 23 percent in 1902 to 29 percent in 1927.

World War I created a crisis in American public finance. Unlike the Civil War, World War I was fought using the technology of the industrial era. Conscription was enacted; 5 percent of the population was in the armed forces. A larger fraction, probably 25 percent, of the nation's output of goods and services was devoted to the war effort.[12] For the first time in American history the federal government found it necessary, and the public generally found it acceptable, to control directly many aspects of the economy. Two reforms initiated just prior to the outbreak of war—creation of the Federal Reserve System and the institution of the personal income tax—made it possible for the Treasury to respond to the fiscal crisis more easily than during the Civil War.

The initial reaction of the American economy to the outbreak of war in Europe was marked by financial panic and a brief recession. European holders of American securities, in a scramble for liquidity, sold heavily on the New York market, putting considerable pressure on the nation's gold reserves. The New York Stock Exchange closed its doors on June 30, 1914, and did not reopen until April 1915. The recession was short-lived as orders for war material and agricultural products poured in from the belligerents. American exports expanded about six-fold within a three-year period. Europeans paid for these exports by liquidating American securities, shipping gold to the United States, and using the proceeds of bond sales to the American public. For the first time America became a net creditor to the rest of the world.

American neutrality became increasingly difficult to maintain as the British intercepted cargos bound for neutral ports, and as the Germans initiated submarine attacks on American ships. In the summer of 1916, Congress authorized more spending for the Army and the Navy, increased

[12] The estimate is taken from Simon Kuznets, *National Product in Wartime* (New York: National Bureau of Economic Research, 1945), p. 102. *See also* John Maurice Clark, *The Costs of the World War to the American People* (New Haven: Yale University Press, 1931) and Charles Gilbert, *American Financing of World War I* (Westport, Conn.: Greenwood Publishing Corporation, 1970).

personal and corporate income taxes, and introduced a federal estate tax. Taxes were increased again in March 1917, and the Treasury was authorized to borrow by selling short-term certificates of indebtedness to the Federal Reserve System. Thus some initial preparations were made, but the Treasury was unready to meet the magnitude of the fiscal problem that followed the declaration of war on April 6, 1917. The problem, in essence, was to reallocate resources from the private sector to the public sector.

The broad outlines of World War I finance can be seen in Figures 10.1 and 10.3. Tax receipts increased mostly as a result of higher tax rates, but partly because of expanded tax bases reflecting the growth in gross national product. For the first time, personal and corporate income taxes were the predominant source of revenue. By 1919 the highest marginal personal income tax rate was set at 77 percent; the same marginal rate applied to corporate income as an excess profits tax with rates up to 65 percent was added to the basic rate of 12 percent. In all, taxes covered about one-third of total expenditures that expanded about 25-fold over their prewar level. As a consequence the Treasury debt rose from less than $1 billion in 1914 to over $25 billion by the end of 1919. Money creation through the issuance of greenbacks was not resorted to, but the borrowing techniques used by the Treasury, plus the monetary policy followed by the Federal Reserve System, amounted to the same thing. The Treasury embarked on a series of short-term borrowings from the commercial banks, and long-term issues—Liberty Bonds—sold with enthusiasm to the public. As Secretary of the Treasury McAdoo put it, "We went direct to the people; and that means to everybody—to businessmen, workmen, farmers, bankers, millionaires, schoolteachers, laborers. We capitalized on the profound impulse called patriotism."[13] Savings stamps in denominations as low as twenty-five cents were issued. As the Treasury spent the proceeds of short-term borrowing from the banks the money supply was increased; it about doubled between 1914 and 1919. Adequate reserves resulting from the influx of European gold and supportive Federal Reserve policy enabled the banks to buy these issues without contracting their loans to the private sector. Indeed the Treasury encouraged individuals to borrow from the banks in order to purchase Liberty Bonds.[14] The net effect was inflationary. Effective demand for goods and services emanating from the private sector was not curtailed sufficiently to prevent prices from rising; the price level was about twice as high in 1919 as it had been in 1914.

The federal government did not rely solely upon the market system to

---

[13] Cited in Studenski and Krooss, *op. cit.*, p. 289.

[14] In all there were four Liberty Bond series between 1917 and 1918 totaling $17 billion, and a $4.5 billion Victory Loan floated in 1919; interest rates ranged between 3.5 percent and 4.75 percent. Terms to maturity varied and the income from some was exempt from taxation.

reallocate resources. In July of 1917 the War Industries Board was created. The Board, headed by Bernard M. Baruch, established a system of priorities, directing scarce raw materials and intermediate products to the production of war goods at the expense of consumer goods. Many products ranging from boxcars to pocket knives were standardized by decree. Baruch found it easier to deal with industry-wide associations than individual firms; in effect, the government encouraged joint action by corporations that was considered illegal under the antitrust acts. By the war's end, the Board was regulating the production of some 30,000 products. Many other agencies were added. Herbert Hoover's Food Administration fixed wheat prices and campaigned for consumer restraint with slogans like "meatless Tuesdays." The Fuel Administration introduced daylight savings time. In December 1917, the government took over the operation but not the ownership of railroads.

This experience with widespread government involvement in the economy had a profound and lasting effect even though practically all of the wartime apparatus was quickly dismantled after the Armistice. Americans learned that their economy could be controlled by government to serve clearly perceived national needs. When the next major crisis struck—the Depression of the 1930s—it is little wonder then that many of the World War I agencies served as a model for new programs of government action. The Reconstruction Finance Corporation initiated by President Hoover early in 1932 was a copy of the War Finance Corporation. Roosevelt's National Recovery Administration was similar to the War Industries Board. Many of the individuals who administered these wartime agencies returned to government service during the Depression. As World War II followed on the heels of the Depression, full-scale mobilization of the economy was planned with the experience of World War I as a guide.

There was a sharp, but brief, depression and deflation following the end of World War I as the economy adjusted to peacetime conditions. As expected, both taxes and expenditures were quickly reduced. During the long boom of the 1920s, federal receipts exceeded expenditures and budgetary surpluses were used to reduce the outstanding debt. Despite the avowed desires of the postwar Republican administrations for a "return to normalcy," federal expenditures did not fall to their prewar level; they equalled about 3 percent of gross national product in the late 1920s.

SOME MEASUREMENTS OF THE PUBLIC SECTOR SINCE 1929

The year 1929 marks a convenient dividing point in this review of the growth of the public sector in the United States. The Great Depression began in that year and there followed, in the 1930s, many major reforms affecting the relationship between the federal government and the private sector of the economy. Since this period of public sector growth is widely known, we need not dwell on the subject at length. From this time on we can be more precise about the dimensions of the public sector in terms of financial aggregates since regularly published data from national income accounts are available.

Since the Depression, the number of governments in the United States has decreased, as shown in Table 10.1.[15] The decline in the number of

Table 10.1 The Number of Governments in the United States

	1942	1952[a]	1957[a]	1962	1967
Total	155,116	116,807	102,392	91,236	81,304
United States	1	1	1	1	1
State	48	50	50	50	50
Local	155,067	116,756	102,341	91,185	81,253
Counties	3,050	3,052	3,050	3,043	3,049
Municipalities	16,220	16,807	17,215	17,997	18,051
Townships	18,919	17,202	17,198	17,144	17,107
School Districts	108,579	67,355	50,454	34,676	21,782
Special Districts	8,299	12,340	14,424	18,323	21,264

[a] Includes Alaska and Hawaii

SOURCES: Bureau of the Census, *Statistical Abstract of the United States, 1951* (Washington, D.C.: Government Printing Office, 1951), p. 347; Bureau of the Census, *Census of Government, 1962,* Vol. 1, Governmental Organization (Washington, D.C.: Government Printing Office, 1963), p. 1; and Bureau of the Census, *Census of Governments, 1967: Governmental Units in 1967* (Washington, D.C.: Government Printing Office, 1967), p. 1.

governments since 1942 is dramatic, and is primarily accounted for by the consolidation of many small school districts. The number of special districts, such as water, irrigation, and soil conservation, has been steadily growing. One reason for the growth in the number of special districts is the constitutional limitations on spending and borrowing imposed on state and local governments during the 1840s, 1870s, and 1930s. New governmental units, not subject to these limitations, are often easier to create than old laws are to repeal.

There is no single index showing the growing economic importance of government activity since 1929. We have prepared some charts to illustrate

[15] The Bureau of the Census defines a government as "an organized entity which in addition to having governmental character, has sufficient discretion in the management of its own affairs to distinguish it as separate from the administrative structure of any other governmental unit." See *Census of Governments, 1967: Governmental Units in 1967* (Washington, D.C.: Government Printing Office, October 1967), p. 1. The *Census of Governments* is taken every five years and contains detailed information on state and local governments.

SOURCE: *Economic Report of the President, 1970* (Washington, D.C.: Government Printing Office, 1970), p. 202.

Figure 10.4 Gross national product and government purchases of goods and services, 1929–1969.

some of the many ways in which particular aspects of government activity can be measured.[16] The growth of government purchases of goods and services, as recorded in the national income accounts, is often referred to as an indication of the expanding role of government. These data are shown, along with the growth of gross national product, in Figure 10.4. Government purchases of goods and services include those of state and local governments;

[16] The *Economic Report of the President,* which contains the Report of the Council of Economic Advisors, is published annually by the Government Printing Office and is probably the most widely read public document devoted to economic policy. The tables in the statistical appendix are a convenient secondary source of many types of economic data. Data for the remainder of this section are taken from that source.

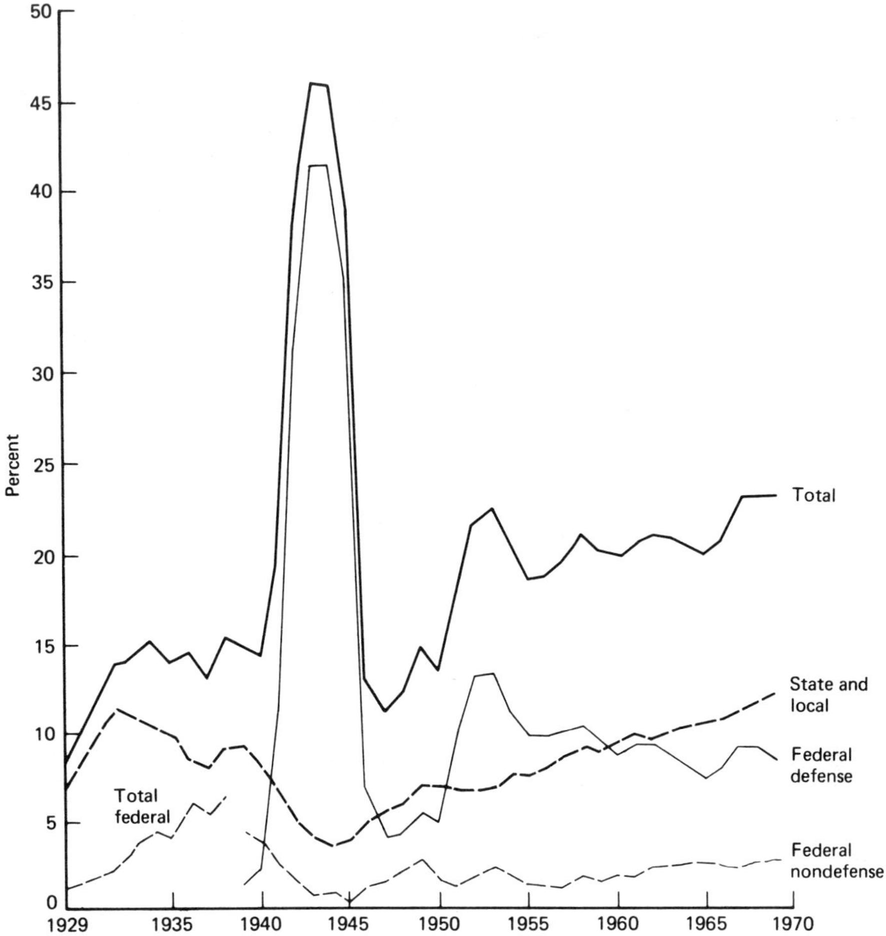

SOURCE: *Economic Report of the President, 1970* (Washington, D.C.: Government Printing Office, 1970) p. 177.

Figure 10.5 Government purchases of goods and services, by type, as a percent of gross national product, 1929–1969.

federal purchases may be categorized as defense and nondefense. These separate types of government purchases are shown as percentages of gross national product in Figure 10.5. Although total government purchases represent a large portion of gross national product (23 percent in 1969), this is an inadequate indicator of the economic impact of governments. Government transfer payments, although not included in purchases of goods and services, are an important component of personal income and affect the ability of households to demand goods and services. As indicated by Figure 10.6, government transfer payments as a percent of personal income have risen from 1 percent in 1929 to 8 percent in 1969. Personal taxes (primarily in-

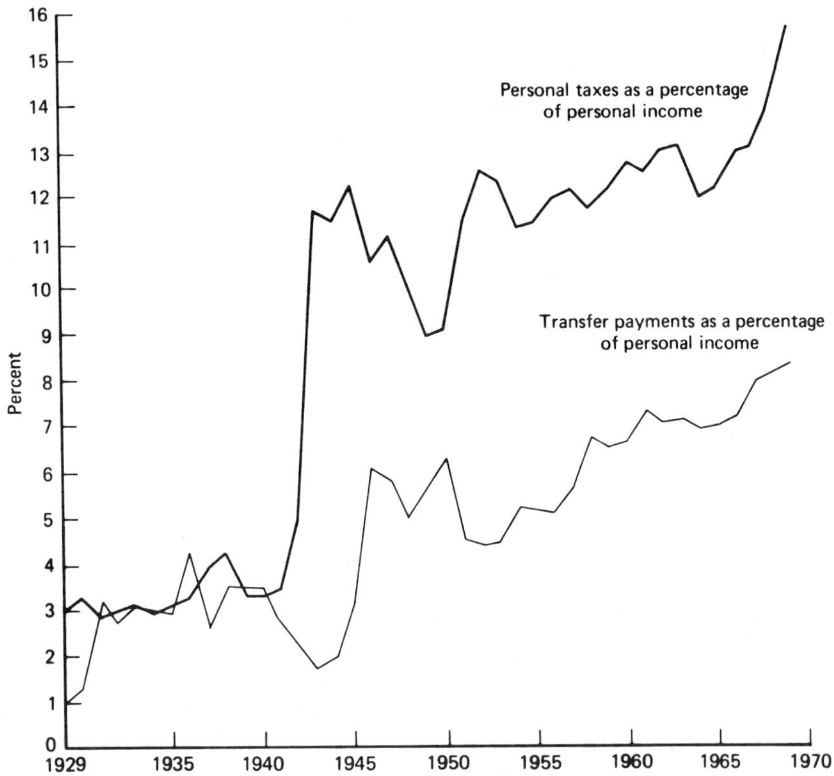

SOURCE: *Economic Report of the President, 1970* (Washington, D.C.: Government Printing Office, 1970) pp. 193, 194.

Figure 10.6 Personal taxes and government transfer payments to persons, as a percent of personal income, 1929–1969.

come taxes) also affect the ability of households to demand goods and services; they are also shown as a percent of personal income in Figure 10.6.

Employment data are presented in Figure 10.7 as an alternative way of looking at the relative importance of government. Total government employment and its separate components—armed forces, federal civilian, and state-local—are shown as percentages of the total labor force. These figures for government employment include the employees of public enterprises, such as the post office and municipally owned utilities.[17] Throughout the 1929–1969 period, total government employment was a smaller percentage of the total labor force than government purchases of goods and services were of

[17] The federal budget annually contains a discussion of federal employment. *See* "Civilian Employment in the Executive Branch," Analysis H, *Special Analyses, Budget of the United States, Fiscal Year 1971* (Washington, D.C.: Government Printing Office, 1970), pp. 99–107.

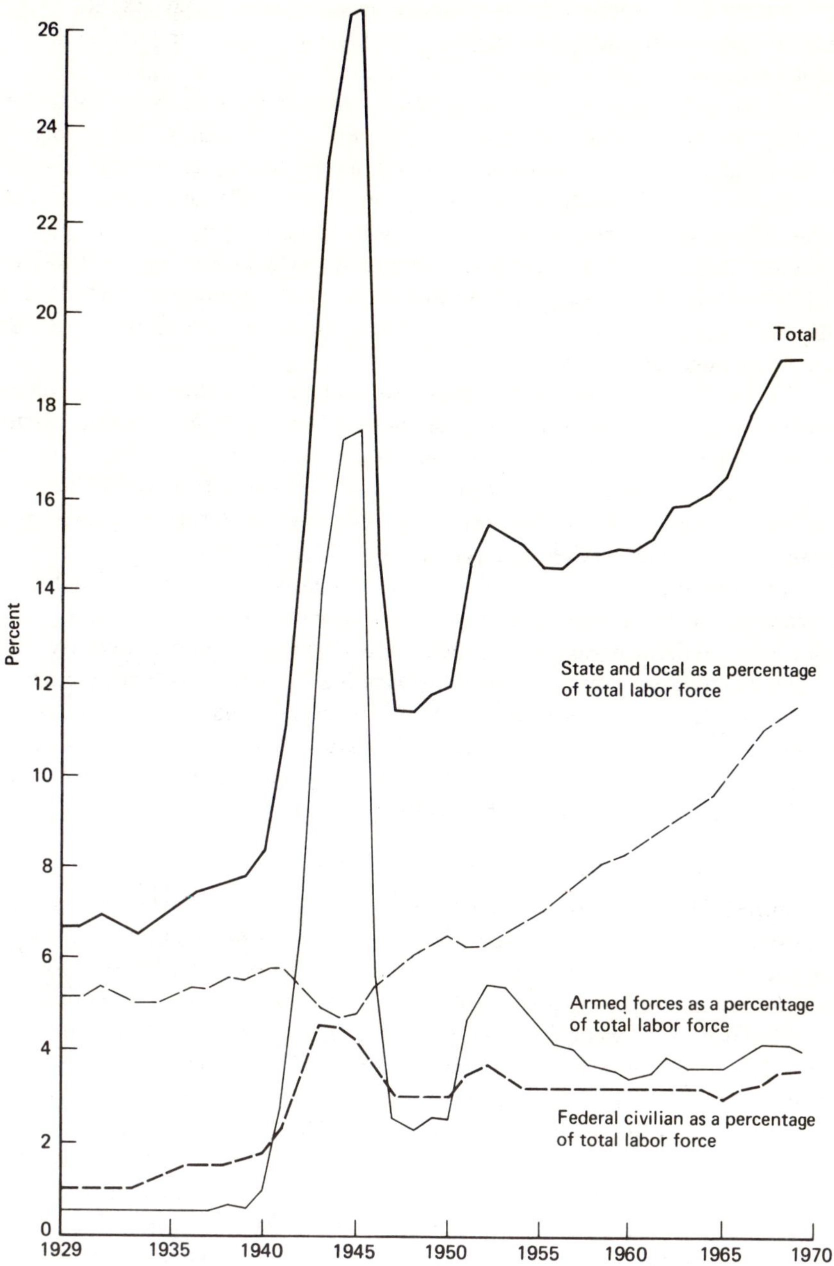

SOURCE: *Economic Report of the President, 1970* (Washington, D.C.: Government Printing Office, 1970) pp. 202, 208.

Figure 10.7 Government employment, by type, as a percent of the labor force, 1929–1969.

gross national product. This is because government purchases are partly made to compensate public employees, and partly to pay for purchases from businesses.

Government indebtedness is typically a matter of interest in discussions of public economic policy. Frequently the debt of the federal government is shown in relation to gross national product, as the ability to service this debt is in some sense related to the aggregate size of the economy. The net debt of the federal government is shown as a percentage of gross national product in Figure 10.8.[18] This net debt is also shown as a percentage of total net indebtedness of all households, businesses, and governments. The debt of state and local governments has been an increasing portion of total net debt during the postwar period.

Numerical measures of the absolute and relative size of government economic activity, such as those presented in Figures 10.4–10.8, are usually used to convince the reader of what he already knows: Government activity now is larger than in 1929. Measures such as these cannot, however, be taken as sufficient indicators of government's economic importance. Public purchases of goods and services may comprise relatively small fractions of gross national product, while the entire economy is nonetheless controlled by the government. In the United States, municipal zoning ordinances or the rulings of state and federal regulatory agencies affect private economic activity. The number of civil servants employed by zoning commissions and regulatory agencies, or the purchases made by these agencies, cannot be used as indexes of their economic importance. Although data from national economic accounts and government budgets cannot quantify economic importance, they do provide the raw material for informed discussion and analysis of public policy.

The effects of World War II are seen dramatically in each of these five figures. The economy had not fully recovered from the Depression when the war broke out. In that sense, then, the problem of resource reallocation was not as severe as it was in World War I because unemployed labor and other resources could be used to meet the demands of the war effort. The unemployment rate went from 17.2 percent in 1939 to 1.2 percent in 1944, while civilian employment went from 45.8 million to 54 million, and the armed forces were increased from 370 thousand to 11.4 million. Women entered the labor force in growing numbers. Household consumption, measured in constant dollars, actually increased by about 16 percent between 1939 and 1944, despite the fact that about 42 percent of the gross national product was being devoted to military purposes. This should not suggest that restraints were not needed to prevent consumers from competing with the

---

[18] Part of the federal government debt is held (owned) by federal agencies. Debt held outside the federal government (owned by the public) is called net federal debt. See Chapters 11 and 12 for a more complete discussion.

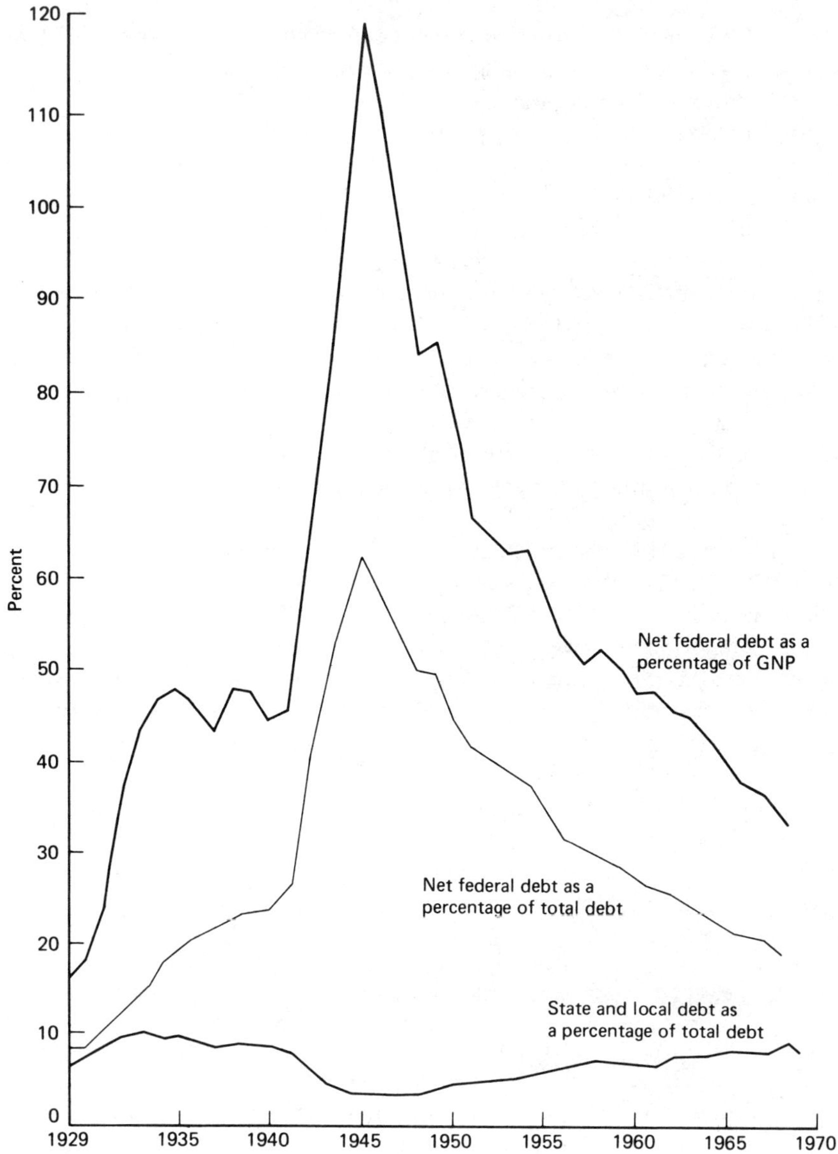

SOURCE: *Economic Report of the President, 1970* (Washington, D.C.: Government Printing Office, 1970) p. 248.

Figure 10.8 Net federal debt as a percentage of gross national product, and net federal and state-local debts as a percentage of total net debt, 1929–1969.

government for goods and services. Indeed a far more comprehensive set of controls was used than in World War I. Many consumer goods were rationed and there were widespread price controls administered by the Office of Price Administration. By 1943 rationing applied to about 95 percent of the nation's food supply. Taxes were increased each year between 1940 and 1944; the system of withholding personal income taxes was introduced in 1943. Congress set the highest marginal personal income tax rate at 91 percent and enacted an excess corporate profits tax with a 95 percent rate. Personal taxes, mainly federal income taxes, reached 12 percent of personal income in 1945. Higher percentages have been common since the Korean War (see Figure 10.6). Congress was reluctant to raise personal income taxes sufficiently to absorb excess purchasing power; in addition to the obvious political unattractiveness of such a measure it was argued that higher taxes would lessen the incentive for laborers to work long hours or migrate to higher paying defense jobs. The net result of rationing, the nonavailability of consumer durables, and federal tax policy was to "force" consumers to save. Saving equaled 25 percent of disposable personal income in 1943 and 1944, compared to a normal rate of 6–7 percent. The failure to absorb more consumer income through taxation resulted in some inflation despite price controls. The consumer price level rose 28 percent between 1940 and 1945.

Taxes of all types amounted to about 46 percent of wartime federal expenditures. The rest was financed by borrowing; the net federal debt increased from $44.8 billion in 1940 to $252.5 billion in 1945. About one-quarter of the increase was accounted for by increased individual holdings, mostly in the form of nonmarketable savings bonds. The Federal Reserve System cooperated with the Treasury's debt operations by pegging interest rates on marketable issues at rates ranging from .375 percent on Treasury bills to 2.5 percent on long-term bond issues.

At the end of the war consumers held large amounts of liquid financial assets, including federal securities, that they used to sustain high levels of spending in the initial postwar years. That consumer spending was in a large part responsible for avoiding a major postwar depression such as the one after World War I.

EXPLAINING THE GROWTH OF THE PUBLIC SECTOR

What interpretation can be given to the historical evidence concerning the growth of the public sector? Apart from periods of major warfare, the size of the public sector, measured in terms of expenditures, in the United States has tended to grow rather steadily, not only in absolute terms but also, in the twentieth century, relative to gross national product. Since the experience of many other countries is similar, a general proposition that, as levels of real income rise people will want to spend a greater proportion of that income on public goods, has long been found in the public finance literature. This proposition has come to be called *Wagner's Law* after the late nineteenth century German economist who first formulated it explicitly.[19]

---

[19] Adolf Wagner, "Three Extracts on Public Finance," in Richard A. Musgrave and Alan

Another approach to this problem is to examine the level and composition of public expenditures among political subdivisions—states, cities, countries, or school districts—at a particular point in time. The variables that, on *a priori* grounds, one would expect to influence municipal spending for police protection, health, welfare, parks, streets and highways, and so on, would certainly include levels of income and the density, size, racial composition, and age distribution of the population. Many cross-section studies have been made; a few findings are common to most all of them.[20] As to be expected, on the basis of Wagner's Law, the higher the level of income in a jurisdiction, the higher the level of per capita spending for most government services. There appear to be both economies and diseconomies of scale; very small jurisdictions, school districts with fewer than 500 pupils, for example, spend relatively more (abstracting from the influence of all other variables) than moderate and large size jurisdictions. Very large units of local government, such as the largest cities, spend more in per capita terms for most government services (again abstracting from the influence of other explanatory variables such as income). Some studies have found the educational level of parents to be an important factor in explaining variations in per pupil expenditures among school districts. The spending of any subordinate political jurisdiction is, of course, heavily influenced by the grants-in-aid that it receives from higher jurisdictions; studies of this type must include grants-in-aid as an explanatory variable in order to reach valid conclusions. This is a subject to which we will return in Chapter 20 dealing with intergovernmental fiscal relations.

T. Peacock (eds.), *Classics in the Theory of Public Finance* (New York: The Macmillan Company, 1958).

[20] For a good example of this literature, *see* Alan K. Campbell and Seymour Sachs, *Metropolitan America: Fiscal Patterns and Government Systems* (New York: The Free Press, 1967).

11

THE PUBLIC SECTOR IN NATIONAL ECONOMIC ACCOUNTS

In a modern economy all economic activity is carried on by households, businesses, or governments. Data reflecting this activity must be organized before they can be interpreted meaningfully. Household budgets or personal income tax returns summarize a family's economic behavior; income statements or balance sheets depict the economic condition of a firm. Similarly, a government budget is a means of organizing economic data. Such accounts permit economic analysis, whereas a chronological listing of transactions would simply overwhelm.

Economic data can be aggregated in a wide variety of ways, including combining accounts for households, businesses, or governments. Examples of such aggregation are the annual summary of federal personal income tax returns compiled by the Internal Revenue Service, or the quinquennial censuses of manufacturing or governments. *National economic accounts* are aggregations of economic data for all households, businesses, and governments.

The four major sets of national economic accounts for the United States are national income accounts, flow of funds accounts, the balance of payments account, and input-output tables. They differ in that each describes a particular type of economic activity: Current production and the generation of income, financial asset transactions, international transactions and interindustry product flows, respectively.[1] A clear understanding of the treatment of the public sector in these accounts is essential because the economic activity of governments looms so large in contemporary America. This chapter is designed to provide such an understanding by describing systematically the treatment of the public sector in the four major national economic accounts.

All four of these accounts are related in that some specific entries in each account are conceptually related to items in the other accounts. These relationships are most clearly seen in the national income accounts, flow of funds accounts, and balance of payments account. The public sector in these three accounts is discussed first using 1969 data. Input-output tables are conceptually related to the other accounts but are not published annually; we use 1963 input-output data—the most recent data available—in the final section of the chapter.

The data in the four national economic accounts are designed to sum up the economic behavior of literally millions of households, businesses, and governments during a single year. The accuracy of these accounts is, in part, a function of the raw material that statisticians have to work with. The American economy, or any other advanced economy, generates masses of raw statistical data that are usually a by-product of some governmental activity. Voluminous and well-enforced tax laws produce a wealth of fairly accurate information, and government regulation of industries yields data on the be-

[1] Of these four, the balance of payments account is the oldest, dating back to 1922. The other three national economic accounts are largely the result of concern over the economic problems of the Depression and World War II. *See* M. Yanovsky, *Social Accounting Systems* (Chicago: Aldine Publishing Co., 1965) for an introduction to national income accounts, flow of funds accounts, and input-output tables. Yanovsky compares and contrasts the accounts used in several nations. A standard work on national income accounting is Richard Ruggles and Nancy D. Ruggles, *National Income Accounts and Income Analysis*, 2d ed. (New York: McGraw-Hill, 1956). For an introductory treatment of national income accounting and the flow of funds accounts, *see* John P. Powelson, *National Income and Flow-of-Funds Analysis* (New York: McGraw-Hill, 1960). For a detailed explanation of the balance of payments account, see *The Balance of Payments Statistics of the United States: Review and Appraisal*, Report of the Review Committee for Balance of Payments Statistics to the Bureau of the Budget (Washington, D.C.: Government Printing Office, 1965).

Although regularly published national economic accounts are a product of the twentieth century, the utility of such accounts was recognized as early as the eighteenth century. The French physiocrat, Francois Quesnay, attempted to depict the flow of products and expenditures between social classes in his *Tableau Economique* (1758). *See* Joseph A. Schumpeter, *History of Economic Analysis* (New York: Oxford University Press, 1954), pp. 223–43.

havior of these industries.[2] The accuracy of the aggregative data depends, therefore, on the accuracy of these underlying data, which, for the most part, depends, in turn, on the accuracy with which records are kept in the private sector, particularly by businesses. Because public policy decisions and private plans are often made on the basis of data taken from national economic accounts, concern over their accuracy cannot be ignored. The point at which to begin any consideration of the accuracy of these data is Oscar Morganstern's classic, *On the Accuracy of Economic Observations*.[3] We do not investigate this issue here nor do we attempt to describe the specific estimating procedures used to develop data for the national economic accounts.

The four national economic accounts each have their own conceptual frameworks within which data are organized. We assume that the reader has some familiarity with the national income accounts but that he will be less familiar with the others; for that reason we devote some attention to the basic conceptual framework of flow of funds, balance of payments, and input-output analysis. The main focus is always on the treatment of the public sector within the accounts. References are made to some of the literature devoted to a more thorough discussion of these accounts. Most of the tables that appear in this chapter present the full detail contained in the primary sources, even when all entries are not fully discussed in the text. Full bibliographic references to the primary sources are given. The terms under which government data are classified are italicized at the point where they are defined.

Acquiring familiarity with the national economic accounts and the treatment of the public sector in them certainly is not the most pleasant task in a student's career. Despite its importance, students—and even authors—often have difficulty working up enthusiasm for what is inherently a tedious analysis of intricate detail. The best mental set to adopt is one characterized by a green eye shade and sleeve garters.

THE PUBLIC SECTOR IN THE NATIONAL INCOME ACCOUNTS

National income accounts are the most important and most widely used system of national economic accounts. The National Bureau of Economic Research and the Department of Commerce pioneered both the develop-

---

[2] In addition to the national economic accounts, the federal government publishes reams of economic data. For a guide to these sources, see *Statistical Services of the United States Government*, Office of Statistical Standards, Bureau of the Budget (Washington, D.C.: Government Printing Office, 1968), and for a directory of personnel responsible for the compilation of data, see *Federal Statistical Directory,* Office of Statistical Standards, Bureau of the Budget (Washington, D.C.: Government Printing Office, 1967).

[3] 2d ed. (Princeton, N.J.: Princeton University Press, 1963).

ment of the conceptual framework of these accounts and the derivation of statistical estimates in the United States during the 1930s.[4] The revolution in macroeconomic theory resulting from the work of John Maynard Keynes heavily influenced the development of the basic framework of the national income accounts. When Keynes wrote *The General Theory of Employment, Interest and Money*,[5] he could not draw upon national income accounts for empirical illustration of his theoretical argument. In part, the difficulty a contemporary reader has in following the reasoning in the *General Theory* is traceable to the reader's prior, basic familiarity with national income accounts and their absence from Keynes' work. Although Keynes' thinking influenced the structuring of national income accounts, it is also true that the nature of the accounts has, necessarily, influenced the subsequent development of empirically based macroeconomic analysis.

Data from the national income accounts make the headlines. They are used by business groups, government officials, and academicians to judge the overall performance of the economy. Argument in support of, or in opposi-

[4] The National Bureau's work was directed by Simon Kuznets; his book, *National Income and Its Composition 1919–1938* (New York: National Bureau of Economic Research, 1941), is a classic in this field. The Department of Commerce first published estimates of national income in 1935; these estimates were for the years 1929–1934. The Office of Business Economics in the Department of Commerce has become the official source of national income accounts data for the United States. Preliminary estimates are published quarterly in the January, April, July, and October issues of the *Survey of Current Business.* These preliminary figures are revised and the final estimates for both the year and each quarter are presented in the July issue of the *Survey of Current Business* of the following year. Further amendments in the estimates are often made. For example, a preliminary estimate of $739.5 billion for gross national product in 1966 was published in the *Survey of Current Business,* January 1967. In July the final figure was revised to $743.3 billion, and a year later a further revision was made, $747.6 billion. As of July 1970, gross national product in 1966 was reported as $749.9 billion. For a discussion of preliminary and revised national income accounts data, *see* Rosanne Cole, *Errors in Provisional Estimates of Gross National Product* (New York: Columbia University Press, 1970). The entire set of accounts going back to 1929 has been revised several times, most recently in 1965, in light of further refinements in their conceptual framework and the availability of additional basic data. The following Commerce Department publications are essential references for definitions, discussions of the conceptual framework of the official accounts, and detailed analysis of revisions: *National Income*, 1954 Edition, a supplement to the *Survey of Current Business*; *U.S. Income and Output*, a supplement to the *Survey of Current Business* (1958); and *Survey of Current Business,* August 1965. For the complete set of data through 1965 see *The National Income and Product Accounts of the United States, 1929–1965: Statistical Tables*, a supplement to the *Survey of Current Business* (1966). Both the League of Nations and the United Nations sponsored the development of national income accounts, on a consistent basis, for all member countries. The assessment of United Nations dues is based on each member's gross national product.

[5] (New York: Harcourt, Brace & World, Inc., 1936.)

U.C.W. ABERYSTWYTH LIBRARY

tion to, major changes in public economic policy is often based on projected effects measured in the framework of the national income accounts. This is particularly true with respect to monetary and fiscal policies. Clearly, every student of economic affairs must be familiar with the basic framework of these accounts and the place of the public sector within them. Running through the following exposition are three major issues regarding the treatment of the public sector in the national income accounts: the measurement of government activity, the presence of public enterprises, and the effects of government receipts and expenditures on the income of individuals.

Gross national product. The most familiar national income data are presented in the first column of Table 11.1. Here *gross national product*, the market value of all final goods and services produced during the year, is decomposed into the four major uses of final output: consumption, invest-

Table 11.1 **Gross National Product, 1969**

	Billions of Current Dollars	Implicit Price Deflators (1958=100)	Billions of Constant (1958) Dollars
Gross national product	931.4	128.1	727.1
Personal consumption expenditures	577.5	123.5	467.7
Durable goods	90.0	106.0	84.9
Nondurable goods	245.8	122.2	201.2
Services	241.6	133.1	181.6
Gross private domestic investment	139.8	—	111.3
Fixed investment	131.4	126.2	104.1
Nonresidential	99.3	122.8	80.8
Structures	33.8	141.1	24.0
Producers' durable equipment	65.5	115.1	56.9
Residential structures	32.0	137.7	23.3
Nonfarm	31.5	137.8	22.8
Farm	.6	132.3	.4
Change in business inventories	8.5	—	7.2
Nonfarm	8.0	—	6.8
Farm	.4	—	.4
Net export of goods and services	1.9	—	.2
Exports	55.5	114.6	48.5
Imports	53.5	111.1	48.2
Government purchases of goods and services	212.2	143.5	147.8
Federal	101.3	133.9	75.7
National defense	78.7	—	—
Other	22.5	—	—
State and local	110.8	153.7	72.1

SOURCE: *Survey of Current Business,* July 1970, Tables 1.1, 1.2, 8.1.

ment, net exports of goods and services, and government purchases of goods and services. The term gross national product is defined to include only newly produced, final goods and services. By final we mean that the value of all intermediate products—outputs of one firm that are used as inputs by another firm—is excluded.

A clear understanding of the category *government purchases of goods and services* is essential. It refers to purchases of labor services from households and to purchases of goods and services from businesses. Several types of government spending are not included in this figure. All government transfer payments, such as social security benefits and welfare payments, are excluded because the payments are not made to compensate individuals for contributing supplies of factor services to the current output of goods and services. Interest payments made by governments are excluded on the grounds that the payments are not compensation to the owners of capital used in current production. Both the purchase of land by a government and the acquisition of financial assets, such as a veteran's mortgage, are excluded. An additional type of public spending not included in government purchases of goods and services is the payments made by public enterprises to cover current operating expenses. *Government enterprises* are defined as the agencies of government, both federal and state-local, whose operating costs are to a substantial extent covered by the sale of goods and services or the receipt of interest income. The Post Office and public power systems are typical examples. In essence, then, the current operations of government enterprises are treated as if they were private businesses. The value of the goods and services they produce is in part included in personal consumption expenditures; most of the remainder represents an intermediate product purchased by other businesses.[6] Other government agencies, in the aggregate, are referred to as *general government*. State universities and public parks, where the fees and admissions collected cover only a nominal part of the operating costs, are part of general government because they are not intended to be self-supporting. Their fiscal operations are reflected in the government purchases of goods and services category. Often this figure for government purchases of goods and services is used as a measure of the size of government in the economy or, when compared to gross national product, as an indication of the relative magnitude of the public sector. Of course, such usage of the national income accounts overlooks the aspects of government activity, such as regulatory policy and transfer payments, that do not absorb goods and services.

Citizens of the twentieth century no longer agree with Adam Smith that "The sovereign, for example, with all the officers both of justice and war who

---

[6] See lines 78 and 79 for government enterprises in the 1963 input-output table, Table 11.20.

serve under him, the whole army and navy, are unproductive laborers. They are the servants of the public, and are maintained by a part of the annual produce of the industry of other people."[7] We all do recognize, however, that some government purchases of goods and services contribute more directly to our welfare than do other purchases. The national income accounts make no distinctions; the salaries of all government employees are included. If, for example, the number of government employees needed to administer an educational program were reduced, and if these employees became public school teachers, gross national product would be unaffected (assuming no change in salaries), yet we would all agree that citizen welfare had been increased.

The division between federal and state and local government purchases of goods and services was about equal in 1969. *Grants-in-aid* are payments from one level of government to another. When federal grants-in-aid are used by state and local governments to purchase goods and services, the expenditures are recorded as state and local government purchases rather than as federal purchases. The separate listing of federal government purchases of goods and services for national defense purposes should be taken as only a rough approximation of the magnitude of defense expenditures. Essentially, it is a problem of classification. The practice is to adopt the system of listing expenditures in federal government budget documents. To Department of Defense expenditures (less expenditures for certain civilian activities, such as river and harbor improvements made by the Army Corps of Engineers) are added purchases by a few other agencies, the most important of which is the Atomic Energy Commission. All purchases of goods and services by that agency are classified as part of national defense, even though some of these purchases are for essentially civilian purposes.[8]

No government expenditures are included in *gross private domestic investment,* hence the term private. Even when governments purchase what are essentially capital goods—roads or office buildings—they are classified as part of government purchases of goods and services and not as investment. When government owned capital is leased to private producers, common in the aerospace industry and others, using gross private domestic investment data as a measure of capital formation is faulty. Between 1940–65 as much as $45 billion of privately utilized capital goods went uncounted because

---

[7] Adam Smith, *The Wealth of Nations* (New York: Modern Library, Inc., 1937), p. 315.

[8] *The Budget of the United States Government, Fiscal Year* (Washington, D.C.: Government Printing Office, 1970), *1971,* pp. 81–89. Expenditure figures from the *Budget* are not strictly comparable with the figures in the national income accounts, primarily because the former are reported on a fiscal year basis whereas the latter are for calendar years. See the discussion of Table 12.9.

they were originally acquired by the federal government.[9] This is also the case when the plant and equipment of government enterprises is expanded: If a privately owned utility builds a new power plant, it is recorded as a part of gross private domestic investment; if a publicly owned power plant is constructed, it is recorded as a part of government purchases of goods and services rather than as investment, even though operating expenses are not classified as government purchases.[10]

Personal consumption expenditures, expressed in per capita terms, are often used as a measure of the welfare of individuals. It should be clearly understood, however, that this measure takes no account of the government services that, in some sense, are consumed by individuals. For example, the welfare of families is surely enhanced by the availability of public education. Although not all government purchases of goods and services will be interpreted by individuals as directly contributing to their personal well-being, this factor cannot be overlooked in interpreting data from the national income accounts.

Even if agreement could be reached on what specific government purchases of goods and services contribute to personal welfare, the problem of interpretation would not be solved. The difficulty is one of attaching dollar figures to the value of government services. When a government agency renders a service, its value is recorded as the sum of purchases made from private business and the compensation of government employees. No account is taken of the rental value of government owned real estate, nor is any attempt made to charge interest or depreciation on publicly owned capital. Another problem of valuation arises with defense expenditures. The value of services rendered by servicemen is equated to the compensation they receive. Men who are conscripted and paid military salaries generally receive less than the compensation they would earn in the private sector. To this extent, the real cost of national defense is understated. Estimates of the increased budgetary costs of an entirely volunteer armed services totaling 2.65 million men range from $4 to $8 billion.[11]

[9] Robert J. Gordon, "$45 Billion of U.S. Private Investment Has Been Mislaid," *American Economic Review*, June 1969. *See also* a comment by George Jaszi and a reply by Gordon, *American Economic Review*, December 1970.

[10] Of course, we are describing the national income accounting system used in the United States. A socialist state, where the majority of new capital goods are acquired by state-owned enterprises, would treat this matter differently. In discussions of economic growth, attention often is focused on the proportion of gross national product devoted to investment. Any international comparisons on this point must make appropriate adjustments in the national income accounts of different countries in order to achieve comparability. M. Yanovsky, *op. cit.*, chapter II.

[11] Walter Y. Oi, "The Economic Cost of the Draft," and Stuart H. Altman and Alan E. Fechter, "The Supply of Military Personnel in the Absence of a Draft," *American Economic Review*, May 1967.

Constant dollar measurement. When comparisons are made between gross national product for two different years, adjustments must be made for changes in prices. This would be a simple matter (and many statisticians would be unemployed) if all prices changed in the same direction and to the same degree. Because this is never the case—some prices are going up, some are going down, and variation in prices is the rule rather than the exception—price indexes must be used to deflate current dollar magnitudes so that gross national product and its component parts for any two or more years can be more accurately compared. Column three in Table 11.1 presents gross national product for 1969 expressed in 1958 dollars. The second column lists the price indexes implied by the adjusted figures.[12] The *implicit price deflator* of 128.1 for gross national product means that the goods and services produced in 1969 had a money value 28.1 percent higher than if they had been produced in 1958. The implicit price deflator for government purchases of goods and services is higher than that for any other component of gross national product. Since the value of goods and services produced by the public sector itself can be measured only by the compensation of general government employees, the implicit price deflator for this part of total government purchases reflects only rising wage and salary levels for public employees.

The influence of rising compensation payments for public employees on the implicit price deflator for total gross national product is better illustrated by Table 11.2, where gross national product is divided according to sector of origin. The private sector, including public enterprises, produces all final products used for consumption, gross private domestic investment, net exports of goods and services, and some of the goods and services purchased by governments. The general government sector produces goods and services using the labor services of public employees as the only factor input. The difference between the value of the product produced in the public sector and government purchases of goods and services is equal to government purchases from the private sector: $212.2 billion less $103.6 billion equals $108.6 billion for 1969. As indicated in column two of Table 11.2, the implicit price deflator for the output of the general government stood 70.8 percent higher in 1969 than in the base period year 1958. During the same period the average gross weekly earnings in all nonagricultural industries

[12] The term *implicit price deflator* is used because these indices are constructed by adding up constant dollar values for subcategories—of, say, personal consumption expenditures on durable goods—and then dividing this sum into the relevant current dollar figure. The price indexes used to estimate constant dollar values for the individual subcategories are primarily compiled for other purposes, such as the consumer and wholesale price indexes. There are some curious blanks in column two of Table 11.1. The Office of Business Economics does not list the implicit price deflator for gross private domestic investment, but since both current and constant dollar magnitudes are published, any reader can divide 139.8 by 111.3 and derive the implicit price deflator.

***Table 11.2* Gross National Product by Sector, 1969**

	Billions of Current Dollars	Implicit Price Deflators (1958=100)	Billions of Constant (1958) Dollars
Gross national product	931.4	128.1	727.1
Private	827.8	124.2	666.4
Business	795.4	123.1	646.0
Nonfarm	767.9	123.4	622.5
Farm	27.5	116.9	23.6
Households and institutions	28.1	171.9	16.4
Rest of the world	4.3	——	4.0
General government	103.6	170.8	60.7

SOURCE: *Survey of Current Business,* July 1970, Tables 1.7, 1.8, 8.4.

increased 52 percent.[13] The smaller increase in the implicit price deflator for the business sector (123.1) results from productivity changes. Compensation of private business employees can increase at a faster rate than the prices of goods and services produced in that sector because of offsetting increases in productivity. If the compensation of auto workers increases by 5 percent, and if the number of automobiles produced per worker also increases by 5 percent—because of technological change, better capital goods, improved education of the workers, or whatever the ultimate source of improved productivity—auto prices can remain unchanged.[14] The nature of the services rendered by public employees prevents any comparable measurements of productivity increases to offset rising wage rates, even though there is evidence of increasing units of output per employee, over time, in some types of government activity.[15] What this means is that the implicit price deflator for gross national product is biased in an upward direction by the implicit price deflator for government purchases of goods and services. The effect of this

13 *Economic Report of the President* (Washington, D.C.: Government Printing Office, 1970), p. 212.

14 Profits in this situation could also increase by 5 percent. Productivity increases occur in the production of most of the goods and services that governments buy from the private sector; hence the deflator for government purchases of goods and services (143.5 — Table 11.1) is considerably lower than the deflator for general government (170.8 — Table 11.2).

15 John W. Kendrick, "Exploring Productivity Measurement in Government," *Public Administration Review,* June 1963. Kendrick refers to evidence of increasing productivity for certain government agencies where output can be measured in physical terms, such as the checkwriting function of the Treasury. For some types of government activity, like the State Department, the mind boggles at the thought of measuring productivity changes.

bias is reflected in the difference between the deflator for gross national product, 128.1 in 1969, and the deflator for private product, 124.2. This latter deflator is a better measure of overall changes in the price level.[16]

National income. The logic of national income accounting is based on the correspondence between the value of final output and the income received by the suppliers of factors of production. The correspondence, however, is not precise. The term *national income* is used to denote the total income received by the suppliers of factors of production. Several adjustments must be made to show the precise relationship between gross national product and national income; these are shown in Table 11.3.

Table 11.3 **Relation of Gross National Product, National Income, and Personal Income, 1969 (Billions of dollars)**

Gross national product		931.4
Less:	Capital consumption allowances	78.8
Equals:	Net national product	852.5
Less:	Indirect business tax and nontax liability	85.2
	Business transfer payments	3.5
	Statistical discrepancy	−4.6
Plus:	Subsidies less current surplus of government enterprises	1.0
Equals:	National income	769.5
Less:	Corporate profits and inventory evaluation adjustment	85.8
	Contributions for social insurance	53.5
	Wage accruals less disbursements	——
Plus:	Government transfer payments to persons	61.5
	Interest paid by government (net) and by consumers	28.9
	Dividends	24.6
	Business transfer payments	3.5
Equals:	Personal income	748.8

SOURCE: *Survey of Current Business,* July 1970, Table 1.9.

Current output of goods and services requires the use of a vast stock of capital goods, some of which are destroyed, wear out, or become obsolete

[16] The argument that we have just made with respect to adjusting the product produced in the general government sector for changes in prices also applies to the production of households and institutions within the private sector (see Table 11.2). Production by households and institutions is almost entirely equal to the compensation of domestic servants and the employees of nonprofit institutions.

during any given year. The value of such capital consumption cannot be estimated precisely. What is known, however, is the amount that businesses attribute to depreciation and treat as a current expense item in their bookkeeping. The *capital consumption allowance* entry in Table 11.3 is made up almost entirely of the aggregate of these depreciation allowances. *Depreciation* is a charge against the value of current output for which there is no corresponding factor payment; hence capital consumption allowances must be subtracted from the gross national product in order to calculate the *net national product;* this is the first step in deriving an estimate of national income. Although no estimate is made for depreciation of publicly owned capital, the public sector has a very significant influence on the estimation of capital consumption allowances. This influence is a by-product of the tax laws. Given the conceptual difficulties in determining the precise value of capital used in the process of production, the Office of Business Economics finds it convenient to define depreciation for national income accounting purposes the same way the Internal Revenue Service and the Internal Revenue Code define it for tax purposes. Any change in tax laws or administrative interpretation that permits businesses to take larger depreciation allowances tends to reduce net national product relative to gross national product. Such changes, usually called accelerated depreciation, generally have the effect of stimulating investment. In 1954 and 1962 major changes in the tax laws affecting depreciation were made for just this reason.

The major deduction from net national product in the calculation of national income is *indirect business taxes.* Sales and excise taxes collected from businesses are of this nature. On the presumption that they are fully shifted forward, these taxes are included in the value of final products in deriving the estimate of gross national product, but are not a factor payment. All property taxes, whether paid by businesses or households, are included in indirect business taxes. Because an imputation for the rental value of owner-occupied housing is included in gross national product, property taxes paid by homeowners should be deducted in order to estimate the imputed factor payment that they receive.

For national income accounting purposes, the current operations of government enterprises are, as just indicated, treated as a part of the private business sector. Subsidies are paid by governments to some private businesses and public enterprises. When subsidies are made, output valued at current market prices, less purchases of intermediate products, is less than value added. Hence subsidies must be added when national income is derived from gross national product. Conversely, the surpluses of public enterprises are netted out because no factor payments (profits) are made to government-owned capital. These surpluses are netted out of the figure for *subsidies less current surplus of government enterprises* that appears in Table 11.3.

Personal income. The relationship between personal income and national income is also shown in Table 11.3, and again the public sector has an influence. *Personal income* is the current income of households from all sources, including transfer and interest payments received from governments. The contributions made by both employers and employees to social insurance programs, like the social security system and public employee retirement plans, are excluded from personal income. By subtracting corporate profits from, and adding dividends to, national income to arrive at an estimate of personal income, the national income accountants are in effect subtracting corporate income taxes and retained earnings. By changing corporate income taxes, the public sector can influence the amount of corporate after-tax profits that are available to be paid out as dividends or for use as retained earnings.

Table 11.4 **Personal Income and Its Disposition, 1969 (Billions of dollars)**

Personal income	748.8
Wage and salary disbursements	509.0
Commodity-producing industries	197.4
Manufacturing	157.5
Distributive industries	119.7
Service industries	87.6
Government	104.0
Other labor income	27.6
Proprietors' income	66.8
Business and professional	50.4
Farm	16.3
Rental income of persons	21.9
Dividends	24.6
Personal interest income	59.6
Transfer payments	65.0
Old-age, survivors, disability, and health insurance benefits	32.9
State unemployment insurance benefits	2.1
Veterans benefits	8.3
Other	21.6
Less: Personal contributions for social insurance	26.0
Less: Personal tax and nontax payments	117.3
Equals: Disposable personal income	631.5
Less: Personal outlays	593.9
Personal consumption expenditures	577.4
Interest paid by consumers	15.6
Personal transfer payments to foreigners	.7
Equals: Personal saving	37.6

SOURCE: *Survey of Current Business*, July 1970, Table 2.1.

Thus, corporate income taxes have an effect on the relationship between national income and personal income.

The sources of personal income are listed in Table 11.4.[17] The primary component is *wage and salary disbursements*, of which payments by governments constituted 20.4 percent in 1969. These government wage and salary disbursements include payments to employees of government enterprises. Wage and salary disbursements is a different accounting concept from employee compensation.[18] The major types of transfer payments are listed separately in this table, as are personal contributions for social insurance.

Government transfer payments. Practically all transfer payments to persons are paid by government—$61.6 billion out of a total of $65.1 billion in 1969. The specific types of government transfer payments are shown in Table 11.5. Hospital and medical insurance benefits (Medicare) appeared for the first time in 1966. In total, these government transfer payments made up about 8 percent of personal income in 1969.

Disposable personal income. *Disposable personal income* is the part of personal income that is available for spending by households. Disposable personal income equals personal income less *personal tax and nontax payments*, as indicated in Table 11.4. This latter term is defined as taxes levied against individuals, their income, and their property that are not deductible as expenses of business operations, and other general government revenues from individuals excluding federal proprietary receipts (see Chapter 12). Purchases from government enterprises are excluded, but fees levied in connection with a government activity (tuition payments to state universities, for example) are included. Property taxes on housing are not included; these are treated as indirect business taxes. Taxes on personal property, such as household furniture, are included. Here the role of the public sector is obvious: Higher personal taxes reduce disposable personal income.

Government budgets. The budget of the federal government and all state and local governments combined is shown within the framework of

---

[17] Personal income is the only account for which monthly estimates are made by the Office of Business Economics and published in the *Survey of Current Business*. Quarterly and annual estimates of personal income in each state are also published.

[18] In the terminology of national income accounting, compensation of employees includes (in addition to wage and salary disbursements, supplements to wages, and salaries) employer contributions for social insurance and contributions to private pension, health, and welfare funds; compensation for injuries; directors' fees; pay of the military reserve; and a few minor items. The entry *other labor income* in Table 11.4 constitutes supplements to wages and salaries less employer contributions to social insurance.

Table 11.5 **Government Transfer Payments to Persons, 1969 (Millions of dollars)**

Total government transfer payments to persons	61,561
Federal government	50,030
Benefits from social insurance funds	40,047
Old-age, survivors, and disability insurance benefits	26,381
Hospital and medical insurance benefits	6,582
State unemployment insurance benefits	2,149
Railroad retirement insurance benefits	1,597
Railroad unemployment insurance benefits	37
Federal civilian pensions	2,560
Veterans life insurance	741
Military pension, disability, and retirement payments	7,486
Other veterans benefits	797
Other	1,700
State and local governments	11,531
Benefits from social insurance funds	3,631
Government pensions	3,275
Cash sickness compensation	356
Direct relief	6,640
Special types of public assistance	6,170
General assistance	470
Other	1,260

SOURCE: *Survey of Current Business,* July 1970, Table 3.9.

national income accounts in Table 11.6.[19] On the receipts side, the payments that make up the *personal tax and nontax receipts* item in Table 11.4 are shown in some detail in Table 11.6. Personal tax receipts are recorded when taxes are actually paid, whereas corporate income taxes and indirect business taxes are recorded on an accrual basis. *Federal grands-in-aid* appear as a receipt item for state and local governments and as an expenditure item for the federal government. On the expenditures side, *purchases of goods and services* are clearly distinguished from transfer payments. The figure for purchases is the same one that appears in Table 11.1, whereas the figure for transfers combines transfer payments to persons, listed as a component of personal income (see Table 11.3), and net transfers to foreigners, which appears in the balance of payments account (see lines 29 and 30, Table 11.15). Purchases of goods and services are shown in three parts: compensation of

[19] The relationship between the federal budget as it appears here in the national income accounts and the statement found in *The Budget of the United States Government* is examined in Chapter 12. The classification of receipts and expenditures in the national income accounts is not identical to the concepts used by the Bureau of the Census in the *Census of Governments* or in their series of publications on government finance.

***Table 11.6* Government Receipts and Expenditures, 1969 (Billions of dollars)**

	Federal	State and Local	Total
Receipts	200.6	118.3	318.9
Personal tax and nontax receipts	95.9	21.4	117.3
Total receipts before refunds	106.8	——	106.8
Income taxes	103.1	10.0	113.1
Estate, death, and gift taxes	3.6	1.0	4.6
Motor vehicle licenses	——	1.4	1.4
Property taxes	——	1.1	1.1
Other taxes	——	.3	.3
Nontaxes	.1	7.5	7.6
Less: Tax refunds	10.9	——	10.9
Corporate profits tax accruals	39.2	3.5	42.7
Indirect business tax and nontax accruals	19.1	66.1	85.2
Total accruals before refunds	19.4	——	19.4
Excise and sales taxes			
Federal	15.9	——	15.9
Liquor	4.7	——	4.7
Tobacco	2.1	——	2.1
Other	9.1	——	9.1
State	——	25.1	25.1
General	——	13.3	13.3
Gasoline	——	5.9	5.9
Liquor	——	1.3	1.3
Tobacco	——	2.1	2.1
Local	——	2.4	2.4
Customs duties	2.4	——	2.4
Motor vehicle licenses	1.4	——	1.4
Property taxes	——	30.9	30.9
Other taxes	——	6.6	6.6
Nontaxes	1.1	2.2	3.3
Less: Tax refunds	.3	——	.3
Contributions for social insurance	46.5	7.1	53.6
Federal grants-in-aid	——	20.2	20.2
Expenditures	191.3	118.9	310.2
Purchases of goods and services	101.3	110.8	212.1
Compensation of employees	42.0	61.5	103.5
Structures (excluding construction force account compensation)	3.1	24.8	27.9
Other purchases	56.1	24.5	80.6
Addendum: Construction force account compensation	.2	.6	.8
Transfer payments	52.1	11.5	63.6
To persons	50.0	11.5	61.5
To foreigners (net)	2.1	——	2.1
Grants-in-aid to state and local governments	20.2	——	20.2
Net interest paid	13.1	.1	13.2
Subsidies less current surplus of government enterprises	4.6	−3.6	1.0
Surplus (+) or Deficit (−)	+9.3	−.6	+8.7

SOURCE: *Survey of Current Business*, July 1970, Tables 3.1 and 3.3.

Table 11.7 **Government Expenditures by Type and Function, 1969 (Millions of dollars)**

	Federal Government					State and Local Governments			
	Total	Purchases of goods and services	Transfer payments and net interest paid	Grants-in-aid to state and local governments	Subsidies less current surplus of government enterprises	Total	Purchases of goods and services	Transfer payments and net interest paid	Less: Current surplus of government enterprises
Total	191,317	101,339	65,220	20,159	4,599	118,921	110,838	11,675	3,593
National defense	81,549	78,763	2,547	428	—189	566	566	——	——
Space and technology	3,953	3,905	——	48	——	——	——	——	——
General government	18,659	2,896	15,720	135	—92	13,913	10,138	3,839	64
International affairs and finance	2,628	575	2,050	5	—2	——	——	——	——
Education	4,558	1,014	385	3,156	3	48,022	47,363	659	——
Health, labor, and welfare	52,020	3,935	37,856	10,220	9	33,689	26,466	7,125	—98
Veterans benefits and services	8,435	1,793	6,631	18	—7	70	24	46	——
Commerce, transportation, and housing	9,780	3,541	21	5,368	850	18,580	22,146	——	3,566
Agriculture and agricultural resources	6,970	2,384	3	254	4,329	1,179	1,172	7	——
Natural resources	2,765	2,533	7	527	—302	2,902	2,963	——	61

SOURCE: *Survey of Current Business*, July 1970, Table 3.10.

employees (the same figure appears in Table 11.2), structures, and other purchases. The latter two represent purchases from the private sector. Because some public employees work on the building of new structures, the value of new structures is reported net of the *construction force account compensation* item that represents the compensation of these employees. This adjustment is made to avoid the double counting that would arise if the full value of the structures were reported along with the compensation of all general government employees. *Net interest paid* is net in the sense that all interest payments received by governments are subtracted from interest payments made by governments rather than reported separately as a receipt item. In some cases, one government agency receives interest payments from another, such as when the social security trust fund receives interest payments from the Treasury on United States government securities that are held in the trust fund; these payments are netted out. The figure for subsidies less current surplus of government enterprises also appeared in Table 11.3. As Table 11.6 shows, government enterprises of state and local governments, in the aggregate, generated surpluses. The difference between the receipts and expenditures listed in Table 11.6 constitutes the surplus or deficit in the government budgets as set forth in the national income accounts.[20]

Additional information on government spending—by type and by function—is presented in Table 11.7. As shown, the largest part of transfer payments is classified under the functional category of health, labor, and welfare; net interest payments are classified under general government. The public enterprises of state and local governments earn, in the aggregate, surpluses; almost all these surpluses are generated by publicly owned utilities and toll roads and are classified under the commerce, transportation, and housing category. The *Survey of Current Business* presents this picture of government activity in more detail by specifying about 50 functional subcategories.

Saving and investment. The basic structure of national income accounting reflects the equality of aggregate saving and total investment. Table 11.8 shows this for 1969. *Gross private saving* is equal to the part of disposable personal income that is not spent on outlays (see Table 11.4), and to the part of business receipts from the sale of final output that is not paid out for factor services or taxes. *Undistributed corporate profits* and *capital consumption allowances* are the major sources of savings by businesses. As just

[20] It must be emphasized that the surplus or deficit in the federal government budget put in the conceptual framework of national income accounts is not equal to the surplus or deficit in the *Budget of the United States Government* (see Chapter 12 for details). In 1969 (calendar year) the federal budget in the national income accounts showed a $9.3 billion surplus while the *Budget of the United States Government* in fiscal 1969 shows a deficit.

Table 11.8 Sources and Uses of Gross Saving, 1969 (Millions of dollars)

Gross private saving	134,950
Personal saving	37,641
Undistributed corporate profits	23,875
Corporate inventory valuation adjustment	—5,424
Corporate capital consumption allowances	49,752
Noncorporate capital consumption allowances	29,106
Wage accruals less disbursements	——
Government surplus or deficit (—), national income and product accounts	8,654
Federal	9,303
State and local	—649
Gross investment	138,934
Gross private domestic investment	139,819
Net foreign investment	—885
Statistical discrepancy	—4,670

SOURCE: *Survey of Current Business,* July 1970, Table 5.1.

indicated, tax rates and treatment of depreciation for tax purposes are the ways in which the public sector can affect business saving. The government sector can also save; *government surpluses* are part of aggregate savings, whereas *government deficits* are a negative component of aggregate savings. As indicated in Table 11.8, the surplus of $8.7 billion in 1969 for all governments combined (see Table 11.6) is added to gross private saving in showing the equality of saving and investment. *Gross investment* adds net foreign investment to gross private domestic investment (see Table 11.1). *Net foreign investment* is equal to the balance on goods, services, and unilateral transfers (Table 11.15, line 31) as measured in the balance of payments account.[21]

The national income accounts provide essential information on the behavior of the public sector—discussion of most policy issues necessarily takes place in terms of these data—yet this information is by no means complete. Many transactions between the public and private sectors are not included, and for that reason we now turn to a consideration of the flow of funds accounts.

[21] Net foreign investment in Table 11.8 is equal to net exports of goods and services (Table 11.1) less personal transfer payments to foreigners (Table 11.4) and government transfer payments to foreigners (Table 11.6).

THE PUBLIC SECTOR IN THE FLOW OF FUNDS ACCOUNTS

The flow of funds accounts focus on financial transactions among the sectors of the economy, in contrast with the measurement of income and product flows in the national income accounts.[22] During a year the net result of the virtually infinite number of financial transactions will be changes in the aggregate financial assets and liabilities of each sector in the economy. In part, these changes in assets and liabilities are associated with the production of current output, but transactions in existing assets also contribute to these changes. The flow of funds therefore encompasses a broader range of economic phenomena, including the transactions of financial institutions, than do the national income accounts. A deeper understanding of the operations of the American economy can be gained by careful study of the data provided in the flow of funds accounts. In particular, these accounts aid the analysis of monetary policy, government deficits, and federal debt management policy.[23] These aspects of public economic policy involve transactions in financial assets between and among the sectors of the economy. Our task here, of course, is more limited: To discuss the place of the federal and state-local governments in these accounts.

The basic concepts underlying flow of funds accounting can be illustrated with the aid of Table 11.9. We divide our model economy into four sectors: households, businesses, the government, and commercial banks. These sectors are arrayed across the horizontal dimension of Table 11.9. The entries in the last column are taken from the national income accounts for this economy, showing the equality of aggregate saving and investment. Saving is a source of funds for a sector. The first line shows household, business, and the government saving; the negative figure for the government indicates a deficit in the government's budget (in the national income accounts) for the time

---

22 The pioneering effort in the development of flow of funds accounts was made by Morris A. Copeland; see *A Study of Moneyflows in the United States* (New York: National Bureau of Economic Research, 1952). The Board of Governors of the Federal Reserve System encouraged research in this area that culminated in *Flow of Funds in the United States: 1939–1953* (Washington, D.C.: Board of Governors of the Federal Reserve System, 1955). The conceptual framework adopted by the Federal Reserve System differed to some extent from that developed by Copeland. The Federal Reserve System has become the official source of these data and has revised the accounts several times since 1955. They are published on a current basis in the *Federal Reserve Bulletin*, and both quarterly and annual estimates are made. The best single source to see for definitions of terms and explanations of conceptual points beyond what is presented here is *Flow of Funds Accounts, 1945–1968* (Washington, D.C.: Board of Governors of the Federal Reserve System, 1970).

23 For a discussion of the uses of flow of funds analysis, see *The Flow-of-Funds Approach to Social Accounting: Appraisal, Analysis, and Applications*, National Bureau of Economic Research, Studies in Income and Wealth 26 (Princeton, N.J.: Princeton University Press, 1962).

Table 11.9 Model Flow of Funds Matrix

	Households		Businesses		Government		Commercial Banks		National Saving and Investment
	Uses	**Sources**	**Uses**	**Sources**	**Uses**	**Sources**	**Uses**	**Sources**	
Saving		77		25		—2			100
Investment	20		80						100
Net financial investment	57		—55		—2				
Financial uses (net)	67		1		2				
Financial sources (net)		10		56		4			
Demand deposits	7		—1					6	
Government securities	4		2			4	—2		
Corporate bonds	56			56					
Mortgages		10			2		8		

period in question. Investment is a use of funds by a sector. Real investment is undertaken by households and businesses, as shown in the second line. Net financial investment (line 3) is the excess of saving over real investment; a sector making investments in excess of its saving incurs negative net financial investment. The financial assets of one sector are the liabilities of another. In flow of funds accounting, acquisition (liquidation) of an asset is a positive (negative) use of funds; issuance (retirement) of a liability is a positive (negative) source of funds. A sector uses funds to acquire financial assets (limited in this model to demand deposits, government securities, corporate bonds, and mortgages). The entries in the fourth line—financial uses (net)—equals the sum of the change in each sector's holding of these financial assets during the time period covered. For example, here the business sector drew down its holdings of demand deposits by 1 (line 6) and increased its holdings of government bonds by 2 (line 7); thus financial uses (net) equals 1. Households in our model issued additional mortgages of 10 (line 9), constituting a liability for that sector. These mortgages were acquired by other sectors (commercial banks and the government) that used funds to acquire them. Financial sources (net) (line 5) sums for each sector its change in liabilities during the period. Focusing on the government sector, we see a budget deficit of 2 and the acquisition of mortgages of 2 being financed by issuing government securities of 4. Households increased their holdings of government securities by 4, businesses by 2, and commercial banks decreased their holdings by 2. The flow of funds matrix shows how the government finances a budget deficit (or surplus) and the acquisition of financial assets. It also shows the net result of transactions in government securities among sectors. Both types of information are important in analyzing the impact of the public sector in financial markets. With this introduction, we can now turn to the actual flow of funds accounts for the United States.

The matrix. The *flow of funds matrix* for 1969 is presented here as Table 11.10. The horizontal dimension of this most basic flow of funds account arrays a broader set of economic sectors than in our model matrix. Households (including nonprofit organizations), nonfinancial businesses (including both incorporated and unincorporated business), and general funds of state and local governments are presented separately and combined as the *private domestic nonfinancial sector;* the federal government appears as a separate sector.[24] The *financial sectors* are shown combined and then in-

[24] State and local governments comprise all political subdivisions of the United States, including the District of Columbia, and all corporations, enterprises, debt-issuing

Table 11.10 Summary of Flow of Funds Accounts for 1969 (Billions of dollars)

	Transaction Category \ Sector	Private Domestic Nonfinancial Sectors: Households		Business		State and Local Governments		Total		United States Government	
		U	S	U	S	U	S	U	S	U	S
1	**Gross saving**		**146.6**		**81.8**		**−5.6**		**222.8**		**7.8**
2	Capital consumption		82.7		66.5				149.2		
3	Net saving (1–2)		63.9		15.2		−5.6		73.6		7.8
4	**Gross investment (5 + 10)**	**137.3**		**74.7**		**−7.5**		**204.4**		**8.6**	
5	Private capital expenditures	116.8		111.1				227.9			
6	Consumer durables	89.8						89.8			
7	Residential construction	22.0		10.2				32.2			
8	Plant and equipment	5.0		92.8				97.8			
9	Inventory change			8.0				8.0			
10	**Net financial investment (11–12)**	**20.5**		**−36.4**		**−7.5**		**−23.4**		**8.6**	
11	**Financial uses, net**	**50.2**		**25.5**		**1.9**		**77.7**		**7.0**	
12	**Financial sources**		**29.8**		**62.0**		**9.4**		**101.1**		**−1.6**
13	Gold and official foreign exchange									1.4	
14	Treasury currency										.3
15	Demand deposits and currency										
16	Private domestic	3.4		.5		2.2		6.0			
17	U.S. government									1.1	
18	Foreign										
19	Time and savings accounts	11.3						−4.1			
20	At commercial banks	3.3		−7.8		−7.5		−12.0		−.1	
21	At savings institutions	8.0						8.0			
22	Life insurance reserves	4.5						4.5			.1
23	Pension fund reserves	15.8						15.8			1.6
24	Interbank items[1]										
25	Credit market instruments	18.7	31.4	11.4	48.1	7.2	8.9	37.3	88.3	2.6	−3.6
26	Corporate shares	−4.3			4.3			−4.3	4.3		
27	U.S. government securities	13.1		−1.4		4.2		15.8		−1.3	−3.6
28	State and local obligations	3.8		2.3		.1	8.5	6.1	8.5		
29	Corporate and foreign bonds	4.9			12.1	2.8		7.7	12.1		
30	Home mortgages	−.5	16.0		−.5	.2		−.3	15.5	.1	−.1
31	Other mortgages	1.8	1.1		10.8			1.8	11.9	.6	
32	Consumer credit		9.3	1.8				1.8	9.3		
33	Bank loans n.e.c.		2.0		12.5				14.5		
34	Other loans		2.9	8.7	8.9		.4	8.7	12.3	3.2	
35	Security credit	−.8	−2.4					−.8	−2.4		
36	To brokers and dealers	−.8						−.8			
37	To others		−2.4						−2.4		
38	Taxes payable				.8				.8	1.0	
39	Trade credit		.4	17.3	11.4		.5	17.3	12.3	.9	−.3
40	Equity in noncorporate business	−4.8			−4.8			−4.8	−4.8		
41	Miscellaneous claims	2.1	.3	4.2	6.5			6.3	6.8	.1	.4
42	Sector discrepancies (1–4)	9.4		7.1		1.9		18.4		−.8	

SOURCE: *Federal Reserve Bulletin*, May 1970, p. A 70.

Financial Sectors																	
Total		Federally Sponsored Credit Agencies		Monetary Authorities		Commercial Banks		Private Non-bank Finance		Rest of the World		All Sectors		Dis-crep-ancy	National Saving and Investment	
U	S	U	S	U	S	U	S	U	S	U	S	U	S	U		
	3.9		**.1**		*		**3.7**		**.1**		**.6**		**235.1**		**234.5**	1
	1.4						.7		.6				150.6		150.6	2
	2.6		.1		*		.9		—.5		.6		84.5		83.9	3
2.2		*		*		**2.7**		**—.5**		**3.7**		**218.9**		**16.3**	**225.6**	4
1.4						.6		.8				229.2		5.9	229.2	5
												89.8			89.8	6
												32.2			32.2	7
1.4						.6		.8				99.2			99.2	8
												8.0			8.0	9
.8		*		*		**2.1**		**—1.3**		**3.7**		**—10.4**		**10.4**	**—3.7**	10
78.2		**9.2**		**4.1**		**16.9**		**48.0**		**10.1**		**173.0**			**6.5**	11
	77.4		**9.1**		**4.1**		**14.9**		**49.3**		**6.5**		**183.4**		**10.1**	12
—.1				—.1						—1.0	.3	.3	.3			13
*				*								*	.3	.2		14
	6.6				3.3		3.3					7.7	6.6			15
.4	5.9	*			2.8		3.1					6.4	5.9	—.6		16
	.5				.6		—.1					1.1	.5	—.6		17
	.2				—.1		.3			.2			.2			18
—.1	—3.0							—.1				—3.0	—3.0			19
—.1	—11.0						—11.0	—.1		1.2		—11.0	—11.0			20
*	8.0							*	8.0			8.0	8.0			21
	4.5								4.5			4.5	4.5			22
	14.2								14.2			15.8	15.8			23
.9	.9			*	.4	1.0	.5					.9	.9			24
77.3	31.0	8.9	8.8	4.2		14.9	4.3	49.3	17.9	1.9	3.5	119.2	119.2			25
12.8	5.5						*	12.8	5.6	1.5	.2	10.0	10.0			26
—8.0	9.1	—.4	9.1	4.2		—11.2		—.5		—1.1		5.5	5.5			27
2.4						1.4		1.0				8.5	8.5			28
6.8	1.7					—.4	.1	7.2	1.6	.5	1.2	14.9	14.9			29
15.6	*	3.9				2.6		9.2	*			15.4	15.4			30
9.5		.6				2.3		6.5				11.9	11.9			31
7.5						3.3		4.2				9.3	9.3			32
16.4	2.1					16.4			2.1		—.3	10.4	16.4			33
14.3	12.5	4.8	—.3	*		.5	4.2	9.0	8.6	1.0	2.4	27.2	27.2			34
—3.8	—2.2					—1.2		—2.6	—2.2	—.2	—.2	—4.8	—4.8			35
—1.2	—2.2					—1.2			—2.2	—.2		—2.2	—2.2			36
—2.6						*		—2.6			—.2	—2.6	—2.6			37
	.3				*		.2		.1			1.0	1.1	.1		38
.3								.3		1.0	.4	19.5	12.4	—7.1		39
												—4.8	—4.8			40
3.2	25.1	.3	.5		.4	2.3	17.5	.7	6.9	7.0	2.5	16.6	34.9	18.3		41
1.7						1.0		.6		—3.1		16.3		16.3	8.9	42

* Less than $50 million

dependently as federally sponsored credit agencies, monetary authorities (primarily the Federal Reserve System), commercial banks, and nonbank financial institutions (including state and local government employee retirement funds).[25] The *federally sponsored credit agencies* sector consists of five types of specialized lending institutions that had originally been created by, and are owned, to varying extents, by the federal government. The federal government's equity has been fully retired and they are now excluded from the federal *Budget* as private institutions. These agencies finance their lending activities mainly through issues of their own debt securities. The agencies are: federal home loan banks; Federal National Mortgage Association; federal land banks; federal intermediate credit banks; and banks for cooperatives. This sector was added to the flow of funds accounts for the first time in 1970 and the accounts for previous years revised accordingly. A sector for the *rest of the world* is presented in order to account for financial transactions, both private and government, between the United States and all foreign countries. The last column of the matrix shows *national saving and investment.* The major difference between this statement and the reconciliation of saving and investment in the national income accounts (see Table 11.8) is that the flow of funds accounts treat the acquisition of consumer durables (line 6) as part of *gross investment,* whereas in the national income accounts these acquisitions are part of consumption spending.

The vertical dimension of the matrix shows transaction categories. For each sector, data are presented in terms of uses (U) and sources (S) of funds. For example, households used $11.3 billion in funds to acquire additional deposits in time and savings accounts (line 19) and received $16.0 billion as a source of funds from the sale of mortgages on homes (line 30). For each sector, the difference between total financial uses of funds (line 11) and total financial sources of funds (line 12) is defined as *net financial investment* (line 10). For any one sector, this figure may be either positive or

---

authorities, and trust funds operated by these subdivisions, except employee retirement funds which are treated as a component of the 'private nonbank finance' sector. The basic data for the sector are the aggregates in the *Census of Governments.*

U.S. government includes the agencies and funds that are in the federal government's *Budget,* except the District of Columbia. Included are the Exchange Stabilization Fund, employee retirement funds, and all corporations that are wholly or partly owned by the federal government. Many of these agencies operate lending programs and a few issue their own debt to the public separate from Treasury securities.

[25] Detailed data for several distinct types of nonbank financial institutions (savings and loan associations, mutual savings banks, life insurance companies, private pension plans, state and local government employee retirement funds, other insurance companies, finance companies, security brokers and dealers, and open-end investment companies) are presented in the *Federal Reserve Bulletin,* but they are not reproduced here. Separate statements for farm and noncorporate nonfinancial businesses and corporate nonfinancial businesses (combined in Table 11.10) are also published.

negative; that is, households in 1969 added $20.5 billion more to their financial assets than they added to their liabilities, and nonfinancial businesses added $36.4 billion more to their liabilities than to their financial assets. Within the domestic economy, most additional liabilities (sources of funds) are acquired as financial assets (uses of funds) by other sectors. The balance would be precise (ignoring discrepancies in the data) if no transactions with the rest of the world took place. Net financial investment for all sectors of the economy combined represents, therefore, the balance of financial transactions with the rest of the world. During 1969, the rest-of-the-world sector had a net financial investment of $3.7 billion, meaning that the rest of the world acquired $3.7 billion of the additional financial assets that represent liabilities of the American economy. In the last column of Table 11.10 this figure appears as the net financial investment component of national savings and investment. The figure is conceptually equal to the estimate of net foreign investment in the national income accounts (see Table 11.8) minus the errors and omission item in the balance of payments (see Table 11.15).[26]

Line 27 of Table 11.10 is of particular interest because it shows changes during the year in holdings of United States government securities.[27] Such information is essential in assessing the impact of monetary and fiscal policy, or in analyzing the implications of debt management techniques. The federal government had a surplus in its budget (following the national income accounts concept) during calendar year 1969, most of which appears in the flow of funds matrix as a $7.8 billion component of gross saving (line 1).[28] This saving on the part of the federal government was used to acquire $7 billion of financial assets (line 11) and to reduce its outstanding liabilities by $1.6 billion (line 12). The total outstanding amount of U.S. government securities issued by the federal government (line 27) was reduced by $3.6 billion; since federally sponsored credit agencies issued $9.1 billion of new securities, the net increase in U.S. government securities during 1969 was $5.5 billion as indicated in line 27 of the all sectors column. Households and state and local governments added to their holdings of U.S. government

---

[26] Some flow of funds data may not be identical with their counterparts in other accounts, as these flow of funds data were published prior to publication of the revised national income and balance of payments accounts.

[27] U.S. government securities consist of all Treasury issues, including savings bonds, foreign currency series, and other nonmarketable issues; agency issues by the Tennessee Valley Authority, Export-Import Bank, and Federal Housing Administration and loan participation certificates sold by the Export-Import Bank and Government National Mortgage Association; and issues by federally sponsored credit agencies, a separate financial sector.

[28] For an explanation of the distinction between the surplus concept in the national income accounts and the gross saving concept in the flow of funds accounts see the discussion of Table 11.11.

securities, no doubt in response to the high interest rates that prevailed during 1969, and commercial banks reduced their holdings as they increased bank loans (line 33).

State and local governments increased their indebtedness by $8.5 billion during the year (line 28), and most of these additional securities were acquired by the household and business sectors. Because one of these governments may hold the securities of another, a figure appears in the uses column for state and local governments indicating that the holding of these types of obligations by state and local governments increased by $.1 billion during 1969.

Some other lines in Table 11.10 merit attention. The *gold and official United States foreign exchange* category (line 13) shows changes in the United States government's stock of international reserve assets—gold, convertible currencies, SDRs, and the gold tranche position with the International Monetary Fund—part of which is held by the United States government sector and part by the monetary authorities sector. Decreases in stocks of reserve assets during the year would be represented by negative entries in a sector's uses of funds column, whereas additions would be shown as positive entries. Table 11.10 shows that the United States government had a net increase in its holdings of reserve assets of $1.4 billion during 1969, whereas the monetary authorities decreased their reserve asset holdings by $.1 billion. The sum of these ($1.3 billion) is the total change in United States holdings of official reserve assets during 1969 and is equivalent to the balance of payments entry in Table 11.15, line 46. The rest-of-the-world column in Table 11.10 shows a — $1 billion use of funds as the United States acquired reserve assets from foreigners; this corresponds to the United States gold inflow recorded in Table 11.15, line 47. As the United States government and monetary authorities acquired additional foreign currencies and an increased gold tranche position in the International Monetary Fund, a $.3 billion source of funds was provided to the rest-of-the-world sector; this acquisition of the rest-of-the-world's liabilities provides the United States with additional international reserve assets, and as these reserve assets were acquired the balance of payments debits recorded in Table 11.15, lines 49 and 50, were incurred. The combination of these rest-of-the-world sources and uses of funds, as recorded in Table 11.10, line 13, is the 1969 change in United States holdings of official international reserve assets recorded in the United States government and monetary authorities columns of Table 11.10 and in Table 11.15, line 46.

The transaction category *Treasury currency* (line 14) primarily represents fractional coins. As a source of funds for the United States government, the $.3 billion largely represents the seigniorage on new coins minted during the year. Line 17 shows United States government demand deposits and currency, often referred to as the *Treasury cash balance.* Changes in this balance represent a use of funds for the federal government and a source of funds for the monetary authorities (Federal Reserve System) and commercial bank sectors. New federal lending to other sectors is shown in line 34. Because such lending results in the acquisition of an asset by the federal government, it is listed in the "uses of funds" column for that sector. The total amount of new lending is distributed among the sources columns for most of the other sectors because these are the sectors that borrowed from the federal government. This lending activity is discussed in greater detail in Chapters 12 and 21. *Taxes payable,* line 40, are a use of funds for both the federal and state-local government sectors and a source of funds for the financial and nonfinancial corporations that owe accrued tax liabilities.

Sources and uses of funds by the United States government and state and local governments sectors. Additional information on financial transactions involving governments can be found in the more detailed sector statements published as a part of the flow of funds accounts. For each sector in the flow of funds matrix accounts are prepared giving *sector statements of sources and uses of funds.* Table 11.11 presents these statements for the United States government, state and local governments, and federally sponsored credit agencies. The first group of entries (lines 1–11) for the United States government is a summary statement of expenditures and receipts for the federal sector in the national income accounts (see Table 11.6). *Net surplus* (line 11) is the same as the surplus (or deficit) entry in the national income accounts, and would record negative figures in years when the federal budget, in terms of national income accounts, were in a net deficit position. The concept *gross saving* (line 13) is unique to the flow of funds accounts. For the United States government sector, gross saving is equal to the net surplus minus insurance and retirement credits, that is, credits accrued by the household sector in government life insurance, government employee retirement, and railroad employee retirement programs administered by the federal government (social security is not included in this category). Gross saving for the state and local government sector is similarly defined, where line 2 refers to government employee retirement systems.[29] Gross saving in each of the government sectors would just equal their net financial investment (lines 14 and 4, respectively) were it not for the discrepancies that creep into these data.

The federal government owns financial assets in tax and loan accounts (deposits in commercial banks) and in deposits in the Federal Reserve

[29] The accruals appear as uses of funds for the household sector in the flow of funds matrix (see line 23, Table 11.10).

Table 11.11 Sector Statements of Saving and Investment, 1969 (Billions of dollars)

	Category	Amount
I	U.S. GOVERNMENT	
1	Total receipts, NIA basis	201.5
2	Personal taxes	95.6
3	Corporation profits tax accruals	40.2
4	Indirect taxes	18.8
5	Insurance receipts	46.9
6	Total expenditures, NIA basis	192.0
7	Goods and services	101.9
8	Grants and donations	36.8
9	Net interest	13.1
10	Insurance benefits	40.3
11	Net surplus, NIA basis	9.4
12	Less: Insurance credits to households	1.7
13	Equals: Gross saving	7.8
14	Net financial investment	8.6
15	Net acquisition of financial assets	7.0
16	Demand deposits and currency	1.1
17	Credit market instruments	2.6
18	Special agency securities	—1.3
19	Mortgages	.7
20	Other loans	3.2
21	Excess of tax accruals over receipts	1.0
22	Other financial assets	2.3
23	Net increase in liabilities	—1.6
24	U.S. government securities	—3.6
25	Savings bonds—households	—.4
26	Direct excluding savings bonds	—.9
27	Budget agency securities	—2.4
28	Life and retirement reserves	1.7
29	Other liabilities	.4
30	Discrepancy (13–14)	—.8
II	STATE AND LOCAL GOVERNMENTS—GENERAL FUNDS	
1	Net surplus, NIA basis	—.6
2	Less: Retirement credit to households	5.0
3	Equals: Gross saving	—5.6
4	Net financial investment	—7.5
5	Net acquisition of financial assets	1.9
6	Currency and demand deposits	2.2
7	Time deposits	—7.5
8	Credit market instruments	7.2
9	U.S. government securities	4.2
10	Direct	2.0
11	U.S. government agency securities	2.2
12	State and local securities	.1
13	Corporate bonds	2.8

***Table 11.11* (continued)**

		Category	Amount
		Net financial investment (continued)	
	14	Home mortgages	.2
	15	Tax receivables	——
	16	Net increase in liabilities	9.4
	17	Credit market borrowing	8.9
	18	State and local obligations	8.5
	19	Short term	4.1
	20	Other	4.4
	21	U.S. government loans	.4
	22	Trade debt	.5
	23	Discrepancy (7–8)	1.9
III		STATE AND LOCAL GOVERNMENT EMPLOYEE RETIREMENT FUNDS	
	1	Net acquisition of financial assets	5.0
	2	Demand deposits and currency	—.1
	3	Credit market instruments	5.0
	4	U.S. government securities	—.1
	5	Direct	—.3
	6	U.S. government agency securities	.2
	7	State and local obligations	—.1
	8	Other credit market instruments	5.2
	9	Corporate bonds	3.0
	10	Corporate stock	1.8
	11	Mortgages	.4
	12	Other	.1
IV		FEDERALLY SPONSORED CREDIT AGENCIES	
	1	Current surplus	.1
	2	Net increase in assets	9.2
	3	Credit market instruments	8.9
	4	U.S. government securities	—.4
	5	Residential mortgages	3.9
	6	Farm mortgages	.6
	7	Other loans	4.8
	8	To cooperatives	.2
	9	To farmers	.6
	10	To savings and loans	4.0
	11	Net increase in liabilities	9.1
	12	Credit market instruments	8.8
	13	Agency securities	9.1
	14	U.S. government loans	—.3
	15	Miscellaneous liabilities	.4

SOURCE: *Federal Reserve Bulletin*, May 1970.

System.[30] An increase in this Treasury cash balance would represent a net acquisition of financial assets. During 1969 an increase was registered in the *demand deposits and currency* category (line 16) that mainly reflected an increase in the Treasury cash balance (line 17, Table 11.10). Of more significance is the acquisition of credit market instruments by the federal government (lines 17–20). These assets of the federal government are liabilities of the private sectors: mortgages and other loans acquired as a consequence of various federal credit programs. The category *other financial assets* (line 22) refers mainly to nonconvertible foreign currencies and the official foreign exchange position of the Treasury.

The net increase in federal government liabilities (line 23) largely takes the form of additional United States government securities outstanding and held outside the federal government (see line 27, Table 11.10). The *budget agency securities* listed here comprise nonguaranteed agency issues and loan participations. Primary examples of the former are the securities sold by the Government National Mortgage Association and the Federal Housing Authority. The latter, loan participations, are issued by the Export-Import Bank and the Government National Mortgage Association as trustees for five federal departments and agencies; blocks of direct loans by the agencies to the private sector are pooled, and certificates of participation (loan participations) in these pools are sold to private investors.

The *net acquisition of assets* by state and local governments (lines 5–15) primarily reflects investing short-term working capital and the reserves of enterprises and trust funds other than public employee retirement systems. Working capital is kept in the form of demand deposits held in accounts with commercial banks, interest-bearing time deposits in commercial banks, and short-term United States government securities. The withdrawal of $7.5 billion from time deposits (line 7) shows the shift of funds to other types of assets yielding higher interest returns. State and local government employee retirement systems are shown as a separate sector in Table 11.11. Their reserves are invested in United States government securities, state and local government obligations, and other assets. Unlike the reserves of social insurance programs administered by the federal government, all of which

---

[30] Households and businesses pay their federal taxes and purchase United States government securities by writing checks against their demand deposits in commercial banks. When these checks are presented to those banks for payment, household or business demand deposits are reduced and the United States government's tax and loan account is increased. As the Treasury shifts deposits from tax and loan accounts to the Federal Reserve System, commercial bank reserves are reduced. Treasury payments to the public in the form of checks drawn on Federal Reserve Banks increase commercial bank reserves as these checks are deposited. The use of tax and loan accounts prevents public payment to the Treasury from having a disruptive effect on the commercial banking system.

are invested in United States government securities or federal agency issues, reserves of state and local government employee retirement systems are in part invested in private securities (lines 9–11).

The primary element in the *net increase in the liabilities* of state and local governments (lines 16–22) is the net expansion in the amount of state and local government bonds outstanding (line 20).[31] Short-term borrowing by state and local governments primarily takes the form of tax anticipation loans from commercial banks, which are subsequently redeemed out of future tax collections (line 19). The expansion in short-term debts outstanding was particularly large in 1969, reflecting the unwillingness or inability of many state and local governments to sell long-term securities during a period of high interest rates. Like households and corporations, state and local governments may purchase goods on credit; the figure reported as the net increase in *trade debt* (line 22) is associated with such purchases.

Funds raised and advanced in U.S. credit markets. Table 11.12 summarizes the flow of funds through the credit markets, indicating the extent of intermediation in those markets. Financial institutions are often referred to as intermediaries between savers, who supply funds to the credit markets, and investors, who raise funds in those markets. These institutions, which collectively form the financial sectors of the flow of funds accounts, are supplied funds by the private nonfinancial sectors mainly in the form of deposits (Part III, lines 3–5) and contributions to insurance and pension reserves (Part III, line 17). New deposits were unusually small in 1969 ($1.4 billion) because of restrictive monetary policy and because suppliers of funds sought new holdings of credit market instruments carrying high yields; new deposits equaled $44.3 billion in 1968. The private nonfinancial sectors also supply funds directly to the credit markets by acquiring additional holdings of credit market instruments (Part III, lines 8–11 or Part II, lines 15–19). In some cases the credit market instruments thus acquired are sold out of the portfolios of financial institutions. This was particularly the case in 1969 with respect to U.S. government securities (Part III, line 9); the private nonfinancial sectors supplied $15.8 billion as they purchased U.S. government securities, only a part of which (see Table 11.10, line 27) were newly issued. Part II of Table 11.12 shows, in lines 6–13, the financial sector advancing funds, and Part I shows the funds raised by the private nonfinancial sectors by type (lines 5–20) and by sector (lines 22–25). The federal government raises funds (Part I, lines

---

[31] These securities are often collectively referred to as *municipal bonds.* There are two basic types of municipal bonds, both of which are included here: *general obligation bonds* are liabilities backed by the taxing power of the issuing government; *revenue bonds* are backed by the revenue-generating capacity of a particular government enterprise, such as a toll road.

Table 11.12 **Summary of Funds Raised and Advanced in U.S. Credit Markets, 1969 (Billions of dollars)**

		Transaction Category, or Sector	Amount
I		FUNDS RAISED, BY TYPE AND SECTOR	
	1	Total funds raised by nonfinancial sectors	88.2
	2	U.S. government	—3.6
	3	Public debt securities	—1.3
	4	Budget agency issues	—2.4
	5	All other nonfinancial sectors	91.9
	6	Capital market instruments	53.6
	7	Corporate equity shares	4.5
	8	Debt capital instruments	49.1
	9	State and local government securities	8.5
	10	Corporate and foreign bonds	13.3
	11	Mortgages	27.4
	16	Other private credit	38.3
	17	Bank loans not elsewhere classified	14.2
	18	Consumer credit	9.3
	19	Open market paper	3.3
	20	Other	11.3
	21	Borrowing sector	91.9
	22	Foreign	3.5
	23	State and local governments	8.9
	24	Households	31.4
	25	Nonfinancial business	48.1
II		FUNDS ADVANCED DIRECTLY IN CREDIT MARKETS	
	1	Total funds raised	88.2
		Advanced directly by	
	2	U.S. government	2.6
	3	Federally sponsored credit agencies (net)	.1
	4	Funds advanced	8.9
	5	Less funds raised in credit market	8.8
	6	Federal Reserve System	4.2
	7	Commercial banks (net)	9.4

2–4) and acts as a financial intermediary (Part II, line 2). Federally sponsored credit agencies are also financial intermediaries that both raise funds in the credit markets through the sale of securities and advance funds by making loans or by buying private securities (Part II, lines 3–5).

Principal financial transactions. The focus of Table 11.13 is on the principal types of financial transactions: net increases in demand deposits and currency holdings, net increases in time and savings accounts, net issues and acquisitions of United States government securities, net issues and purchases of other securities, net lending and acquisition of mortgages, and net

***Table 11.12* (continued)**

	Transaction Category, or Sector	Amount
10	Private nonbank finance	31.0
11	Savings institutions (net)	10.3
12	Insurance	22.3
13	Finance, not elsewhere classified (net)	—1.6
14	Foreign	2.0
15	Private domestic nonfinancial	38.9
16	Business	11.4
17	State and local governments	7.2
18	Households	18.7
19	Less net security credit	—1.6
III	SOURCES OF FUNDS SUPPLIED TO CREDIT MARKETS	
1	Total borrowing by nonfinancial sectors	88.2
	Supplied directly and indirectly by private domestic nonfinancial sectors	
2	Total	40.3
3	Deposits	1.4
4	Demand deposits and currency	5.5
5	Time and savings accounts	—4.1
8	Credit market instruments (net)	38.9
9	U.S. government securities	15.8
10	Private credit market instruments	21.5
11	Less security debt	—1.6
	Other sources	
12	Foreign funds	10.4
15	Change in U.S. government cash balance	.4
16	U.S. government loans	2.6
17	Private insurance and pension reserves	18.7
18	Sources not elsewhere classified	15.8

SOURCE: *Federal Reserve Bulletin*, May 1970. The original numbering of transaction categories has been maintained though some categories have been omitted.

borrowing through bank loans not elsewhere classified. Federal government deposits (Part I, line 2) increased over the year; state and local government holdings of banking system liabilities (line 7) also increased. The federal government does not hold time or savings accounts, but state and local governments do and, on a net basis, they decreased their holdings (Part II, line 4) during the year. The change in United States government securities outstanding, by type of security, is given in Part III, lines 2–6.

Information concerning the net acquisition of United States government securities is essential in analyzing problems in monetary policy and debt management. This information is provided in Part III, lines 7–23. The net

Table 11.13 Principal Financial Transactions, 1969 (Billions of dollars)

		Transaction Category, or Sector	Amount
I		DEMAND DEPOSITS AND CURRENCY	
	1	Net increase in banking system liability	6.6
	2	U.S. government deposits	.5
	3	Money supply	6.1
	4	Domestic sectors	5.9
	(7)	State and local governments	2.2
	10	Rest of the world	.2
II		TIME AND SAVINGS ACCOUNTS	
	1	Net increase—Total	—3.0
	2	At commercial banks—Total	—11.0
	(4)	State and local governments	—7.5
	7	At savings institutions	8.0
III		U.S. GOVERNMENT SECURITIES	
	1	Total net issues	5.5
	2	Household savings bonds	—.4
	3	Direct excluding savings bonds	—.9
	4	Budget agency issues	—.4
	5	Sponsored agency issues	9.1
	6	Loan participations	—1.9
	7	Net acquisitions, by sector	5.5
	8	U.S. government (agency securities)	—1.3
	9	Sponsored credit agencies	—.4
	12	Federal Reserve System	4.2
	13	Foreign	—1.1
	14	Commercial banks	—11.2
	15	Direct	—9.4
	16	Agency issues	—1.8
	17	Nonbank finance	—.5
	18	Direct	—2.3
	19	Agency issues	1.8
	20	Private domestic nonfinancial	15.8
	21	Savings bonds—Households	—.4
	22	Direct excluding savings bonds	8.1
	23	Agency issues	8.1
IV		PRIVATE SECURITIES	
	1	Total net issues, by sector	27.9
	(2)	State and local governments	8.5
	7	Net purchases	27.9
	(10)	State and local governments	2.9
V		BANK LOANS, NOT ELSEWHERE CLASSIFIED	
	1	Total net borrowing	16.4

( ) indicates detail.

SOURCE: *Federal Reserve Bulletin,* May 1970. The original numbering of transaction categories has been maintained though some categories have been omitted.

acquisition of United States government securities by each sector is indicated, and some detail as to types of securities is given. For example, Federal Reserve System holdings of United States government securities, of all types, increased by $4.2 billion (line 12) during the year. Note that only households make net acquisitions of savings bonds (line 21), as the law limits the holding of these nonmarketable securities to households. The net acquisition of United States government securities is negative for some sectors, either for all of these securities or for some types. This occurs when holdings are reduced as some outstanding United States government securities are sold by one sector to another, or when a sector fails to buy new United States government securities as maturing issues are redeemed. State and local governments issue a part (Part IV, line 2) of the total net issue of private securities. State and local governments also make net purchases (line 10) of private securities.

Financial assets and liabilities. The final type of statement found in the flow of funds accounts is presented here as Table 11.14, where balance sheet entries are reported. For each sector (the same sectors that form the horizontal dimension of Table 11.10) estimates for total financial assets and liabilities as of the end of 1969 are shown. Because only financial assets and liabilities are recorded, it is not necessary that the total of these assets equal the total of these liabilities for each sector. The net acquisition of assets and liabilities for the federal government and state and local government sectors recorded in Table 11.11 were added to the balance sheet figures for the end of 1968 to derive the estimates given in Table 11.14 for these two government sectors. For both sectors, total financial liabilities exceed total financial assets, though in neither case is the aggregate value of financial assets insignificant. As is to be expected, the household sector holds far more financial assets than liabilities.

Several of the transactions categories in Table 11.14 are of particular interest. The nation's gold stock (line 3) is treated in the flow of funds as an asset of the monetary authorities; the stock held by the rest-of-the-world sector is defined as all gold held for monetary purposes in other countries. The distribution of ownership of United States government securities is shown by line 20. The total amount of these securities outstanding as of the end of 1969 is $317.6 billion; of this amount $30.6 billion is a liability of the federally sponsored credit agencies and the rest is a liability of the federal government. This listing is on a net basis; the amounts held in federal trust accounts have been deducted. Of the total, $22.9 billion was held by state and local governments and $57.2 billion was held by the monetary authorities (Federal Reserve System). Note that $11.4 billion was held abroad. The distribution of the ownership of state and local government obligations is shown in line 21. None of these securities were held by

Table 11.14 Financial Assets and Liabilities, December 31, 1969 (Billions of dollars)

	Sector / Category	Private Domestic Nonfinancial Sectors								United States Government	
		Households		Business		State and Local Governments		Total			
		A	L	A	L	A	L	A	L	A	L
1	Total financial assets	1807.9		421.3		64.0		2293.3		98.8	
2	Total liabilities		460.7		673.5		142.2		1276.4		331.8
3	Gold									1.5	
4	Official foreign exchange									.8	
5	IMF position									2.4	
6	Treasury currency										5.3
7	Demand deposits and currency										
8	Private domestic	114.7		47.2		12.2		174.1			
9	U.S. government									7.7	
10	Foreign										
11	Time and savings accounts	370.9						399.6			
12	At commercial banks	155.4		17.0		11.6		184.1		.3	
13	At savings institutions	215.5						215.5			
14	Life insurance reserves	124.7						124.7			7.3
15	Pension fund reserves	210.8						210.8			25.2
16	Interbank claims										
17	Credit market instruments	960.5	439.6	71.0	445.4	37.9	136.6	1069.4	1021.6	53.8	288.6
18	Corporate stock	749.3						749.3			
19	Debt instruments									.1	287.0
20	U.S. government securities	105.0		13.0		22.9		140.9			
21	State and local government securities	41.1		6.3		2.2	132.2	49.7	132.2		
22	Corporate and foreign bonds	25.4			147.6	10.3		35.7	147.6		
23	Home mortgages	12.6	260.4		2.5	2.5		15.1	262.8	6.1	1.6
24	Other mortgages	27.1	18.9		139.0			27.1	157.9	3.0	
25	Consumer credit		122.5	28.5				28.5	122.5		
26	Bank loans NEC		19.6		113.7				133.3		
27	Other loans		18.2	23.2	42.6		4.4	23.2	65.2	44.5	
28	Security credit	2.6	12.0					2.6	12.0		
29	To brokers and dealers	2.6						2.6			
30	To others		12.0						12.0		
31	Taxes payable				21.2	2.3		2.3	21.2	20.9	
32	Trade credit		4.5	198.2	126.0		5.7	198.2	136.2	7.3	4.8
33	Miscellaneous	23.7	4.7	88.0	80.8			111.7	85.4	4.1	.6

SOURCE: Board of Governors of the Federal Reserve System.

Financial Sectors										Rest of the World		Total		
Total		Federally Sponsored Credit Agencies		Monetary Authority		Commercial Banks		Private Nonbank Finance						
A	L	A	L	A	L	A	L	A	L	A	L	A	L	
1338.1		36.1		80.0		456.8		765.2		112.1		3842.2		1
	1252.2		35.2		80.0		427.5		709.6		131.0		2991.4	2
10.4				10.4						29.2		41.0		3
2.0				2.0							2.8		2.8	4
—.1				—.1							2.3		2.3	5
6.8				6.8								6.8	5.3	6
	221.5				48.9		172.7					202.2	221.5	7
15.5	209.7	.2			46.5		163.1	15.3				189.6	209.7	8
	6.9				2.0		5.0					7.7	6.9	9
	4.9				.4		4.6			4.9			4.9	10
.8	409.0							.8					409.0	11
.1	192.8						192.8	.1		8.4			192.8	12
.8	216.3							.8	216.3				216.3	13
	117.4								117.4				124.7	14
	185.5								185.5				210.8	15
33.7	33.7			3.6	29.4	30.0	4.2					33.7	33.7	16
1209.0	151.2	35.4	30.6	57.2		403.8	6.5	712.5	114.0	34.8	49.2	2367.0	1510.5	17
136.9	48.3							136.9	48.3	18.6		904.7	48.3	18
														19
165.2	30.6	2.3	30.6	57.2		64.3		41.4		11.4			317.6	20
82.5						60.2		22.3					132.2	21
146.4	22.7					1.5	2.3	144.9	20.3	1.2	13.0		183.3	22
245.6	2.5	11.0				41.1		193.5	2.5				266.9	23
127.8		6.8				29.2		91.9					157.9	24
94.0						48.2		45.8					122.5	25
152.9	13.1	15.3				152.9			13.1		6.5		152.9	26
57.6	34.1			.1		6.4	4.2	35.8	29.8	3.7	29.7		129.0	27
19.6	10.4					10.6		9.0	10.4	.4	.3		22.7	28
7.4	10.4					6.5		.9	10.4	.4			10.4	29
12.3						4.1		8.2			.3		12.3	30
	2.0				.2		.8		1.1			23.2	23.2	31
3.8								3.8		3.7	5.6	212.9	146.5	32
36.6	121.4	.5	1.1		1.5	12.3	50.5	23.7	64.8	30.7	70.8	183.0	278.3	33

the federal government or the monetary authorities; only a small part, $2.2 billion, of the $132.2 billion total was held within the state and local government sector. The total amount of outstanding federal loans to state and local governments is shown as $4.4 billion (line 27).

The flow of funds data that we have described are valuable to the student of public policy. Acquisition of financial assets and issuance of liabilities by governments have a profound impact on capital markets and financial institutions. If, for example, the federal government issues a large volume of new securities to finance a deficit, it makes a difference in terms of the financial impact on the rest of the economy whether those securities are acquired by households, commercial banks, or the Federal Reserve System. Textbooks in the area of monetary economics treat this matter in all its theoretical detail; the flow of funds accounts provide the basic data. If one is interested in credit conditions in the mortgage markets, one can tell from the flow of funds accounts how significant federal lending programs are as a source of funds for this purpose. These are the types of economic issues where a knowledge of the public sector in the flow of funds accounts is helpful. We turn now to a more detailed description of how public sector activity affects America's balance of payments with the rest of the world.

THE PUBLIC SECTOR IN THE BALANCE OF PAYMENTS ACCOUNT

Households, businesses, and governments are parties to international transactions. A *balance of payments account* is a systematic recording of all of these transactions with other nations. The public sector appears in the American balance of payments account because the United States government makes expenditures abroad and receives payments from abroad. In addition, there are international transactions in United States government securities, some of which are initiated by the government itself.

The American balance of payments account for 1969 is given in Table 11.15.[32] Balance of payments *credits* arise when a nation receives an international payment; *debits* are incurred when a nation makes an international payment. The sum of the credits recorded in Table 11.15 equals the sum of

[32] The American balance of payments account is compiled and reported quarterly by the Department of Commerce in the March, June, September, and December issues of the *Survey of Current Business*. It is also reported, with a slightly different format, in the *Federal Reserve Bulletin*.

Throughout this section, when United States is an adjective it refers to the United States (federal) government, and when United States is a noun it refers to the entire American economy, public and private. To minimize confusion, we always refer to American balance of payments and not United States balance of payments.

the debits; the sum of the credits recorded in lines 1–62 exceeds the sum of the debits by $2924 million, and the accounting equality of credits and debits is obtained by adding line 63, *errors and omissions,* of minus this amount. The presentation in Table 11.15 is merely a recording of transactions categories (defined to encompass all international transactions) and does not include any entry that is designated as a balance of payments surplus or deficit. Striking such a balance requires interpretation of these transactions and their classification into two categories. The sum of the transactions in the first category, including errors and omissions in the American account, is the balance of payments surplus or deficit. The second category comprises transactions that are interpreted as settling, or financing, this surplus or deficit. It is important to emphasize that no data other than those contained in Table 11.15 are included in American accounts showing balance of payments surpluses or deficits; deficits and surpluses are merely interpretations of these data. As the following discussion points out, Americans are uncertain about their interpretation of these data, and two accounting concepts of the balance of payments surplus or deficit are thus reported.[33]

The balance of payments surplus or deficit measured on a *liquidity* basis is the concept preferred by Walther Lederer, Chief of the Balance of Payments Division, Office of Business Economics, United States Department of Commerce. The Department of Commerce is the United States government agency officially responsible for collecting, compiling, and reporting the balance of payments statistics. This measure of the American balance of payments shows a deficit of $7221 million in 1969 and is reported, along with the items interpreted as settling this deficit, in the upper portion of

---

[33] This book was in press when, in June 1971, the Department of Commerce introduced several new measures of surpluses and deficits into the official American balance of payments reports. Because of changing circumstances in the international commercial and financial communities at the start of the 1970s, the usefulness of the liquidity measure of the balance of payments was questioned; although still published, this balance of payments measure has been relegated to a minor position in the official reports. However, the accounting issues raised in this book continue to pertain to the interpretation of balance of payments data. For a full discussion of the new balance of payments concepts and tabulation of their surpluses and deficits during the 1960s *see* David T. Devlin, "The U.S. Balance of Payments Revised Presentation," *Survey of Current Business,* June 1971. For discussion of the changing environment within which analysts devised these new concepts *see* Gottfried Haberler and Thomas D. Willett, *A Strategy for U.S. Balance of Payments Policy* (Washington, D.C.: American Enterprise Institute, 1971); Ronald I. McKinnon, *Private and Official International Money: The Case for the Dollar* (Princeton, N.J.: International Finance Section, Department of Economics, Princeton University, 1969); and Laurence B. Krause, "A Passive Balance of Payments Strategy for the United States," *Brookings Papers on Economic Activity,* No. 3, 1970.

Table 11.15 **U.S. International Transactions, 1969[1] (Millions of dollars)**

	(Credits +; debits —)	
1	Exports of goods and services	56,273
2	Excluding transfers under military grants	55,514
3	Merchandise, adjusted, excluding military	36,473
4	Transfers under military sales contracts	1,515
5	Transfers under military grants, net	759
6	Transportation	3,131
7	Travel	2,058
8	Fees and royalties from direct investments	1,369
9	Other private services	1,753
10	Other U.S. government services	376
	Income on U.S. investments abroad:	
11	Direct investments	5,639
12	Other private assets	2,267
13	U.S. government assets	932
14	Imports of goods and services	—53,564
15	Merchandise, adjusted, excluding military	—35,835
16	Military expenditures	—4,850
17	Transportation	—3,608
18	Travel	—3,390
19	Private payments for other services	—709
20	U.S. government payments for other services	—710
	Income on foreign investments in the United States:	
21	Private payments	—3,686
22	U.S. government payments	—777
23	Balance on goods and services (lines 1 and 14)	2,709
24	Excluding transfers under military grants (lines 2 and 14)	1,949
25	Unilateral transfers, net; transfers to foreigners (—)	—3,594
26	Excluding military grants	—2,834
27	Private remittances	—784
28	Military grants of goods and services	—759
29	Other U.S. government grants	—1,644
30	U.S. government pensions and other transfers	—406
31	Balance on goods, services, and unilateral transfers (lines 23 and 25, or 24 and 26)	—885
32	Transactions in U.S. private assets (net); increase in assets (—)	—5,374
33	Direct investments	—3,070
34	Foreign securities newly issued in the United States	—1,667
35	Redemptions	478
36	Other transactions in foreign securities	—305
	Claims reported by U.S. banks:	
37	Long-term	330
38	Short-term	—871

Table 11.15 **(continued)**

	(Credits +; debits −)	
	Claims reported by U.S. residents other than banks:	
39	Long-term	—424
40	Short-term	155
41	Transactions in U.S. government assets, excluding official reserve assets (net); increase in assets (—)	—2,184
42	Loans and other long-term assets	—3,477
43	Foreign currencies and other assets	89
	Repayments on credits:	
44	Scheduled	1,291
45	Nonscheduled (including sales of foreign obligations to foreigners)	—87
46	Transactions in U.S. official reserve assets (net); increase in assets (—)	—1,187
47	Gold	—967
48	SDR	—
50	Convertible currencies	814
50	Gold tranche position in IMF	—1,034
51	Transactions in foreign assets in the United States (net); increase in foreign assets (U.S. liabilities) (+)	12,554
52	Direct investments	832
53	U.S. securities other than Treasury issues	3,112
54	Long-term liabilities reported by U.S. banks	—676
	Other liabilities reported by U.S. private residents other than banks	
55	Long-term	642
56	Short-term	140
	Nonmarketable liabilities of U.S. government, including medium-term securities and long-term obligations payable prior to maturity only under special conditions:	
57	Associated with specific transactions	138
58	Other medium-term securities and long-term obligations	—41
59	U.S. Treasury marketable or convertible bonds and notes	—167
60	Deposits and money market paper held in the United States	8,575
61	Balance on transactions in U.S. and foreign liquid and non-liquid assets, including reserves (lines 32, 41, 46, and 51)	3,809
62	Allocation of special drawing rights (SDR)	—
63	Errors and omissions, net	—2,924

[1] Line 48 appeared in the U.S. Balance of Payments account for the first time in June 1970. SDRs were first distributed on January 7, 1970, and from that time constitute a fourth type of international reserve asset. No SDRs are shown for 1969.

SOURCE: *Survey of Current Business*, June 1970, pp. 34–35.

Table 11.16. The second concept of the American balance of payments surplus or deficit is measured on the basis of *official transactions* and is the concept recommended by the Bernstein Committee in its 1965 report.[34] The official settlements accounting concept records an American surplus of $2708 million for 1969 and is reported, along with the transactions that are interpreted as settling this surplus, in the lower portion of Table 11.16. Before turning to an analysis of public sector transactions in the balance of payments account, we digress to consider these two interpretations of balance of payments surpluses and deficits.[35]

Measuring surpluses and deficits. Examination of Table 11.16 reveals that both the liquidity and the official settlements concepts of the balance of payments record transactions in government owned reserve assets (Table 11.15, line 46) as settlement items (Table 11.16, lines 5 and 19). Transactions in reserve assets, including gold, are traditionally regarded as a means of settling balance of payments surpluses or deficits. Other settlement transactions are at the heart of disagreements regarding measurements of American balance of payments surpluses and deficits, and are responsible for the differences between the liquidity and the official settlements measures.

The transactions recorded in Table 11.15, lines 59 and 60, are together designated as *liquid liabilities to all foreigners* in Table 11.16, line 10. These liquid liabilities to all foreigners, plus transactions in reserve assets, constitute the settlement items under the liquidity concept of the balance of payments account. Transactions in *United States Treasury marketable or convertible bonds and notes* (Table 11.15, line 59) record a balance of payments debit for 1969. This debit means that, during 1969, foreigners decreased their holdings of marketable and convertible bonds and notes issued by the United States Treasury; as foreigners were paid for these securities a debit was recorded in the American balance of payments. The transactions

---

[34] *The Balance of Payments Statistics of the United States: Review and Appraisal*, Report of the Review Committee for the Balance of Payments Statistics to the Bureau of the Budget (Washington, D.C.: Government Printing Office, 1965). This committee is known as the Bernstein Committee, after its chairman, Edward M. Bernstein, and the report is hereafter referred to as the Bernstein Report. Chapter 4 of the Bernstein Report discusses government transactions in the balance of payments account. *See also* Joint Economic Committee, 89th Congress, 1st session, *The Balance of Payments Statistics*, Parts 1, 2, and 3 (Washington, D.C.: Government Printing Office, 1965). *Special Analyses: Budget of the United States, Fiscal Year 1968* (Washington, D.C.: Government Printing Office, 1967) contains an analysis entitled "International Transactions of the Federal Government."

[35] For a discussion of the distinction between the liquidity and official settlements concepts of the American balance of payments, *see* the Bernstein Report, especially chapter 9, and Richard Cooper, "The Balance of Payments in Review," *Journal of Political Economy*, August 1966.

Table 11.16 U.S. Balance of Payments, 1969*
(Millions of dollars)

4	Balance on liquidity basis measured by increase in U.S. official reserve assets and decrease in liquid liabilities to all foreigners; decrease in net assets (—) (lines 5 and 10, with sign reversed)	—7,221
5	U.S. official reserve assets (Table 11.15, line 46); increase (—)	—1,187
6	Gold	—967
7	SDR	—
8	Convertible currencies	814
9	IMF gold tranche position	—1,034
10	Liquid liabilities to all foreigners (Table 11.15, lines 59 and 60); decrease (—)	8,408
11	To official agencies	—525
12	To commercial banks	9,434
13	To other foreign residents and unallocated	—441
14	To international and regional organizations	—60
18	Balance on official reserve transactions basis—measured by increase in all U.S. official reserve assets and decrease in liquid and certain nonliquid liabilities to foreign official agencies (lines 19 through 21, with sign reversed)	2,708
19	U.S. official reserve assets (line 5); increase (—)	—1,187
20	Liquid liabilities to foreign official agencies (portion of line 11) decrease (—)	—525
21	Certain nonliquid liabilities to foreign official agencies; decrease (—)	—996
22	Liabilities reported by U.S. private residents (Table 11.15, portion of line 54)	—834
23	Liabilities reported by U.S. government (Table 11.15, portions of lines 57 and 58)	—162

* This presentation is identical with that in the *Survey of Current Business,* except that lines 1, 2, 3, 15, 16, and 17 have been omitted. These lines dealt with seasonal adjustments or quarterly data and are not relevant to this presentation, which contains only annual data.

SOURCE: *Survey of Current Business,* June 1970, pp. 42–43.

recorded as *deposits and money market paper held in the United States* (Table 11.15, line 60) arose when foreigners increased their demand and time deposits in American banks (bank liabilities to foreigners), or when foreigners increased their holdings of short-term financial liabilities of Americans (money market paper), including short-term United States government securities. As foreigners increased their holdings of these short-term American liabilities, they made payments that were recorded as American balance of payments credits. The total of these two types of transactions, giving a 1969 balance of payments credit equal to $8408 million, is the

Table 11.17 U.S. Liquid Liabilities to Foreigners (Millions of dollars)

		Total During 1969	Amounts Outstanding March 31, 1970
1	Liquid liabilities to all foreigners (Table 11.15, lines 59 and 60; Table 11.16, lines 10 through 14)	8,408	43,233
2	To foreign official agencies	—525	15,747
3	Central banks and governments	—514	14,737
4	Demand deposits	—231	1,445
5	Time deposits	1,044	3,400
6	Other private obligations, mainly money market paper	818	2,892
	U.S. government obligations		
7	Short-term securities and other obligations	—1,903	6,191
8	Payable in U.S. dollars	—1,642	5,989
9	Payable in foreign currencies	—261	202
10	Bonds and notes, marketable	—79	380
11	Bonds and notes, nonmarketable, convertible	—163	429
12	Payable in U.S. dollars	—25	—
13	Payable in foreign currencies	—138	429
14	International Monetary Fund	—11	1,010
15	To foreign commercial banks	9,434	22,369
	(To foreign branches of U.S. banks)	(7,172)	(12,153)
16	Demand deposits	6,631	15,105
17	Time deposits	723	1,962
18	Other private obligations, mainly money market paper	2,090	5,281
19	U.S. government short-term securities	—10	21
20	To other foreign residents and unallocated	—441	4,301
21	Demand deposits	—88	1,766
22	Time deposits	—388	1,610
23	Other private obligations, mainly money market paper	—50	361
	U.S. government obligations		
24	Short-term securities	21	88
25	Bonds and notes	64	476
26	To international and regional organizations not included above	—60	816
27	Demand deposits	—10	81
28	Time deposits	—30	136
29	Other private obligations, mainly money market paper	119	219
	U.S. government obligations		
30	Short-term securities	—150	330
31	Bonds and notes	11	50

SOURCE: *Survey of Current Business,* June 1970, p. 52.

settlement item shown in Table 11.16, line 10. It is also given in the left-hand column of Table 11.17 along with a listing of the types of transactions that were involved. The transactions recorded in Table 11.17, line 2, show that foreign official agencies decreased their holdings of short-term United States government securities, money market paper, and deposits in American banks by $525 million during 1969. The entries in lines 15, 20, and 26, Table 11.17, sum to $8933 million; this is the amount by which foreign commercial banks, private citizens, and businesses and international organizations (excluding the International Monetary Fund) increased their holdings of these American liabilities. Bank deposits, short-term United States government securities, and similar assets are highly liquid in the sense that they may quickly be converted to cash without much likelihood of capital loss. Under existing institutional arrangements, foreign banks, citizens, and international organizations could convert their assets in the United States to a foreign currency by selling these American liabilities to a foreign central bank or government that could, in turn, present them as payment for American reserve assets. Thus, liquid liabilities to all foreigners (Table 11.16, line 10) represent foreign claims against the United States that could readily be presented for payment in American gold and other reserve assets; the Department of Commerce believes that all such items should be interpreted as transactions settling the surplus or deficit. The ability of the United States government to protect the dollar in the sense of maintaining a stable exchange rate for the dollar relative to other currencies rests upon its holding reserves (an asset that is an international acceptable means of payment) that may be utilized to buy dollars when there is downward pressure on the foreign exchange rate. Although these liquid liabilities to foreigners are not being offered for sale, to depress the price of the dollar on the international exchanges, they could be, and the Department of Commerce sees them as a claim against American reserve assets; the Department of Commerce records them as a settlement item in the American balance of payments. Over the course of many years, foreigners have accumulated balances in American banks and holdings of other American liquid liabilities. The accumulated total of these balances, as of December 31, 1969, is shown in the right-hand column of Table 11.17. This total shows that, at the end of 1969, foreigners held over $43 billion of liquid American liabilities, and that approximately $16 billion of these were held by foreign central banks, governments, and the International Monetary Fund (line 2).

The Bernstein Committee argued that this accounting of surpluses and deficits was faulty. Americans as well as foreigners could precipitate a run on the dollar by making deposits in foreign banks or by making purchases of foreign liabilities. These American payments to foreigners (balance of payments debits) could come easily into the hands of foreign official institutions and hence be presented for redemption in American reserve assets. Thus, simply looking at liquid liabilities to foreigners does not adequately reflect the strength or weakness of the dollar. Many of these liabilities to foreigners are held privately because they represent a secure, income-earning asset or because, in the case of bank balances, they are regularly used for making international payments. Much of the world's international trade is paid for with dollars (the dollar is a "vehicle currency") and dollar balances are thus held by foreign banks, firms, and individuals to finance their international commerce. The right-hand column of Table 11.17 shows that at the end of 1969, foreign commercial banks and individuals had noninterest-bearing demand deposits of $16.9 billion in American banks (lines 16 and 21) and time deposits of nearly $4 billion (lines 17 and 22). Private foreigners voluntarily acquire and hold these American liabilities, and it is not clear that transactions in them should be interpreted as settling balance of payments surpluses and deficits.[36]

The official settlements measure of balance of payments surpluses and deficits interprets transactions in reserve assets and *all* American liabilities to foreign official monetary institutions as settlement items. Transactions by private foreigners in American liquid liabilities are included in the surplus or deficit to be financed; transactions in short-term United States liabilities by foreign official institutions are interpreted as financing the surplus or deficit and are recorded in Table 11.16, line 20, and in Table 11.17, lines 2–14. In addition, certain nonliquid United States liabilities held by foreign monetary institutions are included in the official settlements balance as settlement transactions, they are recorded in Table 11.16, lines 21–23, and are parts of the transactions recorded in Table 11.15, lines 54, 57, and 58. The Bernstein Committee's rationale for this inclusion was that all assets held abroad by monetary authorities are international reserves, and transactions in reserve assets are typically treated as financing imbalances. Those transactions recorded in Table 11.16, line 22, are part of the transactions recorded in Table 11.15, line 54; they indicate that foreign official institutions decreased their holding of long-term, nonliquid American liabilities by $834 million during 1969. As this American liability to foreign official institutions was reduced,

---

36 Discussion of the private sector demand for an international means of payment may be found in Richard N. Cooper, *The Economics of Interdependence* (New York: McGraw-Hill, 1968), and H. Robert Heller, "The Transactions Demand for International Means of Payment," *Journal of Political Economy*, January-February 1968. The discussion in the text becomes even more clouded when the eurodollar market is considered. A eurodollar is created when a non-American bank accepts deposits denominated in dollars and then makes dollar loans. Dollar time deposits are accepted in some foreign commercial banks that then make dollar loans; such loans are loans of eurodollars. Ultimately, many eurodollars are owned by foreign official institutions that make placements in the eurodollar market to reap the high interest rates available there. Thus, some of the demand deposits reported in Table 11.17, line 16, are owned by foreign official institutions.

a balance of payments debit was incurred. The transactions recorded in Table 11.16, line 23, are taken from Table 11.15, lines 57 and 58; they show that foreign official institutions decreased their holding of nonmarketable (and thus nonliquid) United States government liabilities by $162 million during 1969 giving rise to an American balance of payments debit.[37]

These two concepts of balance of payments surpluses and deficits do not exhaust the possibilities. Whatever the concept being employed, it reflects an interpretation of the available data recording the nation's international transactions; making this interpretation is difficult and is as much an art as it is a science.[38] With this discussion of balance of payments surpluses and deficits as background, we now turn to a consideration of the measurement of the public sector in the American balance of payments account. A nation's balance of payments account is often analyzed in terms of current account, capital account, and settlement item debits and credits, and the following discussion is so divided. The *current account* records transactions for goods, services, and unilateral transfers; the *capital account* records transactions in financial assets. Balance of payments surpluses and deficits are measured in terms of the balance of credits and debits on the current and capital accounts. When the sum of the current and capital account credits is greater than the sum of the debits, the nation is said to have a balance of payments surplus, and, conversely, when the sum of the debits exceeds the sum of the credits, the nation is said to have a deficit. Transactions interpreted as settling balance of payments accounts then finance this surplus or deficit. In the analysis that follows we discuss balance of payments settlement items utilizing the liquidity concept. This is done because we do not then have to divide the discussion of any line items in Table 11.15; this expediency should not be interpreted as a judgment regarding the preferred accounting concept.

Current account. The United States government gives rise to several

---

[37] The principal component of this transaction is the United States government's acquisition, from foreign official institutions, of Export-Import Bank certificates of participation and special United States government securities issued on a negotiated basis in previous years. These latter securities, payable either in dollars or foreign currencies, had been issued to foreign monetary authorities in lieu of their making purchases of American reserve assets. They were made payable in convertible foreign currencies to guarantee the foreign government against capital loss in the event the United States were to devalue the dollar prior to their maturity date. For details on Table 11.16, line 23, see *Survey of Current Business*, June 1970, Table 5, lines B-11, B-14, B-16, C-2, and C-4.

[38] Charles P. Kindleberger, *International Economics,* 4th ed. (Homewood, Ill.: Richard D. Irwin, Inc., 1968), chapter 24, has a discussion of additional techniques. *See also* "Measuring Equilibrium in the Balance of Payments," *Journal of Political Economy*, November-December 1969.

current account credit items in the balance of payments. *Transfers under military sales contracts* (line 4) are American earnings because the Department of Defense exports goods and services. Here the United States government exports goods that it previously purchased from the private sector of the American economy.[39] *Transfers under military grants* (line 5) are credits that result from the export of military goods by the Department of Defense, which also grants the buyer the funds with which to make the purchase (recorded as the debit item in line 28). *Other U.S. government services* (line 10) are sales of goods and services to foreigners by federal agencies other than the Department of Defense. Finally, the United States government, like the private sector, receives current income on its outstanding foreign investments. This credit is recorded in the balance of payments account as *Income on U.S. investments abroad: U.S. government assets* (line 13).

The United States government also makes current account payments for goods and services that are debit items in the American balance of payments. Since World War II substantial numbers of American troops have been stationed abroad.[40] These troops spend part of their earnings off base, and the maintenance and provision of foreign military bases require some direct United States government expenditures abroad. These official and nonofficial expenditures are balance of payments debits that are classified as *military expenditures* (line 16) in the balance of payments account. The military base itself is treated as an extension of the American economy abroad and servicemen's on-base expenditures and supplies provided directly from the United States do not enter the balance of payments account. *U.S.*

---

[39] Line 4 does not include private-sector sale of military goods for export; such exports are included in *merchandise exports, excluding military* (line 3). Whether or not a transaction is classified as military in the balance of payments account depends on who is a party to the transaction: Whenever the Department of Defense is a party to the transaction (not including licensing), the transaction is military (including some transactions of the Atomic Energy Commission), and whenever the Department of Defense is not a party to the transaction (although it may license the transaction), the transaction is nonmilitary, even if, for example, the transaction is between an American armaments producer and the Canadian Department of National Defense. This distinction also pertains to the discussion of line 15.

Line 24 (*balance on goods and services*) is identical with net exports of goods and services in Table 11.1. Department of Defense purchases that are subsequently sold abroad (and enter the national income accounts as a component of net exports of goods and services) are not included as part of government purchases of goods and services in Table 11.1. This is because receipts from the sale of government property are treated as proprietary receipts from the public in the federal budget and are offset against expenditures, as explained in the discussion of Table 12.1. This accounting practice avoids double counting such transactions in the national income accounts.

[40] In 1968 the United States government had 1,171,000 servicemen stationed abroad and 211,424 civilian employees overseas; *The Statistical Abstract of the United States, 1969* (Washington, D.C.: Government Printing Office, 1969), pp. 256, 399.

government payments for other services (line 20) are the civilian equivalent of military expenditures, but also include some direct United States government imports of foreign goods. United States government and state-local government domestic purchases of imported goods that were imported by the private sector are not separately enumerated in the balance of payments account, but are included in *merchandise, adjusted, excluding military* (line 15). Finally, part of the United States government's debt is owned by foreigners, and current interest payments on foreign-owned securities are the debit item *income on foreign investments in the United States: U.S. government payments* (line 22).

Two types of transfer payments abroad are made by the United States government. The first of these—*military grants of goods and services* (line 28) and *other U.S. government grants* (line 29)—is foreign aid payments where there is no obligation for repayment (making these a current account rather than a capital account transaction). Such transfers are a debit item in the American balance of payments account: They lead to a balance of payments credit if the transferred funds are used by their recipient to buy American exports.[41] Military grants lead directly to Department of Defense exports (line 5); private sector exports that are financed with nonmilitary foreign aid are recorded in the balance of payments account as a *merchandise export* (line 3). The United States government also makes transfers to persons living abroad, such as social security payments or pensions for former government employees; these transfers are the debit item *U.S. government pensions and other transfers* (line 30).[42]

Capital account. Some United States government transactions involve financial assets. When the United States government makes an international loan it acquires an asset in the form of the borrowing nation's promise to repay; this is recorded as a debit in the American balance of payments account as the borrower receives a current payment.[43] *Loans and other long-*

---

[41] Increasingly in the 1960s the United States government required that foreign aid grants be expended in the United States. *See*, for example, *Special Analyses: Budget of the United States, Fiscal Year 1968* (Washington, D.C.: Government Printing Office, 1967), Special Analysis M. It is estimated (*Survey of Current Business*, June 1970, Table 5, lines A26–A34) that of the $5032 million in United States government nonmilitary international grants and loans (Table 11.15, lines 29, 42, 43) in 1969, $4286 billion was spent in the United States.

[42] Line 31—*balance on goods, services, and unilateral transfers*—is identical with *net foreign investment* in the national income accounts (see Table 11.8). On the basis of current transactions completed in 1969, Americans acquired claims on foreigners (debits) that exceeded foreign acquisitions of claims on Americans (credits) by $885 million. On balance this means that as a result of current account transactions, foreigners were indebted to Americans by $885 million.

[43] When a foreign loan is made, the borrower is obligated to repay, and the borrower's

term assets (line 42) in the American balance of payments account records United States government net lending. When the United States government spends previously acquired foreign currencies (nonconvertible), a balance of payments credit is recorded as assets are liquidated. Such asset liquidation is recorded in line 43 of the 1969 balance of payments account.[44] Subsequent repayment of loans constitutes a credit in the American balance of payments account and is recorded as *repayments on credits: scheduled and non-scheduled* (lines 44 and 45). Scheduled repayments occur when loans are repaid as specified at the time the loan was made; nonscheduled repayments occur when the loan is repaid at some other time. A decrease in (export of) United States government assets gives rise to a payment by foreigners that is a credit in the American balance of payments account (line 44). The current interest payments on outstanding United States government loans are the balance of payments credit previously discussed in connection with line 13.

Many foreigners own assets in the United States. Whenever there is a decrease in foreign asset holdings in the United States, this gives rise to an international transaction that is an American balance of payments debit. Conversely, when foreigners acquire assets from Americans, their payment is an American balance of payments credit. These foreign-owned assets may be in a variety of forms, including liabilities of the United States government. Some of these transactions in United States government liabilities are recorded as capital accounts transactions in lines 57 and 58.[45] Line 57 shows that there was a net increase in United States government liabilities to foreigners associated with specific transactions. These specific transactions

---

promise to repay (liability) is held (imported) by the lender as an asset. But as the lender acquires this asset, he makes a current payment that is a debit. When the loan is repaid, the transaction is reversed: As the borrower liquidates his obligation to repay, the lender surrenders (exports) an asset as he receives payment that is a credit. Thus, when the lender increases his asset holdings he incurs a debit, and when the lender decreases his asset holdings he receives a credit.

[44] Additional detail on these transactions may be obtained from *Survey of Current Business*, June 1970, Table 5. Most of the assets recorded in line 43 are nonconvertible foreign currencies and arise from agricultural exports under PL480. *Special Analyses: Budget of the United States, Fiscal Year 1970* (Washington, D.C.: Government Printing Office, 1969), Special Analysis H, "Foreign Currency Availabilities and Uses." This article discusses United States Government holdings of, and transactions in, foreign currencies.

[45] Additional detail on the types of transactions included in lines 57 and 58 may be found in *Survey of Current Business*, June 1970, Table 5, parts B and C. These items were discussed earlier in connection with the official settlements measure of balance of payments surpluses and deficits. It is noted that line 53, *U.S. securities other than the Treasury issues*, records securities issued in the United States by other than the United States government and that are owned by foreigners; line 53 could include state and local government securities.

are primarily related to military sales contracts. The net balance of payments credit arose in 1969 because payments by foreign governments exceeded deliveries of goods and services; the excess of payments over deliveries constitutes an increase in American liabilities. Line 58 indicates that there was a decrease in United States government liabilities to foreigners in certain nonmarketable securities that gave rise to a debit in the American balance of payments as the United States government reduced this liability.[46]

Settlement items. Table 11.16 shows that the United States had a balance of payments deficit, measured on a liquidity basis, of $7221 million in 1969. Balance of payments accounting on a liquidity basis records transactions in marketable United States government securities (liabilities of the United States government) as a settlement item. Line 59, *U.S. government marketable or convertible bonds and notes,* shows that during 1969 foreigners decreased their holdings of United States government securities (decreased their asset holdings in the United States), giving rise to a debit in the American balance of payments. These international transactions in United States government securities by and large do not directly involve the United States government as a participant in the transaction but, because the ownership of securities is a factor in managing the national debt and because interest paid on securities held by foreigners enters the balance of payments account as a United States government payment (line 22), this item is important in a study of the public sector.[47] Additional United States government securities—Treasury bills—are traded internationally; they are part of the money market paper whose international transactions are recorded in line 60. Finally, the United States government, like other national governments, owns reserve assets that are acceptable as settlement items of last resort in bringing a nation's international payments into balance. In 1969 these assets were monetary gold, convertible foreign currencies, and the nation's gold tranche position with the International Monetary Fund (lines 47, 49, and 50). Thus, in 1969 the United States government bought (imported)

---

[46] These nonmarketable securities are issued by the Treasury on a negotiated basis and by the Export-Import Bank. They are not associated with any specific transaction in goods and services.

[47] In the 1960s, international transactions in United States government securities did sometimes directly involve United States government participation as, in order to protect the United States stock of monetary gold, foreign governments and central banks with excess accumulation of dollars were officially asked to purchase United States government securities rather than gold. In some cases special nonmarketable securities denominated in a foreign currency were issued. These are Roosa bonds, named after former Undersecretary of the Treasury Robert Roosa, who was responsible for their creation. Transactions in them are recorded in line 58.

some monetary gold from foreign governments, resulting in a $967 million debit in the American balance of payments. At the same time, the United States government decreased its holdings of convertible foreign currencies giving rise to a $814 million balance of payments credit. Finally, as the United States increased its gold tranche position with the International Monetary Fund a $1034 million balance of payments debit was incurred.

Conclusion. The preceding discussion shows that the United States government participates in many types of international transactions that affect the American balance of payments. All the current and capital account United States government transactions involved direct participation of the United States government, with the exception of the part of military expenditures (line 16) and U.S. government payments for other services (line 20), that are the estimated expenditures abroad of American servicemen and United States government civilian employees. Summing these United States government current and capital account entries for 1969 gives credits of $5100 million and debits of $12,751 million. Some of these debit items, notably military grants and other tied foreign aid and development loans, lead directly to merchandise exports. Because the United States government enters into international transactions that may significantly affect the American balance of payments, the formulation of public revenue and expenditure policy at the national level may be important to achieving balance of payments equilibrium.[48] This balance of payments impact of the United States government is quite aside from the impact of tariffs, taxes on international capital flows (such as the interest equalization tax), and regulatory public economic policies (such as quotas and voluntary limitations on direct foreign investment), which may also have a significant balance of payments impact by directly affecting the level of private capital flows and merchandise trade.

This discussion of the United States government in the balance of payments account has not attempted to relate these United States government international transactions to specific sources of revenue or types of outlays as they appear in *The Budget of the United States Government.* Yet this relationship clearly exists. Any international transaction in which the United States government directly participates is recorded in the *Budget,* although specifically identifying these relationships is usually difficult.

[48] *See* Leonard Dudley and Peter Passell, "The War in Vietnam and the United States Balance of Payments," *Review of Economics and Statistics*, November 1968; and the testimony of Passell and Assistant Secretary of Defense Robert C. Moot before the Joint Economic Subcommittee on International Exchange and Payments (Washington, D.C.: Government Printing Office, January 1969), for a discussion of the direct and indirect impact of military spending for Vietnam on the United States balance of payments.

THE PUBLIC SECTOR IN INPUT-OUTPUT TABLES

Since World War II, input-output analysis has developed as an additional means of national economic accounting.[49] Before we examine the public sector as it appears in the 1963 input-output table, a brief introduction to the technique of input-output analysis seems appropriate.

The basic elements of input-output analysis. Input-output analysis divides the national economy into industries and sectors of final demand. Each industry produces an output that may be distributed to other industries and itself as an input, and to the sectors of final demand. A simple, hypothetical, input-output table for a single year is shown in Table 11.18 for an

Table 11.18 **Input-Output Table with Household and Public Sector Final Demand (Dollars)**

From \ To	A	M	Households	Public Sector	Total
A	100	200	500	200	1000
M	400	400	1000	200	2000
Labor (Households)	500	1400	0	100	2000
Total	1000	2000	1500	500	

economy where there has been no investment (and thus no capital is used as a factor of production) or foreign trade, and where, therefore, households and government are the only final demand sectors. Two industries are designated: industry A (agriculture) and industry M (manufacturing). Labor is the economy's only income earning input, and thus all value added—gross

[49] Input-output analysis was pioneered by Wassily Leontief. For an introduction to the literature on this subject, *see* his *The Structure of the American Economy, 1919–1939* (New York: Oxford University Press, 1953); *Studies in the Structure of the American Economy* (New York: Oxford University Press, 1953); and *Input-Output Economics* (New York: Oxford University Press, 1966). For a somewhat less technical discussion of input-output analysis, *see* the following four articles by Leontief in *The Scientific American*, "Input-Output Economics," October 1951; "The Economic Effects of Disarmament," April 1961; "The Structure of Development," September 1963; and "The Structure of the U.S. Economy," April 1965. For additional discussion, *see* Hollis B. Chenery and Paul G. Clark, *Interindustry Economics* (New York: John Wiley & Sons, 1959); Robert Dorfman, Paul Samuelson, and Robert Solow, *Linear Programming and Economic Analysis* (New York: McGraw-Hill, 1958), chapters 9 and 10; and Chiou-Shuang Yan, *Introduction to Input-Output Economics* (New York: Holt, Rinehart and Winston, 1969).

national product—is due to the sale of labor services by households to industries A and M and to the public sector.[50] All the economy's gross national product is absorbed by households and the public sector.

The entries in the first row of Table 11.18 show that industry A utilized \$100 of its output itself (seed-corn for example); \$200 of its output went to industry M; \$500 of its output went to households; and \$200 of its output went to the public sector. Industry M delivered \$400 of its output to industry A; utilized \$400 of its output itself (for example, manufactured steel used in automobile production); and sold \$1000 of its output to households and \$200 to the public sector. Thus, the gross output of industries A and M, \$1000 and \$2000, respectively, was used as an input in one of these industries, or was purchased by one of the final demand sectors. Finally, labor is shown as having sold \$500 of labor services to A producers, \$1400 to M producers, and \$100 to the public sector. The total value of labor services sold (\$2000) is equivalent to value added in the economy and equals gross national product.

The column entries in Table 11.18 show the inputs to each industry and the product composition of demand in each of the final demand sectors. Thus, industry A acquired \$100 of A inputs from itself, \$400 of M inputs from M, and \$500 of labor inputs from households. Industry M utilized \$200 of A inputs, \$400 of M inputs, and \$1400 of labor services. The value of the inputs to industries A and M, \$1000 and \$2000, respectively, is equal to the total value of the output produced in each of the two industries: The value of an industry's inputs must equal the value of that industry's output. Finally, households purchased \$500 of A goods and \$1000 of M goods, while the public sector absorbed \$200 of A and M goods and used \$100 of labor services to produce \$100 of public services. The sum of the values utilized by households and the public sector (\$1500 and \$500 respectively) is \$2000, and is equal to total value added or gross national product.[51] Because the public sector absorbed \$500 of the gross national product, households must have paid \$500 in taxes from their \$2000 income if the public sector's budget was balanced.

Input-output tables have value beyond that of mere description of interindustry relationships. During the period for which Table 11.18 was

---

[50] Households could also sell labor services to other households; an example of such a transaction might be the service of a babysitter or a maid. This type of transaction is deliberately omitted from Table 11.18 to illustrate the fact that there is no need for all spaces in the input-output table to be filled with positive entries.

[51] This input-output table illustrates the distinction between the gross output of an industry and that industry's contribution to gross national product. In industry A, for example, gross industry output (\$1000) is partially used as an intermediate product (\$300) and is partially used in the final demand sectors where it is counted as part of gross national product (\$700).

compiled, \$100 of A as an input was used to produce \$1000 of A as an output. This means that, on the average, \$0.10 worth of A was used as an input to produce each \$1 of A as an output. Similarly, \$0.40 worth of M and \$0.50 worth of labor was required for each \$1 of A produced. Summing these input requirements shows that \$1 of inputs from three sources was required to produce \$1 of output. Using this procedure, a table of input-output coefficients was compiled and is shown in Table 11.19. Table 11.19 was derived by dividing each entry in a column of inputs in Table 11.18 by the corresponding row (output) total. *Input-output coefficients* give the average input requirements per dollar of output for each of the economy's products.

Table 11.19 **Input-Output Coefficients (Dollars/Dollars)**

From \ To	A	M
A	.10	.10
M	.40	.20
Labor	.50	.70
Total	1.00	1.00

If it is assumed that these input-output coefficients remain constant from one period to the next, a powerful tool is available that may be used for a detailed analysis of the economy under a variety of final demand conditions.[52] The total demand for any product is the sum of the demands for that product in its various uses. Products A and M each have four possible uses: as an input in the two industries and in the two final-demand sectors. The total demand for product A may thus be written as

$$A = .1A + .1M + D_{HA} + D_{GA} \qquad [11.1]$$

where the variables A and M denote gross output of the industries A and M, and the independent variable D denotes dollars of final demand. The first subscript attached to D designates the sector—households, H, or government, G—making the final demand, and the second subscript specifies which product is demanded; D_{HA} is household final demand for product A. Equation (11.1) states that for each dollar's worth of A produced, \$0.10 of A is demanded as an input for that output; for each dollar's worth of M produced, \$0.10 of A is demanded as an input; and for each dollar's worth

[52] The constancy of the input-output coefficients is debated. See the sources cited in note 49 for a discussion of this problem. Analysis may also be based on projected changes in the coefficients.

of A delivered to households or government, \$1.00 of A is demanded. Similarly, total demand for product M may be written as

$$M = .4A + .2M + D_{HM} + D_{GM} \qquad [11.2]$$

Collecting the A terms in Equation (11.1) and the M terms in Equation (11.2) and solving (11.1) and A and (11.2) for M gives

$$A = .111M + 1.11D_{HA} + 1.11D_{GA} \qquad [11.3]$$

$$M = .5A + 1.25D_{HM} + 1.25D_{GM} \qquad [11.4]$$

Now, if we suppose that household and government demands are set autonomously, Equations (11.3) and (11.4) have two unknown dependent variables—A and M—and may be solved simultaneously to give the gross output requirements of sectors A and M as a function of the final demands of households and government; thus

$$A = .147D_{HM} + .147D_{GM} + 1.175D_{HA} + 1.175D_{GA} \qquad [11.5]$$

$$M = 1.323D_{HM} + 1.323D_{GM} + .588D_{HA} + .588D_{GA} \qquad [11.6]$$

The coefficients on the independent variables in Equations (11.5) and (11.6) have the following meanings: In order to support the delivery of one dollar of product M to final demand by either households or government, \$.147 of A and \$1.323 of M must be produced; in order to support the delivery of one dollar of product A to final demand, \$1.175 of A and \$.588 of M must be produced.

Analytically, equations like (11.5) and (11.6) have great potential. Suppose the public sector decided to increase its expenditures on M goods by \$1000. The interindustry structure of this economy suggests that in response to this increase in public sector demand the output of the A industry would have to increase by \$147 and the output of the M industry would have to increase by \$1323. If sufficient unutilized capacity existed in these industries, this increase in public sector demand could be met without cutting back demand elsewhere in the economy. But if capacity limits did not permit these increases in output, the public sector would either have to cut back on some of its other expenditures, increase taxes in order to reduce household demand, or introduce rationing in order to limit total demand to the levels dictated by the productive capacity of the economy.[53] Input-output analysis not only

[53] This analysis may be carried a step further to consider the constraint imposed on this economy by a finite labor force. The total demand for labor is the sum of the demand for labor in industries A and M and in the production of public goods and services by the public sector. The labor input-output coefficients in Table 11.19 indicate that

serves as a type of national economic accounting, but also has analytical value in planning public economic policy.

The 1963 input-output table. Empirical input-output tables have been constructed for the American economy. Unlike the other national economic accounts discussed in this chapter, input-output tables are not available quarterly, or even annually. Because of the data problems involved in specifying interindustry product flows, construction of these tables has been possible for only those years in which there was a *Census of Manufactures.* Table 11.20 gives portions of the United States input-output table for 1963.[54] The industries that make large sales to the public sector are listed in Table

---

per dollar of A produced, \$.50 of labor is required as an input, and per dollar of M produced, \$.70 of labor is required as an input. Public sector output is valued at factor cost. Thus, the total value of labor demanded in this economy is given by

$$L = .5A + .7M + D_{GL} \qquad [11.7]$$

where D_{GL} is the value of gross national product produced in the public sector. Substituting Equations (11.5) and (11.6) into Equation (11.7) and collecting the final demand terms give labor demand as

$$L = D_{HM} + D_{GM} + D_{HA} + D_{GA} + D_{GL} \qquad [11.8]$$

The unitary coefficients on the independent variables in Equation (11.8) indicate that in order to support the delivery of \$1.00 worth of either product to final demand, or the production of \$1.00 worth of goods and services by the public sector, \$1.00 worth of labor is required as an input. In this simple system such a result is expected because all value added is added by labor, and value added is identically equal to gross national product, all of which is delivered to final demand. Thus, if there is an increase in government demand for M goods equal to \$1000, there must be people willing to furnish \$1000 of additional labor services; if this labor is not forthcoming, cutbacks will have to be made somewhere in the economy.

[54] *See* "Input-Output Structure of the U.S. Economy: 1963," *Survey of Current Business*, November 1969, pp. 16–47. This input-output table designates 87 different industries and 6 final demand sectors. The actual specification of industries is at the discretion of the input-output accountant but is done in a way that places all the economy's economic activity into some category of industrial activity. For the concepts and conventions adopted in the 1963 study, *see* Office of Business Economics, *Input-Output Structure of the U.S. Economy: 1963*, Vols. I, II, and III, United States Department of Commerce (Washington, D.C.: Government Printing Office, 1969). These volumes contain a set of disaggregated input-output tables specifying the relationships among 367 industries and 10 final demand sectors. Input-output tables are also available for 1919, 1929, and 1939 in Leontief, *The Structure of the American Economy, 1919–1939, op. cit.*; for 1947, in W. Duane Evans and Marvin Hoffenburg, "The Interindustry Relations Study for 1947," *Review of Economics and Statistics*, May 1952; and for 1958, in "The Transactions Table for the 1958 Input-Output Study and Revised Direct and Total Requirements Data," *Survey of Current Business*, September 1965.

Table 11.20 Selected Interindustry Transactions, 1963 (Millions of dollars)

	FROM \ TO	Personal Consumption Expenditure (1)	Gross Private Fixed Capital Formation (2)	Net Inventory Change (3)	Net Exports (4)	Federal Government Purchases (5)
11	New construction	—	46,151	—	2	4,010
12	Maintenance and repair construction	—	—	—	—	1,414
13	Ordnance and accessories	181	—	–26	197	5,300
14	Food and kindred products	49,921	—	583	1,648	317
26	Printing and publishing	3,160	—	109	163	117
27	Chemicals and selected chemical products	394	—	88	1,160	1,036
31	Petroleum refining and related industries	8,232	—	177	678	711
51	Office, computing, and accounting machines	88	1,615	41	317	448
53	Electric industrial equipment and apparatus	22	1,862	23	343	423
56	Radio, TV, and communication equipment	2,089	1,924	151	366	4,686
59	Motor vehicles and equipment	15,381	5,671	611	1,386	663
60	Aircraft and parts	49	446	342	857	7,532
61	Other transportation equipment	980	1,465	46	165	1,124
62	Scientific and controlling instruments	403	673	56	373	405
65	Transportation and warehousing	8,946	574	152	3,040	1,320
66	Communications; except radio and TV broadcasting	5,542	485	—	43	341
68	Electric, gas, water, and sanitary services	11,358	—	—	30	264
69	Wholesale and retail trade	80,791	4,858	325	1,735	728
71	Real estate and rental	53,878	1,224	—	397	162
72	Hotels; personal and repair services except automobiles	12,074	—	—	4	361
73	Business services	2,967	—	—	199	1,981
77	Medical, educational services, and nonprofit organizations	29,335	—	—	32	1,416
78	Federal government enterprises	888	—	—	90	115
79	State and local government enterprises	638	—	—	—	198
80A	Directly allocated imports	6,004	166	21	–12,320	2,649
84	Government industry	—	—	—	—	24,449
	Total (all inputs)	375,540	80,510	5,329	5,812	64,115

Table 11.20 (continued)

State-Local Government Purchases (6)	Total Final Demand 1–6 (7)	Gross Industry Output (8)	Federal Government Purchases: Defense (9)	Federal Government Purchases: Other (10)	State and Local Government Purchases: Education (11)	State and Local Government Purchases: Health Welfare and Sanitation (12)	State and Local Government Purchases: Safety (13)	State and Local Government Purchases: Other (14)	
15,356	65,519	65,519	1,776	2,234	3,068	1,419	147	10,182	[11]
3,510	4,924	19,794	943	471	736	184	37	2,553	[12]
2	5,654	6,302	4,070	1,229	—	—	2	—	[13]
488	52,957	74,263	167	149	96	221	96	75	[14]
450	3,999	16,283	197	−80	297	29	3	121	[26]
206	2,885	16,893	965	71	24	100	14	68	[27]
301	10,100	21,837	660	52	147	46	42	66	[31]
111	2,619	3,925	331	117	81	7	1	22	[51]
61	2,733	6,495	375	448	11	3	—	45	[53]
116	9,332	12,440	4,290	396	29	65	8	13	[56]
644	24,357	40,031	615	48	37	110	356	356	[59]
−1	9,226	14,317	6,773	760	—	—	—	—	[60]
30	3,811	4,894	985	139	—	—	16	14	[61]
118	2,028	4,280	316	89	34	77	2	5	[62]
682	14,715	39,215	1,168	152	332	98	43	209	[65]
344	6,755	13,495	301	40	59	62	32	192	[66]
860	12,513	29,660	368	−105	581	22	28	229	[68]
114	88,551	120,613	603	125	−179	137	46	111	[69]
478	56,140	83,887	75	87	47	55	2	375	[71]
163	12,603	15,370	267	94	−126	67	44	178	[72]
962	6,108	35,945	1,609	371	204	138	83	537	[73]
723	31,506	33,160	848	567	−10	647	18	67	[77]
182	1,276	5,864	93	21	21	59	8	95	[78]
21	858	7,236	12	186	12	3	2	3	[79]
3	−3,477	—	1,945	704	—	—	—	3	[80A]
30,581	55,029	55,029	18,501	5,947	17,421	4,253	3,573	5,332	[84]
59,082	590,839								[Total]

SOURCE: *Survey of Current Business*, November 1969, pp. 34–35, and *Input-Output Structure of the U.S. Economy: 1963*, Vol. I, Transactions Data for Detailed Industries: A Supplement to the *Survey of Current Business, 1969*, United States Department of Commerce, Office of Business Economics (Washington, Government Printing Office, 1969).

Table 11.21 **Total Requirements, 1963, from Selected Industries Per Dollar of Delivery to Final Demand in Industries 11, 13, 56, 60 (Dollars/Dollars)**

FROM \ TO		New Construction 11	Ordnance and Accessories 13	Radio, TV, and Communications Equipment 56	Aircraft and Parts 60
11	New construction	1.00000	—	—	—
13	Ordnance and accessories	.00053	1.03253	.01036	.01868
20	Lumber and wood products, except containers	.08342	.00789	.00798	.00437
27	Chemicals and selected chemical products	.02278	.01817	.01922	.01654
31	Petroleum refineries and related industries	.03160	.01073	.00995	.01176
32	Rubber and miscellaneous plastic products	.01539	.02589	.01911	.01459
36	Stone and clay products	.10439	.00412	.00437	.00716
37	Primary iron and steel manufacturing	.09410	.06616	.04011	.06801
38	Primary nonferrous metals	.05693	.09180	.06188	.09819
40	Heating, plumbing, and structural metal products	.09825	.00335	.00178	.00218
41	Stamping, screw machine products, and bolts	.00755	.01696	.02973	.02298
42	Other fabricated metal products	.02856	.01949	.02716	.02730
47	Metalworking machinery and equipment	.00367	.01681	.01449	.03440
50	Machine shop products	.00244	.02136	.00608	.05714
56	Radio, TV, and communications equipment	.00283	.07090	1.08689	.06157
57	Electronic components and accessories	.00168	.03478	.18301	.02318
60	Aircraft and parts	.00182	.36639	.02194	1.19862
62	Scientific and controlling instruments	.00546	.01524	.00872	.02296
65	Transportation and warehousing	.07079	.03132	.03081	.03439
68	Electric, gas, water, and sanitary services	.02585	.02132	.01922	.02309
69	Wholesale and retail trade	.11590	.04632	.06138	.04905
70	Finance and insurance	.02074	.01481	.01350	.01396
71	Real estate and rental	.03018	.02121	.02737	.02101
73	Business services	.07255	.04482	.04942	.04647
78	Federal government enterprises	.00491	.00524	.00524	.00847
79	State and local government enterprises	.00672	.00428	.00409	.00463
80	Gross imports of goods and services	.03107	.02694	.04018	.02810
81	Business travel, entertainment, and gifts	.01482	.01890	.01966	.02077

SOURCE: *Survey of Current Business*, November 1969, Table 3, pp. 42–47.

11.20 along with the six sectors of final demand and gross industry output.[55] In addition there is a disaggregation, in columns 9–14, of final demand from the federal and state-local government sectors. This latter detail, available for the first time in the 1963 tables, indicates the impacts that different types of government spending have on the rest of the economy. Negative figures in these columns indicate sectors where government was a net seller of goods. For example, the federal government sold $80 million of printing and publishing, more than it purchased for nondefense purposes, primarily through the Government Printing Office (column 10, row 26). State and local governments were net suppliers of hotel-type educational services as they rented dormitory rooms to students at state and municipal universities (column 11, row 72).

Total final demand shown in Table 11.20, column 7—$591 billion—is identically equal to 1963 gross national product; input-output tables are constructed to achieve this result. Combined state-local and federal government absorption of gross national product in 1963 was $123 billion (column 5 plus column 6). The public sector appears three times as product-originating industries. Industries 78 and 79 are government enterprises and are identical with the public enterprises discussed earlier in this chapter. Gross output of the public enterprises is substantially larger than their deliveries to final demand, indicating that the majority of their output is absorbed as an intermediate product. Examination of the column for industry 68—electric, gas, water and sanitary services—in the full input-output tables shows that this industry received inputs valued at $3841 million from the state-local government enterprises. This is primarily because publicly owned utilities sell some of their output to private distributors for sale to consumers. The federal government's public enterprise exports are primarily earnings from operation of the Panama Canal. Industry 84 is the compensation of public employees, all of which is absorbed by the federal and state-local governments as a component of final demand. Table 11.20 illustrates that a substantial part of government purchases of goods and services is through direct public production, which appears in the national economic accounts as the compensation of public employees. Further examination of Table 11.20 reveals that construction (rows 11 and 12) and the products of defense and aerospace related industries (rows 13, 56, and 60) are the major types of public sector purchases from the private sector.

Coefficients showing the direct and indirect input requirement from certain industries needed to support one dollar of delivery to four types of final demand are given in Table 11.21.[56] These coefficients are equivalent to

---

[55] The criterion used in making this selection was that the industry made combined sales to the federal and state-local governments in excess of $500 million. The public enterprises, industries 78 and 79, are also included.

[56] Except for industries 78 and 79—government enterprises—production industries listed

the coefficients on the independent final demand variables in Equations (11.5) and (11.6). The four final demand industries were chosen because they are industries from which the public sector makes substantial purchases. Table 11.21 suggests that if the public sector were to change its purchases from private industry, the impact on any one industry would vary depending on the type of public sector demand that is changed. For example, a $1 billion increase in construction spending (industry 11) would increase total demand for the output of industry 38—primary nonferrous metals—by $56.9 million; a $1 billion increase in demand, if spent on ordnance (industry 13), would increase total demand for the output of industry 38 by $91.8 million; if $1 billion were spent on radio, television, and communications equipment (industry 56), total demand for the output of industry 38 would increase by $61.9 million; if $1 billion were instead spent on aircraft and parts (industry 60), total demand for the output of industry 38 would increase by $98.2 million. Industry 38 is not listed in Table 11.20 because the public sector does not make substantial direct purchases from this industry. But because primary nonferrous metals are an input to products demanded by the public sector, public sector activity has an important effect on the level of demand for primary nonferrous metals. Knowledge of these relationships can be helpful in the planning of public economic policy.

---

in Table 11.21 were selected because for at least one of the four final demand products the direct and indirect input requirement per dollar of final demand was greater than $.02.

12

THE BUDGET OF THE UNITED STATES GOVERNMENT

Fiscal records of the federal government exist as far back as 1789.[1] Receipt and expenditure estimates have been set forth in a single budget document for the coming fiscal year only since the 1920s, as provided for in the Budget and Accounting Act of 1921. The Budget Act, among other provisions, created the Bureau of the Budget as an executive agency directly responsible to the President.[2] The duties of the

[1] Bureau of the Census, *Historical Statistics of the United States* (Washington, D.C.: Government Printing Office, 1960), p. 711.

[2] Arthur Smithies, *The Budgetary Process in the United States*, Committee for Economic Development Research Study (New York: McGraw-Hill, 1955), chapters 3 and 4, gives a history of the budgetary process; *see also* Charles G. Dawes, *The First Year of the Budget of the United States* (New York: Harper & Row, Publishers, 1923) for the first Budget Director's account of the initial work of the Bureau of the Budget.

A fiscal year runs from July 1 of the previous year to June 30 of the designated year. Federal government finances were switched from a calendar year basis to a fiscal year basis in 1843. Since budget data are reported in fiscal rather than calendar years, reconciliation of data in this chapter with that taken from national economic accounts in Chapter 11 is difficult.

Bureau of the Budget were assumed by the newly created Office of Management and Budget when President Nixon reorganized the Executive Branch in the spring of 1970. Prior to the 1920s, individual revenue measures and numerous appropriation bills were considered separately by a large variety of Congressional committees. After the completion of each fiscal year, statements of receipts and expenditures were drawn up by the Treasury Department in accordance with the Constitutional dictate that "a regular Statement and Account of the Receipts and Expenditures of all public Money shall be published from time to time" (Article 1, section 8). Since the presentation of the first budget for the fiscal year 1923, the format and conceptual framework of the budget have been changed only a few times. A major change in both format and conceptual framework was made with the presentation of the federal budget for fiscal year 1969. This chapter is devoted to an exposition of the conceptual framework of *The Budget of the United States Government, Fiscal Year 1971* and an interpretation of the data that it contains.[3] The task is important because many discussions of federal government activity are buttressed with these data rather than with data from national economic accounts.

THE BUDGET

A one-page summary statement taken from the 1971 *Budget* is presented here as Table 12.1. Data estimates based on the administration's proposed budget for fiscal year 1971 appear in the last column of this table. It is also traditional to present in the *Budget* for a particular fiscal year data estimates for the previous fiscal year—the fiscal year that is only half over when the *Budget* is presented—and actual data for the most recently completed fiscal year. These two sets of summary data appear in the first two columns of Table 12.1. The presentation of data for the three fiscal years is carried throughout the *Budget* since Congress and the public are usually interested in making comparisons between projected fiscal activity and recent experience. These summary data are grouped into three main parts—budget authority, receipts and outlays, and budget financing—and are discussed in turn.[4]

---

[3] This is the basic budget document. It is hereafter referred to as the *Budget*. There are three additional budget documents: *Special Analyses, Budget of the United States, Fiscal Year 1971*, which contains detailed discussions of special aspects of the *Budget; Appendix: The Budget of the United States Government, Fiscal Year 1971*, which has over 1000 pages devoted to budgetary minutia; and *The Budget in Brief, Fiscal Year 1971*, which is a condensation designed for the layman. All these were published by the Government Printing Office in January 1970. For an analysis of the 1971 *Budget* by a former Director of the Budget, *see* Charles L. Schultze, *Setting National Priorities: the 1971 Budget* (Washington, D.C.: The Brookings Institution, 1970).

[4] These are three new concepts that appeared for the first time in the 1969 *Budget*. The

Table 12.1 **Budget Summary (Millions of dollars)**

Description	1968 Actual	1969 Actual	1970 Estimate	1971 Estimate
BUDGET AUTHORITY (LARGELY APPROPRIATIONS):				
Available through current action by Congress:				
Previously enacted		133,213	133,854	—
Proposed in this budget		—	5,095	148,113
Available without current action by Congress		75,860	84,018	86,706
Deductions for offsetting receipts[a]		−12,905	−13,916	−16,788
Total budget authority		196,167	209,051	218,030
RECEIPTS, EXPENDITURES, AND NET LENDING:				
Expenditure account:				
Receipts		187,792	199,386	202,103
Expenditures (excludes net lending)		183,080	194,985	200,088
Expenditure account surplus		4,712	4,401	2,014
Loan account:				
Loan disbursements		13,117	9,489	8,604
Loan repayments		11,640	6,589	7,921
Net lending		1,476	2,900	683
Total budget:				
Receipts		187,792	199,386	202,103
Outlays (expenditures and net lending)		184,556	197,885	200,771
Budget surplus		3,236	1,501	1,331
BUDGET FINANCING				
Net repayment of borrowing to the public (—)		−1,044	−2,583	−1,200
Other means of financing		−2,192	1,082	−131
Total budget financing		−3,236	−1,501	−1,331
OUTSTANDING DEBT, END OF YEAR:				
Gross federal debt	369,769	367,144	374,734	382,503
Held by the public	290,629	279,483	278,483	277,283
Memorandum				
OUTSTANDING LOANS, END OF YEAR:				
Direct loans:				
Loan account	39,843	29,496	32,395	33,078
Expenditure account	15,459	17,360	19,826	20,751
Guaranteed and insured loans	97,618	105,097	107,566	119,949
Government-sponsored agency loans	10,862	27,209	38,455	46,619

[a] These consist of interfund and intragovernmental transactions and proprietary receipts from the public.

SOURCE: *The Budget of the United States Government, Fiscal Year 1971,* p. 539.

Budget authority. No federal government spending can legally take place unless *budget authority* exists for that particular type of spending. All budget authority comes from Congressional action in accordance with Article 1, section 8, of the Constitution: "No money shall be drawn from the Treasury, but in Consequence of Appropriations made by Law." Budget authority for any one fiscal year arises from the enactment of appropriation bills that permit federal government agencies to incur obligations requiring the Treasury to pay out money, either in the current fiscal year or in some future fiscal year. Before an appropriation bill may be enacted, an *authorization act* must be passed. The authorization bills go through the substantive committees of the Congress; for example, a program of federal aid to education, usually including a funding ceiling, would go through the House Committee on Education and Labor and the Senate Committee on Labor and Public Welfare, and then be passed by both houses and signed by the President. *Appropriations* for the authorized program are considered separately by the Senate and House Appropriations Committees, which may recommend funding the program at or below the ceiling specified in the substantive act. Often programs are authorized for which no appropriations are made. Only after appropriation bills are enacted does budget authority exist.[5] In the event that an agency's appropriation bill has not been passed by the start of the fiscal year, Congress usually enacts a *continuing resolution* that permits the agency to operate as before but without undertaking any new programs included in the proposed budget authority.

---

new format and conceptual framework of the *Budget* were recommended in *Report of the President's Commission on Budget Concepts* (Washington, D.C.: Government Printing Office, 1967). This commission is known as the Kennedy Commission after its chairman, David M. Kennedy (who subsequently became President Nixon's Secretary of the Treasury), and the Commission's *Report* contains detailed discussion of various federal fiscal activities and the method of reporting these activities in the *Budget*. See also *Staff Papers and Other Materials Reviewed by the President's Commission* (Washington, D.C.: Government Printing Office, 1967) for materials consulted by the Kennedy Commission. For a comparison of new and old budget concepts, see *Budget of the United States Government, Fiscal Year, 1969* (Washington, D.C.: Government Printing Office, 1968), pp. 464–472. For a systematic discussion of the old budget concepts, *see* Joseph Scherer, "A Primer on Federal Budgets," *Federal Reserve Bank of New York, Monthly Review*, April 1965.

5 The semantics are bound to confuse at this point. The measures that pass through the substantive committees are called authorizations, but budget authority stems only from appropriations. The entire budgetary process is quite complex and highly political. For an analysis of the process, *see* Richard F. Fenno, Jr., *The Power of the Purse: Appropriations Politics in Congress* (Boston: Little, Brown, 1966) or Aaron Wildavsky, *The Politics of the Budgetary Process* (Boston: Little, Brown, 1964). The budgetary process and related topics are also discussed in *The Federal Budget as an Economic Document*, Joint Economic Committee, 87th Congress, 1st session (Washington, D.C.: Government Printing Office, 1962).

Most of the budget authority recommended for a particular fiscal year requires current Congressional action (see Table 12.1). Of the $218 billion recommended in the 1971 *Budget,* $148.1 billion must be enacted by Congress. An additional $86.7 billion of budget authority is available without current Congressional action as a consequence of *permanent appropriations.* Such appropriations include authority to make interest payments on the public debt and to spend out of trust funds for social security payments, unemployment insurance compensation, and grants-in-aid to the states for the interstate highway system.[6] The sum of these two types of recommended budget authority is reduced by certain interfund and intragovernmental transactions and proprietary receipts from the public. The purpose of deducting *interfund and intragovernmental transactions* (estimated at $11.3 billion in fiscal 1971) is to avoid overstating the amount of budget authority for payment to the public. For example, authority for Commerce Department payments to the Post Office (interfund) and authority for Commerce Department contributions to the federal government employees retirement funds (intragovernmental) are deducted. *Proprietary receipts from the public* (estimated to be $5.5 billion in fiscal year 1971) are primarily revenues derived from sale or use of government property and are deducted in order to arrive at total budget authority; such receipts are also netted out of the reported figures for outlays.[7] Receipts from the lease of grazing rights on the public domain are an example of the deductions.

In addition to budget authority for the coming fiscal year, the Congress is also requested to enact *supplemental appropriations* for the current fiscal year. Thus, in the *Budget* for 1971 there is $5.1 billion of budget authority proposed for fiscal 1970 as a supplement to the $133.9 billion of budget authority enacted for 1970 during the previous session of Congress.

The total budget authority reported in Table 12.1 includes authority for public enterprises to spend amounts in excess of their receipts. *Public enterprises* are the business-type activities of the federal government that generate receipts to cover their expenses. Major examples are the Tennessee Valley Authority, the Commodity Credit Corporation, and the Government National Mortgage Association. Any outlay by a public enterprise in excess of its receipts requires budget authority and only to this extent are public enterprises reflected in Table 12.1.

---

[6] In 1956 the establishment of a trust fund to finance the construction of interstate highways, with receipts from gasoline and other motor-vehicle-related excise taxes, resulted from a Congressional decision to exclude this type of spending from the annual appropriation procedure. Congressional leaders feared turning the interstate highway program into a public works "pork barrel."

[7] Table 12, "Offsetting Receipts by Type," *The Budget, Fiscal Year 1971,* pp. 555–557, and chapter 7 of the Kennedy Commission *Report.*

Receipts and outlays. The second major part of Table 12.1 summarizes receipts and outlays. Actual and estimated *receipts* are largely tax revenues received by the Treasury and exclude the proprietary receipts and public enterprise receipts referred to before. A detailed presentation of budget receipts is given in Table 12.5. *Expenditures* are also reported net of proprietary receipts and public enterprise receipts. On this net basis, then, expenditures represent checks issued by the Treasury other than checks representing loan disbursements in the loan account. The presentation of the *loan account* is one of the major innovations of the new budget format, and it records federal government activity as a financial intermediary; this will be explained later in connection with Table 12.7. *Loan repayments* are deducted from *loan disbursements* to arrive at *net lending*. The memorandum at the bottom of Table 12.1 shows the total amount of loans outstanding in the loan account. Net lending, estimated at $.7 billion in fiscal year 1971, will increase total federal direct loans outstanding from $32.4 billion to $33.1 billion. The memorandum also shows the total amount of private loans outstanding that are either guaranteed or insured by some agency of the federal government (see Table 12.7).

Outlays equal expenditures plus net lending.[8] The relationship between budget authority and outlays for fiscal year 1971 is shown in Figure 12.1. New budget authority totaling $218 billion is recommended for fiscal year 1971, and total outlays are estimated at $200.8 billion. These outlays are made partly on the basis of budget authority enacted for fiscal year 1971, and partly on the basis of authority enacted in previous fiscal years. A portion of the authority for fiscal year 1971 will carry over as unspent authorizations for outlays in future fiscal years. Some of the unspent authorizations enacted in prior years will not be used for outlays in fiscal year 1971 and will carry over into future fiscal years. Some budget authority enacted in prior fiscal years expires because outlays for the purpose specified in the appropriation act were not made within the time limit set by Congress. This sometimes occurs when the cost of a specified item is less than the amount appropriated by Congress.

Two important steps—*apportionment* and *obligation*—occur in the budgetary process between the appropriation of new budgetary authority

---

[8] Budget outlays are not equal to the gross payments from the federal government to the public. This is because public enterprises and federal lending are included in the *Budget* on a net basis. The estimated amount of netting for these two types of transactions for fiscal year 1971 is $24.6 billion and $10.9 billion, respectively; see *Special Analyses, Fiscal Year 1971*, Tables B.5 and E.2. In addition, an estimated $5.5 billion in proprietary receipts from the public are offset against expenditures as discussed before. If these amounts were added to budget outlays, estimated federal payments to the public for fiscal year 1971 would be $241.8 billion. This amount does not include such payments as refunds for overpayment of taxes.

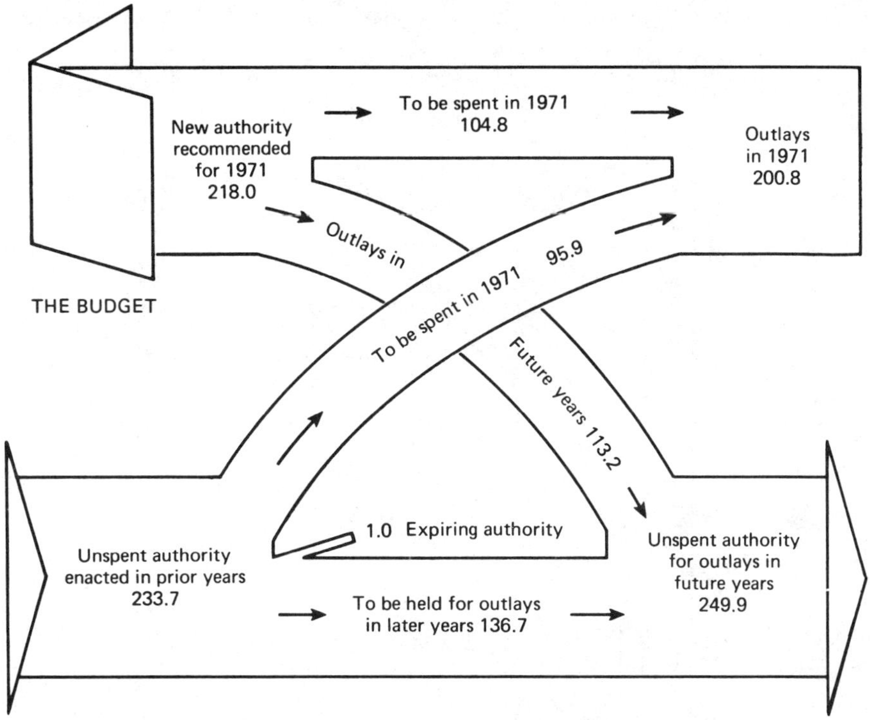

SOURCE: *The Budget of the United States Government, Fiscal Year 1971* (Washington, D.C.: Government Printing Office, 1970), p. 545.

Figure 12.1 1971 Budget—Relation of budget authority to outlays (billions of dollars).

and the outlay of Treasury funds. The Office of Management and Budget, usually on a quarterly basis, apportions budget authority to the individual government agencies. By this means the executive branch has the power, only seldom used, to hold the level of new obligations below that intended by Congress. These apportionments limit the ability of the agencies to incur obligations, that is, to firmly commit the federal government to make an outlay at some future date. For example, after Congress appropriates budget authority for a new weapons system, the Department of Defense may enter into a contract with a supplier only after an apportionment has been received from the Office of Management and Budget. That contract represents an obligation. The corresponding outlay takes place only when *progress payments* are made to the supplier or when final payment is made on delivery of the weapons system. A considerable period of time may elapse, up to several years, between the appropriation of budget authority and the outlay.[9]

[9] The total amount of obligations estimated to be incurred during fiscal year 1971 is $207 billion. See *The Budget, Fiscal Year 1971,* p. 546.

Table 12.2 **Budget Authority and Outlays by Function, Fiscal Year 1969**
(Millions of dollars)

Description	Budget Authority			Outlays		
	Expenditure Account	Loan Account	Total	Expenditure Account	Loan Account	Total
National defense	80,058	*	80,058	81,244	4	81,240
International affairs and finance	2,842	—	2,842	3,422	363	3,785
Space research and technology	3,991	—	3,991	4,247	—	4,249
Agriculture and agricultural resources	7,300	703	8,003	5,829	393	6,221
Natural resources	2,245	2	2,246	2,123	7	2,129
Commerce and transportation	9,998	169	10,167	7,914	−41	7,873
Housing and community development	2,759	592	3,351	1,060	900	1,961
Education and manpower	6,923	402	7,325	6,607	219	6,825
Health	12,359	7	12,366	11,696	*	11,696
Income security	45,209	−641	44,568	38,041	−641	37,399
Veterans benefits and services	7,489	206	7,695	7,438	202	7,640
Interest	15,791	—	15,791	15,791	—	15,791
General government	2,807	75	2,866	2,786	80	2,882
Undistributed intragovernmental payments:						
Employer share, employee retirement	−2,018	—	−2,018	−2,018	—	−2,018
Interest received by trust funds	−3,099	—	−3,099	−3,099	—	−3,099
Total	194,652	1,315	196,167	183,080	1,476	184,556

* Less than $500 thousand.

SOURCE: *The Budget of the United States Government, Fiscal Year 1971*, pp. 540, 558–583.

Budget financing. Outlays must be financed by the exercise of the sovereign power of the federal government to tax, borrow, or create money. *Budget financing* is required to the extent that outlays differ from budget receipts. When outlays exceed budget receipts, there is a *budget deficit;* conversely, when budget receipts exceed outlays, there is a *budget surplus.*

A change in outstanding federal government debt held by the public or a change in the Treasury cash balance are the primary means of budget financing. The estimated budget surplus of $1.3 billion for fiscal year 1971 is expected to be financed almost entirely by reducing the public debt. As shown by Table 12.1, budget deficits or surpluses can also be financed by other means (see the discussion of Table 12.6). If there is a budget deficit rather than a surplus, total budget financing would be positive. The additional data in Table 12.1 show the gross amount of federal debt outstanding and the amount held by the public.[10] Federal debt not held by the public is held by the government itself in various trust funds and public enterprise accounts. An increase of $7.8 billion in the gross amount of outstanding federal debt is estimated for fiscal year 1971; the public's holdings will decrease by an estimated $1.2 billion, and $9 billion will be acquired by federal trust funds and public enterprise accounts.[11] The estimated decrease during fiscal year 1971 from $278.5 billion to $277.3 billion in federal debt held by the public equals the estimated retirement of securities held by the public—$1.3 billion—as the surplus is financed. Budget financing is discussed further in connection with Table 12.6.

The *Budget* by function and agency. In the budget documents, both budget authority and outlays are reported by function. These data are presented here as Table 12.2, showing the expenditure and loan accounts separately; to economize on space and to present figures roughly comparable to the data for the 1969 calendar year used in Chapter 11, only the actual figures for fiscal year 1969 are shown. Budget authority and outlays by agency are presented in Table 12.3. Neither of these breakdowns of federal spending distinguishes among expenditures that constitute purchases of goods and services, transfer payments, and federal aid to state and local

---

[10] The federal debt held by the public corresponds to the $287 billion liability of the United States government as reported in Table 11.14 for December 31, 1969. This figure differs from the $279.5 billion reported in Table 12.1 for June 30, 1969, in part because of the six-month difference in the reporting date, and in part because the flow of funds accounts treat holdings of public enterprise accounts as part of the holdings of the nonfinancial business sector.

[11] Table C-4, *Special Analyses, Fiscal Year 1971. See also* Table 12.6 in this book for information on the holding of outstanding debt.

Table 12.3 **Budget Authority and Outlays by Agency, 1969 (Millions of dollars)**

Department or other unit	Budget Authority 1969 Actual	1970 Estimate	1971 Estimate	Outlays 1969 Actual	1970 Estimate	1971 Estimate
Legislative branch	307	354	391	277	341	368
The Judiciary	110	127	132	109	125	130
Executive Office of the President	32	38	46	31	39	45
Funds appropriated to the President	4,875	5,058	5,000	4,967	4,818	4,184
Agriculture	9,176	8,797	8,577	8,330	8,407	7,953
Commerce	941	1,017	1,170	854	1,087	1,014
Defense—military	76,970	73,484	70,798	77,877	76,505	71,191
Defense—civil	1,282	1,199	1,301	1,268	1,270	1,411
Health, Education, and Welfare	51,237	57,637	64,803	46,594	52,670	59,653
Housing and Urban Development	3,013	4,640	2,997	1,529	2,776	3,317
Interior	967	1,889	4,510	837	1,164	913
Justice	544	848	1,127	515	743	985
Labor	4,613	4,947	5,826	3,475	4,232	5,563
Post Office	1,209	1,438	583	920	1,247	382
State	426	449	490	437	447	473
Transportation	7,392	7,902	11,185	5,970	6,673	7,048
Treasury	16,944	19,112	19,077	16,924	19,107	19,066
Atomic Energy Commission	2,616	2,224	2,363	2,450	2,461	2,411
General Services Administration	338	368	40	425	454	28
National Aeronautics and Space Administration	3,991	3,735	3,330	4,247	3,886	3,400
Veterans Administration	7,665	8,595	8,878	7,669	8,657	8,455
Other independent agencies	6,636	10,608	9,172	3,969	6,397	6,844
Allowances for:						
Revenue sharing			275			275
Civilian and military pay increases		175	1,400		175	1,400
Contingencies		500	1,200		300	900
Undistributed intragovernmental transactions:						
Employer share, employee retirement	–2,018	–2,307	–2,366	–2,018	–2,307	–2,366
Interest received by trust funds	–3,099	–3,781	–4,273	–3,099	–3,781	–4,273
Total budget authority and outlays	196,167	209,051	218,030	184,556	197,885	200,771
MEMORANDUM						
Portion available through current action by Congress	133,213	138,948	148,113	87,087	90,262	92,798
Portion available without current action by Congress	75,860	84,018	86,706	24,115	27,726	28,826
Outlays from obligated balances				50,049	51,998	52,490
Outlays from unobligated balances				36,210	41,815	43,445
Deductions for offsetting receipts:						
Intrabudgetary transactions	–8,714	–9,704	–11,250	–8,714	–9,704	–11,250
Proprietary receipts from the public	–4,192	–4,211	–5,538	–4,192	–4,211	–5,538
Total budget authority and outlays	196,167	209,051	218,030	184,556	197,885	200,771

SOURCE: *The Budget of the United States Government, Fiscal Year 1971,* p. 541.

Table 12.4 Federal Aid to State and Local Governments, 1969 (Millions of dollars)

By Agency	
Executive Office of the President	*
Funds appropriated to the President:	
Economic Opportunity programs	1,406.5
Other (primarily Appalachia)	162.2
Department of Agriculture	1,534.0
Department of Commerce	150.4
Department of Defense:	
Military	34.4
Civil	17.7
Department of Health, Education, and Welfare	10,123.8
Department of Housing and Urban Development	1,109.3
Department of the Interior	401.7
Department of Justice	28.4
Department of Labor	629.3
Department of State	6.3
Department of Transportation	4,401.6
Treasury Department	115.3
Veterans Administration	14.5
National Capital Region[a]	92.0
Other	27.5
Total outlays for federal aid	20,254.9
By Function	
National defense	40.1
International affairs and finance	6.1
Agriculture and rural development	807.2
Natural resources	517.9
Commerce and transportation	4,710.1
Community development and housing	1,669.8
Education and manpower	4,063.5
Health	3,192.7
Income security	4,937.7
Veterans benefits and services	14.5
General government	295.0
Total, grants and shared revenues	20,254.9

[a] Includes federal payments to the District of Columbia.
* Less than $50,000.

SOURCE: *Special Analyses, Budget of the United States, Fiscal Year 1971*, pp. 222, 230–235.

governments. This information is contained in the national income accounts (see Tables 11.6 and 11.7).[12] The distribution by function has been included

[12] The spending of federal monies abroad does not appear explicitly in the *Budget*. *Special Analyses, Fiscal Year 1970* contains a section on "foreign currency availabilities and uses"; these data relate to line 43 in the balance of payments, Table 11.15.

Table 12.5 Budget Receipts by Source (Millions of dollars)

	1969 Actual	1970 Estimate	1971 Estimate
Individual income taxes (net)	87,249	92,200	91,000
Withheld	70,182	77,400	77,000
Other	27,258	27,600	28,000
Refunds	−10,191	−12,800	−14,000
Corporation income taxes (net)	36,678	37,000	35,000
Corporation taxes	38,338	38,900	37,000
Refunds	−1,660	−1,900	−2,000
Employment taxes (trust funds) (total)	34,236	38,914	42,842
Unemployment taxes (trust funds) (total)	3,328	3,340	3,335
Premiums for other insurance and retirement (trust funds) (total)	2,353	2,551	2,931
Excise taxes (net)	15,222		17,520
Manufacturers' excise taxes (total)	6,575	6,980	7,584
Federal funds			
Gasoline	28	28	28
Proposed legislation	—	7	45
Passenger automobiles	1,864	1,825	1,730
Proposed legislation	—	—	260
All other	51	58	68
Trust funds			
Gasoline	3,171	3,331	3,482
Proposed legislation	—	−5	−21
Diesel fuel used on highways	219	245	269
Proposed legislation	—	—	122
Use-tax on certain vehicles	129	132	137
Proposed legislation	—	—	137
Other motor vehicle related taxes (total)	1,343	1,399	1,457
Alcohol tax (total)	4,482	4,690	5,170
Tobacco taxes (total)	2,136	2,095	2,148
Documents and retailers' excise tax (repealed) (total)	1	—	—

in the *Budget* in recent years because most functions involve the activities of several agencies. For example, the functional category, international affairs and finance, involves three departments, six independent agencies, and some funds appropriated to the President.[13] The budget authority and outlays of the Central Intelligence Agency and the National Security Agency are not reported separately in the *Budget*. Rumors current in Washington

[13] *The Budget, Fiscal Year 1971*, p. 559.

***Table 12.5* (continued)**

	1969 Actual	1970 Estimate	1971 Estimate
Excise taxes (net) (continued)			
Miscellaneous excise taxes (total)	1,783	1,976	2,524
General and toll telephone teletype service	1,316	1,470	1,360
Proposed legislation	—	—	300
Transportation of persons by air	224	265	300
Proposed legislation	—	25	245
Jet fuel (proposed legislation)	—	2	18
International departure tax (proposed legislation)	—	3	29
Waybill tax (proposed legislation)	—	5	44
Fuel used on inland waterways (proposed legislation)	—	—	4
Wagering taxes, including occupational taxes	5	5	5
Sugar tax	108	110	112
Coin-operated gaming devices	12	14	15
Interest equalization tax	110	70	50
Foreign insurance policies	18	18	18
Tax on foundations	—	—	35
All other miscellaneous excise taxes	5	5	5
Undistributed depository receipts and unapplied collections	244	199	94
Refunds	—16	—16	—16
Estate and gift taxes (net)	3,491	3,500	3,600
Customs (net)	2,319	2,260	2,260
Miscellaneous receipts (total)	2,916	3,681	3,614
Miscellaneous taxes	52	60	69
Deposit of earnings Federal Reserve System	2,662	3,250	3,350
Fees for permits, regulatory, and judicial services (total)	123	131	158
Other miscellaneous receipts	78	240	38
Total budget receipts	187,792	199,386	202,103
Federal funds	143,329	149,579	147,600
Trust funds	52,009	58,141	64,107
Intragovernmental transactions	—7,547	—8,335	—9,605

SOURCE: *Budget of the United States Government, Fiscal Year 1971*, pp. 551–553.

have it that these amounts are disguised in the budgets for other federal agencies. The only mention made of the CIA in the 1971 *Budget* refers to the expenditure of $58,000 in fiscal year 1969, and $39,000 in fiscal year 1970, for construction of a classified printing facility.

Over 10 percent of federal government outlays in fiscal year 1969 was for *federal aid to state and local governments.* In turn, this aid was equal to about 18 percent of state and local government revenues. Both percentages increased significantly during the 1960s.[14] Table 12.4 describes federal aid by function and by agency. Practically all of this aid takes the form of *grants-in-aid* to states and localities; the remainder, about 1 percent of the total, is shared revenue. The interstate highway program accounts for the largest single grant-in-aid expenditure. In all, there were, as of January 1, 1967, 379 separate authorizations for major grant-in-aid programs.[15]

Budget receipts. Budget outlays for any fiscal year are financed primarily out of budget receipts. A detailed breakdown, although not as detailed as that contained in the *Budget* itself, is presented in Table 12.5. Estimated receipts for fiscal years 1970 and 1971 are based on assumptions about the future level and composition of gross national product. The 1971 *Budget* includes the following account of these assumptions:

Economic Assumptions
(Calendar years, billions of dollars)

	1968 Actual	1969 Preliminary	1970 Estimate
Gross national product	865.7	932.3	985
Personal income	687.9	747.1	800
Corporation profits before tax	91.1	94.3	89

SOURCE: *The Budget, Fiscal Year 1971,* p. 65.

Note that no projection is given for the calendar year 1971, even though the first six months of that year are a part of fiscal year 1971, and receipts are estimated for the full fiscal year. These gross national product estimates, made by the Council of Economic Advisors, reflect the taxing and spending plans incorporated in the *Budget.*

Most budget receipts are general revenues that may be used to finance any type of federal outlay; they are known as *federal funds.*[16] Some budget receipts, however, are *trust funds.* Trust fund monies are raised from special

[14] *Special Analyses, Fiscal Year 1971,* pp. 219–235. *See also* Table 11.6.

[15] Advisory Commission on Intergovernmental Relations, *Fiscal Balance in the American Federal System,* Vol. 1 (Washington, D.C.: Government Printing Office, October 1967), p. 151.

[16] The federal funds of the Treasury should not be confused with federal funds traded between commercial banks. Federal funds in the banking sense are transactions in reserves between commercial banks and are totally unrelated to the federal funds of the Treasury.

taxes, are accounted for separately from general Treasury receipts, and may be spent only for a specific purpose. The major trust funds in the 1960s are the social security fund and the interstate highway fund. The social security fund derives its revenue primarily from employment taxes, and makes outlays only for benefits authorized under the Social Security Act. The interstate highway fund raises revenue from excise taxes on gasoline and other motor-vehicle–related tax bases, and makes grant-in-aid payments to the states to finance the interstate highway system. Any excess of receipts over outlays in the trust funds must be used to buy United States government securities.

The tax items in Table 12.5 are largely self-explanatory.[17] Receipts for fiscal years 1970 and 1971 from individual and corporate income taxes were estimated in view of the personal and corporate income tax legislation contained in the Tax Reform Act of 1969 (see Chapter 17). The tax changes embodied in this act are estimated to increase federal revenues by $3.8 billion in fiscal year 1970 and by $2.4 billion in 1971.[18] Receipts from employment taxes are estimated for 1971 on the basis of tax rate increases scheduled for January 1, 1971. The documents tax and the retailers' excise taxes (sometimes referred to as luxury taxes) on jewelry, furs, cosmetics, and leather goods were repealed in 1965, and by fiscal year 1970 they produced no revenue. The miscellaneous excise tax on fuel used on inland waterways is proposed for enactment in the fiscal year 1971 *Budget*; hence, no figures are reported for fiscal years 1969 and 1970. The administration remains ever hopeful; a similar proposal has been in the *Budget* every year since 1964. The most important miscellaneous receipt of the federal government comes from the deposit of earnings by the Federal Reserve System. The Federal Reserve System held, at the end of December 1969, $57.2 billion of United States government securities (see Table 11.14) acquired over the years largely as a consequence of open market operations. The interest paid by the Treasury on these securities is the major source of income of the Federal Reserve System and greatly exceeds the System's expenses. The excess, equal to about 90 percent of the System's interest receipts, is returned to the Treasury. The deposit of these earnings equals about 15 percent of total interest payments made by the Treasury (see Table 12.2). Fees for permits, regulatory, and judicial services are treated as a budgetary

---

17 The Internal Revenue Service annually publishes a wealth of data based on various types of tax returns. Two such publications are *Statistics of Income: Individual Income Tax Returns* and *Corporation Income Tax Returns*. For a discussion related to the estimation of budget receipts, *see* "The Responsiveness of Federal Personal Income Taxes to Income Change," *Survey of Current Business*, December 1969, pp. 32–45.

18 In subsequent fiscal years the Tax Reform Act of 1969 is expected to result in a net loss in federal revenues as compared with what collections would have been without this legislation. See *The Budget of the United States Government, 1971*, pp. 66–68.

Table 12.6 Budget Financing and Outstanding Debt (Millions of dollars)

BUDGET FINANCING

	1969 Actual	1970 Estimate	1971 Estimate
REPAYMENT OF BORROWING TO THE PUBLIC (—):			
Increase or decrease (—) in debt held by the public:			
Nonbank investors	—4,611	—	—
Commercial banks	—8,400	—	—
Federal Reserve banks	1,865	—	—
Subtotal, decrease (—) in debt held by the public	—11,146	—1,000	—1,200
Reclassification of debt and investments of enterprises[a]	10,102	—1,583	—
Net repayment of borrowing to the public	—1,044	—2,583	—1,200
OTHER MEANS OF FINANCING (OR DISPOSITION OF SURPLUS (—)):			
Decrease or increase (—) in available cash and monetary assets	—2,212	—	—
Increase or decrease (—) in liabilities for:			
Checks outstanding, etc.	—443	137	—41
Deposit fund balances	159	270	—500
Transactions, other than debt, not applied to surplus of the current year:			
Seigniorage on coins	233	307	310
Other	71	368	100
Subtotal, other means of financing	—2,192	1,082	—131
Total, financing transactions (equal to surplus (—))	—3,236	—1,501	—1,331

[a] These transactions consist of: (a) the credits resulting from conversion of three mixed ownership enterprises, formerly a part of the budget, to private ownership, outside the budget totals in fiscal year 1969, and the later redemption of trust fund investments in their securities, and (b) the charges resulting from the reclassification, in fiscal year 1970, of certificates of interest of the Commodity Credit Corporation, from their status as an evidence

receipt rather than as a proprietary receipt offset against expenditures, because these charges are a consequence of the exercise of sovereign power and not the result of a commercial transaction.[19]

Budget financing. As was indicated before in the discussion of Table 12.1, the term *budget financing* refers to the fiscal action that must be taken when outlays differ from receipts. Budget financing is described in more

[19] Kennedy Commission, *Report,* chapter 7.

Table 12.6 **(continued)**

OUTSTANDING DEBT, END OF YEAR

	1968 Actual	1969 Actual	1970 Estimate	1971 Estimate
GROSS FEDERAL DEBT:				
Public debt (issued by Treasury)	345,369	352,895	362,127	370,297
Agency debt (issued by agencies)	24,399	14,249	12,607	12,206
Total gross federal debt	369,769	367,144	374,734	382,503
HOLDINGS BY GOVERNMENT AGENCIES (—):				
Public debt	—76,138	—84,815	—93,790	—102,902
Agency debt	—3,001	—2,846	—2,461	—2,318
Total, federal debt held by the public	290,629	279,483	278,483	277,283

DEBT SUBJECT TO PUBLIC DEBT LIMIT, END OF YEAR

	1968 Actual	1969 Actual	1970 Estimate	1971 Estimate
Public debt (issued by Treasury)	345,369	352,895	362,127	370,297
Notes issued by Treasury to International Monetary Fund (not in debt above)	2,209	825	825	825
Agency and District of Columbia debt subject to general limit on public debt	3,819	3,847	3,171	2,060
Portion of public debt not subject to limit (—)	—654	—636	—430	—425
Total, debt subject to public debt limit[b]	350,743	356,932	365,693	372,757

of the sale of assets to status as a debt of the Corporation. The enterprises converted to private ownership were: Federal National Mortgage Association; banks for cooperatives; and federal intermediate credit banks.

[b] The applicable limitations are: June 30, 1968, $358 billion; July 1, 1968 to April 6, 1969, $365 billion; April 7, 1969 to June 30, 1970, $377 billion; and July 1, 1970 to June 30, 1971, $365 billion.

SOURCE: *The Budget of the United States Government, Fiscal Year 1971,* pp. 548–549.

detail in the first part of Table 12.6. Ordinarily, *borrowing from the public* is the principal means of budget financing when the budget is in deficit, and a reduction in the total amount of debt held by the public usually occurs when the budget is in surplus. Borrowing from the public is broken down into three categories. During the 1969 fiscal year, holdings of government securities by the Federal Reserve banks increased, whereas commercial banks and nonbank investors decreased their holdings of these securities.[20]

[20] As was indicated in Chapter 11, the flow of funds accounts provide more complete information on holdings of and transactions in U.S. government securities by the public.

Debt retirement during fiscal year 1969 decreased the public's holdings of federal securities from $290.6 to $279.5 billion, as shown in the second part of Table 12.6.[21] This amount is only a portion of the *gross federal debt.* Most of the federal debt is issued by the Treasury and is usually called the *public debt.* The second portion of Table 12.6 and footnote *b* to that table describe the relationship between these various debt concepts and the statutory ceiling on the public debt. Following the Kennedy Commission recommendation, President Nixon, in February 1969, requested that Congress redefine the debt ceiling to apply only to the part of the federal debt held by the public. Congress refused. A small amount of the gross federal debt is issued by independent federal agencies and is called *agency debt.* Some federal agencies, including the Commodity Credit Corporation, the Export-Import Bank, and the Government National Mortgage Association, are authorized to borrow funds from which they make loans.[22] Most agency borrowing is not guaranteed by the federal government; thus the total federal debt subject to the legal debt ceiling is less than the gross federal debt. Agency debt also includes the *participation certificates* sold by the Export-Import Bank and the Government National Mortgage Association.[23] Participation certificates are issued as shares in a pool of outstanding agency loans, and interest on the certificates is paid from collections on these loans. The sale of such securities brings additional revenue to the issuing agency, thus permitting the agency to increase its loans outstanding. Although the gross federal debt decreased by $2.7 billion, debt held by the public decreased by a larger amount—$11.1 billion—during fiscal year 1969. The balance—$8.4 billion—was acquired by the trust funds and public enterprises that invest their surpluses in United States government securities.

Seigniorage is an additional means of budget financing. The term is a feudal one referring to the right of the seignior (lord) to mint coins. The cost of the metals used in the minting of coins is exceeded by the face value of the coins, and this difference, essentially a profit to the Treasury, is called *seigniorage.* Formerly, seigniorage was treated as a budget receipt; following

---

[21] This particular measure of debt retirement is deceptively large. During 1969 the Federal National Mortgage Association and several other federal agencies were reorganized as private corporations. Thus, their debts, largely certificates of participation, ceased to be debts of the United States government. Excluding debt retirement stemming from reclassification of these agencies during 1969, $1044 billion of United States government securities held by the public were retired as shown at the top of Table 12.6.

[22] Such borrowing to make loans is sometimes referred to as *backdoor spending* because Congress does not appropriate the monies, and outlays are thus made without budget authority. *See 1961 Congressional Quarterly Almanac* "Backdoor Spending Issue," (Washington, D.C.: Congressional Quarterly, Inc., 1961), pp. 159–161.

[23] *See* Kennedy Commission, *Report*, pp. 54–55, for discussion of participation certificates. *See Treasury Bulletin* for detail on participation certificates and interest-bearing agency security issues.

the recommendation of the Kennedy Commission, it is now treated as a means of budget financing.[24] Changes in asset holdings are a means of financing outlays that differs from current receipts. Increasing the *Treasury cash balance* (available cash and monetary assets) absorbed receipts during fiscal 1969.[25] This balance is held both in Federal Reserve banks and in tax and loan accounts in commercial banks.[26] Changes in liabilities may also finance budgetary imbalances. Between July 1, 1968 and June 30, 1969, the value of uncashed checks drawn on the United States Treasury account decreased by $443 million. Had there not been this decrease in checks outstanding during fiscal year 1969, the Treasury cash balance would have increased by an additional $443 million. However, because the checks were cashed, without there being a corresponding budget outlay during the fiscal year, the accounting of them is similar to the accounting of debt retirement: Both entail reductions in liabilities. During fiscal year 1969 there was an increase of $159 million in United States government deposit fund liabilities.[27] As these liabilities were incurred during fiscal year 1969, the Treasury cash balance increased for reasons not associated with budget financing. This entry is made, then, essentially to adjust the reported change in cash balances.

This completes our discussion of the basic budgetary process and the

---

[24] Kennedy Commission, *Report,* pp. 57–58. Seigniorage in fiscal years 1966 and 1967 exceeded estimated seigniorage in fiscal years 1968 to 1971. This is because new "sandwich" coins were being issued to replace dimes, quarters, and half-dollars with high silver content in the mid-1960s; the volume of new coins minted, and hence seigniorage, was unusually high.

[25] In fiscal year 1967, the Budget deficit was $8.8 billion. This was partially financed by drawing down Treasury cash balances by $4.9 billion. The increase in these balances during fiscal years 1968 and 1969 was perhaps to be expected because the United States government, like a business, requires working cash balances where it banks.

[26] The change in the Treasury cash balance cannot be reconciled with data provided in the monthly *Treasury Bulletin* because of definitional differences. The *Treasury Bulletin* also contains detailed information about the outstanding federal debt (maturities, ownership, yields, refunding operations) and other federal government financial data. The Treasury also issues a *Daily Statement* that summarizes the day's transactions. *The Annual Report of the Secretary of the Treasury, 1955*, pp. 275–84, discusses the Treasury's use of tax and loan accounts.

[27] Deposit funds are special accounts for monies "held by the Government as banker or agent for others" (Kennedy Commission, *Report*, p. 97). *Combined Statement of Receipts, Expenditures, and Balances of the United States Government for the Fiscal Year Ended June 30, 1969*, gives detail on the deposit fund accounts. An example of a deposit fund account is withheld state and territorial income taxes. Compensation of federal employees is a budget outlay. If state or territorial income taxes are withheld, employees' paychecks are less than budget outlays, and the difference is recorded as an increase in this deposit fund balance and is a federal government liability to a state or territorial government. Payment of these monies draws down the Treasury cash balance for reasons not associated with budget outlays at the time of payment.

summary budget statements. In the balance of this chapter there is a more thorough treatment of two types of federal fiscal activities—credit programs and public enterprises—and a discussion of the federal budget in the national income accounts.

FEDERAL CREDIT PROGRAMS

Agency debt, including participation certificates, is incurred largely to support federal lending programs, although some lending is supported directly by budgetary receipts. Net lending, out of the loan account, was summarized in Table 12.1 and reported by function in Table 12.2. Additional information on federal lending activity during fiscal year 1969 is recorded in Table 12.7. The first two columns show loan disbursements and loan repayments by agency and program. Note that the difference between disbursements and repayments from the loan account is the amount recorded as an outlay in Table 12.1. The third column in Table 12.7 shows the total amount of outstanding loans at the end of fiscal year 1969.

Some lending activity is included in the expenditure account because "these programs comprise foreign loans made largely on noncommercial terms and other loans where the terms of the loan contract make repayment in certain respects contingent rather than mandatory."[28] For example, the Commodity Credit Corporation makes loans to farmers accepting crops, valued at support prices, as collateral. Only if market prices rise above the support level will the farmer repay the loan, receive the return of his collateral, and sell the crop on the open market. Hence, repayment is contingent on market conditions. For many years this type of lending activity has been a central part of the federal farm program; because repayment of these loans is not expected on a regular basis, the lending activity logically belongs in the expenditure account. The lending activity listed in the loan account represents the federal government functioning as a financial intermediary.[29] The federal government uses budget receipts, borrowings, and loan repayments to extend credit, largely to the private sector.[30] Of the $13.1 billion

---

[28] *Special Analyses, Fiscal Year 1971*, p. 67. *See* Kennedy Commission, *Report*, chapter 5.

[29] "Most Federal loan programs include at least some element of subsidy. In fact, if this were not true, serious question could be raised about the appropriateness of such activities being conducted by the Federal Government rather than private financial institutions" (Kennedy Commission, *Report*, p. 51). This issue is discussed in more detail in "Feasibility of Explicit Recognition of the Interest Subsidy in Connection with Separate Budgeting of Loans," in *Staff Papers and Other Materials Reviewed by the President's Commission, op. cit.*, pp. 335–48. The Commission recommended that these implicit subsidies be carried in the *Budget* as an expenditure item. This recommendation, as of mid-1970, has not been adopted.

[30] The loans represented in Table 12.7 do not include loans repayable in foreign cur-

Table 12.7 **Federal Credit Programs, 1969 (Millions of dollars)**

Agency or Program	Current: Dis-burse-ments	Current: Repay-ments	Outstanding: Direct Loans	Outstanding: Guar-anteed and Insured Loans
EXPENDITURE ACCOUNT				
Funds appropriated to the President:				
Military assistance	77	19	226	55
Economic assistance	957	139	723	216
Agriculture: Commodity Credit Corporation	2,620	1,801	2,647	666
Health, Education and Welfare	201	1	225	—
Treasury Department	55	46	15	—
Other programs	9	12	—	—
Total, expenditure account	3,919	2,018	3,837	937
LOAN ACCOUNT				
Funds appropriated to the President:				
Office of Economic Opportunity	9	12	13	—
Agriculture:				
Commodity Credit Corporation	221	137	221	—
Rural Electrification Administration	402	172	470	—
Farmers Home Administration	1,765	1,444	489	895
Commerce:				
Economic Development Administration	50	8	76	10
Maritime Administration	1	8	1	142
Health, Education, and Welfare	100	5	14	687
Housing and Urban Development:				
Renewal and housing assistance	842	618	681	1,987
Metropolitan development	48	4	45	—
Federal Housing Administration	297	277	355	14,429
Government National Mortgage Association	2,439	1,883	2,557	—
Federal National Mortgage Association	249	72	782	—
Interior	17	5	14	4
General Services Administration	28	23	28	—
Veterans Administration:				
Housing loans and guarantees	327	138	359	4,017
Insurance policy loans	150	86	150	—
District of Columbia	108	43	110	—
Export-Import Bank	1,668	1,303	1,298	1,723
Farm Credit Administration:				
Banks for cooperatives	1,059	934	1,059	—
Federal intermediate credit banks	2,872	3,158	2,872	—
Federal Home Loan Bank Board	36	15	38	*
Small Business Administration	208	225	248	470
Other agencies or programs	88	12	87	2
Obligations of federally sponsored enterprises	132	1,058	132	—
Total, loan account	13,117	11,640	12,099	24,366
Grand total	17,036	13,659	15,936	25,303

* Less than $500 thousand.

SOURCE: *Special Analyses, Budget of the United States, Fiscal Year 1971*, pp. 69 and 72.

of new loan disbursements made from the loan account in fiscal year 1969, $921 million were loans to state and local governments.[31]

Federal activity in the nation's credit markets is not limited to making direct loans. A variety of federal agencies guarantee and insure loans made by private lenders to certain types of private borrowers. The total amount of federally guaranteed and insured loans outstanding at the end of fiscal year 1969 is shown in the last column of Table 12.7. Most of these loans are associated with the residential housing industry.

PUBLIC ENTERPRISES

The fiscal activity of federal public enterprises enters the budget only on a net basis; only outlays and budget authority in excess of receipts appear in the *Budget*. The gross operations of these public enterprises are reflected in Table 12.8. The Commodity Credit Corporation and the Post Office together account for about half of the gross outlays. The receipts do not include the proceeds of borrowing (either through participation certificates or otherwise), nor do the expenditures include the repayment of borrowing. The receipts shown in Table 12.8 are generally from the public. They also include some transactions (amounting to $3.1 billion) from within the federal government, for example, sales of agricultural commodities held in the inventories of the Commodity Credit Corporation to other federal agencies for programs such as foreign aid and school lunches. The sales of Tennessee Valley Authority power to federal agencies, and payments by all agencies to the Post Office for postal services, are other examples of such intragovernmental receipts included in Table 12.8.[32] The difference between the gross outlays and receipts of the public enterprise funds—$8.4 billion—is the public enterprise component of the total budget outlays reported in Table 12.1. Postal reform legislation enacted in 1970 will have the eventual effect of removing the Post Office from the *Budget*. The legislation provides for the creation of a quasi-private postal corporation. A few of the public enterprise funds have receipts in excess of gross outlays, permitting them to either repay their former borrowings or to make loans to the Treasury by purchasing United States government securities.

---

rencies or those made by federal land banks and federal home loan banks, which are privately owned, federally sponsored institutions. The total outstanding amount of loans repayable in foreign currencies was $5.9 billion at the end of fiscal year 1968, *Special Analyses, Fiscal Year 1970*, p. 100. The federal land banks and federal home loan banks had $6 billion and $4.9 billion, respectively, in loans at the end of fiscal year 1968, *ibid.*, p. 67.

[31] Note *Special Analyses, Fiscal Year 1971*, p. 235, for a listing of such loans.

[32] *Special Analyses, Fiscal Year 1969*, p. 24.

Table 12.8 Public Enterprise Fund Transactions, 1969 (Millions of dollars)

Description	Applicable Receipts	Gross Outlays
Funds appropriated to the President:		
Economic assistance	104	935
Other	235	460
Agriculture:		
Commodity Credit Corporation	3,918	8,247
Farmers Home Administration	1,549	1,817
Federal Crop Insurance Corporation	47	55
Commerce	184	166
Defense:		
Military	10	23
Civil (Panama Canal Company)	167	159
Health, Education, and Welfare	23	122
Housing and Urban Development:		
College housing loan fund	139	341
Urban renewal fund	315	887
Low-rent public housing fund	278	630
Government National Mortgage Association	1,652	1,652
Federal Housing Administration	1,684	1,819
Other	63	102
Interior	49	92
Labor	284	280
Post Office	6,353	7,273
Transportation	24	168
Treasury	*	*
General Services Administration	*	*
Veterans Administration	701	799
Other independent offices:		
Export-Import Bank	1,596	1,842
Farm Credit Administration	96	4
Federal Home Loan Bank Board:		
Federal Savings and Loan Insurance Corporation	362	74
Other	20	19
Small Business Administration	317	416
Tennessee Valley Authority	430	617
United States Information Agency	*	*
Total	20,600	28,997
Receipts from the public	(17,543)	
Receipts from other accounts	(3,147)	

* Less than $500 thousand.

SOURCE: *Special Analysis, Budget of the United States, Fiscal Year 1971, p. 23.*

THE FEDERAL BUDGET IN THE NATIONAL INCOME ACCOUNTS

Thus far in this chapter we have discussed the measurement of federal fiscal activity as it appears in *The Budget of the United States Government.* In Chapter 11 we discussed the national income accounts, and Table 11.6 gave data on the federal government as it is recorded in the national income accounts; that presentation is known as the federal budget in the national income accounts. Aside from the fact that the data of this chapter are for fiscal years, whereas the data in the national income accounts are for calendar years, there are conceptual differences between the *Budget* and the national income accounts that result in different amounts of federal government receipts and expenditures being recorded. Table 12.9 reconciles

Table 12.9 Relationship of the Budget to the Federal Sector in the National Income Accounts, 1969 (Billions of dollars)

Receipts	
Total budget receipts	187.8
Government contribution for employee retirement (grossing)	2.1
Other netting and grossing	1.3
Adjustment to accruals	1.7
Other	—.2
Federal sector, NIA receipts	192.7
Expenditures	
Total budget outlays	184.6
Loan account	—1.5
Financial transactions in the expenditure account	—1.0
Government contribution for employee retirement (grossing)	2.1
Other netting and grossing	1.3
Defense timing adjustment	.7
Dollar expenditures to finance agricultural exports	—.3
Other	.9
Federal sector, NIA expenditures	186.7

SOURCE: *Special Analyses, Budget of the United States, Fiscal Year 1971*, p. 15.

the *Budget* with the federal budget in the national income accounts. The receipt and expenditure totals on a national income basis in Table 12.9 are equivalent to the federal receipt and expenditure totals in Table 11.6, the difference resulting from the fiscal year versus the calendar year means of reporting. Expenditures in the federal budget in the national income accounts exclude the net lending component of outlays in the *Budget* because these are financial asset transactions rather than income or product flows. Total compensation of employees, including fringe benefits paid by employers, are recorded in the national income accounts. The federal government's contribution to government employee retirement funds and insurance programs is an intragovernmental transaction and is offset against expenditures in the *Budget*. In fiscal year 1969 these contributions amounted to $2.1 billion and must be added to both receipts and expenditures in moving from the *Budget* to the federal budget in the national income accounts.[33] Table 12.9 shows additional netting and grossing of $1.3 billion in fiscal year 1969 that must be added to both receipts and expenditures; a major component of this amount is the life insurance program operated by the Veterans Administration. In the national income accounts corporate income tax and indirect business tax receipts are recorded on an accrual basis (corporate income tax liabilities, for example, are recorded when the income subject to tax is earned rather than when the Treasury collects the revenue), and defense purchases are recorded at the time of delivery rather than on a checks-issued basis. Thus, we have the $1.7 billion adjustment for accrued receipts and the $.7 billion defense timing adjustment for expenditures. A major recommendation of the Kennedy Commission was that all budget receipts and outlays be recorded on an accrual basis. Outlays would be recorded as accrued at the time production or work takes place rather than at the time of disbursement of monies or of delivery of goods. As discussed in Chapter 16, accrual recording of federal outlays would better measure the real macroeconomic impact of federal government spending on the economy, for expenditures will be recorded at the time resources are committed to production for government and are thus unavailable for use elsewhere in the economy.

The *Budget* includes some loans in the expenditure account because they are not made on commercial terms. The loans were described in connection with Table 12.4. Some of these noncommercial loans, primarily foreign economic assistance and a few of the transactions of the Commodity Credit Corporation (CCC), are international payments that do not lead to an income or product flow in the United States; they amounted to $1 billion in fiscal year 1969 and are excluded in measuring the federal budget in the national income accounts. Most CCC nonrecourse loans, however, are domestic transactions that lead to the acquisition of agricultural commodities by the CCC; these transactions are treated as purchases of goods and services in recording the federal budget in the national income accounts. When agricultural products are exported under Title I of PL480, a private exporter may receive payment in a foreign currency. The export transaction

---

[33] *See* the *Budget, 1971*, pp. 555–57, for detail on these retirement and insurance fund interfund and intragovernmental receipts.

is recorded in the national income accounts as part of net exports of goods and services (Table 11.1). PL480 provides that the federal government will purchase this foreign currency from the exporter, and this dollar expenditure is a budget outlay. Such outlays, which amounted to $.3 billion in fiscal year 1969, are merely asset transactions and must be subtracted to avoid double counting in the federal budget in the national income accounts.

Finally, there are a series of additional adjustments that are needed to reconcile the *Budget* with the federal budget in the national income accounts. These are primarily adjustments in expenditures. In fiscal year 1969, they amounted to $.9 billion and included disbursement of the foreign currencies just described, nondefense timing adjustments, and transactions in United States government assets, such as public land.

APPENDIX TO CHAPTER 12

BUDGET ESTIMATES COMPARED WITH ACTUAL DATA

The budget requests sent to Congress are for new obligational authority, as pointed out in the discussion of Table 12.1. Assuming the requested amount of budget authority and given knowledge of the balances of obligated and unobligated budget authority from previous fiscal years, the Office of Management and Budget estimates budget receipts and expenditures. Table 12.10 gives estimated and actual budget receipts, expenditures, and surplus or deficit for fiscal years 1966–1971 for the federal budget in the national income accounts.[34] Examination of the data in Table 12.10 reveals that estimates of receipts and expenditures were usually less than their actual amounts during each of these years. The major exception to this pattern is receipts for fiscal year 1968; this revenue estimate was based on the assumption that Congress would enact a 6 percent surtax on personal and corporate income tax liabilities for that fiscal year; the legislation was not enacted. In addition to the tax legislation that is assumed when revenue estimates are prepared, estimates of tax receipts are also made on the basis of a projection of gross national product. During these years, estimated gross national product has always been less than actual gross national product, thus making estimated receipts less than actual receipts.[35] Actual expenditures usually exceed their estimate in each

[34] The federal budget in the national income accounts is used for this comparison because it has been compiled without change in definition, for several years. Data from other budget concepts are not available in a consistent series for recent years.

[35] The accompanying table of estimated and actual gross national product (for calendar years) helps explain why actual receipts were usually above their estimated level. For a discussion of budget projections, *see* Gerhard Colm and Peter Wagner, *Federal Budget Projections* (Washington, D.C.: Brookings Institution, 1966).

	Estimated	Actual
1965	660	681.2
1966	722	743.3
1967	787	789.7
1968	846	865.7
1969	921	932.3 (preliminary)

SOURCE: *The Budget of the United States Government, Fiscal Years 1966–1971.*

***Table 12.10* Federal Budget in the National Income Accounts, Estimated and Actual Data**
(Billions of dollars, fiscal years)

		Receipts	Expenditures	Surplus or Deficit
1966	Estimate (January 1965)	121.0	127.0	—6.0
	Actual	132.6	132.3	+0.3
1967	Estimate (January 1966)	142.2	142.7	—0.5
	Actual	147.6	155.1	—7.5
1968	Estimate (January 1967)	167.1	169.2	—2.1
	Actual	161.1	172.4	−11.3
1969	Estimate (January 1968)	182.5	185.0	—2.5
	Actual	192.7	186.7	+6.0
1970	Estimate (January 1969)	202.3	199.6	+2.7
	Estimate (January 1970)	201.8	198.1	+3.6
1971	Estimate (January 1970)	205.4	203.8	+1.6

SOURCE: *Budget of the United States Government, Fiscal Years, 1966–1971.*

of these fiscal years. This is in large measure because of consistent underestimation by the Department of Defense of the costs of the Vietnamese War. The estimates of expenditures for fiscal year 1969 made in January 1969 are reasonably close to the estimates made one year earlier; this may in large part be because of the condition imposed when Congress enacted the 10 percent surtax on personal and corporate income tax liabilities in July 1968. Congress enacted ceilings that required the administration to cut budget outlays (see Chapter 17).

In 1967, the Joint Economic Committee of the Congress began the practice of holding midyear reviews of the budget.[36] By holding hearings in late summer on the budget for the fiscal year beginning the previous July 1, the Committee seeks to make the Congress and the public aware of the economic implications of tax and expenditure legislation enacted by the current session of Congress. The Committee also seeks to review changes in underlying economic conditions that may affect the assumptions upon which the budget estimates, originally presented to Congress by the administration the previous January, were made. This review procedure was initiated in response to a feeling on the part of many congressmen that they were not fully apprised of the changes in Vietnam spending during the 1967 fiscal year. Information presented by the Office of Management and Budget at these hearings is of critical importance to economists trying to analyze the impact of the federal budget; without this information they would be forced to work with data from the January estimates.

---

[36] Joint Economic Committee, Congress of the United States, *August Review of the 1968 Budget* (Washington, D.C.: Government Printing Office, 1967), and *Summer Review of the 1969 Budget* (Washington, D.C.: Government Printing Office, 1968).

TAX EXPENDITURES

The federal government makes *tax expenditures* through its tax system by excluding certain types of income from the personal and corporate tax bases, by granting additional personal exemptions to certain classes of individuals, by permitting deductions and tax credits, and through other special features of the tax laws (see Chapter 13). These expenditures result because federal revenue is reduced by each of these provisions; additional tax expenditures have the same effect on the overall budget surplus or deficit as additional budget outlays. Tax expenditures can be used to further policy objectives, just as regular expenditures and lending activity are directed toward specific goals. The difference is that tax expenditures are not reviewed annually by the Congress, the Office of Management and Budget, or the public at large. Many specific tax expenditures have been a part of the federal tax system for many years; they come to be called loopholes when the connection between the policy objective and the specific tax provision becomes tenuous. Economists as well as politicians and taxpayers have long been aware of this dimension of public policy. The first major effort to record systematically tax expenditures using the conceptual framework of the budget appeared in the *Annual Report of the Secretary of the Treasury, 1968*.[37] The analysis was extended to cover the tax expenditures implicit in the 1970 budget in the testimony of Secretary of the Treasury Joseph W. Barr before the Joint Economic Committee, January 17, 1969.[38] On June 2, 1970, Murray L. Weidenbaum, Assistant Secretary of the Treasury for Economic Policy, in testimony before the Subcommittee on Economy in Government of the Joint Economic Committee, presented similar data for fiscal year 1969; he used the term *tax aids* instead of tax expenditures, perhaps as a means of differentiating a Republican report from a Democratic one.

As examples of tax expenditures, we present Table 12.11, for the functional category health and welfare. Here estimates are presented for the revenue loss to the Treasury resulting from exemptions, exclusions, and deductions designed to promote health and welfare. These estimates lack the precision of recorded budget outlays, but their relative magnitudes are impressive. Total tax expenditures, by function, are shown in Table 12.12 for most of the categories of budget outlays listed in Table 12.2; estimated tax expenditures as a percent of actual budget outlays are also given. For the functional categories, commerce and transportation and community development and housing, tax exenpditures exceeded budget outlays for fiscal year 1969.[39]

---

[37] For a discussion of the many and vexing conceptual problems involved in estimating the amount of foregone revenue associated with particular tax expenditures, *see* Boris I. Bittker, "Accounting for Federal 'Tax Subsidies' in the National Budget," *National Tax Journal,* June 1969.

[38] *The 1969 Economic Report of the President*, Hearings before the Joint Economic Committee, Part 1, 91st Congress, 1st session (Washington, D.C.: Government Printing Office, 1969).

[39] For an analysis of tax expenditures in the housing area *see* Henry Aaron, "Income Taxes and Housing," *American Economic Review*, December 1970.

Table 12.11 **Tax Expenditures for Health and Welfare, 1968 and 1969 (Millions of dollars)**

	1968	1969
Disability insurance benefits	—	100
Aged, blind, and disabled:		
Additional exemption, retirement income credit and exclusion of OASDHI for aged	2,300	2,700
Additional exemption for blind	10	10
Exclusion for sick pay	85	95
Exclusion of unemployment insurance benefits	300	325
Exclusion of workmen's compensation benefits	150	180
Exclusion of public assistance benefits	50	50
Exclusion for employee pensions	3,000	4,000
Deduction for self-employed	60	135
Exclusion of other employee benefits:		
Premiums on group term life insurance	400	400
Accident and death benefits	25	25
Medical insurance premiums and medical care	1,100	1,400
Privately financed supplementary unemployment benefits	25	15
Meals and lodging	150	165
Exclusion of interest on life insurance savings	900	1,000
Deductibility by individuals of charitable contributions (other than education) including untaxed appreciation	2,200	3,000
Deductibility of medical expenses	1,500	1,600
Deductibility of child and dependent care expenses	25	25
Deductibility of casualty losses	70	80
Standard deduction	3,200*	3,600*
Total	15,550	18,905

* In the absence of the 10 percent standard deduction and most itemized nonbusiness deductions, the minimum standard deduction as presently structured would be taken by all taxpayers, and its revenue cost would be relatively large. Under present treatment, the minimum standard deduction, in keeping with its objectives, is claimed almost entirely by low income taxpayers, and its revenue cost is $300 million. The revenue estimate assumes the minimum standard deduction is designed to assist only low income taxpayers. The minimum standard deduction is regarded in this analysis as related to the system of personal exemptions and thus a part of the structure of an income tax system based on ability to pay, rather than as a tax expenditure.

SOURCE: *The 1969 Economic Report of the President,* Hearings before the Joint Economic Committee, Part 1, 91st Congress, 1st session (Washington, D.C.: Government Printing Office, 1969), p. 41, and "Statement by the Honorable Murray L. Weidenbaum Assistant Secretary of the Treasury for Economic Policy before the Subcommittee on Economy in Government of the Joint Economic Committee," Department of the Treasury, 1970.

Table 12.12 **Tax Expenditures by Function, 1968 and 1969**

Description	Estimated Amount (Billions of dollars) 1968	1969	Percent of Budget Outlays 1968	1969
National defense	.5	.6	1	1
International affairs and finance	.4	.4	9	10
Agriculture and agricultural resources	.9	1.0	15	16
Natural resources	1.6	1.8	94	83
Commerce and transportation	7.8	9.2	98	117
Community development and housing	4.0	4.8	98	125
Health and welfare	15.6	18.9	36	39
Education and manpower	.7	.8	10	12
Veterans benefits and services	.6	.6	9	8

SOURCE: *The 1969 Economic Report of the President,* Hearings before the Joint Economic Committee, Part 1, 91st Congress, 1st session (Washington, D.C.: Government Printing Office, 1969), pp. 34–42, and "Statement by the Honorable Murray L. Weidenbaum Assistant Secretary of the Treasury for Economic Policy before the Subcommittee on Economy in Government of the Joint Economic Committee," Department of the Treasury, 1970.

The $600 personal exemption and the minimum standard deduction taken by low income families are not treated as tax expenditures because these features of tax law are thought to reflect the desired degree of progression in the rate structure. For 1968 the revenue loss to the Treasury from the preferential tax treatment of capital gains was estimated to range between $5.5 billion and $8.5 billion; this tax expenditure cannot be distributed among the functional categories. In addition to the federal grants-in-aid to state and local governments shown in Table 12.4, the deduction of nonbusiness state and local taxes and the exemption of interest on state and local government securities resulted in tax expenditures of $4.2 and $2 billion, respectively, in 1969. Again, these amounts cannot be readily assigned to functional categories.

These systematically presented data on tax expenditures provide some much-needed additional information concerning the total impact of the federal budget.[40] Year to year changes in tax expenditure magnitudes, either because of economic growth or through legislative actions, substantially affect the size of the budget deficit (or surplus) and the expansionary (or restrictive) course of the economy. These data will probably be incorporated into the budget documents in future years.

---

[40] State and local governments also make tax expenditures but no estimates have been made of the magnitudes involved.

13

THE FEDERAL TAX SYSTEM

All citizens pay some federal taxes. The most frugal recluse is likely to purchase some products manufactured by corporations subject to the corporate income tax, even if he earns no income subject to personal income and payroll taxes, and buys no products whose price includes federal excise taxes or tariffs. The complexity of our contemporary economy is mirrored—perhaps to the extent of distortion—by the Internal Revenue Code, the administrative interpretation of that Code made by the Internal Revenue Service, and the judicial interpretation embodied in the decisions of the U.S. Tax Court and other federal courts. Many astute and well-paid lawyers and accountants devote their professional lives to the search for new ways of tax avoidance, showing clients how to minimize their tax liabilities.[1] Hardly a session of Congress goes by without passage of some major tax legislation: The rate structure

[1] *Tax avoidance*, or using all the appropriate loopholes and securing favorable rulings from the Internal Revenue Service and decisions from the courts, is quite legal and not to be confused with *tax evasion*—the illegal failure to pay tax liabilities.

is changed, the definition of the tax base modified, new loopholes opened, and old ones darned. In addition to major legislation whose course is followed in the headlines, many bills are introduced in Congress each year to make minor, technical revisions in the tax laws. We cannot attempt a complete description of the federal tax system, nor can we provide a taxpayer's guide.[2] Instead, the major features of the federal tax system as it exists in the early 1970s are considered and analyzed in the terms of the concepts of allocative efficiency and distributive equity developed in Chapters 7 and 8. Several possibilities for tax reform are discussed, and some empirical literature on redistribution through the federal tax and expenditure process is reviewed.

PERSONAL INCOME TAXATION

The base. Tax liabilities are determined by a combination of tax bases and tax rates. The base for the federal personal income tax, *taxable personal income,* commands our attention first, holding the discussion of rates until later in this section. The definition of taxable personal income is both complex and controversial; the complexity stems from the many ways in which individuals arrange their financial affairs, and the controversy follows from questions of economic efficiency and equity that characterize any particular definition. The income concepts employed in the Internal Revenue Code are

---

[2] For a more detailed treatment see the following volumes in the Studies of Government Finance series published by the Brookings Institution: David J. Ott and Allan H. Meltzer, *Federal Tax Treatment of State and Local Securities*; Stephen L. McDonald, *Federal Tax Treatment of Income from Oil and Gas*; Harold M. Groves, *Federal Tax Treatment of the Family*; John F. Due (ed.), *The Role of Direct and Indirect Taxes in the Federal Revenue System*; Richard Goode, *The Individual Income Tax*; Lawrence B. Krause and Kenneth W. Dam, *Federal Tax Treatment of Foreign Income*; Carl S. Shoup, *Federal Estate and Gift Taxes*; Joseph A. Pechman, *Federal Tax Policy*, rev. ed.; Gerald R. Jantscher, *Trusts and Estate Taxation*; Martin David, *Alternative Approaches to Capital Gains Taxation*; and Arnold C. Harberger and Martin J. Bailey (eds.), *The Taxation of Income from Capital.* Also see these volumes in the series of Fiscal Studies sponsored by the National Bureau of Economic Research: Dan Throop Smith and J. Keith Butters, *Taxable and Business Income*; Lawrence H. Seltzer, *The Nature and Tax Treatment of Capital Gains and Losses*; Daniel M. Holland, *The Income Tax Burden on Stockholders*; C. Harry Kahn, *Personal Deduction in the Federal Income Tax*; Daniel M. Holland, *Dividends Under the Income Tax*; C. Harry Kahn, *Business and Professional Income Under the Personal Income Tax*; and Norman B. Ture, *Accelerated Depreciation in the United States, 1954–60.* One can keep abreast of current developments in the area of federal taxation through the various tax guides published by Research Institute of America, Commerce Clearing House, and Prentice-Hall. Detailed data derived from actual tax returns are made available by the Internal Revenue Service in their *Statistics of Income* series. Hearings and compendiums published by the House Ways and Means Committee are also valuable sources of information and opinion.

related, but by no means identical, to those in national income accounts.[3] The most inclusive concept ever proposed as a measure of personal income for tax purposes is attributed to Henry Simons.[4] He argued that an individual's (or household's) consumption, plus changes, including accrued changes, in net wealth during an accounting period constituted the proper base for an income tax. Alternatively this concept can be interpreted as meaning that one's ability to pay taxes is measured by that amount of consumption that could be undertaken during the year and still maintain one's wealth at its initial level. Most economists subscribe to this definition in principle. The tax base that has emerged in practice diverges considerably from Simon's norm. The divergence results from three factors: the exclusion from taxation of income from certain sources, personal exemptions, and allowable deductions. Each is examined in turn.[5]

Personal receipts necessary to cover expenses incurred as the taxpayer earned his income are not income and are excluded from personal income taxation. The cost of a workman's tools, the office expenses of the self-employed, and the entertainment of customers are included in this category. The basic rationale is clear on equity grounds as business expenses must be subtracted from receipts to determine income, but the dividing line between legitimate business expenses and personal consumption is fuzzy. For example, moving expenses are excluded—the costs of commuting to work are not. Educational expenses incurred as a condition of employment or to maintain competency in one's job can be excluded—educational expenses incurred to qualify for a better job cannot.

Some types of income are excluded from federal personal income taxation. On equity grounds sick pay and welfare payments, including social security benefits, are excluded. Insurance benefits and a portion of pension fund payments are excluded on the grounds that they represent a repayment to the taxpayer of income set aside in prior years and on which he was previously taxed. The first $100 of dividend income is excluded as a sop to those who argue that dividend income has already been taxed at the corporate level, and that inclusion of dividend income represents inequitable

---

[3] Joseph A. Pechman, *op. cit.*, p. 272, gives a detailed reconciliation of aggregate personal income as recorded in the national income accounts, with aggregate adjusted gross income. For 1968 personal income was $688.7 billion and adjusted gross income equaled $599.7 billion.

[4] *Personal Income Taxation* (Chicago: University of Chicago Press, 1938).

[5] A further issue is the definition of the taxable unit: Is the person or the household the taxpaying unit, and if the household, how should the income of separate members of the household be treated?

For a discussion of many of these definitional issues, *see* Boris I. Bittker, Charles O. Galvin, Richard A. Musgrave, and Joseph A. Pechman, *A Comprehensive Income Tax Base? A Debate* (Branford, Conn.: Federal Tax Press, Inc., 1968).

double taxation. As explained in more detail below, interest income from state and local government securities is excluded, income from extractive industries is not fully taxable, and only a portion of net long-term capital gains are included in the definition of taxable personal income. Most income in kind—in particular, the rental value of owner occupied housing—is excluded, more on practical than philosophic grounds. It would require an army of tax assessors to determine the implicit income received by each taxpayer who grows some of his own food, mows his lawn, or is taken to lunch by a salesman. Only in clear-cut cases of income in kind provided by an employer, such as rent-free housing, is such income subject to tax.

The taxpayer's total receipts minus such exclusions is called *adjusted gross income*. Exemptions and deductions are subtracted from adjusted gross income to derive taxable personal income.

From 1948 to 1969 a taxpayer was permitted to deduct a $600 personal exemption for himself plus an additional $600 personal exemption for each of his dependents from his adjusted gross income in computing his taxable income. Additional personal exemptions of $600 were permitted for a taxpayer or spouse who was age 65 or over and/or was blind. The personal exemption is often defended on the grounds that it represents the minimum income needed for subsistence, and equity requires that it be excluded from taxation. If this is its purpose, equity then requires that the size of the exemption be adjusted as price levels change. This, in fact, was done by the Tax Reform Act of 1969; the personal exemption was increased, by steps, to $750 from 1970 to 1973. This increase in the personal exemption is, however, proportionately less than the inflation that has occurred since 1948. Since enactment of the personal income tax in 1913, Congress has changed the size of the personal exemption several times as shown in Table 13.1, column 2. The role of the personal exemption in determining the broadness of the tax base may be seen by considering the number of returns with taxable income, recorded in Table 13.1, column 3. During World War II, the size of the personal exemption was significantly reduced and the number of taxable returns increased. It was only then that the personal income tax base was broadened to make the majority of the population subject to personal income tax liabilities. This was accomplished primarily through adjustment in the size of the personal exemption, although rising personal incomes also played a role as shown in column 4. For calendar year 1967, 198 million personal exemptions were claimed on federal income tax returns (including those returns without any taxable income). Of these, 8.4 million were second exemptions claimed by those age 65 or over, and .1 million were second exemptions taken by the blind. Subtracting these 8.5 million second exemptions that represent double counting leaves 189.5 million persons claimed as exemptions on 1967 income tax returns. The estimated population of the United States as of July 1, 1967, was 199.1 million. Thus, all but

Table 13.1 Federal Personal Income Tax Data

Year (1)	Personal Exemptions (2) Single	Personal Exemptions (2) Married Couple	Returns Taxable (Millions) (3)	Per Capita Personal Income (4)	Tax Rates[1] First Bracket Rate (Percent)	Tax Rates[1] First Bracket Amount of Taxable Income (Thousands) (5)	Tax Rates[1] Top Bracket Rate (Percent)	Tax Rates[1] Top Bracket Taxable Income Over (Thousands) (6)	Personal Income Tax Receipts (Millions) (7)
1913	$3000	$4000	Na	Na	1.000	$20.0	7.00	$ 500	$ 28
1914	3000	4000	Na	Na	1.000	20.0	7.00	500	41
1915	3000	4000	Na	Na	1.000	20.0	7.00	500	68
1916	3000	4000	.4	Na	2.000	20.0	15.00	2000	173
1917	1000	2000	2.7	Na	2.000	2.0	67.00	2000	692
1918	1000	2000	3.4	Na	6.000	4.0	77.00	1000	1128
1919	1000	2000	4.2	Na	4.000	4.0	73.00	1000	1270
1920	1000	2000	5.5	Na	4.000	4.0	73.00	1000	1075
1921	1000	2500	3.6	Na	4.000	4.0	73.00	1000	719
1922	1000	2500	3.7	Na	4.000	4.0	56.00	200	861
1923	1000	2500	4.3	Na	3.000	4.0	56.00	200	662
1924	1000	2500	4.5	Na	1.500	4.0	46.00	500	704
1925	1000	3500	2.5	Na	1.125	4.0	25.00	100	735
1926	1000	3500	2.5	Na	1.125	4.0	25.00	100	732
1927	1000	3500	2.4	Na	1.125	4.0	25.00	100	831
1928	1000	3500	2.5	Na	1.125	4.0	25.00	100	1164
1929	1000	3500	2.5	705	.375	4.0	24.00	100	1002
1930	1000	3500	2.0	625	1.125	4.0	25.00	100	477
1931	1000	3500	1.5	531	1.125	4.0	25.00	100	246
1932	1000	2500	1.9	401	4.000	4.0	63.00	1000	330
1933	1000	2500	1.7	374	4.000	4.0	63.00	1000	374
1934	1000	2500	1.8	427	4.000	4.0	63.00	1000	511
1935	1000	2500	2.1	474	4.000	4.0	63.00	1000	657
1936	1000	2500	2.9	535	4.000	4.0	79.00	5000	1,214
1937	1000	2500	3.3	575	4.000	4.0	79.00	5000	1,093
1938	1000	2500	3.0	526	4.000	4.0	79.00	5000	726
1939	1000	2500	3.9	555	4.000	4.0	79.00	5000	891
1940	800	2000	7.4	593	4.400	4.0	81.10	5000	1,441
1941	750	1500	17.5	719	10.000	2.0	81.00	5000	3,815
1942	500	1200	27.6	911	19.000	2.0	88.00	200	8,823
1943	500	1200	40.2	1106	19.000	2.0	88.00	200	14,449
1944	500	1000	42.4	1194	23.000	2.0	94.00	200	16,216
1945	500	1000	42.7	1223	23.000	2.0	94.00	200	17,050
1946	500	1000	37.9	1246	19.000	2.0	86.45	200	16,076
1947	500	1000	41.6	1327	19.000	2.0	86.45	200	18,076
1948	600	1200	36.4	1434	16.600	2.0	82.13	200	15,442
1949	600	1200	35.6	1389	16.600	2.0	82.13	200	14,538
1950	600	1200	38.2	1501	17.400	2.0	91.00	200	18,375
1951	600	1200	42.6	1657	20.400	2.0	91.00	200	24,228
1952	600	1200	43.9	1736	22.200	2.0	92.00	200	27,803
1953	600	1200	45.2	1806	22.200	2.0	92.00	200	29,431
1954	600	1200	42.6	1787	20.000	2.0	91.00	200	26,666
1955	600	1200	44.7	1881	20.000	2.0	91.00	200	29,614
1956	600	1200	46.3	1980	20.000	2.0	91.00	200	32,732
1957	600	1200	46.9	2050	20.000	2.0	91.00	200	34,394
1958	600	1200	45.7	2074	20.000	2.0	91.00	200	34,336
1959	600	1200	47.5	2166	20.000	2.0	91.00	200	38,645
1960	600	1200	48.1	2219	20.000	2.0	91.00	200	39,464
1961	600	1200	48.6	2268	20.000	2.0	91.00	200	42,225
1962	600	1200	50.1	2371	20.000	2.0	91.00	200	44,903
1963	600	1200	51.3	2457	20.000	2.0	91.00	200	48,204
1964	600	1200	51.3	2581	16.000	.5	77.00	200	47,153
1965	600	1200	53.7	2750	14.000	.5	70.00	100	49,530
1966	600	1200	56.7	2982	14.000	.5	70.00	100	56,087
1967	600	1200	58.7	3161	14.000	.5	70.00	100	62,920
1968	600	1200	61.3	3420	14.000	.5	70.00	100	76,579
1969	600	1200	Na	3676	14.000	.5	70.00	100	Na
1970	625	1250	Na	Na	14.000	.5	70.00	100	Na

[1] Single taxpayer.
Na: Not available.

about 5 percent of the persons in the United States in 1967 were recorded for income tax purposes; most of the unrecorded were over 65.[6]

Deductions from adjusted gross income are permitted in computing taxable personal income in order to advance both the allocative and equity goals of public policy. Contributions to churches, schools, and other nonprofit organizations are deductible based on the belief that the expenditures of these organizations are socially desirable and that the community benefits from allocation of additional resources to them.[7] If, for example, a taxpayer is subject to a 50 percent marginal personal income tax rate, making a $1000 contribution to his alma mater results in only a $500 out-of-pocket expense since the deductible contribution reduces his taxable income and thus reduces his tax liability by $500. Because the tax mechanism partially subsidizes deductible contributions, as the federal government makes tax expenditures, the total size of such contributions may be increased; whenever funds are being raised by nonprofit organizations their solicitors usually point out this feature of the tax laws. Interest paid on a home mortgage and medical and dental expenses (in excess of 3 percent of adjusted gross income) are deductions that are sometimes defended on the basis of social desirability. Home ownership gives the citizen a stake in his community thus encouraging good citizenship; medical care not only enhances the quality of the patient's life but also has the third party benefit of reducing the likelihood of the spread

---

SOURCE: Columns 1, 2, 5, and 6: *The Federal Tax System: Facts and Problems, 1964,* Joint Economic Committee, 88th Congress, 2d Session (Washington, D.C.: Government Printing Office, 1964), pp. 214–215 and 233. Column 3: *Statistics of Income, 1965, Individual Income Tax Returns,* U.S. Treasury Department, Internal Revenue Service (Washington, D.C.: Government Printing Office, 1967), p. 209. Column 4: *The National Income and Product Account of the United States, 1929–1965, Statistical Tables,* A Supplement to the Survey of Current Business, U.S. Department of Commerce, Office of Business Economics (Washington, D.C.: Government Printing Office, 1966), p. 156. Column 7: *Historical Statistics of the United States, Colonial Times to 1957,* U.S. Department of Commerce, Bureau of the Census (Washington, D.C.: Government Printing Office, 1960), pp. 714 and 715, and *Historical Statistics of the United States, Continuation to 1962 and Revisions*, U.S. Department of Commerce, Bureau of the Census (Washington, D.C.: Government Printing Office, 1965), p. 97.

[6] For these data and many others pertaining to the federal income tax, see *Statistics of Income, Individual Income Tax Returns, 1967* (Washington, D.C.: Government Printing Office, 1969).

[7] Deductions reduce the size of the tax base. As a result tax rates must be higher than in the absence of deductions in order to raise a given amount of revenue. Thus, when one citizen takes an income tax deduction, other citizens' tax liabilities are increased. This argument was used by a Maryland atheist in her 1964 effort to persuade the Supreme Court to declare unconstitutional the deductibility of contributions to churches. The Court recognized the argument as valid, thus acknowledging the atheist's increased income tax liability. The Court at the same time refused to declare this provision of the Internal Revenue Code unconstitutional; it argued that church expenditures yielded third party benefits from which even the atheist benefited, like it or not, and as a result the Court saw no reason to prohibit this deduction.

of communicable disease and thus should be encouraged. On the other hand, equity considerations are often important determinants of deductions; medical and dental expenses up to 3 percent of total income are regarded as normal, but those in excess of 3 percent are presumed to reflect serious illness and equity requires that the taxpayer in ill health receive relief since these extraordinary expenditures reduce his ability to pay taxes. One-half the cost of medical insurance is deductible directly. State and local taxes paid are also deductible from adjusted gross income in computing taxable personal income. This deduction, in some instances at least, was required for equity reasons prior to 1964 because the marginal federal income tax rate (91 percent) plus some marginal state income tax rates exceeded 100 percent. Few would argue that equity requires taxing income at more than a 100 percent marginal rate.

Itemizing deductions requires keeping extensive records and the compliance cost of such record keeping may be high.[8] Since all taxpayers are eligible to claim some deductions in computing their tax base (we all pay some state taxes, for example), the Internal Revenue Code, prior to 1971, permitted taxpayers to claim a *standard deduction* equal to 10 percent of their adjusted gross income (not to exceed $1000, however) in lieu of itemizing deductions. Recognizing the compliance costs of itemizing deductions and the fact that rising incomes and prices during the postwar years caused more and more taxpayers to itemize deductions, the Tax Reform Act of 1969 provided for an increase, by stages during 1971, 1972, and 1973, in the standard deduction to 15 percent of adjusted gross income with $2000 being the maximum.

Although best known as a stabilization measure (see Chapter 17), the Revenue Act of 1964 contained a number of features primarily intended to promote tax equity. Among these is the *minimum standard deduction.* In

---

[8] In Chapter 4 we warned that efficiency might be inappropriately measured by looking at expenditures of an agency rather than the total, economy-wide cost of an activity. The more records that must be kept by the taxpayer, the smaller will be the enforcement costs borne by the Internal Revenue Service, and conversely. One estimate is that the compliance costs of filing 1964 individual income tax returns, including imputed value of the taxpayer's labor time, was $1.3 billion. *See* "The Private Costs of Filing Individual Income Tax Returns," in Arthur B. Willis (ed.), *Studies in Substantive Tax Reform* (Chicago: American Bar Association, 1969), chapter 9.

The costs to the federal government of collecting its revenues is small. In fiscal year 1969 the expenditures of the Internal Revenue Service were .52 percent of total federal budget tax receipts. (Computed from the *Budget of the United States Government, 1971,* pp. 65 and 419.) By contrast, the collection cost of a well-administered local property tax would probably exceed 1 percent of revenue due to the expense of proper assessment. Dick Netzer, *Economics of the Property Tax* (Washington, D.C.: The Brookings Institution, 1966), pp. 174–176. The compliance costs incurred by the payer of property taxes are, however, virtually zero.

Table 13.2 **Personal Income Tax Deductions, Taxable Returns With Itemized Deductions, 1966**

Adjusted Gross Income Classes	Number of Returns	Total Deductions		Specific Deductions as a Percent of AGI			
		Amount (Millions)	Percent of Adjusted Gross Income	Medical Expenses	Taxes Paid	Interest Paid	Contributions
Under $2000	317	$ 157	31.2	10.1	8.5	2.9	5.9
$2000 under $3000	849	573	26.4	8.3	7.0	3.5	4.7
$3000 under $4000	1324	1,160	24.9	7.2	6.7	4.0	4.1
$4000 under $5000	1703	1,767	22.9	5.9	6.3	4.5	3.8
$5000 under $6000	2170	2,641	22.0	4.7	6.0	5.4	3.4
$6000 under $7000	2254	3,421	20.6	3.6	5.9	5.7	3.1
$7000 under $8000	2737	4,113	20.0	2.9	6.1	6.0	2.8
$8000 under $9000	2679	4,416	19.4	2.7	6.0	6.0	2.8
$9000 under $10,000	2337	4,205	18.9	2.3	6.0	6.0	2.7
$10,000 under $15,000	6551	13,691	17.3	1.7	5.9	5.5	2.6
$15,000 under $20,000	1842	5,007	15.9	1.4	5.8	4.6	2.6
$20,000 under $50,000	1479	6,186	14.6	1.3	5.6	3.5	2.8
$50,000 under $100,000	211	2,002	14.3	0.9	5.3	3.1	3.3
$100,000 under $200,000	40	883	16.7	0.7	5.3	3.4	4.9
$200,000 under $500,000	9	548	19.6	0.4	5.1	3.8	7.4
$500,000 under $1,000,000	2	207	20.0	0.1	4.7	3.5	9.3
$1,000,000 or more	0.6	268	20.2	0.07	4.1	2.4	11.8

SOURCE: *Statistics of Income, 1966, Individual Income Tax Returns,* Internal Revenue Service, U.S. Treasury Department (Washington, D.C.: Government Printing Office, 1968), pp. 54 and 60.

1964 Americans were becoming increasingly aware of poverty in the United States, and federal poverty guidelines formally defined a family of four with annual income less than $3000 as poor. Reflecting the belief that it was inequitable for the poor to incur federal income tax liabilities, the minimum standard deduction was introduced into the Internal Revenue Code: The taxpaying family, in lieu of itemizing deductions or taking the 10 percent standard deduction, may take a basic $200 deduction plus an additional $100 deduction for each personal exemption to which the family is entitled. Thus, a family of four was entitled to a minimum standard deduction equal to $600; when subtracted from adjusted gross income along with the family's $2400 personal exemption, taxable income was zero and the family incurred no federal income tax liability. The Tax Reform Act of 1969 increased the size of the minimum standard deduction to a fixed amount of $1000 as of 1972. This benefits all families of less than eight members and was specifically intended to remove about 5 million low income families from the tax rolls.

Some data are presented in Table 13.2 on the major types of nonbusiness deductions taken by taxpayers who itemized their deductions in 1966. Although not explicitly indicated, some taxpayers with a positive amount of adjusted gross income have sufficient deductions to reduce their taxable personal income to zero. Total deductions as a percent of adjusted gross income decline through all adjusted gross income classes up to the $100,000 level and increase in the four highest classes. Not surprisingly contributions are the most important deductions for high income taxpayers.

Rates. The federal personal income tax rests on a schedule of progressive rates. Progression is built into federal income taxation by a rising schedule of marginal tax rates applied to successive increments of taxable personal income. Thus, as shown in Table 13.3, column 2, for the schedule of income tax rates in effect since 1965, the first $500 of taxable income is taxed at a 14 percent rate, the second $500 at a 15 percent rate, the third $500 at a 16 percent rate, and so on, and all taxable income in excess of $100,000 is taxed at a 70 percent rate.[9] It is important to understand that these rising marginal tax rates are applied only to successive increments of taxable income; thus, a taxpayer incurs a $70 tax liability on his first $500 of taxable income (14 percent rate), a $75 tax liability on his second $500 of taxable income (15 percent rate), and an $80 tax liability on his third $500 of tax-

---

[9] Effective April 1, 1968, Congress enacted a 10 percent surtax computed as a percent of the tax liability. The surtax was reduced to 5 percent on January 1, 1970, and was repealed as of June 30, 1970. Since the basic tax rates were not modified (and low income taxpayers were, in fact, exempted on equity grounds), the surtax is not further considered in this chapter. It is discussed as a means of stabilization policy in Chapter 17.

Table 13.3 Income Tax Rates, 1965–1970

(1) Tax Rate (percent)	(2) Single For Taxable Income		(3) Married (Joint Return) For Taxable Income		(4) Unmarried Head of Household For Taxable Income	
	Over	But not over	Over	But not over	Over	But not over
14	$ 0	$ 500	$ 0	$ 1,000	$ 0	$ 1,000
15	500	1,000	1,000	2,000		
16	1,000	1,500	2,000	3,000	1,000	2,000
17	1,500	2,000	3,000	4,000		
18					2,000	4,000
19	2,000	4,000	4,000	8,000		
20					4,000	6,000
22	4,000	6,000	8,000	12,000	6,000	8,000
25	6,000	8,000	12,000	16,000	8,000	10,000
27					10,000	12,000
28	8,000	10,000	16,000	20,000		
31					12,000	14,000
32	10,000	12,000	20,000	24,000	14,000	16,000
35					16,000	18,000
36	12,000	14,000	24,000	28,000	18,000	20,000
39	14,000	16,000	28,000	32,000		
40					20,000	22,000
41					22,000	24,000
42	16,000	18,000	32,000	36,000		
43					24,000	26,000
45	18,000	20,000	36,000	40,000	26,000	28,000
46					28,000	32,000
48	20,000	22,000	40,000	44,000	32,000	36,000
50	22,000	26,000	44,000	52,000	36,000	38,000
52					38,000	40,000
53	26,000	32,000	52,000	64,000	40,000	44,000
55	32,000	38,000	64,000	76,000	44,000	50,000
56					50,000	52,000
58	38,000	44,000	76,000	88,000	52,000	64,000
59					64,000	70,000
60	44,000	50,000	88,000	100,000		
61					70,000	76,000
62	50,000	60,000	100,000	120,000	76,000	80,000
63					80,000	88,000
64	60,000	70,000	120,000	140,000	88,000	100,000
66	70,000	80,000	140,000	160,000	100,000	120,000
67					120,000	140,000
68	80,000	90,000	160,000	180,000	140,000	160,000
69	90,000	100,000	180,000	200,000	160,000	180,000
70	100,000	—	200,000	—	180,000	—

SOURCE: *Statistics of Income, 1965, Individual Income Tax Returns,* U.S. Treasury Department, Internal Revenue Service (Washington, D.C.: Government Printing Office, 1967), p. 169.

U.C.W. ABERYSTWYTH LIBRARY

able income (16 percent rate). On a \$1500 taxable income the total tax liability is \$225; this is a 15 percent average rate of tax on total taxable income and is less than the 16 percent rate that applies at the margin. Similarly, the taxpayer with over \$100,000 in taxable income incurs tax liabilities at the 70 percent rate only on that part of his taxable income that exceeds \$100,000. He also incurs some tax liability at the lower rates and, irrespective of the height of his taxable income, his total tax liability, as a percent of taxable income, will always be less than 70 percent.

The schedule of tax rates applicable for single and married taxpayers is different as shown in Table 13.3, columns 2 and 3. Even if only one spouse received income, as long as they file a joint return, a couple may pay taxes as though husband and wife each received half of the family's taxable income and incurred separate tax liabilities on their respective shares. Because of the progressive rate structure, *income splitting,* as this provision is called, enables a couple to reduce substantially its total tax liability. Consider a single and a married taxpayer, each of whom has a \$100,000 taxable income. The bachelor incurs a \$55,490 tax liability whereas the married man's liability is only \$45,180. As shown in Table 13.3, column 4, single taxpayers who qualify as heads of households pay taxes at a third set of rates that accords to them approximately half of the tax advantages derived by married as compared with single taxpayers. Because many considered the tax treatment of single individuals as inequitable, the Tax Reform Act of 1969 modified the rate schedules for single taxpayers and heads of households. As of 1971 a new schedule of rates requiring that single taxpayers never pay over 20 percent more taxes than a married taxpayer with the same income was enacted; the schedule of rates for heads of households was made to fall halfway between the new schedule for single taxpayers and the schedule for married taxpayers.

The schedules of personal income tax rates have been changed several times since the tax was first enacted. As shown in Table 13.1, columns 5 and 6, income tax rates were at first modest (when compared with today's rates) and the brackets to which these rates applied were wide. Rapidly growing revenue requirements to finance World War II led to increased income tax rates and narrower brackets to which those rates applied. The personal income tax was democraticized and became the principal source of federal government tax revenue.

There were 58.9 million income tax returns with taxable income for calendar year 1967.[10] Each of these returns included taxable income taxed at the 14 percent marginal rate; for successively higher marginal rates fewer and fewer returns incurred any liabilities. All 58.9 million returns with tax-

---

[10] The data referred to in this paragraph come from *Statistics of Income, 1967: Individual Income Tax Returns, op. cit.*, p. 85.

able income generated some revenue at the 14 percent marginal rate, whereas only 5295 returns generated any tax at the 70 percent tax rate. The adjusted gross income reported on these 58.9 million taxable returns was $475 billion, and taxable income was $303 billion. About 90 percent of the income tax base and 80 percent of the tax revenue generated were at tax rates of 25 percent or less. Only about 3 percent of the tax base and 7 percent of the tax revenue generated were at marginal rates of 50 percent or above. This is a matter of considerable importance because it implies that major revenue changes require adjustment of the lower marginal rates, or broadly based changes in the definition of the tax base—variation in the personal exemption, for example. With a tax base of $46.2 billion, varying the 14 percent rate will have a substantial impact on federal government revenues. Top marginal rates are relatively unimportant as a source of revenue, and significant revenue variation can hardly be accomplished by adjustment in them. With a tax base of only $784 million, increasing or decreasing the 70 percent rate will barely change total federal government revenue collections. The resulting impact on the disposable income of the 5295 taxpayers who incur liabilities at this rate may be considerable; equity objectives principally govern such tax rate variations.

The Revenue Act of 1964 reduced the lowest bracket tax rate from 20 percent to the present 14 and 15 percent rates on the first $2000 of taxable income (for married couple filing joint return). This part of the income tax reduction, affecting all taxpayers, was at the core of the administration's stabilization program. At the same time, the top bracket rate was reduced from 91 percent to 70 percent. This latter reduction was of little consequence as a revenue measure and hence of minor importance as part of the stabilization program; the change was made on the belief that marginal rates of personal income tax as high as 91 percent (which at that time were the highest anywhere in the world) were inequitable. As a continuing reflection of this belief, the Tax Reform Act of 1969 provided that no taxpayer, after 1971, be required to pay more than 50 percent of his *earned* taxable income in federal personal income taxes.

Horizontal equity, as a canon of taxation, requires that equals be taxed equally, but over what time span is equality to be measured? Progressive tax rates make this issue important, for if tax liabilities are incurred annually, the taxpayer receiving his income in uneven flows will incur higher tax liabilities than a taxpayer who has the same total income received in equal annual installments. This might be the case of the novelist who produces a best seller every five years as compared with a salaried writer on the staff of a literary magazine. Suppose the novelist receives a $100,000 taxable income in his year of publication but has no other income during a five-year period; also assume the salaried writer receives a $20,000 taxable income per year for each of five years. Suppose both are single and are taxed at the rates given in Table 13.3, column 2. In his year of publication the novelist incurs a $55,490 personal income tax liability. The salaried writer incurs a $6,070 annual tax liability equaling $30,350 over a five-year period. Thus, over this period these writers earn the same income and might be judged equal; horizontal equity would then require that they incur equal tax liabilities but, because of progression in the tax rates, this does not occur. The novelist pays tax on the last $80,000 of income at rates ranging from 48 percent to 69 percent while the salaried writer pays tax on his equivalent $80,000 of income at rates ranging from 14 percent to 45 percent. In recognition of such violations of horizontal equity, income averaging was permitted by the Revenue Act of 1964 and further liberalized by the Tax Reform Act of 1969. *Income averaging* permits the taxpayer with markedly uneven income flows to treat his income over a five-year period as though it were received in equal annual installments.

Tax liabilities may be reduced by *tax credits*. The major tax credits are for certain amounts of retirement income, foreign income taxes paid, and the investment of tax credit (discussed in the next section in connection with corporate income taxes). Tax credits for other purposes are often proposed. Tax credits differ from exemptions and deductions in that they reduce tax liabilities rather than taxable personal income. An exclusion, deduction, or exemption of $100 reduces a taxpayer's liability by less than the full $100 of reduced tax liability he receives as a result of a $100 tax credit. The value of exclusions, deductions, and exemptions depends on the taxpayer's marginal tax rate.

An appraisal. The rate structure of the federal personal income tax is progressive but these rates are applied to taxable rather than total income. The belief is widely held that the tax structure should be evaluated with reference to total income rather than the tax base. Empirical evidence regarding the effective tax rate on adjusted gross income, by income class, is given in Table 13.4. Tax liabilities as a share of adjusted gross income are shown in column 4; effective tax rates are progressive. Measuring the degree of progression is somewhat arbitrary and is surely a function of how the income brackets are defined. Without attempting to define the degree of progression, we note that it is the low and middle income taxpayer who faces rapidly rising effective tax rates; these are taxpayers who derive the majority of their income from the sale of labor services.

As explained at the beginning of this section, adjusted gross income is a qualified portion of the taxpayers' total receipts. Probably the most important qualification pertains to the treatment of the profit income derived from the sale of assets. Profits from the sale of assets held less than six months are taxed as ordinary income. Profits from the sale of assets held more than six months are known as long-term *capital gains*, and their treatment for

Table 13.4 **Effective Tax Rates, Taxable Returns 1967**

Adjusted Gross Income Classes	Adjusted Gross Income (Millions) (1)	Amended Gross Income (Millions) (2)	Tax Liability (Millions) (3)	Effective Rate of Tax on Adjusted Gross Income (Percent) (4)	Effective Rate of Tax on Amended Gross Income (Percent) (5)
Under $1000	$ 586	$ 592	$ 5	0.9	0.8
$1000 under $2000	7,454	7,492	374	5.0	5.0
$2000 under $3000	10,901	10,961	793	7.3	7.2
$3000 under $4000	17,170	17,317	1,384	8.1	8.0
$4000 under $5000	22,380	22,528	1,914	8.6	8.5
$5000 under $6000	27,357	27,547	2,430	8.9	8.8
$6000 under $7000	33,271	33,476	3,066	9.2	9.2
$7000 under $8000	37,879	38,096	3,563	9.4	9.4
$8000 under $9000	37,812	38,068	3,766	10.0	9.9
$9000 under $10,000	36,296	36,500	3,775	10.4	10.3
$10,000 under $15,000	124,171	125,138	14,627	11.8	11.7
$15,000 under $20,000	46,762	47,544	6,562	14.0	13.8
$20,000 under $50,000	54,914	56,956	10,282	18.7	18.0
$50,000 under $100,000	17,162	18,596	5,054	29.5	27.2
$100,000 under $200,000	6,736	7,923	2,509	37.2	31.7
$200,000 under $500,000	3,619	4,822	1,504	41.6	31.2
$500,000 under $1,000,000	1,383	2,058	605	43.7	29.4
$1,000,000 or more	1,590	2,512	707	44.5	28.1

SOURCE: *Statistics of Income, 1967, Individual Income Tax Returns,* Internal Revenue Service, U.S. Treasury Department (Washington, D.C.: Government Printing Office, 1969), pp. 7 and 39. Amended gross income is computed by adding to adjusted gross income the net long-term capital gains (column 9 minus column 3, page 39), which were not included in adjusted gross income.

income tax purposes is controversial. Taxpayers own assets such as securities, real estate, paintings, and sculpture. The difference between the value of these assets when acquired and sold constitutes a capital gain (or loss) for their owner.[11] Capital gains clearly constitute income to the taxpayer; only a portion of these gains is included in the tax base, the mechanism being as follows. The taxpayer computes 50 percent of his capital gains; this amount constitutes the capital gains that qualify as a tax base. He may then either (1) add this half of capital gains to his income from other sources in computing adjusted gross income, or (2) he may compute his capital gains tax

[11] Capital losses may be fully deducted from capital gains and the resulting net capital gains is the concept dealt with in the text. Fifty percent of losses in excess of gains, up to $1000, may be deducted from income from other sources in computing taxable personal income.

liability as 50 percent of this base and the resulting tax liability is then added to his tax liability on income from all other sources to yield his total tax liability.[12] Since only half of capital gains is in a tax base, the effective rate of tax on capital gains income will be half the tax rate on income from other sources or, because of the second alternative, 25 percent. Thus, adjusted gross income, as defined by the Internal Revenue Service, includes only half of the capital gains income earned by those taxpayers who pay taxes on these gains under the first option and none of the capital gains income earned by those taxpayers who pay taxes on these gains under the second option. In 1967 the value of capital gains not included in adjusted gross income was $10.3 billion and this amount, when added to adjusted gross income, gives *amended gross income.*

Tax liabilities as a share of amended gross income are shown in Table 13.4, column 5; the effective rate structure becomes regressive for incomes above $200,000. This regressivity is attributable to the special treatment accorded capital gains. For adjusted gross incomes below $20,000, the effective tax rate on adjusted and amended gross incomes is nearly the same because citizens in the lower income brackets derive virtually all of their adjusted gross income from the sale of labor services. The gap between effective tax rates on adjusted and amended gross incomes widens as incomes rise because capital gains income increases in importance. This regressivity in the income tax structure is reinforced when the exclusion from federal income taxation of interest paid on state and local government securities is considered. At the end of 1969 the value of municipals outstanding was $132.2 billion, and $41.1 billion of these were held by households (see Table 11.14). Interest paid to households on these securities was over $1 billion. Such securities are held almost exclusively by high income citizens, and if amended gross income could be further refined to reflect this income flow, the degree of regressivity shown in Table 13.4 would be greater yet. The rationale for excluding interest on municipals from federal income taxation is that by doing so, their attractiveness to buyers will increase and the cost of debt service to state and local governments will be reduced. This is, in fact, the case; in the 1960s the yield difference on Aaa rated municipals and Aaa rated corporate bonds was in the vicinity of 1.5 percent.[13] If the federal government had elected to subsidize state and local borrowing rather than to make tax expenditures, municipals would then compete with

---

[12] As a result of the Tax Reform Act of 1969, use of this alternative computation is limited to the first $50,000 of long-term capital gains. Capital gains in excess of this amount are taxed under the first procedure.

[13] *Federal Reserve Bulletin,* May 1970, Table A 34. *See also,* David J. Ott and Allan H. Meltzer, *Federal Tax Treatment of State and Local Securities* (Washington, D.C.: Brookings Institution, 1963), especially chapter 3. Differences in the degree of risk may also be responsible for this yield difference.

corporate securities, increasing debt-service costs by $15 per year per $1000 bond. However, for each bond outstanding, taxpayers would receive, for example, $70 in taxable interest income. If we make the assumption that this interest income would be received by taxpayers in the 50 percent marginal bracket, tax receipts from these interest payments would total $35. Thus, tax expenditures are a more costly means of subsidizing state and local government interest payments because the revenue lost by the federal government exceeds the saving in interest charges to state and local governments. This fact, coupled with its implications for vertical equity, make this provision of the tax laws a target for reform. The target was missed in 1969.

Much of the debate over federal tax policy centers on capital gains. Few would deny they are income and eligible for income taxation, although the fact that they escape taxation altogether in some nations suggests that even this point is questioned. Ideally, the economist would have capital gains income recorded on an accrual basis with tax liabilities incurred in the year of accrued gain. This is impractical since many assets are not regularly marketed—paintings, for example—and making appraisals of their value would be arbitrary and inefficient. Furthermore, if assets had to be liquidated in order to meet tax liabilities, serious equity questions would arise. Thus, the current practice of taxing capital gains upon realization (for example, sale) appears necessary. Why, however, should these gains be taxed at special rates?

One viewpoint is that equity requires special treatment of capital gains because income flows are large in the year when gains are realized. Horizontal equity requires equal treatment of equals, and the progressive rate structure means that if capital gains are taxed at ordinary rates the taxpayer with large realized capital gains income in one year (that had accrued over many years) will incur a larger, long-run tax liability than the taxpayer with the same income received in equal annual installments. However, most high income taxpayers have capital gains income in each year, and the unevenness of their flow is not a relevant issue. To the extent it is, income averaging resolves this problem.

It is argued that high marginal income tax rates destroy incentives and, as an inducement for taxpayers to save and especially to supply risk capital, they must be able to reap and retain substantial returns on their savings. Since, the argument continues, investment is required for economic growth, the special treatment of capital gains stimulates the flow of funds into investment and is therefore socially desirable. There is some evidence to show that the special treatment of capital gains induces savers to hold assets that will appreciate in market value rather than assets producing annual flows as interest or dividends.[14] It is not clear, however, that allocating savings to

---

[14] J. Keith Butters, Lawrence E. Thompson, and Lynn L. Bollinger, *Effects of Taxation:*

firms that yield asset value appreciation rather than current incomes flows to security holders is a socially preferred allocation of resources. Two issues are at hand then: What is the effect of capital gains taxation on the allocation of savings between types of assets, and what is the effect of capital gains taxation on the total amount of savings to be allocated? We see that the answer to the first question is uncertain. To answer the second requires knowledge of who saves, what portion of their savings is affected by tax treatment of capital gains, and what would be done with these savings in the absence of special treatment of capital gains.[15]

In a society that believes equity is promoted by progressive income taxation, the special tax treatment of capital gains can be questioned. Arguments are, however, advanced for these provisions and available evidence leaves the analyst uncertain as to their relative merits. To a degree, capital gains taxation is an issue because of the high marginal tax rates on income from other sources; if the Internal Revenue Code were revised to provide full taxation of capital gains as ordinary income, the income tax base would be increased and the same amount of revenue could be raised from this expanded base at lower tax rates. For 1960 Richard Goode estimated that with full taxation of capital gains, all tax rates could have been cut by 4 percentage points and the degree of progression would have been substantially increased. If tax rates were reduced, leaving the degree of progression unchanged, substantial reductions could alternatively be made in the higher marginal rates;

Investments by Individuals (Boston: Harvard University Graduate School of Business Administration, 1953). Of course, the existence of special treatment of capital gains may induce firms to alter their management practices to produce capital gains returns to owners rather than current income flows; expansion of the firm through financing of investment from retained earnings will have this effect, for assets, and therefore stock values, increase without any increase in the number of equities outstanding.

[15] Related to this question is the whole problem of the effect of taxation on incentives. We saw in Chapter 7 that a theoretical case may be made for income taxation adding to or destroying work incentives. Empirical studies of this question conclude that taxation has no discernible effect on work incentives although high income taxpayers may try to incur deductible business expenses in order to avoid taxes. *See* Robin Barlow, Harvey E. Brazer, and James N. Morgan, *Economic Behavior of the Affluent* (Washington, D.C.: Brookings Institution, 1966), and "A Survey of Investment Management and Working Behavior Among High-Income Individuals," *American Economic Review*, May 1965; T.H. Sanders, *Effects of Taxation on Executives* (Boston: Harvard University Graduate School of Business Administration, 1951); C.H. Hall, *Effects of Taxation on Executive Compensation and Retirement* (Boston: Harvard University Graduate School of Business Administration, 1951); George Break, "Income, Taxes, Wage Rates, and the Incentive to Supply Labor Services," *National Tax Journal*, December 1953; R. Davidson, "Income Taxes and Incentives," *National Tax Journal,* September 1953; Lowell E. Gallaway, "Negative Income Tax Rates and the Elimination of Poverty," *National Tax Journal*, September 1966; and D. B. Fields and W. T. Stanbury, "Income Taxes and Incentives To Work: Some Additional Empirical Evidence," *American Economic Review*, June 1971.

the lower are marginal rates of tax on high incomes, the weaker these arguments for special treatment of capital gains become.[16]

CORPORATE INCOME TAX

Taxable corporate income is basically defined as the gross receipts of the corporation reduced by the expenses incurred producing those receipts. Receipts include the proceeds from sales plus whatever dividend or interest income the corporation receives, 50 percent of the corporation's capital gains (with no limitation on the amount of losses which may be offset), and any other receipts.[17] The cost of producing these receipts includes wages, salaries, rent, and interest as payments to factors of production; purchases of raw materials and manufactured inputs; state and local taxes; charitable contributions (within limits); and advertising expenditures. All these are straightforward deductions and are not further considered in this section. In addition, depreciation (or capital consumption) allowances and depletion allowances in extractive mineral industries are permitted deductions; these provisions are controversial and are taken up in detail as the discussion develops. Dividends paid on the equity capital of the corporation are not deductible; to the extent that dividends represent a normal return to equity capital, the Internal Revenue Service's definition of profit differs from the economist's definition used in earlier chapters. Thus, the base for the corporate income tax is the economic profit of corporations subject to certain qualifications; these qualifications are a source of controversy.

The schedule of corporate income tax rates is much simpler than the schedule of personal income tax rates. Since 1965 the basic rate has been 22 percent with a 26 percent surtax on all profits in excess of $25,000; thus small corporations are favored, reflecting the traditional American ideal of the small businessman; the large corporation is basically taxed at a 48 percent rate.[18] These corporate income tax rates reflect the tax reduction in the Revenue Act of 1964; this reduction reversed the trend for increasing corporate income tax rates, as illustrated in Table 13.5.[19] During World War II corporate income tax rates were increased and supplemented by an ex-

---

[16] For a discussion of this point, *see* Richard Goode, *The Individual Income Tax* (Washington, D.C.: The Brookings Institution, 1964), pp. 199–204.

[17] The Tax Reform Act of 1969 increased the effective rate of tax on the long-term capital gains of corporations from 25 to 30 percent.

[18] From January 1, 1968, until June 30, 1970, corporations were also subject to the surtax.

[19] The corporate income tax was enacted prior to adoption of the 16th Amendment and was upheld by the Supreme Court. The tax was assessed on the privilege of doing business as a corporation with the amount of profit taken as a measure of the privilege.

Table 13.5 **Corporate Income Tax—Rates and Base**

Calendar Year	Corporate Income Subject to Maximum Rate is That Income Over	Maximum Rate (Percent)
1909–13	$ 5,000.00	1.00
1913–15	—	1.00
1916	—	2.00
1917	—	6.00
1918	2,000.00	12.00
1919–21	2,000.00	10.00
1922–24	2,000.00	12.00
1925	2,000.00	13.00
1926–27	2,000.00	13.00
1928	3,000.00	12.00
1929	3,000.00	11.00
1930–31	3,000.00	12.00
1932–35	—	13.75
1936–37	40,000.00	15.00
1938–39	25,000.00	19.00
1940	38,565.89	24.00
1941	38,461.54	31.00
1942–45	50,000.00	40.00
1946–49	50,000.00	38.00
1950	25,000.00	42.00
1951	25,000.00	50.75
1952–63	25,000.00	52.00
1964	25,000.00	50.00
1965–70	25,000.00	48.00

SOURCE: *The Federal Tax System: Facts and Problems, 1964,* Joint Economic Committee, 88th Congress, 2d Session (Washington, D.C.: Government Printing Office, 1964), p. 265.

cess profits tax designed to increase effective tax rates (on taxable profits) to 80 percent. During the Korean War, corporate income tax rates were raised and supplemented by a 30 percent excess profit tax subject to the ceiling that the effective rate of tax not exceed 70 percent.

All factor payments except dividend payments on equity capital are deductible expenses in computing the corporate income tax base. This special treatment of one type of capital income is the source of several controversies centering around the belief that dividend income is taxed twice—once as it is received by the corporation and again as it is received by shareholders—and is inequitable. Also, double taxation is claimed to discourage equity financing by corporations. With respect to double taxation of dividend income it is important to know whether or not the tax is shifted—this issue is discussed shortly. If shifting of the tax occurs the double taxation argument is invalid. Based on the implicit assumption that the corporate income tax is not shifted, the inequitable double taxation argument is often voiced and is reflected in the Internal Revenue Code. Between 1954 and 1964 personal income taxpayers were permitted to exclude the first $50 of dividends from adjusted gross income and to take a tax credit against their personal income tax liability equal to 4 percent of all additional dividends. In 1964 this credit was reduced to 2 percent, and in 1965 it was eliminated. At the same time the dividend exclusion was increased to $100.

Division of financing between debt and equity is a different but related issue. With a 48 percent corporate income tax rate, to produce a 5 percent after-tax yield on a $1000 bond requires $50 in before-tax earnings; to produce a 5 percent after-tax yield on a $1000 equity requires that the corporation earn $96.15 before taxes. Thus, corporations may prefer debt to equity financing but management experts warn against excessive financing in fixed commitment obligations such as bonds. Because reliance on excessive debt financing is unsound management policy, it does not appear to occur; sale of equities remains the principal external source of new financing for corporations.[20]

The costs of capital goods—plant and equipment—are clearly business expenses to be subtracted from receipts as taxable corporate profits are computed. Since assets yield factor services over many years their full cost may not be subtracted during those years in which they are acquired. Instead, assets must be depreciated during their useful life, and the annual depreciation charge is the deductible capital expense in computing the corporate income tax base.[21]

Since 1954 three major depreciation schedules have been used. These are illustrated in Table 13.6 assuming a $10,000 asset with a 10-year useful life. *Straight-line depreciation*, the means primarily used prior to 1954, permits the corporation to write off asset acquisition costs in equal annual installments over the asset's life; as shown in column 1, one-tenth of the asset's acquisition value is deductible as the annual capital expense. In 1954 the Internal Revenue Code was modified to permit two additional depreciation schedules. First, the *200 percent of declining balance method* permits the corporation to take capital charges on the undepreciated balance at twice the rates permitted by straight-line depreciation. Thus, 20 percent of the asset's value—$2000—is the first year's depreciation charge and the undepreciated balance is $8000; in the second year 20 percent of this balance—$1600—is the capital charge, as shown in column 2. Finally, the *sum of the years digits* depreciation method permits the corporation to sum the asset's years

[20] Joseph A. Pechman, *Federal Tax Policy, op. cit.*, pp. 119–20, and *The Federal Tax System: Facts and Problems, op. cit.*, pp. 58–59.

[21] Depreciation, for tax purposes, is based on acquisition rather than replacement cost. The firm is permitted to recover the amount actually spent on factors of production rather than the amount needed to replace those factors.

Table 13.6 **Comparison of Depreciation Methods, $10,000 Asset**

	Straight-line (1)		200 Percent Declining Balance (2)		Sum of the Years-Digits (3)	
Year	Annual Charge	Cumulative Charges	Annual Charge	Cumulative Charges	Annual Charge	Cumulative Charges
1	$1000	$1,000	$2000	$2000	$1818	$1,818
2	1000	2,000	1600	3600	1636	3,454
3	1000	3,000	1280	4880	1455	4,909
4	1000	4,000	1024	5904	1273	6,182
5	1000	5,000	819	6723	1091	7,273
6	1000	6,000	655	7378	909	8,182
7	1000	7,000	[a]655	8033	727	8,909
8	1000	8,000	655	8688	545	9,454
9	1000	9,000	655	9343	364	9,818
10	1000	10,000	655	9998	182	10,000

[a] Switch to straight-line for years 7 through 10 authorized so that total depreciation will equal the cost of the asset. Cumulative charges do not add to $10,000 because of rounding.

SOURCE: *The Federal Tax System: Facts and Problems, 1964,* Joint Economic Committee, 88th Congress, 2d Session (Washington, D.C.: Government Printing Office, 1964), p. 90.

of useful life and compute capital charges in each year as that year is a share of the sum of the digits. Thus, the sum of the digits in our example is 55—equal to 10 + 9 + 8 . . . + 1—and the first year's depreciation charge is 10/55 of the asset's value, as shown in column 3.

Determining the asset's useful life is difficult but essential to computing depreciation charges. Prior to 1934 the corporation was generally free to declare any reasonable life. In 1934 this procedure was tightened by the Internal Revenue Service with the issue of *Bulletin F,* which specified useful lives for many assets. While not binding on the corporation, *Bulletin F* did establish a pattern that many believed set asset lives too long; incentives to invest were presumed to have been dampened because, in general, longer depreciation periods reduce rates of return. In 1954 the 200 percent of declining balance and sum of the years digits methods of *accelerated depreciation* were permitted, and in 1962 *Bulletin F* was supplemented by new guidelines that accorded assets useful lives some 30 to 40 percent shorter. These means of accelerated depreciation were coupled with the investment tax credit in 1962, as part of the Kennedy Administration's program to achieve full employment by encouraging the allocation of additional resources in investment, thereby increasing the investment component of aggregate demand. The investment tax credit as a stabilization measure is discussed in Chapter 17.

There is no question that depreciation charges are appropriate when the corporate tax is assessed on an income base; accelerated depreciation is at the core of controversy regarding this feature of the tax laws. On equity grounds the objection is raised that when capital consumption allowances are taken before capital consumption itself occurs, the taxpayer is enabled to postpone his tax liability and this is inequitable. However, others argue that assets depreciate more rapidly in their early years than in later years. Except for products such as automobiles, where style changes make old models quickly obsolete, it is not clear why this should be the case. On the other hand, if accelerated depreciation is an effective means of promoting policy objectives, such as increased rates of economic growth, this consideration perhaps takes precedence over other issues.

Far more controversial are mineral depletion allowances. As extractive properties yield their product they are exhausted (just as assets depreciate), and the Internal Revenue Code permits mineral industry producers to recover their capital costs through depletion allowances rather than depreciation. Under the *percentage depletion* method persons or firms engaged in extractive industries may deduct a fixed percentage of their annual gross receipts from extractive properties in computing their tax base, subject to the limitation that depletion deductions may not exceed 50 percent of net income in each year. However, depletion deductions may be taken in each year and there is no limitation on the total amount that may be deducted over a period of years. Thus firms may take depletion allowances that exceed the costs of developing the extractive properties. In addition, immediate depreciation write-offs for some exploration and development costs are permitted. The 1969 schedule of depletion rates by industry is given in Table 13.7, and the amount of depletion claimed in 1966 by size of firm and by industry is given in Table 13.8. Large firms take the most depletion, and the petroleum and natural gas industries are the principal beneficiaries.

It is estimated that the tax saving to corporations taking percentage depletion rather than depreciation is about $1.3 billion per year.[22] This being the case, a substantial misallocation of resources may result since for the same after-tax rate of return in extractive and other industries, the before-tax rate of return in extractive industries may be less.[23] Thus, by encouraging the allocation of resources to extractive industries, the tax mechanism is promoting reduced rates of return. On the other hand, proponents of depletion allowances argue that ordinary corporate income taxation does not

---

[22] *The 1969 Economic Report of the President*, Part I, Joint Economic Committee, 91st Congress, 1st Session (Washington, D.C.: Government Printing Office, 1969), p. 36. This tax saving by corporations is an annual revenue loss to the Treasury as this tax expenditure is made.

[23] Arnold Harberger, "The Taxation of Mineral Industries," *Tax Revision Compendium*, House Committee on Ways and Means, 86th Congress, 1st Session (Washington, D.C.: Government Printing Office, 1959); Paul Davidson, "Policy Problems of the Crude Petroleum Industry," *American Economic Review*, March 1963, and comments and reply, *American Economic Review*, March 1964.

Table 13.7 Depletion Rates

1969 Rate (Percent)	1970 Rate (Percent)	Industries
27.5	22	Oil and gas wells.
23	22	Sulfur, uranium, asbestos, bauxite, cobalt, lead, manganese, mercury, nickel, platinum, thorium, tin, titanum, tungsten, and zinc.
15	14	Certain clays, asphalt, vermiculite, and metals not covered by (2) above.
10	10	Asbestos (if not covered by (2) above), coal, lignite, and salt.
5	5	Brick and tile clay, gravel, sand, clam and oyster shells, peat, pumice, sand, scoria, shale, rough stone, and certain brine well products.
15	14	All other minerals except soil, sod, dirt, turf, water, or mosses, or minerals from sea water, the air, or similar inexhaustible sources.

SOURCE: *The Federal Tax System: Facts and Problems, 1964,* Joint Economic Committee, 88th Congress, 2d Session (Washington, D.C.: Government Printing Office, 1964) pp. 107–108, and *Wall Street Journal,* December 22, 1969.

account for different degrees of risk among industries, that oil and gas exploration, for example, is particularly risky, and that underallocation of resources to these industries would result in the absence of the special treatment accorded by depletion allowances. The evidence of especially large risk in oil and natural gas development is uncertain. Even if substantial risk is present, however, the preponderance of depletion allowances accrue to large firms (see Table 13.8) and the full loss offset against other revenues accorded to corporations should enable them to self-insure.

Equity questions are often raised when depletion is considered. First, recovery of capital costs in nonextractive industries is limited to actual outlays; depletion allowances permit the firm to recover more than its initial outlays, often in the first year of operation. Is this equitable?[24] Second, as

[24] A 1969 ruling of the Tax Court shows how the depletion allowances can be used to generate profits in a most unusual case. The Court "ruled that a geothermal steam well qualifies for the percentage depletion and other tax benefits granted oil and gas wells." Its ruling involved a firm that vents underground steam in the Geysers area near San Francisco and uses the steam to drive electric generators. The Court decided that the product of the well was indeed steam (not merely heat), and that steam

Table 13.8 **Depletion Deductions, Corporate Income Tax Returns, 1966 (Millions of dollars)**

By Size of Total Assets	
Total	3,860.9
Zero	6.1
$1–50,000	—
50,000–100,000	.02
100,000–250,000	.07
250,000–500,000	.3
500,000–1,000,000	1.5
1,000,000–5,000,000	15.9
5,000,000–10,000,000	10.8
10,000,000–25,000,000	31.5
25,000,000–50,000,000	53.4
50,000,000–100,000,000	108.3
100,000,000–250,000,000	164.6
250,000,000 or more	3,468.4
By Industrial Groups	
Total	3,860.9
Agriculture, forestry, and fisheries	1.2
Mining	691.0
Crude petroleum and natural gas	514.8
Contract construction	2.8
Manufacturing	2,902.4
Petroleum refining and related industries	2,377.6
Transportation, communication, electric, gas, and sanitary services	145.1
Wholesale and retail trade	33.3
Finance, insurance, and real estate	82.4
Services	2.8

SOURCE: *Statistics of Income, 1966, Corporation Income Tax Returns* (Washington, D.C.: Government Printing Office, 1970), pp. 186–194, line 61.

we saw in the previous paragraph, depletion allowances seem to provide benefits principally to the large corporation. Finally, we often read of the millionaire who incurs no tax liability; this is usually because he owns municipal bonds or extractive properties eligible for depletion.[25]

is a gas in the ordinary meaning of the word. Further, it found that the steam was taken from a natural subterranean reservoir of fixed capacity and was thus being depleted. The case was a gas, all right, three of the seven judges said in dissent. "This is depletion run riot," they declared. The law rules out percentage depletion for water, and they found it hard to accept "a 27.5 percent bonanza for water vapor." *The Wall Street Journal*, August 6, 1969.

[25] Because of this inequity, the Tax Reform Act of 1969 introduced the *minimum income tax*. Many types of income, including income from mineral depletion allowances (but excluding interest paid on municipal bonds), would qualify for taxation at a 10 per-

The proponents of percentage depletion for oil and natural gas argue, when all else fails, that it is essential for national defense. In order to guarantee our independence and freedom from "fuel blackmail" during a national emergency, this line of economic activity should be encouraged so that our domestic capacity will make us self-sufficient. But why merely extractive industries? Certainly, steel, aircraft, chemicals, and electronics are equally important for national defense, and by this rationale they should also receive special treatment. Even if the argument is valid, the granting of mineral depletion allowances for extractive properties abroad is absurd since their products would not be available during periods of national emergency. On balance, your authors have no sympathy with the arguments advanced for percentage depletion allowances. The tax treatment of capital costs in these industries should be essentially similar to that in other industries. To the economist with the perspective of the whole economy in mind they seem to promote misallocation of resources and inequity in the distribution of income, as well as being costly of revenue to the federal government. Depletion allowances were a major topic of debate as the Tax Reform Act of 1969 was drafted. As a result of this debate, mineral depletion allowances, especially in the petroleum industry, were reduced as shown in Table 13.7.

The shifting and incidence of the corporate income tax is an important yet uncertain issue. As we saw in Chapter 7, from a theoretical stance the tax may be wholly or partially shifted forward, absorbed by the owners of the corporation, or shifted backward to factors of production depending on the assumptions made by the analyst. Several empirical studies have been made to determine the shifting and incidence of the corporate income tax; rather than systematically comparing analytic methods and data we summarize several conclusions and make a few observations. Krzyzaniak and Musgrave, in a study of short-run shifting using data for 1935–42 and 1948–59, found that the corporate tax was more than 100 percent shifted forward for tax increases, and that this forward shifting was not fully reversed for tax reductions.[26] A second study of short-run shifting by R. J. Gordon, resting on data for 1924–62, concludes that there is no short-run shifting of the tax, but leaves open the question of long-run shifting in a general equilibrium model.[27] Arnold Harberger, in a study of long-run shifting, found that the corporate income tax was substantially borne by capital owners.[28]

---

cent rate when a wealthy taxpayer receives substantial income from preferential sources.

[26] Marian Krzyzaniak and Richard A. Musgrave, *The Shifting of the Corporate Income Tax* (Baltimore: The Johns Hopkins Press, 1963).

[27] R. J. Gordon, "The Incidence of the Corporate Tax," *American Economic Review,* September 1967.

[28] Arnold C. Harberger, "The Incidence of the Corporate Income Tax," *Journal of*

The contradictions that these studies afford stem from uncertainty about the goals of firms and the interpretation of the data used in analysis. Our discussion of shifting and incidence in Chapter 7 formally dealt with profit-maximizing and sales-maximizing behavior; other models could also be considered. Empirical studies will differ as analysts base their work on different sets of assumptions. Whatever assumptions are made about the goal of firms, more than the corporate income tax affects the attainment of that goal; demand conditions, technological changes, raw material prices, and wage rates also affect prices, profits, and rates of return. These other factors do not remain constant during a period of time for which the effects of the corporate income tax are being investigated. No wonder that empirical investigations of the shifting and incidence of the corporate income tax do not yield a uniform set of results.

The empirical evidence, therefore, seems no more helpful than theoretical analysis in determining the shifting and incidence of the corporate income tax. Many feel, despite any analysis or evidence, that shifting of the tax must occur, based on a belief in the nonprofit-maximizing behavior of corporations. The only conclusion we can draw is that more evidence must be compiled before we can clearly know the shifting and incidence of the corporate income tax.

It is sometimes argued that the corporate income tax should be wholly or partially replaced with a tax on value added.[29] One point of view on this issue is that the corporate income tax is basically a tax on the equity capital of corporations, thus leading firms to substitute other factors for equity capital, and that replacement of the corporate income tax with a tax on value added would be more neutral since it falls equally on all factor services.[30] Since competition, subject to different degrees of risk, is expected to make after-tax rates of return on homogenous factors equal throughout the economy, a tax that falls primarily on equity capital must make its before-tax rate of return higher in taxed lines of activity, resulting in misallocation of resources and reduction in total social product. For 1953–55 the economy-wide loss from this type of inefficiency was estimated at $1.5 billion annually.[31] If the recommended tax substitution were made, it is argued, the after-tax rate of return on capital investment would increase, stimulating

---

Political Economy, June 1962. *See also* John G. Cragg, Arnold C. Harberger, and Peter Mieszkowski, "Empirical Evidence on the Incidence of the Corporate Income Tax," *Journal of Political Economy*, December 1967.

29 *A Better Balance in Federal Taxes on Business* (New York: Committee for Economic Development, 1966).

30 For the argument that the corporate income tax falls on equity capital, *see* Harberger, "The Incidence . . . ," *op. cit.* For the neutrality argument, *see* Carl Shoup, "Tax Reform in Japan," *Proceedings of the National Tax Association*, 1949.

31 *The Federal Tax System: Facts and Problems, op. cit.*, pp. 55–57.

investment. At the same time, consumption would be moderated by the price increases resulting from a forward shifted value-added tax. This reallocation of resources would stimulate economic growth and would thus be consistent with an often stated goal of national economic policy. Both these arguments assume that the corporate income tax is not shifted and, as we have seen, this is uncertain. This tax substitution is sometimes recommended on balance of payments grounds as well (see Chapter 22).

This tax substitution is often opposed on equity grounds. It is argued that the corporate income tax has been capitalized and its repeal would lead to windfall capital gains (already taxed at inequitably low rates) to corporate shareowners. Again, the argument assumes the corporate income tax is not shifted. Furthermore, the value-added tax is seen as similar to a retail sales tax and, as shown in Chapter 14, retail sales taxes are regressive. Thus, the value-added tax is viewed by critics as regressive, inequitable, and an improper replacement for the corporate income tax. Again, however, an assumption is made about the incidence of the corporate income tax and this assumption is not based on firm evidence. Finally, we note that much of the regressivity in retail sales taxes stems from the fact that many items are excluded from the tax base; if the value-added tax were levied on all types of economic activity much of the equity objection might disappear. With our present knowledge, the safest conclusion seems to be recognition that reasonable arguments do exist for such a tax substitution, but they rest on assumptions about tax incidence which must be further investigated before policy prescriptions are drawn.

PAYROLL TAXES

Payroll taxes were added to the federal revenue system with enactment, in 1935, of Old Age Survivors and Disability Insurance (social security) and unemployment insurance. These programs are financed by taxes based on the wages and salaries of covered persons and are thus termed *payroll taxes*. Our purpose here is to consider these programs only from a revenue point of view; issues related to social security and unemployment insurance as a whole are considered in Chapter 19. Our discussion in this section is confined to social security taxes.

When social security taxes were originally levied their base was the first \$3000 of wages and salaries received by persons entitled to benefits; this amount has since increased to \$7800, as shown in Table 13.9. The tax is assessed on both the employee and his employer, the tax rate being equal for each. This rate, which in 1971 was 5.2 percent of the tax base, has been substantially increased since first enactment. For self-employed taxpayers the rate is 1.5 times the employer or employee rate.

With the tax base so broadly defined, this tax is likely to be neutral as

Table 13.9 **Social Security Taxes**

Year	Base	Rate for Both Employee and Employer (Percent)
1937–49	$3000	1.000
1950	3000	1.500
1951–53	3600	1.500
1954	3600	2.000
1955–56	4200	2.000
1957–58	4200	2.250
1959	4800	2.500
1960–61	4800	3.000
1962	4800	3.125
1963–65	4800	3.625
1966–67	6600	4.125
1968–70	7800	4.800
1971	7800	5.200

SOURCE: *The Federal Tax System: Facts and Problems, 1964,* Joint Economic Committee, 88th Congress, 2d Session (Washington, D.C.: Government Printing Office, 1964), p. 174, and *Budget of the United States Government* (Washington, D.C.: Government Printing Office, various years).

concerns employee behavior. Since there are few uncovered areas of employment, the employee may not change occupation to avoid the tax, and the incidence of the employee's share of employment tax liabilities most likely falls on the employee. If, however, unions or individual workers negotiate wage contracts on the basis of their perceptions of real disposable income, employment taxes, which reduce disposable income, may lead to increased wage demands; shifting may therefore occur. Since the tax rate is constant, effective employment tax rates are proportional for citizens with wage and salary incomes that do not exceed the limits of the tax base, and regressive for those citizens who receive nonlabor income or whose labor income exceeds the limits of the tax base.

The incidence of the employer's share of payroll tax liabilities is more difficult to appraise. Employers will perceive this tax as a cost associated with engaging labor services; as such it increases labor costs relative to the cost of other factor services and may lead to factor substitution. As this happens smaller amounts of labor will be employed and unemployment will rise. As unemployment rises, competition for jobs may, in a static model, drive wages downward or, in a dynamic model, prevent wages from rising over time by as much as would have been the case in the absence of the tax. To the extent this happens, the employer's share of the tax is shifted backward to labor and the full tax incidence falls on the employee. Alternatively, with increased labor costs resulting from employment taxes, employers will perceive increased marginal and average production costs and may wholly or partially shift the tax forward. Unless social security benefits lead to sufficient increases in demand (shift in the demand curve), with increased product prices, smaller amounts of factors will be employed as quantity demanded decreases (movement along an unshifted demand curve), and all factors will experience rising unemployment. As unemployed factors compete for jobs their prices will fall and the employer share of the tax may be shifted backward to all factors of production. From a theoretical stance we see that the employer share of employment taxes may be shifted either forward or backward, or, under certain types of sales-maximizing behavior, absorbed by the firm. Empirical evidence shows payroll taxes to be regressive.[32]

Since payroll tax rates increased substantially during the 1950s and 1960s the liability on the low income taxpayer, as a share of his income, has risen. We saw earlier in the chapter that emerging concepts of equity in the 1960s required that the poor be relieved of federal income tax liabilities; the minimum standard deduction is evidence of this. At the same time as this innovation was made and personal income tax rates were being reduced, social security tax rates were increased so that the poor taxpayer saw his combined federal income and payroll tax liabilities as a share of income rising.[33] As a result, some suggest that the social security tax be abolished and social security payments instead be funded from general revenues obtained from increased personal income taxation. The incidence of tax liabilities would be altered and the equity of the federal tax system would be improved in the opinion of those who perceive equity being promoted by progressive taxation. In addition, to the extent that payroll taxes frustrate the maintenance of full employment, because they cause substitution of other factors for labor, this tax revision is desirable.

FEDERAL COMMODITY TAXATION

The United States government relies less heavily on commodity taxes than do the national governments of other Western nations.[34] Despite this,

[32] R. R. Hansen, "Social Security Taxes: Regressive or Progressive," *National Tax Journal*, June 1966; E. C. Harvey, "Social Security Taxes: Regressive or Progressive," *National Tax Journal*, December 1966; and John A. Brittain, "The Incidence of Social Security Payroll Taxes," *American Economic Review*, March 1971.

[33] Since 1964 the family of four with less than a $3000 income has incurred no federal income tax liability. In 1964, using the rates in Table 13.9, the social security liability was 3.625 percent of this income while in 1971 it had risen to 5.2 percent. For further discussion of this issue, *see* Mary W. Smelker, "The Impact of Federal Income and Payroll Taxes on the Distribution of After-Tax Income," *National Tax Journal*, December 1968.

[34] Jacob A. Stockfish, "International Comparisons of Direct and Indirect Taxes," *Ex-*

excises constitute an important source of revenue. As part of a program of tax reduction in the 1960s, most of the federal excise taxes left over from World War II were repealed in 1965. The repealed excise taxes had been levied at the retail level on admissions and such products as leather goods, furs, cosmetics, and jewelry, and at the manufacturer's level on household appliances and such selected items as matches, light bulbs, phonograph records, revolvers. The major products remaining subject to federal excise taxation are shown in Table 13.10 along with the rates prevailing in 1970. As may be

***Table 13.10* Selected Excise Tax Rates, 1970**

Automobiles	7 percent
Tires	10¢/pound
Gasoline	4¢/gallon
Cigarettes	$4/thousand
Liquor	
Hard	$10.50/proof gallon
Beer	$9.00/barrel
Telephone	10 percent

SOURCE: Subcommittee on Fiscal Policy, Joint Economic Committee, *The Federal Tax System: Facts and Problems 1964* (Washington, D.C.: Government Printing Office, 1964).

seen from this table, both specific and *ad valorem* excise taxes are used. Under existing law (1970) the automobile and telephone and telegraph excise taxes are scheduled for repeal in 1973. Barring additional legislative action, federal excise taxes will then be based on only alcoholic beverages and tobacco, and on fuels and other transport-related items. The latter revenues are largely earmarked for financing parts of the nation's transportation network and may be said to be assessed on the benefit principle.

We saw in Chapter 7 that both the profit-maximizing and the sales-maximizing firm, under most circumstances, may be expected to partially or fully shift excise taxes forward to consumers. The belief is widespread that such shifting does occur and this is supported by empirical evidence. Brownlee and Perry, for instance, found that most product prices fell by nearly the full amount of the excise tax reduction in 1965 giving support to the belief that shifting does occur.[35] Thus, the incidence of excise taxes may be said

cise Tax Compendium, Committee on Ways and Means, 88th Congress, 2d Session (Washington, D.C.: Government Printing Office, 1964), and Richard A. Musgrave, *Fiscal Systems* (New Haven: Yale University Press, 1969).

35 Oswald Brownlee and George L. Perry, "The Effects of the 1965 Excise Tax Reduction on Prices," *National Tax Journal*, September 1967. *See also* F. O. Woodard and Harvey Siegelman, "Effects of the 1965 Federal Excise Tax Reduction Upon the

to fall on the buyer of the taxed product and the following appraisal of excise taxes assumes this incidence.

Excise taxes, and consumption taxes in general, are defended on several grounds. The volume of consumption may be regarded as a proxy variable for ability to pay, and by this approach to taxation consumption is a suitable tax base. However, many believe the minimum income needed for subsistence should escape taxation. To the degree these are society's beliefs, consumption is a poor measure of ability to pay. Examination of the range of products subject to federal excise taxation shows, however, that the products included in the tax base tend not to be necessities, and as a measure of ability to pay, consumption of these products may be a suitable tax base. Because federal fuel and transport-related excise taxes are largely earmarked for expenditure on the nation's transportation system, these excise taxes may be said to be assessed on the benefit principle. Without passing any judgment on the appropriateness of current rates, we conclude that, by the benefit principle, these transportation-related excise taxes are proper. In addition, sumptuary taxes are sometimes levied to promote society's regulatory goals with respect to morally offensive products; while this rationale perhaps typified society's views in earlier years, in the last third of the twentieth century it is difficult to defend tobacco and alcoholic beverage excise taxes on this ground and others must be found. The ability to pay approach may be some help, but a more compelling case may be made to assess these taxes on allocative grounds to cover the social costs associated with their use. Whatever else may be said, the demand for tobacco and alcohol is undoubtedly quite inelastic, and excise taxes do little to discourage their consumption. As shown in Table 12.5, they constitute an important source of revenue for the federal government and are likely to be retained.

On allocative grounds excise taxation may be objectionable though in the American case this argument, if applicable, largely applies to pre-1965 excise taxation. Because of their forward shifting, product prices are increased and, if taxed products are inputs in a manufacturing process, input costs of production rise. This may lead to an economically wasteful reallocation of resources as nontaxed inputs are substituted for taxed inputs. In addition, the resulting change in relative product prices may reduce welfare (see Chapter 7, Figure 7.3). Finally, this method of taxation may have an impact on the international competitiveness of products; this is further discussed in connection with the border tax issue in Chapter 22.

On equity grounds consumption taxes are often scorned because they

---

Prices of Automobile Replacement Parts—A Case Study in Tax Shifting and Pyramiding," *National Tax Journal*, September 1967; Harry L. Johnson, "Tax Pyramiding and the Manufacturers' Excise Tax Reduction of 1954," *National Tax Journal*, September 1964; and John F. Due, "The Effect of the 1954 Reduction in Federal Excise Taxes Upon the List Price of Electrical Appliances," *National Tax Journal*, September 1954.

are regressive. This argument is developed in the next chapter. We briefly note here that this regressivity arises because the poor spend larger shares of their income on taxed products than the rich; since the tax base depends on spending, commodity taxation is regressive. Prior to 1965 this charge was valid for federal excise taxes, as is empirically illustrated in Table 13.12, line 8, and was part of the reason for the excise reductions in the mid-1960s. With the narrow excise tax base of the 1970s we do not believe this is any longer an issue: there are considerations other than equity that pertain to taxation, and even though empirical analysis would continue to show the transportation-related, alcohol, and tobacco excises as regressive, further tax reform in this area is not required.

Specific excise tax rates based on weight, volume, or count constitute different percentage amounts of product values. The $10.50 per proof gallon spirits excise tax falls more heavily on cheap than expensive liquor; liquor taxes as a share of income thus constitute a greater percent of the poor imbiber's income than the rich imbiber.[36] Cigarettes are taxed by count. When the cigarette excise was first enacted several low price brands were driven off the market because of the relative price change that resulted. Thus, on both equity and allocative efficiency grounds, *ad valorem* excises are preferred to specific excise taxes.

ESTATE AND GIFT TAXATION

Estate and gift taxes yield only modest amounts of revenue to the federal government but may be important from the viewpoint of distributive equity. In a society that believes all are equal before the law and that each citizen should be judged on his own merits, many hold that estate and gift taxation is just because it limits the transfer of wealth from generation to generation and promotes these democratic ideals. Andrew Carnegie favored estate taxes as a means of stimulating incentives: "The parent who leaves his son enormous wealth generally deadens the energies of the son, and tempts him to lead a less useful and less worthy life than he otherwise would."[37] On the other hand, many believe estate and gift taxes destroy the

[36] Over 50 percent of the retail price of hard liquor consists of federal, state, and local excise taxes which are intended to be assessed on the consumer although the liability is the distributor's. Bottle breakage in stores thus destroys only modest amounts of economic goods but the financial cost to the dealer is large because of the inclusion of taxes in the product's value. To avoid these losses many package stores retain the necks of broken bottles—if the revenue stamp is not broken consumption is presumed not to have occurred and the dealer may obtain an excise tax refund. A special note for the clumsy reader: if you, after making a retail purchase, inadvertently break an unopened liquor bottle and the revenue stamp on the neck remains intact, try returning the neck to a dealer; many will give you a refund.

[37] *Gospel of Wealth*, cited in Pechman, *Federal Tax Policy*, rev. ed., *op. cit.*, p. 186.

incentive to accumulate wealth, thus reducing the incentive to save, and hinder economic growth by cutting off the flow of funds to finance investment.

The estate tax base is the total value of the decedent's estate reduced by a $60,000 exemption and certain deductions including, for example, charitable bequests, funeral expenses, settlement costs, and any claims outstanding against the deceased at the time of death. In addition, 50 percent of an estate transferred to one's spouse is exempt from the estate tax base. Credits for certain state inheritance and estate taxes are allowable deductions against the federal estate tax liability. The schedule of federal estate tax rates is given in Table 13.11. The rate schedule is progressive and may be interpreted as reflecting the belief that transfer of enormous wealth from generation to generation is inequitable.

Table 13.11 **Federal Estate and Gift Tax Base and Rates**

Tax Base	Estate Tax Rate (Percent)	Gift Tax Rate (Percent)
0 to $5000	3	2.25
$5000 to $10,000	7	5.25
$10,000 to $20,000	11	8.25
$20,000 to $30,000	14	10.50
$30,000 to $40,000	18	13.50
$40,000 to $50,000	22	16.50
$50,000 to $60,000	25	18.75
$60,000 to $100,000	28	21.00
$100,000 to $250,000	30	22.50
$250,000 to $500,000	32	24.00
$500,000 to $750,000	35	26.25
$750,000 to $1,000,000	37	27.75
$1,000,000 to $1,250,000	39	29.25
$1,250,000 to $1,500,000	42	31.50
$1,500,000 to $2,000,000	45	33.75
$2,000,000 to $2,500,000	49	36.75
$2,500,000 to $3,000,000	53	39.75
$3,000,000 to $3,500,000	56	47.25
$3,500,000 to $4,000,000	59	42.00
$4,000,000 to $5,000,000	63	44.25
$5,000,000 to $6,000,000	67	50.25
$6,000,000 to $7,000,000	70	52.50
$7,000,000 to $8,000,000	73	54.75
$8,000,000 to $10,000,000	76	57.00
$10,000,000 and over	77	57.75

SOURCE: *The Federal Tax System: Facts and Problems, 1964,* Joint Economic Committee, 88th Congress, 2d Session (Washington, D.C.: Government Printing Office, 1964), pp. 159 and 162.

In order to promote distributive equity, the federal estate tax is coupled with the federal gift tax. The gift tax liability is borne by the giver and is based on the value of the gift; the gift tax rate is 75 percent of the estate tax rate. The first $3000 to any one recipient annually is excluded from the gift tax base; if both husband and wife make gifts the annual exclusion per recipient is $6000. In addition, a total cumulative lifetime exclusion of $30,000 per recipient applies; this exclusion totals $60,000 when a gift is made by a couple. Since up to $60,000 in tax exempt gifts may be transferred to each recipient, a couple with five children may, over a ten-year period transfer $300,000 tax free, whereas if $300,000 were transferred to the same recipients at the time of the death of their parents, a federal estate tax liability would have been incurred on a $240,000 base.

At least two means of avoiding estate taxation, other than by gift, are available. The first of these is the trust; the second is the charitable foundation. Property put into trust is not subject to estate taxation and, upon termination of the trust, transferred wealth again escapes taxation. Thus, by creating a trust and surrendering control of wealth into the hands of a trustee for a period of years, the wealthy may provide for the outright transfer of their property into another generation without any estate tax liability being incurred. The charitable foundation also enables the wealthy to escape estate taxation. Charitable bequests are deductible expenses in computing the estate tax base. If a family-owned enterprise is incorporated with nonvoting preferred stock and voting common stock outstanding, the nonvoting preferred shares may be donated to a charitable foundation and claimed as a deduction in filing estate tax returns. Income from the property is lost to the donor, but control is not transferred, and often it is control rather than ownership that is economically important. On equity grounds both these means of avoiding estate taxation are questioned and are frequently cited as areas for tax reform.

REDISTRIBUTION VIA THE TAX AND EXPENDITURE PROCESS

In earlier chapters we discussed public expenditures and welfare. As citizens perceive benefits from public expenditures their real income rises; as they perceive costs their real income falls. As taxes are raised, those who bear the incidence find their disposable money income, and hence their real income, reduced. Ideally, real income would be measured in welfare units, but for empirical work this is impossible. Analysts investigating the expenditure process can attempt to identify those actually affected by expenditures and assume that consumption of these expenditures is perceived as beneficial, with the value of the benefit being equal to the public expenditure. The incidence of taxes may be studied and costs may be seen falling on those who bear the incidence. Comparison of these dollar measures of benefits and costs, showing either positive or negative net benefits, may be taken as a measure of redistribution through the tax and expenditure process.

This measure of redistribution entails several obvious shortcomings. Our personal welfare function [see Equation (1.2)] was constructed to make one citizen's welfare a function of the welfare of others; thus, a citizen who pays taxes to finance transfer payments may see this as welfare increasing, although the dollar measure shows negative net benefits since costs are positive and benefits nonexistent. Because empirical studies can only assign benefits to those who consume expenditures, redistribution measured in terms of the share of public expenditures consumed and changes in welfare are not the same. Empirical assignment of benefits may differ from citizen readings of benefits; all citizens consume nuclear weapons, and the expenditures for these will be assigned to all as benefits although some citizens perceive the expenditure of public monies to finance them as welfare decreasing. Finally, citizens may be unaware of many of the benefits they reap from public expenditures and, if taxes are shifted, also unaware of costs; as this occurs redistribution measured in dollar amounts will bear no relationship to citizen perceptions of the impact of the public sector on their well-being. With these problems in mind we examine empirical evidence on redistribution through the tax and expenditure process.

A Tax Foundation study measured the incidence of federal taxes and expenditures by income class in 1965.[38] These measures are shown in Table 13.12. In any study of this type many assumptions are required; we briefly summarize the more important of these. *General benefit expenditures* (line 1) refers to expenditures that all citizens consume—such as national defense, foreign affairs, the space program, and conservation. *Individual benefit expenditures* (line 4), by contrast, are such items as interest payments on government securities, agricultural subsidies, social security benefits, and the pensions of retired government employees, where identifiable citizens are presumed to be the sole beneficiaries of the expenditures. Individual benefit expenditures were allocated to income classes in accordance with distribution of their recipients by income class. General benefit expenditures were allocated to income classes 50 percent on the basis of the distribution of families

[38] *Tax Burdens and Benefits of Government Expenditures by Income Class, 1961 and 1965* (New York: Tax Foundation, 1967). A study by W. Irwin Gillespie found similar results and will not be discussed here; *see* "Effect of Public Expenditures on the Distribution of Income," in Richard A. Musgrave (ed.), *Essays in Fiscal Federalism* (Washington, D.C.: The Brookings Institution, 1965), pp. 112–86. *See also* John H. Adler, "The Fiscal System, the Distribution of Income, and Public Welfare," in Kenyon E. Poole (ed.), *Fiscal Policies and the American Economy* (Englewood Cliffs, N. J.: Prentice-Hall, 1951); A. M. Carter, *The Redistribution of Income in Postwar Britain* (New Haven: Yale University Press, 1955); and O. H. Brownlee, *Estimated Distribution of Minnesota Taxes and Public Expenditure Benefits* (Minneapolis: University of Minnesota Press, 1960).

Table 13.12 **Federal Taxes and Expenditures as a Percent of Family Income—1965**

	Income Class									
	Under $2000	$2000 to 2999	$3000 to 3999	$4000 to 4999	$5000 to 5999	$6000 to 7499	$7500 to 9999	$10,000 to 14,000	$15,000 and over	Total
Expenditures										
1 General benefit expenditures	34.5	19.9	15.8	13.3	11.9	10.7	9.5	8.4	7.0	11.6
2 National defense and international affairs	26.2	15.1	12.0	10.1	9.0	8.1	7.2	6.4	5.3	8.8
3 Other	8.3	4.8	3.8	3.2	2.9	2.6	2.3	2.0	1.7	2.8
4 Individual benefit expenditures	44.8	26.1	15.8	7.9	6.3	4.9	4.3	4.3	4.0	7.9
5 Total	79.3	46.0	31.6	21.2	18.2	15.6	13.8	12.7	11.0	19.5
Taxes										
6 Individual income	1.9	3.1	4.5	6.4	6.9	7.7	8.8	10.0	16.1	8.3
7 Corporate income	4.5	4.3	5.5	3.6	3.9	3.4	3.4	5.3	10.9	4.6
8 Excise and customs	3.3	3.1	3.3	3.1	3.0	2.8	2.6	2.4	1.5	2.7
9 Estate and gift	—	—	—	—	—	—	—	—	4.6	.5
10 Social insurance	3.2	3.4	3.8	4.1	4.0	3.8	3.5	3.3	1.7	3.5
11 Total	13.0	14.0	17.1	17.3	17.9	17.8	18.4	21.1	34.9	19.6
Redistribution										
12	6.10	3.28	1.85	1.23	1.02	0.88	0.75	0.60	0.32	0.99

SOURCE: *Tax Burdens and Benefits of Government Expenditures by Income Class, 1961 and 1965* (New York: Tax Foundation, Inc., 1967), pp. 20 and 21.

by income classes and 50 percent by the share of total income found in each income class. The rationale behind this assumption is that, on the one hand, all benefit equally from national defense (allocation by family) but, on the other hand, the larger your income the more you have to defend (allocation by income).

The incidence of the personal income tax (line 6) was assumed to fall entirely on the taxpayer, while excise and customs receipts (line 8) were assumed to be fully shifted forward to consumers. The federal estate and gift tax (line 9) was assumed to be borne entirely by those in the highest income class. The corporate income tax (line 7) was assumed to be 50 percent shifted forward, the remainder falling on share owners. The employee share of social security and unemployment insurance taxes (line 10) was assumed to fall on the employee; the employer's share was assumed fully shifted forward to consumers. The income classes were measured by family money income after payment of all federal, state, and local income and personal property taxes.

The incidence of benefits was found to be regressive (line 5). Regressive here means in favor of the lower income groups in the sense that the value of benefits as a percent of income falls as income rises. For general benefit items (lines 1–3), this is due to the allocation of half the expenditures to income class on the basis of families. Because of the skewed income distribution in the United States, any study that gives substantial distributive weight to population, by income class, will always yield this pattern. The regressive incidence of individual benefit expenditures (line 4) is due to social security benefits that, with but few exceptions, are received by low income families (see Chapter 19). Thus, the incidence of the distribution of benefits from federal expenditures, as a share of disposable income, favors low income families.

The incidence of federal taxes is shown to be progressive (line 11). As expected, the personal income tax (line 6) is progressive because of the rate structure.[39] The corporate income tax (line 7) is progressive in the high income brackets because of the assumption that 50 percent of the incidence of the tax falls on stockholders who tend to be in high income brackets. Excise taxes and customs (line 8) are regressive as is expected for commodity taxes; this would also be the case for the corporate income tax if full forward shifting had been assumed. Social security taxes (line 10) are first progressive and then, as expected in the higher income brackets, regressive. The initial progression in this tax is because the lowest income brackets contain many poor agricultural workers who were not covered in

[39] Regressivity due to the special treatment of capital gains does not show up in the high income brackets in Table 13.12 because the highest income class includes all families with incomes over $15,000 and because the income classes are measured after taxes. Compare Table 13.12, line 6, with Table 13.3.

1965 and many elderly persons who have withdrawn from the labor force. As income rises, the share of heads of families who are employed and who are also covered by social security increases, and thus the social security tax appears progressive for incomes below $5000 as the incidence of the employee share of the tax offsets the regressive element introduced by the assumption that the employer's share is fully shifted forward and reflected in commodity prices.

To obtain a measure of redistribution through the federal tax and expenditure process, we divide the incidence of benefits (line 5) by the incidence of taxes (line 11) with the results shown in line 12. For the lowest income class the value of the benefits derived from federal expenditures is 79.3 percent of their income, while federal taxes are 13 percent of that income. Thus, for each dollar paid in taxes the Tax Foundation found that families in this income class received $6.10 worth of benefits from expenditures. By contrast, taxpayers in the highest income bracket received $.32 worth of benefits for each dollar of taxes paid. Presuming the statistical accuracy of these results we should inquire if the redistributive pattern here shown is equitable. A firm answer to this question is impossible because of the personal nature of equity judgments, but a few questions may be raised. First, while redistribution clearly appears to occur, is this the right amount or should redistribution be greater or smaller than measured here? Second, these measures say nothing about the absolute levels of citizen well-being in any of the income classes; can equity and equitable redistribution be measured without also making reference to existing standards of living in each income class and their changing pattern over time? Third, should equity judgments be based on total measures, or should one also look at the distribution of the various components of the total? Suppose, for example, one is dedicated to progressive taxation; does that mean that regressive excises must be eliminated from the tax structure despite the fact that the total tax system has the desired characteristics?

In Chapter 1 we discussed individual welfare and set out an individual's welfare function containing public expenditures as one of the independent variables. Clearly expenditures by government bear on the well-being of the governed, and ideally the benefits from these expenditures would be included in measures of welfare and considered in discussion of distributive equity. The Tax Foundation's study, and others like it, are important because they attempt to consider public expenditures along these lines. Although they imperfectly measure the impact of public expenditures on real income, they are important as contributions to understanding these issues.

14

STATE AND LOCAL GOVERNMENT REVENUES

State and local governments had over $100 billion in budget receipts in 1969. Besides those receipts obtained as grants-in-aid, which are considered in Chapter 20, state and local government revenues are largely derived from taxation, user charges, and fees, as shown in Table 14.1. Commodity taxation is the principal source of state government revenue, and property taxes provide the largest share of local government receipts. In addition many states and localities collect personal and corporate income taxes. After an examination of state and local income taxes that parallels our previous discussion of federal income taxes, we consider sales and property taxes. Other state and local taxes, user charges, and fees are then briefly surveyed.[1]

---

[1] For a survey of state and local government finances, *see* James A. Maxwell, *Financing State and Local Governments,* rev. ed. (Washington, D.C.: The Brookings Institution, 1969). For details, *see* Advisory Commission on Intergovernmental Relations, *State and Local Taxes: Significant Features, 1967–1970* (Washington, D.C.: Government Printing Office, 1969). Throughout this chapter the District of Columbia is treated as a local rather than as a state government.

The chapter concludes with evidence concerning redistribution through state and local government taxes and expenditures.

INCOME TAXATION

Consideration, in Chapter 7, of the allocative effects of taxation showed that nonneutral taxes are a variable in the calculus of decision makers. As long as a tax is uniform throughout a jurisdiction its allocative effects will not influence locational decisions within the jurisdiction. When taxes differ from one jurisdiction to another, however, they may influence locational decisions as among jurisdictions and in this respect may also be non- As long as a tax is uniform throughout a jurisdiction its allocative effects will not influence locational decisions within the jurisdiction. When taxes differ from one jurisdiction to another, however, they may influence locational decisions as among jurisdictions and in this respect may also be nonneutral. This issue was not raised in connection with federal taxation since federal taxes are uniform throughout the nation. The American population is highly mobile between city and suburb, within a metropolitan area, as well as among regions of the nation; this mobility makes it possible for businesses and individuals to shop for the optimal community in which to locate. Taxes and public expenditures are likely to play a role in these locational decisions. Citizens will not merely attempt to minimize their tax liabilities; high taxes and good schools, highways, and community services may be found together. However, for those communities providing roughly equivalent benefits from state and local expenditures, the rational citizen may locate where taxes are lowest. Government officials are thus concerned lest high taxes on corporations induce firms to locate elsewhere. Hence state and local corporate income tax receipts are relatively small. At the same time, municipalities fear that taxation of their residents' income will spur movement to the suburbs. Despite this fear, over 3000 cities have adopted personal income or payroll taxes in the face of acute revenue needs. Studies have been made to determine the impact of taxation on locational decisions; the evidence does not suggest that taxes are an important locational variable since tax differences between jurisdictions are often small, or reflect differences in public expenditures. Other factors, such as proximity to employment and costs of housing, usually loom larger. Businessmen give first consideration to such factors as availability of labor, transportation facilities, and closeness to markets and raw material supplies. Despite the lack of evidence that taxes are a locational variable, states and municipalities do worry about this issue and sometimes exempt new industries from taxation for a number of years.[2]

---

[2] John F. Due, "Studies of State-Local Tax Influences on Location of Industry," *National*

Approximately 18 percent of state tax revenues are derived from personal income taxes, and an additional 8 percent from corporate income taxes, as indicated by Table 14.1; these percentages have been growing since World War II and will continue to increase in the future. At the start of 1970, 40 states levied taxes on personal incomes and 43 states taxed corporate incomes. For state and municipal personal and corporate income taxes, the base is taxable income, computed in much the same manner as federal income taxes. The tax bases often differ, however, because of particular features of state and local tax laws.[3] Personal income tax rates are proportional in a few states but are typically progressive, with the highest marginal rate being 14 percent. Some states with high marginal rates permit deduction of federal income taxes in calculating the tax base. A general observation may be made here concerning administrative efficiency. Three states—Alaska, Nebraska, and Vermont—assess their personal income taxes as a percent of the taxpayer's federal income tax liability. This is administratively efficient from the taxpayer's viewpoint, and is preferred to the procedure in other states where separate schedules of personal exemptions and deductions make two sets of tax computations necessary as federal and state tax returns are filed. The Internal Revenue Service might even be made the collection agency for state or local income taxes saving these governments the expenses associated with tax collections. If state or local income tax liabilities were based on the federal income tax base or liability, changes in the federal tax base or rates would result in windfall revenue gains or losses for those governments who would then have to enact rate changes themselves. This drawback does not, however, appear to negate the gains that would accrue from the adoption of a standard nationwide set of definitions for income tax purposes.

COMMODITY TAXATION

Approximately 60 percent of state government tax receipts are derived from commodity taxation. Motor fuel, tobacco, and alcoholic beverage excise taxes provide almost half the commodity tax revenues. Motor fuel tax rates ranged from 5 to 9 cents per gallon in 1969. Most of the receipts are

---

Tax Journal, June 1961, and Advisory Commission on Intergovernmental Relations, *State-Local Taxation and Industrial Location* (Washington, D.C.: Government Printing Office, 1967).

[3] Only when a corporation does all of its business in a single state would its entire income form the state corporate income tax base. In general, the portion of sales, employment, or property holding in a state are the criteria upon which state tax laws prorate the corporate income tax base. For one study of this, with special reference to North Carolina, *see* Charles E. Ratliff, Jr., *Interstate Apportionment of Business Income for State Income Tax Purposes* (Chapel Hill: University of North Carolina Press, 1962).

Table 14.1 State and Local Government Revenue, by Source 1968–1969 (Thousands of dollars)

Source	Total	State	Local
Total revenue	[a]132,153	77,584	[a]79,274
Total general revenue	[a]114,550	67,312	[a]71,943
Intergovernmental revenue	19,153	17,775	26,082
From federal government	19,153	16,907	2,245
From states	([a])	—	23,837
From local governments	([a])	868	([a])
Revenue from own sources	113,001	59,809	53,192
General revenue from own sources	95,397	49,537	45,861
Taxes	76,712	41,931	34,781
Property	30,673	981	29,692
Individual income	8,908	7,527	1,381
Corporation income	3,180	3,180	([b])
Sales and gross receipts	26,519	24,050	2,470
General sales and gross receipts	14,038	12,443	1,595
Selective sales and gross receipts	12,481	11,606	875
Motor fuel	5,681	5,644	37
Alcoholic beverages	1,297	1,246	51
Tobacco products	2,153	2,056	97
Public utilities	1,231	763	468
Other	2,119	1,897	222
Motor vehicle and operators licenses	2,841	2,685	157
Death and gift	996	996	([c])
All other	3,594	2,512	1,082
Charges and miscellaneous general revenue	18,686	7,606	11,080
Current charges	13,305	5,460	7,845
Education	5,184	3,091	2,093
School lunch sales	1,284	—	1,284
Institutions of higher education	3,306	3,041	264
Other	595	50	545
Hospitals	2,665	786	1,879
Sewerage	684	—	684
Sanitation other than sewerage	220	—	220
Local parks and recreation	236	—	236
Natural resources	273	189	84
Housing and urban renewal	546	8	538
Air transportation	433	33	400
Water transport and terminals	252	71	181
Parking facilities	151	—	151
Other	2,663	1,282	1,380
Miscellaneous general revenue	5,381	2,146	3,235
Special assessments	491	19	472
Sale of property	314	56	258
Interest earnings	2,255	1,083	1,172
Other	2,321	988	1,333
Utility revenue	5,931	—	5,931
Liquor stores revenue	1,909	1,663	245
Insurance trust revenue	9,764	8,609	1,155

— Represents zero or rounds to zero.

[a] Duplicate transactions between levels of government are excluded.

[b] Minor amount included in individual income tax figures.

[c] Minor amount included in 'All other' taxes.

SOURCE: U.S. Department of Commerce, Bureau of the Census, *Governmental Finances in 1968–1969* (Washington, D.C.: Government Printing Office, 1970), p. 20.

earmarked for highway construction and maintenance; hence gasoline taxes are assessed on the benefit principle.[4] State cigarette taxes ranged, in 1969, from 2.5 to 13 cents per pack. Many cities add taxes of their own. As a result of tax differentials, the smuggling of cigarettes became widespread during the 1960s. Differentials in state and local taxes on alcoholic beverages induce the thirsty to buy in low tax jurisdictions.

At the start of 1970, 45 states levied retail sales taxes.[5] All retail sales taxes are *ad valorem* taxes. In 1970 rates ranged from 2 to 6 percent, with a modal rate at 3 percent. Unlike excise taxes, *ad valorem* taxes must be used because retail sales taxes are assessed on many different products and enumeration of separate specific rates for each product would be administratively inefficient. Even the most casual observation of retail practices suggests that retail sales taxes are shifted forward to consumers. The base for retail sales taxes typically does not include the value of personal services, financial transactions, or real estate; thus the services of the academician, beautician, lawyer, and physician are exempt. These are items to which citizens devote increasing shares of their income as income rises. Because the tax base absorbs a decreasing share of income as income rises, the effective rate of sales taxation is regressive. In order to promote equity in sales taxation many jurisdictions exempt, or tax at preferentially lower rates, necessities such as food and drugs. Even with such exemptions, empirical evidence, as presented in Table 14.4, line 5, shows commodity taxation to be regressive.[6] To offset this regressivity a few states have introduced a tax

---

[4] The traditional rural control of many state legislatures call this allegation into question since a larger portion of motor fuel excise tax revenues is raised in urban centers than is expended there. Some states have magnificent rural highways while city streets are in disrepair. As evidence of the benefit intent we note that farmers may obtain refunds of federal and state gasoline taxes; the presumption is that farm machinery is not driven on highways.

The earmarking of highway user taxes has come under question in view of the needs in urban areas to finance balanced transportation systems. The Advisory Commission on Intergovernmental Relations has recommended that greater flexibility in the use of these funds be permitted. *See* the Commission's report, *State Aid to Local Governments* (Washington, D.C.: Government Printing Office, 1969).

The literature on highway finance and transport problems is voluminous. For two studies, *see* John R. Meyer, *et al., The Urban Transportation Problem and Public Policy* (Cambridge: Harvard University Press, 1965), and W. Owen, *The Metropolitan Transportation Problem* (Washington, D.C.: The Brookings Institution, 1966). *See also* Roger Sherman, "A Private Ownership Bias in Transit Choice," *American Economic Review,* December 1967.

[5] Local sales taxes are sometimes assessed separately from the state tax. In other instances state sales tax legislation permits a local option whereby the local government is permitted to impose its tax for joint collection with the state tax, the state acting as revenue agent and making the tax payment to the local government.

[6] A number of additional studies yield the same empirical findings. *See* Richard A. Musgrave, *et al.,* "Distribution of Tax Payments by Income Groups: A Case Study for 1948," *National Tax Journal,* March 1951; "The Incidence of the Tax Structure and

credit against state personal income tax liabilities, for sales taxes paid. A taxpayer whose income is so low he has no state income tax liability receives a cash refund.

The regressivity of the retail sales tax leads many to question its vertical equity. Sales taxes also may be questioned on horizontal equity grounds. Although many would agree that equals should be taxed equally, fewer would concur that determining equals for tax purposes should be done on the basis of consumption; yet those citizens who consume equal quantities of products included in the sales tax base incur equal sales tax liabilities although their incomes may be substantially different.[7] Two families with the same income will incur unequal sales tax liabilities if one family is larger than the other because large families must devote a greater share of their income to consumption. Families with uninsured losses due to natural disasters will incur larger sales tax liabilities than others with the same income, as will the newly married couple first setting up its household.

Retail sales taxes have their defenders. First, even if equity requires that public policy favor the poor, does this mean that regressive taxes should be eliminated? We raised this issue at the end of Chapter 13 and will return to it in the final section of this chapter when we again consider redistribution through the taxes and expenditures of governments. Second, some argue that each level of government—federal, state, and local—in a federal system should have separate bases from which they derive their tax revenues.[8] Thus, since the federal government has largely preempted income taxation, and local governments property taxation, sales remain as the proper tax base for state governments in the American federal system. This viewpoint is not widely held. Finally, since all reap some benefits from government expenditures, it is argued that equity requires all to incur some tax liabilities as these benefit-rendering expenditures are financed; since income taxation tends to exempt the lowest income groups, they should pay taxes on other bases, such as consumption.

If commodity taxes are to be used, collection at the retail level is

Its Effect on Consumption," in Joint Economic Committee, 84th Congress, 1st Session, *Federal Tax Policy for Economic Growth and Stability* (Washington, D.C.: Government Printing Office, 1955); James R. Beaton, "Family Tax Burdens by Income Levels," *National Tax Journal,* March 1962; George A. Bishop, "Tax Burden by Income Class," *National Tax Journal,* March 1961; G. N. Rostvold, "Distribution of Property, Retail Sales, and Personal Income Tax Burdens in California," *National Tax Journal,* March 1966; and D. G. Davies, "An Empirical Test of Sales Tax Regressivity," *Journal of Political Economy,* 1959.

[7] Reed R. Hansen, "An Empirical Analysis of the Retail Sales Tax with Policy Recommendations," *National Tax Journal,* March 1962.

[8] James M. Buchanan, *The Public Finances,* 3rd ed. (Homewood, Ill.: Richard D. Irwin, Inc., 1970), pp. 363 and 379. The issue is discussed in George F. Break, *Intergovernmental Fiscal Relations in the United States* (Washington, D.C.: The Brookings Institution, 1967), chapter 2.

probably most efficient. A manufacturer's sales tax or wholesale tax would entail fewer collection points and might thus be easier to enforce. However, in the American economy, where most retail establishments regularly keep good records, enforcement is hardly a problem; this consideration is superseded by the advantages of a single-stage retail tax as compared with either single or multistage taxes at other than the retail level. To the extent commodity taxes change relative prices, their allocative effects are minimized by taxation at the retail level; if pyramiding would ordinarily occur retail sales taxation is particularly helpful. Retail taxes are not assessed on products to be exported, and fall on imported and domestically produced products equally; thus the border tax issue does not arise (see Chapter 22). Collecting single-stage commodity taxes below the retail level would entail higher tax rates to generate the same revenue, because the value of the tax base at the manufacturer's or wholesaler's level is less than at the retail level. If tax avoidance and political objection to taxes are a function of tax rates rather than liabilities, economic efficiency as well as the welfare-maximizing actions of public officials dictate retail sales taxation. Conversely, if citizens are unaware of taxes assessed below the retail level, from the public officials' viewpoint just the opposite conclusion applies. On balance, if commodity taxes are to be part of a nation's revenue system, their assessment at the retail level seems preferred.

PROPERTY TAXATION

The property tax is the principal source of local government revenue. As may be seen from Table 14.1, local governments in 1969 derived over 80 percent of their tax receipts from this source. The base for property taxation is the value of assets such as residential and business real estate, household furniture, business inventories, and bank balances. Since real estate constitutes the most important base for property taxation, the discussion of this section is confined to taxes on this base.

Basing taxes on property values requires that valuations or assessments be made. Recently sold real estate or newly constructed buildings have current market values reflected by their sale price or construction cost, but how are untraded properties to be appraised?[9] Local officials are typically as-

[9] Acquisition values may not be a suitable guideline; suppose a manufacturer constructs a building large enough to permit the assembly of aircraft. The resale value of this facility may be far less than its initial cost if its only alternative employment is for indoor tennis courts. It is often argued that land values should be taxed more heavily than the value of buildings and other improvements so as to promote more efficient land use and encourage the making of improvements. For a discussion of this issue *see* David Holland (ed.), *The Assessment of Land Value* (Madison, University of Wisconsin Press, 1971). The *single tax*, proposed in the nineteenth century by Henry George, was to be a tax on only land values.

signed the responsibility for making property value judgments. They may be assisted by state assessors, and are often limited by state-imposed guidelines designed to make assessment procedures uniform throughout the state. Earlier in this century state governments also relied heavily on property taxes, and a few still receive a limited amount of revenue from this source. Most states assess properties such as railroads and public utilities that overlap local jurisdictions; these properties are then placed on local tax rolls at the state-assessed value. Those states that make substantial grant-in-aid payments to local governments, primarily to support primary and secondary education, often use assessed property values as a basis for allocating funds; hence they have an interest in uniform assessment practices.

Some jurisdictions claim that properties are assessed at 100 percent of their fair or true market value, while others deliberately make assessments at other than 100 percent of these values. The 1967 *Census of Governments* reported a nationwide average ratio of assessed values to market values of 30.8 percent for locally assessed ordinary real estate in 1966; the ratio ranged from a high of 77 percent in Kentucky to a low of 4.6 percent in South Carolina.[10] Thus, while each jurisdiction makes judgments regarding the value of the tax base, effective rates will depend on how assessed values relate to market values; making direct rate comparisons from one jurisdiction to another is impossible without also understanding how assessment procedures differ.

Estimates of property tax rates that may be meaningfully compared on a state by state basis are available. They show that for the United States as a whole, the effective property tax rate was 1.4 percent of true property values in 1960; the highest effective rates were in Massachusetts and Maine at 2.4 percent, and Alabama had the lowest effective rate, equal to .5 percent.[11] For single family houses in the 59 largest cities, median effective tax rates in 1966 ranged from a low of .92 percent in Birmingham, Alabama, to a high of 4.06 in Newark, New Jersey.[12]

More than one government may levy taxes on the assessed value of a particular property since the boundaries of many of the nearly 80,000 units of local government in the United States overlap. Once the tax base has been determined by assessment, various local taxing authorities set tax rates to meet their revenue needs from the property tax base.[13] In many jurisdictions

---

10 Bureau of the Census, *1967 Census of Governments,* Vol. 2, *Taxable Property Values* (Washington, D.C.: Government Printing Office, 1968).

11 Advisory Commission on Intergovernmental Fiscal Relations, *Measures of State and Local Fiscal Capacity and Tax Effort* (Washington, D.C.: Government Printing Office, 1962), p. 125.

12 Bureau of the Census, *Taxable Property Values, op. cit.*

13 Property often is not reassessed for years even if it is improved or sold. If, to a degree, property ownership reflects ability to pay, this is a potential source of inequity, for two properties of equal market value may be assessed for substantially different amounts.

the ability to raise revenues from property taxes is limited by state constitutional or statutory limits on tax rates that can be charged by a local government. These limitations often lead to the formation of new, overlapping units of government—special districts with the authority to levy property taxes and expend funds for limited purposes such as water districts, sewer districts, mosquito abatement districts, and so on.

It is sometimes argued that property taxes are equitable because ownership of wealth is an indicator of ability to pay. Property taxes, in fact, are not wealth taxes for they are assessed on only limited types of assets and it is not clear that ownership of real estate is a reasonable measure of ability to pay. Persons have to live somewhere; ownership of housing may reflect ability to pay as measured by income during that part of a citizen's life when housing was purchased, but this is certainly not the case for the retired homeowner. In this instance home ownership reflects a former rather than a current income position, and payment of property taxes is often difficult for the pensioner.[14] The property tax is also defended on the benefit principle. Such local services as police and fire protection may be said to protect property and the value of property thus measures benefits received. When we remember that the major local expenditure is for education, the benefit-based case for property taxation is weakened. Unshifted property taxes are expected to be capitalized, reducing asset values. However, to the extent the property tax is assessed on the benefit principle, municipal services are included in the value of property and the net result of local property taxation and expenditure may be to increase property's market value.

By almost universal agreement the property tax is regressive. The data given in Table 14.4, line 6, show this to be the case. The assumption behind this finding is that business property taxes are fully shifted forward thus giving a regressive pattern as they are distributed to income classes on the basis of consumption. Taxes on housing are assumed to be borne by the resident for both owner-occupied and rental units; since the income elasticity of demand for housing is low, this component of the property tax is also regressive.[15] Separate estimates of the effective rates of property taxation on owner-occupied and rental housing, by income class, are given in Table 14.2; the regressive pattern of this tax is clearly revealed in these data.

---

[14] As property tax rates have risen since World War II, the hardship imposed by increased tax liabilities on fixed-income elderly citizens has sometimes been recognized. Some communities permit elderly citizens to continue to live in their homes when taxes are in arrears, but a lien is attached to the property and the property is sold for the benefit of the state upon the death of the owner rather than passing to the decedent's heirs. Some jurisdictions grant special property tax exemptions to the elderly, usually on the first few thousand dollars of assessed value.

[15] Dick Netzer, *Economics of the Property Tax* (Washington, D.C.: The Brookings Institution, 1966), p. 57.

***Table 14.2* Effective Rates of Property Taxation as a Percent of Income, by Income Class for Owner-Occupied and Rental Units, 1959–1960**

Income Class	Effective Rate (Percent)	
	Owner Occupied	Renter Occupied
Less than $2,000	6.43	8.49
$2,000–$3,000	4.53	3.92
$3,000–$4,000	3.70	2.95
$4,000–$5,000	3.25	2.47
$5,000–$7,000	3.11	2.06
$7,000–$10,000	2.81	1.75
$10,000–$15,000	2.55	1.62
Over $15,000	2.29	1.35
All Classes	2.91	2.40

SOURCE: Dick Netzer, *Economics of the Property Tax* (Washington, D.C.: The Brookings Institution, 1966), pp. 50 and 52.

Property taxes will affect industries differently as the tax is or is not shifted, and as taxable property is a factor of production; electric and gas utilities are heavily taxed while airlines, by contrast, largely escape property taxation, as shown in Table 14.3. As property taxes fall unevenly on industries they may, if fully shifted forward, lead to changes in relative product prices and, if not shifted, have differential impacts on rates of return. In either case they are nonneutral, and allocative effects may result that must be determined and considered as the property tax is evaluated.

Many types of property are excluded from the tax base. Constitutionally, one government may not assess taxes on another.[16] Thus communities in which federal installations are located, such as military bases or federal offices, may not assess taxes on one of the community's principal employers; similarly, state office buildings or university facilities are not taxable by the communities in which they are located. In addition, the property of nonprofit organizations is typically excluded from the tax base; yet churches, colleges and universities, and charitable organizations often occupy valuable properties in the center of cities that, if devoted to other uses, would produce considerable amounts of revenue. At the same time, government properties and the properties of nonprofit organizations do, to the extent property can, benefit from public expenditures and these benefits must be financed. The federal government does make payments to local school systems on the basis of the number of children of federal employees attending school. In some

[16] In 1819 this issue was decided by the Supreme Court in the case of *McCulloch* v. *Maryland*.

Table 14.3 **Property Taxes as a Percent of National Income Originating in industry, by Industry—1957**

	Property Taxes as Percentage of National Income Originating
Electric and gas utilities	11.6
Pipelines	7.0
Telephone and telegraph	5.8
Railroads	4.9
Air transportation	0.04

SOURCE: Dick Netzer, *Economics of the Property Tax* (Washington, D.C.: The Brookings Institution, 1966), p. 26.

instances nonprofit organizations voluntarily make payments in lieu of taxes to the jurisdiction in which they are located. Many communities are reconsidering exemptions from their property tax base.

OTHER STATE AND LOCAL TAXES

A variety of other taxes are assessed by state and local governments. Among these are severance, estate, gift, and inheritance taxes; payroll taxes to finance unemployment compensation insurance; and taxes on asset transactions such as the purchase of real estate or securities. In addition, states license automobiles and drivers, thereby producing considerable revenue as shown in Table 14.1. Each of these taxes is briefly considered in this section.

Severance taxes are levied on extractive industries by some states, often in lieu of corporate income or property taxes. The rationale of the severance tax is that mineral properties are the heritage of all; therefore, everyone should benefit from the exhaustion of natural resources. Severance taxes are thus based on the quantity or value of minerals extracted. It is sometimes charged that the property tax has the undesired allocative effect of encouraging excessively rapid cutting of timber or mining of properties in order to reduce property values and, hence, tax liabilities. To the extent this occurs, severance taxes may be a useful substitute as tax liabilities depend only on current extractions rather than total asset values. However, as the level of activity in extractive industries fluctuates over the business cycle, severance taxes are an unstable source of state government revenue. Presuming that severance taxes are shifted forward, most of these tax liabilities can be exported outside the state imposing the tax. The political attractiveness of such taxes is obvious.

States levy employment taxes to finance unemployment insurance benefits. These taxes are assessed on the basis of the payroll of covered employees, with the tax liability being the employers'. The rates paid by individual employers vary according to each employer's record of employment instability. The maximum rate in 1970 was 3.1 percent. The shifting, incidence, and allocative effects of this payroll tax may be viewed in the same light as the employer's share of social security.

States, as well as the federal government, levy estate and gift taxes; in addition some states tax inheritances. At the beginning of this century many states did not have estate taxes; some states were competing for wealthy residents by exempting their wealth from taxation at death. The provisions of the federal estate tax law were partially in response to this condition; in the 1920s a credit against the federal estate tax liability was permitted for certain state estate and inheritance taxes. The intent of this legislation was to induce all states to adopt estate taxes and end their competition.

Governments at all levels tax a variety of asset transactions and the legal documents associated with them. The recording of deeds and automobile titles is taxed in many jurisdictions. New York state imposes a tax ranging from 1 cent to 4 cents per share on stock transactions; New York City, in 1968, also planned to do so until the New York Stock Exchange threatened to leave the city rather than submit to additional taxes. The Philadelphia Stock Exchange did move to the suburbs when that city instituted a tax based on security transactions.

State governments license automobiles and their drivers. Operator license fees are primarily for regulatory purposes and rates are generally set to cover the cost of examining applicants and processing permits. Auto tags, on the other hand, yield revenue usually earmarked for expenditure on highway construction and maintenance, and are assessed on the benefit principle. Some automobile license fees are based on the value of the vehicle, thus introducing the ability to pay principle.

State and local governments assess a variety of miscellaneous taxes on many different bases. A license is required to do business as a physician, barber, or electrician; these license fees are probably aimed more at regulation than revenue, the license being issued to all who can certify their competence to perform the trade. Other license fees, such as those required to operate taxicabs, liquor stores, and retail outlets are primarily designed to regulate entry into the industry, although they also produce some revenue. Many jurisdictions levy gambling taxes; assessments on race track bets are particularly common. Nevada's gambling taxes are an important source of revenue. Massachusetts levies a 5 percent tax on restaurant meals costing one dollar or more; the proceeds are earmarked for old age assistance. Many states tax hotel and motel accommodations on the grounds that out-of-state guests benefit from the state's services and should make a contribution toward their provision. Finally, penalty assessments, primarily fines for traffic violations and other criminal acts, are a source of state and local government revenues.

USER CHARGES AND FEES

Examination of Table 14.1 shows that state and local governments in 1968–1969 received over $13 billion of budget receipts from charges, and an additional $6 billion as operating revenue from municipally owned utilities. These receipts are commonly called user charges or fees. *User charges* are those receipts, assessed on the benefit principle, that are designed to cover the full cost of providing a particular government service. This is true of the sale of electricity, for example, where beneficiaries are easily identified, and commonly held standards of equity require that the user should pay the full cost. On the other hand, *fees* are charges upon direct users of public facilities and services that are not designed to cover the full cost of providing that public service, often because substantial third party benefits are present; this is the case, for example, with receipts from institutions of higher education, school lunch sales, and hospitals.

In Chapter 3 we saw that efficient allocation of resources requires that price be set equal to marginal cost. However, when marginal cost is decreasing or is zero, such pricing will not provide a return to the private producer adequate to cover his total costs. Thus, quite aside from any third party benefits, efficiency may require that facilities such as parks and recreational areas be provided by government. However, when congestion occurs charges are required to allocate resources; thus free admission to a municipal picnic area on weekdays and a fee on weekends may be the efficient means of providing these services. Similarly, on-street parking in business districts is typically not metered during after-business hours and on holidays because it is not scarce; during business hours parking space is limited; fees are a means of rationing that also yield some revenue.

Although not a tax or a user charge, some states and municipalities derive revenue from the operation of liquor stores. This occurs where private outlets are prohibited and state stores are granted a monopoly position. This procedure is primarily intended as a regulatory device, but the profits from operation may be an important source of revenue. To the extent profits are earned from the retailing of alcoholic beverages (or any other public service), the buyer is, in a sense, being taxed.

REDISTRIBUTION VIA STATE AND LOCAL TAXES AND EXPENDITURES

At the end of Chapter 13 we discussed a number of problems involved in determining the incidence of public expenditures, and then examined some

Table 14.4 State and Local Taxes and Expenditures as a Percent of Family Income, 1965

	Income Class									
	Under $2000	$2000 to 2999	$3000 to 3999	$4000 to 4999	$5000 to 5999	$6000 to 7499	$7500 to 9999	$10,000 to 14,999	$15,000 and Over	Total
Expenditures										
1 General benefit expenditures	11.7	6.8	5.4	4.6	4.1	3.6	3.3	2.9	2.3	4.0
2 Individual benefit expenditures	18.0	12.2	9.0	7.9	7.1	6.2	5.0	4.4	2.9	6.4
3 Total	29.7	19.0	14.4	12.5	11.2	9.8	8.3	7.3	5.2	10.4
Taxes										
4 Individual and corporate income	.6	.6	.8	.9	.9	.9	1.1	1.2	2.2	1.1
5 Sales, excise, and so on	6.1	5.5	5.6	5.3	5.1	4.8	4.4	4.0	2.6	4.6
6 Property	6.9	5.2	4.7	4.2	4.2	3.8	3.5	3.3	2.4	3.8
7 Death and gift	—	—	—	—	—	—	—	—	1.3	.1
8 Social insurance	1.5	1.4	1.4	1.4	1.3	1.3	1.2	1.1	.7	1.2
9 Total	15.1	12.7	12.6	11.8	11.5	10.8	10.1	9.6	9.1	10.8
Redistribution										
10	1.97	1.50	1.14	1.06	0.97	0.91	0.82	0.76	0.57	0.96

SOURCE: *Tax Burdens and Benefits of Government Expenditures by Income Class, 1961 and 1965* (New York: Tax Foundation, Inc., 1967), pp. 20 and 21.

empirical evidence on redistribution through the federal tax and expenditure process. Evidence taken from the Tax Foundation's study on redistribution through state and local taxes and expenditures is given in Table 14.4. The assumptions for analysis of state and local taxes and expenditures are the same as those given in Chapter 13. The additional assumption needed to explain the property tax incidence was given earlier in this chapter. The state and local tax system is regressive; this was expected since the principal sources of state and local government tax revenues—property and commodity taxes—are regressive. Of greater interest, however, is the analysis of expenditures, for the incidence of state and local expenditure benefits appears to be highly regressive (Table 14.4, line 3). Regressive here means in favor of the lower income groups in the sense that the value of the benefits as a percent of income falls as income rises. As expected, this is the case for general benefits because 50 percent of these expenditures were distributed by population. This pattern is reinforced by the treatment of educational expenditures as an individual benefit that is allocated to income classes on the basis of the distribution, by income class, of children under age 18. Since the poor tend to have larger families than the more affluent, this allocation distributes substantial benefits to the low income classes (line 2), and gives a highly regressive pattern to the distribution of benefits from state and local government expenditures (line 3). This assignment of educational expenditures probably overdistributes benefits to the low income classes. There clearly are some third party benefits from primary and secondary education. Just as clearly, the pupil benefits from his education. Basing the allocation on the distribution of the school-age population is not obviously inappropriate.

Dividing the incidence of benefits (line 3) by the incidence of taxes (line 9) gives the Tax Foundation's measure of redistribution through state and local government taxes and expenditures, as shown in line 10. This measure of redistribution shows, on the average, that for each dollar of taxes paid to state and local governments by the lowest income citizens, $1.97 of benefits were received in exchange; the highest income citizens received 57 cents of benefits for each tax dollar. Thus, the state and local government tax and expenditure process appears to favor the poor, although to a lesser degree than the federal process.

These measures of redistribution are important inputs to serious consideration of equity and public policy. We fully recognize the difficulties in making and interpreting these empirical results and do not presume to suggest an amount of redistribution that is just. What we note here is that, while the state and local taxation is regressive, redistribution appears to result. In making judgments on equity should each and every component of the public sector be evaluated in the light of a single equity criterion or should the entire public sector be evaluated? On equity grounds one frequently hears criticism of commodity and property taxes because they are regressive; if the benefits that they finance are even more regressive should these taxes be judged inequitable? We think not. Both public revenues and expenditures affect individual welfare. Traditionally, the incidence of benefits from public expenditures has seldom been formally considered, and equity has been viewed from the incidence of taxes alone. Public policy would be better formed if analysis of equity moved away from narrow consideration of the incidence of taxes and instead focused on the broader concept of citizen welfare.

15

FISCAL POLICY MODELS

Fiscal policy has been a topic of scholarly dispute and public discussion only since the Keynesian revolution of the 1930s. Fiscal policy has, nonetheless, existed ever since taxes joined death as certainties in this world. In Chapter 2 fiscal policy was defined as the use of public expenditures and revenues to affect macroeconomic stability. Our reason for suggesting that fiscal policy dates from the first appearance of a public sector in history is that the combined impact of expenditures and receipts has a macroeconomic effect even if this is not the avowed goal of public authorities.[1]

Implicit fiscal policy is the combined impact of public sector expenditures and revenues when the goal of economic policy concerns resource

---

[1] The principles of modern fiscal policy have proven useful in analyzing historical situations where stabilization was not thought of as a goal of public policy. *See,* for example, Alexander Balinsky, *Albert Gallatin: Fiscal Theories and Policies* (New Brunswick, N.J.: Rutgers University Press, 1958) and Lewis H. Kimmel, *Federal Budget and Fiscal Policy, 1789–1958* (Washington, D.C.: The Brookings Institution, 1959).

allocation or equity rather than stabilization. An obvious example is national defense spending which absorbed about 10 percent of gross national product in the 1960s. Such spending is undertaken to allocate resources; the consequent fiscal policy impact may be recognized, welcomed, or counteracted, but in any event clearly exists. Progressive income taxes reflect societal attitudes toward equity in the distribution of income, but also affect the stability of the relationship between personal income and disposable personal income. State and local governments do not consciously pursue stabilization as a goal but their sizable expenditures and receipts cannot help but affect the stability of macro-economic variables. For example, reductions in state and local government expenditures in response to dwindling receipts complicated the problem of achieving stability during the 1930s.

The federal government may explicitly vary either receipts or expenditures or both in an attempt to influence the economy's stability. *Explicit fiscal policy* usually requires Congressional action to initiate or expand expenditure programs or to change tax rates or bases. The Civilian Conservation Corps and the Works Progress Administration, both of which were begun in the 1930s and terminated as military demand restored full employment during World War II, illustrate the explicit use by Congress of expenditures to stabilize the economy. The Revenue Act of 1964 is an instance of Congressional action designed primarily to reduce unemployment and stimulate economic growth by reducing taxes. In addition to Congressional measures, some explicit fiscal policy moves can be made at the discretion of the President. An administration has far more discretionary power to vary expenditures than to influence revenues. Once monies have been appropriated, the executive branch, through the apportionment powers of the Office of Management and Budget, and other means, may vary the timing of obligations and outlays in response to stabilization requirements. For instance, highway building, military construction, and other public works may be accelerated or postponed. On the revenue side, the executive may authorize the sale of some publicly owned financial or real assets without the expressed consent of Congress. However, increases or decreases in federal tax revenues may not be initiated at the discretion of the President, for tax rates or tax bases may be changed only by Congress. Granting this power to the President has often been suggested as a desirable reform in the United States fiscal system.[2]

Some taxes and expenditure programs comprise *automatic fiscal policies*. By this we mean that tax receipts tend to vary directly and expenditures inversely with changes in gross national product. The automatic fiscal policy features of particular taxes and expenditure programs are sometimes ex-

---

[2] In 1967 Congress did grant the President authority to vary the interest equalization tax within a specified range. Because of the special nature of this tax (see Chapter 22), it is unlikely that this action will be taken as a precedent for extending the President's power by permitting discretionary changes in other tax rates.

plicitly designed but more commonly are implicit by-products of legislation. As gross national product and personal income increase, receipts from personal income taxes rise whereas, by contrast, property taxes remain constant. The same short-run increase in gross national product will result in reduced transfer payments. Such automatic changes in public revenues and expenditures affect macroeconomic variables but do not necessarily promote stability at a full employment level. This matter is taken up in Chapters 16 and 17.

This chapter is devoted to the development of four macroeconomic models that explicate the impact of explicit or implicit fiscal policies on the economy. In these models the level of gross national product in current dollars, Y, has been taken as the primary dependent variable, although the goals of fiscal policy are usually formulated in terms of real income, price level, and employment variables. Thus, the variables in terms of which the goals of fiscal policy are expressed do not appear explicitly in these models. Specification of the relationships among the money value of gross national product and the employment, price level, and real income variables is beyond the scope of this book, but a few comments are in order.[3]

The variable Y—as used in these models and, indeed, in practically all public discussion of fiscal policy—is economic shorthand for infinite combinations of real incomes and price levels. Furthermore, for any one level of gross national product, the shares of consumption, investment, and government goods and services may differ. Within each of these classifications of aggregate output the specific composition of goods and services may also vary.

A fiscal policy action's most obvious effect on employment comes as changes in Y cause changes in real gross national product. For instance, with constant prices and unchanged technology, any increase in Y will result from the greater real output made possible by augmented resource employment. Alternative fiscal policy actions having the same effect on Y may, however, have quite different impacts on employment: Increasing the compensation of public employees because of increased public employment and increasing government purchases from corporations will usually result in different changes in employment. Conversely, using fiscal policy to alter the product mix, while holding the level of employment and technology constant, may change gross national product. If, for example, the public sector acted as employer of last resort, stable full employment of labor, by definition, would be achieved. As public employment absorbed workers laid off by corporations, gross national product would fall reflecting the economy's failure to utilize fully corporate plant and equipment, and other nonlabor resources. The welfare implications of fully employed labor resources are, from a

---

[3] For a standard theoretical treatment of this problem, *see* Gardner Ackley, *Macroeconomic Theory* (New York: Macmillan, 1961), chapter 14.

societal viewpoint, usually of more concern than the implications of idle plant capacity; hence employment objectives are typically stated in terms of a labor variable.

The Phillips curve is a useful pedagogic device for discussing the relationship between labor employment and the price level.[4] The *Phillips curve,* as illustrated in Figure 15.1, suggests an inverse relationship between the

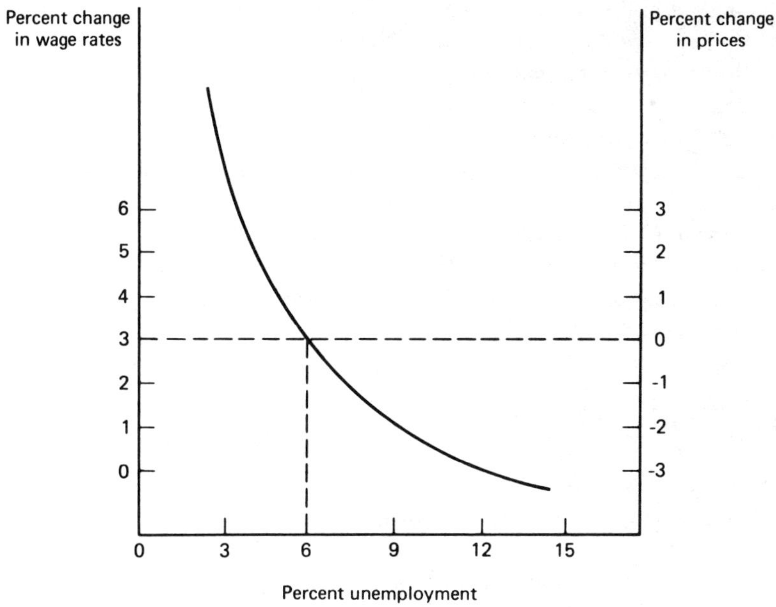

Figure 15.1 The Phillips Curve.

rate of unemployment and the rate of increase in wage rates: When unemployment is high employers are under less pressure to increase wage rates than when unemployment is low. If the rate of increase in money wage rates equals the rate of increase in labor productivity, higher wages can be paid with unchanged product prices; labor costs and profits per unit of output would remain constant. If the rate of increase in wage rates exceeds (is less

[4] A. W. Phillips, "The Relation Between Unemployment and the Rate of Change in Money Wage Rates in the United Kingdom, 1862–1956," *Economica,* November 1958. For a review of the subsequent literature, *see* George L. Perry, *Unemployment, Money Wage Rates, and Inflation* (Cambridge, Mass.: The M.I.T. Press, 1966). *See also* Charles C. Holt, *et al., The Unemployment–Inflation Dilemma: A Manpower Solution* (Washington, D.C.: The Urban Institute, 1971); H. I. Liebling and A. T. Cluff, "U.S. Postwar Inflation and Phillips Curves," *Kyklos,* 1969; and George L. Perry, "Changing Labor Markets and Inflation," *Brookings Papers on Economic Activity,* **3**:1970.

than) the rate of growth of productivity, prices rise (fall), assuming that the division of corporate income between wages and profits remains constant. Figure 15.1 has been drawn using an assumed annual increase in labor productivity of 3 percent. Therefore the right-hand scale, measuring change in prices, has been set three percentage points above the left-hand scale. The price level would remain unchanged at the point where a 6 percent rate of unemployment is associated with a 3 percent rate of increase in money wage rates. This Phillips curve indicates downward pressure on prices when unemployment exceeds 6 percent and, conversely, upward pressure at rates of unemployment below 6 percent. This form of analysis is often used to illustrate the conflict between the employment and price level goals of fiscal policy. As the fiscal policy models that follow are developed, policy makers' concern for these real output, price, and employment objectives should be kept in mind even though the major dependent variable of the models is the money value of gross national product. After establishing a theoretical basis for analyzing fiscal policy actions we turn, in Chapters 16 and 17, to some of the problems of formulating fiscal policy, and a survey of American fiscal policy since World War II.

MODEL I

In simple Keynesian macroeconomic analysis, the money value of gross national product, Y, is equal to the sum of the money values of final demands. In a closed economy (no international transactions) these final demands consist of private sector demand by households for consumption, C, and by businesses for investment, I, and the demand of the public sector for goods and services, G. Algebraically,

$$Y = C + I + G \qquad [15.1]$$

The money value of gross national product is equal to the gross national income generated in the production of that product. In this first model all gross national income is received by the household sector as personal income. There are only three ways in which the household sector can dispose of personal income: Consumption spending, C, payment of taxes, T, and household saving, S_H; therefore,

$$Y = C + T + S_H \qquad [15.2]$$

The levels of investment and government spending on goods and services are taken as autonomous, I_o and G_o, as are household taxes, T_o. Consumption is assumed to be a function of disposable personal income, Y_D, where

$$Y_D = Y - T_o \qquad [15.3]$$

and

$$C = C_o + k(Y_D) \qquad [15.4]$$

C_o is an autonomous component of household demand, and k is the household sector marginal propensity to consume disposable personal income. It is assumed that $0 < k < 1$.

Substituting Equation (15.3) into (15.4) and (15.4) into (15.1), and solving for Y, yields

$$\overline{Y} = \frac{1}{1-k}\,(C_o + I_o + G_o - kT_o) \qquad [15.5]$$

where $\overline{Y}$ is the *equilibrium value of money gross national product*. The first element to the right of the equal sign in Equation (15.5), $1/1 - k$, is the familiar multiplier. In an algebraic sense the full amount of autonomous consumption, investment, and government spending on goods and services is multiplied in the creation of aggregate demand. Aggregate demand is reduced by the imposition of taxes. Because the marginal propensity to consume, k, is assumed to be less than one, taxes, T_o, reduce aggregate demand by a smaller amount, kT_o. It is this latter amount that, when multiplied, reduces aggregate demand by $(1/1 - k)(kT_o)$.

Geometrically, Equation (15.5) may be illustrated as in Figure 15.2. The money value of gross national product is measured on the horizontal axis; aggregate demand is measured on the vertical axis. OX is a 45° line indicating all the possible points of equality between the money value of gross national product supplied and the sum of final demands in the three sectors, $C + I + G$. The vertical intercept OQ is given by the expression $C_o + I_o + G_o - kT_o$ in Equation (15.5). The slope of the aggregate demand schedule, $C + I_o + G_o$, is, in this model, determined by and equal to the marginal propensity to consume disposable personal income, k. The intersection of the aggregate demand schedule and the 45° line, OX, determines the equilibrium money value of gross national product, $\overline{Y}$.

An equilibrium value of money gross national product is one where the income flow is equal to the product flow. The meaning of this in accounting terms was made clear in Chapter 11. Since there are only three possible dispositions of the flow of income—consumption, C, household saving, S_H, and taxes, T_o—the condition for equilibrium is

$$C + T_o + S_H = C + I_o + G_o \qquad [15.6]$$

Substracting consumption from both sides of Equation (15.6) gives

$$T_o + S_H = I_o + G_o \qquad [15.7]$$

Household saving is the difference between disposable personal income and consumption spending:

$$S_H = (Y - T_o) - C \qquad [15.8]$$

Figure 15.2 Determination of the equilibrium level of the money value of gross national product.

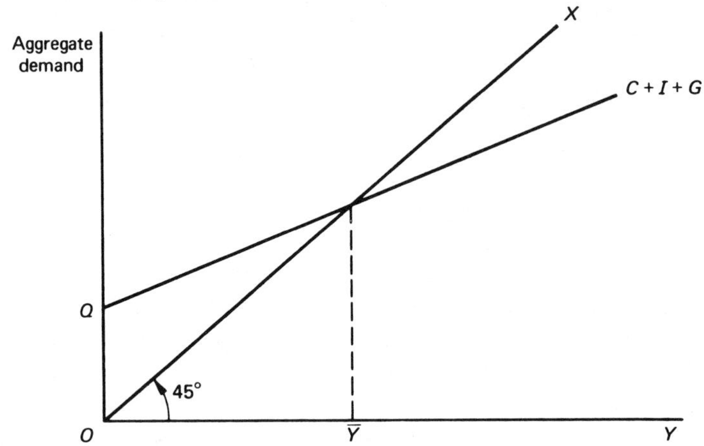

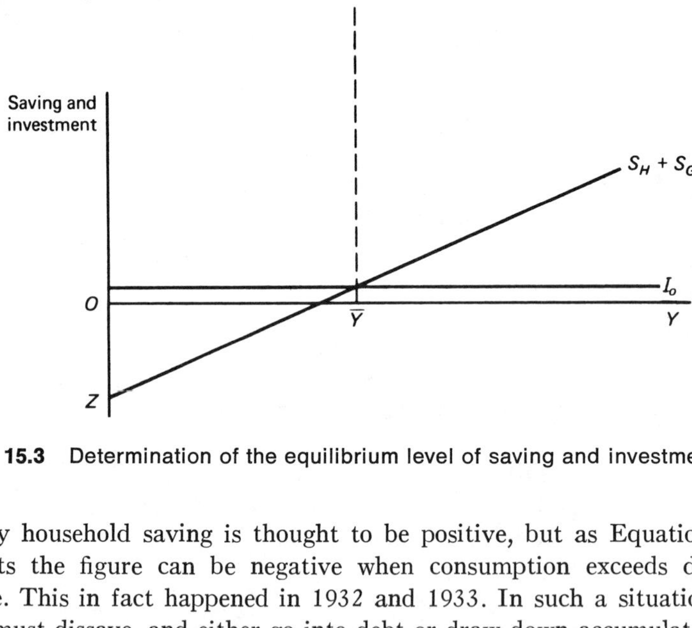

Figure 15.3 Determination of the equilibrium level of saving and investment.

Usually household saving is thought to be positive, but as Equation (15.8) suggests the figure can be negative when consumption exceeds disposable income. This in fact happened in 1932 and 1933. In such a situation households must dissave, and either go into debt or draw down accumulated assets.

The public sector in any economy may save by expending an amount less than revenues. In accounting terms these savings are referred to as a surplus in the public sector budget. When public expenditures exceed revenues in the public sector budget it is said to be in deficit. Therefore public sector saving may be negative or positive. In the context of this model, public sector saving is defined as

$$S_G = T_o - G_o \qquad [15.9]$$

Subtracting G_o from both sides of Equation (15.7) and substituting Equation (15.9) into Equation (15.7) restates the equilibrium condition as

$$S_H + S_G = I_o \qquad [15.10]$$

The equilibrium condition expressed in Equation (15.10) can be illustrated as in Figure 15.3. Here saving and investment are measured on the vertical axis and the money value of gross national product is again measured on the horizontal axis. The saving function, $S_H + S_G$, has a negative intercept, OZ, equal to $OQ - I_o$ in Figure 15.2, and a slope of $1 - k$.[5] The expression $1 - k$ is the marginal propensity to save disposable personal income. The saving function intersects I_o, the function illustrating autonomous investment, at the same value for $\bar{Y}$ as was determined in Figure 15.2.

This equilibrium money value of gross national product may not be consistent with the price level and employment goals of public policy. Any money value of gross national product may result from a variety of combinations of price and real output levels. If the policy goal is to increase real output and employment (assuming output and employment move in tandem), an increase in Y will represent movement toward that goal as long as the price level remains constant (or increases proportionately less). Conversely, in a situation where labor is fully employed and plant and equipment are utilized to capacity, a decrease in Y may represent a fall in the price level without any change in real output and employment (or proportionately smaller decreases in real output and employment).

A change in public sector expenditures, ΔG_o, or revenues, ΔT_o, will lead to a change in the equilibrium money value of gross national product, $\Delta \bar{Y}$. In this model these effects may be expressed algebraically as

$$\Delta \bar{Y} = \frac{1}{1-k}(\Delta G_o) \qquad [15.11]$$

and

$$\Delta \bar{Y} = -\frac{1}{1-k}(k\Delta T_o) \qquad [15.12]$$

Equation (15.11) indicates that $\bar{Y}$ will change (increase or decrease) by an amount equal to the multiplier, $1/1 - k$, times the change (increase or decrease) in autonomous government spending on goods and services. Equation (15.12) states that $\bar{Y}$ will change (decrease or increase) by an amount equal

[5] As was stated above, it is assumed that $0 < k < 1$. This constraint on the value of k is a necessary condition for a stable equilibrium value for $\bar{Y}$ in this model. In geometric terms, this constraint on the marginal propensity to consume assures that the aggregate savings function will have a positive slope as the marginal propensity to save is also greater than zero and less than one.

to the multiplier times the product of the marginal propensity to consume and the change (increase or decrease) in autonomous taxes. A simultaneous change in public expenditures and revenues may be expressed as a combination of Equations (15.11) and (15.12)

$$\Delta\overline{Y} = \frac{1}{1-k}(\Delta G_o) - \frac{1}{1-k}(k\Delta T_o) \qquad [15.13]$$

If the public sector balances its budget at the margin, by increasing or decreasing taxes and expenditures by the same amount, that is, $\Delta G_o = \Delta T_o$, then $\overline{Y}$ will change by an amount equal to the change in taxes and expenditures. Substituting ΔG_o for its equivalent ΔT_o in Equation (15.13), and factoring ΔG_o from each term on the right-hand side of that equation yields

$$\Delta Y = \Delta G_o\left[\frac{1}{1-k} - \frac{k}{1-k}\right] = \Delta G_o\left[\frac{1-k}{1-k}\right] = \Delta G_o \qquad [15.14]$$

This result is known as the *balanced-budget theorem;* it states that if the public sector changes its expenditures and matches this by a corresponding change in taxes, then the equilibrium value of money gross national product will change by the full amount of the change in government spending but not by any multiple.[6] For example, suppose that an economist is employed as a government consultant but at the same time a tax, ΔT_o, equal to his consulting fee, ΔG_o, is levied on households. The money value of gross national product will first increase by the value of the consultant's services, ΔG_o. The consultant will then increase his consumption by the amount $k\ (\Delta G_o)$, and his saving by the amount $(1 - k)(\Delta G_o)$. Simultaneously, households subject to the new tax will decrease their consumption by the amount $k(\Delta T_o)$ and their savings by the amount $(1 - k)(\Delta T_o)$. The net effect of increasing taxes and government spending is to leave aggregate household consumption and saving unchanged. Thus, $\overline{Y}$ will change only by the amount of change in government spending.

The results of changes in public expenditures and taxes that have been algebraically stated in Equations (15.11) through (15.14) may also be illustrated geometrically. An increase in government expenditures, as in Equation (15.11), would shift the intercept *OQ* in Figure 15.2 upward by an amount equal to ΔG_o. The slope of the aggregate demand schedule would remain unchanged and the point of intersection of the schedule with the 45° line would shift to the right by an amount equal to $(1/1 - k)(\Delta G_o)$. Similarly, in Figure 15.3 the intercept *OZ* would shift downward, the slope of the aggregate saving function would remain unchanged, and the point of inter-

[6] Note that the public sector budget must be balanced at the margin but not necessarily balanced in the aggregate for this theorem to hold: That is, $\Delta G_o = \Delta T_o$, but G_o need not equal T_o.

section with the investment function would shift to the right. An increase in taxes would shift the intercept OQ in Figure 15.2 downward by an amount equal to $k\Delta T_o$, and in Figure 15.3 the intercept OZ would shift upward by the same amount. The slopes of the aggregate demand and saving schedules again remain unchanged; the equilibrium level of money gross national product in both Figures 15.2 and 15.3 would shift to the left by an amount equal to $(1/1-k)(k\Delta T_o)$. When both expenditures and taxes are changed the intercepts change by an amount equal to $\Delta G_o - k\Delta T_o$. In the case of the marginally balanced budget, the intercept would change by an amount equal to $(1-k)(\Delta G_o)$, and the horizontal shift in the points of intersection that determine $\overline{Y}$ would equal ΔG_o.

MODEL II

This fiscal policy model differs from the first only by the inclusion of autonomous transfer payments, P_o, along with expenditures on goods and services as a component of total public spending. As in the first model, the money value of gross national product equals gross national income, all of which is again received by the household sector as personal income. The household sector in this second model also receives transfer payments as a component of personal income. Personal income now equals $Y + P_o$. Adding P_o to both sides of the aggregate demand Equation (15.1) gives

$$Y + P_o = C + I_o + G_o + P_o \qquad [15.15]$$

Since there are only three ways in which the household may utilize personal income, Equation (15.2) may be rewritten as

$$Y + P_o = C + T_o + S_H \qquad [15.16]$$

Disposable personal income is now defined as

$$Y_D = (Y + P_o) - T_o \qquad [15.17]$$

Consumption remains a function of disposable personal income

$$C = C_o + k(Y_D) \qquad [15.18]$$

Substituting Equation (15.17) into (15.18), and (15.18) into (15.15), and solving for Y, yields

$$\overline{Y} = \frac{1}{1-k}(C_o + I_o + G_o + kP_o - kT_o) \qquad [15.19]$$

Equation (15.19) differs from (15.5) in that the level of $\overline{Y}$ is increased by an amount equal to $1/1-k(kP_o)$. The geometric representation of Equation

(15.19) would be the same as in Figure 15.2 except that the intercept OQ would be higher by an amount equal to kP_o.

An equilibrium value of money gross national product in this second model is one where the income flow of Equation (15.16) equals the product flow of Equation (15.15), therefore,

$$C + T_o + S_H = C + I_o + G_o + P_o \quad [15.20]$$

Subtracting consumption from both sides of Equation (15.20) gives

$$T_o + S_H = I_o + G_o + P_o \quad [15.21]$$

Household and government saving must now be redefined as

$$S_H = [(Y + P_o) - T_o] - C \quad [15.22]$$

and

$$S_G = T_o - (G_o + P_o) \quad [15.23]$$

Subtracting $G_o + P_o$ from both sides of Equation (15.21) and substituting Equation (15.23) into (15.21) again gives the equilibrium condition

$$S_H + S_G = I_o \quad [15.24]$$

illustrated in Figure 15.3. In this case, however, the aggregate saving function is shifted downward by $k(P_o)$.

Changes in taxes and government expenditure on goods and services have the same impact on the equilibrium level of money gross national product $\overline{Y}$ as in the previous model [see Equations (15.11) and (15.12)]. Changes in transfer payments affect $\overline{Y}$ as follows:

$$\Delta\overline{Y} = \frac{1}{1 - k} (k\Delta P_o) \quad [15.25]$$

A comparison of Equations (15.11) and (15.25) indicates that changes in transfer payments have a smaller impact on $\overline{Y}$ than do changes in government spending on goods and services. The difference in impact is attributable to the fact that recipients of transfer payments save a fraction, $1 - k$, of this component of their personal income. A dollar of transfer payments results in less than a dollar of demand for consumer goods and services, whereas a dollar spent directly by the public sector on goods and services results in a full dollar of final demand.[7] Following the same procedure used to derive the balanced budget theorem, when $\Delta P_o = \Delta T_o$,

---

[7] The multiplier for changes in government expenditures for goods and services and for transfer payments is the same. Making these expenditures in equal amounts has a different impact on $\overline{Y}$, not because of multiplier differences, but because not all of the transfer payment is spent to create an initial addition to aggregate demand equal to the government's outlay.

$$\Delta\overline{Y} = \frac{1}{1-k}(k\Delta P_o) - \frac{1}{1-k}(k\Delta T_o) = 0 \qquad [15.26]$$

Taxing Peter to make a transfer payment to Paul has no net effect on the equilibrium value of money gross national product as long as Peter and Paul have the same marginal propensity to consume.[8]

To illustrate this model the following numerical values for the parameter k and autonomous variables in Equation (15.19) are assumed:

Autonomous Variables	Parameter
$C_o = 5$	$k = .9$
$I_o = 10$	
$G_o = 10$	
$P_o = 10$	
$T_o = 15$	

Substituting these values into Equation (15.19) and solving for $\overline{Y}$ yields

$$\overline{Y} = 10(20.5) = 205$$

The value of the multiplier in this example, $1/1 - .9$, is determined by the single parameter k. The equilibrium values for the other dependent variables are:

$$\begin{aligned} Y_D &= 200 \\ C &= 185 \\ S_H &= 15 \\ S_G &= -5 \end{aligned}$$

and the equilibrium condition that total saving equals investment is satisfied. Public sector saving is negative; its budget is in deficit.

To illustrate this model further, five variations of the numerical example follow. Each variation takes the values of the autonomous variables given above and introduces specific changes, keeping the value of k equal to .9.

Variation 1: Government expenditures on goods and services increase. Suppose G increases from $G_o = 10$ to $G_o = 15$, then

$$\begin{aligned} \overline{Y} &= 255 \\ Y_D &= 250 \\ C &= 230 \\ S_H &= 20 \\ S_G &= -10 \end{aligned}$$

[8] For a more complete treatment and empirical investigation of this point, *see* Harold Lubell, "Effects of Redistribution of Income on Consumers' Expenditures," *American Economic Review,* March 1947.

As expected on the basis of Equation (15.11), the equilibrium value of Y increases by an amount equal to the multiplier times the change in government expenditures on goods and services, or

$$\Delta\overline{Y} = \frac{1}{1-k}(\Delta G_o) = 10(5) = 50$$

Because T_o remains constant, the public sector deficit goes up by the full amount of the increased spending on goods and services. The equilibrium condition that total saving equals investment is satisfied due to the increased saving of the household sector.

Variation 2: Taxes increase. If T_o increases from $T_o = 15$ to $T_o = 20$ then

$$\begin{aligned} \overline{Y} &= 160 \\ Y_D &= 150 \\ C &= 140 \\ S_H &= 10 \\ S_G &= 0 \end{aligned}$$

The public sector budget is now balanced but the equilibrium value of money gross national product has fallen by $\Delta\overline{Y} = -45$, as specified in Equation (15.12).

Variation 3: Government expenditures on goods and services and taxes increase by an equal amount. Here Variations 1 and 2 are combined, $\Delta G_o = \Delta T_o = 5$, and

$$\begin{aligned} \overline{Y} &= 210 \\ Y_D &= 200 \\ C &= 185 \\ S_H &= 15 \\ S_G &= -5 \end{aligned}$$

This is the case of the marginally balanced budget [see Equation (15.14)]; $\Delta\overline{Y} = \Delta G_o = \Delta T_o = 5$. The only dependent variable that changes is $\overline{Y}$. The deficit in the public sector budget is unaffected.

Variation 4: Transfer payments increase. If $\Delta P_o = 5$, then

$$\begin{aligned} \overline{Y} &= 250 \\ Y_D &= 250 \\ C &= 230 \\ S_H &= 20 \\ S_G &= -10 \end{aligned}$$

The increase in transfer payments results in $\Delta\overline{Y} = 45$, as given by Equation (15.25); this increase in $\overline{Y}$ is less than the increase that resulted from a like change in spending on goods and services as illustrated in Variation 1. Variation 4 shows a change in household saving offset by a change in the public sector deficit, and the equilibrium condition remains satisfied.

Variation 5: Transfer payments and taxes increase by an equal amount. This final case is a combination of Variations 2 and 4 where $\Delta P_o = \Delta T_o = 5$ and

$$\begin{aligned} \overline{Y} &= 205 \\ Y_D &= 200 \\ C &= 185 \\ S_H &= 15 \\ S_G &= -5 \end{aligned}$$

This variation illustrates Equation (15.26),

$$\Delta\overline{Y} = \frac{1}{1-.9}[.9(5)] - \frac{1}{1-.9}[.9(5)] = 0$$

Comparing Variations 3 and 5 clearly illustrates the differential impact on the equilibrium money value of gross national product of the two types of public sector expenditures.

MODEL III

With the exception of a few minor sources of revenue, modern governments do not set taxes at autonomous levels. Most taxes are functionally related to levels of income; as the level of income increases tax receipts go up as long as tax rates remain unchanged. Such is the case even where the tax base is not income per se, as in the case of sales and excise taxes. The third fiscal policy model drops autonomous taxes, T_o, and introduces taxes as a linear function of taxable personal income. Since all gross national income is received as a component of personal income by the household sector and since the transfer payment component of personal income is assumed to be exempt from taxation, we may write

$$T = tY \qquad [15.27]$$

where the parameter t is the proportional tax rate. The definition of disposable income expressed by Equation (15.17) must now be modified as

$$Y_D = (Y + P_o) - tY = (1 - t)Y + P_o \qquad [15.28]$$

As in the previous models, consumption remains a function of disposable income, Equation (15.18), and the money value of gross national product equals the sum of the final demands for that product, Equation (15.15). Substituting Equation (15.28) into Equation (15.18), and (15.18) into (15.15), and solving for Y, yields

$$\overline{Y} = \frac{1}{1 - k(1 - t)} (C_o + I_o + G_o + kP_o) \qquad [15.29]$$

The second element to the right of the equal sign in Equation (15.29) differs from the corresponding element in Equation (15.19) because there are no autonomous taxes in this model. The new expression for the multiplier is $1/1 - k(1 - t)$. With a positive tax rate, a second leakage is introduced into the aggregate income flow, thus reducing the numerical value of the multiplier. In the previous model the production of an additional dollar of gross national product generated a dollar of personal income of which the fraction k was spent on consumption by the initial recipient of that dollar. In this model the production of an additional dollar of gross national product also results in the generation of a dollar of personal income but that dollar is taxed. The remaining fraction of that dollar, $1 - t$, represents an addition to the initial recipient's disposable income. The fraction of taxable personal income spent on consumption will equal $k(1 - t)$. The fraction $k(1 - t)$ is the marginal propensity to consume taxable personal income. The value of the marginal propensity to consume disposable personal income remains unchanged at k, but for purposes of determining the multiplier the marginal propensity to consume must be specified in terms of the relationship between consumption and the money value of gross national product.

Geometrically, Equation (15.29) may be illustrated in Figure 15.2. The slope of the aggregate demand schedule is equal to the marginal propensity to consume taxable personal income, Y, and is, in this model, equal to $k(1 - t)$. Any variation in t, given a constant k, would change the slope of the aggregate demand schedule. The intercept OQ is equal to $C_o + I_o + G_o + kP_o$. Figure 15.3 can be used to illustrate the equilibrium condition for this model. The equality of aggregate saving and investment occurs at a level of money gross national product determined by the intersection of these two functions. Just as the slope of the aggregate demand schedule was lowered by introducing a second leakage, the slope of the aggregate saving function is raised and is equal to $1 - k(1 - t)$, the marginal propensity to save taxable personal income. Taxable personal income, in this model, equals the money value of gross national product.[9]

[9] The necessary condition for stability of $\overline{Y}$ is that $0 < k(1 - t) < 1$. In the previous models it was necessary that k be positive and less than one; this is no longer an algebraic necessity though it remains reasonable as an economic assumption. If consumers insist on spending more than their marginal increments of disposable income,

New equations are necessary to show the effects of changing government expenditures on goods and services or transfer payments:

$$\Delta\overline{Y} = \frac{1}{1 - k(1 - t)} (\Delta G_o) \qquad [15.30]$$

$$\Delta\overline{Y} = \frac{1}{1 - k(1 - t)} (k\Delta P_o) \qquad [15.31]$$

The only difference between these two equations and (15.11) and (15.25) is attributable to the change in the value of the multiplier. Geometrically, changes in G_o and P_o would still be shown as shifts in the intercepts of Figures 15.1 and 15.2; assuming no change in the value of k and a positive tax rate, the resulting changes in $\overline{Y}$ for any specific ΔG_o or ΔP_o would be less than in the previous models because of the lesser slope of the aggregate demand function and the greater slope of the aggregate saving function.

A change in tax rates affects the equilibrium value of money gross national product by changing the slopes of the aggregate demand and saving functions and hence the value of the multiplier. The effects of such a change may be expressed as

$$\Delta\overline{Y} = -\frac{k(C_o + I_o + G_o + kP_o)}{[1 - k(1 - t_2)][1 - k(1 - t_1)]} \Delta t \qquad [15.32]$$

where t_1 is the original tax rate, and t_2, equal to $t_1 + \Delta t$, is the new tax rate.[10]

The policy of balancing the budget at the margin would require that

---

the government may promote stability by taxing personal income at a sufficiently high rate, presuming of course that government spending on goods and services does not increase in response to the receipt of additional taxes.

[10] Equation (15.32) is derived in the following manner

$$\Delta\overline{Y} = \overline{Y}_2 - \overline{Y}_1 \qquad [15.32a]$$

$$\overline{Y}_1 = \frac{1}{1 - k(1 - t_1)} (C_o + I_o + G_o + kP_o) \qquad [15.32b]$$

$$\overline{Y}_2 = \frac{1}{1 - k[1 - (t_1 + \Delta t)]} (C_o + I_o + G_o + kP_o) \qquad [15.32c]$$

Substituting (15.32b) and (15.32c) into (15.32a), and collecting terms, yields

$$\Delta\overline{Y} = \frac{-k\Delta t}{\{1 - k[1 - (t_1 + \Delta t)]\}\{1 - k(1 - t_1)\}} (C_o + I_o + G_o + kP_o) \qquad [15.32d]$$

Substituting t_2 for $t_1 + \Delta t$ in the denominator and expressing $\Delta\overline{Y}$ as a function of Δt yields Equation (15.32).

the change in tax rates be sufficient to yield a change in tax receipts equal to the change in government expenditures on goods and services. As in the case where changes in autonomous taxes match changes in public expenditures on goods and services, the balanced-budget multiplier is equal to one[11]

$$\Delta\overline{Y} = \Delta G_o = \Delta T \tag{15.33}$$

Geometrically, such a change in tax rates and government expenditures would shift the intercepts in Figures 15.2 and 15.3 by an amount equal to ΔG_o, and change the slope of the aggregate demand schedule by $-k\Delta t$ and the slope of the aggregate saving schedule by $k\Delta t$.

Model III is now illustrated with a numerical example based on the following values for the independent variables and parameters:

---

[11] The balanced-budget multiplier where taxes are proportional to income is derived as follows

$$\Delta\overline{Y} = \overline{Y}_2 - \overline{Y}_1 \tag{15.33a}$$

where $\overline{Y}_1$ is the original equilibrium level of money gross national product, and $\overline{Y}_2$ the new equilibrium level. Since

$$\overline{Y}_1 = C_o + k[(\overline{Y}_1 - t_1\overline{Y}_1) + P_o] + I_o + G_o \tag{15.33b}$$

and

$$\overline{Y}_2 = C_o + k[(\overline{Y}_2 - t_2\overline{Y}_2) + P_o] + I_o + G_o + \Delta G_o \tag{15.33c}$$

and since

$$\Delta G_o = \Delta T = t_2\overline{Y}_2 - t_1\overline{Y}_1 \tag{15.33d}$$

Equation (15.33a) may be rewritten as

$$\Delta\overline{Y} = \frac{\Delta t\overline{Y}_1}{1 - \Delta t - t_1} \tag{15.33e}$$

Equation (15.33e) was reached by substituting (15.33d) into (15.33c), and then (15.33c) and (15.33b) into (15.33a), with $t_2 = t_1 + \Delta t$, and $\overline{Y}_2 = \overline{Y}_1 + \Delta\overline{Y}$. Substituting (15.33e) into (15.33d) yields

$$\Delta t = \frac{(1 - t_1)\Delta G_o}{Y_1 + \Delta G_o} \tag{15.33f}$$

This expression specifies the change in tax rates necessary to marginally balance the public sector's budget for any given change in government expenditures on goods and services. Substituting (15.33f) into (15.33e), in effect solving Equations (15.33d) and (15.33e) simultaneously, proves Equation (15.33).

Independent Variables	Parameters
$C_o = 8$	$k = .9$
$I_o = 10$	$t = .2$
$G_o = 20$	
$P_o = 20$	

These values can then be substituted into Equation (15.29) with the result that

$$\overline{Y} = 3.57(56) = 200$$

With $\overline{Y} = 200$ the values for the other dependent variables are

$$C = 170$$
$$T = 40$$
$$S_H = 10$$
$$S_G = 0$$

The value of the multiplier, 3.57, is smaller than in the previous examples despite using the same value, .9, for the marginal propensity to consume disposable personal income. This reduction is traceable to the addition of income taxes as a leakage in the system. The example has been constructed with the public sector budget initially in balance.

Variation 1: Tax rates are reduced. In an attempt to increase the money value of gross national product, the public sector may adopt an explicit fiscal policy of cutting taxes by reducing the tax rate. Changing the tax rate from $t = .2$ to $t = .15$, and retaining the values of all other independent variables and parameters as given in the basic example, the resulting change in $\overline{Y}$ is determined using Equation (15.32), as

$$\Delta\overline{Y} = -\frac{.9(56)}{[1 - .9(.85)][1 - .9(.8)]}(-.05) = 38.3$$

Alternatively, using Equation (15.29), the new equilibrium value of money gross national product, $\overline{Y}_2$, is

$$\overline{Y}_2 = 4.26(56) = 238.3$$

The new values for the other dependent variables are

$$C = 208.3$$
$$T = 35.7$$
$$S_H = 14.3$$
$$S_G = -4.3$$

The equilibrium condition that saving equals investment is met as the public sector deficit is treated as a negative component of aggregate saving. The increase in $\overline{Y}$ is due to the increase in the value of the multiplier, reflecting the lower tax rate. In comparison to the basic example, the tax rate in Variation 1 has been reduced by 25 percent, yet tax receipts have fallen by less than 25 percent as the new, lower tax rate is applied to a larger tax base, $\overline{Y}_2$.

Variation 2: Government spending on goods and services is increased and the public sector budget is balanced at the margin. The public sector may wish to increase its expenditures on goods and services and generate sufficient additional tax receipts to finance the increase in expenditures. Starting with the basic example, suppose $\Delta G_o = 25 = \Delta T$. For ΔT to equal 25 the necessary change in the tax rate is derived from Equation (15.33f).

$$\Delta t = \frac{.8(25)}{200 + 25} = .089$$

Adding this change in the tax rate to the original tax rate and using the new level of government expenditures to solve Equation (15.29) gives

$$\overline{Y}_2 = 2.88(81) = 225$$

This confirms the balanced-budget theorem stated in Equation (15.33). Solving for the new values of the other independent variables gives

$$\begin{aligned} C &= 170 \\ T &= 65 \\ S_H &= 10 \\ S_G &= 0 \end{aligned}$$

Even the simple model used here illustrates the potential conflict between policy goals. If, for allocative purposes, taxes and expenditures are increased by equal amounts, such a policy will have an implicit effect on macroeconomic variables as the money value of gross national product rises.

MODEL IV[12]

Discussion and controversy concerning fiscal policy range over a broader spectrum of specific governmental actions than can be analyzed with models like I, II, and III. Changes in expenditures on goods and services, transfer payments, and household taxes cannot adequately depict all the major fiscal policy measures that might be used by a central government. Our purpose in

---

12 This section may be omitted without any loss of continuity.

this section is to develop a macroeconomic model with enough variables and parameters to permit analysis of additional types of policy actions. The framework of this model has been copied from the design of national income accounts.

There are in fact many governments, at different levels, but since only central governments pursue explicit fiscal policy we continue to make the assumption that the public sector consists of one government. This government makes transfer payments to households and two separate types of expenditures on goods and services: Compensation for the factor services rendered by public employees, and purchases from corporations. The public sector derives revenues from three different tax bases in the form of personal income taxes, corporate income taxes, and indirect business taxes. A major step toward greater reality is taken by dividing the private sector into two parts—households and corporations. Corporations invest, pay taxes, and make two types of factor payments to households: Compensation of employees, and dividends. These factor payments plus the compensation of public employees and government transfer payments comprise aggregate personal income. Households make consumption purchases of goods and services from corporations, pay income taxes, and save. These consumption expenditures are functionally related to disposable personal income. Investment is a function of corporate cash flow, the internal funds available to firms from current operations. Other sectoral relationships certainly exist, such as transactions in financial assets, but, in striking a compromise between pedagogic utility and completeness, these relationships have been excluded from this model.[13]

Model IV is based on the simplified version of the national income accounts presented in Table 15.1. The symbols used in the algebraic statement of the model are listed in this table. The numerical values are derived from an illustration of the model presented later in the chapter. The first account in Table 15.1 may be expressed in its familiar algebraic form

$$Y = C + I + G_o \qquad [15.34]$$

Government expenditures on goods and services are autonomously determined. Both consumption and investment are functions of other macroeconomic variables. The absence of any final demand reflecting net exports of goods and services stems from the assumption of a closed economy.

---

[13] For more complete, empirically based models, *see* Frank de Leeuw and Edward Gramlich, "The Federal Reserve-MIT Econometric Model," *Federal Reserve Bulletin,* January 1968; James S. Duesenberry, Gary Fromm, Laurence R. Klein, and E. Kuh, (eds.), *The Brookings Quarterly Econometric Model of the United States Economy* (Chicago: Rand McNally, 1965); and Michael K. Evans and Laurence R. Klein, *The Wharton Econometric Forecasting Model* (Philadelphia: University of Pennsylvania Press, 1967).

Table 15.1 Simplified National Income Accounts

	Symbols	Numerical Values
I GROSS NATIONAL PRODUCT OR EXPENDITURE		
Gross national product equals	Y	648.77
Consumption plus	C	400.46
Investment plus	I	108.31
Government expenditures on goods and services	G_o	140.00
(Government expenditures on goods and services equals Government purchase from corporations plus	G_C	70.00
Compensation of government employees)	W_G	70.00
II NATIONAL INCOME BY TYPE OF INCOME		
National income equals	NI	531.99
Compensation of employees plus	W	416.49
(Compensation of employees equals Compensation of corporate employees plus	W_C	346.49
Compensation of government employees)	W_G	70.00
Corporate profits	R	115.50
(Corporate profits equals Corporate income taxes plus	T_C	46.20
Dividends plus	D	32.72
Retained earnings)	RE	36.58
III RELATION OF GROSS NATIONAL PRODUCT, NATIONAL INCOME, AND PERSONAL INCOME		
Gross national product	Y	648.77
Less capital consumption allowance equals	A	58.39
Net national product	NNP	590.38
Less indirect business taxes equals	T_B	58.39
National income	NI	531.99
Less corporate income taxes	T_C	46.20
Less retained earnings	RE	36.58
Plus government transfer payments equals	P_o	50.00
Personal income	PI	499.21
IV SOURCES AND DISPOSITION OF PERSONAL INCOME		
Compensation of employees plus	W	416.49
(Compensation of employees equals Compensation of corporate employees plus	W_C	346.49
Compensation of government employees)	W_G	70.00
Dividends plus	D	32.72
Government transfer payments equals	P_o	50.00
Personal income	PI	499.21
Less personal income taxes equals	T_H	89.84
Disposable personal income	Y_D	409.37
Less consumption equals	C	400.46
Personal saving	S_H	8.91

Consumption is a function of disposable personal income. The definition of this latter variable, given in the fourth national income account of Table 15.1, is

$$Y_D = W + D + P_o - T_H \qquad [15.35]$$

Personal income consists of compensation of employees, W, dividends, D, and government transfer payments, P_o. Household taxes, T_H, derive solely from a personal income tax. Existing law exempts most government transfer payments from personal income taxation, thus P_o is excluded from the tax base and

$$T_H = t_H(W + D) \qquad [15.36]$$

where t_H is the proportional tax rate on taxable personal income. Substituting Equation (15.36) into Equation (15.35) gives

$$Y_D = (1 - t_H)(W + D) + P_o \qquad [15.37]$$

or

$$Y_D = y_H(W + D) + P_o \qquad [15.38]$$

The household tax rate, t_H, is a parameter of this model with its complement, $y_H = 1 - t_H$, being the fraction that disposable taxable income is of taxable personal income. Table 15.2 lists and defines this model's parameters and their complements in those cases where the use of complements simplifies the algebraic derivation of the model. The numerical values will be referred to later.

Households are likely to have different marginal propensities to consume disposable income from the three separate sources of personal income. We assume $k_p > k_W > k_D$ where these are the marginal propensities to consume transfer payments, disposable employee compensation, and disposable dividends respectively. The consumption function may hence be specified as

$$C = C_o + k_W y_H W + k_D y_H D + k_p P_o \qquad [15.39]$$

or

$$C = C_o + k_W y_H (W_C + W_G) + k_D y_H D + k_p P_o \qquad [15.40]$$

where C_o is an autonomous component of consumption. The W_G and P_o elements of Equation (15.40) are independent variables autonomously set by the public sector. The W_C and D elements are dependent variables that are functionally related to national income produced by corporations.

To derive national income produced by corporations we start with Account III in Table 15.1 which shows national income, NI, equal to gross national product less capital consumption allowances and indirect business taxes, $Y - (A + T_B)$. Both capital consumption allowances and indirect

Table 15.2 **Fiscal Policy Model Parameters and Complements**

	Symbols: Parameter	Symbols: Complement	Numerical Values
Marginal propensity to consume disposable employee compensation ($y_H W$)	k_W		.90
Marginal propensity to consume disposable dividends ($y_H D$)	k_D		.50
Marginal propensity to consume transfer payments (P_o)	k_P		.95
Proportional rate of tax on taxable personal income ($W + D$)	t_H		.20
The fraction disposable taxable income is of taxable personal income ($W + D$)		$y_H = (1 - t_H)$	.80
Proportional rate of tax on corporate profits $[p(Y - A - T_B - W_G)]$	t_C		.40
The fraction after-tax corporate profits are of corporate profits $[p(Y - A - T_B - W_G)]$		$y_C = (1 - t_C)$	.60
The fraction indirect business taxes are of gross national product (Y)	t_B		.09
The wage share of national income produced by corporations ($Y - A - T_B - W_G$)	w		.75
The profit share of national income produced by corporations ($Y - A - T_B - W_G$)		$p = (1 - w)$	.25
The marginal rate of dividend payment out of after-tax corporate profits $[y_C\, p(Y - A - T_B - W_G)]$	d		.40
The fraction capital consumption allowances (depreciation) are of gross national product (Y)	a		.09
The fraction national income is of gross national product (Y)		$n = (1 - a - t_B)$	.82
The marginal propensity to invest out of corporate cash flow ($E + A$)	i		.30

business taxes are assumed to be constant fractions, a and t_B respectively, of gross national product, or

$$A = aY \qquad [15.41]$$

and

$$T_B = t_B Y \qquad [15.42]$$

Part of national income, W_G, is produced in the public sector; hence, national income produced by corporations is equal to $Y - A - T_B - W_G$.

Compensation of corporate employees, W_C, is functionally related to national income produced by corporations

$$W_C = w(Y - A - T_B - W_G) \qquad [15.43]$$

where w is the wage share of national income produced by corporations.[14] The dividend relationship is less direct than for wages because dividends are paid out of after-tax corporate profits. Corporate profits, R, are equal to national income produced by corporations less compensation of corporate employees—which equals the profits share, p, of national income produced by corporations—or

$$R = Y - A - T_B - W_G - W_C = p(y - A - T_B - W_G) \qquad [15.44]$$

These profits are taxed at the proportional rate t_C; hence corporate income taxes, T_C, are expressed as

$$T_C = t_C p(Y - A - T_B - W_G) \qquad [15.45]$$

After-tax profits, E, are given by subtracting Equation (15.45) from Equation (15.44)

$$E = (1 - t_C)p(Y - A - T_B - W_G) = y_C p(Y - A - T_B - W_G) \qquad [15.46]$$

where y_C is the complement of t_C. Dividends may now be written as

$$D = D_o + dE \qquad [15.47]$$

where d is the marginal rate of dividend payments out of after-tax corporate profits. An autonomous element of dividend payments is included in Equation (15.47) as corporations typically do not increase (decrease) dividends proportionately as corporate profits rise (fall). All the terms that appear in the consumption function, Equation (15.40), have now been specified.

The gross investment component of gross national product is taken as a function of corporate cash flow—the sum of after-tax corporate profits and capital consumption allowances. Thus

$$I = I_o + i(E + A) \qquad [15.48]$$

where i is the marginal propensity to invest, and I_o is an autonomous com-

---

[14] The assumption that w is a constant share of national income produced by corporations is convenient; it also has some empirical and theoretical validity as demonstrated by the constancy of the wage shares in the national income accounts and studies based on the Cobb-Douglas production function. In terms of the notation used in this chapter, the Cobb-Douglas production function would be of the form $Y - A - T_B - W_G = L^w K^p$, where L is the labor force employed by corporations, K is the stock of capital, and $w + p = 1$. The literature dealing with Cobb-Douglas production functions is voluminous. One valuable source is Richard R. Nelson, "Aggregate Production Functions and Medium Range Growth Projections," *American Economic Review*, September 1964.

ponent of investment. The logic of national income accounting demands that capital consumption allowances be included to reflect the value of capital used up in the process of production. Since the appropriate amount cannot be known with precision, the estimates reported in the national income accounts are based on the amount of depreciation claimed on business tax returns. A modification of the tax laws regarding depreciation affects capital consumption allowances and thus the availability of cash that can be used by firms for investment or other purposes. Similarly, any change in the corporate tax rate will affect after-tax profits, the other component of corporate cash flow.[15] By expressing investment as a function of corporate cash flow, this component of aggregate demand may respond to explicit fiscal policy actions.[16]

Specifying the autonomously determined government component of final demand as

$$G_o = G_C + W_G \qquad [15.49]$$

we are now ready to solve Equation (15.34) for Y, the level of money gross national product. After making the appropriate substitutions and collecting terms, the equilibrium value of money gross national product $\overline{Y}$, is given by

$$\overline{Y} = \left[\frac{1}{1 - k_W y_H w n - k_D y_H d y_C p n - i(y_C n p + a)}\right] [C_o + k_D y_H D_o$$

$$+ k_p P_o + I_o + G_C + W_G + p W_G (k_W y_H - k_D y_H d y_C - i y_C] \qquad [15.50]$$

[15] Using the notation of this model, the following represents a consolidated profit and loss statement for corporations:

Gross corporate receipts	$Y - W_G = C + I + G_C$
Less corporate employee compensation	W_C
Less depreciation	A
Less indirect business taxes	T_B
Corporate profits	R
Less corporate profits taxes	T_C
After-tax corporate profits	E
Plus depreciation	A
Corporate cash flow	$E + A$
Less dividends	D
Corporate saving	S_C

This statement shows how changes in both A and T_C affect the internal availability of funds for investment and other purposes.

[16] Specification of investment functions in macroeconomic models is difficult. For a review of the topic, *see* Robert Eisner and Robert Strotz, "The Determinants of Business Investment," *Impacts of Monetary Policy,* Commission on Money and Credit Research Monographs (Englewood Cliffs, N.J.: Prentice-Hall, 1963). An obvious shortcoming of this investment function is the exclusion of any monetary variable such as the interest rate. No accelerator principle is at work.

where $n = 1 - a - t_B$.[17] The first element to the right of the equal sign in Equation (15.50) is the multiplier, and the second element contains the autonomous terms being multiplied. The terms C_o, I_o, and G_C, all represent autonomous purchases directly from corporations, and the total amount of these purchases is multiplied. Autonomous dividend payments are taxed, and only a fraction of the resulting disposable income is spent. Nontaxable autonomous government transfer payments are not wholly spent. Thus autonomous dividends and transfer payments result in autonomous consumption purchases from corporations equal to $k_D y_H D_o$, and $k_p p_o$, respectively, which are multiplied. Unlike transfer payments, the compensation of public employees, W_G, is a direct component of gross national product as this compensation represents, and is equal to, the value of product produced by the public sector. The full amount of this spending is multiplied, and an additional amount of consumer spending, also multiplied, is associated with the compensation of public employees. This additional spending, represented by the unwieldy term $pW_G(k_W y_H - k_D y_H d y_C - i y_C)$, arises because compensation of public employees has a different effect on gross national product than an equal amount of purchases from corporations.[18]

Now consider the multiplier in Equation (15.50). This multiplier, like any multiplier, is in the basic form

$$\frac{1}{1 - \text{the marginal propensity to spend gross national product}}$$

Because all government spending in this model is autonomously determined, the terms in the denominator of the multiplier reflect only economic behavior within the private sector. The first parametric term in the denominator of the multiplier is the marginal propensity to consume gross national product

---

[17] The necessary substitutions are made in four steps:

1) Substitute Equations (15.41) and (15.42) into (15.43) and (15.46), setting $1 - a - t_B = n$, and substitute (15.41) into (15.48).
2) Substitute Equation (15.46) into (15.47) and (15.48).
3) Substitute Equations (15.43) and (15.47) into (15.40).
4) Substitute Equations (15.40), (15.48), and (15.49) into (15.34).

[18] The entire term $pW_G(k_W y_H - k_p y_H d y_C - i y_C)$ has a relatively small value. It is positive in the numerical example that follows and will remain positive as long as $k_W y_H > (k_p y_H d y_C - i y_C)$, which is to be expected. Verbally the term is explained as follows: Had an amount equal to W_G been purchased from corporations, profits equal to pW_G would have accrued. This amount when received instead by public employees is taxed, and the remaining income is spent at the rate k_W. This additional consumer spending, $pW_G k_W y_H$, is multiplied. Two negative amounts are also multiplied—the consumption spending that would have occurred, $pW_G k_D y_H d y_C$, had dividend payments been associated with pW_G, and the marginal increment of investment, $pW_G i y_C$, that would have been made had an amount equal to pW_G accrued to corporations.

based on the compensation of employees.[19] The second parametric term is the marginal propensity to consume gross national product based on dividend payments. The final parametric term is the marginal propensity to invest gross national product based on corporate cash flow.

As in all macroeconomic models, for a particular level of money gross national product to be an equilibrium level, the aggregate saving and investment schedules must intersect at that level, or

$$S = I \tag{15.51}$$

The aggregate investment schedule is given by Equation (15.48); the aggregate saving schedule is the summation of the separate saving schedules of households, S_H, corporations, S_C, and the public sector, S_G, or

$$S = S_H + S_C + S_G \tag{15.52}$$

where

$$S_H = [y_H(W + D) + P_o] - C \tag{15.53}$$

$$S_C = E + A - D \tag{15.54}$$

$$S_G = T - (G_o + P_o) \tag{15.55}$$

The term T in Equation (15.55) designates aggregate tax receipts

$$T = T_H + T_B + T_C \tag{15.56}$$

For there to be a stable value for $\overline{Y}$, the denominator of the multiplier must be greater than zero and less than one. Alternatively this constraint may be expressed as

$$0 < [k_W y_H wn + k_D y_H d y_C pn + i(y_C np + a)] < 1$$

where the bracketed term is the marginal propensity to spend gross national product.[20] The second element to the right of the equal sign in Equation (15.50)—the amount being multiplied—must be positive, though any single term, such as C_o or I_o, might equal zero or be negative.

A numerical example. A numerical example based on this fiscal policy model is now presented. The values assumed for the autonomous, independent variables are presented in Table 15.3; the values of the parameters were

[19] This marginal propensity might more conventionally be expressed as $(1 - s_W)(1 - t_H)(1 - p)(1 - a - t_B)$, where s_W is the marginal propensity to save disposable employee compensation. All parameters in this expression represent leakages between an increment of gross national product and an increment of consumption.

[20] Additional constraints are that $w + p = 1$, and that $0 < n < 1$. Other parameters might take on values less than zero or greater than one as long as the overall constraint stated in the text is fulfilled.

Table 15.3 **Autonomous Independent Variables**

Variable	Symbol	Numerical Value
Autonomous consumption	C_o	40
Autonomous dividends	D_o	5
Autonomous investment	I_o	70
Autonomous government purchases from corporations	G_c	70
Autonomous compensation of government employees	W_G	70
Autonomous government transfer payments to households	P_o	50

listed in Table 15.2. These values when substituted into Equation (15.50) yield

$$\overline{Y} = 2.1114(307.27) = 648.77$$

This value for $\overline{Y}$, along with calculated values for the other dependent variables, was given in Table 15.1. The numerical value of the marginal propensity to spend gross national product is .5264, and hence the multiplier is 2.1114. This value for the multiplier is small even though the marginal propensity to consume disposable personal income from its major source—employee compensation—is relatively large, .9. This model's many leakages in addition to household saving are responsible for the low value of the multiplier.

To show that the equilibrium condition specified in Equation (15.51) is fulfilled, total saving and its components can be computed using Equations (15.46), (15.52), (15.53), (15.54) and (15.55), and the numerical values listed in Tables 15.1 and 15.2.

$$\begin{aligned} S_H &= 8.91 \\ S_C &= 94.97 \\ S_G &= 4.43 \\ \hline S &= 108.31 = I \end{aligned}$$

The positive value for S_G indicates a surplus in the public sector budget. Investment, all of which is undertaken in this model by corporations, exceeds corporate saving. In effect investment absorbs the saving of households and the public sector. One possible disposition of the government surplus (public sector saving) would be to redeem outstanding government bonds held by households (that is, retire some of the public debt). The cash thus received could then be used by households to purchase new securities issued by corporations.[21]

An implicit fiscal policy is embodied in this numerical example: The combined effect on $\overline{Y}$, and the other dependent variables, of the values selected for the publicly determined independent variables and parameters. The effects of an explicit change in fiscal policy can be calculated by altering the value of any one of these autonomous variables, G_C, W_G, and P_o, or parameters, t_H, t_C, t_B, and a. Examples of such calculations are presented in Table 15.4; for the set of calculations associated with each of seven explicit fiscal policies, only the indicated independent variable or parameter has been changed and all other independent variables and parameters retain

Table 15.4 Illustrations of Alternative Fiscal Policies

Dependent Variables	Original Fiscal Policy	Fiscal Policy Actions (1) $\Delta G_C = +10$	(2) $\Delta W_G = +10$	(3) $\Delta P_o = +10$	(4) $\Delta t_H = +.02$	(5) $\Delta t_C = -.10$	(6) $\Delta t_B = -.01$	(7) $\Delta a = +.01$
C	400.46	410.22	412.87	419.24	385.35	407.71	408.09	394.89
I	108.31	109.66	109.36	109.59	107.27	112.64	109.16	109.70
G_o	140.00	150.00	150.00	140.00	140.00	140.00	140.00	140.00
Y	648.77	669.88	672.23	668.83	632.62	660.35	657.25	644.59
W_C	346.49	359.47	353.42	358.84	336.55	353.62	356.64	339.09
W_G	70.00	70.00	80.00	70.00	70.00	70.00	70.00	70.00
D	32.72	33.76	33.28	33.71	31.93	38.00	33.53	32.13
P_o	50.00	50.00	50.00	60.00	50.00	50.00	50.00	50.00
PI	499.21	513.23	516.70	522.55	488.48	511.62	510.17	491.22
T_H	89.84	92.65	93.34	92.51	96.47	92.32	92.03	88.24
T_C	46.20	47.93	47.12	47.84	44.88	35.36	47.55	45.21
T_B	58.39	60.29	60.50	60.19	56.93	59.43	52.58	58.01
T	194.43	200.87	200.96	200.54	198.28	187.11	192.16	191.46
S_H	8.91	10.36	10.49	10.80	6.66	11.59	10.05	8.09
S_C	94.97	98.43	97.91	98.25	92.32	103.94	96.95	100.15
S_G	4.43	.87	.96	.54	8.28	−2.89	2.16	1.46
S	108.31	109.66	109.36	109.59	107.27	112.64	109.16	109.70
Value of the Multiplier	2.1114	2.1114	2.1114	2.1114	2.0610	2.1547	2.1390	2.0978

[21] Debt retirement changes the composition of household assets—more cash and less securities—and is not an income flow to households. Since household consumption, savings, and taxes are functionally related to income only, such debt retirement would not affect these variables. Thus, even though households might purchase new corporate securities with the proceeds acquired from public debt retirement, it is the public sector and not households that has currently saved.

the original values given in Tables 15.2 and 15.3. Each of these policy actions is discussed in turn.[22]

Fiscal policy actions (1), (2), and (3) all involve increasing government expenditures by ten; since no parameter is changed, the value of the multiplier remains unchanged. Of the three actions, increasing the compensation of public employees has the greatest impact on gross national product, and increasing transfer payments the least, although this latter action has the greatest impact on personal income and consumption. With the original fiscal policy, the budget of the public sector had a surplus of 4.43; in each case where expenditures are increased by ten the surplus declined by a lesser amount because tax receipts increase as the size of each tax base responds to the expansion of $\overline{Y}$.

Increasing the household tax rate by 10 percent, as in fiscal policy action (4), reduces the value of the multiplier because a leakage has been increased. This change also reduces the amount being multiplied despite the retention of all original values for the autonomous variables. These two effects combine to reduce the level of gross national product. Corporate profit and indirect business tax receipts decline in response to the reduction in their tax bases; despite the fall in taxable personal income, household tax receipts increase due to the rate change. On balance, total tax revenue rises as does the surplus in the public sector budget. A tax increase of this sort might be appropriate in a period of inflationary pressure.

In a period of stagnation and unemployment, an explicit policy of reducing the corporate tax rate might be pursued as illustrated by fiscal policy action (5). The 25 percent reduction in the corporate tax rate reduces the size of a leakage and hence increases the value of the multiplier. Investment is stimulated and gross national product increases. As the tax bases respond to the increase in $\overline{Y}$, corporate tax collections fall by less than 25 percent and household and indirect business taxes increase. The net effect is, however, to reduce aggregate tax revenues and put the public sector budget into deficit.

The fiscal policy action (6) involves reducing the rate of indirect business taxation which also has the effect of increasing the size of the multiplier. Gross national product expands solely because of the change in the value of the multiplier; the parameter t_B in no way affects the amount being multiplied. Total tax receipts decline slightly as rising personal income and corporate profit taxes partially offset falling indirect business tax receipts.[23]

[22] For an empirically based discussion of simulating fiscal policy action using a large-scale econometric model (The Brookings Quarterly Econometric Model of the United States with over 300 equations), *see* Gary Fromm and Paul Taubman, *Policy Simulations with an Econometric Model* (Washington, D.C.: The Brookings Institution, 1968).

[23] We have now discussed changes in both expenditures and taxes. The balanced-budget

Modifying the tax laws to permit corporations to depreciate assets over a shorter period of time has the effect, in this model, of increasing the value of the parameter a. Such a change is illustrated by fiscal policy action (7). The usual rationale for accelerated depreciation is the stimulation of investment. In this example the increase in the rate of depreciation has that effect but also results in a reduction in gross national product. By increasing the rate of depreciation, national income as a share of gross national product is reduced. Since corporate wages are functionally related to national income rather than gross national product, consumption as a fraction of gross national product falls. Increasing the parameter a reduces, on balance, the value of the multiplier.[24] As one would expect, corporate saving increases in response to this change in the rate of depreciation.

Possible modifications of the model. The impact of the explicit fiscal policy actions analyzed above is expressed, in each case, by comparing one set of equilibrium values for dependent variables with an initial set. Nothing was said about the movement of these variables through time. These exercises in comparative statics do not permit analysis of automatic fiscal policy or the lead and lag times associated with explicit and implicit fiscal policy. Dynamic relationships within the private sector, such as an accelerator that specifies investment as a function of changes in the level of a macroeconomic variable, cannot be handled with comparative statics. A dynamic fiscal policy model using either difference equations (where time is treated in discrete segments) or differential equations (where time is treated continuously) must be used to cope with such problems.

Even in the context of a comparative statics model the specification of the public sector could be further elaborated. On the expenditure side, government spending may be related to other variables rather than set autonomously. A part of such spending, particularly transfer payments, could be expressed as a function of the difference between actual and full-employment levels of gross national product. Some government spending might be functionally related to the level of gross national product to reflect the income elasticity of demand for public goods and services. On the revenue

---

theorem cannot be easily applied. The effect on the various dependent variables will be different depending on which of the three taxes is changed. Also, the balanced-budget multiplier will not be equal to unity due to the four different marginal propensities to consume gross national product. For further discussion of this point, *see* Richard A. Musgrave, *The Theory of Public Finance* (New York: McGraw-Hill, 1959), pp. 438–41 and 465–66.

[24] The denominator of the multiplier element in Equation (15.50) may be rewritten as $[1 - (1 - a - t_B)(k_W y_H w + k_D y_H d y_C p + i y_C p) - ia]$ to show more clearly the impact of the parameter a on the value of the multiplier. If alternative values of the other parameters were assumed, an increase in the parameter a might have the effect of increasing the value of the multiplier, and hence $\overline{Y}$.

side, including progressive personal income taxes would make household taxes a nonlinear, increasing function of taxable personal income. Payroll taxes could be introduced with compensation of employees as the tax base. A state-local component of the public sector, with its own tax and expenditure functions, and which receives grants-in-aid from the federal government, could be built into a model.

The private sector is divided into only two parts, households and corporations, in Model IV. The national income accounts include a third part—unincorporated businesses. The incomes generated by proprietorships and partnerships, including farmers, are reflected in this segment of the national income accounts. In our model this source of income has been implicitly included in corporate profit and wage payments but could be separately specified. Unincorporated business income might be treated as part of personal income and taxed at personal income tax rates, consistent with the general provisions of the Internal Revenue Code. After-tax personal income from this source would be associated with a relatively low marginal propensity to consume, since the owners of unincorporated businesses typically finance some investment directly out of their personal saving.

The extensive postwar theoretical and empirical literature concerning household behavior suggests modifications of the consumption function used in this model. Quarterly data from the national income accounts show that the relationship between consumption and current income is not as stable as indicated by long-run, time series data. The major focus of the postwar consumption function literature has been on the need to reconcile short-run observations with long-run trends, and to reconcile cross-section studies of family budgets with aggregate relationships. Two types of solutions to these problems have been proposed. One attempts to perfect the definitions of consumption and income and then specify an aggregate consumption function using the new definitions. The other attempts the necessary reconciliation by introducing additional explanatory variables, such as asset holdings, and sometimes by dividing aggregate consumption into component parts, such as durables and nondurables.[25]

Modifications may also be made in the treatment of corporations. Investment may be divided into the three major parts delineated in the national income accounts—producers' plant and equipment, inventory change, and residential housing—and separate investment functions specified. Plant and equipment spending could remain a function of cash flow, inventory change made a function of consumption spending, and investment in residential housing functionally related to disposable personal income. In

---

[25] Two general surveys of this literature are available: Robert Ferber, "Research on Household Behavior," *American Economic Review,* March 1962; and M. J. Farrell, "The New Theories of the Consumption Function," *The Economic Journal,* December 1959.

addition, the interest rate, as a financial variable, should be included in the investment function in accordance with the assumption that the profit calculus of entrepreneurs establishes an inverse relationship between investment and the rate of interest.

In 1962 the United States instituted an investment tax credit designed to stimulate investment in producers' plant and equipment. This feature of the tax laws permitted corporations to take an amount equal to 7 percent of qualified investment as a credit against their corporate profit tax liability. Such a credit serves to increase corporate cash flow and might be incorporated into a more detailed model.[26]

A further step toward reality would be to drop the assumption of a closed economy and include net exports of goods and services as a component of aggregate demand, as is the practice in national income accounting. A new parameter, the marginal propensity to import, would be added to the denominator of the multiplier. Such a step would be essential in developing a fiscal policy model for one of the many nations where imports and exports are relatively large fractions of gross national product. An additional source of tax revenue could be introduced by making tariff receipts a function of imports. The public sector might also make foreign aid-type transfer payments that would not be a component of domestic personal income.

Models such as those presented in this chapter provide a necessary, but not sufficient, theoretical background for analysis of fiscal policy. Explicit consideration must also be given to the timing of the macroeconomic impact of government receipts and expenditures and the ensuing multiplier processes. Budget deficits and surpluses must be financed. These subjects are taken up in the following chapter.

---

[26] One possible way to include the investment tax credit in Model IV is to rewrite Equation (15.46), which specifies after-tax earnings of corporations, as

$$E = y_C p(Y - A - T_B - W_G) + .07qI \qquad [15.46a]$$

where q is the fraction of total investment that qualifies for the investment tax credit. Investment, as specified by Equation (15.48), would increase as the tax credit increased the value of E.

16

THE MACROECONOMIC IMPACT OF PUBLIC EXPENDITURES AND REVENUES

To appraise fiscal policy in an economy as complex as that of the United States of the 1970s certainly requires the analysis made possible by the use of economic models. Policy makers utilize models, and many of these contain far more intricate specifications of economic relationships than those discussed in Chapter 15. Selection of an appropriate model is only the beginning of the analyst's task. Once a model is built data must be collected and parameters estimated. More importantly results must be interpreted as the basis for policy recommendations. Two major issues pertaining to the interpretation of the macroeconomic impact of public expenditures and revenues are considered in this chapter. First, what is the macroeconomic impact of federal budget deficits and surpluses? Second, what is the timing of the impact of federal expenditures, receipts, and fiscal policy actions?

Budget imbalances must be financed and the means of financing determines their macroeconomic impact. Budget deficits, for instance, are incurred when government outlays exceed budget receipts; outlays are made when checks are drawn against the Treasury cash balance. If the Treasury possesses an adequate cash balance, this stock of assets may be drawn down as a deficit is financed; otherwise the Treasury must borrow from the public. Conditions prevailing in financial markets, and the monetary policy actions of the Federal Reserve System, determine the impact of both drawing down Treasury cash balances and Treasury borrowing from the public. Similarly, budget surpluses must be financed. This financing may be accomplished by the Treasury increasing its cash balance or reducing its liabilities by retiring some United States government securities held by the public. Conditions prevailing in financial markets and the actions of the Federal Reserve System also determine the impact of financing a surplus.

The timing of federal expenditures and receipts must be considered from several viewpoints. Government expenditures and tax receipts were included in the fiscal policy models of Chapter 15 and their multiplier effects were shown. No consideration was given, however, to when their impact on aggregate demand occurs. Does a federal highway construction program, for instance, affect aggregate demand when monies are appropriated, when they are obligated, or when budget outlays occur? When does the multiplier effect bear on aggregate demand? In addition, the timing of explicit fiscal policy actions is important; the macroeconomic consequences of these actions, if they are to promote stability, must occur at the appropriate time. Mistimed stabilization measures may serve to aggravate economic instability.

There is an implicit fiscal policy embodied in the receipts and expenditures of state and local governments. In addition, fiscal policy actions of the federal government may alter state and local government receipts and expenditures; this chapter concludes with a brief consideration of the relationship of state and local governments to fiscal policy.

FINANCING FEDERAL BUDGET DEFICITS AND SURPLUSES

The conventional wisdom of the intelligent layman, and the oft-cited opinions of the professional economist, support the belief that budget deficits expand and surpluses contract the aggregate level of economic activity.[1] At first glance this seems a logical enough proposition. When deficits are incurred, the government is injecting more spending into the economy than is

[1] Throughout this chapter and the next we refer to expansionary and contractionary policies rather than inflationary and deflationary policies. Inflation and deflation are most often understood to refer to price level changes rather than increases and decreases in the economy-wide level of economic activity. By expansionary policies we mean to include policies that increase real output at constant prices, as well as policies that increase prices at unchanged levels of real output, and combinations of the two. Contractionary policies also refer to both real and price changes.

extracted with taxes, user charges, and fees, and increased aggregate demand should result. By contrast, in the event of a budget surplus, government is making less expenditures than could have been financed with its budget receipts, and thus the public sector, on balance, must be promoting a reduction in aggregate demand. Upon closer scrutiny this position is less obvious. The balanced-budget theorem showed that balanced budgets are likely to be expansionary. More importantly, budget imbalances must be financed. Changes in the Treasury cash balance and net borrowing from the public are the principal means of financing imbalances in the federal budget. This section is organized to consider first deficit financing and then surplus financing; in each case change in the Treasury cash balance is discussed prior to net borrowing from the public.

Deficit financing. Most Treasury cash balances are held in tax and loan accounts at commercial banks until they are needed to fund disbursements; at that time they are transferred to Treasury's accounts at Federal Reserve Banks (see Table 17.3). Assuming commercial banks are fully loaned-up, transfer of monies from tax and loan accounts to the Treasury's Federal Reserve accounts reduces the money supply as commercial banks lose reserves; the disbursement of these monies from the Treasury's Federal Reserve accounts reverses this monetary effect and, on balance, the result of drawing down the Treasury's tax and loan account balances to finance expenditures is to leave the money supply unchanged.[2] If the deficit is financed by drawing down the Treasury's accounts with Federal Reserve banks, the money supply is increased, commercial banks acquire additional reserves, and further expansion of aggregate demand may result as the economy's liquidity increases. Since drawing down the Treasury cash balance permits public spending to occur without any simultaneous reduction in private expenditures, financing a deficit by this means should lead to an economy-wide increase in aggregate demand.

Budget deficits are usually financed by borrowing from the public. If newly issued United States government securities are acquired by the

[2] The money supply is usually understood to comprise coin and currency outside the banking system, plus demand deposits in commercial banks except those of the federal government. Thus, Treasury deposits in tax and loan accounts are not usually treated as part of the money supply. When the sequence described in the text occurs, the drawing down of tax and loan accounts and the concomitant increase in private sector balances technically does increase the money supply. Since no change in commercial bank reserves results there is no multiple effect on the money supply as may occur when reserves change in a commercial banking system with fractional reserves. We regard such transactions as leaving the money supply unaffected although this treatment is at variance with its technical definition. For the Federal Reserve System's definition of the money supply, *see* the *Federal Reserve Bulletin,* September 1970, p. A 17.

Federal Reserve System, or if they are bought by commercial banks with their excess reserves, new money is created. When budget outlays in excess of receipts from taxes, user charges, and fees are financed by money creation, public expenditures certainly exceed the reduction in private expenditures that result from raising these revenues, and an increase in aggregate demand results. In this case budget deficits are expansionary.

An increase in aggregate demand may not result if financing a deficit entails borrowing funds that otherwise would have been used to finance spending within the private sector. When this occurs, deficit financing and taxation have similar impacts on private sector demand; both serve to reduce private spending. If the Treasury sells securities in competition with corporate issues, savers may buy public issues rather than the new issues of corporations. Thus public spending is financed, but private investment is less than it otherwise would have been, and the deficit does not increase aggregate demand.[3]

Surplus financing. Budget surplus must also be financed. Surpluses are realized when taxes, user charges, and fees exceed outlays; but what disposition is made of this excess of collections over disbursements? If the Treasury elects to increase its cash balance in tax and loan accounts, there will be no change in the money supply as balances are transferred from private to public ownership. As long as budget receipts would otherwise have been used to finance private sector spending, the budget surplus leads to a reduction in aggregate demand and is contractionary. If the Treasury increases its deposits with Federal Reserve Banks, the commercial banking system loses reserves; provided the commercial banking system is fully loaned-up, the money supply contracts and this means of surplus financing is even more contractionary.

A surplus is usually financed by reducing the federal debt held by the public. If the Treasury retires securities held by the Federal Reserve System, surplus financing leads to a reduction in the money supply; in this event budget surpluses are contractionary. But if the Treasury retires securities held by the nonbank public, it is not at all clear that contraction results. Government securities are financial assets of their owners. When government securities held by the nonbank public are retired their owners'

---

[3] In March 1970, the Treasury ceased issuing $1000 Treasury bills. Their denomination was increased to $10,000. Although administrative efficiency was cited, the principal reason for the change was that the Treasury had been competing for funds that otherwise would have been utilized in the private sector, and this competition was unwanted. In view of the high Treasury bill rates prevailing at that time, individuals were withdrawing funds from savings and loan and passbook savings accounts where interest rates were lower and buying Treasury bills, thus decreasing the availability of funds in the home mortgage market.

portfolios now contain fewer government securities and larger cash balances. Cash balances produce no income and their owners can be expected to buy income earning assets instead. If the volume of newly issued corporate securities is just sufficient to absorb saving from current income, conversions of these cash assets to holdings of securities will have the effect of bidding up security prices rather than supplying funds to finance additional private investment.[4] But if the supply of newly issued corporate securities exceeds what can be absorbed by current private saving at unchanged interest rates, asset holders may buy these securities with the cash obtained from the retirement of government securities.[5] In this latter case the effect of the budget surplus is to permit the financing of a greater volume of private investment than would otherwise have been possible. In the event of budget surpluses, the public sector has provided for saving out of current national income. The act of reducing the debt held by the public changes the composition of the assets in the portfolios of private asset holders but does not constitute current saving in the private sector; rather, through the budget surplus, the public sector saves, and, by retiring the debt held by the public, makes this saving available to the private sector where it may or may not be used to expand aggregate demand. Debt retirement is not necessarily contractionary.

Relationship between monetary and fiscal policies. The policy actions of the Federal Reserve System must also be considered in any discussion of financing federal budget imbalances. Federal Reserve System open market transactions in United States government securities are a principal means by which the monetary authorities pursue their policy objectives. Although they also depend upon commercial bank response, open market operations are likely to affect both the rate of interest and the availability of money, and may, at the same time, directly support the activities of the fiscal authorities. Open market purchase of government securities, by increasing the demand for them, raises their price; as security prices rise their yield to maturity falls and interest rates are reduced. Federal Reserve security purchases serve to increase commercial bank reserves, and with fractional reserve banking may result in a yet greater increase in the money supply. Open market purchase of United States government securities supports expansionary fiscal policies. Similarly, contractionary open market operations call for sales of United States government securities. Increasing their supply on the market decreases their price, thereby increasing their yield to

---

4 As security prices rise yields decrease. Lower yields, by lowering the cost of borrowing, may lead to an increase in newly issued corporate securities.

5 In the absence of this, or some other sources of purchasing power, the excess of new security supply over current saving would drive up security yields and serve to decrease their supply at higher rates of interest.

maturity; as yields rise interest rates increase, dampening aggregate demand. As the Federal Reserve System sells United States government securities, commercial bank reserves are reduced and the resulting decrease in the money supply is contractionary. If securities sold from the Federal Reserve System's portfolio are acquired by the Treasury as it finances a surplus, then a contractionary fiscal policy is directly supported by the monetary authorities.

Such complementarity of fiscal and monetary policies need not occur. At the same time fiscal authorities are pursuing contractionary policies, the Federal Reserve System might make open market purchases of securities to lower interest rates, increase the money supply, and have an expansionary impact. Such seemingly contradictory policies might be desirable in the face of a conflict of goals for public economic policy. Suppose the economy contains inflationary pressures at the same time it is experiencing an unsatisfactorily slow rate of economic growth. Moderation of aggregate demand is required for stabilization purposes, while the allocation of additional resources to investment is required for economic growth. Budget surpluses obtained by additional taxes on households, coupled with low interest rates and readily available credit to encourage additional investment in plant and equipment, may advance attainment of both policy objectives. It is desirable that the monetary and fiscal authorities cooperate in any stabilization program, and that each take actions that complement the actions of the other.

THE TIMING OF THE IMPACT OF PUBLIC EXPENDITURES

Accurately gauging the timing of the impact of government expenditures is important in formulating fiscal policy. One approach to understanding this problem is discussed here.[6] The macroeconomic impact of a defense procurement contract might involve the following sequence of events. Upon letting the contract—that is, upon the obligating of monies—the contractor with tool-up for production, order raw materials, hire workers, and let subcontracts. As production commences and payrolls are met, the contractor will borrow the working capital needed to defer these costs. During this

[6] This approach was first suggested by Murray Weidenbaum. *See* "The Timing of the Economic Impact of Government Spending," *National Tax Journal,* March 1959. *See also* Murray Weidenbaum, "Impact of Vietnam on the American Economy," *Economic Effect of Vietnam Spending,* Hearings Before the Joint Economic Committee, 90th Congress, 1st Session (Washington, D.C.: Government Printing Office, 1967); and Harvey Galper, "The Timing of Federal Expenditure Impacts," and Edward M. Gramlich, "Measures of the Aggregate Demand Impact of the Federal Budget," in *President's Commission on Budget Concepts, Staff Papers and Other Materials Reviewed by the President's Commission* (Washington, D.C.: Government Printing Office, 1967).

time, resources are committed to the production of goods that will subsequently be delivered to the government and are unavailable for use elsewhere in the economy. The national income accounts will record an increase in gross private domestic investment as the defense contractor accumulates inventories; there will be a reduction in inventories and an increase in government purchases of goods and services as the Department of Defense takes delivery. At the time this budget outlay is made no net change in aggregate demand will be recorded; the increase in aggregate demand occurs as the inventories are accumulated. Any multiplier process induced by the public spending begins to affect aggregate demand as production workers spend their earnings during the time of production and inventory accumulation. Upon delivery, the contractor may discharge workers, and upon payment he will retire the loan taken to cover operating costs.

The recording of expenditures in budgets and in the national income accounts thus does not coincide with the timing of the real impact of government spending. Over periods of time when spending on goods and services remains constant, this discrepancy in timing is relatively unimportant, but during periods of rapid increase or decrease in government purchases from businesses, the timing of the real impact may be important to the formulation of macroeconomic stabilization policy. Recording outlays on an accrual basis in both budgets and national income accounts would better reflect the timing of the impact of federal spending. To the extent that progress payments are made on some purchases, budget outlays are recorded on an accrual basis at the present time.[7]

Government expenditures for goods and services are multiplied. Suppose the value of the multiplier is 2.5. This means that for each dollar of government expenditures on goods and services, $2.50 of gross national product is generated. The timing of the impact of government expenditures just discussed refers to when government expenditures themselves contribute to aggregate demand; the additional spending implied by the multiplier is not made by government and will add to aggregate demand in periods subsequent to the initial government expenditures. In response to a government contractor paying wages and salaries in January, for instance, workers will make consumption expenditures in February, and the merchants who make these sales may then pay wages and salaries, thus permitting their employees

---

[7] As may be inferred from Tables 12.2 and 12.3, and as is shown in Table 11.20, defense related purchases are the primary type of federal government purchases from businesses. At the request of the Joint Economic Committee, the Department of Defense began to issue monthly, in June 1967, *Selected Economic Indicators* which gave data on contracts let, obligations incurred and outstanding, expenditures, and other items, in order to permit better economic analysis of the impact of defense spending on the economy. This series was superseded by *Defense Indicators*, published monthly by the Department of Commerce beginning in June 1968.

to make consumption expenditures in March. This process continues until ultimately, in response to an initial dollar of government expenditure, $1.50 of household consumption expenditures occur and total additional expenditures equal $2.50. Planning stabilization policy requires consideration of the timing of multiplier effect of changed government expenditures for goods and services. Quite apart from the timing of the impact of government purchases there is the question of their impact on particular industries. Input-output tables help answer this type of question.

TIMING OF EXPLICIT FISCAL POLICY ACTIONS

For explicit fiscal policies to be effective as stabilization measures it is essential that their impact be felt when economic instability exists. Expansionary policies must have their impact when the economy is depressed, and contractionary policies must reduce aggregate demand when the economy is inflated. Mistimed stabilization policies hinder the attainment of policy objectives by depressing aggregate demand during periods of unemployment, or by adding to aggregate demand while inflation is a problem. The timing of explicit fiscal policy actions is often discussed in the context of a recognition lag and an implementation lag. The *recognition lag* is the time that elapses between the onset of economic instability, and the realization that this instability exists and that fiscal policy actions are required. The *implementation lag* is the period of time that then elapses between the recognition of the need for policy action and the impact of whatever policy actions are taken.

Before explicit fiscal policies may be enacted their need must be recognized. Unless forecasted, unemployment or inflation must first develop before the need for corrective action is realized; whatever policy actions are adopted will be initiated later than is desirable. By contrast, if employment or inflationary problems have been forecast, explicit stabilization policies could be adopted in their anticipation and economic instability moderated or prevented. The length of the recognition lag may serve to determine the seriousness of a recession or inflation.

Once the need for explicit fiscal policies is recognized they must be formulated and implemented. Time elapses between recognition and implementation because explicit fiscal policies generally require Congressional action. Mustering the required legislative authority is time-consuming. The administration has some leeway in the letting of new contracts and the apportionment of monies, but even when discretionary action is quickly taken, stabilization goals may not be advanced because the impact of changing public expenditures is subject to uncertain timing.

Expenditure variations requiring legislative authorization are unlikely to result in effective stabilization in all but the most severe recession or inflation. Even if a set of public expenditure projects were fully planned for immediate submission to Congress or the administration were able to identify "nonessential" expenditures that could be cut back, the time required to obtain Congressional action is probably so great that economic conditions would change before the explicit policy's impact could be felt. Serious conflicts among policy goals may arise. If public expenditures are justified on allocative or distributive grounds, should the decision to make these expenditures be determined by the phase of the business cycle? If they are not justified on either allocative or distributive grounds should they be made merely to increase the level of aggregate demand?

Tax changes, rather than expenditure changes, therefore, are more suitable as a means of taking explicit fiscal policy actions. The macroeconomic impact of a personal income tax change begins to be felt almost immediately through variation in personal income tax withholdings. Increases or decreases in lower bracket personal income tax rates, with corresponding changes in the withholding rate, may, within a week or two, be reflected in the disposable income of wage earners. It is reasonable to expect that changes in disposable paychecks will quickly have some impact on the level of aggregate demand. Thus, although the recognition lag is the same for both expenditure and tax changes, and although both require time for legislative enactment, tax changes can have a shorter implementation lag than expenditure measures. Discretionary fiscal policy actions are best accomplished through variation in revenues.[8]

The President, at the start of the 1970s, does not possess the discretionary authority to vary tax rates or bases for stabilization purposes. Setting tax rates and specifying tax bases remain the jealously guarded prerogative of Congress. Presidential authority to vary personal and corporate income tax rates within a specified range for stabilization purposes is a desirable fiscal reform. Congress might grant the President, in consultation with designated members of his Cabinet and selected committeemen in Congress, authority to increase or decrease personal and corporate income tax rates by 5 percentage points for a period not to exceed 12 months; extension of these rate changes beyond the 12-month period would then require the explicit consent of Congress. Granting the President this discre-

[8] Small and temporary changes in personal taxes may have a negligible impact on consumption if households base their spending on their perceptions of long-run income. The *permanent income hypothesis* is that households make consumption expenditures on the basis of the expected value of their lifetime disposable income rather than on the basis of their actual disposable income in any particular time period. *See* Milton Friedman, *A Theory of the Consumption Function,* National Bureau of Economic Research (Princeton, N.J.: Princeton University Press, 1957). This consideration may have played an important role in determining the impact of the 10 percent surtax in the last part of the 1960s.

tionary authority would mean that once the need for explicit fiscal policy action is recognized it may be quickly implemented. Congress would continue to retain control over the structure of the tax mechanism and basic long-term changes in tax rates, including those required for stabilization purposes.

AUTOMATIC FISCAL POLICY

At the time budgets are prepared no one expects public expenditures and receipts to be precisely at their estimated level. *Automatic fiscal policies* are changes in public expenditures and receipts stemming from changes in the aggregate level of economic activity; no new legislation or additional administrative actions are required. To the degree that economy-wide changes in the level of economic activity are predictable, so are the resulting automatic changes in public expenditures and receipts. For example, as the rate of unemployment rises unemployment insurance benefits and welfare payments increase; with weakness in labor markets, the elderly may have difficulty maintaining employment and retire, thus causing an increase in social security payments. Conversely, as the rate of unemployment falls, welfare payments and unemployment insurance benefits decrease; as labor markets tighten, some older workers may postpone retirement and others may even reenter the labor force thus reducing social security benefits. These expenditure changes occur automatically; no discretionary action is required on the part of public officials.

Budget receipts, even more than expenditures, fluctuate automatically. During recessions personal income weakens, as does the volume of sales, and corporate profits decline; as this happens the personal income, sales, and corporate income tax bases are affected and, with unchanged tax rates, receipts fall below their expected levels. Conversely, as recovery progresses and economic growth occurs, personal income, the value of sales, and corporate profits increase, and unchanged tax rates automatically yield additional revenues. The automatic growth in public revenues attributable to the expanded tax bases that result from economic growth is known as the *fiscal dividend*.[9]

These automatic fiscal policies are commonly referred to as *automatic stabilizers*—automatic changes in either receipts, expenditures, or both, that serve to advance the stabilization objectives of public economic policy. We prefer to regard these policies as automatic fiscal policies rather than as automatic stabilizers, because under some circumstances they may be

---

[9] These automatic increases in government revenues were considered in a different light in Chapter 9 where we saw that additional spending may receive legislative authorization each year without enactment of new revenue measures.

destabilizing and hinder the attainment of policy objectives. Specifically, accepting the position that budget deficits are expansionary, in a less than fully employed economy budget deficits are the proper fiscal policy for advancing full employment objectives. As the economy expands toward full employment, the fiscal dividend yields additional budget receipts and, if expenditures are not correspondingly adjusted, the budget deficit is automatically reduced and may even be changed into a budget surplus. In the 1960s this changed budget position came to be called *fiscal drag*. Fiscal drag prior to reaching full employment serves to hinder the attainment of full employment; hence the fiscal dividend may be destabilizing.

Automatic fiscal policies, unlike explicit fiscal policies, do not rely on recognition of their need and the granting of authority for their implementation. They quickly influence aggregate demand and, providing they are stabilizing, may better serve to advance policy objectives than explicit fiscal policies that are subject to recognition and implementation lags, as well as errors of judgment on the part of policy makers. Several studies have been made of automatic fiscal policies in the postwar years.[10] They conclude that automatic fiscal policies have contributed to the postwar economic stability of the American economy. Especially during recessions, automatic reductions in federal tax receipts and increases in expenditures served to moderate the downturns, making the recessions milder than they otherwise would have been.

STATE AND LOCAL GOVERNMENTS AND FISCAL POLICY

State and local government securities are not bought and sold by the Federal Reserve System. As these governments finance surpluses or deficits it is less likely that the money supply will be affected than when federal budget imbalances are financed. Thus state and local government borrowing directly competes with funds sought by the private sector and may be expected to lead to reductions in private investment; it is not clear that state and local government deficits will be expansionary. Conversely, as these governments retire their debts, private asset holders have cash rather than securities in their portfolios, and if an adequate volume of newly issued private securities is forthcoming, state and local government surpluses will not be contractionary. Despite these considerations, and despite the fact that state and local governments cannot reasonably pursue explicit fiscal policies, an implicit fiscal policy is embodied in their combined receipts and expenditures.

State and local governments have many restrictions on their authority

---

[10] Wilfred Lewis, Jr., *Federal Fiscal Policy in the Postwar Recessions* (Washington, D.C.: The Brookings Institution, 1962), chapters 2 and 3, and Peter Eilbott, "The Effectiveness of Automatic Stabilizers," *American Economic Review,* June 1966.

to borrow and, by and large, their borrowing is limited to financing capital outlays. On a year-by-year basis these governments, in combination, are therefore more likely to have a balanced budget than the federal government. If we presume the state and local government sector budget is balanced, the balanced-budget theorem shows their combined receipts and expenditures to be expansionary. Over time, as citizens demand additional goods and services, the state and local government sector will expand; there is an ever greater expansionary impact of their augmented receipts and expenditures. During recessions tax bases decline or expand slowly, and if tax rates are not increased the expenditures of state and local governments may decline, although stabilization policy requires additional increments to aggregate demand. During the 1930s tax bases actually decreased, state and local government receipts declined, and were matched by corresponding reductions in expenditures. Thus, while this sector's budget tended to remain in balance, the balance was struck at reduced levels and the expansionary impact of state and local government balanced budgets was diminished at precisely that time when the opposite effect was needed.[11]

Federal fiscal policy actions sometimes have an impact on state and local governments. Perhaps the most direct impact comes through variation in federal grants-in-aid; they constitute approximately 20 percent of the budget receipts of state and local governments and any variation will directly affect their expenditures. For example, the interstate highway system is financed from federal motor vehicle-related excise taxes; these monies are used to make grants-in-aid to state governments that contract for highway construction. When contractionary policies are required, the federal government often postpones construction expenditures, including highway expenditures.

Expansionary federal fiscal policies serve to increase the rate of growth of tax bases and hence the rate at which state and local expenditures may increase. Similarly, contractionary fiscal policies decrease the rate of growth of tax bases and slow the growth of state and local expenditures. The adjustment of state and local governments to federal fiscal policy actions is an additional automatic fiscal policy that will complement explicit federal policy

---

[11] Obtaining data on the surplus or deficit position of state and local governments is difficult. State and local government employee retirement funds buy federal government and corporate securities; these are asset transactions that are offset against the issue of new state and local government securities when these governments are recorded in national income accounts. Thus, summing the annual surpluses and deficits of state and local governments in the postwar years shows that, on the basis of their recording in national income accounts, their budgets were approximately in balance from 1945 to 1968. During that same period their combined indebtedness increased from $13.4 billion to $128.6 billion. *Economic Report of the President, 1970* (Washington, D.C.: Government Printing Office, 1970), pp. 248 and 257.

actions if there are no lags between changes in state and local receipts and changes in their expenditures. The existence of lags may be a source of instability.

Monetary policy actions in pursuit of stabilization goals are usually accompanied by changes in interest rates, and interest rates affect state and local government expenditures. The input-output data in Chapter 11 showed the importance of state and local government construction expenditures. These projects are often financed from the sale of bonds. When interest rates rise, as part of a contractionary monetary policy, the cost of borrowing funds is increased, and state and local governments sometimes postpone new bond issues, thereby delaying the corresponding expenditures. Conversely, expansionary monetary policies are often accompanied by falling interest rates leading to accelerated borrowing and construction expenditures by state and local governments.

17

FISCAL POLICY SINCE WORLD WAR II

Since the 1930s, first economists and then politicians and the public-at-large have come to understand that the expenditures and revenues of government, which formerly had been seen only from the vantage of allocative and distributive goals, affect the economy's macroeconomic stability. What a contrast there is between Franklin Roosevelt's 1932 campaign dictum that the cure for the Depression was belt tightening and restoration of a balanced federal budget, and President Kennedy's deliberate planning of budget deficits to promote greater economic growth during the comparatively prosperous 1960s. By the end of the 1960s most, if not all, citizens recognized that fiscal policy and macroeconomic stability were related. Debate persisted, however, regarding the efficacy of discretionary stabilization policies and the power of fiscal policy as compared with monetary policy. Among those who see fiscal policy as an effective means of advancing stability goals, differences remain regarding the technique and timing of explicit fiscal policy actions. Our purpose in this chapter is to chronicle and critique fiscal policy in the postwar years.[1] The chapter is organized to consider fiscal policy in each of several periods into which the postwar years are often divided. Discussion of policy must be preceded by a consideration of measuring instability and full employment.

Postwar business cycles. Students of economic activity have discerned four major cycles in the postwar life of the American economy. The first reached a peak in November 1948; the downturn ran to a trough in October 1949, and the expansion lasted throughout the Korean War and peaked in July 1953.[2] The second cycle declined from this peak to a trough in August 1954 and rose to a new peak in July 1957. From this peak the third cycle reached a trough in April 1958 and experienced a short expansion to a peak in May 1960. The trough of the fourth cycle occurred in February 1961, and a long expansion ran throughout the remainder of the 1960s. Many different statistical indicators are examined in the measurement of the business cycle; two of these are shown in Figure 17.1. Quarterly data (at seasonally adjusted annual rates) for gross national product in constant, 1958, dollars are shown; the movement in this series approximates the dating of the four postwar business cycles. We have argued throughout this volume, however, that personal welfare is the proper object of economic study; we are interested in the level of real gross national product because it has implications for the well-being of citizens. While many variables bear on welfare, being employed is certainly a key factor. Thus, quarterly unemployment data are also given in Figure 17.1. This series clearly shows the rate of unemployment increasing during downturns and falling during periods of expansion.

Since price stability as well as the level of employment is a frequent object of stabilization policy, the gross national product deflator is also

---

[1] Throughout the chapter data pertaining to the federal budget and the combined budgets of state and local governments are taken from the national income accounts unless otherwise noted. The data are for calendar years unless fiscal year data are specified.

There are a number of works dealing with postwar economic policy. Two surveys are Wilfred Lewis, Jr., *Federal Fiscal Policy in the Postwar Recessions* (Washington, D.C.: The Brookings Institution, 1962), and Herbert Stein, *The Fiscal Revolution in America* (Chicago: University of Chicago Press, 1969). The annual *Economic Report of the President* is a valuable document for those interested in knowing the administration's views on economic policy in any year. Three former Chairmen of the Council of Economic Advisors have published their views on economic policy: Authur F. Burns, *Prosperity Without Inflation* (New York: Fordham University Press, 1955); Walter W. Heller, *New Dimensions of Political Economy* (New York: W.W. Norton and Co., 1966); and Arthur Okun, *The Political Economy of Prosperity* (Washington, D.C.: The Brookings Institution, 1970).

[2] The dating of these cycles is taken from Alvin H. Hansen, *Business Cycles and National Income*, Expanded ed., (New York: W.W. Norton and Co., 1964), p. 611.

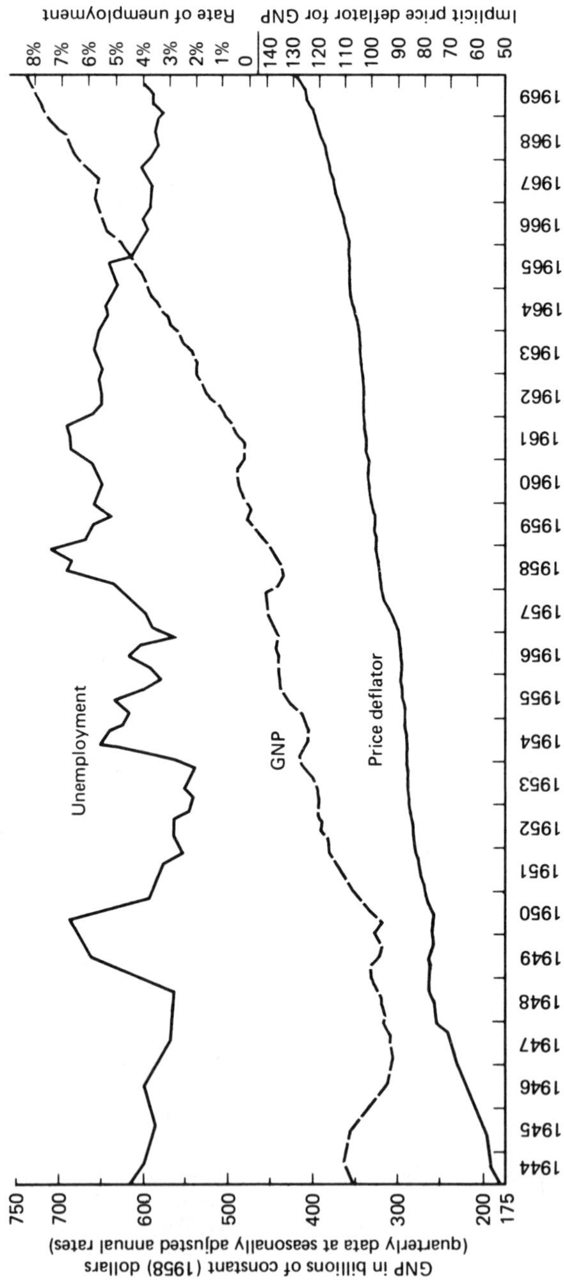

SOURCES: *Monthly, Labor Review*, 1949-1969. *The National Income and Product Accounts of the U.S.*, 1929-1965, a supplement to the *Survey of Current Business*, 1966. *Economic Report of the President*, 1971 (Washington, D.C.: Government Printing Office, 1970).

Figure 17.1 Gross national product in constant dollars, unemployment, and the price level, 1944–1969.

shown in Figure 17.1. The discussion of fiscal policy that follows examines public expenditures and revenues during these four cycles. Throughout, our intention is not to analyze any one of these cycles in all its details; instead our focus is on the way in which fiscal policy contributed to, or served to counteract, these cyclical movements.

Measuring full employment. The measurement of those variables in terms of which economic stability is customarily measured must be considered before the record of fiscal policy may be appraised.[3] What constitutes full employment of the labor force? With the definitions used in the United States, persons who have given up seeking employment are not counted as unemployed. They are totally disregarded in these data since they are not counted as members of the labor force. The welfare implications of this are important; an area may appear to have a low level of unemployment despite the fact that many of its citizens are impoverished. Those who are seasonally unemployed, those between jobs, and second-household income earners, are counted as unemployed when they are out of work and seeking employment. In a very obvious sense they are unemployed and should be so counted, but the welfare implications of their unemployment are quite different from a situation where all members of a household are unable to find work. Few believe that the object of public economic policy should be to reduce the percentage rate of unemployment to zero, but what positive rate is to be interpreted as full employment? During World War II the rate of unemployment fell from its depression era level of 17 percent in 1939 to between 1 and 2 percent of the civilian labor force, and during the Korean War the rate of unemployment fell below 3 percent. The economy was fully employed during these years; whatever unemployment remained is often termed either frictional unemployment (those between jobs, for instance) or structural unemployment that cannot be cured by short-run increases in the level of aggregate demand. Intensive job training and counseling of individuals are required to reduce structural unemployment.

---

[3] The Joint Economic Committee has held hearings on the technique and responsibility for various statistical series and issued reports on these data. See *Measuring Employment and Unemployment*, Hearings Before the Subcommittee on Economic Statistics, Joint Economic Committee, 88th Congress, 1st Session (Washington, D.C.: Government Printing Office, 1963); *Improved Statistics for Economic Growth*, Subcommittee on Economic Statistics, Joint Economic Committee, 89th Congress, 2nd Session (Washington, D.C.: Government Printing Office, 1966); *The Coordination and Integration of Government Statistical Programs*, Hearings Before the Subcommittee on Economic Statistics, Joint Economic Committee, 90th Congress, 1st Session (Washington, D.C.: Government Printing Office, 1967); and *Productivity, Prices and Incomes*, Joint Economic Committee, 89th Congress, 2nd Session (Washington, D.C.: Government Printing Office, 1967). See also *Economic Report of the President, 1970* (Washington, D.C.: Government Printing Office, 1970), pp. 147–56.

Table 17.1 **Unemployment by Type (Percentage rates)**

Year	All Workers	By Sex and Age			By color		By Selected Groups			
		Both Sexes, 16–19 years	Men, 20 years and over	Women, 20 years and over	White	Negro and Other Races	Experienced Wage and Salary Workers	Married Men	Full-time Workers	Blue-collar Workers
1960	5.5	14.7	4.7	5.1	4.9	10.2	5.7	3.7	—	7.8
1961	6.7	16.8	5.7	6.3	6.0	12.4	6.8	4.6	6.7	9.2
1962	5.5	14.7	4.6	5.4	4.9	10.9	5.6	3.6	—	7.4
1963	5.7	17.2	4.5	5.4	5.0	10.8	5.5	3.4	5.4	7.3
1964	5.2	16.2	3.9	5.2	4.6	9.6	5.0	2.8	4.8	6.3
1965	4.5	14.8	3.2	4.5	4.1	8.1	4.3	2.4	4.2	5.3
1966	3.8	12.8	2.5	3.8	3.4	7.3	3.5	1.9	3.4	4.2
1967	3.8	12.8	2.3	4.2	3.4	7.4	3.6	1.8	3.5	4.4
1968	3.6	12.7	2.2	3.8	3.2	6.7	3.4	1.6	3.1	4.1
1969	3.5	12.2	2.1	3.7	3.1	6.4	3.3	1.5	3.1	3.9

SOURCE: *Economic Report of the President, 1970* (Washington, D.C.: Government Printing Office,1970), p. 205.

The rate of unemployment was debated in the 1960 Presidential campaign. John F. Kennedy promised to reduce the rate of unemployment to 3 percent. Very shortly after his inauguration President Kennedy redefined his interim full employment objective as 4 percent of the civilian labor force unemployed. Public economic policy in the 1960s looked to 4 percent of the labor force unemployed as a target for stabilization policy, and 4 percent came to be regarded by many as the norm.

For many purposes unemployment data should be disaggregated to show unemployment by type. Such data for the 1960s are shown in Table 17.1. The welfare implications of teenage unemployment are undoubtedly different from the implications of unemployed married men (at the head of households), and these disaggregated data show the levels of unemployment for these two groups to be substantially different. As Americans became aware of the problems of minority groups and formulated public policies to improve their economic condition, these disaggregated data became important inputs to policy discussions. The data in Table 17.1 clearly show differences in the rates of unemployment for the white and nonwhite segments of the American population.

Labor is only one factor of production that imposes capacity limitations on the economy's output. Equally important is the economy's capital stock; plant and equipment may be fully employed or there may be idle capacity. Measuring business plant capacity and its degree of utilization is difficult; do we define capacity in terms of a 40-hour or 168-hour week, for instance?[4] Despite such problems, measures of capacity utilization are compiled and published by the Federal Reserve System. These measures are shown in Table 17.2 along with the index of industrial production. When capacity utilization reaches 90 percent the economy's capital stock is usually considered to be fully employed. The index of industrial production rose throughout the 1960s with particularly rapid growth during 1964, 1965, and 1966. The series on percent capacity utilization in manufacturing shows an increase from 1961 to 1966 as the United States recovered from the 1961 recession; with over 90 percent capacity utilization in 1966 there was full employment of capital as well as labor in that year. In the years after 1966 capacity utilization rates fell despite a continuing increase in industrial production and unemployment rates of less than 4 percent. This is because

---

[4] For literature on this issue, *see* Frank de Leeuw, "The Concept of Capacity," *Journal of the American Statistical Association*, December 1962; Peter Gajeski, "Manufacturing Capacity Measures and Current Economic Analysis," *American Statistical Association*, 1964; Frank de Leeuw, "The Demand for Capital Goods by Manufacturers," *Econometrica*, July 1962; Frank de Leeuw, Frank E. Hopkins, and Michael D. Sherman, "A Revised Index of Manufacturing Capacity," *Federal Reserve Bulletin*, November 1966; and Jared J. Enzler, "Manufacturing Capacity: A Comparison of Two Sources of Information," *Federal Reserve Bulletin*, November 1968.

Table 17.2 **Business Indicators**

	Index of Industrial Production (1957–59 = 100)	Capacity of Utilization in Manufacturing (Percent)
1960	108.7	80.6
1961	109.7	78.5
1962	118.3	82.1
1963	124.3	83.3
1964	132.3	85.7
1965	143.4	88.5
1966	156.3	90.5
1967	158.1	85.3
1968	165.5	84.5
1969	172.8	81.7

SOURCE: *Federal Reserve Bulletin,* July 1970, p. A62.

net private domestic investment in producers' durables added to the nation's capital stock more rapidly than industrial output expanded.

THE EMPLOYMENT ACT OF 1946

Although the late 1930s saw economic recovery from the depths of the Depression, full employment was not achieved until the 1940s when military spending increased aggregate demand and hence the demand for labor; simultaneously, conscription and growth in the size of the armed forces led to decreases in the supply of civilian labor.[5] At the end of the war, concern was widespread that decreased military expenditures and manpower requirements would cause the rate of unemployment to rise again. The specter of renewed depression haunted political leaders. The Full Employment Act of 1945 was introduced into Congress (and passed by the Senate) at the start of 1945.[6] This bill, Section 2, parts b and c, contained the provision that

> all Americans able to work and seeking work have the right to useful, remunerative, regular, and full-time employment, and it is the policy of

[5] The civilian labor force decreased from 55.6 million at the end of 1940 to 53.9 million at the end of 1945, while the size of the armed forces increased from .5 million to 11.4 million; there can be no doubt that this increase in the size of the armed forces worked to decrease the supply of civilian labor. For employment data, see *Economic Report of the President, 1970* (Washington, D.C.: Government Printing Office, 1970), p. 202.

[6] For references to the concern with postwar employment and the politics of the Full Employment Act of 1945 and the Employment Act of 1946, *see* Stephen K. Bailey, *Congress Makes a Law: The Story Behind the Employment Act of 1946* (New York: Columbia University Press, 1950).

> the United States to assure the existence at all times of sufficient employment opportunities to enable all Americans . . . to exercise this right; . . . it is essential that continuing full employment be maintained in the United States.

Many in Congress and the business community were uneasy about the Full Employment Act; they questioned the consistency of a government obligation to guarantee employment opportunities with traditional American principles of free enterprise in a market economy. The measure was defeated; the Employment Act of 1946 was enacted instead. The Employment Act's declaration of policy is milder and commits the federal government only "to use all practical means . . . to foster and promote . . . conditions under which there will be afforded useful employment for those able, willing, and seeking to work . . . ." The Employment Act also obligates the President to submit to Congress annually an economic report, *The Economic Report of the President,* setting forth a program to meet the Act's objectives. To aid the President in this task, the Council of Economic Advisors was established. In addition, the Joint Economic Committee of Congress was created "to make a continuing study of matters related to the economic report; [and] to study means of coordinating programs in order to further the policy of this Act." The Joint Economic Committee, unlike most Congressional committees, has no legislative functions; its primary purpose is to keep the Congress informed on economic issues.[7]

POSTWAR READJUSTMENT

Military spending at the height of World War II absorbed over 40 percent of gross national product; over 11 million Americans were members of the armed forces. Cessation of hostilities was thus certain to create economic

[7] The Joint Economic Committee holds hearings on many economic issues and these hearings are important to the student of public economic policy. As required by the employment act itself, the Joint Economic Committee holds annual hearings on *The Economic Report of the President*; since the mid-1960s the Joint Economic Committee has held annual hearings on the midyear review of the federal budget, and studied the implications of that budget for economic conditions. Several volumes of hearings stand out as important collections of papers dealing with federal tax and expenditure policy: see *Federal Tax Policy for Economic Growth and Stability*, Joint Economic Committee, 84th Congress, 1st Session (Washington, D.C.: Government Printing Office, 1955); and *Federal Expenditure Policy for Economic Growth and Stability*, Joint Economic Committee, 85th Congress, 1st Session (Washington, D.C.: Government Printing Office, 1957). See also *Staff Report on Employment, Growth and Price Levels* (Eckstein Report), Joint Economic Committee, 86th Congress, 1st Session (Washington, D.C.: Government Printing Office, 1959).

strains. This was particularly true because the United States in 1945 did not foresee her military commitments of the 1950s and 1960s, and political pressures made it imperative to demobilize the citizen army quickly. The size of the armed forces decreased from 11.4 million at the end of 1945 to 1.6 million at the end of 1947; defense expenditures for goods and services fell to less than 4 percent of gross national product. Many women left the labor force, as did elderly workers who had postponed their retirement; but with the release of approximately 10 million men from the armed forces it is hardly surprising that civilian unemployment rose from 1.9 percent in 1945 to 3.9 percent in 1947. That it did not rise yet further, especially in the face of rapidly declining federal expenditures for goods and services, is attributable to strong investment and consumer demand during those years. Given the magnitude of the adjustment that was occurring, even though the rate of unemployment did rise, few saw this as a sign of economic weakness. During the demobilization, most wartime wage and price controls were removed and prices increased substantially; inflation rather than unemployment became the principal concern. Households had postponed consumption spending during the war and their wartime saving permitted substantial postwar expenditures. This household demand plus investment demand coincided to provide an inflationary environment during a period when industry was switching from military to civilian production.

Federal taxes as well as expenditures were reduced at the war's end. Personal and corporate income tax rates were reduced in 1946 increasing the disposable income of households and the after-tax profits of corporations. Tax reduction, by increasing the purchasing power of the private sector, undoubtedly contributed to the postwar inflation. Both the federal and state and local government budgets were in surplus positions in 1946–1948. Net federal debt held outside federal trust funds and the Federal Reserve System declined by nearly $40 billion between 1945 and 1948; there was virtually no change in the value of United States government securities held by the Federal Reserve System (see Table 17.3). Financing of these federal surpluses supplied federal saving to the private sector; it is doubtful that these surpluses were contractionary. Despite the tax reductions of 1946, federal budget surpluses were explicitly sought. President Truman believed that the public debt should be reduced; what better time for this than in a period of high tax receipts and rapidly decreasing expenditures? The administration's motivation for budget surpluses was not primarily to advance macroeconomic stability; debt reduction per se was the object of policy.

Throughout the early postwar years there was continuing Congressional pressure for further tax reductions. Two tax reduction measures were enacted but vetoed by President Truman who considered them inconsistent with his debt retirement objective. With the postwar inflation, however, sizable fiscal dividends arose; receipts ran well ahead of their expected level.

Year	Treasury Cash Balance			Public Debt							
					Held By						
							Private Investors				
	Total	In Federal Reserve Banks	In Tax And Loan Accounts	Total Gross Debt	Federal Government Accounts	Federal Reserve Banks	Total	Commercial Banks	Other Corporations	Individuals
1944	22.2	1.3	20.3	230.6	19.0	18.8	192.8	76.7	21.4	53.1
1945	26.0	1.7	24.0	278.1	23.9	24.3	230.0	90.8	22.2	64.0
1946	3.5	.7	2.6	259.1	27.4	23.3	208.4	74.5	15.3	64.1
1947	3.1	.9	1.0	256.9	30.8	22.6	203.6	68.7	14.1	65.7
1948	4.2	1.1	2.0	252.8	33.7	23.3	195.8	62.4	14.8	65.5
1949	4.7	.8	2.6	257.1	35.9	18.9	202.4	66.8	16.8	66.3
1950	4.2	.7	2.3	256.7	35.0	20.8	199.9	61.8	19.7	66.3
1951	4.3	.3	2.7	259.4	39.3	23.8	196.3	61.5	20.7	64.6
1952	6.1	.4	4.4	267.4	42.9	24.7	199.8	63.4	19.9	65.2
1953	4.6	.3	3.4	275.2	45.4	25.9	203.8	63.7	21.5	64.8
1954	5.2	.6	3.5	278.8	46.7	24.9	207.1	69.2	19.1	63.5
1955	4.5	.4	3.0	280.8	49.0	24.8	207.0	62.0	23.2	65.0
1956	4.4	.4	3.0	276.6	51.2	24.9	200.5	59.5	18.7	65.9
1957	4.6	.5	3.1	274.9	52.8	24.2	197.8	59.5	17.7	64.9
1958	5.0	.4	3.5	282.9	52.1	26.3	204.5	67.5	18.1	63.7
1959	5.6	.5	4.2	290.8	51.4	26.6	212.7	60.3	21.4	69.4
1960	6.4	.5	5.2	290.2	52.8	27.4	210.0	62.1	18.7	66.1
1961	6.5	.5	5.2	296.2	52.5	28.9	214.8	67.2	18.5	65.9
1962	7.6	.6	6.1	303.5	53.2	30.8	219.4	67.1	18.6	66.0
1963	7.4	.9	5.6	309.3	55.3	33.6	220.5	64.2	18.7	68.2
1964	7.3	.8	5.4	317.9	58.4	37.0	220.5	63.9	18.2	69.8
1965	6.6	.7	4.5	320.9	59.7	40.8	220.4	60.7	15.8	72.1
1966	6.0	.4	4.1	329.3	65.9	44.3	219.1	57.4	14.9	74.6
1967	5.6	1.1	4.3	344.7	73.1	49.1	222.4	63.8	12.2	74.0
1968	4.7	.7	3.9	358.0	76.5	52.9	228.6	65.4	11.5	75.3
1969	5.3	1.3	3.9	368.2	89.0	57.2	222.0	56.1	15.8	79.4

SOURCE: *Federal Reserve Bulletin*, various issues, and *Economic Report of the President, 1970* (Washington, D.C.: Government Printing Office, 1970), p. 233.

U.C.W. ABERYSTWYTH LIBRARY

In April 1948, a further personal tax rate reduction was enacted, accompanied by an increase in the size of the personal exemption; the tax reduction was made retroactive to the start of 1948. This tax cut, and the refunds made in mid-1949, served to bolster disposable personal income and consumption spending during the 1949 recession. At the time the tax reduction was enacted few saw a recession on the horizon, and stabilization objectives were not foremost in lawmakers' minds. These countercyclical fiscal policy actions were not primarily aimed at promoting stabilization goals; their timing as stabilization measures was coincidental.

Increased military expenditures associated with the Berlin Airlift in 1949–1950, and the outbreak of the Korean conflict in June 1950, occurred during the recovery from the first postwar recession. These expenditure increases, made for allocative reasons, must be deemed an implicit fiscal policy that was stabilizing. Falling rates of unemployment during the early 1950s from the trough in 1949 are partially attributable to the increased aggregate demand arising from additional military expenditures. During this same period, the size of the armed forces was increased, having the complementary effect of reducing the civilian labor force.

In 1949, the federal budget was in a deficit position and the size of the public debt increased; at the same time the Federal Reserve System decreased its holdings of United States government securities as a monetary policy action to stem inflation. The federal government borrowed from the private sector in competition with private users of funds; as a result it is doubtful that the 1949 budget deficit was expansionary. Fiscal and monetary policy actions in 1949 were uncoordinated.[8] In 1950 and 1951 the federal budget was in a surplus position and much of the surplus was financed by increasing the Treasury cash balance; the surplus in these years was stabilizing.[9] As the Korean War progressed, expenditures ran ahead of re-

---

[8] In March 1951 the Treasury and Federal Reserve System, recognizing the need for complementary fiscal and monetary policy actions, reached an accord. During World War II and continuing until this time, the Federal Reserve System acted to support, at relatively low interest rates, the market for United States government bonds. As this arrangement was terminated, long-term interest rates were permitted to rise as a part of monetary policy designed to combat inflationary pressures.

[9] Examination of the Treasury's financial operations as summarized in Table 17.3 reveals that there was a growth in the public debt during 1950 and 1951 but that the Treasury cash balance did not grow until 1952. The seeming contradiction here arises from the fact that we are citing the federal budget as recorded in the national income accounts, and this budget records corporate income tax liabilities on an accrual rather than a cash flow basis. As the economy recovered from the 1949 recession, corporate profits rose as did accrued corporate income tax liabilities, but this did not increase the cash flow to the Treasury until 1951 and 1952. The Treasury cash balance and public debt position reflect actual financial transactions rather than accruals. For the budget data, see *The Economic Report of the President, 1970, op. cit.*, p. 253.

ceipts, and the federal budget was in a deficit position in 1952 and 1953. Congress enacted personal and corporate income tax rate increases and reimposed the corporate excess profits tax; these tax increases were stabilizing during a period of full employment.[10] There was some increase in the Federal Reserve System's holding of United States government securities during these years as the size of the public debt increased; these budget deficits were destabilizing. The federal deficit continued on into the recession year 1954, but since there was a reduction in Federal Reserve System holdings of United States government securities during that year, the deficit's expansionary impact is questionable.

The first postwar business cycle includes the demobilization from a world war and the mobilization associated with the far more limited Korean War. Substantial federal expenditure shifts were made primarily to promote allocative objectives; in some instances the implicit fiscal policy embodied in these allocative decisions was countercyclical, and in others economic instability was aggravated. The whole period was expectedly unsettled as the economy adjusted to years of war and peace. On balance, explicit fiscal policy did a poor job of advancing stabilization objectives.

INFLATION WITH UNEMPLOYMENT IN THE 1950s

Following the Korean Armistice in mid-1953, federal expenditures were sharply reduced and a beginning was made at again reducing the size of the armed forces. This reduction in military expenditures was made for allocative reasons; the implicit fiscal policy was contractionary. With reduced government expenditures for goods and services there was a weakening of aggregate demand, and hence the demand for labor, while reducing the size of the armed forces served to increase the civilian labor force. The rate of unemployment rose during the last half of 1953 and early 1954 as the American economy moved into its second postwar recession.

The new Eisenhower administration, like its predecessor, sought debt reduction. When reenacted in 1951, the excess profits tax had been scheduled for repeal in mid-1953; personal income and excise tax reductions were scheduled for mid-1954. Fearing the charge that it was excessively probusiness, for political reasons the Eisenhower administration wanted business and personal tax reductions to occur at the same time. Repeal of the excess profits tax was postponed at the administration's request until 1954 rather than move the personal income and excise tax reductions up to 1953 where they would coincide with the military expenditure reduction. Although the

[10] Prior to 1950, many had sought to reduce or repeal the manufacturers' and retailers' excise taxes; these pressures were temporarily abandoned during the Korean War and, in some instances, excise tax rates were increased.

federal budget showed a deficit in 1953, the failure to time both expenditure and tax cuts in that year undoubtedly contributed to the recession. When the tax reductions originally scheduled for 1953 and 1954 were enacted, no one could foresee this recession on the horizon. Tax reductions are appropriate stabilization measures during a recession, but the fact that they occurred during this second postwar recession cannot be interpreted as an explicit stabilization policy, especially in view of the administration's decision to delay rather than accelerate their timing.[11]

In the mid-1950s the Eisenhower administration believed inflation to be the nation's principal economic problem. There had been substantial inflation in the first three postwar years and then relatively stable prices until the outbreak of the Korean War. Consumer prices rose rapidly in 1950 and 1951. From 1952 to 1955 prices remained relatively stable, but beginning in 1956 they again began to rise. From 1955 to 1957 the rate of unemployment fell, as recovery from the recession occurred, and fluctuated around 4 percent; it is understandable that with the development of inflationary pressures in 1956 the Eisenhower administration would be more concerned with inflation than unemployment. The rate of unemployment rose to higher levels in 1958 than in either of the previous postwar recessions, and the recovery in 1959 and 1960 was short and incomplete. Although the employment picture improved in these two years, over 5 percent of the civilian labor force remained unemployed. Despite the recession, prices rose in 1958 and the inflation continued in the two years of recovery, 1959 and 1960.

During the 1958 recession several fiscal policy developments served as countercyclical stabilization measures. First, the Soviet launching of Sputnik in 1957 gave stimulus to the American space effort, and expenditures for goods and services thus rose in 1958; this allocative policy was a stabilizing, implicit fiscal policy. Second, with a weakening in the growth of personal income and a fall in corporate profits during the recession, personal and corporate income tax receipts were short of expectations at the same time as expenditures rose. Thus, the federal budget showed a \$10.2 billion deficit during 1958. There was a modest increase in Federal Reserve System holdings of United States government securities during this year and commercial banks made substantial purchases with excess reserves; the 1958 budget deficit was stabilizing (see Table 17.3). The fall-off in revenues that occurred in 1958, and the resulting deficit, was an automatic fiscal policy that was stabilizing.

In 1958 the American economy saw high rates of unemployment (with a peak of 7.6 percent in April), continuing inflation, and the largest peace-

[11] The federal debt was not reduced at this time, despite the postponement of tax reductions, because the recession so contracted tax bases that federal budget surpluses that would have permitted debt retirement did not materialize.

time federal budget deficit in history. To fiscal conservatives in Congress, imbued with the dogma of balanced budgets, 1958 was a disaster. The Republican administration was concerned with the continuing growth of federal spending as an encroachment on the free enterprise economy. These two attitudes combined to hold the line on expenditures without any change in tax rates or bases during 1959 and 1960. Federal expenditures for goods and services remained constant from 1958 to 1960, and total outlays increased but modestly, as such payments as social security benefits rose. With recovery from the recession, personal income and corporate profits rose and federal budget receipts increased. By 1960, the federal budget was in a $3.5 billion surplus despite the fact that well over 5 percent of the civilian labor force remained unemployed.[12]

The swing from the $10.2 billion budget deficit in 1958 to the $3.5 billion budget surplus in 1960 was an automatic fiscal policy.[13] Is such a swing in the federal budget position stabilizing if it has the effect of checking the expansion prior to attainment of policy objectives? Defining objectives, of course, was difficult especially at this time when both inflation and unemployment were present. Still, analysis of the 1960 recession led many to conclude that the fiscal dividend that accrued from 1958 to 1960 was the primary reason for the shortness of the expansion and the downturn in 1960 prior to the attainment of full employment.[14] From this set of events the concept of the full employment surplus evolved as a gauge of fiscal policy. This concept, to which we now turn, dominated the fiscal policy discussions of the 1960s.

THE FULL EMPLOYMENT SURPLUS

The full employment surplus is the federal budget surplus or deficit (as recorded in national income accounts) that would result if the economy were operating at full employment. As this concept was evolved by the Council of Economic Advisors in the early 1960s, full employment was interpreted to mean 4 percent of the civilian labor force unemployed. Computation of the

---

[12] The Eisenhower administration recognized that budget surpluses may lead to an increase in the supply of loanable funds to finance private investment. Increased investment to promote economic growth was sought and the administration argued that its projected budget surplus for "fiscal year 1961 would be helpful in relieving pressure on the supply of funds" to finance that investment. See *Economic Report of the President, 1960* (Washington, D.C.: Government Printing Office, 1960), p. 37.

[13] The size of this changed budget position is even more dramatic if measured with quarterly data at seasonally adjusted annual rates. The federal deficit in the second quarter of 1958 was $12.4 billion and the surplus in the first quarter of 1960 was $7.1 billion.

[14] For a discussion of this position and references to the literature on this subject, *see* Lewis, *op. cit.,* chapter 7, and Stein, *op. cit.,* chapter 14.

full employment budget surplus begins with the projected gross national product upon which actual budget estimates are based. Then, at constant prices, *potential gross national product*—the level of gross national product that would be produced if the economy were fully employed—is estimated. Accounting for the automatic revenue and expenditure changes that would result in this budget if gross national product changed to its potential level, a surplus or deficit in the federal budget is computed; this computation is made on the assumption that no discretionary actions are taken to modify either budget receipts or expenditures. This budget position is the *full employment surplus.*

The Council of Economic Advisors introduced the full employment surplus concept in 1962; their presentation utilized Figure 17.2.[15] Actual

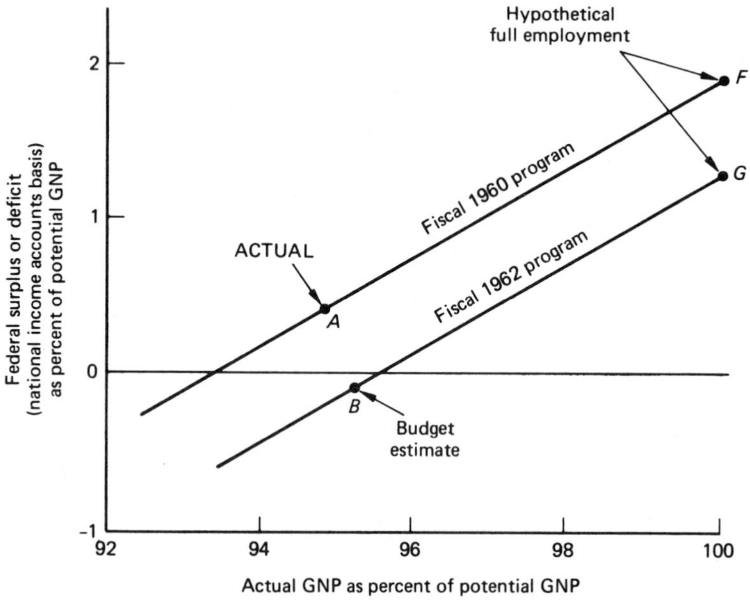

SOURCE: *Economic Report of the President, 1962* (Washington, D.C.: Government Printing Office, 1962), p. 79.

Figure 17.2 Effect of level of economic activity on federal surplus or deficit.

gross national product as a share of potential gross national product is shown on the horizontal axis, and the federal surplus or deficit as a percent of potential gross national product is shown on the vertical axis. The upper schedule in Figure 17.2 shows, at point *A*, that the actual budget surplus in 1960 was .4 percent of potential gross national product, while actual gross

---

[15] *Economic Report of the President, 1962* (Washington, D.C.: Government Printing Office, 1962), pp. 78–81.

national product was only 95 percent of its potential level. Had the economy grown to its full employment level during that year, without any discretionary budgetary action, the federal budget surplus would have been approximately $10 billion, and this full employment surplus would have been nearly 2 percent of potential gross national product, as shown at point *F*. The lower schedule in Figure 17.2 shows that an actual budget deficit was anticipated with less than capacity operation of the economy in 1962 (point *B*); if the economy had operated at its full employment level in 1962 a full employment budget surplus would have accrued that would have been just over 1 percent of potential gross national product, as shown at point *G*. Discretionary fiscal policies affect the height of the schedules shown in Figure 17.2; movements along each schedule reflect automatic fiscal policies as the economy's performance varies.

The basic concept is straightforward although there are substantial statistical difficulties encountered in making the necessary computations.[16] Once the full employment surplus has been computed, what implications can one draw as to its significance? In Chapter 16 we discussed the macroeconomic impact of budget surpluses and deficits and saw that how they are financed is crucial to understanding their effects. The Council of Economic Advisors was cautious and argued as follows:

> The full employment surplus is a measure of the restrictive or expansionary impact of a budget program on over-all demand. Generally speaking, one budget program is more expansionary than another if it has a smaller full employment surplus. . . . If the full employment surplus is too large, relative to the strength of private demand, economic activity falls short of potential. . . . If the full employment surplus is too small, total demand exceeds the capacity of the economy and causes inflation. . . . But whether a given full employment surplus is too large or too small depends on other government policies, as well as on economic circumstances affecting the general strength of private demand.

The Council of Economic Advisors then argued that

> analysis of the budget program in terms of the full employment surplus points to a probable major cause of the incomplete and short-lived nature of the 1958–1960 expansion. . . . The full employment surplus declined

[16] Arthur M. Okun, "Potential GNP: Its Measurement and Significance," *American Statistical Association Proceedings,* 1962, and Arthur M. Okun and Nancy H. Teeters, "The Full Employment Surplus Revisited," *Brookings Papers on Economic Activity* **1**:1970. The relationship between movements in the full employment surplus and changes in real gross national product has also been questioned: *See* the discussion by Norman B. Ture in *Fiscal Policy and Business Capital Formation* (Washington, D.C.: The American Enterprise Institute, 1967), pp. 199–206.

> sharply . . . during the 1957–1958 recession until it reached an estimated $3 billion in the second half of 1958. Thereafter it rose gradually through most of 1959 but then increased sharply to about $12.5 billion in 1960. Thus, whereas the Federal budget contributed to stability during the contraction phase of the cycle and during the first year of expansion, it was altered abruptly in the direction of restraint late in 1959 at a time when high employment had not yet been achieved.[17]

These changes in the full employment surplus just described for 1959 and 1960 result from automatic rather than discretionary changes in the federal budget. The Council believed they were a major cause of the 1960 recession. Yet the Council's own interpretation of budget surpluses and deficits was ambivalent; the 1963 *Report* contains the following: "The experience of the last few years should make it clear that merely to incur deficits is not an appropriate objective of policy. For it is not the deficits as such that provide stimulus. Only reductions in tax rates or increases in expenditures have an actively stimulating role. The passive deficits which are the product of recession or slack, however, have a valuable cushioning function."[18] Thus the Council seems, on the one hand, to have believed that automatic changes in budget positions may substantially affect stability, and, on the other hand, believed that automatic changes serve only as a cushion, and that discretionary policy actions are the key to stabilization. Understanding these issues requires consideration of the means of financing budget imbalances and the precise nature of the revenue and expenditure changes that occur.

THE REVENUE ACT OF 1964

Stabilization policy in the 1960s must be divided into two distinct phases. First, there was the drive toward full employment to the first half of that decade; the dominant feature in that drive was the Revenue Act of 1964. Second, in the latter part of the 1960s the primary concern of stabilization policy shifted to inflation in a fully employed economy; the increased military expenditures associated with the Vietnam War and the debate over the enactment of additional taxes to finance those expenditures dominated stabilization policy discussions. This section examines fiscal policy between 1961 and 1965; the following section considers fiscal policy during the Vietnam War.

The Kennedy administration came to office as the fourth postwar recession reached its lowest point. The civilian labor force unemployed was

---

[17] *Economic Report of the President, 1962* (Washington, D.C.: Government Printing Office, 1962), pp. 80–81.

[18] *Economic Report of the President, 1963* (Washington, D.C.: Government Printing Office, 1963), p. 73.

approaching 8 percent in early 1961; the new administration now had to deliver on its campaign pledge to reduce unemployment. Throughout the last part of the 1950s concern had been mounting about the slow rate of growth in the American economy in comparison with other nations. If private investment could be spurred, full employment could be approached through the increased aggregate demand that additional private investment would entail; greater private investment would also accelerate the rate of economic growth of potential gross national product. Thus, two allocative policy actions were taken in 1961 and 1962 to increase investment in the private sector. First, in April 1961, a 7 percent investment tax credit was proposed; this change in the tax laws was finally enacted by Congress in October 1962. The legislation permitted a firm to take a tax credit against corporate income tax liabilities (or against personal income tax liabilities if the firm were unincorporated) equal to 7 percent of the firm's new investment in depreciable equipment (not plant) in excess of current depreciation allowances; a ceiling on the credit equal to $25,000 plus 25 percent of the remaining income tax liability was set. Second, in 1962 the Internal Revenue Service promulgated new rules governing the depreciation of assets (see Chapter 13); these accelerated depreciation guidelines were intended to further encourage additional investment in plant and equipment. By augmenting the after-tax earnings of businesses, and increasing firms' cash flows, these measures were expected to encourage the allocation of additional resources to investment in producers' plant and equipment. Such allocative measures have their impact over a considerable time span. At the end of 1962 the rate of unemployment still remained high, although the upswing from the recession had begun. During the years 1961–1962 the federal budget was in deficit; a substantial part of the increase in federal borrowing reflected Federal Reserve System purchases of United States government securities and the financing of these deficits was most likely expansionary, thus contributing to the recovery.

Looking forward to 1963, the administration saw the rate of unemployment remaining over 5 percent; as the recovery progressed tax bases would expand and the fiscal dividend was seen reducing the federal deficit. A large full employment surplus was envisioned. In fact, the federal budget in the national income accounts did show a surplus during the last three quarters of 1963. Fiscal drag at less than full employment was seen as hindering the attainment of stabilization objectives. Thus, in January 1963, the administration sent a revenue bill to Congress whose principal feature was a substantial and permanent reduction of personal and corporate income tax rates, specifically not to be accompanied by a parallel reduction in federal expenditures. Seen within the context of fiscal policy model III, Chapter 15, the proposal was to take discretionary action that would increase gross national product by reducing tax rates in order to increase the size of the multiplier; the line was to be held on expenditures so that there would be no offsetting change in the value being multiplied. In the context of the illustration in Figure 17.2, this was a discretionary policy action to shift the budget schedule downward to reduce the full employment surplus.

Debate over the proposed tax measure was long and hard. Several years earlier the Republican administration, and fiscal conservatives generally, had aimed at balancing the federal budget. Now a new administration was deliberately proposing to unbalance the budget for stabilization purposes. This was not easy medicine for many to take. Further, some who agreed that deliberately running budget deficits to promote full employment was the needed policy action preferred the public expenditure rather than the tax reduction route to full employment. They argued on allocative grounds for substantial increases in government expenditures for housing, schools, and hospitals, and that increased public expenditures for these facilities was more desirable than increased consumer expenditures and corporate investment.[19]

After a year's debate the Revenue Act of 1964 was finally enacted in February of that year; this act was primarily intended as a stabilization measure and entailed the personal and corporate income tax reductions during 1964 and 1965 described in Chapter 13. Reduced income tax withholding rates applicable to wages and salaries became effective in March 1964, and this tax reduction measure was quickly able to influence aggregate demand. As Figure 17.1 shows, gross national product rose rapidly during 1964 and 1965 with only slight increases in the gross national product deflator; thus virtually all of the increased gross national product reflected an accelerated rate of growth of real output and, as a result, the rate of unemployment fell throughout 1964 and 1965. In December of 1965 unemployment had fallen to 4.1 percent of the civilian labor force; the avowed employment goal had been attained at the same time as prices remained satisfactorily stable.

Complementing the 1964 reduction in personal and corporate income tax rates was the repeal and reduction of federal excise taxes in 1965. The Johnson administration sought repeal of the World War II retailers' excise taxes, and repeal or reduction in the manufacturers' excise taxes. The only excise taxes unaffected by this bill were those on tobacco, alcoholic beverages, and gasoline (and some other motor vehicle-related excises). This action was a continuation of the stabilization program but was also motivated by allocative efficiency and equity considerations.

When tax reductions were first proposed, Congressional fear over bud-

---

[19] This is often referred to as the social balance argument; J. K. Galbraith, Leon Keiserling, and Michael Harrington were among its proponents. For a sampling of this viewpoint, *see* J. K. Galbraith, *The Affluent Society* (Boston: Houghton Mifflin, 1958), and Leon Keiserling, *Progress or Poverty* (Washington, D.C.: Conference on Economic Progress, 1964).

get deficits was allayed by arguing that the federal revenue loss would be only temporary. By spurring economic growth, tax bases would grow and lower tax rates applied to increased tax bases would enable the federal government during coming years to again restore budget balance without additional tax and expenditure measures being adopted. The administration's argument was correct; the drive to high employment in 1964 and 1965 quickly turned the planned budget deficit to a 1965 budget surplus at higher levels of employment.

Developments during 1961 to 1965 indicate that discretionary fiscal policy actions can be an effective means of promoting stabilization policy goals. While questions may be validly raised over priorities, and whether the tax reduction route to full employment was preferable, the response of the American economy to these tax reductions does show that discretionary policy actions, when carefully planned and sold to Congress and the public, are fruitful. This is the best instance in the postwar years of stabilizing discretionary policies being adopted; the Kennedy and Johnson administrations deserve good marks on this count.

VIETNAM: INFLATION AND FULL EMPLOYMENT

As the American economy approached full employment in 1965, President Johnson ordered a major increase in the American military commitment in Vietnam. As a result federal government expenditures for goods and services rapidly increased and this increase continued during the last half of the 1960s. At the same time, the size of the armed forces grew from 2.7 million in 1965 to 3.5 million in 1968; unemployment fell from an annual rate of 4.5 percent to 3.6 percent of the civilian labor force. Clearly two forces were at work to bring about this reduction in unemployment: the increased aggregate demand due to greater federal purchases of goods and services, and the reduction in the supply of civilian labor due to the increase in the size of the armed forces. The consumer price index had been creeping upward at an annual rate of just over 1 percent from 1958 to 1965, and the wholesale price index had been constant. Beginning in 1965, however, inflation became a matter of concern; during the last half of the 1960s consumer and wholesale prices rose at annual rates of from 3 to 6 percent. This inflation in a fully employed economy illustrates the trade-off expected on the basis of the Phillips curve analysis. The military commitment to and the resulting federal expenditures for Vietnam are one of the most hotly contested policies in all of American history; there is little question, however, that it constituted an implicit fiscal policy that was destabilizing. Most of the discussion that follows in this section deals with the explicit policies proposed and enacted to promote stability during these years.

Recognizing that increased military expenditures for goods and services would be inflationary in a fully employed economy, the Johnson administration took actions to increase budget receipts for stabilization purposes. In January 1966, the Johnson administration requested the retention of automotive and telephone service excise taxes scheduled for repeal under the 1965 excise tax legislation. Additional budget receipts were sought by accelerating the payment of personal and corporate income taxes. Working on the assumption that the Vietnam War would be quickly terminated, the administration saw an opportunity to increase its budget receipts in the short run without having to increase personal and corporate income tax liabilities. Thus, a schedule of graduated withholding rates for personal income taxes was introduced in early 1966; this had the effect of increasing personal income tax payments during 1966 without requiring any increase in personal income tax liabilities. In addition, corporate income tax payments were accelerated and the self-employed were required to make quarterly rather than annual remissions of their social security taxes. These accelerated tax payments were short-run measures designed to absorb liquidity in the private sector, thereby reducing aggregate demand.

To dampen further aggregate demand in the private sector, the 7 percent investment tax credit was suspended in November 1966. This suspension had been proposed several months earlier and in response there was a reduction in private investment.[20] Real gross national product fell slightly in the first quarter of 1967. Monetary policy also played a role. During 1966 the Federal Reserve System pursued a tight money policy; interest rates rose and there was little increase in the total money supply during that year. The investment tax credit was restored in March 1967, and continued in effect until 1969 when it was repealed as part of that year's tax reform package.

As the Vietnam conflict continued, the Johnson administration came to believe that additional tax measures would have to be enacted to advance economic stability. In January 1967, the President announced that he would seek a 6 percent surtax on personal and corporate income tax liabilities. It was not until August of that year that a tax bill was actually sent to Congress; at that time the President requested that the surtax rate be set at 10 percent. The 10 percent surtax was finally enacted in June 1968 and made retroactive to April 1968; it was scheduled to expire on June 30, 1969. Scheduled reductions in the telephone and automotive excise taxes were again postponed. The surtax specifically exempted low income taxpayers from the additional personal income tax liabilities. Despite the enactment of the surtax, coupled with increased withholding rates, inflation continued in the United States. This is not surprising. The lowest income taxpayers, who are least likely to have savings from which to maintain their consump-

---

[20] "Suspension of Tax Credit and Accelerated Depreciation: Estimated Impact on Investment," *Survey of Current Business,* February 1967, pp. 5–6.

tion expenditures, were exempt. More affluent taxpayers knew that the tax increase was temporary and could thus maintain their consumption spending by drawing down savings or by reducing the fraction of their disposable income going to current saving.

The long delay in enactment of the surtax reflected political considerations and debate over the means by which to advance stabilization objectives. Many in Congress were uneasy about raising taxes and would have preferred to have the administration pare expenditures. The administration countered that it had already submitted a "bare-bones" budget; expenditure cuts should be made only on the basis of a clear statement of priorities and objectives drawn up by Congress. At issue, of course, was the practical political consideration that raising taxes is as unpopular as is cutting back already authorized programs; neither Congress nor the administration wanted to act. When the surtax was finally enacted Congress imposed expenditure ceilings for the fiscal year 1969; certain categories of federal expenditures were excluded from this ceiling, and as the administration began serious consideration of cutbacks, Congress authorized additional exceptions in other areas.

The Revenue and Expenditure Control Act of 1968, by which Congress placed a ceiling on federal outlays, was a major departure from standard budgetary procedure. In his 1970 budget message, President Johnson quite properly berated Congress for this action.

> In limiting total outlays, the Congress departed from its traditional procedure of using individual appropriation actions as the primary means of exercising its control over the Federal budget. In contrast with normal practice, the Congress placed direct restrictions on the amount of checks that could be issued or cash disbursements that could be made in the 12-month period ending June 30, 1969.
>
> To implement this new restriction, the executive departments and agencies have had to add to their financial control machinery. In prior years, executive control of the budget was exercised at the stage of placing contracts, hiring personnel, making loan and grant commitments, or incurring some other obligation. These obligations lead, of course, to Federal disbursements, sometimes in the same fiscal year and sometimes in a later fiscal year. Now, in fiscal year 1969, each executive establishment must also exercise direct control over the amount of disbursements it makes within the year.
>
> An inflexible spending ceiling unrelated to the appropriations process forces inefficient or uneconomical practices in carrying out legislatively approved programs. In some cases, national priorities are arbitrarily distorted by the fact that the outlays for some Federal programs are sheltered in basic law from meaningful annual control, and, consequently, compensating reductions have to be made elsewhere.[21]

---

[21] *Budget of the United States Government, Fiscal Year 1970* (Washington, D.C.: Government Printing Office, 1969), pp. 14–15.

The performance of both the administration and Congress regarding fiscal policy during the Vietnam War was faulty. The administration proposed tax increases in January 1967, and then waited until August 1967 to send its tax bill to Congress. In the Congress, primarily under the leadership of Wilbur Mills, Chairman of the House Ways and Means Committee, it was argued that the surtax would be enacted only if the administration would reduce expenditures. Congressman Mills surely understood that taxes are a means of financing expenditures and not a Congressional reward for virtuous behavior; yet the politics of the debate suggested just the opposite. If discretionary fiscal policies are to be effective they must be quickly implemented. In 1967 the Administration perceived the need for action and delayed; once action was proposed Congress delayed again. The climate was not conducive to prompt fiscal policy action. On the positive side, the administration was correct in seeing that stabilization is best promoted through tax rather than expenditure measures.

When the Nixon administration came to office in January 1969, inflation had not been checked; consumer prices were rising at an annual rate of over 5 percent. The rate of unemployment was below 4 percent although the percent capacity utilization of manufacturers' plant and equipment was at less than the full employment level. President Nixon promptly sought retention of the surtax until June 1970, but Congress again hesitated. Many continued to seek expenditure reductions; at the same time, pressure was mounting for income tax reform and some in Congress insisted that a meaningful tax reform bill be included in the legislation to continue the surtax. Congress finally extended the surtax through December 31, 1969; its further continuation at a 5 percent rate from January to June 1970 was incorporated into the tax reform bill in order to force the administration's interest in this legislation. The political interests involved in these fiscal policy actions are obvious; it is questionable, however, whether stabilizing fiscal policy actions can effectively be taken in such an environment.

During 1967 and 1968 there were federal budget deficits of $12.4 billion and $5.3 billion respectively. The Federal Reserve System increased its holding of United States government securities by approximately $8 billion and the Treasury cash balance was reduced as these deficits were financed; these budget deficits undoubtedly contributed to inflation. In 1969, by contrast, the federal budget showed a $9.7 billion surplus. Borrowing from the public fell (excluding the monetary authorities) in 1969 and the Federal Reserve System increased its holdings of government securities. Private investment in 1969 substantially exceeded its 1968 level. As borrowing from the public fell during 1969, the United States government supplied funds to finance private investment; surplus financing in 1969 was not contractionary.

Determining the optimal course for stabilization policy in the last half of the 1960s was difficult. With the growth of military expenditures at the end of 1965, many believed that tax increases were required in the fully employed American economy. Yet, although inflationary pressures were developing, an examination of price data by sector reveals that it was by no means economy-wide. In fact, during 1966 the prices of many consumer durables were either stable or falling, and these sectors are likely to be the first ones affected by an increase in personal income taxes since consumer durable expenditures are easily postponed. Tax increases of either 6 or 10 percent in 1966 might have reduced demand for the output of these industries; since resources released from consumer durable production could not be quickly absorbed in those sectors experiencing rising prices, tax increases at that time might have served to raise unemployment without dampening the inflation. As a complex economy approaches full employment not all sectors become fully employed at the same time. Bottlenecks develop and prices, after all, are the means by which a market economy allocates resources. Across-the-board tax increases, rather than selective controls, may not affect those sectors where bottlenecks have developed and the success of modest tax increases in such an environment is doubtful.

In addition, Phillips curve analysis suggests that price stability comes at the expense of rising unemployment. In the United States of the 1960s this trade-off was the source of a serious policy dilemma. Stated bluntly, the trade-off implies that in order to reduce the rate of inflation the level of unemployed must rise. In the last part of the 1960s the civilian labor force was approximately 80 million; if checking inflation caused a one percent increase in the percent rate of unemployment, then 800,000 citizens would be deliberately made unemployed in order to achieve price stability. There are costs associated with inflation (although it must also be remembered that some, such as debtors, benefit) and hence, benefits associated with its elimination. Who bears the cost of inflation and reaps the benefit of its elimination? This is a particularly important question, for there are substantial costs associated with obtaining price stability. These costs may be seen from two perspectives. From the viewpoint of the total economy there is the reduction in real output that results when employment falls. From the viewpoint of each of those who are made unemployed, the cost is staggering. These considerations are particularly weighty; during the 1960s social unrest surfaced in the United States. Minority groups were seeking to enter the mainstream of American life and their entry depended heavily on their ability to find and maintain employment. Members of minority groups are most likely to become unemployed as unemployment grows; rising unemployment could easily be interpreted as society's breaking faith with these groups and be the cause of justifiable social unrest.

The stabilization policy choices that the United States faced in the last part of the 1960s were particularly difficult ones. The authors believe that greater weight should be given to the employment variable than to the price variable as the object of stabilization policy. When policy conflicts arise this does not mean that we seek inflation; instead, we believe that if moderate inflation can only be eliminated through substantial increases in unemployment then the cost is too high. Policy steps should be taken that will, over a longer time span, alter structural conditions to shift the Phillips curve toward the origin. Structural changes would permit removal of inflationary pressures without a corresponding rise in the rate of unemployment; in the short run the inflation must be tolerated.

The discretionary fiscal policies of the last half of the 1960s, on balance, seem to have failed. Two administrations did state their intention to check inflation and yet were unable expeditiously to accomplish this goal.[22] The greatest failure of fiscal policy during these years, however, stems from the political environment within which it had to be implemented. Irrespective of the correctness of the priorities for stabilization policy in these years, once a stabilization policy was recommended, the administration was remiss in its pursuit and Congress was reluctant to provide the authority for action. If discretionary fiscal policy is to play a key role in promoting economic stability, we are forced to return to an earlier conclusion: the President should be granted the authority to vary personal and corporate income tax rates within a specified range in order that policy actions may be taken promptly once their need is perceived.

---

[22] Without the surtax even larger amounts of inflation would probably have occurred, and to the degree this is the case, fiscal policy succeeded. For a critique of fiscal policy at the end of the 1960s *see* Robert Eisner, "What Went Wrong," *Journal of Political Economy*, May/June 1971 and Robert A. Mundell, *The Dollar and the Policy Mix: 1971* (Princeton, N.J.: International Finance Section, Department of Economics, Princeton University, 1971).

18

PUBLIC DEBTS AND DEBT MANAGEMENT

Government debts are a frequent subject of debate among politicians and among the public. These debates often reflect a preconditioned reaction based on the belief that deficit financing is proper or unsound per se, and the argumentation is not supported by reasoned analysis. What a paradox there is in the thinking of the little old lady who simultaneously insists that deficit spending is immoral and that all true patriots should buy savings bonds. Our purpose in this chapter is not primarily to investigate the reasons for public indebtedness, but rather to examine a number of issues that arise from its existence. What are the implications of public debts for their holders as creditors and governments as debtors; what impact do government securities have on the financial sector of the American economy? The chapter is organized to take up federal government debt separately from state and local government debts, because some of the issues related to government indebtedness are different between these levels of governments; this division should not, however, obscure the fact that government debts are similar irrespective of the level of the debtor government.

FEDERAL GOVERNMENT DEBT

Federal debt, unlike the debts of state and local governments, is generally not created for the explicit purpose of financing capital expenditures.[1] At least four reasons for changes in the federal government's indebtedness may be discerned: First, change in the size of the federal debt is sometimes required for stabilization purposes. Second, deficit financing sometimes occurs because higher taxes to finance necessary expenditures are unacceptable. This occurred in the United States during World War II. Capital expenditures were not being financed and macroeconomic stability did not call for increased aggregate demand. During the war the civilian labor force was being asked to work overtime and women were induced to enter the labor force; most citizens were newly subject to personal income taxation. Personal tax rates were raised and the base was broadened, but tax revenues remained inadequate to finance the total war effort. Raising taxes further, it was feared, would curtail the supply of labor at precisely the time additional labor effort was required. Thus bonds were issued in lieu of even higher taxes, and rationing was used to allocate resources as demand exceeded supply at government controlled prices. Third, budget receipts and outlays sometimes differ from the levels expected at the time budgets are prepared because of fluctuations in the economy's level of activity; unplanned increases or decreases in the size of the public debt may result as these unplanned budget imbalances are financed. Fourth, federal government receipts are subject to seasonal fluctuations while outlays tend to be relatively stable from month to month. Personal income tax receipts, for example, are seasonally high in April as taxpayers file previous year returns and settle their tax liabilities. In months when receipts exceed outlays, maturing federal securities are often not refunded and there is a short-term reduction in the outstanding indebtedness of the federal government.[2]

In Chapter 11 we examined the ownership of government securities. At the end of 1969, $89 billion of the federal debt was held by trust and public enterprise accounts within the federal government itself and another $57 billion was held by the Federal Reserve System. That part of the gross federal debt held outside the government, including holdings by the Federal Reserve System, was shown, by type of owner, in Table 11.14. As shown in Chapter 12, most federal securities are issued by the Treasury and these issues are known as the *public debt* of the federal government. The remainder of this section is concerned only with the interest-bearing component of this

---

[1] Two exceptions come to mind: both the Louisiana Purchase and the construction of the Panama Canal were financed with receipts obtained from bonds sold for the specific purpose.

[2] See any issue of the *Federal Reserve Bulletin* or the *Treasury Bulletin* for data pertaining to this dimension of federal government finance.

public debt.[3] The composition of the interest-bearing public debt of the United States government, by type of security, at the end of 1969 is shown in Table 18.1. There are two basic types of federal interest-bearing securities: those issued to the public and special issues. *Special issues* are securities issued directly to United States government public enterprise accounts and trust funds as they invest their surpluses (public enterprises and trust funds also held public issues of Treasury securities).[4] *Public issues* are both marketable and nonmarketable securities; marketable issues include bills, notes, and bonds.[5] *Treasury bills* have a maturity of one year or less at their time of issue; they carry no coupon rate of interest but instead are sold at a weekly auction.[6] Notes and bonds, by contrast, carry a coupon. *Notes* have a length to maturity of from one to seven years at their time of issue, and *bonds* have maturities at their time of issue in excess of seven years.[7] When the Treasury wishes to sell an issue of notes or bonds, the terms of the issue —price, coupon rate, and length to maturity—are announced to the public and subscriptions invited on or before the announced date of issue. Buyers can subscribe through most commercial banks and brokerage houses. If the issue is oversubscribed, purchasers of large amounts will receive a prorated share of their subscription. If the Treasury misjudges the market so that less than the entire amount of the issue is subscribed for, the Federal Reserve

---

[3] *Noninterest-bearing securities* are primarily of two types: (1) some matured securities have not been presented for redemption by their holders; and more importantly (2), special noninterest-bearing securities have been issued to the International Monetary Fund. The total noninterest-bearing component of the public debt as of December 31, 1969, was $2 billion. *Treasury Bulletin*, March 1970, pp. 22–23. Agency debt is not further considered in this section because it is not included in the data readily available in published form.

[4] At the end of 1969, $23.7 billion of special issues were held by the social security trust fund, $17.9 billion by federal employees' retirement funds, $5.8 billion by the veterans life insurance fund, $3.2 billion by the Railroad Retirement Fund, $10.7 billion by the unemployment insurance trust fund, and $9.7 billion by other funds. *Treasury Bulletin*, January 1970, p. 24.

[5] Certificates, or certificates of indebtedness, are a one-year security sold with a coupon rather than at auction. In the mid-1960s the Treasury abandoned this type of security. Prior to March 1970, all marketable Treasury securities had a $1000 face value. Since March 1970, bills have been issued only in $10,000 denominations.

[6] Bills are typically due on Thursdays. Sometimes the Treasury issues *tax anticipation bills* due on the day corporations are required to make quarterly corporate income tax payments. These bills are commonly bought by corporations who earn interest until they mature and take redemption by submitting the bill in payment of taxes. Commercial banks may buy Treasury bills by making credits to the Treasury's tax and loan account in the commercial bank. With fractional reserve banking this means that the commercial banks must pay only a fraction of the bill's price until the Treasury transfers funds to its Federal Reserve Account for disbursement.

[7] Prior to the mid-1960s notes had maturities of from one to five years and bonds were securities that were issued with more than five years to maturity.

Table 18.1 **Interest-Bearing Public Debt (Millions of dollars)**

End of Fiscal Year or Month	Total Interest-bearing Public Debt	Public Issues: Total Public Issues	Marketable: Total	Marketable: Bills	Marketable: Certif-icates	Marketable: Notes	Marketable: Treasury Bonds	Nonmarketable: Total	Nonmarketable: U.S. Savings Bonds	Nonmarketable: Treasury Bonds Invest-ment Series	Nonmarketable: Depos-itary Bonds	Nonmarketable: Foreign Series Secur-ities[a]	Nonmarketable: Foreign Currency Series Secur-ities[b]	Nonmarketable: Other[c]	Special Issues
1961	285,672	240,629	187,148	36,723	13,338	56,257	80,830	53,481	47,514	5830	117	—	—	19	45,043
1962	294,442	249,503	196,072	42,036	13,547	65,464	75,025	53,431	47,607	4727	138	860	75	25	44,939
1963	301,954	257,153	203,508	47,230	22,169	52,145	81,964	53,645	48,314	3921	103	648	630	29	44,801
1964	307,357	260,729	206,489	50,740	—	67,284	88,464	54,240	49,299	3546	103	392	832	68	46,627
1965	313,113	264,463	208,695	53,665	—	52,549	102,481	55,768	50,043	3256	59	1132	1137	141	48,650
1966	315,431	264,311	209,127	54,929	1,652	50,649	101,897	55,183	50,537	2692	44	817	957	137	51,120
1967	322,286	266,131	210,672	58,535	5,610	49,108	97,418	55,459	51,213	2589	45	624	890	97	56,155
1968	344,401	284,874	226,592	64,440	—	71,073	91,079	58,282	51,712	2516	30	2001	1740	282	59,526
1969	351,729	284,940	226,107	68,356	—	78,946	78,805	58,833	51,711	2459	28	1703	2367	564	66,790
Dec. 1969	366,221	295,213	235,863	80,571	—	85,414	69,878	59,350	51,549	2426	26	1765	1996	1587	71,008

[a] Consists of certificates of indebtedness, Treasury notes beginning January 1963, and Treasury bonds beginning September 1964, sold to foreign governments for U. S. Dolla's.

[b] Consists of the dollar equivalent of Treasury certificates of indebtedness; Treasury bonds beginning October 1962; and Treasury notes beginning November 1966 issued and payable in designated foreign currencies.

[c] Includes Treasury bonds, Rural Electrification Administration series beginning July 1960; retirement plan bonds beginning January 1963; Treasury certificates beginning June 1963; Treasury bonds beginning January 1964; and U. S. savings notes beginning May 1967.

SOURCE: *Treasury Bulletin*, March 1970, p. 23, Table 3.

System will buy the remainder of the issue so as not to embarrass the Treasury. This is, in part, what is meant by saying that one of the functions of the Federal Reserve System is to maintain an orderly market for Treasury securities. Only occasionally in recent years has the Treasury arranged for an entire issue of notes or bonds to be underwritten by a syndicate of investment bankers in the manner most corporate and municipal bonds are marketed.

Since the mid-1960s, as the size of the interest-bearing public debt has grown, the volume of outstanding bills and notes has sharply increased, while the volume of bonds outstanding has declined. This is at least partially attributable to the fact Congress has set an interest rate ceiling of 4.25 percent on United States government marketable bonds. In the fully employed American economy of the late 1960s, market rates of interest exceeded this level and new bond issues were impossible since 4.25 percent bonds could not be marketed at par. Thus as bonds matured they were refunded with bills or notes. In 1971 Congress granted the Treasury authority to sell up to $10 billion of bonds at rates above the ceiling; some 10 year bonds carrying a 7 percent coupon were issued in August 1971.

Congress has also placed a ceiling on the size of the public debt; indebtedness in excess of this ceiling is legally the financial responsibility of the Secretary of the Treasury. This debt ceiling has been increased several times since World War II despite the political unpopularity of doing so. In the absence of expanding the debt ceiling Congress would have to enact tax increases or cut back expenditures, and both these courses of action are often politically even less attractive. Neither the interest nor debt ceilings make any sense; both should be repealed.

The nonmarketable interest-bearing public debt consists primarily of *savings bonds* sold to households; approximately two-thirds of all United States government securities held by households are savings bonds; corporations and financial institutions, rather than households, are the principal buyers of marketable United States government securities. During World War I *liberty bonds* were sold to households as marketable securities; as interest rates rose in the postwar period, the market value of these unmatured securities fell and many bondholders, unacquainted with fluctuations in financial markets, felt cheated by their government. Thus, to protect their buyers against capital loss if interest rates rose, nonmarketable *victory bonds* were issued to help finance World War II; throughout the post-World War II period, savings bonds have remained nonmarketable issues. Savings bonds may be held beyond their due date and continue to accrue interest. Savings bonds are not subject to the interest ceiling that applies to marketable Treasury bonds.

In addition to savings bonds, several other nonmarketable securities are issued. *Nonmarketable treasury bonds* are a special series issued to commercial banks in 1951 in exchange for other securities. They carry a 2.5 percent coupon and are convertible into a 1.5 percent marketable security with a five-year maturity at their owners' option. They are scheduled to mature in 1980. *Depositary bonds* are special issues held by deposit funds (see Chapter 12). As the United States incurred balance of payments deficits in the 1960s foreign governments were sometimes persuaded to buy interest-earning United States government securities rather than monetary gold; some of the securities sold to foreign governments were payable in dollars (foreign series securities) and others were payable in foreign currency (foreign currency series securities) to prevent their buyers from facing capital losses in the event of a devaluation of the dollar; these latter securities are the Roosa bonds discussed in Chapter 11.

Marketable securities have maturity dates specified when the securities are first sold. Table 18.2 gives data on the distribution of marketable United States government securities by maturity and type of owner as of December 31, 1969. These data show the maturity structure of the marketable securities held by United States government agencies and trust funds as well as the Federal Reserve System. Holdings of the United States government securities by state and local governments are of interest. Long-term securities are held by their public employee pension funds; bills are often held as these governments invest that portion of their tax receipts that is in excess of funds needed to finance current outlays when taxes are paid.

Federal government securities are widely held in part because they are regarded as riskless; no one believes the federal government will fail to make scheduled interest and principal payments on its debt. The holder of marketable United States government securities does run the risk that market prices will decline; hence if he wishes to sell before maturity he may suffer a capital loss. Of course, if prices advance, he can sell at a capital gain. This type of risk holds for all types of marketable securities. Many hold federal securities in lieu of cash since cash balances draw no interest income. The government bill market is particularly important in this respect because corporations, financial institutions, state and local governments, and even individuals who periodically have substantial cash balances prefer to hold interest earning bills. There is an active, over-the-counter secondary market in United States government securities, particularly bills, centered in New York City, where a few specialized dealers make markets in these securities. The existence of these markets makes United States government securities highly liquid; that is, a holder can readily sell a security to someone else if he does not wish to hold to maturity.

Whenever federal trust funds and public enterprise accounts are in surplus, their excess of receipts over outlays is invested in United States government securities. Most payments into trust funds commit the federal government to making outlays in future years; this is true, for example, of social

Table 18.2 Ownership of Marketable Securities, By Maturity, December 31, 1969
(Par value in millions of dollars)

		Within 1 Year			1–5	5–10	10–20	Over 20
	Total	Total	Bills	Other	Years	Years	Years	Years
All holders	235,863	118,124	80,571	37,553	73,301	20,026	8358	16,054
U.S. Government agencies & trust funds	16,295	2,321	812	1,509	6,006	2,472	2059	3,438
Federal Reserve Banks	57,154	36,023	22,265	13,758	12,810	7,642	224	453
Held by private investors	162,414	79,780	57,494	22,286	54,485	9,912	6075	12,164
Commercial banks	45,173	15,104	6,727	8,377	24,692	4,399	564	414
Mutual savings banks	2,931	501	149	352	1,251	263	203	715
Insurance companies	6,152	868	419	449	1,808	253	1197	2,028
Nonfinancial corporations	5,007	3,157	2,082	1,075	1,766	63	12	8
Savings and loan associations	3,851	808	269	539	1,916	357	329	441
State and local governments	13,909	6,416	5,200	1,216	2,853	524	1225	2,893
All others	85,391	52,926	42,648	10,278	20,199	4,053	2545	5,665

SOURCE: *Federal Reserve Bulletin*, November 1970, p. A43.

security contributions, veterans life insurance, and the pensions of government employees. Thus, although receipts have exceeded outlays from these funds, at some time in the future, this may not be the case and that part of the debt that is held within the government will either have to be retired or sold to the public. Suppose all the federal budget except a trust fund is in balance. If the trust fund is in surplus, the federal budget is in surplus; the total outstanding debt would not change but the value of securities held by the public would decrease as the trust fund invests its surplus by making purchases of public issues. Conversely when the trust fund is in deficit, the total budget is in a deficit position; gross federal debt remains unchanged but that part of the debt held by the public would increase as the trust fund sells securities to finance its outlays.

Servicing the federal debt. The federal government as a debtor must service its debt. *Debt service* expenses include the interest payments that must be made on outstanding securities and the payments of principal that must be made from budget surpluses if the debt is to be retired, or from the proceeds from the sale of new issues if the maturing debt is to be refunded. Refunding operations are considered as part of debt management in a subsequent section. Interest payments on outstanding securities may be a significant budget outlay. We saw in Chapter 10 that interest payments were the principal federal government expenditure in the early years of our nation's history; in fiscal year 1969 interest outlays by the federal government were $15.8 billion, as shown in Table 12.2.

By making an analogy with households some argue that government budgets must be balanced; the balance need not be annual but surely must be struck over time. Just as the household must limit its expenditures to its income, so must a government limit its expenditures to receipts from taxes, fees, and user charges; just as households must retire any debts they incur, so should government retire its debt. This argument overlooks a fundamental difference between households and governments; household debts are the legal responsibility of the borrower whose lifetime is finite; thus personal debts must be retired during a lifetime. Governments like corporations, by contrast, expect to last forever and thus may carry debts permanently.

Whether or not debts are a source of financial difficulty depends on the debtor's ability to meet interest and principal payments. In the private sector, as a man's income rises he is able to carry larger debts because the income from which he makes interest and principal payments has risen. The same should also be true of governments; as economic growth occurs and tax bases expand, governments have additional revenues available to finance additional expenditures, including debt service expenses. The ability of debtors to carry debt is not a function of size of the debt alone; other expenditure obligations and the level of income from which all expenses must be paid also are important. Thus, a government's ability to carry debt is related to its ability to raise revenue and the other expenditures that it makes; the fact that government debts increase is not, per se, harmful and, conversely, neither is it possible for a government to increase its indebtedness without limit.

Federal government debt as a share of gross national product has declined since World War II although the size of that debt has grown. Over the same period, interest payments as a share of gross national product have not experienced as sharp a decline since interest rates have substantially increased. Federal government *net interest payments,* that is, payments exclusive of those to public enterprise and trust fund accounts, as a percent of gross national product, are given in Table 18.3. In a sense, this may be

Table 18.3 **Federal Government Net Interest Payments**

Calendar Year	Amount (Billions)	As a Percent of GNP
1929	$ .4	.43
1934	.6	.91
1939	.6	.71
1944	2.4	1.15
1949	4.4	1.72
1954	5.0	1.37
1959	6.4	1.33
1964	8.3	1.32
1969	13.1	1.40

SOURCE: Office of Business Economics, U.S. Department of Commerce, *The National Income and Product Accounts of the U.S., 1929–1965, Statistical Tables* (Washington, D.C.: Government Printing Office, 1966), pp. 52–53, and *Survey of Current Business,* March 1970, p. 11.

taken as a measure of the ability for the federal government to carry its debt; whatever the nation's debt service charges are they must be raised by taxes paid from the nation's income. Although taxes clearly could not be raised to one hundred percent of national income, the fact the federal government net interest payments as share of gross national product have not risen since the end of the war, although the size of the debt has increased, is surely reassuring that the debt outstanding at the start of the 1970s is not leading us to national bankruptcy. This is not to say that some substantially larger debt and debt service charge might not be unmanageable and the source of serious financial difficulty for the United States government.

Debt burdens. The implications of a national debt do not end with the requirement that it be serviced. Government securities constitute assets for their owners. If the public expenditures financed from the sale of bonds had alternatively been financed by taxation, the wealth of the private sector would have been less, to the extent that taxpayers reduced their saving, and private absorption of the nation's output would have been less if consumption was cut.[8] Americans have never been forced to buy government securities. Savers voluntarily purchase newly issued government securities rather than acquire other types of assets. As this occurs the availability of funds to finance private investment is reduced; as a result, some new issues of private securities may not be marketed and private investment is reduced. If public securities are being issued to finance capital expenditures, then the nation's stock of public capital is increased and private capital is reduced; in future years the economy as a whole will receive greater output from publicly owned capital goods and less from privately owned capital. By contrast, if public expenditures are for current consumption rather than capital formation, then in the first instance the private capital stock is reduced without any corresponding increase in the stock of public capital and the economy's future productive capacity may be impaired.[9] The effects are altered if the monetary sector, simultaneously with the government issue, creates additional liquidity. As government securities are sold there is then no concomitant reduction in the volume of private securities marketed and, provided the economy's capacity permits both the additional public and private spending without inflation, there will be no reallocation of resources away from private investment.

These considerations all bear on what has traditionally been called the burden of the debt.[10] One view is that the burden of the debt falls on the generation in which the debt is incurred, while another takes the position that the burden must be shifted forward to the generation that services the debt.[11] Both views look at the incidence of debt service charges; the first

---

[8] If sale of bonds makes the wealth of the private sector greater than it would have been had taxes been imposed, then consumption spending in later years may increase due to this wealth effect as higher levels of financial assets encourage household consumption.

[9] During some of the war years, net private domestic investment was negative, thereby diminishing the economy's productive capacity in the postwar years. But, the war was won.

[10] We have refrained from using the term burden since public revenues are typically raised to finance expenditures from which citizens benefit; public revenues are the prices we pay for those things we buy through the public sector. As was also the case with taxation we prefer not to discuss burdens since the term itself implies a judgment that is not the result of analysis.

[11] For the first view, *see* Abba P. Lerner, *The Economics of Control* (New York: Macmillan, 1944), chapter 24; for the second, *see* James M. Buchanan, *Public Principles of Public Debt* (Homewood, Ill.: Richard D. Irwin, 1958). *See also* James M.

sees incidence collectively from a generational viewpoint, while the second sees incidence from the perspective of separate citizens within a generation. In the first view, since debts are presumed to be held by citizens within the jurisdiction of the debtor government, debt service charges are seen as a transfer between one citizen and another; in this sense we owe it to ourselves, and the generation that services the debt is seen surrendering nothing.[12] This first view also sees the generation that buys new issues of government securities burdened by surrendering command over real resources to the government; debt service charges, in this view, involve nothing more than intragenerational transfers of purchasing power and, since the debt servicing generations collectively surrender nothing, no burden is incurred by these generations.

By contrast, the second view examines debt burdens from the vantage point of individual citizens rather than generations of citizens. Since American governments do not compel their citizens to purchase securities, they are competitively sold in financial markets and are voluntarily acquired as citizens purchase financial assets. Hence, the buyer of newly issued government securities cannot be seen incurring any burden as he voluntarily makes his decision; if government securities had not been offered for sale, he would have bought private securities, held cash balances, purchased real assets, or made consumption expenditures. Whatever interest income he derives from government securities as the debt is serviced is the expected return that led him to hold this type of asset rather than another. Any burden associated with government debts must, therefore, be borne by the taxpayer who finances debt service charges. If, instead, expenditures had been financed with taxes, their costs would have fallen on citizens in the taxpaying generation. Thus, in this second view the burden of the debt is shifted forward to taxpayers in the generation when government debts are serviced.

Neither argument considers what use the borrowing government makes of the revenues acquired from the sale of securities. On the basis of a benefit approach it may be suitable for government capital expenditures to be financed by borrowing; those who are taxed to service government debts are incurring costs as they derive benefits from publicly owned capital, and their burden is a perfectly proper method of charging for these services. The prices we pay for telephone service or electricity, for instance, include an amount

---

Ferguson (ed.), *The Public Debt and Future Generations* (Chapel Hill: University of North Carolina Press, 1964).

[12] The distribution of ownership of outstanding federal and state and local government securities was given in Table 11.14, lines 18 and 19. If all taxpayers were bondholders, tax payments to meet debt service charges would be returned to the taxpayers as interest payments. However, since this may not be presumed, some taxpayers may perceive debt service expenditures as imposing real costs from which no benefits are received in exchange.

necessary to cover the interest payments and amortize the debts of the private supplier; just as these prices are not usually spoken of as a burden, neither should such payments on public debts be seen as burdens. This is especially true of the debts of state and local governments, most of which are incurred for the financing of capital expenditures.

When public capital is created resources may be diverted from private capital formation. As this occurs there is a long-run shift away from private toward public provision of goods and services, and future generations may have smaller amounts of private goods and larger amounts of publicly provided goods and services from which to choose.[13] This narrowing of options in the private sector in the debt servicing generation has also been seen as a burden of government indebtedness.

Debt management. Debt management issues are basically different from questions pertaining to the size of the debt. Once a decision had been made to increase a government's indebtedness an additional decision must be made regarding the type and maturity date of the security that will be issued. If public debts are to be reduced a choice must be made regarding which outstanding securities to retire. If a government's debt remains unchanged, maturing securities must be refunded and the type and maturity of the refunding issue must be selected. Probably no government whose debt is significant wants all its outstanding securities to mature simultaneously because refunding a particularly large issue is likely to be more difficult than refunding one of more moderate size, or because running the budget surplus necessary for debt retirement is likely to be financially and politically difficult. Imagine the impact on the nation's financial markets and the Congressional response if the net federal government debt were to be retired or refunded at one time. Decisions regarding the types of securities issued, their maturities, and other related issues, constitute *debt management.*

At least two objectives of debt management are usually discerned. The first is to manage debts to minimize the interest expenses of the debtor government, and the second is to adjust the length to maturity of the debt to affect the economy's liquidity in a manner consistent with stabilization goals. The first of these objectives certainly motivates state and local governments, and is also a possible goal for the federal government; the second objective is limited to the federal government for only national governments pursue explicit stabilization policies. We first consider the objective of minimizing interest costs, returning later in this section to the liquidity question.

---

[13] No implications are intended in this discussion about the efficiency of public as opposed to private investment, and the resulting size of the nation's real product as this substitution occurs.

Throughout most of the post-World War II period, short-term interest rates have been below long-term interest rates. There are reasons to expect this relationship.[14] First, there are considerations of risk and liquidity: the purchase of long-term securities requires the lender to part with funds for an extended period of time if he holds the security to maturity; the holder bears the risk that the market price of the security may decline and he can gain liquidity, that is, sell the security for cash, only by taking a capital loss. Changes in the overall level of interest rates cause long-term bonds to fluctuate in price more than short-term securities, hence long-term securities usually command higher interest rates than short-term issues. Second, if the long-run expectation is for rising interest rates, then long-term rates will exceed short-term interest rates. Finally, the market for U.S. government securities is, to some extent, segmented: some holders (corporations and commercial banks) prefer bills and others (insurance companies) prefer bonds; thus, interest rate differentials in these markets may persist and widen or narrow depending on changes in supply and demand within the short- and long-term markets.

Given the postwar tendency for long-term rates to exceed short-term rates, the federal government might be expected to issue only short-term securities to minimize interest costs. There are several reasons for not following this course of action. Over time both short- and long-term interest rates may rise and fall. Current long-term interest rates, when interest rates are low, may be less than the short-term interest rates that will prevail when interest rates are high; long-term interest rates in the mid- and late-1950s and early 1960s were below the short-term rates that prevailed in the late 1960s, for example. Thus, the objective of minimizing interest costs may require placing the government's debt in long-term securities when interest rates are low in order to avoid the necessity of having to refund the debt in periods of high interest rates. Likewise, in periods of cyclically high interest rates, governments would certainly want to issue short-term securities; not only are their rates below long-term rates but also their early maturity means they may perhaps be refunded at lower rates. In addition, there are administrative costs associated with the frequent refunding operations that occur when a substantial part of the government's debt is in short-term securities.[15] During fiscal year 1968 the value of marketable securities out-

---

[14] The yield curve for U. S. government securities is presented in the monthly *Treasury Bulletin*. Whatever relationship exists between the market yields on securities and their term to maturity is referred to as the *yield curve* or *term structure of interest rates*.

[15] The longest term security of all is the *perpetuity*; such securities never mature and are retired only as the issuing government buys them on the open market. Perpetuities, known as *consols*, were once issued by the British government and some are still outstanding. Modern governments do not issue perpetuities.

standing increased by $15.9 billion; during that same year the Treasury issued new bills and notes valued at $203.5 billion.[16] This excess of new issues over the increase in the face value of outstanding securities represents necessary refunding operations.

The United States Treasury offerings typically are larger than any offerings by corporations or state and local governments. The size of any Treasury issue thus has a significant impact on conditions in and the stability of financial markets. The federal government is concerned with the maturity structure of its marketable securities; excessive activity at any one time may disrupt financial markets. In addition, the shorter the maturity of government securities, the more often government issues must be placed in the security markets. In recognition of the potential impact of new offerings on security markets, and in the face of rising interest rates, *advance refunding* as a technique of debt management was introduced at the end of the 1950s.[17] During World War II many bonds with a 2.5 percent coupon had been issued; as interest rates rose in the postwar years, their owners felt locked-in as liquidation of these securities prior to their maturity date would entail taking capital losses. In order to avoid marketing new issues the Treasury offered to exchange certain unmatured bonds for new bonds or notes with a greater time to maturity. These new securities carried a higher coupon than 2.5 percent but lower than that which would have to be paid on a newly marketed public issue. This offer was attractive to many investors who traditionally like to hold long-term securities (pension funds, for example), and did permit the Treasury marginally to lengthen its debt without having to make new market placements. However, advance refunding occurs at the expense of increased interest payments in the short run; the exchange entails replacing a 2.5 percent coupon (which in some instances had as much as ten years to run) with a higher coupon. With the high interest rates of the last part of the 1960s, the advance refunding of securities that would have matured during this time undoubtedly did reduce Treasury interest costs in the long run; in the absence of ability to forecast long-term interest rates the procedure, however, does validly remain subject to criticism.

A second objective of debt management is to promote macroeconomic stability. The maturity of the debt as a factor influencing the economy's liquidity is the key to advancing this policy goal. Short-term securities are more liquid than long-term securities. Increased liquidity is seen as having a buoyant effect on the economy while reduced liquidity is viewed as a depressant; thus in periods of recession the maturity of the public debt should

---

[16] Computed from *Annual Report of the Secretary of the Treasury for the Fiscal Year Ended June 30, 1968* (Washington, D.C.: Government Printing Office, 1969), pp. 19 and 150–154.

[17] Joseph Scherer, "Advance Refunding: A Technique of Debt Management," in *Essays in Money and Credit* (New York: Federal Reserve Bank of New York, 1964).

be shortened and in periods of inflation the debt should be lengthened.[18] Pursuit of this policy requires debt management actions just the opposite of those required to minimize interest costs, for interest rates tend to rise during an inflationary period and fall in periods of recession.

Debt management may play a domestic stabilization role but should not be overrated. Studies relating the stock of liquid assets to levels of consumption and investment are inconclusive and, in any event, shortening or lengthening the maturity of the public debt will have but small marginal impact on this stock of assets.[19] Balance of payments equilibrium is also a goal of stabilization policy. In 1962 "Operation Twist" was inaugurated whereby the Treasury and Federal Reserve System aimed at nudging up short-term interest rates relative to long-term rates in the belief that short-term capital flows were a principal cause of American balance of payments difficulties; this relative change in interest rates was intended to keep short-term funds at home. Thus, bills were issued in substantially increased amounts with their increased supply, relative to that of other government securities, being designed to nudge up short-term relative to long-term rates.[20] Balance of payments deficits continued despite "Operation Twist."

Quite obviously, fiscal policy, debt management, and monetary policy should all be coordinated to advance national policy objectives. However, placing prime emphasis on cyclical stabilization as the objective of debt management seems unrealistic; in the absence of clear indicators that other

[18] In 1954 the Committee for Economic Development advanced this objective of debt management policy. *See* Committee for Economic Development, *Managing the Federal Debt* (New York: 1954). Data on the average length to maturity are regularly published in the *Treasury Bulletin*. At the end of World War II the average length to maturity of marketable public debt securities was 7 years, 11 months; this had decreased along a fluctuating path to 3 years, 8 months at the end of 1969.

[19] Warren L. Smith, *Debt Management in the United States*, Joint Economic Committee, 86th Congress, 2nd Session (Washington, D.C.: Government Printing Office, 1960).

[20] As indicated in Table 18.1, from 1961 through 1964 the increase in the value of bills outstanding constituted a significant part of the increase in marketable public debt. Bonds could have been issued in greater amounts at this time but were not. That relative interest rates on federal government securities did change during this period is seen in the following data taken from the *Federal Reserve Bulletin*:

Market Yields (Percent)

	3-month bill	Bonds
1962	2.77	3.95
1963	3.16	4.00
1964	3.54	4.15

For the administration's balance of payments program, see *The Economic Report of the President, 1964* (Washington, D.C.: Government Printing Office, 1964), pp. 127–130.

actions are required, it seems reasonable to expect the Treasury to adopt interest expense minimization as the objective of debt management.[21]

STATE AND LOCAL GOVERNMENT DEBTS

Most state and local government borrowing is to finance capital expenditures. In 1968 state and local governments issued a total of $16.4 billion new long-term securities for the following purposes:[22]

Schools	$4.7 Billion
Water and sewer	1.9
Highway, bridge, and tunnel	1.6
Housing	.5
Industrial aid	1.6
Other	6.1

In addition to borrowing to finance capital outlays, state and local governments often incur short-term debts in anticipation of tax receipts. Local governments rely on property taxes that are paid annually or semiannually, although outlays must regularly be made as salaries, for example, are paid. Thus, during the month before taxes are paid, receipts may be less than outlays. If this happens the government must borrow in anticipation of tax receipts. This is usually done by taking a direct loan from a local commercial bank rather than by floating a security issue. Conversely, in the month property taxes are paid receipts exceed outlays; this temporary surplus is often invested by state and local governments if not needed to repay tax anticipation borrowing.[23]

---

[21] It would be a mistake to interpret this goal as being advanced by selling special issues to trust and public enterprise accounts at less than market rates of interest. The smaller the earnings of these funds on their investments, the higher will be payroll taxes, user charges, and so on, and it is not correct to conclude that minimal interest payments and minimal cost are the same thing.

[22] The Daily Bond Buyer, *Statistics on State and Local Government Finance* (New York: 1969), p. 9. *The Daily Bond Buyer* is the best regularly published source of information on municipals. For extended discussion of state and local capital expenditures and their financing, see *State and Local Public Facility Needs and Financing,* Volume I, *Public Facility Needs*, and Volume 2, *Public Facility Financing*, Joint Economic Committee, 89th Congress, 2nd Session (Washington, D.C.: Government Printing Office, 1966).

[23] State and local government general funds owned $2.2 billion of municipal bonds at the end of 1969 (see Table 11.14). Some additional municipal bonds were held by state and local government pension funds. This is financially foolish since these securities, because of their tax exempt status, carry a lower yield than either federal or corporate securities. Since the income of state and local governments is not taxable there is no rational reason why they should hold tax exempt securities.

Many state and local governments may not incur debts without the expressed authorization of the voters. In 1968, $8.7 billion of new long-term municipals were issued as a result of their approval in bond elections; in that same year voters rejected an additional $7.5 billion of new state and local long-term borrowing.[24] Bond elections are an instance where citizens participate directly in the selection of public policies.

State and local government securities are generally of two types: *general obligation bonds* that are payable from and secured by revenues derived from taxes, and *revenue bonds* that are payable from user charges and fees. Revenue bonds are a common means of financing such facilities as toll roads, bridges, water works, and electric plants, where user charges provide the revenues to cover operating costs and amortize the debt. Of the $16.4 billion of new state and local long-term borrowing in 1968, $6.7 billion was accomplished with revenue bonds and the remainder with general obligation securities.[25] State and local government bonds are usually *serial issues*; a fraction of the issue comes due for redemption each year until the entire issue is retired. Underwriting syndicates typically bid for new issues of municipals and are responsible for their marketing. The interest rate on new issues is of considerable concern to state and local governments because their officials are sensitive to the size of their debt service expenses. In some states there are constitutional or statutory limits on the rates of interest that can be paid. Many capital projects may be cancelled or postponed, and these governments sometimes do adjust their borrowing plans because of money market conditions. Primarily because of high interest rates, nearly $1 billion of new bond issues were cancelled or postponed by state and local governments between September 3, 1968, and August 8, 1969.[26]

The combined indebtedness of state and local governments is clearly manageable in an economy whose gross national product is as large as that of the United States in the 1970s. At the start of this decade their annual interest payments exceeded $3 billion; although these interest payments have been rising both absolutely and as a percent of gross national product in the years since World War II, there is no evidence to suggest that interest payments of this amount are unmanageable.[27] This is not, however, true for

---

[24] *Statistics on State and Local Government Finance, op. cit.*, p. 16.

[25] *Ibid.*, p. 5. Of the $16.4 billion of new long-term issues only $ .1 was for refunding operations.

[26] *The Daily Bond Buyer*, August 12, 1969, p. 22. For a discussion of the literature and some empirical findings on the sensitivity of municipal issues to interest rates, *see* Paul McGouldrick, "The Effect of Credit Conditions on State and Local Bond Sales and Capital Outlays Since World War II," in *Public Facility Financing, op. cit.*

[27] State and local government interest payments are shown as only $ .1 billion in Table 11.6 because in national income accounts government interest payments are reported net of interest received. As may be seen from Table 11.14, state and local government general funds, at the end of 1969, held $37.9 billion of credit market instruments

each state and local government separately. Some may have exceeded their ability to service their debt. At the end of the 1960s almost none of the approximately $130 billion of state and local government securities outstanding was in default. Because these governments seldom default precise data are difficult to obtain. One study found only 30 instances of defaults in the post-World War II period; nineteen of these defaults were on revenue bonds where, primarily because of poor planning, the capital facility in its early years did not produce the expected flow of user charges and fees.[28]

(line 17) and $11.6 billion of time deposits at commercial banks (line 12); interest received on these assets, plus interest received on financial assets held by state and local government pension funds, is subtracted from interest paid on state and local government debts to obtain the figure for net interest paid by state and local governments in Table 11.6. See *Survey of Current Business,* July 1970, Table 3.13, for a reconciliation.

[28] Jackson Phillips and Roger Baum, "Post War Default Experience of Municipal Bonds," *Public Facility Financing, op. cit.*

19

MAINTAINING PERSONAL INCOME

During the 1960s Americans became aware that many within their society were impoverished. Recognized in the writings of such authors as Michael Harrington (*The Other America*), President Johnson's War on Poverty, proposals for a negative income tax, and President Nixon's Family Assistance Plan, poverty in America became a gnawing social and political issue. In most instances the American poor could not be considered impoverished by the standards of living in other parts of the world; instead, they were poor by American standards and, as such, were largely outside the mainstream of American life. As awareness of American poverty spread, the seeds of change were sown. The poor themselves, as well as their partisans in government and the private sector, sought amends. Political organization and power often accompanied the poor's quest for economic security; as American society groped for a more equitable distribution of income, the inflexibility of existing institutions sometimes resulted in the politics of confrontation.

In 1968 there were 50.5 million family

units in the United States with a medium income of $8632. In addition, there were 13.8 million unrelated individuals with a median income of $2786. Using the poverty guideline that the first member of a household requires $1500 for subsistence and that $500 is required for each additional member, Table 19.1

Table 19.1 **Number and Money Income (in 1968 prices) of Families and Unrelated Individuals, by Race of Head, 1960 and 1968**

	Families[a]		Unrelated Individuals[b]	
	1960	1968	1960	1968
Total (millions)	37.2	50.5	11.1	13.8
Median income	$4716	$8632	$2021	$2786
With incomes under $3000:				
Number (millions)	9.7	5.2	4.5	4.0
Percent	26.0	10.3	40.9	28.8
Total White (millions)	34.1	45.4	9.6	12.0
Median income	$4916	$8937	$2187	$2952
With incomes under $3000:				
Number (millions)	7.8	4.0	3.7	3.3
Percent	22.8	8.9	38.6	27.2
Total Negro and other races (millions)	3.1	5.1	1.5	1.8
Median income	$2514	$5590	$1332	$1999
With incomes under $3000:				
Number (millions)	1.9	1.2	0.8	0.7
Percent	60.0	22.8	55.2	39.5

[a] The term family refers to a group of two or more persons related by blood, marriage, or adoption and residing together; all such persons are considered members of the same family.

[b] The term unrelated individuals refers to persons 14 years old and over (other than inmates of institutions) who are not living with any relatives.

SOURCE: *Economic Report of the President, 1970* (Washington, D.C.: Government Printing Office, 1970), p. 200.

shows the number of impoverished families and unrelated individuals in the United States.[1] These data show that 10.3 percent of the families and 28.8 percent of the unrelated individuals lived in poverty in 1968. During the 1960s many escaped poverty but, at the start of the 1970s, millions of Americans remained poor.

[1] Robert Lampman, "Approaches to the Reduction of Poverty," *American Economic Review,* May 1965, discusses the poverty guideline. These are the amounts used when President Johnson declared the War on Poverty in 1964; during the course of the 1960s they were frequently revised upward as may be seen in various issues of the *Economic Report of the President.*

The sources of personal income as recorded in the national income accounts were listed in Chapter 11. In 1969, $65.5 billion in transfer payments were received by households and individuals as personal income (Table 11.4). Of these, $61.6 billion were made by governments, as shown in Table 11.5.[2] Retired government employees receive pensions that are government transfer payments, and although certainly important to the pensioner's welfare, pensions hardly qualify as a government program aimed at the elimination or alleviation of poverty. The same applies to some veterans benefits. Therefore, pension fund transfers (including the railroad retirement insurance plan) and veterans benefits are omitted from further consideration in this chapter. The major remaining payments are those made from social insurance funds by the federal government, and direct relief or welfare payments made by state and local governments. By and large these transfer payments, shown in Table 19.2, are made to low income families and individuals, and are one means by which public policy serves to support the personal income of the poor.

Table 19.2 **Government Transfer Payments to Persons, 1969 (Millions of dollars)**

Total government transfer payments to persons	61,561
Federal government	50,030
Old age, survivors, and disability insurance benefits	26,381
Hospital and medical insurance benefits	6,582
State unemployment insurance benefits	2,149
State and local government	11,531
Direct relief	6,640
Special types of public assistance	6,170
General assistance	470

SOURCE: Table 11.5.

Although the discussion that follows concentrates on financial assistance to the poor, other forms must be kept in mind. Maintaining income in the welfare sense, rather than in the cash flow sense of the national income accounts, requires consideration of benefits in kind. Food stamps that the poor may buy for less than their redemption value at retail food outlets, distribution of surplus agricultural commodities, school lunch programs, and subsidized housing all contribute to welfare. In fiscal year 1969 federal outlays for these programs were $1.6 billion.[3] The availability of medical care at

[2] Transfer payments not made by governments are primarily payments from private pension funds. In 1968, 3.8 million citizens received $5 billion of benefits from private pension plans. See *Social Security Bulletin,* April 1970, p. 43.

[3] *Special Analyses: Budget of the United States Government, Fiscal Year 1971* (Washington, D.C.: Government Printing Office, 1970), p. 190.

public health clinics contributes to welfare, as does the provision of special recreational programs, especially during summer months when children are out of school. In addition, such regulatory policies as mine and other industrial safety laws, and minimum wage legislation contribute welfare to some, although they do not require the outlay of public money other than for administration and enforcement.

Aid to farmers through Commodity Credit Corporation "purchase" of crops at support prices is not considered in this chapter although income maintenance was often intended when the support programs were initiated. These programs augment farmers' income, but most of the benefits accrue to the large, and often wealthy, farmer.[4] In 1970 Congress formally addressed itself to the relation between agricultural policy and income, and adopted legislation stipulating that no farmer could receive more than $55,000 of government money per crop per year. As a result many wealthy farmers divided their agricultural holdings into several smaller units, each of which qualified for a $55,000 payment.

Our discussion of personal income maintenance does not examine poverty in detail or lay out its causes. Factors such as discrimination, education, malnutrition, mental retardation, and, of course, un- or underemployment are the root of poverty, but their consideration is beyond the scope of this volume.[5] Rather, our purpose is to look at the principal, existing government income maintenance programs—their financing, benefits, and consequences—and to consider proposals for their reform. As this examination is made, the details of each program are again beyond the reaches of this volume even though such details as denial of welfare payments to families with a man in the house, sale of food stamps in minimum monthly amounts that exceed the available cash of eligible buyers, and procedures under which need for general assistance is determined, have a far-reaching impact. Having made these disclaimers we begin our examination of government transfer payments with the social security system.

SOCIAL SECURITY

Public policies to maintain personal income in the United States are largely an outcome of the 1930s. Prior to this time government employees generally obtained pension rights, workman's compensation laws were widely adopted,

[4] *See* Charles L. Schultze, *The Distribution of Farm Subsidies: Who Gets the Benefits?* (Washington, D.C.: The Brookings Institution, 1971).

[5] For analysis and interpretation of causes of poverty, *see* Lester Thurow, *Poverty and Discrimination* (Washington, D.C.: The Brookings Institution, 1969), chapter 3; K. Boulding, "Reflections on Poverty," in H. P. Miller (ed.), *Poverty American Style* (Belmont, Calif.: Wadsworth Publishing Company, 1966). *See also* Joseph A. Kershaw, *Government Against Poverty* (Washington, D.C.: The Brookings Institution, 1970).

and many states had a variety of programs to provide for the blind, deaf, orphans, and the insane. As our industrial society became increasingly complex, fewer and fewer could regard themselves as truly self-sufficient, though self-sufficiency remained the norm prior to the Depression. Most Americans did not consider government transfer payments proper. The events of the 1930s changed this. Widespread and protracted unemployment clearly demonstrated that the private sector had failed to provide either adequate job opportunities or income, and that some measure of collective responsibility for citizen well-being was required. As a result, legislation was proposed and enacted; President Roosevelt signed the Social Security Act on August 14, 1935.

The Social Security Act established two insurance programs: a federally sponsored program of old age benefits for retired workers, popularly known as social security, and a federal-state program of insurance under which unemployed, but unretired, workers would receive payments. These are *income replacement programs*; one qualifies for benefits when income from another source is lost; the level of benefits largely depends on a prior wage history rather than need. In addition, the Social Security Act provided for several types of categorical assistance; the federal government would make grants-in-aid to state and local governments for aid to the aged, the blind, and dependent children. These are *income support programs,* where benefits to qualified recipients are based on need. This section is divided to consider the social security system first; then unemployment insurance and categorical assistance are discussed. The section concludes with an examination of general assistance, the only major welfare program that is solely supported by state and local governments.[6]

OASDI. As first enacted the social security program was a system of insurance by which covered employees, and their employers, were taxed a fraction of the employee's wage; these taxes were deposited in a trust fund and earmarked for making insurance-type benefit payments to the employee

---

[6] For additional background material and analysis, *see* "Federal Income Security Programs," *Special Analyses: Budget of the United States Government, Fiscal Year 1971* (Washington, D.C.: Government Printing Office, 1970); the President's Commission on Income Maintenance Programs, *Technical Studies* (Washington, D.C.: Government Printing Office, 1970); U.S. Department of Health, Education, and Welfare, Social Security Administration, *Social Security Programs in the United States* (Washington, D.C.: Government Printing Office, 1968); Joseph A. Pechman, Henry J. Aaron, and Michael K. Taussig, *Social Security: Perspectives for Reform* (Washington, D.C.: The Brookings Institution, 1968); John C. Turnbull, C. Arthur Williams, Jr., and Earl F. Cheit, *Economic and Social Security*, 3d ed. (New York: The Roland Press, 1967); and Clair Wilcox, *Toward Social Welfare* (Homewood, Ill.: Richard D. Irwin, Inc., 1969). The monthly *Social Security Bulletin* contains discussion of various welfare issues and data pertaining to trust fund receipts and outlays.

upon his retirement. In 1939, the Act was modified to extend benefits to a covered employee's survivors. In 1956, the Act was further broadened by the creation of a new trust fund to provide disability insurance. As amended, the Social Security Act now provides old age, survivors, and disability insurance, commonly referred to as OASDI. Over the life of the system, benefit payments have been less than taxes deposited; at the start of 1970 the accumulated surplus in the old age, survivors, and disability insurance trust funds was $34.5 billion. When enacted, the Social Security Act covered approximately 50 percent of the labor force. During the life of the Act coverage has been expanded to include farm workers, household servants, and members of the armed forces; the self-employed, employees of state and local governments, and employees of nonprofit organizations may choose social security coverage. At the start of the 1970s nearly all employees other than most civilian employees of the federal government and some state and local government employees were covered by social security, as were a number of the self-employed; approximately 90 percent of the total labor force was covered.

Covered employees (or their survivors) receive benefits upon their retirement or disability. The amount of these benefits and the terms for qualification have changed several times since 1935. Basically, to qualify for maximum benefits at the start of the 1970s one must have earned $50 subject to social security taxes in one-fourth of the calendar quarters since 1950, or since age 21, or for a period of ten years. Persons who are covered for less than these periods or who retire prior to reaching age 65 (62 for women) receive less than the maximum benefits. For those who qualify, benefits are computed on the basis of their average monthly earnings subject to payroll taxation during those years of their employment histories that are counted in computing the benefit base. In 1970 the minimum benefit was $64 per month. Dependent's benefits are in addition to the covered employee's primary benefit. For the employee's spouse the additional benefit is 50 percent of the primary benefit. A sample schedule of monthly benefits is given in Table 19.3. Social security benefits, like most transfer payments, are excluded from personal income taxation.

Since the system's inception in 1935 annual social security benefits have grown to their 1969 level of $26.4 billion. These transfer payments certainly contribute to maintaining the personal income of the elderly and the disabled. Between 1950 and 1964 the real average monthly benefit increased 37 percent as did the average real wage in manufacturing.[7] Thus, as Congress

---

[7] Henry Aaron, "Benefits Under American Social Security," in Otto Eckstein (ed.), *Studies in the Economics of Income Maintenance* (Washington, D.C.: The Brookings Institution, 1967), p. 52.

Table 19.3 Examples of Monthly Cash Payments under Social Security, 1970

Average yearly earnings subject to social security taxation after 1950	$923 or less	$1800	$3000	$4200	$5400	$6600	$7800
1 Retired worker—65 or older; disabled worker—under 65	64.00	101.70	132.30	161.50	189.80	218.40	250.70
2 Wife 65 or older	32.00	50.90	66.20	80.80	94.90	109.20	125.40
3 Retired worker at 62	51.20	81.40	105.90	129.20	151.90	174.80	200.60
4 Wife at 62, no child	24.00	38.20	49.70	60.60	71.20	81.90	94.10
5 Widow at 62 or older	64.00	84.00	109.20	133.30	156.60	180.20	206.90
6 Widow at 60, no child	55.50	72.80	94.70	115.60	135.80	156.20	179.40
7 Disabled widow at 50, no child	38.90	51.00	66.30	80.90	95.00	109.30	125.50
8 Wife under 65 and one child	32.00	51.00	70.20	119.40	164.60	177.20	183.80
9 Widow under 62 and one child	96.00	152.60	198.60	242.40	284.80	327.60	376.20
10 Widow under 62 and two children	96.00	152.60	202.40	280.80	354.40	395.70	434.40
11 One child of retired or disabled worker	32.00	50.90	66.20	80.80	94.90	109.20	125.40
12 One surviving child	64.00	76.30	99.30	121.20	142.40	163.80	188.10
13 Maximum family payment	96.00	152.60	202.40	280.80	354.40	395.60	434.40

SOURCE: Department of Health, Education & Welfare.

liberalized benefit formulas, real average payments grew and kept pace with the earnings of those still in the labor force.

Social security is not without its critics. While benefits are available to the covered employee as a statutory right, this right is conditional upon retirement rather than merely reaching age 65, as is the case when a citizen buys an annuity through a private plan.[8] In 1970 benefits were paid in full for those over 65 whose current earnings were less than $1680 per year. For current earnings over $1680 but less than $2880, one dollar of benefits was withheld for each two dollars of earnings; benefits were reduced by one dollar for each dollar of earnings above $2880. This effectively constituted a 50 percent tax on earnings between $1680 and $2880, and a 100 percent tax up to the limit of social security benefits received, on earnings in excess of $2880. Upon reaching age 72, full benefits were paid regardless of earnings. Income from private pension funds, as well as income from other sources, such as financial assets, is not considered as earnings for purposes of determining benefits; earnings arise from the sale of one's labor service. Thus, the elderly coupon-clipper qualified for full benefits whereas a partially retired craftsman did not. Social security benefits may be inadequate to lift the beneficiary out of poverty as defined by the federal poverty guideline. As may be determined from Table 19.3, many recipients, with no other source of income, would be deemed poor by the 1964 poverty standard. Recipients of social security benefits often seek other types of public assistance as their benefits are inadequate for subsistence. In 1969, 57 percent of those citizens receiving old age assistance were also recipients of social security benefits.[9] Comparison of rows one and five, Table 19.3, shows that a surviving widow, living alone, receives less than an elderly man, living alone. Are these features equitable?

Although some object to compulsory coverage and payroll taxation, virtually all Americans are now covered by social security, and thus a means is provided by which, even if it is inadequate, the income of the elderly is maintained. Nearly universal coverage might not occur were it not compulsory. Despite social security's designation as insurance, it constitutes a tax-transfer mechanism where a current generation of employees is taxed to support the income of a former generation of employees. The insurance aspect of social security is introduced by the presumption that a future generation of employees will do the same for today's taxpayers as they retire; this presumption is supported by the fact that social security benefits are a

---

[8] Unlike private pension plans the beneficiary of social security does not, upon retirement, choose his type of annuity. Neither is there a cash value that is part of his estate. Rather he, his spouse, and dependent children may draw benefits during their lifetime or period of dependency irrespective of the total value of the covered employee's contribution.

[9] "Federal Income Security Programs," *op. cit.*, p. 191.

permanent Congressional appropriation. The equity of the structure of taxes and benefits is often questioned. As shown in Chapter 13, payroll taxes are regressive (disadvantageous to the poor) while the distribution of benefits is also regressive (in favor of the poor). Perceiving the social security system as a tax-transfer mechanism rather than as insurance has led some to question the equity of taxing most heavily a current generation of low income citizens to make transfer payments to an older generation of low income citizens. Those who question the equity of this mechanism suggest the abolition of the social security trust fund, repeal of the separate payroll tax, and financing social security benefits from general revenues obtained with increased personal income taxes.

Medical insurance. In 1965 the Social Security Act was amended to provide medical care for the aged. Two programs were established. First a program of hospital insurance (Medicare) was created to be financed from payroll taxes. Of the 4.8 percent employee and employer payroll tax prevailing in 1970, 0.6 percent was earmarked to finance the program of hospital insurance and 4.2 percent was earmarked to finance OASDI benefits. For those aged 65 and over who do not qualify for OASDI benefits, hospital insurance benefits are provided and financed from general revenues. Thus, all citizens aged 65 and over qualify for hospital benefits even when they are not covered by social security. In addition, the federal government makes grants-in-aid to states for the provision of medical care to those low income citizens who qualify as determined by a means test (Medicaid). The 1965 amendment to the Social Security Act also instituted a voluntary program of supplementary medical insurance to be financed from $4 (1970) monthly premiums paid by those who choose coverage; these premiums are matched by the federal government from general revenues. Although the legal distinctions are not so clearly stated, the Medicare program essentially covers costs incurred for in-hospital treatment, whereas the supplemental insurance program covers such out-of-hospital costs as physicians fees and home nursing care. All medical benefits are limited and, in the case of supplemental insurance benefits, cover 80 percent of reasonable expenses in excess of $50.

These two medical insurance programs are so new that their detailed evaluation is impossible at this writing. There is no question that since the inception of the medical insurance programs the elderly have been receiving health care in increased quantities and, it is frequently alleged, placing a severe strain on medical facilities, as the federal government acted precipitately to increase medical care demand without taking action also to increase supply. This contributed to the rapid increase in the index of medical care prices in the last half of the 1960s. Further, the costs of medical care for the aged, both because of the quantity of benefits provided and the increase in the unit cost of these benefits, far exceeded expectations, leading to an intensive Congressional review of the federal government's role in the delivery of medical care. As this volume goes to press that review is in progress.

Unemployment compensation insurance. Prior to the industrial era nearly all individuals were somehow rooted in agrarian society where they, or at least their family, could hope to be self-sufficient. A concomitant by-product of industrialization was a loss of self-sufficiency as increasingly specialized productive units were created. A member of an industrial and urban society depends on the sale of his labor services for money that may then be exchanged for goods and services. When, for whatever the reason, that flow of money is interrupted the plight of the individual is severe. OASDI benefits were designed to replace the income of those who withdrew from the labor force by virtue of retirement or disability. Unemployment insurance was provided in the Social Security Act to replace the income of the unemployed but unretired members of the labor force while they are involuntarily out of work. Unemployment insurance was established as a state government program, subject to federally specified minimum standards.

Covered employees work for private, profit-oriented firms employing, during 20 or more weeks per year, four or more employees. Agricultural and domestic workers, the self-employed, and the employees of state and local governments and other nonprofit institutions are excluded.[10] Some states, as a result of their own legislation, have extended coverage to more employees than required by the basic federal legislation. Approximately 75 percent of the civilian labor force was covered at the start of the 1970s.

To finance the program the Social Security Act calls for a payroll tax (3.1 percent since 1961), whose liability is the employers', to be levied on the payrolls of qualifying employers. The revenues from this tax are deposited in a trust fund and earmarked for making benefit payments to the employees of these firms in the event they are laid off. To qualify for benefits the employee must have been employed by a covered employer for some period of time (which varies from state to state) prior to becoming unemployed, must be involuntarily separated from his employment (but not fired because of fault on the part of the employee), available and willing to work, and registered as seeking work with a state employment office.

In order to induce the states to take basic responsibility for the program, the federal legislation grants employers a 90 percent tax credit against their federal payroll tax liability for unemployment insurance taxes paid to state governments in support of approved state unemployment insurance plans. Although only Wisconsin had an unemployment insurance program when the Social Security Act was enacted, all states had unemployment insurance plans by 1937. The Social Security Act requires that states deposit their

[10] Federal employees were included by a 1955 amendment to the Act.

receipts with the federal government, but each state's receipts are earmarked for making benefit payments within that state. Federal monies are also provided to cover the administrative costs of the state's program. As first enacted the payroll tax was based on total payrolls; in 1939, the Act was amended so that the tax base was limited to the first $3000 of each employee's wages. This base, by federal standards, was still in effect in 1970. Many states, however, base the tax on a larger base, some as large as $7200. Evidence has accumulated showing that some employers provide more stable employment than do others; legislation has been enacted under which employers with better employment records pay lower rates of payroll taxes than do others.

Federal law does not specify the amount of benefits to be paid; unemployment compensation benefits vary widely from state to state. Benefits generally are computed on the basis of an employment history prior to becoming unemployed. In March 1970, the average national weekly benefit, including dependents' allowances, was $48.39; benefits ranged from a high of $63.04 (Connecticut) to a low of $33.48 (Oklahoma).[11] Benefits are not paid indefinitely. In most states benefits may be obtained for 26 weeks; the range of time over which benefits are available runs from 22 to 39 weeks. During the 1958 and 1961 recessions, special programs of temporary unemployment insurance were provided by acts of Congress; the unemployed in those states that chose to participate could receive benefits beyond the time ordinarily permitted. Benefits under this temporary extension of coverage were financed from trust fund reserves and were replenished by additional employer taxes during the recovery from these recessions. In recession years, when there is a sharp rise in involuntary unemployment, benefit payments are in excess of receipts, drawing down the fund's accumulated balance. In other years payroll tax receipts exceed benefit payments and a surplus is accumulated from which future benefits may someday be financed. In the absence of such widespread unemployment as occurred during the Depression, it seems unlikely that, with the current schedule of payroll tax rates and benefit payments, this accumulated surplus will be depleted. With an accumulated surplus of over $12 billion and because benefits are substantially below the earnings of the employee prior to his job separation, increasing the schedule of unemployment insurance benefits to more adequately maintain family income is appropriate. Extending coverage to a larger fraction of the labor force is also desirable; in the age of campus disorders faculty members have a special interest in this reform.

Categorical assistance. The Social Security Act provided for aid to certain citizens not eligible for, and as supplements to, social security benefits.

---

[11] *Social Security Bulletin,* July 1970, p. 53.

The principal programs were old age assistance, aid to the blind, and aid to families with dependent children. In 1950 additional aid was provided for the permanently and totally disabled. The states administer, determine eligibility, and set the benefit levels for all these programs, subject to federal minimum standards. The federal government participates by providing a fraction (generally 50 percent) of the administrative costs, and a portion, through grants-in-aid, of the benefits paid. Because the states separately determine eligibility and benefit levels it is not surprising that these programs differ widely from one part of the nation to another. The nation-wide average monthly, and the high and low state benefits, per recipient in February 1970, are given in Table 19.4. On the average these benefits are inadequate to lift their recipients out of poverty.

Table 19.4 **Public Assistance: Average Monthly Payment per Recipient, February 1970**

	Old Age Assistance	Aid to the Blind	Aid to the Disabled	Aid to Families with Dependent Children	General Assistance
National average	$75.15	$100.30	$91.05	$45.85	$51.75
High state average	125.00	162.00	136.85	68.15	135.00
	(N.H.)	(Calif.)	(Iowa)	(Mass.)	(N.J.)
Low state average	46.65	54.65	50.80	12.05	3.95*
	(Miss.)	(Miss.)	(Ala.)	(Miss.)	(Ark.)

* Six states—Idaho, Indiana, Kentucky, Nebraska, Nevada, and Vermont—made no general assistance transfers in February 1970.

SOURCE: *Social Security Bulletin*, July 1970, p. 56.

Federal outlays for categorical assistance are financed from general revenues rather than from trust funds. Federal payments, per recipient, are generally determined in accordance with the following formula:

1. 31/37 of the first $37 of the average monthly payment per adult recipient and 5/6 of the first $18 per recipient of aid to families with dependent children.

2. A federal share that ranges from 50 percent to 65 percent of the balance of the monthly payment, up to a maximum of $75 per adult recipient and up to $32 per recipient ($100 per child in a foster home) in aid to families with dependent children.[12]

[12] *Appendix: Budget of the United States Government, Fiscal Year 1971* (Washington, D.C.: Government Printing Office, 1970), p. 438.

The federal share of assistance under part two of the above formula is applied to states in inverse proportion to per capita personal income in the states. Thus, federal participation in these programs defers a larger percent of categorical assistance benefits in poor states than in states with higher per capita incomes. This form of equalization is further discussed in Chapter 20.

In fiscal year 1969 federal outlays for categorical assistance were $3.6 billion, as shown in Table 19.5. They are not recorded as part of federal

Table 19.5 **Federal Outlays for Categorical Assistance, by Type, Fiscal Year 1969 (Billions of dollars)**

Old age assistance	1.2
Aid to the blind	.1
Aid to the permanently and totally disabled	.4
Aid to families with dependent children	1.7
State and local administration	.2
Total	3.6

SOURCE: *Appendix, Budget of the United States Government, Fiscal Year 1971* (Washington, D.C.: Government Printing Office, 1970).

transfer payments to persons in Table 19.2 because these payments are made as grants-in-aid to state governments. Federal participation is included in *special types of public assistance* as recorded for state and local governments in Table 19.2. The federal share of these benefits is over 50 percent.

General assistance. General assistance is financed and administered solely by state and local governments. These programs are found in most states; since there are no federal guidelines or minimum standards they differ widely from state to state and are difficult to characterize. This is a residual assistance category in that state laws typically specify that those who qualify for any of the previously mentioned transfer programs may not qualify for general assistance. As may be seen from Table 19.4, general assistance benefits tend to be less than transfer payments supported with federal monies. The total amount of general assistance provided by the state and local governments in calendar year 1969 was $470 million (see Table 19.2).

One particularly common characteristic of general assistance programs, as well as many state laws with respect to categorical assistance, is noted here. The transfer recipient's benefit is often determined by a social worker's computation of need. The procedure is basically as follows: Monthly food, shelter, and clothing requirements are estimated; from this is subtracted the families' income from other sources. The monthly benefit check is this difference, not to exceed a statutory maximum. This procedure effectively constitutes a 100 percent marginal tax on earnings, as each dollar of earnings leads to a dollar reduction in benefits. This procedure constitutes a disincentive to work, for, unless earnings exceed the total transfer payments, time spent at work does not increase the worker's disposable income.

At the start of the 1970s a few municipalities made transfer payments to the victims of crime. Since crime is a problem of all society it is inequitable that the criminal's victim be required privately to cover the costs incurred as the result of physical injury suffered during an attack. Thus some cities have begun to make transfers to defer medical expenses and lost earnings not recoverable through the victim's insurance.

THE NEGATIVE INCOME TAX[13]

The programs discussed in the previous section, plus some aspects of veterans benefits and various agricultural programs, were the major government supported income maintenance programs in the United States at the start of the 1970s. A noticeable feature of all these programs with the exception of general assistance, which provided a mere $470 billion in 1969 benefits, is that the transfer recipient is not identified by his income alone. A means test is often used to determine eligibility but never is the sole basis for qualification. To qualify for a government transfer payment one, perhaps, must be poor, but he must also be aged, a veteran, a farmer, blind, disabled, and so on. By and large, government transfer payments are not provided to citizens only because they are poor. The negative income tax plans are proposed as a means of maintaining the personal income of citizens distinguished by no characteristic other than their poverty.

The negative tax proposals also stem from the inability of low income

---

[13] For an extended treatment of this subject, *see* Christopher Green, *Negative Taxes and the Poverty Problem* (Washington, D.C.: The Brookings Institution, 1967). *Poverty Amid Plenty*, Report of the President's Commission on Income Maintenance Programs (Washington, D.C.: Government Printing Office, 1969), discusses and proposes a negative tax plan. *See also* Peter A. Diamond, "Negative Taxes and the Poverty Problem," *National Tax Journal*, September 1968; Lowell E. Gallaway, "Negative Income Tax Rates and the Elimination of Poverty," *National Tax Journal*, September 1966; A. James Heins, "The Negative Income Tax, Head Grants, and Public Employment Programs: A Welfare Analysis," *Journal of Human Resources*, Summer 1970; Richard A. Musgrave, Peter Heller, and George E. Peterson, "Cost Effectiveness of Alternative Income Maintenance Schemes," *National Tax Journal*, June 1970; Peter Mieszkowski and James Tobin, "Is the Negative Income Tax Practical?" *Yale Law Journal*, November 1967; M. J. Boskin, "The Negative Income Tax and the Supply of Work Effort, A Comment," *National Tax Journal*, December 1967; and *Industrial Relations*, February 1967, for a collection of papers dealing with negative income taxation.

citizens to benefit from a number of equity based provisions of the personal income tax. Adjusted gross income is reduced by personal exemptions and deductions in computing taxable personal income. There is an equity motive underlying the personal exemption and many deductions, but to benefit from these, adjusted gross income must at least equal their sum. The innovation of the minimum standard deduction in 1964 was designed to exempt from the federal income tax the minimum income necessary to lift a family out of poverty. To benefit from this tax relief, however, it is necessary to receive an adjusted gross income at least as large as the poverty guideline.

Professor Milton Friedman proposes that citizens continue to compute taxable personal income in the present manner. When taxable income is positive a positive tax liability is incurred.[14] But if taxable income is negative—that is, if personal exemptions and deductions exceed adjusted gross income—then a negative tax liability should be incurred on that base, and a transfer payment, equal to that negative tax liability, should be received. Friedman suggests transfer payments equal to 50 percent of negative taxable income. With $600 personal exemptions and the minimum standard deduction, a family of four would receive transfers whenever its adjusted gross income is less than $3000. For each dollar of earnings the transfer is reduced by 50 percent, a lower marginal tax on earnings than applies under most existing transfer programs. The Friedman recommendation is illustrated in Table 19.6, presuming the federal personal income tax base and rates applicable from 1965 to 1969 (exclusive of the 10 percent surtax from which low income taxpayers were exempt). Actual tax liabilities and disposable incomes during 1965–1969 are shown by way of comparison.

Related, but somewhat different, is Professor James Tobin's proposal that the federal government provide family allowances under which every man, woman, and child would be entitled to a $400 transfer payment each year.[15] Thus, a family of four would be guaranteed a $1600 minimum cash flow. Tobin would then apply a $33\frac{1}{3}$ percent marginal tax rate to each dollar of cash receipts from all sources other than the allowance. The Tobin plan is also illustrated in Table 19.6. As long as adjusted gross income (which excludes the allowance) is less than $4800, the family's tax liability is less than its allowance; the family is a net transfer receiver. If disposable income is greater than $4800 but less than $6288.88 the family is a net taxpayer but the allowance and tax liability, in combination, continues to leave disposable income larger than it would be if determined from regular tax bases and rates. In order to guarantee that no family's disposable income be less

---

[14] Friedman was the first to suggest formally the adoption of the negative income tax. *See* his *Capitalism and Freedom* (Chicago: The University of Chicago Press, 1962), chapter 12. He uses the 50 percent tax rate for illustrative purposes only; that rate is not offered as a formal policy recommendation.

[15] "On Improving the Economic Status of the Negro," *Daedalus*, Fall 1965.

Table 19.6 Comparison of Disposable Income by Adjusted Gross Income for a Family of Four: Actual, 1965–1969; The Tobin Plan; and the Friedman Plan*

	1965–1969 Actual		Tobin Plan			Friedman Plan	
AGI	Tax	Disposable Income	Allowance	Tax	Disposable Income	Tax	Disposable Income
$ 0.00	$ 0.00	$ 0.00	$1600.00	$ 0.00	$1600.00	—$1500.00	$1500.00
3000.00	0.00	3000.00	1600.00	1000.00	3600.00	0.00	3000.00
4000.00	140.00	3860.00	1600.00	1333.33	4266.67	140.00	3860.00
4800.00	260.00	4540.00	1600.00	1600.00	4800.00	260.00	4540.00
5000.00	290.00	4710.00	1600.00	1666.67	4933.33	290.00	4710.00
6000.00	450.00	5550.00	1600.00	2000.00	5600.00	450.00	5550.00
6288.88	494.20	5794.68	1600.00	2094.20	5794.68	494.20	5794.68
7000.00	603.00	6397.00	0.00	603.00	6397.00	603.00	6397.00

* Neglecting social security taxes and all other federal, state, and local taxes except the federal personal income tax (without the 10 percent surtax), and assuming that the family does not receive any nontaxable transfer payments other than those that are part of the negative tax plan. The computations of actual disposable income and the Friedman plan are based on the minimum standard deduction when adjusted gross income is $6000 or less and the 10 percent standard deduction when adjusted gross income is greater than $6000.

under this plan than under the actual tax law, Tobin proposes that upon reaching the breakeven income level—in this case \$6288.88—a family renounce its right to the allowance, cease being taxed at the $33\frac{1}{3}$ percent marginal rate, and instead be taxed on the ordinary tax base at regular tax rates.

What would be the budgetary cost of these transfers? The value of unused personal exemptions and deductions on nontaxable personal income tax returns was \$9.6 billion in 1968 (see Table 19.7). Under the Friedman

Table 19.7 **Unused Personal Exemptions and Deductions, Nontaxable Individual Income Tax Returns for 1968**

	Million
1 Number of returns	12.4
2 Personal exemptions claimed	30.2
3 Value of personal exemptions 30.2 × \$600	\$18,120
4 Total deductions	\$7,537
5 Adjusted gross income	\$16,102
6 Taxable income	—\$9,555

SOURCE: *Preliminary Statistics of Income, 1968: Individual Income Tax Returns* (Washington, D.C.: Government Printing Office, 1970), Table 3.

plan the resulting transfer would be \$4.8 billion. This figure overestimates the size of transfer to these citizens since the 30 million exemptions claimed on these nontaxable returns include second exemptions for the nontaxable elderly and blind. On the other hand, this figure underestimates the transfer because not all citizens are claimed as exemptions on personal income tax returns. In 1968, 201.4 million exemptions were taken on all personal income tax returns; of these 8.8 million were second exemptions for those aged 65 and over and .1 million were second exemptions taken by the blind.[16] Subtracting these second exemptions to eliminate double counting, 194.2 million citizens were enumerated on 1968 income tax returns. As of July 1, 1968, the Bureau of the Census estimated the United States population as 199.9 million.[17] Thus, in 1968 approximately 4.7 million poor Americans were not claimed as an exemption on any income tax return. With a \$600 personal exemption and assuming an average \$200 minimum standard deduction for each, their combined personal exemptions and deductions amount to \$3.8 billion. Since these individuals undoubtedly had some income their negative taxable income is somewhat less. On balance, we estimate

[16] *Preliminary Statistics of Income, 1968: Individual Income Tax Returns* (Washington, D.C.: Government Printing Office, 1970), p. 5.

[17] *Statistical Abstract of the United States, 1969*, p. 25.

that the transfer payment base proposed by Friedman was between $10 to $12 billion in 1968; with a 50 percent rate of transfers, from $5 to $6 billion would have been required. The Tobin plan is obviously more expensive; in 1970 its cost would probably have been $15 to $20 billion.[18]

Neither plan, as illustrated in Table 19.6, would lift all the low income transfer recipients out of poverty; neither do most existing government transfer payments if they are the only source of the recipient's income. Thus Tobin proposed his plan as a supplement to existing transfer payments; the only exception to current practice is that he would then include transfer payment income, other than the allowance, as part of adjusted gross income as the recipient's tax liability is computed. To finance the budgetary cost of his program Tobin proposed that the fiscal dividend, for two years, be specifically earmarked for this purpose. Friedman, by contrast, sees his plan as a replacement for all government transfer payments except veterans benefits.[19] Thus, OASDI, categorical assistance programs, and so on, would be terminated, and those receiving income maintenance assistance from government would henceforth receive that assistance only because they are poor and no longer because they are aged, blind, or disabled. In Friedman's view, if the objective is the elimination or alleviation of poverty, then attack poverty as such and identify the beneficiaries of transfer payments only by their income.

It is sometimes argued that negative tax programs, and transfer payments in general, destroy the incentive to work. This issue is discussed with the aid of Figure 19.1. Leisure is measured on the horizontal axis and income is measured on the vertical axis. In the absence of transfer payments a citizen maximizes his welfare at equilibrium *B*, and works *QM* hours in exchange for income *BQ*. With a negative tax plan, he is now provided some minimum income, *MZ*, irrespective of effort; under the Friedman plan *MZ* is $1500 and under the Tobin plan $1600. Henceforth, his trade-off between income and leisure takes *Z* rather than *M* as the origin. With the transfer a citizen is now guaranteed welfare level U_2, and the decision to enter the labor force depends on the budget line *ZWP;* the slope of *ZW* is one-half his wage rate (the slope of *PM*) under the Friedman plan and two-thirds the wage rate under the Tobin plan, and reflects the rate at which leisure may be converted into disposable income. As shown, the transfer recipient enters the labor force and maximizes happiness at *C,* works *DM* hours, and receives disposable income inclusive of transfer equal to *CD*. As a result of the negative tax the citizen illustrated in Figure 19.1 reduces the time spent

[18] *See also* Attiat F. Ott, David J. Ott, and J. Scott Turner, "Simulation of Costs of a Negative Tax Plan and Its Implications for the Poor," in Arthur B. Willis (ed.), *Studies in Substantive Tax Reform* (Chicago: American Bar Association, 1969).

[19] Friedman, *op. cit.*, p. 193. Presumably, the pensions of public employees would also be retained.

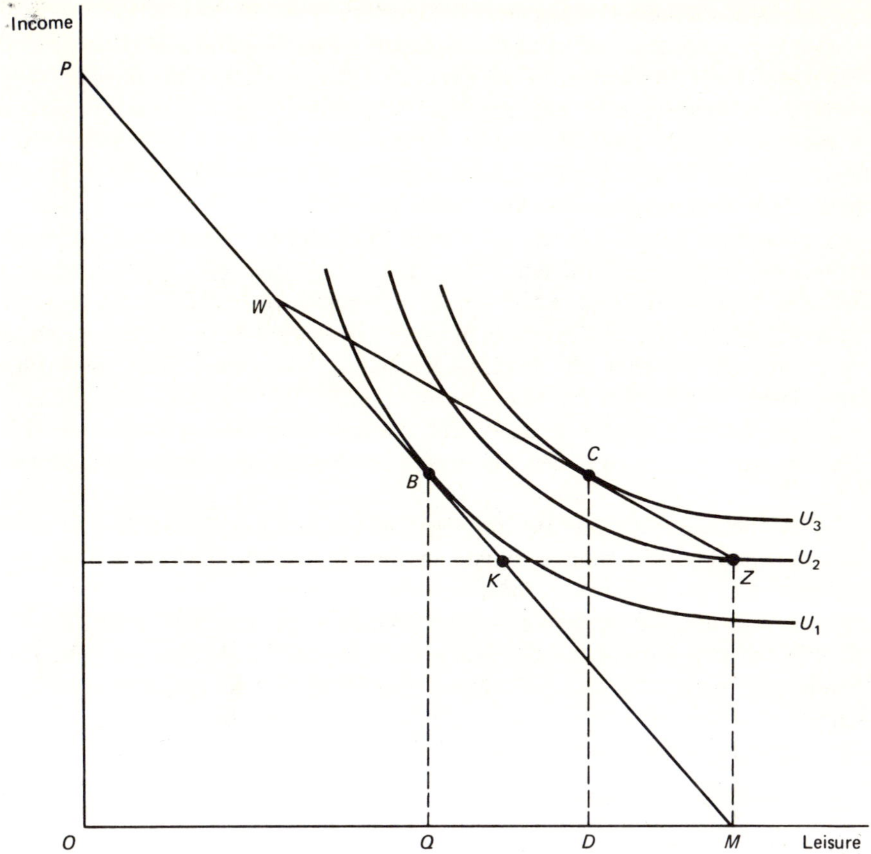

Figure 19.1 Work incentives and the negative income tax.

at work. Figure 19.1 could easily have been constructed to show the negative tax increasing effort as well, but the theoretical possibility that it destroys incentives for those who ordinarily might be expected to be members of the labor force cannot be denied.

Negative tax plans should also be compared with existing programs. Under many programs the transfer recipient's benefit is reduced by one dollar for each dollar of earnings; effectively the transfer recipient faces the budget line *ZKP* shown in Figure 19.1 and, as there illustrated, it is rational behavior to remain outside the labor force at equilibrium *Z*. By contrast with present programs, under which the transfer recipient is subject to a 100 percent marginal tax rate on earnings, the negative tax plans tax earnings at less than 100 percent and may encourage effort as illustrated by equilibrium *C*, as compared with *Z*.

In 1968 the Office of Economic Opportunity established a trial program to ascertain the impact of income maintenance programs on several variables, including work incentives. This program was designed to furnish data pertinent to evaluation of negative tax plans and family assistance programs in general. The preliminary results of the study suggest that rather than being destructive of incentives, the recipients of transfers actually increased their effort as compared with the control group.[20]

There are administrative difficulties with negative tax plans although these may be no more difficult than those associated with other transfers. Perhaps the most difficult is the timing of transfer payments. Since they are designed to alleviate poverty they presumably should be made during those weeks or months when the family's income is low, rather than some time later. Income taxpayers file tax returns in April of each year to settle their accounts for the previous year. Would the poor be expected to file monthly declarations of expected poverty in order to receive their transfer on a current basis?

The definition of income for negative tax purposes must also be considered. Should other transfer payments, pensions, and gifts, for instance, be included as part of income for purposes of computing the transfer base? Should students, having access to soft loans to finance their education, be eligible for transfers? Should the size of transfers be determined solely by family size or should account also be taken of differences in the cost of living? Should wealth be considered in determining eligibility?

FAMILY ASSISTANCE PLAN

Suggesting acceptable alternatives is more difficult than finding fault with transfer programs. The negative tax plans have generated little enthusiasm in the public at large and virtually none in Congress. In an effort to reform the transfer mechanism in the United States, President Nixon, in August 1969, proposed the Family Assistance Plan.[21] The Family Assistance Plan is designed to aid families with dependent children; it would replace

[20] Office of Economic Opportunity, *Preliminary Results of the New Jersey Graduated Work Incentive Experiment* (Washington, D.C.: Office of Economic Opportunity, mimeo, February 18, 1970). *See also* "Current Status of Income Maintenance Experiments," a collection of papers by Harold W. Watts, Mordecai Kurz and Robert G. Spiegelman, and Terence F. Kelly and Leslie Singer, *American Economic Review,* May 1971, pp. 15–38.

[21] For additional discussion of family assistance programs, especially in other nations, *see* Green *op. cit.*; *European Social Security Systems,* Joint Economic Committee, 89th Congress, 1st Session (Washington, D.C.: Government Printing Office, 1965); and *Guaranteed Minimum Income Program Used by Governments in Selected Countries,* Joint Economic Committee, 90th Congress, 2nd Session (Washington, D.C.: Government Printing Office, 1968).

federal categorical assistance programs, especially aid to families with dependent children, and most state general assistance programs.[22] In their place the Family Assistance Plan would provide, for a family of four, $1600 per year throughout the nation; although the political attractiveness of such national uniformity is obvious, its equity is questionable given regional differences in the cost of living.[23] The only qualification for the transfer is that the recipient accept job training and, if available, employment for which he is qualified. Day care centers are proposed so that the mothers of dependent children may enter the labor force. The first $60 of monthly earnings would not be offset against the transfer; for each two dollars of earnings in excess of $60 per month the transfer would be reduced by one dollar. As concerns incentives, this is an improvement over current practice which often taxes earnings at a 100 percent rate. President Nixon estimated that, in its first year of operation, the Family Assistance Plan would require the federal government to make outlays $4 billion larger than would be required under the replaced programs; at the same time there would be some budgetary saving to state and local governments.

It is perhaps excessive to characterize the Family Assistance Plan as providing a guaranteed annual income, since single adults and childless couples are ineligible for benefits, and adults with dependent children must qualify by accepting job training and employment. The plan is particularly interesting because it is a formally proposed legislation, and because almost as a birthright, it guarantees a minimum income to all.[24] The major drawback is that it makes this right conditional on the willingness to accept employment without guaranteeing that employment will be available. In the United States, as well as elsewhere, we are still not prepared to take that step in the direction of human dignity proposed in the Full Employment Act of 1945, under which the declared policy of the United States government would have been to guarantee, "useful, remunerative, regular, and full-time employment" to every American. To what end do we provide job training for marginal entrants to the labor force when, as clearly was the case at the start of the 1970s, seeking price stability entails taking policy actions whose likely result is increasing the rate of unemployment? To what end do we provide incentives to work without also providing the work itself? In the long run, the elimination of poverty must rest on employment, possibly with

---

[22] The Family Assistance Plan does not provide benefits to adults without dependent children; these citizens would continue to receive benefits under existing programs.

[23] In order to preclude this program substitution reducing benefits to some, in the 30 states where current benefits exceed the federal payment under the Family Assistance Plan, the state would be required to make payments to maintain the current benefit level. In all cases states could authorize additional benefits beyond the basic federal payment.

[24] The elderly are provided for with OASDI benefits.

government serving as employer of last resort. The Family Assistance Plan differs from previous American experience but fails to deal with the problem of proverty in its most fundamental form.

SUMMARY

The major income maintenance programs in the United States at the start of the 1970s fail in many instances to lift beneficiaries out of poverty. Eliminating poverty is not the fundamental purpose of these programs; many recipients of social security and unemployment insurance benefits are not poor. There are several reasons for this. First, the underlying work ethic in our society implies that poverty stems from laziness and is the fault of the individual. Thus, the able-bodied do not qualify for transfers. Legislators enact laws that provide for the elderly, the disabled, or dependent children because of their inability to be self-sufficient. Second, eliminating poverty would be expensive; governments are reluctant to impose sufficient taxes to accomplish this objective. Third, the partisans of other policy objectives are better organized politically than are the poor. Thus, available funds are allocated to other purposes.

The negative tax proposals and the Family Assistance Plan show an awareness of shortcomings in existing transfer mechanisms. However, at the level of funding proposed for these reforms, the poor would still be among us.

20

INTERGOVERNMENTAL FISCAL RELATIONS

In the American federal system relationships between governments are varied and complex. States are in many respects sovereign and have power independent of the federal government. Cities, counties, and other units of local government have large measures of autonomy; although they are legally the creatures of state governments, state constitutions and statutes recognize their independence. *Intergovernmental relations* include all aspects of the relationships between the federal government and the states, among the states, between the federal government and localities, between states and localities, and among localities. These aspects may be legal, political, or economic. The laws of one government affect another whether it is a federal law that constrains the actions of school districts, or a state law that determines the authority of a municipality. Political relationships can deteriorate into civil war. Obviously our concern here is with economic relationships—the payments made by one government to another; the conflicts between, and coordination of, taxes imposed by different governments; and the limitations placed by higher levels of governments on the power to collect revenues, make expenditures, and incur debts by lower levels of government. These economic relationships are called *intergovernmental fiscal relations.*[1] Our primary focus in this chapter is on intergovernmental transfers of funds; we discuss the theoretical justifications for such transfers, the major techniques used, and proposals for reform.

Transfers of funds are only a part of intergovernmental fiscal relations. Governments raise funds primarily through taxes and, with a multiplicity of governments, citizens find themselves subject to the taxes of many political jurisdictions. A particular tax base, such as personal income or a piece of real property, may be taxed several times, each time by a different government. Overlapping taxes may be an inherent feature of federalism but they also lead to inequities and administrative headaches for both tax collectors and taxpayers. The man who works in one jurisdiction and lives in another may find that both impose taxes on his income. To avoid inequities the tax laws must be made more complex by the introduction of credits for taxes paid to another jurisdiction.[2] Multistate corporations must pay corporate income taxes in several states on the portion of their income attributable to the business they do in each state. State laws vary with respect to determining what that share is.[3] Smaller businesses find multistate compliance particularly burdensome. In many instances the costs of tax compliance far exceed the tax liabilities involved. Evasion is thought to be widespread.

---

[1] For the best introductory discussion of the subject, *see* George F. Break, *Intergovernmental Fiscal Relations in the United States* (Washington, D.C.: The Brookings Institution, 1967). For a wide-ranging collection of materials, see *Revenue Sharing and Its Alternatives: What Future for Fiscal Federalism?*, Vol. I–III, Joint Economic Committee, 90th Congress, 1st Session (Washington, D.C.: Government Printing Office, 1967).

In 1959 the Advisory Commission on Intergovernmental Relations was created by Congress. The Commission is made up of public officials, representing all levels of government, and private citizens. The Commission and its small staff is charged with giving "continuing attention to intergovernmental problems." Three of its reports are particularly noteworthy: *Measures of State and Local Fiscal Capacity and Tax Effort* (Washington, D.C.: Government Printing Office, 1962); *Fiscal Balance in the American Federal System* (Washington, D.C.: Government Printing Office, 1967); and *State Aid to Local Government* (Washington, D.C.: Government Printing Office, 1969).

[2] New York taxes the income that nonresidents earn in the state but allows a credit against the New York tax liability for taxes paid on the same income to another state. When first enacted, New Jersey residents who worked in New York would have paid that tax since their home state had no income tax. In retaliation, New Jersey enacted an income tax only on the income its residents earned in the state of New York, and set the rates and definition of the tax base in accordance with the New York statute. Now the commuter is taxed in New Jersey on the income he earns in New York and claims that tax as a credit equal to his liability to New York. In essence the tax imposed by New York was captured by New Jersey; the taxpayer pays no more than he did before New Jersey acted but now he pays it to his home state.

[3] Break, *op. cit.,* pp. 55–61.

An overview of intergovernmental transfers of funds was provided in the *1967 Census of Governments*. State and local governments received 16.9 percent of their general revenue from the federal government. The aggregate amount of federal aid was $15.4 billion, all but $1.8 billion being aid to state governments.[4] For individual states, federal aid as a percentage of total state and local government general revenues varied widely as indicated in Table 20.1. The 83.1 percent of aggregate state and local government general

Table 20.1 **Federal Aid, Selected States, 1966–1967**

States	Federal aid as a percent of total state and local government general revenues
Highest ranked states	
Alaska	51.8
Wyoming	31.4
Arkansas	27.8
West Virginia	27.0
Utah	25.9
National average	16.9
Lowest ranked states	
Maryland	12.8
Indiana	12.3
Wisconsin	12.3
New Jersey	11.2
New York	11.1

SOURCE: Bureau of the Census, *Compendium of Government Finances, 1967 Census of Governments*, Vol. 4 (Washington, D.C.: Government Printing Office, 1969), p. 41.

revenue not accounted for by federal aid was raised about equally by states (41.4 percent) and local governments (41.7 percent) from their own sources. States made substantial transfers to local governments ($18.4 billion), comprising distributions of both federal and state funds. About 62 percent of these state transfers to local government were for education. Our analysis of intergovernmental fiscal relations commences with some theoretical explanations for these intergovernmental transfers of funds.

SOME THEORETICAL CONSIDERATIONS

In our earlier discussions of the theory of public finance we often treated the public sector as if it were a single government. As we developed the case

[4] States also received $673 million in transfers from local governments. Table 12.4 showed the distribution of federal aid in fiscal 1969, by agency and by function.

for government expenditures based on the concept of public goods in Chapter 3, no consideration was given to the question of what level of government should provide a particular public good or merit want. American practice is varied. For example, consider the area of education: Hawaii has no local school districts, and the state government has complete responsibility for public elementary and secondary schools. At the other extreme is Nebraska, where in 1966, there were 2322 separate school districts.[5] Recognizing great variations in practice, a few theoretical propositions are, however, relevant.

Efficiency. The activities of state and local governments create externalities in much the same way that private sector activities create externalities. This phenomenon, which some economists refer to as *interjurisdictional spillovers,* establishes a theoretical basis for intergovernmental transfers of funds.[6] A local government, by providing a system of elementary and secondary education, is likely to provide benefits to the residents of other jurisdictions as its citizens emigrate; residents in the particular jurisdiction are likely to benefit as citizens educated elsewhere migrate into that community. In this type of situation, where total benefits are greater than benefits perceived locally, the local government is likely to underspend. A higher level of government, representing a geographically larger constituency, may make payments to the local government in order that more of the public service is produced. Conversely, citizens of a local community are likely to view the costs of a particular public service only in terms of those costs paid out of the local government's budget. Yet, just as a distinction can be made between the private costs and social costs of goods produced in the private sector, the social costs of providing the public service may exceed the amount paid by the local government. Provision of the service can generate diseconomies for those living outside the boundaries of the local government as costs are imposed on them. Social costs stemming from government activity are nowhere more evident than in the air we breath and the water we drink. By burning trash in a municipal incinerator or dump, a city imposes costs on its leeward neighbors. Sewage disposal in a river affects the costs of municipal water systems in downstream communities. Such externalities can justify intergovernmental transfers of funds; they also call for other types of intergovernmental relations—regional planning authorities and regulatory measures.

Economies of scale establish a second theoretical justification for intergovernmental fiscal relations. Some types of government services can be

---

[5] Bureau of the Census, *Governmental Organization, 1967 Census of Governments,* Vol. I (Washington, D.C.: Government Printing Office, 1968), Table 13.

[6] Werner Z. Hirsch, Elbert W. Segelhorst, and Morton J. Marcus, *Spillover of Public Education Costs and Benefits* (Los Angeles: University of California, Institute of Government and Public Affairs, 1964).

provided at lower unit costs and perhaps with improved quality on a large scale than on a small scale. In many instances this phenomenon has led to the creation of *special districts*, units of local government with responsibility for a particular, narrow range of public services, but usually with a geographic jurisdiction spreading over several town, city, and county governments. They have substantially increased in number since the war (see Table 10.1). The special districts are particularly prevalent in the fields of water and transportation. The largest in the country is the New York Port Authority, which provides a wide variety of transportation services on both the New York and New Jersey sides of the port of New York. Its expenditures in 1966 were $210 million, larger than those of several state governments.[7] Special districts raise their own tax revenues and generate income through user charges and fees; some have the power to issue securities, and many receive payments from other units of government. These special districts are able to take advantage of economies of scale. They can, however, easily lose touch with the citizenry, since their officials are usually not elected.

Economies of scale have led to the consolidation of many small units of government, especially school districts. The motive for consolidation is not simply to lower costs but also to improve quality. James B. Conant in *The American High School Today* concluded that, "The number of small high schools must be drastically reduced through district reorganization."[8] He argued that small schools were unable to offer a curriculum broad enough to meet the educational needs of all students. The Conant Report stimulated the trend toward consolidation of school districts. Much has been written about the desirability of consolidating units of local government in metropolitan areas but, by 1970, only in a very few instances had this occurred. Another method of securing economies of scale is for small units of government to contract with larger jurisdictions for the provision of specific services. This is sometimes referred to as the *Lakewood Plan*, named after a southern California suburban community established shortly after World War II that contracted with Los Angeles County for the provision of police and other services.

If citizens have different demands for public goods, welfare may be increased if those with similar demands locate in the same jurisdiction.[9] Those desiring high-level expenditures on public education may flock together in a particular suburb, and those who want more spending on recreational facilities may congregate in another. People can vote with their feet. Differences in incomes as well as tastes may motivate this type of

[7] Bureau of the Census, *Finances of Special Districts, 1967 Census of Governments*, Vol. 4, No. 2 (Washington, D.C.: Government Printing Office, 1969), p. 4.

[8] New York: McGraw-Hill, 1959, p. 40.

[9] *See* Charles M. Tiebout, "A Pure Theory of Local Expenditures," *Journal of Political Economy,* October 1956, for an exposition of this argument.

differentiation of local government units. For example, as high income families locate in a suburb they may choose to tax themselves and spend larger amounts on public services than in surrounding jurisdictions. They may also use zoning ordinances and building restrictions to prevent lower income families from locating in that jurisdiction, feeling that low income families would use public services without paying for their share. The aspect of federalism that encourages variations in the quantity and quality of public services reflecting differences in income raises serious questions of equity.

Equity. During the 1960s conflict clearly emerged between two deeply seated precepts of American political life—equal protection of the laws and autonomy of local governments. Essentially the controversy is over equity in the distribution of public goods. Fragmentation of local governments permits segregation along income lines so that per capita (or per pupil) public spending is very much higher in some areas than in others. Have higher levels of government—the states and the federal government—met the constitutional dictum of equal protection? Court contests over this question developed in the late 1960s with respect to financing public education. For example, the Detroit school board sued the state of Michigan, arguing that the method used to distribute state funds to local school districts resulted in inequitable differences in spending among the various school districts in the state. The method used made payments dependent, in part, upon the assessed value of taxable property per pupil. Detroit, as a central city, must finance many other expenditures from that same tax base. The amount available for school spending is not as great as in suburbs having the same level of assessed value per pupil. Detroit also faces higher costs. Suits of this nature were, in 1970, pending in the courts; the issue they raise is likely to be a prominent one during the 1970s.

The uneven distribution, in a geographic sense, of tax bases constitutes a theoretical justification for making certain types of intergovernmental transfers of funds. On either allocative or equity grounds, certain levels of spending for public services provided by local governments may be desired. Some local jurisdictions will find it much more difficult than others to raise the revenues required, given the tax bases located within their boundaries. Raising revenue can be difficult both because of limited tax bases and because of the concentration of demands for public services placed on certain jurisdictions. An area may be poor in the sense that incomes, retail sales, property values, and other potential tax bases are low, relative to the population. A jurisdiction can also be hard-pressed because of extraordinary demands for public services. Central cities in metropolitan areas typically face this problem. Demands for police protection, transportation facilities, health services, and other services to cope with the many manifestations of what has come to be called the urban crisis, have created "municipal overburden."[10] The situation exists even when tax bases, measured in per capita terms, are relatively high. Some rapidly growing suburban areas face similar fiscal problems, especially when school age children are a particularly large fraction of the total population, and when sewer and water systems must be constructed.

Having considered some theoretical grounds for intergovernmental transfers of funds we now turn to empirical evidence regarding different fiscal patterns, both among states and within states. These differences underlie actual American practice in the area of intergovernmental fiscal relations.

FISCAL CAPACITY AND TAX EFFORT

During the post–World War II years, state and local government receipts and expenditures have grown proportionately more rapidly than those of the federal government. The majority of the increase in these governments' receipts has been derived from their own tax sources. One factor explaining these increased tax receipts is expanded tax bases because of economic growth and, to a lesser extent, inflation. As population increased and per capita incomes rose, sales and income tax bases expanded; as new construction took place and property values increased the property tax base grew. In addition, of course, tax rates have risen and new bases have been taxed, and, as a result, state and local governments have been able to finance substantially increased expenditures.[11] Many question, however, whether or not state and local revenues can adequately continue to expand and finance necessary outlays by these governments; the urban crisis, for example, is a matter of great concern in the 1970s and additional public expenditures are seen as part of the solution. In this section we investigate the fiscal capacity and tax effort of state and local governments to aid in determining whether or not additional public services may be funded from their own resources.

The Advisory Commission on Intergovernmental Fiscal Relations defined fiscal capacity and tax effort as follows: "*Fiscal capacity* is a measure of the combined ability of the State and its local governments to raise tax revenue for financing local government programs, while *tax effort* is a measure of the relationship of the taxes actually collected to fiscal capacity."[12] Irrespective of the tax base, unless assets are liquidated as tax liabili-

---

[10] This term was coined by the Advisory Committee on Intergovernmental Relations; see *Fiscal Balance in the American Federal System, op. cit.,* Vol. 2, "Municipal Fiscal Disparities."

[11] The *critical limit hypothesis* once was offered to suggest that taxes (by all levels of government combined) could not exceed 25 percent of gross national product. This share has long been exceeded throughout the Western world. *See* Colin Clark, "Public Finance and Changes in the Value of Money," *Economic Journal,* December 1945.

[12] *Measures of State and Local Fiscal Capacity and Tax Effort, op. cit.,* p. 87.

ties are met, taxes are paid out of current income and the capacity of a government to raise taxes must be related to income in its jurisdiction. Two income concepts are appropriate. The first is personal income received by residents. Ultimately all tax liabilities are borne by people and, with respect to taxes assessed by state and local governments, their citizens' personal income reflects their capacity to pay. Evidence regarding variations in the pattern of per capita personal income in the United States for 1968 is shown

Table 20.2 **Variation in Per Capita Personal Income, 1968 Selected States and Metropolitan Areas**

	Per Capita Personal Income	
States and Metropolitan Areas	**Amount**	**Percent of U.S. Average**
Five highest states:		
Connecticut	$4303	126
Bridgeport	4399	129
New Haven	4105	120
New York	4141	121
New York	4650	136
Utica–Rome	3140	92
Alaska	4053	118
California	4010	117
San Francisco–Oakland	4809	141
Oxnard–Ventura	2679	78
Illinois	3989	116
Chicago	4439	130
Davenport–Rock Island	3422	100
United States average:	3425	100
Five lowest states:		
West Virginia	2433	71
Charleston	3098	91
Wheeling	2892	85
South Carolina	2391	70
Greenville	3033	89
Charleston	2396	70
Alabama	2365	69
Birmingham	2962	87
Tuscaloosa	2118	62
Arkansas	2315	68
Little Rock	3145	92
Fort Smith	2270	66
Mississippi	2074	61
Jackson	2709	79
Biloxi–Gulfport	2577	75

SOURCE: Bureau of the Census, *Statistical Abstract of the United States, 1970* (Washington, D.C.: Government Printing Office, 1970), pp. 842–887.

in Table 20.2. The range of per capita personal income among the states is from a high of 126 percent of the national average in Connecticut to a low of 61 percent in Mississippi. Variations within states are typically greater than the variation among states. Selected data for Standard Metropolitan Statistical Areas are also shown in Table 20.2; were data available for individual jurisdictions within states they would undoubtedly show even greater variations. The second concept, income produced in a jurisdiction, may also, logically, be taken as a measure of fiscal capacity, but these data are not available on a regular basis, even for states. Estimates made by the Advisory Commission on Intergovernmental Relations for 1959 indicated a wider range of variation among states' per capita income produced than for per capita personal income received.[13]

Fiscal capacity is only one factor affecting the generation of revenue by state and local governments. Equally important is the range of taxes used and the level of tax rates imposed. Although property taxes are in force in all states, not every state uses both an income tax and a retail sales tax. At the local level where property taxes are the major revenue source there are wide discrepancies in assessment practices and rates leading to considerable variation in tax yields. The *1967 Census of Governments* reported data on effective property tax rates for single-family homes in 122 large cities. The median effective tax rate ranged from 0.36 percent to 4.31 percent of market values.[14] A more global estimate of tax efforts can be made by comparing general revenue raised by state and local governments from their own revenue sources with personal income in the state. Such data are shown in Table 20.3 for the five highest ranking and the five lowest ranking states in 1966–67.

A similar measure of tax effort in 1965 is given in Table 20.4 for the nation's thirty-seven largest metropolitan areas. These data give per capita local taxes as a percent of per capita income for the central city in each of these metropolitan areas and for that city's suburbs. The data indicate very different degrees of tax effort from one metropolitan area to another. While there are exceptions, the data also suggest that tax effort is greater in the central city than in the suburban communities. Two forces are at work here which, to a degree, are cause and effect of one another. As middle and high income citizens moved to the suburbs in the 1950s and 1960s, suburban tax bases expanded while those in the cities stagnated or declined; thus tax rates in the cities rose in an effort to maintain municipal services while suburban communities could hold down tax rates as tax bases grew. As tax rates rose, taxes may have played a role as a locational variable stimulating the movement to the suburbs.

These data regarding fiscal capacity and tax effort suggest that some

---

[13] *Ibid.*, pp. 27–28. Other methods for measuring fiscal capacity are also discussed.

[14] Bureau of the Census, *Taxable Property Values*, *1967 Census of Governments*, Vol. 2 (Washington, D.C.: Government Printing Office, 1968), p. 15.

Table 20.3 **Tax Effort, Selected States, 1966–1967**

States	State-local general revenue from own sources in fiscal 1966–1967 as a percent of 1966 personal income
Highest ranked states	
North Dakota	18.4
Wyoming	18.0
New Mexico	16.5
Hawaii	16.4
Arizona	16.3
National average	13.1
Lowest ranked states	
Pennsylvania	11.2
New Jersey	11.2
Connecticut	10.8
Ohio	10.6
Illinois	10.2

SOURCE: Bureau of the Census, *Compendium of Government Finances, 1967 Census of Governments,* Vol. 4 (Washington, D.C.: Government Printing Office, 1969), pp. 73–74.

state and local governments should be able to meet demands for increased spending out of their own tax resources. In other instances, particularly in a number of central cities, attempts to increase local taxes may exacerbate rather than permit the solution of pressing social problems. Even in instances where tax effort is relatively low, the fear that broadening tax bases or increasing tax rates may unfavorably affect locational decisions by individuals and businesses prevents action from being taken.

Variations in fiscal capacity and tax effort would, in the absence of federal aid, result in considerable differences among states and within states in the level and mix of public spending. Even with the system of federal aid prevailing in the late 1960s, considerable variation in the level and mix of state and local government spending persisted. We do not want to suggest that spending patterns should be uniform. Indeed there are good reasons why they should not be. Demographic structures of local populations differ, and the tastes of voters vary. Nonetheless it is widely believed that spending patterns should be altered, for both allocative and equity reasons, through the techniques of intergovernmental fiscal relations. We need not document in full detail the existing patterns of state and local government spending. Data concerning spending to maintain personal income were presented in the previous chapter. We can, however, show the extent of variations in spending in the important area of elementary and secondary education. For the 1969–70 school year, current expenditures per pupil averaged \$783 in

Table 20.4 **Per Capita Local Taxes as a Percentage of Per Capita Income Inside and Outside Central City, 37 Largest Standard Metropolitan Statistical Areas, 1965**

Area	Central City (1)	Outside Central City (2)	Difference (1)–(2)
Los Angeles–Long Beach, California	7.2	9.4	−2.2
San Bernardino–Riverside–Ontario, California	8.1	8.8	−.7
San Diego, California	5.7	6.4	−.7
San Francisco–Oakland, California	7.8	7.7	+.1
Denver, Colorado	6.8	6.1	+.7
Washington, D.C.	9.7	4.2	+5.5
Miami, Florida	8.2	5.5	+2.7
Tampa–St. Petersburg, Florida	6.3	4.4	+1.9
Atlanta, Georgia	5.2	4.0	+1.2
Chicago, Illinois	7.4	4.0	+3.4
Indianapolis, Indiana	6.3	6.0	+.3
Louisville, Kentucky–Indiana	5.2	3.5	+1.7
New Orleans, Louisiana	4.0	2.5	+1.5
Baltimore, Maryland	6.1	4.0	+2.1
Boston, Massachusetts	9.2	6.1	+3.1
Detroit, Michigan	7.0	5.3	+1.7
Minneapolis–St. Paul, Minnesota	7.2	7.1	+.1
Kansas City, Missouri–Kansas	10.2	6.7	+3.5
St. Louis, Missouri–Illinois	6.8	6.4	+.4
Newark, New Jersey	7.7	4.6	+3.1
Paterson–Clifton–Passaic, New Jersey	7.3	5.6	+1.7
Buffalo, New York	5.1	5.2	−.1
New York, New York	8.0	4.9	+3.1
Rochester, New York	6.7	5.3	+1.4
Cincinnati, Ohio–Kentucky–Indiana	6.3	6.2	+.1
Cleveland, Ohio	4.9	5.2	−.3
Columbus, Ohio	7.3	4.2	+3.1
Dayton, Ohio	13.3	6.5	+6.8
Portland, Oregon–Washington	7.5	6.1	+1.4
Philadelphia, Pennsylvania–New Jersey	6.5	4.7	+1.8
Pittsburgh, Pennsylvania	6.9	4.8	+2.1
Providence, Rhode Island	7.0	4.7	+2.3
Dallas, Texas	4.8	3.5	+1.3
Houston, Texas	4.8	6.8	−2.0
San Antonio, Texas	n.a.	n.a.	n.a.
Seattle–Everett, Washington	4.3	5.0	−.7
Milwaukee, Wisconsin	8.2	4.4	+3.8
Unweighted average	7.0	5.4	+1.6
Weighted average	7.6	5.6	+2.0

n.a. = Data not available.

SOURCE: Advisory Commission on Intergovernmental Relations, *Fiscal Balance in the American Federal System,* Vol. 2, Metropolitan Fiscal Disparities (Washington, D.C.: Government Printing Office, 1967), p. 80.

the United States. The state with the highest average, New York, spent $1237 per pupil, almost three times as much as Alabama, the lowest ranking state with a figure of $438. The range among the 15 largest cities was also marked, from a high of $1300 in New York City to a low of $535 in Houston.[15] Variations in per pupil spending among school districts within states is also considerable, though current data are more difficult to come by. Using data for 1959–60, the Advisory Commission on Intergovernmental Relations reported a 3.86 ratio of expenditures per classroom unit between the highest (98th percentile) and lowest (2nd percentile) for all school districts in the United States. The state having the highest ratio (3.96) was Missouri and Nevada had the lowest ratio (1.37). In 25 states the ratio was more than 2.[16] These data on per pupil expenditures are for the costs of inputs and do not necessarily reflect differences in output, as discussed in Chapter 4.

SOME TECHNIQUES OF INTERGOVERNMENTAL FISCAL RELATIONS

When a decision is made at the federal level, on either allocative or equity grounds, to aid state or local governments a choice can be made from a variety of techniques to implement that decision. State governments have the same options when supporting local governments. In this section we discuss the principal techniques of intergovernmental fiscal relations in use in the United States.[17]

Grants-in-aid. Practically all of the direct federal aid to state and local governments takes the form of grants-in-aid. The aggregate amount of such aid ($20.3 billion in fiscal year 1969) was shown in Table 12.4, by agency and by function. About seven-eighths of this total goes to state governments, with the remainder going directly to local units of government. Much of the amount received by a state is, of course, passed on to its political subdivisions. Grants-in-aid tie the recipient government to using the funds for a specific purpose and are thus called *categorical grants*. That purpose may be broadly defined (elementary and secondary education, for example) or narrowly prescribed (educational training for fishermen, for example). *Project grants* are those where recipient governments must apply for funds appropriated for a specific purpose. The Model Cities program is probably the best known example of project grants. *Formula grants* are those where funds are allotted to all qualifying units of government according to an *allotment*

---

[15] U.S. Office of Education, *Statistics of Public Elementary and Secondary Day Schools, Fall 1969* (Washington, D.C.: Government Printing Office, 1970), pp. 27–28.

[16] *State Aid to Local Government*, *op. cit.*, p. 58.

[17] Federal lending to state and local governments is treated in Chapter 21.

formula that divides the pie of funds appropriated among the qualifying governments. Some programs utilize *matching grants*, where the government receiving aid is required to spend from its own sources an additional amount, at least equal to a specified fraction of the grant, for the particular purpose associated with the program. A grant formula is said to contain an *equalization* feature if the amount going to each qualifying government is adjusted to reflect differing fiscal capacities. This is surely not the place to discuss the details of all of the literally hundreds of federal and state grant-in-aid programs; instead we make some general comments about this fiscal technique.

Grant-in-aid programs have proliferated because of their political appeal. They are a specific response to social and economic problems. If public spending is to be directed toward a particular objective, such as employment training for the unemployed, the usual American presumption is that such a program should be conducted by local units of government. If these governments do not meet the problem because they lack fiscal capacity, or because expected benefits are widely diffused beyond the boundaries of their jurisdiction, higher units of government, either state or federal, can respond with a grant-in-aid program. Political leaders who perceive the problem can then point with pride to a specific solution. Constituent groups who benefit more directly from the program argue for its adoption, retention, and expansion. Lobby groups form. If there were a grant-in-aid program for inspection of fish food plants there would surely be a National Association of Fish Food Inspectors who would work closely with the relevant Congressional committees. Reformers have often called for simplification of intergovernmental fiscal relations by substituting larger block grants for many smaller categorical grants dealing with a particular function such as education. *Block grants* require the recipient government to spend the funds for a broadly defined public purpose (education, for example) rather than a narrowly defined purpose (high school library books, for example). These proposals run counter to the obvious vested interests of particular groups, but also are opposed by legislators and bureaucrats in the donor government who want to know precisely where the funds are going.

How does the grant-in-aid affect the spending of the recipient government; does that government substitute grant-in-aid funds for what it would have spent out of its own revenues? Figure 20.1 is helpful in considering questions like these. Here we show a preference map for a recipient government's officials, where each indifference curve represents a series of equally satisfactory budget allocations between the type of public spending being supported by the grant-in-aid and all other types of public spending. With the initial budget constraint shown by line AB, an optimal allocation of spending is achieved at R where OD amount is spent on the particular purpose and OC is spent on all other purposes. If a grant-in-aid equal to RS is received, the recipient government may view its new budget line as EF, and

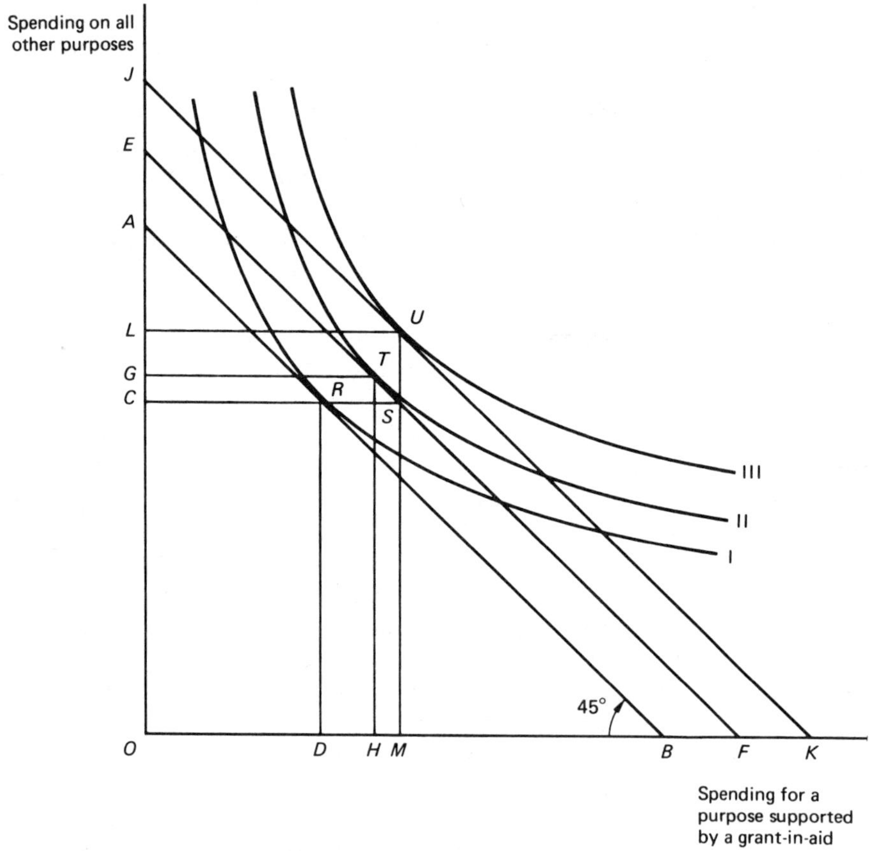

Figure 20.1 Response to a categorical grant-in-aid.

adjust the allocation of spending to *T*. An additional amount, *DH*, less than the grant-in-aid, will be spent on the particular purpose; *CG* additional expenditures will be for other purposes. In essence the recipient government will substitute some of the grant money for spending out of its own sources for the supported purpose. The configuration of indifference curves might be such that *T* would be directly above (or even to the left of) *R* and no more (or even less) would be spent on the supported purpose. If the recipient government's officials wanted to maintain a constant level of satisfaction from total spending they could do so by maintaining the allocation of spending at *R* and reducing revenues from their own sources by an amount, *RS*, equal to the grant received. Such an extreme reaction seems unlikely; nonetheless some reduction in local revenues is a possibility with the final budget line being to the right of *AB* and to the left of *EF*.

The possibility that receipt of a grant-in-aid will lead to substituting grant funds for their own resources, or to a reduction in tax effort on the part of the recipient government, induces grant-making governments to insist upon *maintenance of effort*. In the context of Figure 20.1 this means that the grant, *RS*, is given on the condition that spending for the particular purpose out of the funds of the recipient government be held at $OD = CR$. Then the new allocation of spending is at *S* and all of the grant funds are used as intended. This places the recipient government on a lower indifference curve, passing through *S* (but not drawn), than indifference curve II. Such an allocation may seem inefficient from the viewpoint of the recipient government, but from the vantage point of the grant-giving government, *S* is preferred to *T* because that government perceives added benefits (either on allocative or equity grounds) of spending for that purpose that are not perceived by the recipient government.

Suppose that over time the budget of the recipient government increases with additional revenues raised from its own resources. A new budget line, *JK*, can now be drawn on Figure 20.1. If the terms of the grant-in-aid remain the same, spending for the supported purpose will be kept constant at *OM*, where *OD* is from the resources of the recipient government, and *DM* is from the grant; as long as the point of tangency of an indifference curve with the new budget line lies to the left of a vertical line through point *S*, all of the additions to the budget will be used for other purposes. If an indifference curve is just tangent to *JK* at *U*, then the pattern of spending by the recipient government will be no different than if the grant were received without being tied to spending for a particular purpose. Both points *R* and *U* would be on an expansion path. In the short run, then, a matching grant-in-aid will lead to increased spending for the supported purpose, but in the longer run the allocation of spending is not likely to differ from what would exist under a system of more general aid. The amounts of the categorical grants can of course be increased, and strong efforts made to enforce maintenance of effort provisions. The preferences of local decision makers may also be altered so as to favor particular expenditure purposes.

Many grants-in-aid require grant money to be matched, in a specified ratio, with spending for the supported purpose from own resources by the recipient government. These can be examined with the aid of Figure 20.2. Again the initial constraint is *AB*, and the preferred allocation of spending is at *R*. If an *open-ended* matching grant (which sets no limit on the amount of grant funds) with no maintenance of effort provision is introduced, the recipient government sees a new budget constraint *AE*, as spending out of their own resources for the supported purpose is matched by grant funds in the ratio of *BE:OB*. Decision makers for the recipient government will select a new allocation at *S* where total spending on the supported purpose is $OH = FS$, an increase of *DH*. Spending out of the recipient government's own resources for the supported purpose has, however, declined from *OD* to

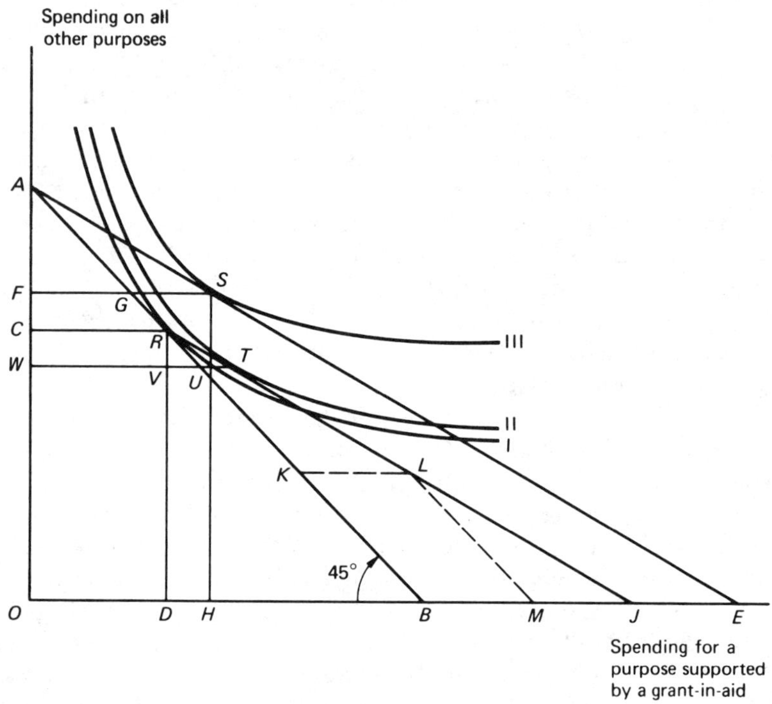

Figure 20.2 Response to a categorical grant-in-aid with a matching provision.

FG; the grant equals *GS*. A maintenance of effort provision implies a budget line of *ARJ* and a new allocation at *T*. The amount of the grant that the recipient government will willingly accept is smaller, *UT*, than in the case where there is no matching provision; additional spending, *VU*, by the recipient government out of its own resources for the supported purpose has been induced at the expense of spending for other purposes. Most matching grants are not open-ended, rather there is a fixed maximum available on a matching basis. If coupled with a maintenance of effort provision, a fixed maximum equal to *KL* results in the budget line *ARLM*. Given this illustration, the recipient government would still view *T* as the preferred allocation, and would not use the maximum grant for which it is eligible.

Figure 20.3 illustrates the case where a government does not respond at all to the availability of a matching grant. The position of indifference curve I with respect to the initial budget line *AB* indicates that *A* is the preferred allocation; all revenues from the recipient government's own sources are spent for other purposes and none for the supported purpose. If the terms of the matching grant are expressed by a new budget line *AC* (for

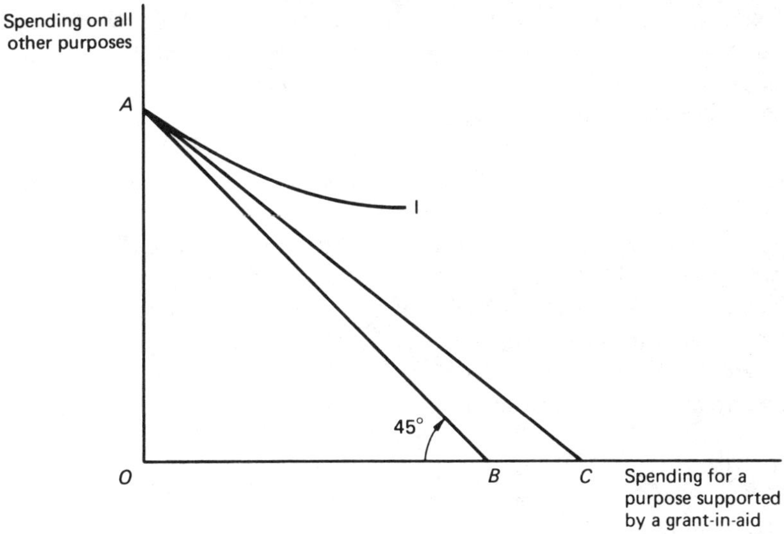

Figure 20.3 No response to a matching grant.

purposes of this illustration the grant can be considered open-ended), the recipient government makes no response, refuses the offer of the grant-in-aid, and retains allocation *A*. Only if the slope of *AC* were less than the slope of the tangent to indifference curve I at *A* would the allocation be altered and some portion of the available grant funds accepted. If decision makers for a recipient government do not see any gain in satisfaction from spending on the supported purpose, they will refuse the grant-in-aid even if no matching funds were required.

Analysis of a grant-in-aid program should not end with an examination of the effects on the spending of recipient governments. Attention must be focused on the fundamental purpose of the program. If it is rat control, the primary question is how many rats have been killed, not just how much is spent. Viewed in the context of program budgeting grants-in-aid can be seen as one of several potential methods of accomplishing a particular objective perceived by the donor government.[18]

The formulas used to allot grant-in-aid funds among eligible governments merit special attention. These should be judged in terms of their consistency with the basic allocative and equity aims of the program. Most formulas distribute funds in a manner that just exhausts the total amount appropriated. In some cases the formulas are specified in authorizing legisla-

[18] Selma J. Mushkin and John F. Cotton, *Functional Federalism: Grants-in-Aid and the PPB System* (Washington, D.C.: State-Local Finances Project of the George Washington University, 1968).

tion, and in other cases the formula is left up to an administrative agency. The simplest of all are those that divide the total according to some measure of need. Thus a federal program to provide manpower training for the unemployed might divide the funds among the states in proportion to each state's share of the nationwide number of unemployed workers. A formula can be made more complex by introducing an equalization provision that gives larger slices of the pie to poorer governments. Per capita personal income is widely used as a measure of fiscal capacity for equalization purposes in federal grant-in-aid programs.[19] How good a measure is it? Interregional differences in the price level distort this measure of fiscal capacity; per capita personal income is relatively high in Alaska and Hawaii but much of this merely reflects higher prices.[20] Assessed property value per pupil is used in many states as a means of measuring fiscal capacity in state grant-in-aid programs to local school districts. Such a technique requires similar assessment practices in all districts. It may also work to the disadvantage of central cities that have many more expenditure needs to be met out of that property tax base. *Variable matching ratios* are used as a means of introducing equalization into matching grant programs; "rich" governments may be required to match grant funds with funds from own sources in a ratio of 1:2 ($1 of grant funds with $2 of own funds), and "poor" governments may be allowed to match grant funds at a 1:1 ratio. Tax effort factors can also be included in allotment formulas, as a reward to governments making a greater than average tax effort. In short, allotment formulas are often quite complex and are not widely understood by either legislators or program administrators. Federal funds may be distributed equitably among states, but state agencies may pass the funds on to local governments in a very inequitable manner. Vigilance is called for to see to it that the formulas used are consistent with the basic purposes of a program.[21]

---

[19] Only a part of the variation in federal aid as a percent of state and local government revenues, shown in Table 20.1, is attributable to equalization. "Excluding Alaska, Hawaii, and the District of Columbia, the correlation between per capita grants and per capita income in 1967 was –0.338. This equalizing effect decreased in 1968 with the correlation coefficient still negative at –0.182." *Special Analyses, Budget of the United States Government, 1971* (Washington, D.C.: Government Printing Office, 1970), p. 278.

[20] The lack of data reflecting interstate differences in the level of prices is a curious gap in the arsenal of federal statistics.

[21] *See* Ralph E. Smith, "Apportionment of Funds Under the Manpower Development and Training Act of 1962," *Journal of Human Resources*, Fall 1968, for a case study.

When funds for one purpose are distributed among states in proportion to the funds they receive for other purposes, strange things happen. Federal aid for technical education (electronic technicians, for example), a program introduced in the late 1950s, was initially distributed among the states partially in proportion to the pounds of fish caught in each state!

Shared revenues. Only about one percent of the total federal aid to state and local governments in 1969 constituted *shared revenues,* tax or other receipts divided in fixed proportions among two or more governments. These were mostly in the natural resources area where state and local governments receive shares of federal receipts from lease payments for use of federally owned land. These payments are not subject to annual review by Congress as are appropriations for grants-in-aid. The proposal for a major program of federal revenue sharing is discussed below.

Revenue sharing is more common at the state and local level where specified shares of state retail sales taxes or gasoline excise taxes are remitted to the local jurisdictions in which they were collected. Such plans may be challenged on equity grounds, as those specific tax bases may be very unevenly distributed among localities.[22] Typically, at both the federal and state levels, shared revenues, unlike grants-in-aid, are unrestricted in their use. Only in a few cases, such as gasoline taxes remitted from states to counties or municipalities, is the use of the funds restricted to a particular purpose.

Tax expenditures. The federal government indirectly assists state and local governments through a system of tax expenditures (see Chapter 12). By making state and local income, property, sales, and gasoline excise taxes deductible in computing federal income tax liabilities, the federal government reduces the net cost to the high income taxpayer who itemizes deductions of these state and local taxes. This may allow state and local governments to generate more revenue from their own sources than would otherwise be the case. The federal government implicitly subsidizes state and local governments by making the interest income from their securities exempt from federal income taxes. The distribution of this subsidy among governments depends, of course, on the amount of debt issued by each state and local government.

A system of credits against federal estate tax liabilities for state estate and inheritance taxes paid was introduced in 1924. Since 1926 the credit has been set at 80 percent; that is, an estate subject to a federal tax can deduct amounts paid on state estate and inheritance taxes up to 80 percent of the federal tax.[23] The primary purpose of this device is to limit interstate competition in the field of death taxes. Each state is encouraged to impose

[22] Shared revenues differ from state administered, but locally imposed taxes. Counties, for example, may impose a surtax on the state personal income tax, or localities may add a percent or two to the state sales tax rate. Shared revenues are established by state actions alone rather than a combination state permission and local action.

[23] For further details *see* James A. Maxwell, *Tax Credits and Intergovernmental Fiscal Relations* (Washington, D.C.: The Brookings Institution, 1962), chapter 2.

taxes at least equal to the amount of the credit. In 1969 the Federal Treasury "lost" $350 million as a result of this credit.[24]

When unemployment insurance was enacted in the 1930s a federal tax was imposed and tax credits equal to 90 percent of the federal liability were granted for state taxes paid. This device was not designed to raise federal revenue but rather to encourage state action. By the middle of 1937, less than two years after the federal act was passed, all of the states had introduced unemployment insurance programs. The 90 percent tax credit proved to be a powerful stimulative device.[25]

FEDERAL REVENUE SHARING: A PROPOSAL FOR REFORM

In 1970 the Nixon administration proposed a system of revenue sharing by which monies equal to a fraction of the federal personal income tax base would be distributed each year among the states, without being tied to particular expenditure purposes. Payments would have totaled $275 million in fiscal year 1971 and have risen to an estimated $4 billion in 1975. The proposal called for state shares to be based on population, with an adjustment for tax effort. Those states making greater tax efforts would receive relatively more funds. A fraction of each state's funds would "pass through" to local jurisdictions. This proposal reflected growing dissatisfaction with the complex system of categorical grants-in-aid, and was viewed as a means of directing a portion of federal fiscal dividends to the state and local governments. A revenue sharing proposal had originated about ten years earlier during the Kennedy administration; it came to be called the Heller-Pechman plan after its proponents, Walter Heller, President Kennedy's Chairman of the Council of Economic Advisors, and Joseph Pechman, Director of Economic Studies at the Brookings Institution.[26] Administration interest in the proposal flagged under the pressures of financing the war in Vietnam, but by 1967 several senators and congressmen from both parties had introduced or supported bills embodying one form or another of federal revenue sharing. President Nixon included it in his 1968 campaign as a major part of what he called "a new federalism." Enactment in 1970 was thwarted, in part because the fiscal dividend was absorbed by spending for other purposes.

Supporting arguments. Revenue sharing is viewed by its proponents as

[24] *Special Analysis, Budget of the United States, Fiscal Year 1971* (Washington, D.C.: Government Printing Office, 1970), p. 222.

[25] Maxwell, *op. cit.*, chapter 3.

[26] Walter W. Heller, *New Dimensions of Political Economy* (New York: W.W. Norton and Co., 1967), chapter 3.

a means of revitalizing American federalism.[27] States would know with certainty the amount they would receive from this source, as revenue sharing would not be subject to the annual appropriations process; funds equal to a specified fraction of the federal personal income tax base would be automatically deposited in a trust fund and then distributed among the states. This is seen as an improvement over the expansion of categorical grant-in-aid programs, the appropriations for which are often uncertain and delayed, making it difficult for recipient governments to plan effectively. Fixing the aggregate amount of revenue to be shared as a fraction of the personal income tax base, rather than income tax receipts, is preferred because the former is not affected by changes in tax rates, and grows at a more stable rate. Automatic growth in the amount distributed among the states would give the states an elastic revenue source, thus easing the continued fiscal pressure that most states and local governments feel as they face increasing demands to raise expenditures but must rely on state and local income taxes or upon less elastic revenue sources, such as sales and property taxes. In a sense, personal income, which forms the base for the federal tax, is as available for taxation at the state and local levels as at the federal level. Proponents of revenue sharing argue, however, that states are constrained in their use of the income tax because the federal government has preempted that revenue source, and because states fear that increasing income taxes will unfavorably affect the locational decisions of individuals. Most local income taxes are difficult and expensive to administer. In addition, poorer states can only tap income within their boundaries. Even without any explicit equalization feature, revenue sharing would have an equalizing effect as the aggregate amount would be distributed among the states on the basis of population.

Many pressing expenditure needs are at the local rather than the state level. To counter the charge that state governments might not pass funds on to local governments in an appropriate manner, proponents of revenue sharing argue that, since the Supreme Court's "one man, one vote" decision, reapportioned state legislatures are more receptive to the needs of urban areas. In recognition of the problem, and to gain political support from big city mayors, proponents of revenue sharing have included specific pass through provisions in their proposals. If adopted, these provisions would guarantee that a portion of funds allotted to a state would automatically pass through the state treasury to urban governments.[28]

---

27 See *Intergovernmental Revenue Act of 1969 and Related Legislation,* Hearings Before the Subcommittee on Intergovernmental Relations of the Committee on Governmental Operations, U.S. Senate, 91st Congress, 2nd Session (Washington, D.C.: Government Printing Office, 1970), for analysis and discussion of a particular proposal.

28 For discussions of state-urban relationships, *see* Alan K. Campbell (ed.), *The States and the Urban Crisis,* The American Assembly, Columbia University (Englewood

Opposition views. The Nixon administration's proposals for revenue sharing were considered during the 1970 session of Congress. It languished in the House Ways and Means Committee as many members felt that the prospects of a substantial budget deficit in fiscal 1971 ruled out any major new expenditure program. There was no fiscal dividend to be shared. Aside from opposition based on temporary budget exigencies, there are more fundamental arguments made by the opponents of revenue sharing.

Some hold that legislatures should not spend money, for whatever purpose they choose, without also having the responsibility of raising sufficient revenues to finance those expenditures. As Congressman Byrnes, the ranking Republican on the Ways and Means Committee, put it,

> The crucial error in revenue sharing is that it encourages irresponsible spending. . . . It does so by removing from one set of legislators the onus of levying taxes to pay for the spending they authorize, thus eliminating the best restraint we have against unjustifiable spending.[29]

Those who subscribe to this view are willing to admit the efficacy of categorical grants-in-aid for either allocative or equity reasons. Under such grants, the federal government, which raises the revenues, also determines the purposes for which those funds are used. With revenue sharing, the federal legislators who suffer the pain of imposing taxes must forego the pleasure of spending. Some would want to cut federal taxes and let the states or cities impose additional taxes if they so choose.

A specific proposal has been offered as an alternative by some opponents of revenue sharing. It calls for a credit against federal personal income tax liabilities for a portion of state and local taxes paid.[30] Plans that would limit the credit to a percentage of state and local income tax liabilities, rather than all state and local taxes, have received the most attention because states would thereby be encouraged to expand their use of income taxes. With a credit for state income taxes, states could increase their income tax collections and taxpayers would pay no more in total income taxes. There are several drawbacks to such proposals. If there is no requirement that states actually increase their taxes, the credit may result simply in tax reductions for some taxpayers. Some states do not have income taxes. States with relatively low fiscal capacity, as measured by taxable personal income, would not benefit as much as states with greater fiscal capacity. Questions of interpersonal

---

Cliffs, N.J.: Prentice-Hall, Inc., 1970); and Walter W. Heller, *et al., Revenue Sharing and the City* (Baltimore, Md.: The Johns Hopkins Press, 1968).

29 *The Wall Street Journal*, August 28, 1970.

30 For examples of such proposals, *see* Committee for Economic Development, *A Fiscal Program for a Balanced Federalism* (New York, 1967), and Maxwell, *op. cit.*, chapters 4 and 7.

equity arise as high income taxpayers who itemize deductions would benefit both from the deduction and the credit, whereas lower income taxpayers who take the standard deduction would benefit only from the credit.

SUMMARY

American intergovernmental fiscal relations need to be improved. The system of federal categorical grants-in-aid has become increasingly cumbersome. Local governments with pressing expenditure needs face a bewildering array of state and federal aid programs. Meeting the terms and conditions of each separate program has placed increasing administrative burdens on both grant-giving and recipient governments. Many individual grant-in-aid programs should be consolidated into block grants for more broadly defined purposes. Such grants must be justified primarily on allocative grounds and the distribution of those funds to states or local governments should be consistent with allocative and equity objectives.

There is a place in the American system of intergovernmental fiscal relations for revenue sharing. Distribution of these funds in proportion to population would serve equity objectives; receipts from revenue sharing would be larger relative to the potential tax base in states having low fiscal capacities than in states having a high fiscal capacity. In many states revenue sharing would relieve the fiscal pressure stemming from rapidly increasing expenditure needs coupled with fears that tax increases at the state or local level would unfavorably affect locational decisions.

Reforms at the state and local level are called for. All states should use both personal income and sales taxes; state income taxes should be closely coordinated with the federal income tax, both to make the taxpayer's compliance easier and, in the interests of equity, to assure full compliance. States should assume responsibility for all property taxes on other than residential property to make these taxes more uniform. The competition among localities using full or partial property tax exemptions to attract industries could be avoided. States should then make more generous, and equitable, payments to local jurisdictions, particularly in support of education. Localities would then be free to finance other expenditures desired by the local citizenry that those citizens are willing to pay for, primarily out of taxes on residential property.

21

FEDERAL CREDIT PROGRAMS

Government credit programs encompass public sector lending and guaranteeing or insuring securities issued by private borrowers. Credit programs, as an aspect of public finance, merit the attention given them in this chapter because of their equity implications and the impact they have on the allocation of resources between consumption and investment, as well as their impact on the composition of aggregate investment. In addition, federal credit programs sometimes have stabilization goals. Although state and local governments embark on some credit programs, these are minor in nature, and because they are not summarized in any single statistical source, are omitted from formal consideration in this chapter. Federal credit programs have already been discussed in Chapter 12 in the context of the *Budget*; Table 12.7 shows loan disbursements and repayments, and outstanding direct and guaranteed and insured loans, for fiscal year 1969. Our focus in this chapter is first on the major issues raised by federal credit programs and then on the programs themselves.

ISSUES

The rationale for federal credit programs. Governments extend loans or guarantee and insure private loans to individuals and firms, instead of making purchases of goods and services or transfer payments, when the objective of public policy entails private sector acquisition of real assets.[1] Two kinds of situations motivate government credit policies: The government acts to remedy apparent imperfections in the functioning of private credit markets and the government has objectives that even a perfectly functioning, private credit market would not achieve.[2]

The first of these rationales implies the existence of "gaps" in the private credit market. Some borrowers might not have access to credit, or would have access only on "unfair" terms, because of their size, location, or intended use of funds. Borrowers might have imperfect knowledge of credit sources or lenders may be unable to assess accurately the degree of risk associated with particular types of loans. There may be lack of effective competition among lenders in some credit markets. For example, farmers in isolated rural areas might be inadequately served by lending institutions, or college students might not be able to borrow to finance their education because banks see high administrative costs associated with such loans and may have no easy means of judging the associated risk. Implicit in this rationale for government credit programs is the premise that the borrower could afford to meet interest and principal payments if only a loan were available upon competitive terms.

The second rationale for credit programs is that the combined social and private benefits of additional credit for a particular purpose are greater than the private costs of credit when private benefits do not exceed private costs; therefore a subsidy is called for. The subsidy usually takes the form of lending at below market interest rates or on more liberal terms to maturity than private lenders would be willing to extend. If, for example, private ownership of housing by low income families is accepted as a policy goal, then a program of low interest rate, long-term lending would be appropriate. Low income families cannot afford the monthly mortgage payments that would result from borrowing at the same interest rates and terms to maturity

---

[1] Although this discussion is put in terms of government loans to private individuals and firms, the federal government also makes loans to state and local governments and foreign governments.

[2] The Report of the Commission on Money and Credit, *Money and Credit: Their Influence on Jobs, Prices, and Growth* (Englewood Cliffs, N.J.: Prentice-Hall, Inc., 1961), chapter 7. Two research volumes prepared for the Commission provide excellent discussions of this whole area of public policy: *Federal Credit Programs* (Englewood Cliffs, N.J.: Prentice-Hall, Inc., 1962) and *Federal Credit Agencies* (Englewood Cliffs, N.J.: Prentice-Hall, Inc., 1962).

that middle and upper income families experience in the private credit market.[3] For an overview of the variety of interest rates and terms to maturity incorporated into federal credit programs at the end of 1969, see Table 21.1. Interest rates below 8.5 percent, the prime rate charged by commercial banks at that time, may be taken as a rough indication of implicit subsidies.

Types of federal credit programs. An arsenal of techniques is available to the federal government in developing credit programs: These include federally sponsored private agencies, such as the Federal National Mortgage Association; direct lending of Treasury funds; guarantees of private loans; and insurance of private loans. The particular weapons selected may be related to policy objectives or may be based upon budgetary considerations. When the rationale for a credit program is the existence of an imperfection in private capital markets, federal sponsorship of a financial institution, by providing an initial capital fund, is an appropriate response. The institution should be able to raise its own funds through the sale of securities to the public, and make loans out of the proceeds, along with making loans out of the initial federal funding and the repayment of prior loans. Administrative expenses can be more than paid for out of interest income, and in time the initial federal capital contribution can be repaid. The lending activity of a federally sponsored private credit agency takes place outside the federal budget.[4] Gaps in the private credit market can also be appropriately met by insurance programs, where the recipient of the private loan pays a premium for the insurance, and the federal agency covers losses to private lenders out of the accumulated premiums, or by guarantee programs where the federal government assumes whatever losses are experienced by private lenders. Insurance and guarantee programs induce private lenders to extend credit at competitive market rates to borrowers who, for some reason, would not be served in the absence of the program. Budget outlays must be made to the extent that insured losses exceed insurance premiums paid, or when guaranteed loans are in default.

Direct lending entails government functioning as a financial intermediary, and is called for when the rationale of a federal credit program requires subsidizing private borrowing. Such lending, net of loan repayments and interest, appears as an outlay in the federal *Budget* requiring an annual appropriation from Congress.[5] With new or rapidly growing loan

---

[3] An obvious alternative policy means would be transfer payments sufficient to allow low income families to meet the private costs of home ownership.

[4] Federally sponsored financial institutions are treated as a separate sector in the flow of funds accounts (see Chapter 11).

[5] The implicit outlay associated with extending loans at less than market rates of interest is not recorded.

Table 21.1 **Interest Rates and Maturities for Major Active Credit Programs Classified by Agency or Program, December 1969**

Agency or Program	Direct Loans: Interest Rate (Percent)	Direct Loans: Maturity (Years)	Guaranteed and Insured Loans: Interest Rate (Percent)	Guaranteed and Insured Loans: Maturity (Years)
EXPENDITURE ACCOUNT				
Funds appropriated to the President:				
Military assistance	7¼–7¾	5–10	9–9½	1–7
Economic assistance	2–4½	5–40	6–9½	5–25
Agriculture: Commodity Credit Corporation	2–5[a]	1–40		
Health, Education, and Welfare	0–6⅜	1–20[b]		
LOAN ACCOUNT				
Office of Economic Opportunity	4⅛	1–30		
Agriculture:				
Commodity Credit Corporation	5–7⅜	½–5		
Rural Electrification Administration	2	35		
Farmers Home Administration	1–7½	1–50	4–7½	5–40
Commerce:				
Economic Development Administration	5¾–6¼	12–40	9–12	3–10
Maritime Administration			8¼–8½	20–25
Health, Education, and Welfare	2½–8	½–40	7	½–15[b]
Housing and Urban Development:				
Renewal and housing assistance	3–6	¼–50	5.6–6.0	¼–40
Metropolitan development	0–5⅜	40		
Federal Housing Administration	0–8½	1–40	3–8½[c]	1–40
Government National Mortgage Association	3–8½	1–40		
Interior	0–8½	0–50	6½–8	5–15
General Services Administration	6¼–7½	8–10		
Veterans Administration:				
Housing loans and guarantees	7½–8½	7–30	7½–8½	7–30
Insurance policy loans	4	([d])		
District of Columbia	0–6¼	½–40		
Export-Import Bank	6	1¼–20	6–10	½–10
Federal Home Loan Bank Board	4–7.2	1–25		
Small Business Administration	3–6⅝	1–30	6–12	1–30

[a] When commodity loan is repaid by forfeiting collateral, no interest is charged. On export loans lower interest is charged during initial grace period.

[b] On student loans, maturities begin when student leaves school and exclude period of military, Peace Corps, or Vista service.

[c] In addition, property improvement loans are insured for 4½ percent to 5½ percent discount per year (or an effective annual rate of 8.8 percent to 10.6 percent), and with maturities of 6 months to 7 years.

[d] Indefinite.

SOURCE: *Special Analyses, Budget of the United States, 1971* (Washington, D.C.: Government Printing Office, 1970).

programs, such appropriations focus attention on the program and its purposes. Similar attention may not be paid to established programs that simply extend new loans as old ones are repaid. Because appropriations appear in the *Budget* for new or growing loan programs, there is an inducement for administrations wishing to minimize budget outlays to substitute interest subsidy payments to private borrowers for direct federal loans. Under such an arrangement only the amount of the subsidy rather than the full amount of the loan appears in the *Budget*.[6] During the late 1960s several loan programs were altered in this manner. Since subsidies, and absorption of losses, are the real cost to the government of direct loan programs; this technique has the advantage of placing only that cost in the *Budget*. There is a drawback, however. When the federal government subsidizes private borrowing, by making payments to lenders equal to the difference between interest payments based on market interest rates acceptable to private lenders and the lower rates paid by eligible borrowers, the success of the government's program is dependent on the cooperation of private lenders.

Macroeconomic impact. Fiscal policy concerns itself primarily with the effect of government receipts and expenditures on aggregate employment and the price level. The influence of credit programs on these macroeconomic variables is seldom discussed. We can offer two possible excuses for this sin of omission. First, the macroeconomic impact of government activity is usually analyzed within the framework of the national income accounts. These accounts do not directly reflect the actions of government credit agencies because these agencies buy and sell financial assets rather than currently produced goods and services. Second, the macroeconomic impact depends on the adjustments within the entire capital market to the actions of the federal credit agencies.[7]

In some cases the extension of credit can have the same impact as government transfer payments.[8] This would be true if the borrower, because he now has cash as he sells a security to the government, purchases goods and services that he would not have purchased in the absence of the federal

---

[6] For a discussion of the treatment of loan programs, especially the subsidy element in such programs, *see* President's Commission on Budget Concepts, *Staff Papers and Other Materials Reviewed by the President's Commission* (Washington, D.C.: Government Printing Office, 1967), pp. 297–345, 380–414.

[7] R. J. Saulnier, Harold G. Halcrow, and Neil H. Jacoby, *Federal Lending and Loan Insurance,* A Study by the National Bureau of Economic Research (Princeton, N.J.: Princeton University Press, 1958), chapter 5.

[8] A loan will have the same type of macroeconomic impact as transfer payments rather than government purchases of goods and services because no factor services are absorbed as the outlay is made. See the discussion of government purchases of goods and services in contrast with transfer payments in Chapter 15.

loan. Had he not received the federal loan would he have financed those same purchases (or a smaller volume of purchases) with credit (probably at less advantageous terms) from private sources? If federal credit merely substituted for private credit, aggregate demand would be unaffected. It would be a mistake to suppose that if all federal credit were halted aggregate demand would decline by a comparable amount. The lack of any precise means to measure the extent of substitution makes it impossible to specify the impact of federal credit programs on aggregate demand. The matter is further complicated by the ways in which federal lending may be financed. Credit agencies may be empowered to lend funds received from interest and principal payments on outstanding loans, monies annually appropriated by Congress, funds borrowed from the Treasury, or funds obtained from the private capital market by the sale of agency debt issues.[9] If agencies simply relend funds received as payments on existing loans, we would expect no change in aggregate demand. If agencies lend funds appropriated by Congress or borrowed from the Treasury, the macroeconomic effect is the same as if transfer payments were being financed. If increased lending results in a budget deficit then the means by which that deficit is financed becomes crucial (see Chapter 16). When agencies borrow in the capital markets to acquire the funds that they then lend, the macroeconomic impact depends on the sources of those funds. If the purchasers of agency securities would have alternatively purchased private securities, then credit may be reallocated within the private sector but no net increase in aggregate demand will result. If agency securities are purchased by commercial banks having excess reserves, both aggregate spending and the money supply will be increased. The same thing would be true if the Federal Reserve System supported the agency issue by making new reserves available to the banking system. Under these circumstances the effect of government lending can be expansionary. Units within the private sector that borrow from federal agencies spend on goods and services rather than stimulation coming from government spending.

Federal credit programs exhibit an implicit fiscal policy that follows from the net macroeconomic impact of the private sector expenditures financed by government loans, and the reductions in spending induced as agencies acquire the funds out of which they make loans. One study of this question concluded that this net impact was stabilizing in two of the first

[9] The distinction between lending funds appropriated by Congress or borrowed from the Treasury is more political than economic. An agency lending out appropriated funds is subjected to annual Congressional review as a part of the appropriations process, but an agency having the permanent authority to borrow, up to some limit, directly from the Treasury is not subject to the same Congressional control. Congress has traditionally been reluctant to grant agencies the power to borrow directly from the Treasury.

four postwar recessions.[10] There is also some tendency for lending activity to increase during a period of inflationary pressures and hence exacerbate the task of achieving price level stability. The demand for credit from federal agencies that do not raise the rate of interest charged on their loans will increase as other interest rates rise and private credit terms tighten. The feelings of potential borrowers that they have a right to federal credit can easily be translated into political pressure aimed at expanding the amount of federal credit available on easy terms.

Federal lending programs can also be viewed as potential tools of explicit fiscal policy. During a period of recession, lending activity can be expanded and, if financed by the sale of Treasury debt to the Federal Reserve System, aggregate demand is thereby enhanced. This avenue for fiscal policy might be favored by those hesitant about increasing government expenditures for goods and services or transfer payments. Lags between the extension of credit and increased spending by recipients are thought to be considerable in, for example, the area of housing; hence, this type of explicit fiscal policy action is subject to considerable uncertainty. During an inflationary period, federal credit agencies could act to decrease the liquidity of the private sector by selling assets (outstanding loans) from their portfolios to the public; the result would be essentially similar to open market sales of government securities by the Federal Reserve System, provided Treasury Federal Reserve Bank cash balances are increased. If proceeds from the sale of government held securities were viewed as a means of financing government purchases of goods and services, there would be no contractionary impact. Because of the impact they have on private capital markets, the lending (and financing) activities of federal credit agencies should be coordinated with monetary policy. Without that coordination, monetary policy actions may be taken that have the effect of counteracting the macroeconomic impact of agency programs.

Credit programs can also affect the stability of the economy through their impact on particular sectors of the economy. If an inflation is in part attributable to imbalances in the structure of the economy, credit policy can be effective in increasing the flow of factor services in particularly acute supply. For example, if so few factor services are being supplied in the area of medical care that rapidly increasing prices result, and if, for some reasons, the flow of credit from private sources to that area is restricted, a program of government lending to construct medical facilities and to finance the education of medical personnel could contribute to moderating the price increases in that sector. Credit programs can also have the opposite effect when the private spending financed through government loans occurs in a sector already

---

[10] George F. Break, *Federal Lending and Economic Stability* (Washington, D.C.: The Brookings Institution, 1965).

beset with bottleneck problems. Saulnier, Halcrow, and Jacoby studied the housing sector in the first few years after World War II and concluded that in large part, federal credit programs aggravated the postwar inflation by driving up construction costs and the prices of existing homes.[11]

PROGRAMS

To supplement the data in Table 12.7 we present Table 21.2, indicating in broad programmatic terms the extent of federal direct loans outstanding at

Table 21.2 **Federal Direct Loans Outstanding, June 30, 1969 (Billions of dollars)**

	Total	Loan Amount	Expenditure Account
Loans to aid			
Agriculture	9.7	8.0	1.7
Housing	7.7	7.7	a
Industry	1.9	7.9	a
Education	4.7	3.4	1.3
State and local governments	1.4	1.3	.1
Foreign loans[b]	19.7	5.7	14.0
Other loans	1.1	1.1	a
Total	46.2	29.0	17.1

[a] Less than $50 million.
[b] In addition foreign currency loans totaling $5.7 billion were outstanding.

SOURCE: *Treasury Bulletin*, December 1969, pp. 171–174.

the end of fiscal 1969.[12] This presentation serves to organize a brief survey of the major federal lending programs.

Agriculture. By virtue of longevity, a discussion of federal lending to farmers should come first. The Federal Land Bank System was inaugurated in 1916 as the first major federal credit program. Twelve regional banks were established that extended mostly long-term loans secured by mortgages on farm real estate through several hundred local Federal Land Bank Associations. The Federal Intermediate Credit Banks and the Banks for Cooperatives were established in 1923 and 1933, respectively, to extend other types of agricultural credit. The three types of institutions collectively comprise the

[11] Saulnier, Halcrow, and Jacoby, *op. cit.*, p. 144. This conclusion has been challenged; see *Federal Credit Programs, op. cit.*, pp. 257–260.

[12] The total direct loans outstanding as listed in Tables 12.7 and 21.2 cannot be easily reconciled because they come from two different sources.

Farm Credit System. The system is federally sponsored, and controlled through a federal agency, the Farm Credit Administration—although these institutions are privately owned as cooperatives by the farmers who borrow from them. Capital from the federal government was initially made available to the system, but by 1968 it had all been repaid. Any net increase in credit outstanding is either financed by the system's earnings or by securities sold to private investors and is not reflected in the *Budget,* and is not part of the balances shown in Table 21.2. At the end of 1969, the Farm Credit System accounted for about 23 percent of the total outstanding farm mortgages; a decade earlier the comparable figure was 20 percent.[13]

In addition to loans extended by the Farm Credit System, several agencies directly extend credit to the agricultural sector as reflected in Tables 12.7 and 21.2. The outstanding loans in the expenditure account are those made by the Commodity Credit Corporation; they are loans in name only, representing the purchase of surplus farm commodities. The major programs in the loan account are those of the Rural Electrification Administration and the Farmers Home Administration. An agency created during the New Deal era, the Rural Electrification Administration extends credit to cooperatives established to provide electricity and, since 1949, telephone service in rural areas. When it was established in 1935, only about 10 percent of the nation's farms were electrified; by 1970 all but about 1 percent of the nation's farms were served with electricity. In 1950 about 38 percent of farms had telephone service; in 1970 the figure was about 83 percent. Slightly over $5 billion in Rural Electrification loans were outstanding at the end of fiscal 1969. These loans are extended at a 2 percent rate of interest—a clear example of subsidizing the cost of borrowing in order to accomplish an allocative and distributive objective. The Farmers Home Administration makes credit directly available for rural housing; $2.7 billion of such loans were outstanding at the end of fiscal 1969, and about an equal amount of private loans for rural housing were insured by the Farmers Home Administration.

Housing. The federal government's role in the nation's housing markets is pervasive. Housing for military personnel and some government employees is constructed with direct federal expenditures. Monetary policy, through its impact on interest rates and credit availability, influences both the construction of new housing and the resale of existing houses. The personal income tax encourages home ownership by making mortgage interest payments and property taxes deductible, and the rapid depreciation of investments in housing influence private investors. Our concern here, of course, is with federal credit programs. We will consider first programs that insure or guarantee

---

[13] *Federal Reserve Bulletin,* various issues.

private loans, then direct lending programs, and finally the activities of federally sponsored institutions.

In 1935, the Federal Housing Administration began a program of insuring home mortgages. An initial objective of the program was to stimulate employment in the construction of new housing, but since World War II the emphasis has been on facilitating the flow of private credit into home mortgages by reducing the risk to the holders of insured mortgages. The borrower pays a 0.5 percent per annum insurance premium on the outstanding principal of his mortgage. The funds accumulated, as premiums have been paid, have been more than sufficient to cover losses. After the end of World War II, the Veterans Administration began a program of guaranteeing low down payment mortgages for veterans. This program has operated at a loss as "the bulk of the loans now outstanding were guaranteed without the collection of fees. A one-time fee is now collected on most of the new loans guaranteed in order to cover part of the costs of the program."[14] The two programs affect a very large part of total mortgage lending. In 1969, FHA and VA mortgages were 22 percent of total nonfarm mortgages outstanding. The figure was as high as 33 percent in 1956. Of the $25 billion of new, nonfarm mortgage commitments in 1969, FHA and VA mortgages accounted for 51 percent of the total; the comparable figure for 1949 was 84 percent.[15] The percentage of new commitments has fluctuated widely primarily because of the effects of FHA and VA interest rate ceilings. As the general level of interest rates rises, fixed FHA and VA rates discourage lenders from extending new insured and guaranteed loans. These ceilings can be varied as a matter of federal policy.[16] There are other regulatory aspects of the FHA and VA programs. Acceptable minimum down payments, maximum terms to maturity, and maximum loan amounts are set. Quality specifications for construction must be met for a property to be eligible for an insured or guaranteed mortgage. These and other features of the FHA and VA programs extend their influence beyond simply the flow of credit into home mortgages.

The federal government acts as a financial intermediary by providing direct loans, or their equivalent, in the form of government purchases of home mortgages. The cumulative extent of this activity is reflected in Table 21.2 as the total amount of outstanding direct loans to aid housing. The major programs do not involve subsidies. These are the Veterans Administra-

---

[14] *Special Analyses, Budget of the United States, 1971* (Washington, D.C.: Government Printing Office, 1970), p. 210.

[15] *Economic Report of the President, 1970* (Washington, D.C.: Government Printing Office, 1970), p. 246; *Flow of Funds Accounts: 1945–1968* (Washington, D.C.: Board of Governors of the Federal Reserve System, 1970), pp. 34–35; and *Federal Reserve Bulletin*, various issues.

[16] *Report of the Commission on Mortgage Interest Rates* (Washington, D.C.: Government Printing Office, 1969).

tion's direct loans to veterans in rural areas, and certain activities of the Government National Mortgage Association. The latter agency makes direct loans on housing of a new and experimental nature, and in urban renewal areas. "In some cases, this budget impact can be reduced through sale of the direct loan to a private investor."[17] Subsidized loans are also made by the Government National Mortgage Association to assist in the construction of housing for low and moderate income families. The Department of Housing and Urban Development makes subsidized loans for housing for the elderly and for the rehabilitation of housing owned by families with low or moderate incomes. Under some programs only subsidies are provided, and the basic capital financing is provided by private investors at market interest rates.

Two federally sponsored institutions are active in the housing field. The Federal National Mortgage Association—which passed from the status of federal agency to privately owned, though federally sponsored, institution in 1968—purchases FHA and VA mortgages with funds obtained by selling its own securities to private investors. It aims to provide liquidity to the mortgage market, as holders of existing mortgages sell to it, and also auctions off the right to sell mortgages to it in the future. In this manner builders of new housing can be assured that mortgages on that housing can be sold even if private financing cannot be acquired. In 1970 the Association was planning to extend its activities to the purchase of conventional mortgages, that is, other than FHA and VA mortgages. The Federal Home Loan Banks similarly raise funds in the private capital market but make advances to savings and loan associations that in turn invest in mortgages. These 12 regional banks act to maintain the liquidity of savings and loan associations experiencing unusual withdrawals of deposits.

The extent of federal activity in the mortgage markets can be assessed, in part, by considering the holdings of federal agencies and sponsored institutions as a percent of total mortgage, outstanding. In 1969 these agencies and institutions combined held about 5 percent of the total amount of mortgages, $425 billion, including farm mortgages, outstanding. It is more important, however, to consider the new commitments of these agencies and institutions as a portion of all new mortgage commitments. In the twenty years between 1949 and 1969, this percentage has fluctuated between less than 1 percent to about 19 percent. The latter figure held in 1969. During the late 1960s when high interest rates prevailed, these agencies about doubled their mortgage holdings; a smaller than usual fraction of private funds went into mortgages because of the attractiveness of other securities with higher yields. It is difficult to interpret this experience. Some private holders of mortgages may have liquidated mortgage holdings by selling

---

[17] *Special Analyses, Budget of the United States, 1971, op. cit.*, p. 211.

to the Federal National Mortgage Association and invested in other securities rather than new mortgages. To finance its acquisition of mortgages, the Federal National Mortgage Association sold its own securities to the public. Perhaps purchasers of those securities would alternatively have purchased new mortgages.

Industry. The Small Business Administration accounts for about 80 percent of the outstanding direct loans listed in Table 21.2 as aid to industry. These loans usually involve an element of subsidy by virtue of a below-market interest rate. Some of these loans are made from the Disaster Loan Fund to aid small firms hit by the effects of natural disasters. Other programs in this area include loans to firms in depressed economic regions, and loans for ship construction. Guaranteed and insured loans are also used for these purposes.

Education. Practically all of the outstanding loans to aid education shown in Table 21.2 are supportive of higher education. The federal government uses loan programs to aid both institutions and students. Most loans to students are carried in the expenditure account; most loans to institutions are for educational facilities and college housing and are included in the loan account.

By the beginning of the 1970s, federal support had shifted from direct loans to interest subsidy payments on loans made by private lenders. These subsidy programs were expected to support $500 million in loans for construction of classrooms, laboratories, and $300 million of newly constructed college housing in fiscal 1971. As part of the post-Sputnik reaction of the late 1950s, the National Defense Education Act was passed which, among other provisions, made direct, low interest, long-term loans to needy university students. In the 1960s a guaranteed student loan program was made available to students of all income levels. While the student is in school the federal government pays the interest on loans made by private lenders. After graduation, the student pays the interest up to a maximum rate of 7 percent. A special allowance—in 1970, 2.25 percent of the principal amount of insured student loans—is paid to lenders when financial market conditions make such payments necessary to induce private lenders to make such loans.[18] If higher education is viewed primarily as an investment in human capital, the benefits of which accrue to the student, then loan programs are an appropriate means of government aid for higher education. Loans would be repaid out of the future income resulting from the education. Subsidized loans, or forgiveness of principal payments, could be provided if students entered careers thought to be particularly needed. Such a policy for women students presents a special problem. Who wants to marry a girl with a negative dowry?

---

[18] *Ibid.*, p. 125.

State and local governments. The federal government, in 1969, lent nearly $1 billion to state and local governments; the extension of new loans was offset by payments of interest and principal by state and local governments to the federal government, making the net outlay by the federal government about $374 million. Table 21.3 shows the distribution of these

Table 21.3 **Federal Loans to State and Local Governments, 1969 (Millions of dollars)**

Program	Disbursements	Net Outlays
Agriculture and rural development	65.4	63.5
Natural resources	7.0	5.7
Commerce and transportation	18.6	17.9
Community development and housing	566.2	92.5
Education and manpower	146.2	121.4
General government (including the District of Columbia)	117.6	72.9
Total	921.0	373.9

SOURCE: *Special Analyses, Budget of the United States, 1971* (Washington, D.C.: Government Printing Office, 1970), pp. 234–235.

disbursements and net outlays by major program area. Lending was a small fraction, about 5 percent in 1969, of total federal aid to state and local governments, and represents about 7 percent of total federal lending (disbursements from the loan account). The largest lending programs were in the fields of housing, urban renewal, and higher education facilities. This is an area where federal lending should be expanded. When the federal government borrows from the public to finance lending to state and local governments, the interest income received by purchasers of the federal securities is fully taxable; if state and local governments borrowed from the federal government at subsidized interest rates, rather than selling tax exempt bonds to the public, federal tax receipts would increase by more than the interest subsidy.

Foreign loans. Most of these loans, summarized in Table 21.2, are rightly listed in the expenditure account as they are mainly loans made on noncommercial terms as a part of foreign economic and military aid programs. Foreign currency loans are also of this nature. There are two major programs reflected here in the loan account. The Credit Commodity Corporation makes short-term foreign loans to finance exports of surplus agricultural commodities. Also included here are $4 billion of direct loans extended by the Export-Import Bank. This federal agency extends dollar credits directly to borrowers outside the United States for purchases of

American goods and services. Disbursements under the loan agreements are made in the United States to the suppliers of the goods and services, and the loans, plus interest, must be repaid in dollars. The intent is to supplement private credit in cases when there are political or commercial risks that private lenders are unwilling to assume. Credit is extended on longer terms than private lenders might be willing to grant. In the 1960s most of these loans were made to borrowers in less developed countries. The Export-Import Bank also guarantees credit extended by private financial institutions in the United States, and foreign financial institutions where such credit is used to purchase American goods and services by foreigners. The Bank has the authority to borrow from the Treasury to finance its operations, but in the 1960s it instead sold its own securities in private capital markets, mostly in the United States but also, to a limited extent, abroad. The lending incorporated in the American foreign aid program and the activities of the Export-Import Bank are examples of the international aspects of public finance, the subject of the next chapter.

22

INTERNATIONAL ASPECTS OF PUBLIC FINANCE

International economic policies affect resource allocation and income distribution among nations and balance of payments stability. Some explicit international economic policies directly entail federal government revenues and expenditures and are an aspect of public finance. These aspects of public finance are considered in this chapter because of their prominence during the postwar era.

International allocative policies alter domestic and foreign resource use from what would obtain in their absence. Any policy that discourages imports, for example, encourages the allocation of domestic resources to the production of import-competing goods, and reduces the allocation of resources abroad for their production. The United States levies tariffs to protect domestic industry from foreign competition and, as such, tariffs constitute an explicit international allocative policy. Foreign aid outlays are also an explicit international allocative policy, as are the loans of the Export-Import Bank.

International distributive policies may be viewed from two perspectives. The first involves those whose subjects are citizens of the policy-making nation. The tax treatment of domestic and foreign source income is a case in point: Federal personal and corporate income taxes are applied to income earned by Americans abroad for equity as well as allocative and stabilization reasons. The other perspective involves international distributive policies between citizens of different nations. International disaster relief such as American food shipments to Biafra at the conclusion of the Nigerian civil war reflects equity considerations. Foreign economic assistance may be based on equity grounds, especially when it is multilaterally provided through international agencies such as the United Nations or the World Bank rather than being bilaterally provided so that the donor nation has some control over the recipient nation.[1] Equity considerations motivate many American Peace Corps volunteers.

International stabilization policies are probably the most familiar (although least understood), because international economic instability is often accompanied by currency speculation and the movement of gold reserve assets that, in the popular imagination, connote crisis. Such crises and their resolutions, as explicit international stabilization policies are adopted, frequently make the headlines and are the subject of extensive journalistic discussion. A nation's international accounts must tend toward balance in the long run. Specifically, those international transactions that are interpreted as causing balance of payments surpluses and deficits must adjust so that credits equal debits. In a world of flexible exchange rates imbalance is self-eliminating. In a world of fixed exchange rates, governments must adopt explicit international economic policies to eliminate the imbalance, or face undesired increases or decreases in their stocks of reserve assets. Especially in the event of balance of payments deficits, these explicit policy actions must be adopted, for stocks of reserve assets are finite and undesired reductions in them may not continue forever. As a result of taking explicit policy actions, debits and credits may balance at greater or lesser total international transactions values than otherwise would obtain; in the limiting case of policies that eliminated all international transactions, balance of payments credits and debits would balance with both equal to zero. The point to note is that balance must be attained in the long run either as the result of explicit policy actions or, in their absence, automatic adjustment.

The persistence of the United States balance of payments deficit in the 1950s and the 1960s must certainly lead some readers to question these

[1] During the 1960s, many proponents of foreign aid who viewed foreign aid from an equity perspective recommended that larger fractions of foreign aid be provided through international agencies because bilateral aid often reflected advancement of the political objectives of the donor rather than the development needs of the less developed nations. *See* Report of the Commission of International Development, Lester B. Pearson, Chairman, *Partners in Development* (New York: Frederick A. Praeger, 1969).

assertions. In fact, the deficit's very persistence should lead the student to question the idea that an account recording deficits per se indicates imbalance. Between 1950 and 1969 the accumulated United States balance of payments deficit, measured on a liquidity basis, was $44.5 billion. During those years the United States stock of international reserve assets declined by $9.1 billion. That foreigners chose to hold United States liquid liabilities rather than international reserve assets suggests that the recording of a balance of payments deficit does not of necessity imply an imbalance that must be corrected.

Many implicit international economic policies stem from the federal government's revenues and expenditures. Allocative policies, such as federal deferral of research and development expenses, have an implicit impact on the international competitiveness of American products.[2] These are sometimes made explicit. At the end of the 1960s federal financing of the research and development costs of an American supersonic transport was defended on the grounds that if the United States did not develop an SST, the American balance of payments would deteriorate: Foreign carriers would purchase the British-French or Soviet SST rather than American subsonic transports, and American carriers, in order to compete, would have to purchase SSTs abroad. Federal taxation of corporate income, as an internal revenue policy, has implicit implications for international capital flows if that tax affects the rate of return on domestic investment. Macroeconomic stabilization measures whose objects are domestic employment or price variables have implicit consequences for the nation's exports and imports. This chapter considers in detail the implicit international economic policy embodied in internal taxes. Nations make compensatory adjustments at their frontiers for internal taxes reflected in product prices. These adjustments, known as border tax adjustments, were an American international economic policy issue at the start of the 1970s. They are the subject of the final section of this chapter.

Our discussion of explicit international economic policies begins, in the next section, with questions related to taxation. This is followed by a look at American international expenditures. Throughout this chapter it is important to remember that there are other means of public economic policy than public finance. Regulatory policies such as quotas, restrictions on international capital flows, and prohibitions on the import of goods originating in

---

[2] For a discussion of research and development as an input in American exports, and the federal role in supporting research and development, *see* William Gruber, Dileep Mehta, and Raymond Vernon, "The R&D Factor in International Trade and International Investment of the United States," and Donald B. Keesing, "The Impact of Research and Development on United States Trade," *Journal of Political Economy*, February 1967. For additional discussion of several explicit and implicit international economic policies, *see* Robert E. Baldwin, *Nontariff Distortions of International Trade* (Washington, D.C.: The Brookings Institution, 1970).

certain nations may be employed.[3] Monetary policy also plays a role. Changes in interest rates, for example, may be designed to alter the yield on domestic securities relative to the yield available abroad, to induce a change in international capital flows. At the start of the 1960s the Federal Reserve System and the Treasury cooperated in "Operation Twist," a policy designed to increase short-term interest rates relative to long-term rates in the hope that American short-term investors would make domestic rather than foreign security purchases.

TAXATION

Tariffs. In fiscal year 1969 the United States government raised $2.3 billion with tariffs (see Table 12.5). Revenue is not the principal reason for tariffs in the 1970s. The government of an industrial nation imposes tariffs for the explicit allocative purpose of discriminating against imports by increasing their prices relative to the prices of import-competing domestic production, so that consumers will substitute domestic for imported goods. The protective tariff is akin to the sumptuary excise tax in its intent. In addition, tariffs may be levied by nations with balance of payments deficits to attain balance in their international accounts.[4]

Private citizens as well as public officials seek tariffs. The owners of factors of production utilized in import-competing industries want protection. Governments protect resources employed in import-competing industries whose output is deemed essential to national security. Private resource owners, not wishing to admit their self-interest, often use the national defense argument when lobbying for protection. If import-competing firms are concentrated in a geographic area, such as the American textile industry in the Southeast, public officials as well as factor owners may seek protection; in

---

[3] The Department of Commerce has promulgated regulations governing direct foreign investments: *See* U.S. Department of Commerce, Office of Foreign Direct Investments, *Foreign Direct Investments, 1970* (Washington, D.C.: Government Printing Office, 1970). The Federal Reserve Board has imposed limitations on foreign lending by banks: *See* "Balance of Payments Program: Revised Guidelines for Banks and Nonbank Financial Institutions," *Federal Reserve Bulletin*, January 1970.

[4] In 1964 the United Kingdom imposed a 15 percent surtax (tariff) on almost all imports for balance of payments reasons. The import surtax was motivated by the goal of obtaining stability in the British balance of payments.

In less developed countries the tariff may have purposes other than altering the allocation of resources. It may be an important revenue measure, especially on administrative efficiency grounds, as the few points of entry into a nation are easily policed making evasion difficult. In addition, the tariff may be levied on equity grounds: If most imports are consumption goods the tariff has much the same effect as a series of domestic excise taxes that may be graduated to tax "luxuries" at higher rates than "necessities."

this case government's object is stabilization rather than allocation, for increased imports may cause unemployment that cannot easily be absorbed. In addition, governments sometimes levy tariffs in order to have something to negotiate with when they request tariff reductions from other nations.

Partial equilibrium analysis, as illustrated in Figure 22.1, helps explain tariffs as a policy instrument. The left-hand panel shows the domestic import-competing sector. In the absence of foreign trade the domestic market would clear at the price P_D; at prices below this level domestic demand exceeds production and this excess demand, if met, must be supplied from imports. The excess of domestic demand over production constitutes the demand for imports, D_I, shown in the center panel. The right-hand panel depicts the foreign export sector. At prices above the market clearing price, P_F, there is an excess of production over consumption that constitutes the foreign supply of exports, S_E, shown in the center panel. Under free trade conditions, S_E is also perceived as the supply of imports to the importing nation, and an international market clearing price, P_1, is established. At that price the traded quantity, Q_1, is equal to the excess of demand over supply, Q_3 minus Q_2, in the importing economy, and the excess of supply over demand, Q_5 minus Q_4, in the exporting economy.

The levying of a protective tariff makes the price paid by the importer, including the tariff, differ from the price received by the exporter. With the levy of a specific tariff, the supply of imports, as perceived in the importing nation, is given by S_I in the center panel of Figure 22.1.[5] The new price in the tariff levying nation is P_2; at that price the quantity Q_6, equal to Q_8 minus Q_7, is imported. The traded quantity Q_6 is supplied by the exporting nation at the price P_3, and is equal to the foreign excess of domestic production over consumption, Q_{10} minus Q_9. The difference in price, P_2 minus P_3, is the per unit amount of the tariff. It is paid by importers to the importing nation's gov-

---

[5] Tariffs may be specific and/or *ad valorem*. At the start of the 1970s, item 319.23 in the United States tariff schedule was the following:

> Woven fabrics, wholly of cotton (continued): suitable for making typewriter ribbon, not fancy or figured, containing yarns the average number of which exceeds 50 but not 140, the total thread count (treating ply yarns as single threads) of which per square inch, counting warp and filling, is not less than 240 and not more than 340, and in which the thread count of either the warp or filling does not exceed 60 percent of the total thread count of the warp and filling: Not bleached and not colored: of numbers 60 to 89—5¢ per pound plus 7.5% ad valorem.

See Office of the Special Representative for Trade Negotiations: ***Report** on United States Negotiations: General Agreement on Tariffs and Trade 1964–1967 Trade Conference, Geneva, Switzerland* (Washington, D.C.: Government Printing Office, 1967), Vol. II, p. 181. This item illustrates a typical item in the U.S. Tariff code. Thousands of such items are enumerated, the item sometimes being so precisely defined that it is exported by only one nation.

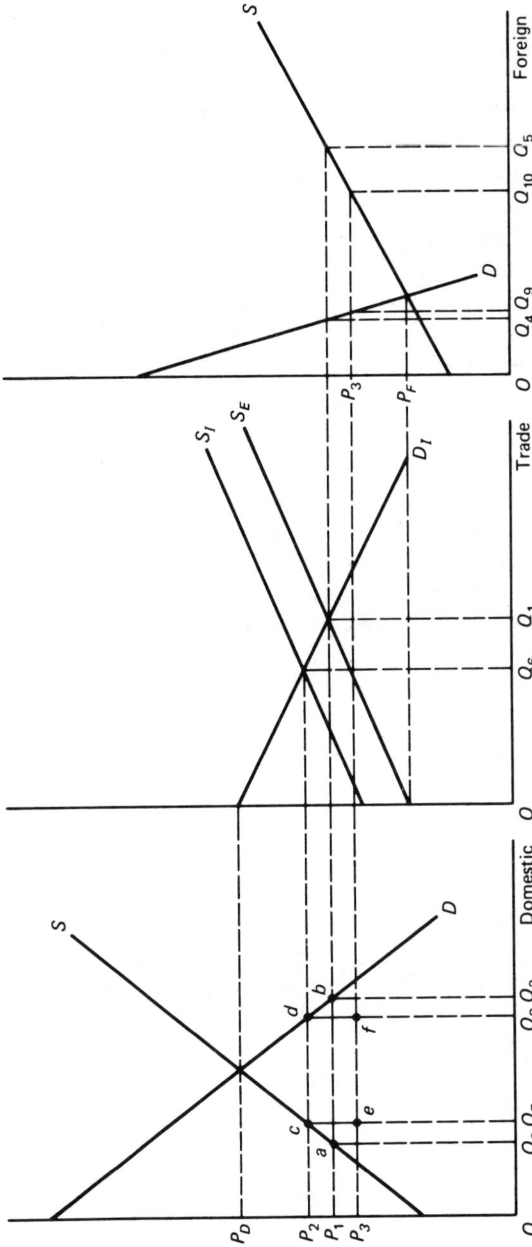

Figure 22.1 Effects of a tariff.

ernment and is not an international payment. The increase in domestic production from Q_2 to Q_7 is an allocative effect of the protective tariff (as is the reduction in foreign production from Q_5 to Q_{10}). Without the tariff, the last unit of domestic production, with a marginal cost equal to P_2, would not be able to compete with an additional unit of imports, with marginal cost equal to P_3. The tariff shelters high cost domestic production from the competition lower cost imports would otherwise provide. Welfare-maximizing owners of factors of production employed in the import-competing sector seek this allocative policy.

The additional purpose of promoting balance of payments stability is also illustrated in Figure 22.1. Under free trade conditions Q_3 minus Q_2, units of imports were bought at the price P_1. The total value of imports was given by the area of the rectangle aQ_2Q_3b, all of which represented a balance of payments debit since the price paid by the importer was also the amount received by the exporter. With the tariff, Q_8 minus Q_7 units of imports are bought. The total amount paid by consumers for imports is given by the rectangle cQ_7Q_8d, but not all of this is an international payment. The amount given by rectangle $cefd$ is tariff revenue. The amount paid to the exporter is given by eQ_7Q_8f; this international payment is less than under free trade conditions. Thus if deficits exist the levy of a tariff may promote balance of payments stability by reducing the nation's international expenditures on imports. Welfare-maximizing public officials, to whom balance of payments deficits are a problem, may seek such policies. Resource owners in import-competing industries often propose tariffs under the guise of seeking balance of payments stability when, in fact, their true motive is the allocative policy of increasing domestic production.

A nation's *terms of trade* are the ratio of its export prices to import prices. The terms of trade express the quantity of imports available per unit of exports. An increase in this ratio is usually referred to as an improvement in the terms of trade; when export prices rise relative to import prices, more imports are earned per unit of exports. It is sometimes argued that nations may levy tariffs to improve their terms of trade.[6] This may be illustrated with the aid of Figure 22.1. Assuming export prices are unaltered, the levy of a tariff reduces the price paid internationally for imports from P_1 to P_3. This fall in import prices gives the desired terms of trade improvement.

However, if the importing nation faces a perfectly elastic supply of imports the results are different. The illustration of Figure 22.1 essentially divides the world into two parts, each of which has enough transactions with the other to have some consequence on prices. Suppose instead a nation takes such a small fraction of an internationally traded product that a reduction in its quantity of imports leaves import prices unchanged. Thus, the supply

---

[6] Paul Prebisch, "Commercial Policy in the Underdeveloped Countries," *American Economic Review*, May 1959.

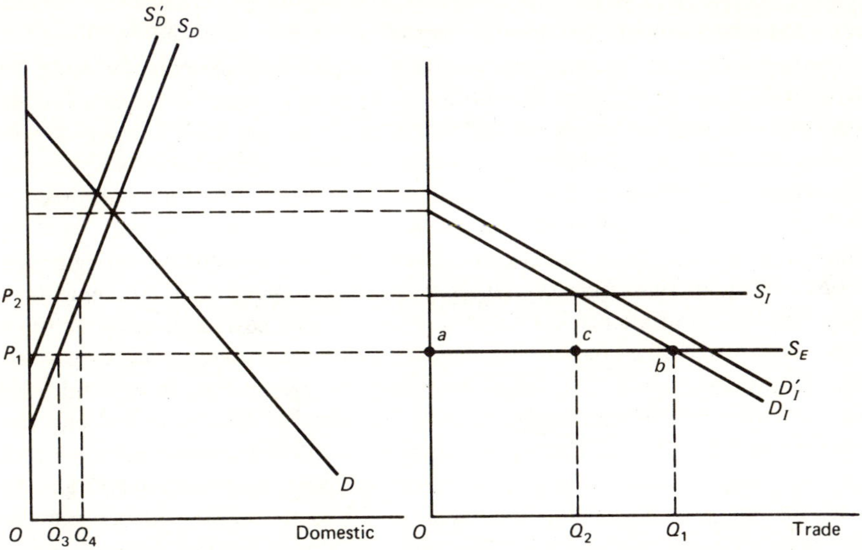

Figure 22.2 Effects of a tariff with a perfectly elastic supply of imports.

of imports is perceived as the horizontal schedule, S_E, in the right-hand panel of Figure 22.2, and the international price of this product is unaltered when a tariff is levied, raising the import supply schedule to S_I. In this case, starting from the free trade quantity of imports, Q_1, the tariff increases the domestic price to P_2, the quantity of imports decreases to Q_2, the nation's international expenditures for imports decrease from $OabQ_1$ to $OacQ_2$, and domestic production increases from Q_3 to Q_4. In these respects a perfectly elastic import supply schedule leaves the previous analytical results unchanged. But now the tariff does not lead to an improvement in the terms of trade, and any benefits that will accrue from that improvement are not available. Nations facing a perfectly elastic import supply function cannot improve their terms of trade by levying tariffs.

If tariffs are levied on inputs they increase input prices and hence the cost of production of final products. In Figure 22.2, the shift in domestic supply of a final product from S_D to S_D' is the result of increased input prices stemming from a tariff on inputs. The demand for the imported final product shifts to D_I'. At the free trade final product price, P_1, the tariff on inputs decreases domestic production and increases imports. In addition, the levy of a tariff on inputs may serve to undo some or all of the protection from the tariff on the final product that caused its price to rise from P_1 to P_2. If the tariff on inputs is high enough, domestic production of the final product under the nation's total tariff structure may be less than it would be under free trade conditions.[7]

---

7 Empirical tariff studies have sought to take account of the effect of tariffs on input

U.C.W. ABERYSTWYTH LIBRARY

Akin to tariffs is the interest equalization tax proposed by President Kennedy in July 1963, and enacted by Congress in September 1964. In the late 1950s and early 1960s foreign investments were seen as the cause of the American balance of payments deficit. In order to approach balance of payments stability, the administration sought to check capital outflows by taxing American portfolio purchase of foreign securities.[8] The rationale was as follows: The yield on American securities was lower than the yield on foreign securities, hence Americans sought the more profitable foreign securities. Many foreign security issuers were also making direct placements in the American capital market because of the lower cost of borrowing there. The interest equalization tax was levied at variable rates, up to 15 percent, on the purchase price of foreign securities, the rate being set to reduce the yield to maturity on a foreign security bought by Americans by one percentage point. Thus, the American buyer of a $1000 European bond with a 5 percent coupon and 20 years to maturity would be taxed $150. For his current outlay of $1150 the American would then receive $50 per year for 20 years and the face value of the bond, $1000, at its maturity, giving an effective yield of approximately 4 percent. This reduction in yield was designed to make American securities more competitive with foreign securities, thereby checking the balance of payments debits arising from portfolio foreign investment.

The interest equalization tax was a success at the same time as it failed (see Table 22.1). Although not enacted until September 1964, the legislation was written to be effective as of the date on which it was proposed, July 18, 1963. The data for the second half of 1963 show that portfolio foreign investment (lines 4 and 6) precipitately declined suggesting that the policy was a success. On balance, however, net capital outflows did not decline (line 1); investors simply sought other types of securities not subject to the interest equalization tax, such as making direct bank loans (line 7). In this respect the policy failed. Despite the fact that the interest equalization tax did not

---

prices as well as the impact of the tariff on final products. *See* Bela Balassa, "Tariff Protection in Industrial Countries: An Evaluation," *Journal of Political Economy*, December 1965. For an empirical investigation of the protective effect of internal taxes as well as tariffs, *see* H.G. Grubel and Bela Balassa, "Nominal Tariffs, Indirect Taxes and Effective Rates of Protection: The Common Market Countries 1959," *Economic Journal*, December 1967.

[8] *Portfolio foreign investment* occurs when Americans buy securities by a foreign corporation in which Americans do not have an "important managerial voice." If an individual or group owns 10 percent of the voting stock, or if 50 percent of the voting stock is owned by Americans collectively, Americans are said to have an "important managerial voice" in the foreign corporation, and transactions in that firm's securities are designated as *direct foreign investment* rather than portfolio in the American balance of payments account. *See* Report of the Review Committee for Balance of Payments Statistics to the Bureau of the Budget, *The Balance of Payments Statistics of the United States* (Washington, D.C.: Government Printing Office, 1965), pp. 62ff, and *Foreign Direct Investments Regulations, 1970, op. cit.*

Table 22.1 **Recorded Private Capital Outflows, 1960–1964 (Millions of dollars*)**

	Type of Capital	1960	1961	1962	Seasonally Adjusted Annual Rates			
					1963		1964	
					First Half	Second Half	First Half	Third Quarter
1	Total net capital outflows	3885	4180	3434	5530	3084	5662	4867
2	Long-term	2537	2624	2881	4478	2668	3164	3655
3	Direct investment	1674	1599	1654	2190	1586	2184	2076
4	New issues of foreign securities	555	523	1076	1858	642	682	564
5	Redemptions	—201	—148	—203	—186	—204	—184	—152
6	Transactions in outstanding securities	309	387	96	302	—204	—268	—148
7	Long-term bank claims	155	136	127	322	1156	614	1044
8	Other long-term claims	45	127	131	—8	—308	136	271
9	Short-term	1348	1556	553	1052	416	2498	1212

* Outflow, +; inflow —.

SOURCE: *Economic Report of the President, 1965* (Washington, D.C.: Government Printing Office, 1965), p. 76.

eliminate the balance of payments deficit, in 1967 the administration sought, and was granted, an extension of the tax with authority to increase its effective rate to 2 percent. In 1969 American purchases of stock in foreign corporations were taxed at an 18.75 percent rate; bonds were taxed at rates ranging from 1.31 to 18.75 percent depending on their length to maturity. The portfolio acquisition of the securities of less developed nations are exempt from the interest equalization tax, as are many Canadian and some Japanese securities.[9]

Taxation of foreign income. Personal and corporate income originating abroad may be taxed there and may also be taxed under American laws. As of 1968, the United States had treaties with 26 nations pertaining to taxation of international income, and several tax treaties were pending. The manner in which foreign source income is taxed may determine where firms base foreign operations, which nations' securities firms and individuals hold, and the direction of international capital flows. Taxation of international income is thus an allocative variable. In addition, equity questions arise if domestic taxes may be avoided by obtaining foreign source income. Stabilization questions are involved if the taxation of foreign source income induces transactions that are a cause of balance of payments instability.[10]

Taxation requires that the taxing government have jurisdiction over the taxpayer. The United States taxes all the income of American based firms, irrespective of the nation in which that income originates, and taxes that portion of the income of foreign based firms that originates in the United States.[11] A firm is said to be based in the United States if it is incorporated there; a firm is based abroad if it is incorporated abroad. Thus, an American firm that operates abroad through foreign branches is entirely based in the United States and its total earnings, even if not repatriated from the foreign branches, comprise the base for the American corporate income tax. If the

---

[9] International Monetary Fund, *20th Annual Report on Exchange Restrictions* (Washington, D.C.: International Monetary Fund, 1969), pp. 496–97.

[10] We are not concerned with international differences in tax structures. Such differences may, however, be important allocative variables. We sometimes hear of the movie star who finds it desirable, for income tax purposes, to be a Swiss rather than an American citizen. The emergence of the international corporation, with plants located throughout the world, may mean that differences in national business taxes will become a more important locational variable. *See* Richard A. Musgrave, *Fiscal Systems* (New Haven: Yale University Press, 1969), and Organization for Economic Cooperation and Development, *Border Tax Adjustments and Tax Structures in OECD Member Countries* (Paris: OECD, 1968).

[11] For background material pertaining to this section, *see* Laurence B. Krause and Kenneth W. Dam, *Federal Tax Treatment of Foreign Income* (Washington, D.C.: The Brookings Institution, 1964); Boris I. Bittker and Laurence F. Ebb, *United States Taxation of Foreign Income and Foreign Persons* 2d ed. (Branford, Conn.: Federal Tax Press, Inc., 1968); and Harold J. Heck, *The International Business Environment* (New York: American Management Association, 1969), chapter 11.

branch's earnings are taxed abroad, a credit for foreign income taxes paid may be taken against the U.S. corporate income tax liability. Subsidiaries of American firms, including wholly owned subsidiaries, are incorporated abroad. Their earnings are not taxable under American laws unless they are repatriated as dividends or other means. As dividends are paid, credits may be taken for foreign income taxes paid. Since corporate income tax rates are lower in many nations than in the United States, this feature of the tax laws may encourage foreign incorporation to avoid taxation. This has been questioned on equity grounds, especially because earnings may never be repatriated or may be repatriated as a capital gain upon liquidation of the subsidiary. Since 1962, the American owners of foreign corporations—owned 50 percent or more by Americans in blocks of 10 percent or more—must treat their share of the corporation's earnings as income for current personal or corporate income tax purposes if the subsidiary is located in a nation where corporate income is taxed at substantially lower rates than in the United States. In this case subsidiaries are treated much like branches for tax purposes. This change in the procedure of taxing foreign source income was made not only for equity reasons but also to diminish the attractiveness of direct foreign investments in order to promote balance of payments stability. This treatment of the earnings of subsidiaries applies only to foreign investments in developed nations. The income of subsidiaries established in developing nations continue to escape taxation; this is consistent with an American policy of promoting economic development.

The personal income tax base treats income from domestic and foreign sources alike. Thus wages and salaries earned abroad, dividends paid by foreign corporations, even if not repatriated, and other foreign source income is included in adjusted gross income. Foreign income taxes paid may be taken as a credit against the American personal income tax liability; the credit may not, however, exceed the amount of domestic taxes that are due on the foreign source income. The major exception to this procedure occurs when an American citizen resides abroad. Residency abroad comprises living outside the United States for a full tax year or for 510 days during 18 consecutive months. In this case the American may exclude the first \$20,000 (\$25,000 after three years) earned outside the United States from adjusted gross income. As a resident of a foreign nation, however, the United States citizen may be subject to the income taxes of that nation. In general, foreign citizens with income in the United States are subject to American personal income taxation.

EXPENDITURES

The federal government makes several types of international expenditures. In 1969 foreign economic assistance totaled \$5 billion (Table 11.15, lines 29, 42, and 43), military assistance was \$0.8 billion (Table 11.15, line

28), and military expenditures abroad were $4.9 billion (Table 11.15, line 16). The government expenditures giving rise to these balance of payments debits are the focus of this section. Additional United States government international expenditures are interest payments on the foreign held United States government debt, the pensions of retired government employees living abroad, and some maintenance expenditures of American embassies. These latter international expenditures do not reflect explicit international economic policies; they are omitted from consideration in this section.

Foreign economic assistance, much of which is known as foreign aid, takes the form of loans and grants.[12] Grants may be either financial or in kind. In some instances this assistance is for genuinely humanitarian purposes, such as the grant of food and medical supplies to Peru after the 1970 earthquake. In other instances, economic assistance is aimed at supporting a government in power in the belief that the continuation of that government serves American interests (as in the case of aid to Vietnam). In still other instances, the aid is a mixture of the two. It is virtually impossible to determine from the *Budget* itself the items that give rise to the balance of payments entries in Table 11.15, lines 29, 42, and 43. The Department of Commerce does, however, break these down by program:[13]

	(Millions of dollars)
Farm product disposal programs	1156
Foreign assistance acts and related programs	2136
Export-Import Bank Act	1258
Capital subscriptions to international and regional organizations, excluding IMF	184
Other assistance programs	257
Other foreign currency assets acquired	350
Less foreign currencies used by U.S. government other than for grants or credits	334
Other (including changes in administrative cash holdings), net	25
	5032

First are agricultural transfers under PL 480. This act has the dual purpose of disposing of American agricultural surpluses and feeding the world's hungry. In some instances these transfers are made as grants (Table

[12] The term foreign aid is not well defined. Sometimes it refers to the economic and military assistance extended by governments either as grants or loans. Other times it refers only to economic grants and loans of governments. Some sources treat private foreign investments as foreign aid. Any comparisons of the amounts of foreign aid provided by different nations must first clarify the definition. When Congress debates foreign aid the economic assistance grants (Table 11.15, line 29) are usually at question although sometimes foreign lending (line 42) is also at issue. American foreign aid is not popularly understood to include the loans of the Export-Import Bank.

[13] *Survey of Current Business*, June 1970, p. 50.

11.15, line 29 debits financing, line 3 credits); in other cases they are loans (line 42 debits to finance, line 3 credits). Transfers under foreign assistance acts include grants and loans, such as loans made as part of the Alliance for Progress. These monies are largely appropriated to the President and their expenditure is tied to the purchase of American goods. Export-Import Bank loans were discussed in the previous chapter. They are extended to foreigners to assist their purchase of American exports. Multilateral foreign aid is included in capital subscriptions to international and regional organizations.

Most American aid is *tied aid,* meaning that the assistance provided by the United States (Table 11.15, lines 29, 42, and 43 debits) must be expended in the United States, giving rise to a merchandise export (Table 11.15, line 3 credit). It is frequently charged that tying aid reduces its real value, for the recipient must buy American exports that are more expensive than similar items produced in other countries. While this is sometimes true, the criticism is probably not valid, for United States policy makers have many policy objectives: Some of these are humanitarian and some are political; there is the economic objective of obtaining balance in the American balance of payments. In the absence of tying aid, the total amount of dollar credits authorized by Congress would probably be reduced. It is probably not true to contend that tying aid reduces the real transfer.

As of June 30, 1969, the outstanding foreign loans of the United States government totaled $19.7 billion denominated in dollars and $5.7 billion denominated in foreign currencies (see Table 22.2). These loans produced the $932 million balance of payments credit for interest payments shown in Table 11.15, line 13. Of the United States foreign dollar loans, those made through the Agency for International Development as part of the economic assistance program and those of the Export-Import Bank are the most numerous. In addition there are substantial Treasury loans outstanding; $1.2 billion of these are outstanding credits granted during World War II and the immediate postwar years. The $3.3 billion of loans and other credits primarily consists of loans extended to the government of the United Kingdom during the 1960s to enable that government to maintain the par value of the pound during times of international currency speculation.

At the end of fiscal year 1969, the United States government held the equivalent of $2.1 billion in foreign currencies, excluding holdings of convertible foreign currencies by the exchange stabilization fund.[14] These foreign currencies are largely inconvertible currencies of less developed nations. A principal means by which they are acquired is through the commercial export of surplus agricultural commodities where the United States accepts payment in the foreign currency. Over the years balances of these currencies have accumulated and these balances have in turn been loaned out by the Agency for International Development, giving rise to the $5.7 billion in

[14] *Treasury Bulletin,* November 1969, p. 127.

Table 22.2 **United States Government Foreign Loans Outstanding, June 30, 1969 (Millions of dollars)**

Type of Loan and Lending Agency	Total	Foreign Currency Loans
Funds appropriated to the President:		
Liquidation of foreign military sales fund	74,098	—
Military assistance credits in liquidation	1,361	—
Agency for International Development:		
Alliance for Progress, development loans	1,856,088	—
Common defense, economic, and triangular trade loans	63,682	3,831,650
Development loans	4,150,770	—
Development loan fund liquidation account	250,321	978,435
Loans to domestic or foreign firms and United States firms in foreign countries	—	170,429
Loans of predecessor agencies in liquidation	1,058,805	694,582
Other loans	516,289	63,555
Agriculture Department:		
Commodity Credit Corporation:		
Long-term export sales credits	1,301,956	—
Short-term export sales credits	299,774	—
Commerce Department:		
Maritime Administration	810	—
State Department:		
Loans to the United Nations	89,406	—
Treasury Department:		
Miscellaneous loans and certain other assets:		
Lend-lease and surplus property	1,216,479	1,877
Loans and other credits	3,313,851	—
Receivable from foreign banking institutions	3,000	—
Atomic Energy Commission:		
Long-term receivables	61,493	—
Export-Import Bank of the United States	5,421,488	—
Total foreign loans	19,679,671	5,740,528

SOURCE: *Treasury Bulletin,* December 1969, p. 173.

foreign currency loans recorded in Table *22.2*. The United States accepts payment for PL 480 agricultural exports and repayment of some foreign loans in foreign currencies so the developing nation will not have to allocate scarce foreign exchange to these purposes. By making agricultural products and credits of local currencies available without requiring foreign exchange expenditures, the United States intends to provide not only agricultural and credit assistance, but also to free foreign exchange for expenditures on other imports, furthering the recipient nation's program of economic development.

Military assistance expenditures are made to support the development of the armed forces of other nations. The monies for military assistance are appropriated to the President; the budget document itself contains no specific designation of the nations receiving military assistance. In fiscal 1969 budget outlays for military assistance were $611 million. During calendar year 1969, $0.8 billion of international transactions recorded in the balance of payments account (Table 11.15, lines 5 and 28) were for military assistance. A precise reconciliation is impossible.

Military expenditures result in a substantial American balance of payments debit (Table 11.15, line 16). In 1970 the United States had over 400 foreign military installations. The most important of these were associated with the presence of American forces in Indo-China, Korea, and Western Europe. At the start of the 1970s all these foreign military commitments were subject to intensive review and many were being reduced. One reason for this cutback was politics, both domestic and foreign, but in addition there were interlocking economic reasons: The budgetary expense that military forces entail and the balance of payments impact these forces have when stationed overseas. In general, the larger the fraction of the military forces overseas the greater the budgetary costs of those forces as they become increasingly distant from their major source of supply. The increased supply cost associated with distance may be partially offset by provisioning foreign military bases from purchases made in foreign economies, but this only serves to aggravate the balance of payments impact of the foreign military presence. Reconsideration of priorities and the balance of payments deficit of the United States coincided, at the start of the 1970s, to bring about a reduction in American foreign military commitments.

BORDER TAX ADJUSTMENTS

An implicit international economic policy arises when a nation's internal taxes affect domestic prices and hence relative domestic and foreign prices. These changes in relative prices have an impact on the nation's commodity exports and imports and the balance of payments. The General Agreement on Tariffs and Trade (GATT) permits governments to assess internal commodity taxes on imports and to excuse or rebate them on exports.[15] Without these adjust-

---

[15] The General Agreement on Tariffs and Trade was created in 1947 as a temporary organization through which nations might begin to reduce their barriers to international trade, pending ratification of the Charter of the International Trade Organization. When the ITO was rejected, GATT continued to function, and in the postwar years has served as the principal international organization concerned with nations' international commercial policies. GATT's purpose is to advance freedom of international trade. One means by which it has sought this objective is through sponsorship of six multilateral negotiating sessions in which tariff reductions, often bilaterally

ments it is alleged that the domestic tax mechanism would discriminate against the products of domestic industry both in home and foreign markets, and this discrimination is undesirable on allocative, equity, and stabilization grounds. Thus, border adjustments are made for commodity taxes to eliminate the discrimination that internal taxation would otherwise entail. Viewed in this manner, border tax adjustments are the obverse of tariffs that are levied for the specific purpose of discriminating in favor of domestic products. This section is organized first to consider the rationale for making border tax adjustments, and then to examine them in the light of proposals for American international economic policy.

Rationale and practice. Our previous discussion of taxation showed that commodity taxes, on both theoretical and empirical grounds, are believed to be shifted forward and reflected in increased product prices. The levy of commodity taxes has the effect of increasing the price of taxed products in the tax-levying nation. If the tax liability is incurred prior to the time of export or import, the taxed product then sells at a higher price relative to foreign products. This relative price change will lead to the domestic substitution of imports for locally manufactured goods, and abroad, buyers will choose less of the taxing nation's exports.

GATT procedures are consistent with this interpretation of the effects of commodity taxation. Article III, section 2 of the Articles of Agreement states that "imports shall not be subject to internal taxes . . . in excess of those applied to like domestic products." Article XVI proscribes export subsidies; what comprises a subsidy is clarified by Annex I to that Article: "The exemption of an exported product from . . . taxes borne by the like product when destined for domestic consumption, or the remission of such . . . taxes in amounts not in excess of those which have accrued, shall not be deemed to be a subsidy." The foundation of the GATT authorization of border tax adjustments is found in these two articles, but in neither case does the Articles of Agreement specify which taxes may be adjusted for as products cross national frontiers. That distinction has arisen from interpretation and administration of the Agreement. At the start of the 1970s border adjustments

negotiated, were widely applied. The most recent tariff negotiating session was known as the Kennedy Round, and was completed in June 1967. For a discussion of the Kennedy Round of tariff negotiations, *see* Ernest H. Pregg, *Traders and Diplomats* (Washington, D.C.: The Brookings Institution, 1970), and Robert E. Baldwin, "Tariff-Cutting Techniques in the Kennedy Round," in Robert E. Baldwin, *et al., Trade, Growth, and the Balance of Payments* (Chicago: Rand McNally and Company, 1965). For a discussion of the origins, purpose, and provisions of the GATT, *see* C. H. Alexandrowicz, *World Economic Agencies* (New York: Frederick A. Praeger, 1962), chapter 9. To keep abreast of current developments in GATT, *see* General Agreement on Tariffs and Trade, *Basic Instruments and Selected Documents*, published irregularly in Geneva.

are made for commodity taxes such as sales and excise taxes, including turnover and value-added taxes. Corporate income, social insurance, and property taxes may not be adjusted for at national frontiers.

In the United States manufacturers of cigarettes, alcoholic beverages, and automobiles are excused from the federal excise tax on that portion of their output they export, and these taxes, as well as any tariffs that also apply, arc assessed on similar products when they are imported. In Western Europe, turnover and value-added taxes are excused or rebated upon exports and are assessed, along with any tariffs that apply, on imports.[16] Making border adjustments for turnover taxes involves an element of arbitrariness, for the nominal rate of tax will have different percentage impacts on price, depending on the number of stages of fabrication and distribution at which turnover tax liabilities are incurred prior to export. The same problem arises in determining the rate at which border adjustments should be made for imports that compete with domestic production.

Some argue that border adjustments should be made for the corporate income tax. In Chapters 7 and 13 we saw that the theoretical and empirical findings on the shifting of this tax are uncertain. If the tax is not shifted, making border adjustments for it would merely disguise protection of import-competing industries and subsidization of exports. If the corporate tax is shifted, recommending border adjustments for it is understandable. Determining the appropriate rate for border adjustments might be difficult and somewhat arbitrary, but probably no more so than in making adjustments for turnover taxes.

Policy. The United States assesses taxes on corporate incomes at higher rates than do many other industrial nations, derives a smaller fraction of its budget receipts from commodity taxes than do most nations, and has had persistent balance of payments deficits during the postwar years.[17] Some firms feel discriminated against because no adjustments are made for the corporate income tax. Some propose making border adjustments for the

---

16 Even in the Common Market, where most tariffs have been eliminated, border tax adjustments are made because the EEC nations have different tax structures that would otherwise be a factor in determining international competitiveness. Further, commodity taxes are sometimes talked of as consumption taxes, and on these grounds it is the taxes of the nation of consumption, rather than the taxes of the nation of production, that should be reflected in product prices.

17 For further discussion of border tax procedures and recommendations for American policy, *see* Harry G. Johnson and Mel Krauss, "Border Taxes, Border Tax Adjustments, Comparative Advantage, and the Balance of Payments," *Canadian Journal of Economics,* November 1970; J. Frank Gaston and William J. J. Smith, *Border Taxes and International Economic Competition* (New York: National Industrial Conference Board, 1969); and Committee for Economic Development, *A Better Balance in Federal Taxes on Business* (New York: Committee for Economic Development, 1966).

corporate income tax to lessen the balance of payments deficit. If such border adjustments cannot be made, under GATT, some have recommended that the United States wholly or partially replace the corporate income tax with a tax on value added and make border adjustments for that tax. Assuming the corporate income tax is shifted forward, these positions at first glance seem reasonable. Closer inspection, however, makes this conclusion questionable.

First, taxes are only one of many government policies that comprise an implicit international economic policy. The provision of social overhead capital and the deferral of research and development expenses, as in the aerospace industry, are also aspects of public finance that are implicit international economic policies. In what respect is it proper to adjust at the border for one type of governmental policy and not for others? The very existence of government is bound to have international economic consequences; netting these out by making border adjustments is impossible.

Second, making border adjustments for the tax component of price implies that the no-tax price is in some respect normatively correct. If the economy were perfectly competitive, and profit-maximizing firms all set prices equal to marginal cost and minimum average total cost, it might be possible to develop such a case but, by and large, prices are not set at this level. Generally prices differ from average costs to yield a margin of profit; profit margins differ from firm to firm within an industry and, on the average, from industry to industry. By what criterion do we specify that the no-tax price should be maintained? Unless the no-tax price is normatively correct, the case for maintaining that price for international transactions is questionable.

Finally, and most important, a nation's balance of payments must always tend toward balance. Striking balance may be done through a variety of policy mixes. Assuming unchanged domestic and foreign prices, quoted in local currency units, devaluation increases the local currency price of imports and reduces the foreign currency price of exports; appreciation reduces the local currency price of imports and increases the foreign currency price of exports. With unchanged exchange rates the same changes between domestic and foreign prices may be accomplished by some combination of tariffs and export subsidies, or by making border tax adjustments. In fact, this was done by the Federal Republic of Germany in 1968 and 1969. At that time Germany was running a balance of payments surplus and appreciation of the mark was widely expected. During the currency speculation of November 1968, Germany, who had been making an 11 percent border adjustment for her 11 percent tax on value added, reduced her rate of border tax adjustment to 7 percent; this policy action had exactly the same impact on relative product prices as would have resulted from a 4 percent appreciation of the mark. In 1969 Germany officially appreciated the mark by 9 percent; at the same time she resumed making border adjustments at the 11 percent rate. Effectively then, Germany changed the price of her goods relative to the price of other nations' goods by 4 percent in 1968, and by an additional 5 percent in 1969, using a combination of exchange rate and border tax adjustment policies.

In view of these considerations who is to say what constitutes discrimination against the products of domestic industry? Even if the corporate income tax is shifted, over the course of many years American international economic policies, as well as the international economic policies of other nations, have adjusted to a pattern of international trade that achieves balance. If the United States were to make adjustments for the corporate income tax, further adjustments in other policy variables would be required. In the short run a competitive and balance of payments advantage might be obtained, but in the long run that is not possible because equality of the balance of payments credits and debits must result. During the course of the 1960s Germany increased her rate of border tax adjustment; prior to 1968 this was a border adjustment for her 4 percent turnover tax. The rate of tax was constant but the border adjustment rate was increased. When Germany shifted to the value-added tax at the start of 1968, her rate of border tax adjustment was increased even further. Over the course of the 1960s Germany moved into a substantial balance of payments surplus position; this is certainly the result of many factors but a contributing factor may have been the increased border tax adjustments she made during that decade. At the end of the decade the appreciation of the mark had the opposite effect on product prices. It is tempting to speculate that without increased border tax adjustment rates during the 1960s the appreciation of the mark in 1969 would not have been needed.[18]

If border adjustments for the corporate income tax cannot be negotiated within GATT, some have proposed that the United States substitute the tax on value added for the corporate income tax so that border tax adjustments can be made. For this to be effective it is necessary that the corporate tax be shifted so that its removal or reduction reduces prices; the levy of the tax on value added will then raise prices to their presubstitution level and making border tax adjustments for it will then give balance of payment advantage. Again, however, this may only happen in the short run, for in the long run additional policy actions will be required to restore balance in the nation's international accounts.

Simply because one nation makes border tax adjustments does not mean that another should make adjustments too, even for the same tax. There

---

[18] For a discussion of German border tax adjustments, *see* Milledge K. Weathers, "Some Implications of GATT Rules Governing the Treatment of Domestic Taxes in International Trade: The Case of Germany Since the Currency Reform of 1948," *National Tax Journal*, March 1970.

are many combinations of policies that will give balance in a nation's international accounts and it is not obvious that one combination is preferred to another. What does seem obvious is that a nation's internal taxes should not be manipulated primarily for balance of payments reasons. There may be many and good reasons for replacing the corporate income tax with a tax on value added. One such reason might be obtaining increased rates of return on corporate investment in order to stimulate economic growth.[19] If this is the best means to obtain that objective, then the tax substitution should be made; border tax adjustments should be made as a consequence only if a balance of payments imbalance results that is not better eliminated by some other policy action. But to substitute taxes primarily for balance of payments advantage should not be done. The internal revenues of a nation should not be manipulated primarily for purposes of international economic policy. Just as few would argue that the tariff, as a tool of international economic policy, should be employed when the modern nation is adopting a revenue measure, so policy variables that are primarily associated with a nation's internal policies should not be manipulated to obtain international economic advantage.

---

[19] If tax substitution does affect rates of return on investment, then an additional balance of payments impact arises due to the effect of rates of return in international capital transactions.

INDEXES

NAME INDEX

SUBJECT INDEX

U.C.W. ABERYSTWYTH
LIBRARY